'Elephant riders must fight with elephant riders,
as one on foot fights a foot soldier'
(*Rāmāyana*, Sanskrit epic, *c.* 3rd C. B.C.)

Attached to force are certain self-imposed imperceptible limitations hardly worth mentioning, known as international law and custom but they scarcely weaken it … Kind-hearted people might … think there was some ingenious way to disarm or defeat an enemy without too much bloodshed, and might imagine that is the true goal of the art of war. Pleasant as it sounds, it is a fallacy that must be exposed: war is such a dangerous business that the mistakes which come from kindness are the very worst.

Clausewitz, *On War*, 1832

Decisions were impacted by legal considerations at every level. [During the Gulf War] the law of war proved invaluable in the decision-making process.

General Colin Powell, US Army
Chairman, Joint Chiefs of Staff

The contemporary law
of armed conflict

Melland Schill Studies in International Law
Series editor Professor Dominic McGoldrick

The Melland Schill name has a long-established reputation for high standards of scholarship. Each volume in the series addresses major public international law issues and current developments. Many of the Melland Schill volumes have become standard works of reference. Interdisciplinary and accessible, the contributions are vital reading for students, scholars and practitioners of public international law, international organisations, international relations, international politics, international economics and international development.

The contemporary law
of armed conflict
second edition

L. C. Green

Juris Publishing

MANCHESTER
UNIVERSITY PRESS

First edition published 1993 by Manchester University Press
Reprinted 1996, 2000

This edition published by
Manchester University Press
Oxford Road, Manchester M13 9NR, UK
www.manchesteruniversitypress.co.uk

British Library Cataloguing-in-Publication Data
A catalogue record for this book is available from the British Library

ISBN   0 7190 5600 4 *hardback*
         0 7190 5601 2 *paperback*

First published in the USA and Canada by Juris Publishing, Inc.
Executive Park, One Odell Plaza, Yonkers, NY 10701

Library of Congress Cataloging-in-Publication Data applied for

ISBN   1-929446-03-9 *hardback*

This edition first published 2000

12 11 10 09 08 07 06 05 04   14 13 12 11 10 9 8 7 6 5

Typeset in Times
by Northern Phototypesetting Co. Ltd, Bolton
Printed in Great Britain
by Biddles, *www.biddles.co.uk*

Contents

Contents

Contents

Contents

Contents

Contents

Contents

Foreword

By her will the late Miss Olive Schill established a fund in memory of her brother, Melland, who was killed in World War I. This fund has supported lectures and publications on many aspects of international law over the past three decades, including the present series of *Melland Schill Studies in International Law*. Olive Schill's bequest was motivated by a desire to contribute to scholarship and learning in international law. She doubtless entertained the hope that such a contribution might increase the role of law in international relations and thereby serve to decrease the likelihood of further devastating armed conflicts.

While she might have been saddened to see the publication in the 1990s of a lengthy work on the contemporary law of armed conflict, she would have appreciated both the necessity for such a body of law, with its roots in antiquity and the teachings of all the major religions, and the value of a careful and lucid exposition of this law, which has seen such considerable development since World War II. There can be few living scholars better equipped to provide an account of the contemporary law of armed conflict than Professor Leslie Green. He is well known to fellow specialists in the field, and to international lawyers generally, through his numerous publications. The present work is the culmination of many years of study, writing and practical experience of this body of law.

Professor Green has based his text on the draft *Manual of Armed Conflict Law* he prepared for the Canadian Department of National Defence. This comprehensive work should prove invaluable to such departments around the world, as well as to serving officers, practising lawyers who have to deal with any aspect of the 'laws of war', and law teachers and their students. The *Melland Schill* series is greatly enriched by Professor Green's monograph.

Gillian M. White
Emeritus Professor of International Law
University of Manchester
August 1993

Preface and acknowledgements

This volume has grown out of the draft *Manual of Armed Conflict Law* that I prepared at the request of the then Judge Advocate General, General Jack Wolfe, for the Canadian Department of National Defence. I am grateful to General Wolfe for permission to use that draft for this purpose.

In preparing the volume I have received encouragement from a number of friends in both Canada and United States government service, especially Commander J. W. Fenrick, D/Law(T) of the Canadian Judge Advocate General's Department, Mr W. Hays Parks, Chief, International Law Branch, International Affairs Division, US Department of the Army, Office of the Judge Advocate General and Captain W. Ashley Roach, US Navy, Office of the Legal Adviser, US Department of State. I should also like to thank Professor Gillian White for reading the manuscript, for preparing the Table of Treaties, and for her very useful suggestions, especially in improving the style.

Although Protocol I of 1977 has not been acceded to by the majority of the leading military powers, since General Colin Powell, Chairman of the US Joint Chiefs of Staff, in his Report to Congress on Coalition operations in the Gulf in 1991, made it clear that the provisions of the Protocol were, for the main part, applied as if they constituted customary law, this book has been written on the same premise. Generally speaking, the line has been taken that Protocol I expresses the law of international armed conflict as it exists today.

Finally, as always, I must thank my wife Lilian for the manner in which she has tolerated my absent-mindedness about other matters while preparing the manuscript of this work.

L. C. G.
October 1992

Preface to the
second edition

During the five years that have elapsed since the publication of the first edition there has been a number of developments affecting the law of armed conflict. Among these have been treaties dealing with the use of specific weapons, such as lasers and anti-personnel mines. In addition, the International Court of Justice has rendered an advisory opinion concerning the use of nuclear weapons. Perhaps more far-reaching has been the establishment of international tribunals which have helped to create a jurisprudence on the criminality of breaches of the law with a process for enforcing that law. Further, they have contributed to clarification of the law as it affects non-international armed conflicts. It has also become necessary to pay some attention to the manner in which the proposed International Criminal Court may replace the need for such *ad hoc* tribunals and make its own contribution to the means for enforcing the law.

Also during this period some countries have produced their own manuals of war law or have sponsored studies directed to that end, while a variety of works devoted to specific aspects of the problem have also become available and, where relevant, these have been taken into consideration.

During my two years as Stockton Professor at the United States Naval War College, where much of the revising was done, I had plenty of opportunity to discuss a number of war law issues that were significant to officers called upon to apply that law in their service activities, and the impact of these discussions has also played a part in the updating of the volume.

Finally, I must thank Manchester University Press for being tolerant regarding deadlines and I must especially take this opportunity to thank my wife Lilian for her patience and good temper while her social life was disrupted and she was left to undertake many obligations which we would normally have shared.

L. C. G., Edmonton, AB
October 1998

Series editor's preface

When Professor Green's book on *The contemporary law of armed conflict* was published in 1993 it was quickly recognised as a classic and authoritative work. Great intellectual authority was combined with linguistic lucidity to produce a readable and informative text. The 1990s have witnessed an explosion of literature and interest in the law of armed conflict. Part of that explosion has been generated by massive and systematic violations of humanitarian law. However, in a more positive sense, there have also been sustained efforts to move international humanitarian law into the mainstream of public international law and to integrate it into the training and education of the military at all levels and in a vastly greater number of countries. Both of these efforts will be assisted by this new edition.

Dominic McGoldrick
International and European Law Unit
University of Liverpool

Abbreviations

A.C.	Appeal Cases (UK)
A.F.P	Air Force Pamphlet (US)
Acton	Acton Reports (UK)
Am. J. Int'l Law	American Journal of International Law
Ann. Dig.	Annual Digest of Public International Law Cases
App.	Appendix
Art.	Article
B. & C.P.C.	British and Colonial Prize Cases
B.F.S.P.	British and Foreign State Papers
Bothe, Partsch and Solf	*New Rules for Victims of Armed Conflicts 1982*
Brit. Y.B. Int'l Law	British Yearbook of International Law
C.C.C.	Canadian Criminal Cases
C.M.R.	Court Martial Reports (US)
C.Rob.	Christopher Robinson's Admiralty Reports (UK)
Can. Y.B. Int'l Law	Canadian Yearbook of International Law
Carnegie tr.	Carnegie Endowment translations of the 'Classics of International Law'
Ch.	Chancery Reports (UK)
Cmd	Command Papers (UK)
Conv.	Convention
Conv. I	Geneva Convention on Wounded and Sick in the Field, 1949
Conv. II	Geneva Convention on Wounded, Sick and Shipwrecked, 1949
Conv. III	Geneva Convention on Prisoners of War, 1949
Conv. IV	Geneva Convention on Civilians, 1949
D.L.R.	Dominion Law Reports (Canada)
Dalhousie L. J.	Dalhousie Law Journal
Denver J. Int'l. Law	Denver Journal of International Law
Dods.	Dodson's Admiralty Reports (UK)

Dougl.	Douglas's King's Bench Reports (UK)
E.R.	English Reports
ENMOD	Convention on Modification of the Environment
Ex.D.	Exchequer Division (UK)
F.2d	Federal Reporter, Second Series (US)
FM27	Field Manual 27, The Law of Land Warfare (US)
F.Supp.	Federal Supplement (US)
G.A.	General Assembly
G.L.R.	Ghana Law Reports
Gen. Ass.	General Assembly
Green, *Essays*	Green, *Essays on the Modern Law of War*, 1984, 1999
Grotius Transactions	Transactions of the Grotius Society
H.C.	House of Commons
HMSO	His Majesty's Stationery Office
Hague Recueil	Recueil des Cours, Académie de Droit International de la Haye
Hague Regs	Hague Regulations annexed to Hague Convention IV, 1907
I.C.J.	International Court of Justice
I.C.L.Q.	International and Comparative Law Quarterly
ICRC	International Committee of the Red Cross
I.L.M.	International Legal Materials
I.L.Q.	International Law Quarterly
I.L.R.	International Law Reports
Int'l Rev. Red X	International Revue of the Red Cross
Israel Y.B.H.R.	Israel Yearbook on Human Rights
Jap. Ann. Int'l Law	Japanese Annual of International Law
K.B.	King's Bench Reports (UK)
L.J.	Law Journal
L.N.T.S.	League of Nations Treaty Series
Land	Geneva Convention I, 1949
M.A.T.	Mixed Arbitral Tribunals (Recueil des décisions)
M.L.R.	Military Law Reports (US)
Manitoba L. J.	Manitoba Law Journal
Maritime	Geneva Convention II, 1949
Mil.Law Rev.	Military Law Review
Mod. Law Rev.	Modern Law Review
NATO	North Atlantic Treaty Organisation
NWP 9	Commander's Handbook on Law of Naval Operations (US)
N.Y. Supp.	New York Supplement Reporter (US)
N.Z.L.R	New Zealand Law Reports

Netherlands Y.B. Int'l Law	Netherlands Yearbook of International Law
P.	Probate, Divorce and Admiralty Reports (UK)
Pr.	Protocol
Ps.w	Prisoners of war
R.I.A.A.	Reports of International Arbitral Awards (UN)
R.I.I.A.	Royal Institute of International Affairs
R.S.C.	Revised Statutes, Canada
Rec. T.A.M.	Recueil des Tribunaux Arbitraux Mixtes
S.A.L.R.	South Africa Law Reports
S.C.	Security Council
SC	Supreme Court (Cape of Good Hope)
S.E. 2d	South Eastern Reporter Second Series (US)
San Remo Manual	San Remo Manual on International Law Applicable in Armed Conflicts at Sea
Schindler and Toman	Schindler and Toman, *The Laws of Armed Conflicts*, 1988
Steward	Steward's Reports (Nova Scotia)
Supp.	Supplement
T.W.C.	Trials of War Criminals (US Nuremberg Series)
UN	United Nations
UNCLOS	United Nations Convention on the Law of the Sea 1982
UNESCO	United Nations Educational, Scientific and Cultural Organisation
U.N.T.S.	United Nations Treaty Series
UNWCC	United Nations War Crimes Commission
WW	World War
War Crimes Reports	UNWCC Law Reports of Trials of War Criminals
Whiteman	Whiteman, *Digest of International Law*
Y.B.I.L.C.	Yearbook of the International Law Commission
Y.B. World Affairs	Yearbook of World Affairs

1

The legality of war and the law of armed conflict

War defined

The International Military Tribunal at Nuremberg held that 'a war of aggression ... is the supreme international crime ... in that it contains within itself the accumulated evil of the whole'.[1] Since there is an 'aggressor' in every war, it would seem that to speak of a 'law of war' is something of a paradox lacking any real substance. It becomes necessary, therefore, to examine this apparent dichotomy and to introduce any study of the law of armed conflict by considering the legality of war. Before doing so, however, it is as well to bear in mind that Cicero maintained '*silent enim leges inter armes*',[2] while Clausewitz[3] went so far as to assert that 'since war is an act of force, there is no logical limit in the application of force ... attached to force are certain self-imposed imperceptible limitations hardly worth mentioning, known as international law and custom, but they scarcely weaken it. [K]ind-hearted people might ... think there was some ingenious way to disarm or defeat an enemy without bloodshed, and might imagine that this is the true goal of the art of war. Pleasant as it sounds, it is a fallacy that must be exposed: war is such a dangerous business that the mistakes which come from kindness are the very worst ...'.

It is generally accepted, though perhaps not with complete accuracy, that the earliest modern writer on the law of war is Grotius who, in his *De Jure Belli ac Pacis*, published in 1625, stated that 'war is the state or situation of those who dispute by force of arms'[4] and for any war to be 'called just ... it is not enough that it be made between Sovereigns, but it must be undertaken by public Declaration, and so that one of the Parties declare it to the other'.[5] Even though such a declaration

---

[1] HMSO, Cmd 6964 (1946), 13; 41 Am. J. Int'l Law (1947), 172, at 186.

[2] 'laws are inoperative in war', *Pro Milone*, IV, xi.

[3] *Vom Kriege* (On War), 1833, Eng. tr. Howard and Paret, 1976, Bk. I, ch.1, ss. 2, 3, 75.

[4] Bk I, ch. I, s. II, 1; Eng. tr. (1738), 2; Carnegie tr. (1925), 33.

[5] *Ibid.*, Bk III, ch. III, s. V; 552; 633. Grotius points out that this rule was already to be found in Josephus, *Antiquities of the Jews*, 1st century, XV, 3.

may have been issued, a war would only be just,[6] that is to say lawful, 'where the Methods of Justice cease'[7] and only by war of the 'Right of Self Defence ... [for] if a Man is assaulted in such a Manner that his Life shall appear in inevitable Danger, he may not only make War upon, but may very justly destroy the Aggressor'.[8] Moreover, this right exists when the threat is not actual, but appears imminent, for 'if a Man takes Arms, and his Intentions are visibly to destroy another, the other may very lawfully prevent his Intentions'.[9] He also suggested that war in defence of property was permissible,[10] and conceded that while 'supreme Powers have not only a Right of Self-Defence, but of revenging and punishing Injuries ... [so] that they may lawfully prevent an Insult which seems to threaten them, even at some considerable Distance; not directly ... but indirectly, by punishing a Crime that is only begun',[11] nevertheless

> I can by no Means approve ... that by the Law of Nations it is permitted to take up Arms to reduce the growing Power of a Prince or State, which if too much augmented, may possibly injure us[12] ... Neither can I admit ... that even those who have given just Cause to take up Arms against them, may lawfully defend themselves ... But he who has offended another, ought first to offer him such a Satisfaction, as by the judgment of any honest Man shall be thought sufficient; and if that be refused, he may in Conscience defend himself.[13]

The views expressed by Grotius owed much to natural law concepts, but as such ideas became less philosophically significant, and states paid more attention to the Machiavellian precept 'that war is just that is necessary',[14] so the idea of measuring the legality of war by its justness disappeared, other than by appeals to morality and one's own conviction that one's cause was just. Machiavelli had himself maintained,[15] almost foretelling the view of the World Court on the use of nuclear weapons,[16] that 'when the entire safety of one's country is at stake, there should be

---

[6] For discussion of some of the issues concerning the 'justness' of a conflict, see Waltzer, *Just and Unjust Wars*.

[7] Grotius, *De Jure Belli*, Bk II, ch. I, s. II, 1: 129; the Carnegie tr. says 'where judicial settlement fails', 171.

[8] *Ibid.*, s. III; 131; 172. See, below, discussion on use of nuclear weapons, especially in light of the ICJ opinion on *Legality of the Threat or Use of Nuclear Weapons* (1996).

[9] *Ibid.*, s. V; 132; 173. For a modern discussion of 'anticipatory self-defence', see Dinstein, *War, Aggression and Self Defence*, 182–7, 190, 244.

[10] *Ibid.*, s. XIII; 139–40; 182.

[11] *Ibid.*, s. XVI; 141; 184.

[12] *Ibid.*, s. XVII; 141; 184.

[13] *Ibid.*, s. XVIII, 1, 2; 141; 185. For a recent analysis of the just-war concept, see Coates, *The Ethics of War*, 1997.

[14] *Thoughts of a Statesman*, vol. 2.

[15] *Discourses*, Bk III, ch. xi.

[16] *Legality of the Threat or Use of Nuclear Weapons* [1996] ICJ 226 '... the Court cannot conclude definitively whether the threat or use of nuclear weapons would be lawful or unlawful in an extreme case of self-defence, in which the very survival of the State would be at stake.'

no consideration of just or unjust, merciful or cruel, praiseworthy or disgraceful; on the contrary, putting aside every form of respect, that decision which will preserve her liberty must be followed completely'. This self-description of the justness of one's cause may be seen as recently as April–May 1982, during the Falklands War, both the Archbishop of Canterbury and the Cardinal Archbishop of Westminster were describing the British cause in that conflict as 'just'.[17] Even though there has been a general retreat from such descriptions as the legitimate ground for resort to war, the need for a declaration has been embodied in treaty law,[18] and this treaty still subsists even though most recent conflicts have commenced without such a declaration.

Criminalising war: Napoleon

It was not until the defeat of Napoleon that any attempt was made to declare war or those resorting to it as illegal or criminal:[19]

> after having been formally declared by the Congress of Vienna to be an international outlaw for having invaded France in violation of the Treaty of Paris of 1814,[20] Napoleon was actually deported to St. Helena. By the Convention of 11th April 1814, entered into between Austria, Prussia, Russia and Napoleon, the latter agreed to retire to Elba. After his escape and re-entry into France with an armed force, the Congress of Vienna on 13th March, 1815, issued a declaration that by having violated his agreement Napoleon had 'destroyed the sole legal title upon which his existence depended … placed himself outside the protection of the law, and manifested to the world that it can have neither peace nor truce with him'. The Powers declared that Napoleon had put himself outside 'civil and social relations, and that as Enemy and Perturbator of the World, he has incurred liability to public vengeance'. Had the Powers followed the recommendation of Field Marshal Blücher, Napoleon would have been shot on sight as one who … was an 'outlaw'.

Instead, following his surrender after Waterloo he was handed over to the British who exiled him to St. Helena, a decision made on political not legal grounds, but reflecting the view that his resort to war in breach of treaty was criminal.

---

[17] *The Times* (London), 30 Apr. 1982; 3, 8 May 1982.

[18] Hague Convention III, 1907, Schindler and Toman, *The Laws of Armed Conflicts*, 57.

[19] UNWCC, *History of the United Nations War Crimes Commission*, 242, n. 1(c); see also Glueck, 'The Nuremberg Trial and aggressive war', 59 Harvard Law Rev., (1946), 396, 399.

[20] Cp. London Charter, 1945, (Schindler and Toman, 911), Art. 6(a) 'Crimes against peace: namely, planning, preparation, initiation or waging of a war of aggression, or a war in violation of international treaties, agreements or assurances.'

Criminalising war: the Treaty of Versailles

The treatment of Napoleon served as a precedent for the decision of the Principal Allied and Associated Powers at the end of World War I when considering the treatment to be accorded to those responsible as authors of that war. The Commission set up by the Preliminary Peace Conference was of opinion that:[21]

> On the special head of the breaches of the neutrality of Luxembourg and Belgium, the gravity of these outrages upon the principle of the law of nations and upon international good faith is such that they should be made the subject of a formal condemnation by the Conference. On the whole case, both the acts which brought about the war and those which accompanied its inception, particularly the violation of Belgium and Luxembourg, it would be for the Peace Conference, in a matter so unprecedented, to adopt special measures, and even to create a special organ to deal as they deserve with the authors of such acts.

Here we have a precursor of what by the London Charter establishing the Nuremberg Tribunal in 1945 became known as the criminality of war of aggression.[22] Ultimately, the Allied and Associated Powers embodied this recommendation in Article 227 of the Treaty of Versailles, 1919:[23]

> The Allied and Associated Powers publicly arraign William II of Hohenzollern, formerly German Emperor, for a supreme offence against international morality and the sanctity of treaties. A special tribunal will be constituted to try the accused, thereby assuring him the guarantees essential to the right of defence. It will be composed of five judges, one appointed by each of the following Powers: namely, the United States of America, Great Britain, France, Italy and Japan [the Principal Allied and Associated Powers]. In its decision the tribunal will be guided by the highest motives of international policy, with a view to vindicating the solemn obligation of international undertakings and the validity of international morality. It will be its duty to fix the punishment which it considers should be imposed.

It is important to note that while the treaty does not talk here of crimes against international law, but of 'a supreme offence against international morality and the sanctity of treaties', it clearly indicates that such a war constitutes a crime. Moreover, when the German delegation protested at the inclusion of this article in the treaty, the Allied and Associated Powers formally stated[24] that the war was:

> the greatest crime against humanity and the freedom of peoples that any nation calling itself civilised, has ever consciously committed ... a crime deliberately against the life and liberties of the people of Europe ... [However,] the public arraignment

---

[21] Report, 19 Mar. 1919, 14 Am. J. Int'l Law (1920), 117.

[22] See n. 20 above.

[23] 12 B.F.S.P. 1; 13 Am. J. Int'l Law (1919), Supp.; 2 Israel, *Major Peace Treaties of Modern History 1648–1967*, 1265.

[24] UNWCC, *History of the United Nations War Crimes Commission*, 240.

under Article 227 framed against the German ex-Emperor has not a juridical character as regards its substance, but only in its form. The ex-Emperor is arraigned as a matter of high international policy, as the minimum of what is demanded for a supreme offence against international morality, the sanctity of treaties and essential rules of justice. The Allied and Associated Powers have desired that judicial forms, a judicial procedure and a regularly constituted tribunal should be set up in order to assure to the accused full rights and liberties in regard to his defence, and in order that the judgment should be of the utmost solemn character.

While the tribunal was to be judicial in character it was not instructed to apply any rules of law, but simply 'to be guided by the highest motives of international policy' in order to vindicate the validity of 'international morality'. How this would have helped to establish the illegality or criminality of war will never be known since The Netherlands government refused to hand the ex-emperor over for trial.

Criminalising war: the League of Nations

A more definite attempt to prevent war is to be found in the Covenant of the League of Nations.[25] Article 11 states that 'Any war or threat of war, whether immediately affecting any of the Members of the League or not, is hereby declared a matter of concern to the whole League, and the League shall take any action that may be deemed wise and effectual to safeguard the peace of nations.' The parties undertook to submit disputes to arbitration, judicial settlement or consideration by the League, and Article 16 of the Covenant provided that 'should any Member of the League resort to war in disregard of its covenants … it shall *ipso facto* be deemed to have committed an act of war against all Members of the League', which would then proceed to apply sanctions against the wrongdoer. While sanctions might be considered as a punishment, they are not in the nature of a criminal penalty, but merely indicate the action which would be taken by the League in response to a breach of treaty. League members soon realised that the provisions in the Covenant were not adequate in practice and that some attempt should be made to strengthen its provisions by way of criminalising the resort to aggressive war. In 1923 the League Assembly drew up a draft Treaty of Mutual Assistance[26] which solemnly proclaimed 'that aggressive war is an international crime' with the Parties undertaking that 'no one of them will be guilty of its commission'. By way of penalty, an aggressor would be required to carry:

the whole cost of any military, naval or air operations … including the reparation of all material damage caused by operations of war … up to the extreme limit of [the

---

[25] The Covenant is in fact Chapter I of the Treaty of Versailles.
[26] Ferencz, *Defining International Aggression*, vol. 1, 77, Arts 1, 10.

State's] financial capacity [and] the amount payable ... by the aggressor shall ... be a first charge on the whole of the assets and revenues of the State.[27]

Thus, the 'criminal' penalty arising was purely financial and fell to be borne by the state as such. There was no suggestion that there might be any sort of personal liability in connection with such aggression. Although 29 states expressed willingness to accept this treaty, difficulties with regard to the definition of aggression resulted in its remaining a mere draft.

Since the United States did not belong to the League, an American committee proposed in 1924 a Draft Treaty of Disarmament and Security which would not depend on League Council action for its enforcement, and decisions as to whether the treaty had been breached or not would be made by the Permanent Court of International Justice, for although the United States had not become a party to the Court's statute the bench included an American lawyer. This draft[28] reproduced the language of the 1923 draft treaty as to the criminality of aggressive war and provided that 'a State engaging in war for other than purposes of defence commits the international crime' of aggressive war. As with its predecessor, sanctions were directed against the offending state, whereby 'all commercial, trade, financial and property interests of the aggressor shall cease to be entitled, either in the territory of the other signatories or on the high seas, to any privileges, rights or immunities accorded by international law, national law or treaty'. This proposal, though considered by the League Assembly, too remained a draft and it was followed by the equally abortive Geneva Protocol for the Pacific Settlement of International Disputes adopted by the League Assembly in 1924.[29] According to its preamble 'a war of aggression constitutes a violation of [the] solidarity [of the members of the international community] and an international crime ... and [with a view to] ensuring the repression of international crimes'; the parties forswore war save by way of 'resistance to acts of aggression or when acting in agreement with the Council or the Assembly of the League or Nations in accordance with provisions .of the Covenant and of the present Protocol'. As before, no provision was made for anything in the way of personal criminal liability. The Committee established by the League to examine the draft was of opinion,[30] foretelling Article 51 of the Charter of the United Nations,[31] that:

---

[27] After the Gulf War, 1991, the Security Council adopted Resolution 687 (30 I.L.M., 847) 'reaffirm[ing] that Iraq is liable under international law for any direct loss, damage ... or injury to foreign Governments, nationals and corporations as a result of Iraq's unlawful invasion and occupation of Kuwait', and created a fund to be administered by an International Commission for this purpose.

[28] Ferencz, *International Aggression*, 124.

[29] *Ibid.*, 132.

[30] *Ibid.*, 140, 141.

[31] Art. 51: 'Nothing in the present Charter shall impair the inherent right of individual or collective self-defence if an armed attack occurs against a Member of the United Nations, until the Security Council has taken the measures necessary to maintain international peace and security.'

the prohibition affects only aggressive war. It does not, of course, extend to defensive war. The right of legitimate self-defence continues, as it must, to be respected. The State attacked retains complete liberty to resist by all means in its power any act of aggression of which it may be the victim. Without waiting for the assistance which it is entitled to receive from the international community, it may and should at once defend itself with its own force. Its interest are identified with the general interest.

Nevertheless, the Protocol never came into force.

In 1927 the League Assembly adopted a declaration concerning wars of aggression, 'being convinced that a war of aggression can never serve as a means of settling international disputes, and is, in consequence, an international crime … declares that all wars of aggression are, and shall always be, prohibited'. Since this was only a declaratory resolution of the Assembly it lacked even the economic sanctions that were to be found in other proposals.

Early in 1928 the Sixth International Conference of American States adopted a resolution[32] that 'war of aggression constitutes an international crime against the human species … and all aggression is considered illicit and as such declared prohibited', but the resolution contained no sanctions provisions and as a resolution lacked any effective obligatory force.

The Pact of Paris

Since the United States was not a member of the League and had become, by virtue of its being among the victors in 1918, a power to be considered, it is important to note that in 1927 resolutions were introduced into the Senate by Senators Capper and Borah calling for the 'outlawry' of war condemning it as 'a public crime under the law of nations'. In the meantime, Secretary of State Kellogg was negotiating with Foreign Minister Briand of France, and from these negotiations there developed the Pact of Paris, also known as the Kellogg–Briand Pact, or the General Treaty for the Renunciation of War, 1928.[33] By this instrument the parties 'condemn recourse to war for the solution of international controversies, and renounce it as an instrument of national policy in their relations with one another' and commit themselves never to seek to settle their disputes other than by peaceful means. The Pact makes no reference to possible sanctions, but in its preamble it states that 'any signatory which shall hereafter seek to promote its national interests by resort to war should be denied the benefits furnished by this Treaty'.[34]

To some extent it may be said that the first attempt to give substance to the 'punitive' provision in the Pact of Paris is to be found in the Stimson Doctrine of

[32] Royal Institute of Int'l Affairs, *Documents on International Affairs 1928* (1929), 194.
[33] Ferencz, *International Aggression*, 190.
[34] For some of the views concerning the effect of the Pact, see Green, 'Cicero and Clausewitz or Quincy Wright: The Interplay of Law and War', ch. II of *Essays*, 1999.

7

non-recognition propounded by the United States Secretary of State in response to the Japanese attack on China:[35] 'The American Government ... does not intend to recognise any situation, treaty, or agreement which may be brought about by means contrary to the covenants and obligations of the Pact of Paris ...' This was followed by a League Assembly resolution[36] stating that it is 'incumbent upon the members of the League of Nations not to recognise any situation, treaty, or agreement brought about by means contrary to the Covenant of the League of Nations or the Pact of Paris'. An attempt to provide further and perhaps more effective sanctions was taken by the International Law Association, a non-governmental but influential body of international lawyers, in 1934 when it adopted the Budapest Articles of Interpretation.[37] After stating that a party cannot release itself from the Pact by denunciation or non-observance, the Articles provided that in the event of a resort to armed force or war by one party against another, third States could, without breaking any rule of international law, deny the aggressor any of the rights normally attaching to a belligerent in its relations with neutrals, nor was a neutral obliged to observe towards such an aggressor any of the duties of a neutral. At the same time, third States could legally supply the victim with any assistance it might require, including armed forces. Finally, 'a violating State is liable to pay compensation for all damage caused by a violation of the Pact to any signatory State or its nationals'. However, the Budapest Articles did not make any reference to criminality, although they are often construed as having done so.

In addition to these multilateral efforts to control aggression and condemn it as a crime, there was a series of bilateral treaties seeking to do the same,[38] and it was the breach of many of these to which Germany was a party that, together with the Pact of Paris, formed the basis for the charge of preparing or waging aggressive war lodged against the major war criminals of the European Axis at Nuremberg.[39]

The United Nations Charter

Despite the fact that the inter-war period showed that the system created by the League Covenant as supplemented by the various resolutions and treaties concerning aggression and the criminality of aggressive war had failed, no attempt was made to improve the situation in the Charter of the United Nations, even though the opening statement in the preamble expresses the determination of 'the peoples of the United Nations ... to save succeeding generations from the scourge of war, which twice in our lifetime has brought untold sorrow to mankind'. The

---

[35] Hackworth, 1 *Digest of International Law*, 334.
[36] *Ibid.*, 335.
[37] Report of Thirty-eighth Conference, 66; 29 Am. J. Int'l Law (1935) 92; Harvard Research, Draft Convention on Aggression, 33 Am. J. Int'l Law (1939), Supp., 825, n. 1.
[38] *Ibid.*, 867–71.
[39] Indictment, ch. III, Charges V–XXVI.

underlying principle of the Covenant is reproduced in Article 1 of the Charter wherein the first purpose of the United Nations is stated to be:

> to maintain international peace and security, and to that end: to take effective col-
> lective measures for the prevention and removal of threats to the peace, and for the
> suppression of acts of aggression or other breaches of the peace, and to bring about
> by peaceful means, and in conformity with the principles of justice and international
> law, adjustment or settlement of international disputes or situations which might
> lead to a breach of the peace.

To that end, the members are obligated by Article 2(4) to 'refrain in their international relations from the threat or use of force against the territorial integrity or
political independence of any state'. It would thus appear that a resort to force
which does not involve such a threat might not infringe the commitment.[40] Moreover, by Article 51 the Charter preserves the:

> inherent right of individual or collective self-defence if an armed attack occurs
> against a Member of the United Nations, until the Security Council has taken the
> measures necessary to maintain international peace and security. Measures taken in
> the exercise of this right of self-defence[41] shall be immediately reported to the Secu-
> rity Council and shall not in any way affect the authority and responsibility of the
> Security Council ... to take at any time such action as it deems necessary to main-
> tain or restore international peace and security.[42]

In accordance with Chapter VII of the Charter if there should be any threat to the
peace or act of aggression the Security Council is given the power, which is subject to the exercise of the veto by any one of the five permanent members,[43] 'to
make recommendations or decide what measures shall be taken ... to maintain or
restore international peace and security', and by Articles 41 and 42 these measures
may be of an economic or military character. However, as with the Covenant and
all other agreements seeking to control aggression, there is no suggestion that any
individual responsible for resorting to aggression shall be subject to criminal proceedings. However, in view of the atrocities committed during the conflicts consequent upon the break-up of the former Yugoslavia and during the civil war in

---

[40] See, e.g., Green, 'Rescue at Entebbe: legal aspects', 6 Israel Y.B.H.R. (1976), 312;
on the rescue of nationals, generally, see Ronzitti, *Rescue of Nationals Abroad*, 1985, and
Dinstein, *op.cit.*, 226–30.

[41] There is much debate whether the 'inherent right' is available against a threatened
attack or only after an attack has been launched, and in its decision on *Military and Paramilitary Activities in and against Nicaragua* [1986] I.C.J. 14, the World Court expressly
declined to comment on 'the issue of the lawfulness of a response to the imminent threat
of armed attack since [this] has not been raised', at 103. See also comments on 'anticipatory' and 'interceptive' self-defence, in Dinstein, *War, Aggression and Self-Defence*,
Green, 'Armed conflict, war and self-defence', in *Essays*, 1999, ch. III.

[42] For the actions of the Security Council in relation to Iraq's attack upon Kuwait in
1990, see Resolutions 660–78, 686–712, 29 and 30 I.L.M., resp.; see also Green, 'The Gulf
"War", the UN and the law of armed conflict', 28 *Archiv des Völkerrechts* (1991), 369.

[43] Charter, Art. 27(3).

Rwanda, the Security Council decided that action was necessary under Chapter VII and authorised the despatch of military forces as well as the establishment of *ad hoc* war crimes tribunals. In 1999, in the light of atrocities committed by the Yugoslav authorities against dissidents in Kosovo province, and anticipating a veto by Russia and/or China, NATO, without any resort to the Security Council, made a series of demands upon Yugoslavia. When these were rejected, NATO, in the name of humanity, instituted a series of aerial-bombing raids against Serbia. It announced its intention to try the Yugoslav leaders responsible with crimes against humanity.

While the Charter restricts the right to resort to measures of a warlike character to those required by self-defence, its provisions only relate to the *jus ad bellum*. Once a conflict has begun, the limitations of Article 51 become irrelevant. This means there is no obligation upon a party resorting to war in self-defence to limit his activities to those essential to his self-defence. Thus, if an aggressor has invaded his territory and been expelled, it does not mean that the victim of the aggression has to cease his operations once his own territory has been liberated. He may continue to take advantage of the *jus in bello*, including the principle of proportionality, until he is satisfied that the aggressor is defeated and no longer constitutes a threat. However, when authorising action in 1991 against Iraq following its invasion of Kuwait, the Council's decision only related to the 'liberation' of Kuwait and not any further action against Iraq proper once this had been achieved.

The London/Nuremberg Charter

It is clear, therefore, that the Charter does not *per se* declare war to be illegal or criminal, but merely a breach of treaty subject to the sanctions embodied in that treaty. However, at the time the Charter was signed the parties thereto were aware of the fact that a tribunal was about to be established which would adjudicate on the personal criminality of politicians alleged to have been responsible for waging or planning to wage a war of aggression. It may be assumed, therefore, that at least for some of them there would have been a connection between the wording in the Charter and that in the document which eventually became known as the London Agreement for the Prosecution and Punishment of the Major War Criminals of the European Axis,[44] especially as drafts of that instrument were already under discussion at San Francisco at the same time as the Charter of the United Nations was being drawn up.[45]

The Constitution of the International Military Tribunal appended to the London Agreement was endowed[46] with

[44] Ferencz, *International Aggression*, 406; Schindler and Toman, *op.cit.*, 911.
[45] *Ibid.*, 362 *et seq.*
[46] Art. 6.

the power to try and punish persons who, acting in the interests of the European Axis countries, whether as individuals or as members of organisations, committed [in addition to war crimes and crimes against humanity] CRIMES AGAINST PEACE: namely, planning, preparation, initiation or waging of a war of aggression, or a war in violation of international treaties, agreements or assurances, or participation in a common plan or conspiracy for the accomplishment of any of the foregoing ... [and] leaders, organisers, instigators and accomplices participating in the formulation or execution of a common plan or conspiracy to commit any of the foregoing crimes are responsible for all acts performed by any persons in execution of such plans.

Moreover,[47] departing completely from former customary international law which recognised the immunity from suit of a head of state or diplomatic representative anywhere but in accordance with the terms of his own national law, 'the official position of defendants, whether as Heads of State or responsible officials in Government Departments, shall not be considered as freeing them from responsibility or mitigating punishment'. In view of this provision, the Tribunal had no option but to find that 'a war in violation of international agreements or assurances' amounted to a crime carrying personal liability in respect of those deciding upon such warlike activities, regardless of the fact that any such treaty omitted to declare a war in breach thereof criminal, or to postulate any punishment if it did so declare.

The Nuremberg Judgment

In its Judgment, the Tribunal stated that

the charges that the defendants planned and waged aggressive wars are charges of the utmost gravity. War is essentially an evil thing. Its consequences are not confined to the belligerent states alone, but affect the whole world. To initiate a war of aggression, therefore, is not only an international crime; it is the supreme international crime differing only from other war crimes in that it contains within itself the accumulated evil of the whole.[48]

The Court then traced the historic development of Nazi policy leading to the annexation of Austria and Czechoslovakia, and then the various acts of aggression from the invasion of Poland through to the attack on the Soviet Union and the declaration of war against the United States. It then referred briefly to the various treaties that had been broken including the Kellogg Pact and drafts which, as has been pointed out, never came into effect, but which were used as indicative of the general attitude toward the criminality of aggressive war. As to the Kellogg Pact itself, the Tribunal stated[49] that:

[47] Art. 7.

[48] HMSO, Cmd 6964 (1946), 13; 41 Am. J. Int'l L. (1947), 186; Ferencz, *International Aggression*, 452.

[49] *Ibid.*, 39–41; 218–20; 486–8.

11

the question is what was the legal effect of this Pact? The nations who signed the Pact or adhered to it unconditionally condemn recourse to war for the future as an instrument of policy, and expressly renounce it. After the signing of the Pact, any nation resorting to war as an instrument of national policy breaks the Pact. In the opinion of the Tribunal, the solemn renunciation of war as an instrument of national policy necessarily involves the proposition that such a war is illegal in international law; and that those who plan and wage such a war, with its inevitable and terrible consequences, are committing a crime in so doing. War for the solution of international controversies undertaken as an instrument of international policy certainly includes a war of aggression, and such a war is therefore outlawed by the Pact … But it is argued that the Pact does not expressly enact that such wars are crimes, or set up courts to try those who make such wars.

The Court then pointed out that Hague Convention IV[50] prohibiting certain means and methods of warfare does not declare any act to be criminal, although tribunals have exercised criminal jurisdiction over those breaching such prohibitions.[51] Moreover, many such prohibitions had been enforced long before the adoption of the Convention in 1907 and, it is submitted, that the Court perhaps paid insufficient attention to the fact that state practice had, almost since feudal times,[52] regarded such acts as criminal. The judgment continued:

in the opinion of the Tribunal, those who wage aggressive wars are doing that which is equally illegal, and of much greater moment than a breach of one of the rules of the Hague Convention. In interpreting the words of the Pact, it must be remembered that international law is not the product of an international legislature, that such international agreements as the Pact of Paris have to deal with general principles of law, and not with administrative matters of procedure. The law of war is to be found not only in treaties, but in the customs and practices of states which gradually obtained universal recognition, and from the general principles of justice[53] applied by jurists and practised by military courts. This law is not static, but by continual adaptation follows the needs of a changing world. Indeed, in many cases treaties do no more than express and define for more accurate reference the principles of law already existing. The view which the Tribunal takes of the true interpretation of the Pact is supported by the history which preceded it.

Much of that history indicates that states, while prepared to pay lip-service to the condemnation of war as criminal, were not prepared to follow their verbal condemnation by legal enactment. For the Tribunal to parade in its support a series of resolutions, draft treaties or municipal decisions punishing actual breaches of the law of war lends little support to the view that there was substantial evidence to support the Tribunal's approach to the Pact. Nor does one derive much comfort from the assertion that:

---

[50] Schindler and Toman, *The Laws*, 63.

[51] See, e.g., UNWCC, *Law Reports of Trials of War Criminals*, vols I–XV.

[52] See, e.g., Keen, *The Laws of War in the Late Middle Ages*, chs III, IV; Contamine, *War in the Middle Ages,* 284–92.

[53] See Martens clause in Preamble to Hague Convention IV (Schindler and Toman, *op.cit.*, 70).

all these expressions of opinion, and others that could be cited, so solemnly made, reinforce the construction which the Tribunal placed upon the Pact of Paris, that resort to a war of aggression is not merely illegal, but is criminal. The prohibition of aggressive war demanded by the conscience of the world, finds its expression in the series of pacts and treaties to which the Tribunal has just referred.

It is interesting to recall that, despite its condemnation of the crime against peace as the supreme crime, the Tribunal failed to sentence to death any of the accused found guilty of this crime alone, and not of the 'lesser' war crimes or crimes against humanity.

It may be argued that the entire commentary by the Tribunal as to the nature of the Pact of Paris as well as the extensive interpretation applied thereto were really *obiter dicta* and unnecessary to the judgment. The Pact of Paris is, in law, a treaty like any other treaty, and the Tribunal's Charter expressly stated that war in breach of treaty was a crime and to be treated as such by the Tribunal. However, subsequent to the Judgment there have been constant statements by commentators, both political and legal, to the effect that the Tribunal's comments regarding the Pact are expressive of good law. Whether this is so is now irrelevant, for there can be no doubt that the community of nations accepts the view that the Tribunal in its Judgment correctly defined wars of aggression and in breach of the Pact of Paris as criminal acts carrying personal liability. Evidence of this may be seen in the literal adoption of the words of the Nuremberg Judgment in this regard by the International Military Tribunal for the Far East,[54] accompanied by the comment that 'with the foregoing opinion of the Nuremberg Tribunal and the reasoning by which they are reached the Tribunal is in complete accord'.

The United Nations and the concept of aggression

In 1946, the General Assembly at its first session adopted a resolution[55] affirming 'the principles of international law recognised by the Charter of the Nuremberg Tribunal and the judgment of the Tribunal'. This was followed by a further resolution[56] instructing the International Law Commission to 'formulate' these principles, which it duly did at its second session in 1950,[57] reaffirming that crimes against peace are 'punishable as crimes under international law … [That] any person who commits an act which constitutes a crime under international law is responsible therefor and liable to punishment', regardless of whether any such punishment is postulated by international law and denying to an accused any defence based on his status as a head of state. In a later Report on State Responsibility the International Law Commission stated that 'an international crime may

[54] Ferencz, *International Aggression*, 545–6.
[55] Gen. Ass. Res. 95(I), Schindler and Toman, *The Laws*, 921.
[56] Gen. Ass. Res. 177(II). 2, Y.B.I.L.C. (1950), 374; Schindler and Toman, *The Laws*, 923.
[57] 2, Y.B.I.L.C. (1950), 374; Schindler and Toman, *The Laws*, 923.

result ... from a serious breach of an international obligation – finally amended to add here the words "of essential importance"[58] – for the maintenance of international peace and security, such as that prohibiting aggression', but it contained no provision concerning sanctions, criminal punishment or personal liability. The Commission has now adopted a Draft Code of Crimes against the Peace and Security of Mankind[59] and this expressly provides that aggression, threats of aggression and intervention constitute crimes carrying personal liability by those responsible, whether as superiors or subordinates. The most important concrete development since Nuremberg is the General Assembly Resolution defining aggression.[60] This definition listed a series of acts which would amount to aggression, but did not include any reference to war in breach of treaty, although Article 4 stated that 'the acts enumerated are not exhaustive and the Security Council may determine that other acts constitute aggression under the provisions of the Charter'. Under Article 5 'a war of aggression is a crime against international peace. Aggression gives rise to international responsibility'. However, if what would normally be regarded as aggression under the resolution is committed in the name of 'self-determination, freedom and independence', Article 7 removes the slur of criminality.

The General Assembly definition, like its precursors, is silent as to the means of punishing the international crime of aggression, the reason being that, in connection with the Code of Offences against the Peace and Security of Mankind it was hoped that these issues would be dealt with in a statute for an International Criminal Court. Although the draft postulates the need for a fair trial it does not provide for the establishment of an international criminal tribunal. Presumably, it was intended that trial would be by national tribunals. In 1998, however, a treaty constituting the Statute for an International Criminal Court was adopted,[61] with jurisdiction over genocide, crimes against humanity, war crimes and aggression, without providing any definition of the latter, not even mentioning the General Assembly's Resolution. Jurisdiction would arise if the Prosecutor referred the matter to the Court on his own initiative or such matter had been referred to him by the Security Council. The Court is 'complementary' to national tribunals and so does not possess jurisdiction if a national tribunal has already been or is likely to become seised of the case, unless the tribunal in question is 'unable or unwilling genuinely to prosecute'.[62] Despite the absence of any definition of aggression, it remains clear that criminality for this offence rests with senior political or military authorities. It cannot extend to the ordinary member of the armed forces who participate in a war of aggression since they merely carry out the order to fight

---

[58] 2, Y.B.I.L.C., (1979), 91, Art. 19(3)(a); Art. 19(a), 37 I. L. M. 1998, 440, 447.
[59] 11 Sept. 1991, 30 I.L.M., 1584.
[60] Res. 3314 (XXIX) 1974, Ferencz, *International Aggression*, vol. II, 565.
[61] A/CONF. 183/9, 17 July 1998.
[62] Unfortunately, the United States has declared its determined opposition to become a party to the treaty.

promulgated by their political or military masters to wage war in the name of their country, a decision to which they have made no contribution.

The law of war

In view of the clearly established criminality of war it might be queried whether there is any scope for a law of war, for it seems inconsistent to assert that a criminal procedure may be conducted in accordance with a legal regime. In fact the ban on resort to war only relates to the decision to wage such a war, the *jus ad bellum*. The purpose of what is known as the law of war – *jus in bello* – is to reduce the horrors inherent therein to the greatest extent possible in view of the political purpose for which war is fought, namely to achieve one's policies by victory over one's enemy.

From earliest times it was recognised that war should not be a campaign directed at the ultimate extermination of the enemy. Thus, writing about the fourth century BC, Sun Tzu in *The Art of War*[63] stated:

> generally in war the best policy is to take a state intact; to ruin it is inferior to this. Do not put a premium on killing. To capture the enemy's army is better than to destroy it; to take intact a battalion, a company or a five-man squad is better than to destroy them. For to win one hundred victories in one hundred battles is not the acme of skill. To subdue the enemy without fighting is the acme of skill.

In biblical times, too, unless the war was undertaken at the express command of God, some measure of mercy was demanded from the Israelites.[64] During feudal times military codes were frequently published ordaining punishment for members of one's own force who committed what would today be described as crimes against humanity, while the orders of knighthood developed their own codes of chivalry.[65]

These may have been the views in early times, but Tolstoy writing in 1862 probably was correct in describing the attitude of many fighting men when he had Prince Andrew on the eve of the Battle of Borodino, 1812, comment 'They preach at us about the laws of warfare, chivalry, flags of truce, humanity to the wounded and what not ... But this is only throwing dust in each other's eyes ... [W]e are to listen to a rhodomontade about the rules of war and generosity towards our enemy! ... There are lies enough in the world as it is. War should be taken as a hard fact; not as a game; otherwise it becomes a mere pastime for the idle and frivolous ...'[66]

---

[63] Eng. tr. Griffith, 1963, (III), 'Offensive strategy', 77.

[64] See, e.g., Roberts, 'The Judaic sources of and views on the laws of War', 37 Naval Law Rev. (1988) 221; Green, 'The Judaic contribution to human rights', 28 Can. Y.B. Int'l Law (1990).

[65] See, e.g., works by Keen, Contamine, and ch. 2 below.

[66] *War and Peace*, Garnett tr., 1904, vol. III, ch. VII.

The law *in nascendi*

Coming to more recent times, only a year after Tolstoy wrote the above, we find that Lieber, often regarded as the first to promulgate an acceptable modern code,[67] wrote[68]

> War … by no means absolves us from all obligations toward the enemy, on various grounds. They result in part from the object of war, in part from the fact that the belligerents are human beings, that the declaration of war is, among civilised nations, always made upon the tacit acknowledgement of certain usages and obligations, and partly because wars take place between masses who fight for others, or not for themselves only.

A somewhat similar view is expressed in the Final Protocol of the Brussels Conference of 1874 which drew up a Project of an International Declaration concerning the Laws and Customs of War:[69]

> It had been unanimously declared [at St. Petersburg in 1868] that the progress of civilisation should have the effect of alleviating, as far as possible, the calamities of war; and that the only legitimate object which States should have in view during the war is to weaken the enemy without inflicting upon him unnecessary suffering … [The states now gathered possess] the conviction … that a further step may be taken by revising the laws and general usages of war, whether with the object of defining them with greater precision, or with the view of laying down, by a common agreement, certain limits which will restrain, as far as possible, the severities of war. War being thus regulated would involve less suffering, would be less liable to those aggravations produced by uncertainty, unforeseen events, and the passions excited by the struggle; it would tend more surely to that which should be its final object, *viz.*, the re-establishment of good relations, and a more solid and lasting peace between the belligerent States.

In 1880 the Institute of International Law adopted its *Oxford Manual of the Laws of War on Land*:[70]

> suitable as the basis for national legislation in each State, and in accord with both the progress of juridical science and the needs of civilised nations … By so doing, [the Institute] believes it is rendering a service to military men themselves. In fact so long as the demands of opinion remain indeterminate, belligerents are exposed to painful uncertainty and to endless accusations. A positive set of rules, on the contrary, if they are judicious, serves the interests of belligerents and is far from hindering them, since by preventing the unchaining of passion and savage instincts – which battle always awakens, as much as it awakens courage and manly virtues – it strengthens the discipline which is the strength of armies; it also ennobles their patriotic mission

---

[67] Instructions for the Government of Armies of the US in the Field, General Orders No. 100, 1863, Schindler and Toman, *The Laws*, 3.

[68] *Political Ethics*, vol. 2 (1839), 657.

[69] Schindler and Toman, *The Laws*, 25

[70] *Ibid.*, 35.

in the eyes of the soldiers by keeping them within the limits of respect due to the rights of humanity. But in order to attain this end it is not sufficient for sovereigns to promulgate new laws. It is essential, too, that they make these laws known among all people, so that when a war is declared, the men called upon to take up arms to defend the causes of the belligerent States, may be thoroughly impregnated with the special rights and duties attached to the execution of such a command.

Humanitarian law

When the powers met at The Hague, first in 1899 and then in 1907, to write down what could be agreed upon as the *jus in bello*, that is to say the laws and customs of war, they gave expression to these same high ideals in the preamble to what is now Hague Convention IV.[71] The preamble refers to their

> desire to serve [even in war] the interests of humanity and the ever increasing requirements of civilisation. Thinking it important, with this object, to revise the laws and general customs of war, either with the view of defining them more precisely, or of laying down certain limits for the purpose of modifying their severity as far as possible ... [T]hese provisions, the wording of which has been inspired by the desire to diminish the evils of war, as far as military requirements permit,[72] are intended to serve as a general rule of conduct for the belligerents in their mutual relations and in their relations with the inhabitants [of enemy territory]. It has not, however, been found possible at present to concert regulations covering all the circumstances which arise in practice ... Until a more complete code of the laws of war has been issued, the High Contracting Parties deem it expedient to declare[73] that, in cases not included in the Regulations adopted by them, the inhabitants and the belligerents remain under the protection and the rule of the principles of the law of nations, as they result from the usages established among civilised peoples, from the laws of humanity, and the dictates of the public conscience.

---

[71] *Ibid.*, 67.

[72] It should be noted that the rules embodied in this and similar documents have been drafted in the light of military needs and are adapted thereto. This means that, normally speaking, they cannot be evaded by recourse to alleged military necessity or *raison de guerre*. Nevertheless, not all military commanders were willing to accept these restrictions. Thus, Admiral Lord Fisher referring to the Convention, in words similar to those used by Tolstoy, fulminated 'The humanizing of War! You might as well talk of the humanizing of Hell. When a silly ass got up at the Hague and talked about the amenities of civilized warfare and putting your prisoners' feet in hot water and giving them gruel, my reply, I regret to say, was considered totally unfit for publication. As if war could be civilized. If I'm in command when war breaks out I shall issue my order – "The essence of war is violence. Moderation in war is imbecility. Hit first, hit hard, and hit everywhere."' Bacon, *Lord Fisher*, 1929, vol. 1, 120–1.

[73] This declaration – and the sentiments expressed therein even if not in identical language – is known as the Martens Clause, after the Russian delegate to the 1899 Conference, where he propounded it.

The application of these latter principles is declared by the Geneva Conventions of 1949[74] to remain effective in any conflict, even though a party has denounced the Conventions. Finally, the same reservation regarding 'the protection and authority of the principles of international law derived from established custom, from the principles of humanity and from the dictates of public conscience' appears in Article 1 of Protocol I, 1977.[75]

It is clear that the principles of humanitarian law are to apply in any conflict, and regulate the conduct of the man in the field. He is not concerned with the legality of the war in which he is engaged,[76] nor does it matter whether the Security Council or any other body has declared that war to be criminal. While it is normally considered that no man shall benefit from his crime, it should be borne in mind that 'the maxim *ex injuria jus non oritur* often yields to the rival principle, *ex factis jus oritur*',[77] so that even those responsible for waging an aggressive war, as well as those who in their conduct of hostilities commit breaches of the law of war are still protected by the *jus in bello,* for:

> it is not only the abandonment of the humanitarian rules in the strict sense of the word [those relating to the treatment of persons *hors de combat*] which must necessarily deprive the conduct of hostilities of essential restraints. Most rules of warfare are, in a sense, of a humanitarian character inasmuch as their object is to safeguard, within the limits of the stern exigencies of war, human life and some other fundamental human rights and to make possible a measure of intercourse between enemies ... [Thus, t]he belligerent occupant, even if he is the aggressor, is entitled to exact from the civilian population the obedience ... due to him under international law. To say that the population is at liberty to differentiate between the 'lawful' and 'unlawful' occupant in the matter of obedience owed to him, is, in effect, to free the occupant of the obligation to treat the population, in such circumstances, in accordance with international law. He cannot be expected to treat as non-combatants inhabitants who claim the right to commit against him direct or indirect acts of hostility and who are not organised in a manner entitling them according to international law to be treated as lawful combatants[78] ... It is pertinent to refer to an extreme example of the consequence of the view that the guilty belligerent cannot rely on the laws of war. That view, when pushed to its rigid logical consequences, leads to the conclusion that the typical manifestation of belligerent action in war, namely the killing of lawful combatants, is a criminal act of murder ... Its corollary would seem to be that members of armed forces of the belligerent waging an unlawful war would be liable for murder if captured.[79]

[74] I (Wounded and Sick); II (Wounded, Sick and Shipwrecked); III (Prisoners of War); IV (Civilians), Schindler and Toman, *The Laws*, 373 *et seq.*, Arts 63, 64, 142, 158, resp.

[75] Protocol I Additional to the Geneva Conventions relating to the Protection of Victims of International Armed Conflict, Schindler and Toman, *The Laws*, 621. Its continued validity has been most recently confirmed in the World Court's *Nuclear* opinion.

[76] See, e.g., *Levy* v. *Parker* (1973) 1 *Military Law Reporter* 2130.

[77] Lauterpacht, 'Rules of warfare in an unlawful war', in Lipsky (ed.), *Law and Politics in the World Community*, 89, 92.

[78] See ch. 6 below.

[79] Lauterpacht, 'Rules of Warfare', 93–4, 96.

This is clearly contrary to the provisions of the Geneva Convention of 1949 on the Treatment of Prisoners of War,[80] Article 1 of which obligates the parties 'to respect and to ensure respect for the present Convention in all circumstances', while the preamble to Protocol I asserts that the 1949 Conventions and the Protocol are to 'be fully applied in all circumstances … without any adverse distinction based on the nature or origin of the armed conflict or on the causes espoused by or attributed to the Parties to the conflict'. The various decisions of the *ad hoc* tribunals for the former Yugoslavia and Rwanda amply illustrate this fact.[81]

[80] Schindler and Toman, *The Laws*, 423 – a similar provision is to be found in each of the three remaining 1949 Conventions.
[81] See chs 18, 19 below.

2

The history and sources of the law of armed conflict[1]

The position in antiquity

As pointed out in chapter 1, it has been recognised since earliest times that some restraints should be observed during armed conflict. Already in the Old Testament there are instances of limitations ordained by God. Thus we read in Deuteronomy,[2] for example, that when attacking heathen tribes among the inhabitants of Canaan the Israelites were enjoined that while they might eat the fruit from captured orchards, they were not to destroy the actual trees themselves, and Maimonides commenting upon this bluntly stated that the destruction of fruit trees for the mere purpose of afflicting the civilian population was forbidden.[3] Similarly, in the Book of Kings we are told[4] that when Elisha was asked by the king whether he should slay his prisoners, the prophet replied: 'Thou shalt not smite them: wouldest thou smite those whom thou hast taken captive with thy sword and with thy bow? Set bread and water before them, that they may eat and drink and go to their master. And he prepared great provision for them: and when they had eaten and drunk, he sent them away and they went to their master.' Moreover, the Israelites were enjoined:[5]

---

[1] For a general survey, see Green, 'The law of war in historical perspective', in Schmitt, *The Law of Military Operations*, 1998, 39–78.

[2] Deuteronomy, XX, 19–20.

[3] Roberts, 'Judaic sources of and views on the laws of war', 37 Naval Law Rev. (1988), 21, 231.

[4] Kings, VI, 22–3. This should be compared with the action of the Emperor Franz Joseph, Colonel in Chief of the First King's Dragoon Guards, who in 1914 sent a letter to the regiment to the effect that 'the Emperor wished the regiment to know that he was most distressed that his regiment and his country should be in a state of war, and went on to explain that he had given orders to all his troops that should any officer or man of the KDG be so unfortunate as to be taken prisoner, he was to be regarded as a personal guest for the duration of hostilities', letter by Major T. J. D. Holmes to *The Times* (London) 24 Jul. 1984.

[5] Deuteronomy, XX, 10–14.

when thou comest nigh unto a city to fight against it, then proclaim peace unto it. And ... if it make thee answer of peace, and open unto thee, then ... all the people that is found therein shall be tributaries unto thee. And if it will make no peace with thee, but will make war against thee, then shalt thou besiege it: And when the Lord thy God hath delivered it into thine hands, thou shalt smite every male thereof with the edge of the sword: But the women, and the little ones, and the cattle, and all that is in the city, even all the spoil thereof, shalt thou take unto thyself; and thou shalt eat the spoil of thine enemies.

Sun Tzu maintained[6] that in war one should attack the enemy armies, and 'the worst policy is to attack cities. Attack cities only when there is no alternative'. In ancient India the sacred writings sought to introduce some measure of humanitarianism. The Mahabharata[7] states that 'a King should never do such an injury to his foe as would rankle the latter's heart', and went on to ordain that a sleeping enemy should not be attacked, while 'with death our enmity has terminated',[8] thus rejecting desecration of the corpse. Moreover, it prohibited the killing of those suffering from any natural, physical or mental incapacity, and 'he is no son of the Vrishni race who slayeth a woman, a boy or an old man'.[9] The Code of Manu was promulgated around the same era and provides[10] that 'when the king fights his foes in battle, let him not strike with weapons concealed, nor with barbed, poisoned, or the points of which are blazed with fire ... These [latter] are the weapons of the wicked'. In ancient India it was considered that war should be conducted on a basis of equality and proportionality prevailing between the contestants, 'a car-warrior should fight a car-warrior. One on horse should fight one on horse. Elephant riders must fight with elephant riders, as one on foot fights a foot soldier'.[11]

According to Homer[12] the ancient Greeks considered the use of poison on weapons to be anathema to the gods, and among the city states

temples and priests and embassies were considered inviolable ... Mercy ... was shown to helpless captives. Prisoners were ransomed and exchanged. Safe-conducts were granted and respected. Truces and armistices were established and, for the most part, faithfully observed ... Burial of dead was permitted; and graves were unmolested. It was considered wrong and impious to cut off or poison the enemy's water supply, or to make use of poisoned weapons. Treacherous stratagems of every description were condemned as being contrary to civilised warfare.[13]

[6] *The Art of War*, c. 4th century BC, III, 'Offensive strategy', 78.

[7] Epic Sanskrit poem based on Hindu ideals, probably composed between 200 BC and 200 AD.

[8] Cited Armour, 'Customs of warfare in ancient India', 7, 71, 81, 77.

[9] *Ibid.*, 76.

[10] Bühler, *The Laws of Manu*, 230, Tit. VII, 90.

[11] Armour, 'Customs of warfare', n. 7, 74. In more recent times, it has been suggested that if a sophisticated force is engaged with one not so advanced, the former should only use weapons available to the latter.

[12] *The Odyssey*, Bk I, lines 260–3 ed. Lattimore (1965), 34.

[13] Phillipson, *The International Law and Custom of Ancient Greece and Rome*, vol. 2, 21–3.

With the Romans the practices in war:

> varied according as their wars were commenced to exact vengeance for gross viola-
> tions of international law, or for deliberate acts of treachery. Their warlike usages
> varied also according as their adversaries were regular enemies ... or uncivilised
> barbarians and bands of pirates and marauders ... [T]he belligerent operations of
> Rome, from the point of view of introducing various mitigations in the field, and
> adopting a milder policy after victory, are distinctly of a progressive character. They
> were more regular and disciplined than those of any other ancient nation. They did
> not as a rule degenerate into indiscriminate slaughter and unrestrained devastation
> ... The sanctions of *ius sacrum*, apart from those of positive law, also operated in the
> law of war ... The *ius belli* imposed numerous restrictions on barbarism, and con-
> demned all acts of treachery ... [According to Livy,] there were laws of war as well
> as peace, and the Romans had learnt to put them into practice not less justly than
> bravely ... The Romans [says Cicero] refused to countenance a criminal attempt
> made on the life of even a foreign aggressor.[14]

By the 7th century some of these principles had spread to the Islamic world and
the Caliph Abu Bakr commanded his forces,[15] 'let there be no perfidy, no false-
hood in your treaties with the enemy, be faithful to all things, proving yourselves
upright and noble and maintaining your word and promises truly'. The leading
Islamic statement on the law of nations written in the ninth century to some extent
reflects principles laid down in the Old Testament, with its ban on the killing of
women, children and the old,[16] or the blind, the crippled and the helpless insane.[17]
Insofar as cities under siege were concerned, the attitude[18] was similar to that laid
down in Deuteronomy. While fighting was in progress between the *dar al-Islam*
(the territory of Islam) and the *dar al-harb* (the rest of the world, also known as
the territory of war), 'Muslims were under legal obligations to respect the rights
of non-Muslims, both combatants and civilians.'[19] In accordance with the teachings of the Prophet, booty of war did not belong to the individual who had taken

---

[14] *Ibid.*, ss. 110–11. During the United States operations against Panama – Operation
'Just Cause' – 1989, the US put a price on the head of Noriega, then head of the Panaman-
ian Government and forces. Similarly, in Somalia in 1993 the UN put a price on the head
of General Aidid, one of the faction leaders. It was disclosed in 1998 that during WW II
Churchill had instructed plans to be prepared for the assassination of Hitler, but these were
never put into operation.

[15] *C.* AD 634, Alib Hasan Al Muttaqui, *Book of Kanzul'umman*, vol. 4 (1979), 472; see
also, *The Islamic Law of Nations* (Shaybani's Siyar, *c.* early 9th century), tr. Khadduri
(1966), s. 1711.

[16] *The Islamic Law*, ss. 29–31, 47, 81. While it had been anticipated during the Gulf War,
1991, that women members of the force would be accorded the courtesies of Islam, in fact
many of those in the US forces captured by Iraq were subjected to torture or other ill-treatment, *The Times* (Life and Times) 12 Jun. 1992. See, however, Cornum, *She Went to War*,
1992.

[17] *Ibid.*, ss. 110–11.

[18] *Ibid.*, ss. 1, 55.

[19] *Ibid.*, Khadduri, Intro., 13.

it but was to be shared in accordance with set rules.[20] Moreover, 'the prisoner of war should not be killed, but he may be ransomed or set free by grace',[21] but if it was considered that killing prisoners would be advantageous to the Muslims, then they should be killed, although this would not be so if they became Muslim,[22] in which case they were to be regarded as booty and divided among the captors. However, if there was substantial Muslim evidence that the prisoners had been awarded safe-conducts they were to be allowed to go free.[23] Whereas the Israelites were told not to destroy the animals of the enemy nor to set fire to his land,[24] Islam permitted the inundation or burning of a city, even though there might be protected persons, that is to say, women, children, the aged or the sick, or even Muslim inhabitants, who would be destroyed in the process.[25]

The Middle Ages and chivalry

By the Middle Ages the power of the Church was such that it was able to forbid Christian knights from using certain weapons as hateful to God. Thus, in 1139 the Second Lateran Council condemned the use of the crossbow and arc, a view that coincided with the concepts of chivalry which regarded such weapons as disgraceful, since they could be used from a distance thus enabling a man to strike without the risk of himself being struck.[26] In the same way, darts and catapults were anathemised by the *Corpus juris canonici*, 1500, 'in order to reduce as far as possible the engines of destruction and death',[27] although by 1563 these and other weapons capable of sending 'men ... to perdition by the hundreds' were in common use.[28] In fact, the feudal knights were aware of what they knew as the 'law of chivalry', a customary code of chivalrous conduct that controlled their affairs and which was enforced by arbitrators specially appointed or, in the case of England and France, by Courts of Chivalry.[29] In 1307 special military courts were trying

[20] *Ibid.*, ss. 2–38, 54–60, 148–371.

[21] *Ibid.*, s. 44 (n. 85 says this is based on Koran XLVII, 5).

[22] During the civil war in Afghanistan there were reports that Russian soldiers supporting the government captured by the *mujahudin* were frequently killed if they refused conversion.

[23] *The Islamic Law,* ss. 55, 95–109.

[24] Josephus, *Contra Apion*, II, 29.

[25] *The Islamic Law*, ss. 22, 112–23.

[26] Draper, 'The interaction of Christianity and chivalry in the historical development of the law of war,' 5 Int'l Rev. Red X (1965), 3, 19.

[27] Belli, *De Re Militari et Belli Tractatus* (1563), Pars. III, Cap. III, 29 (tr. Carnegie (1936), 186). See also *The Alexiad of Anna Comnena*, tr. Sewter (1969), 316–17: 'The crossbow is a weapon of the barbarians ... a truly diabolical machine.'

[28] Belli, *De Re Militari*. See also Gardot, 'Le Droit de la Guerre dans l'Œuvre des Capitaines Français du XVIe Siècle', 72 *Hague Recueil* (1948), 397, 416.

[29] See, e.g., Keen, *The Laws of War in the Late Middle Ages* (1965), 27; see also his *Chivalry*, 1984; see also Contamine, *War in the Middle Ages*, Eng. tr. (1984), 270–7; and generally, Ward, *The Foundation and History of the Law of Nations in Europe*, vol. II (1795), ch. XIV, 'Of the influence of chivalry'.

allegations of breach of parole.[30] In view of the fact that many knights with their groups of followers were prepared to serve in the army of the ruler who paid them most, the problem of parole was of some significance. It was the system whereby a captive was given his freedom in return for a promise not to take up arms against his captor. This promise could be general and permanent in character, for a particular war, or in a specified geographic area or until a ransom had been paid.[31] These rules of chivalry, however, only regulated the behaviour of the knights and could be enforced by commanders of any nationality. They were so generally recognised that as early as 1370 at the siege of Limoges, when the English commander had issued orders that no quarter was to be given, three French knights who had been captured appealed to John of Gaunt and the Earl of Cambridge:[32] 'My lords we are yours: you have vanquished us. Act therefore to the law of arms',[33] and their lives were spared and they were treated as prisoners. By way of contrast, reference might be made to the reaction of the Venetians at the use of firearms – 'In 1439, when the army of Bologna, using a new handgun, killed a number of plate-armoured Venetians, feeling ran so high at this disregard for the game of war, that the victorious Venetians massacred all prisoners who had stooped so low as to use this "cruel and cowardly innovation", gunpowder. It would, unchecked, they said, make fighting a positively DANGEROUS profession.'[34] By the time of Elizabeth the principles of the 'law of arms' were so well established that in *Henry V*, Shakespeare[35] has Fluellen say 'Kill the boys and the luggage! 'Tis expressly against the law of arms: 'tis as arrant a piece of knavery as can be offer'd.' By 1434 the Constable of France was trying a variety of *écorcheur* captains for war crimes,[36] and in 1474 Peter of Hagenbach was tried by a tribunal made up of representatives of the Hanseatic League for having administered occupied territories in a fashion that was contrary to 'the laws of God and of man' and was executed, regardless of his plea of obedience to the commands of his lord.[37]

[30] Keen, *The Laws of War*, 34.

[31] See, e.g., Brown, 'Prisoner of war parole: ancient concept, modern utility', 156, Mil. Law Rev. 1998, 200.

[32] Keen, *The Laws of War*, 1.

[33] See, e.g., Squibb, *The High Court of Chivalry*, 1997, 166. 'Cases concerning prisoners of war were described as being determined according to the law of arms' – n. 6, *Tatesham* v. *Garenserres* (1351), *Lydell* v. *Louthre* (1359).

[34] Treece and Oakeshott, *Fighting Men – How Men Have Fought Through the Ages*, 1963, 207–8.

[35] Act 4, Scene 7, lines 1, 5–10. The statement is made in connection with Henry's order at Agincourt to kill the French prisoners by way of reprisal for the slaughter of the 'boys'. Shakespeare bases his account on Holinshed's *Chronicles*, but a somewhat different version is given by Vattel, *Le Droit des Gens* (1758), Liv. III, ch. VIII, s. 151 (tr. Carnegie (1916), 85–6); see, on this, Green, 'International criminal law and the protection of human rights', in Cheng and Brown (eds), 116, 117–18. See also Meron, *Henry's Wars and Shakespeare's Laws*, 1993.

[36] Literally, 'skinner', armed bands of free companies, Keen, *The Laws of War*, 192; see also 97–100.

[37] See Schwarzenberger, *International Law*, vol. 2, *The Law of Armed Conflict*, ch. 39.

The rules of chivalry did not apply to foot soldiers who were under the regime established by national military codes, with military commanders possessing 'rights of justice' over their own men, and as early as the reign of Richard ll,[38] 1385, clear orders were issued delimiting these powers. This process was facilitated by the early fifteenth century when all men-at-arms had to be included in an official muster, subject to a disciplinary code, including rules with regard, for example, to the taking and distribution of booty,[39] forbidding pillage and the destruction of private property. Richard's code also postulated respect for priests, women, children, the infirm and others. Respect for women was general among the knights. During the sixteenth century senior French knights were adamant in protecting the modesty of women found in surrendered cities,[40] and by the Ordinance promulgated by Coligny violence against women was punishable by death.[41] The principle for the protection of women was so well established that Gentili stated in 1612[42] that 'to violate the honour of women will always be held to be unjust', and he quoted as evidence of this the view of Alexander: 'I am not in the habit of warring with prisoners and women.' By the seventeenth century, England had a full system of Articles of War[43] regulating the behaviour of the armed forces, forbidding, among other things, marauding of the countryside, individual acts against the enemy without authorisation from a superior, private taking or keeping of booty, or private detention of an enemy prisoner. Similar codes existed in Switzerland and in Germany.[44] Of these codes it has been said that, combined with the rules of international law they form 'le meilleur frein pratique pour imposer aux armées le respect d'un *modus legitimus* de mener les guerres'.[45]

Precursors of Geneva

It was not only through the medium of military codes or the rules of chivalry that rudimentary rules for the conduct of war were developing. While, during the Crusades, religious hatreds tended to lead to the total destruction of the enemy, by the twelfth century the Knights of the Order of St. John had established a hospital in Jerusalem for the care of the sick as well as for injured Crusaders, and by the sixteenth century they had established themselves as the Sovereign Order of Malta, with their members known as Knights Hospitallers. At the same time, writers

[38] Winthrop, *Military Law and Precedents*, App. II, 1412.
[39] Estatutz et custumes en l'ost', c. *Black Book of Admiralty*, ed. Twiss, vol. 1, 453–4.
[40] Gardot, *Le Droit de la Guerre*, 452–3.
[41] *Ibid.*, 469, c. Fourquevaux, *La Discipline militaire*, (1592).
[42] *De Jure Belli*, Lib. II, cap. xxi (tr. Carnegie (1933), 257, 251).
[43] Laws and Ordinances of Warre (1639) (Clode, *Military Forces of the Crown*, vol. 1, App. VI).
[44] See Gardot, *Le Droit de la Guerre*, 467–8.
[45] de Taube, 'L'apport de Byzance au développement du droit international occidental', 67 *Hague Recueil* (1939), 237.

were beginning to assert that doctors, often in clerical orders, enjoyed a special immunity. Thus, Bartolus maintained, during the first half of the fourteenth century, that they were immune from seizure, and Belli[46] used this as a basis for his own comments on the role of doctors during war: 'persons of doctors may not be seized, and they may not be haled to court or otherwise harassed; consequently, attendants may not search them for the carrying of arms'. By the time of Louis XIV careful attention was being given to the need to provide for the care of the wounded, and by a decree of 1708[47] there was established a permanent medical service 'à la suite des armées et dans les places de guerre'. Prior to this, the care of the wounded depended upon the predilections of individual commanders who often had their own personal physicians attached to their staff. Even before Louis XIV had established his medical service, the regiments of Gustavus Adolphus had four surgeons, while the Armada was accompanied by medical personnel, although these only looked after their own. However, principles of chivalry were still commonly observed and during the siege of Metz, 1552–53, François de Guise summoned the great French surgeon Ambroise Pará 'to succour the abandoned wounded soldiers of the enemy and to make arrangements for their transport back to their army'.[48]

Towards the end of the seventeenth century the first tentative arrangements were being made for reciprocal care of wounded in the field, and:

> in 1679 a convention was signed between the Elector of Brandenburg, for the league of Augsburg, and the Count of Asfield, who commanded the French forces [providing] for a mutual respect towards both hospitals and wounded ... [The] convention made in 1743, between Lord Stair on behalf of the Pragmatic army and the Marshal Noailles for the French during the Dettingen campaign bound both sides to treat hospitals and wounded with consideration. Noailles, when he felt that his operations might cause alarm to the inmates of the hospitals at Techenheim, went so far as to send word that they should rest tranquil as they would not be disturbed. A fuller and more highly developed type of agreement was that signed at L'Ecluse in 1759 by the Marshal de Brail, who commanded the French, and Major-General Conway, the British general officer commanding. The hospital staff, chaplains, doctors, surgeons and apothecaries were not ... to be taken prisoners; and, if they should happen to be apprehended within the lines of the enemy, they were to be sent back immediately. The wounded of the enemy who should fall into the hands of their opponents were to be cared for, and their food and medicines should in due course be paid for. They were not to be made prisoner and might stay in hospital safely under guard. Surgeons and servants might be sent to them under the general's passport. Finally, on their discharge, they were themselves to travel under the same authority and were to travel by the shortest route.[49]

Despite such arrangements, in 1764 'Chamousset ... referred with regret to the

---

[46] Belli, *De Re Militari*, n. 26, Part VII, ch. III, 34 (tr. 187).
[47] Butler and Maccoby, *The Development of International Law*, 134.
[48] *Ibid.*, 187 n. 28.
[49] *Ibid.*, 149–50.

thousands of lives which had been sacrificed when, as a result of military operations, the forced and hurried evacuation of hospitals had become necessary in order to save the wounded from falling into enemy's hands. Péyrilhe in 1780 proposed international recognition of the principle that the wounded should not be made prisoners of war and should not enter into the balance of exchanges.'[50] However, it was not until after the experiences of Florence Nightingale in the Crimea and the *Souvenir de Solferino*, published by Henri Dunant in 1862, reporting on what he had seen at the Battle of Solferino in 1859, that steps were taken to give effect to Péyrilhe's suggestion.[51]

Apart from arrangements of the kind just mentioned, other customs were developing. During the Hundred Years War it was possible to distinguish among *guerre mortelle*, war to the death, *bellum hostile*, a war between Christian princes and in which prisoners could ransom themselves, *guerre guerriable*, fought in accordance with the feudal rules of chivalry, and the truce, which indicated a temporary cessation of hostilities when the wounded and dead might be collected, and a resumption thereafter was considered a continuation of an ongoing armed conflict and not the commencement of a new one.[52] Each of these had its own rules, but they were rules[53] of honour rather than laws or principles of humanitarianism. In such conflicts, unless it was one in which no quarter was to be given, and this was indicated by the raising of a red pennant, prisoners and others, for example, heralds, enjoying immunity carried a white wand or even a piece of white paper in their head-dress, were frequently allowed to move freely under safe-conducts which often enabled them to be employed as messengers between the rival armies.[54]

In medieval conflict the capture of cities was of major importance and could be effected either by an instrument of surrender or by siege and assault. If surrender was effected by agreement, the inhabitants were treated in accordance with the terms of that agreement, but if the city was taken by assault there were no legal restrictions concerning the treatment of the inhabitants, although churchmen were often spared. However, the commanders of the besieging forces often instructed their followers to spare women and children. Siege required peculiar weapons, both offensive and defensive,[55] and as siege became less frequent and these

---

[50] *Ibid.*, 150–1.

[51] For a general account of 'War law and the medical profession', see Green, *Essays*, 1999, ch. XIV.

[52] The Arab–Israeli conflict has continued since the establishment of Israel with the original cease-fire and armistice agreements being constantly breached. Dinstein suggests that 'A number of rounds of hostilities between Israel and the Arab countries … are incorrectly adverted to as "wars". Far from qualifying as separate wars, these were merely inconsecutive time frames of combat, punctuated by extended cease-fires, in the course of a single on-going war', *War, Aggression and Self Defence*, 56.

[53] See Stacey, 'The age of chivalry', in Howard, *The Laws of War*, 1994, 27, 32 *et seq.*

[54] See, generally, Gentili, *De Jure Belli*, Lib. II, cap. XVII, XVIII (tr. 216–40).

[55] See, e.g., Contamine, *War in the Middle Ages*, 102–6, 193–207, 211–12.

weapons therefore of less value, they tended to be regarded as illegal. Perhaps the best example of these is boiling oil, often a defensive weapon against those attempting to make use of scaling ladders. This is not to say that refinements of such weaponry have not been developed to suit more modern needs. Similarly, as the dress of those involved in conflict changed from the heavy metal armour[56] of knights riding similarly apparelled horses, so weapons like the iron club, the mace, the axe, the ball-and-chain, the halberd, the glaive, the partisan and the military fork have all fallen into desuetude, and their use today would almost certainly be regarded as unlawful.[57]

War: a public activity

Until after the Thirty Years War, 1618–48, the natural condition among the European powers tended to be one of war rather than peace, and the early writings on the law of nations were primarily concerned with describing the law of war, the relations between States during such periods, and the duties of soldiers, rather than with the relations that would exist during peace time. Even the great work of Grotius, who is frequently referred to as 'the father of international law', reflects this fact in its title: *De Jure Belli ac Pacis (Concerning the Law of War and Peace)*, 1625. However, there were many works written before Grotius and in these the emphasis on the law of war is even more marked.[58] Each of these works outlined what the author considered should be the law governing war and made use of examples from mythology and classical history, as well as from more recent battles, but by and large their writings reflected the general practice of their day. It is in these writings that we find much of the evidence as to what now constitutes the customs of war and the customary law regulating armed conflict.

The Thirty Years War was terminated by the Treaty of Westphalia, 1648, and by that time the nature of the relations between fighting men had changed. War was no longer a matter of personal relations between princely commanders, with the individual soldier entering into a personal contract of service with his commander, or with the prisoner being in a master-servant relation to his captor. War had become a matter between sovereigns only, and for a legally recognised armed conflict to exist there had to be a hostile contention by means of armed

[56] See, e.g., Erasmus, *Bellum* [1515], Imprint Soc., ed. (1972), 17, Green, *Essays*, 1985, 155.

[57] See, e.g., *The German War Book,* Morgan, ed. (1915), 66. Both the British *Manual of Military Law*, Part III, *The Law of Land Warfare*, para. 110, and the US *Law of Land Warfare*, FM 27, para. 34, refer to lances with barbed heads as unlawful. See also Green, 'What one may do in conflict – then and now', Delissen and van Reesema, *International Human Rights Law: Theory and Practice*, 269.

[58] E.g., Legnano, *De Belli, De Represaliis et De Duello,* Belli, *De Re Militari et Bello,* Ayala, *De Jure et Officiis Bellicis et Disciplina Militari.*

forces carried on between States[59] and most frequently they were fought by standing armies supplemented as necessary. By then, too, the old distinction between just and unjust wars[60] had disappeared and it had become accepted that any war conducted by a Christian prince was clearly just,[61] although both Suarez and Vitoria had some reservations concerning Spanish claims in regard to the colonisation of the new world.[62]

The first modern codes

The first modern attempt to draw up a binding code for the conduct of an armed force in the field was that prepared by Professor Francis Lieber of the United States, promulgated as law by President Lincoln in 1863[63] during the American Civil War. This Code, though only binding upon United States forces, was based on what Lieber regarded as the generally accepted law of his day. It prescribed,[64] among other things: that

> military necessity does not admit of cruelty – that is, the infliction of suffering for the sake of suffering or for revenge[65] ... the unarmed citizen is to be spared in person, property, and honour as much as the exigencies of war will admit ... protection of the inoffensive citizen of the hostile country is the rule ... The United States acknowledge and protect, in hostile countries occupied by them, religion and morality; strictly private property; the persons of the inhabitants, especially those of women: and the sacredness of domestic relations. Offenses to the contrary shall be rigorously punished ... All wanton violence committed against persons in the invaded country ... all robbery ... or sacking, even after taking a place by main force, all rape, wounding, maiming or killing of such inhabitants, are prohibited under the penalty of death ... Crimes punishable by all penal codes, such as arson, murder, maiming, assaults, highway robbery, theft, burglary, fraud, forgery, and rape, if committed by an American soldier in a hostile country against its inhabitants, are not only punishable as at home, but in all cases in which death is not inflicted, the severer punishment shall be preferred.

The rules embodied in the Lieber Code were so consistent with accepted practice that Lieber's hope that 'it will be adopted as basis for similar works by the Eng-

[59] See, e.g., Bordwell, *The Law of War between Belligerents*, ch. IV – he takes the Dutch Wars of Louis XIV, 1672–78, as *the dies a quo*.

[60] See ch. 1 above.

[61] See, e.g., Shafirov, *A Discourse concerning the Just Causes of the War between Sweden and Russia: 1700–1721*.

[62] See, e.g., Scott, *The Catholic Conception of International Law*; see also Green and Dickason, *The Law of Nations and the New World*, 39–47, 50–4, 192–8.

[63] Instructions for the Government of Armies of the US in the Field, General Orders, 24 Apr. 1863, Schindler and Toman, 3; see also Baxter, 'The first modern codification of the law of armed conflict', 29 Int'l Rev. Red X (1963), 171.

[64] Arts 16, 2, 37, 44, 47.

[65] See, e.g., Green, '"Unnecessary suffering", weapons control and the law of war', *Essays*, 1999, ch. IX.

lish, French and Germans'⁶⁶ soon came to fruition, and between 1870 and 1893 similar manuals or codes were issued by Prussia, 1870; The Netherlands, 1871; France, 1877; Russia 1877 and 1904; Servia, 1878; Argentina, 1881; Great Britain, 1883 and 1904; and Spain, 1893.⁶⁷

Although such codes were issued by national authorities, there was no agreed international document laying down rules and principles governing warfare among the European states, in which group may be included the United States and the newly independent Latin American Republics. The rules embodied in these national codes or in the writings of acknowledged international law authorities, to the extent that they expressed agreement, constitute the customary international law⁶⁸ of armed conflict, and to the extent that they have not been overruled by treaty or expressly rejected by a state, especially one considered a significant military power, they are as obligatory as any other rules of international law.⁶⁹

Inter-state concern begins

The first inter-state agreement aimed at restraining the undesirable effects of armed conflict was drawn up at the end of the Crimean War by the signatories of the peace treaty terminating that war in 1856.⁷⁰ This was confined to the law of maritime warfare and forbade the issue of letters of marque to privateers, stated that a naval blockade would only be legal if effective, and granted immunity to enemy goods on neutral ships and neutral goods on enemy ships, unless such goods constituted contraband. Of more general significance was the Geneva Convention of 1864 for the amelioration of the wounded in armies in the field,⁷¹ signed only a year after the founding conference of the Red Cross,⁷² and which recognised the special distinctiveness and immunity of the red cross and of personnel wearing this insignia. A clarificatory document was signed in 1868⁷³ which sought to extend the protection of the red cross to naval warfare, but the document never received a single ratification. The 1864 Convention was amended or revised by the later Geneva Conventions of 1906, 1929 and 1949,⁷⁴ and by the Protocol of

⁶⁶ Letter to Gen. Halleck, c. Holland, *The Laws of War on Land*, 72. See also Doty, 'The United States and the development of the laws of war', 156 Mil. Law Rev. 1998, 224; Carnahan, 'Lincoln, Lieber and the laws of war: the origins and limits of the principle of military necessity', 92 Am. J. Int'l Law 1998, 213.
⁶⁷ Holland, *op.cit.*, 72–3.
⁶⁸ On customary law, see, e.g., D'Amato, *The Concept of Custom in International Law.*
⁶⁹ See, e.g., Akehurst, 'The hierarchy of the sources of international law', 47 Brit. Y.B. Int'l Law (1974–75), 273; Villiger, *Customary International Law and Treaties*, esp. Part III.
⁷⁰ Declaration of Paris, Schindler and Toman, 787.
⁷¹ *Ibid.*, 270.
⁷² Resolutions of Geneva International Conference, *ibid.*, 275.
⁷³ *Ibid.*, 285.
⁷⁴ *Ibid.*, 301, 325, 339, 373, 401, 423, 495.

1977[75] additional to those Conventions. These Conventions are generally described as the Geneva Law regarding armed conflict and constitute a body of humanitarian law governing the treatment and protection of those *hors de combat*, civilians and other non-combatants.

In 1863 Russia had invented a bullet which exploded on contact with a hard object and was intended for use against ammunition wagons, but in 1867 the bullet was modified so as to explode on contact with soft objects.[76] The Russian Government considered this to be an inhumane weapon and called a conference at St. Petersburg which drew up a declaration[77] forbidding the use of any projectile weighing less than 400 grams, which was either explosive or charged with fulminating or inflammable substances. This Declaration was of general application and therefore of significance for both land and sea warfare. From the point of view of the development or purpose of the law of armed conflict, the statement adopted explaining the reason for the promulgation of the Declaration of St. Petersburg is perhaps more significant than its substance:

> the progress of civilisation should have the effect of alleviating as much as possible the calamities of war; the only legitimate object which states should endeavour to accomplish during war is to weaken the military forces of the enemy; for this purpose it is sufficient to disable the greatest possible number of men; this object would be exceeded by the employment of arms which uselessly aggravate the sufferings of disabled men, or render their death inevitable; the employment of such arms would, therefore, be contrary to the laws of humanity.

However, the Declaration contained an all-participation clause so as to become ineffective in any conflict in which any of the belligerents was not a party thereto, regardless of whether it played an active role in the fighting.

Precursors of Hague Law

In contrast to the Geneva Law is the law concerning means and methods of conducting actual military operations in armed conflict. This is generally known as the Law of The Hague, although it had its origin in a conference of fifteen European states called to Brussels in 1874 at the invitation of Czar Alexander II of Russia.[78]

---

[75] *Ibid.*, 621. Although described as additional to the Geneva Conventions, Parts III and IV of Protocol I are more related to the Hague Law.

[76] Invented by Great Britain at Dum-Dum near Calcutta. There was a general belief that ordinary bullets, although they might kill, were ineffective in stopping 'the onrush of a hardy and fanatical savage', and in 1903 Holland (letter to *The Times*, 2 May) was maintaining that the use of such bullets was not unlawful insofar as the UK and US were concerned, *Letters on War and Neutrality* (1909), 53. However, the UK 'withdrew Dum-Dum bullets during the South African War, and it is to be taken for granted that Great Britain will not in future make use of them in a war with *civilised* Powers', Oppenheim, *International Law*, vol. 2, 119 (italics added).

[77] Declaration of St. Petersburg, Schindler and Toman, 101.

[78] *Ibid.*, 25.

This confirmed the principles underlying the St. Petersburg Declaration, and, being convinced that 'a further step may be taken by revising the general usages of war, whether with the object of defining them with greater precision, or with the view of laying down, by a common agreement, certain limits which will restrain, as far as possible, the severities of war', drew up a Project of an International Declaration concerning the Laws and Customs of War.[79] The hope was expressed that 'war being thus regulated would involve less suffering, would be less liable to those aggravations produced by uncertainty, unforeseen events, and the passions created by the struggle; it would tend more surely to that which should be its final object, *viz.*, the re-establishment of good relations, and a more solid and lasting peace between the belligerent States'. But not all the States which signed the Brussels Protocol were willing to ratify the Project. However, the Project to a great extent formed the basis of the *Manual of the Laws of War on Land* drawn up by the Institute of International Law[80] at its Oxford Conference, 1880.[81]

In its Preface, the *Manual* states that:

> independently of the international laws existing on this subject, there are certain principles of justice which guide the public conscience, which are manifested even by general customs, but which it would be well to fix and make obligatory ... Since 1874 [Brussels] ideas, aided by reflection and experience, have had time to mature, and because it seems less difficult than it did then to trace rules which would be acceptable to all peoples.

But the Institute did not consider that the Manual should be embodied into a treaty, for this 'might be premature or at least very difficult to obtain'. However, the *Manual* could serve as a basis for national legislation and was:

> in accord with both the progress of juridical science and the needs of civilised armies. Rash and extreme rules will not, furthermore, be found therein.[82] The Institute has not sought innovations in drawing up the Manual; it has contented itself with stating clearly and codifying the accepted ideas of our age so far as this has appeared allowable and practicable.

The Institute also, for the first time, emphasised the need for dissemination and education so far as the law of armed conflict is concerned, for:

> in order to attain [the] end [aimed at] it is not sufficient for sovereigns to promulgate new laws. It is essential, too, that they make these laws known among all people, so that when a war is declared, the men called upon to take up arms to defend the causes

---

[79] *Ibid.*, 67.

[80] The Institute is an unofficial but highly respected body of leading scholars, whose eminence leads to their resolutions and proposals receiving the highest respect and often form the basis for draft agreements submitted to governments.

[81] Schindler and Toman, 35.

[82] By this comment the Institute touches upon a problem that has confronted every effort to enact rules intended to modify the rigours of war – the need to effect a compromise between the ideals of the humanitarian and the needs of the military, see above, ch. 1, text to note 72.

of the belligerent States, may be thoroughly impregnated with the special rights and duties attached to the execution of such a command.

The Hague Law

The promulgation of the Brussels Declaration and the adoption and publication by the Institute of its *Manual* helped to move governments towards the adoption of an international treaty concerning the conduct of armed conflict. Again at the initiative of the Czar, twenty-six countries met at The Hague in 1899 and adopted Conventions and Declarations which underlie that part of the law of armed conflict still known as the Law of The Hague. The Declarations related to a ban on the launching of projectiles and explosives from balloons or by other similar methods,[83] which was only intended to last for five years and was replaced in 1907 by a further Declaration[84] prohibiting the discharge of projectiles and explosives from balloons which was intended to subsist until the convening of a third Hague Conference which has never been held; a ban on the use of projectiles, the only object of which is the diffusion of asphyxiating or deleterious gases;[85] and a ban on the use of bullets which expand or flatten easily in the human body, such as bullets with a hard envelope, of which the envelope does not cover the core or is pierced with incisions.[86] Although not all the great powers ratified or formally accepted these Declarations,[87] the general view is that they are expressive of rules of customary law. The importance of customary law in the law of armed conflict is explained by the United States Department of the Army Field Manual on the *Law of Land Warfare*,[88] 'although some of the law has not been incorporated in any treaty or convention to which the United States is a party, this body of unwritten or customary law is firmly established by the custom of nations and well defined by recognised authorities on international law ... The unwritten or customary law of war is binding upon all nations'.

More important than the Declarations adopted at the 1899 Hague Conference was the Convention (II) with Respect to the Laws and Customs of War on Land,[89] to which was annexed a set of regulations seeking to spell out the rules of law

[83] Schindler and Toman, 201 – this is the first attempt to lay down any principles concerning aerial warfare.

[84] *Ibid.*

[85] *Ibid.*, 105.

[86] *Ibid.*, 109 – this was aimed at Dum-Dum bullets, see n. 76 above. Many municipal police forces now use a soft-nosed or explosive bullet, contending that it is more effective, less likely to pass through the victim's body or ricochet, thereby endangering others.

[87] Thus, the US acceded to none of these, although it did to the 1907 Declaration on Projectiles from Balloons; while the UK declined to accede to the 1899 Balloons Declaration, but accepted that of 1907.

[88] *Law of Land Warfare*, n. 57 above, paras. 4(b), 7(c).

[89] Schindler and Toman, 63 – this was replaced by Hague Convention IV, 1907.

concerning the conduct of warfare on land. While the Hague Regulations of 1899 clearly constitute the first codification of the laws and customs of war accepted by the powers in a binding multilateral document, the draftsmen were aware that their code did not cover 'all the circumstances which occur in practice'. With this in mind they emphasised that the regulations were not exhaustive and that, to the extent that they were silent, customary law would continue to govern. They expressed this understanding by way of the Martens Clause, specifying the 'principles of the law of nations, as they result from the usages established between civilised nations, from the laws of humanity, and the dictates of the public conscience'.

A further conference was held at The Hague in 1907, again at the initiative of the Czar, and this, apart from amending Hague Convention II of 1899 and reiterating the Declaration concerning the discharge of projectiles from balloons, adopted ten other Conventions concerning warfare, including the opening of hostilities,[90] naval warfare,[91] and the rights and duties of neutrals.[92] Each of these Conventions contains an all-participation clause, rendering its application null should any of the belligerents in a conflict not be a party to the relevant Convention. This makes the concept underlying the Martens Clause of greater significance than might otherwise have been the case, for it provides for the continued relevance of customary law when treaty law is not applicable. In practice, belligerents sometimes adopted the policy that when the belligerent non-party to the Convention was insignificant from the point of view of the subject-matter of the Convention, they would nevertheless continue to apply the Convention as between themselves.[93] Moreover, to the extent that any of the provisions in the Hague Regulations or any of the Conventions are now considered to be declaratory of customary law[94] or are regarded as having developed into customary law, they will be applicable and the wording found in the particular Convention will be treated as expressing what is considered to be the rule of customary law.[95]

[90] Convention III, *ibid.*, 57.
[91] Conventions VI–XII, *ibid.*, 791 *et seq.*
[92] Convention V, XIII, *ibid.*, 941, 951.
[93] See, e.g., *The Möwe* [1951] P. 1, and *The Blonde* [1922] 1 A.C. 313, for the application of Hague Convention VI, 1907 (Status of Merchant Ships at Outbreak of Hostilities), though Serbia and Montenegro were not parties.
[94] E.g., Art. 4 affirming that prisoners of war are in the power of the enemy government and not the soldier capturing them; Art. 7 – the holding government is obliged to maintain prisoners; Art. 12 – prisoners breaking parole may be punished if recaptured; Art. 22 – the means of injuring the enemy is not unlimited; Art. 23 – the ban on the use of poison and of denying quarter; Art. 32 – protection of one carrying a flag of truce, etc. Not all military commanders were 'happy' with these humanitarian principles, see comment by Admiral Lord Fisher, ch. 1 above.
[95] See, e.g., *Nuremberg Judgment*, 1946. 'Several of the belligerents in the recent war were not parties to this Convention … [B]y 1939 these rules laid down in the Convention were recognised by all civilised nations, and were regarded as being declaratory of the laws and customs of war.' HMSO, Cmd 6964 (1946), 65; 41 Am. J. Int'l Law (1947), 172, 248–9.

Although to a great extent the Fourth Hague Convention relative to the Laws and Customs of War on Land reproduced the provisions of its 1899 precursor, it introduced a principle regarding enforcement. By Article 3 of the Convention 'a belligerent party which violates the provisions of the Regulations shall, if the case demands, be liable to pay compensation. It shall be responsible for all acts committed by persons forming part of its armed forces'. Neither the Convention nor the annexed regulations, however, made any provision for the prosecution of individuals who disregarded or breached the regulations. Prior to the establishment of the International Military Tribunal in 1945, trials of such persons for war crimes were conducted by national tribunals[96] applying customary international law,[97] the Regulations,[98] or in the case of their own personnel the national military or criminal code.[99] The only difference Nuremberg has made is that war crimes trials held since have referred to and applied the principles stemming from the judgment of that Tribunal.[100]

Of the substantive provisions of both the 1899 and 1907 versions of the Regulations, the most important is Article 1 which, until the adoption of Protocol I in 1977,[101] defined the belligerents to whom the Regulations applied. Its purview extends to armies, militia units and volunteer forces, provided they are commanded by a person responsible for his subordinates, have a fixed distinctive

[96] In the case of the German trials held at Leipzig after World War I against German accused, these were in accordance with Art. 228 of the Treaty of Versailles.

[97] See, e.g., German trial of Captain Fryatt, 1916, for attempting to ram a German U-boat while captain of a merchant ship (Garner, *International Law and the World War*, vol. 1, 407). Nurse Cavell, who, in breach of her protected status as a medical person, assisted in the escape of allied soldiers, was not tried for a war crime, but for a breach of the German Military Penal Code to which she was not strictly liable (*ibid.*, vol. 2, 97). See also *The Llandovery Castle*, in which officers of a U-boat were sentenced by a German tribunal for, 'contrary to international law', firing upon and killing survivors of an unlawfully torpedoed hospital ship (Cameron, *The Peleus Trial*, App. IX); trial of Eck – *The Peleus Trial*, 1945 (*ibid.*); *Klein*, 1945, for killing allied civilian nationals contrary to international law (1 UNWCC, *Law Reports of Trials of War Criminals*, 46), *etc.*

[98] See, e.g., *Drierwalde Case*, 1946, *ibid.*, 81, killing captured RAF personnel contrary to Art. 23(c).

[99] *Müller's Case and Neumann's Case*, 1921, at Leipzig (Cmd 1422, 26, 36), guilty of ill-treating prisoners of war contrary to German Penal Code and Military Penal Code; see also US trials of personnel accused of crimes against prisoners or enemy civilians during the Korean and Vietnam conflicts, e.g., *US* v. *Keenan* (1954) 14 C.M.R., 742; *US* v. *Calley* (1969–71; 1973) 46 C.M.R. 1131, 48 C.M.R. 19, 1 Mil. Law Reporter, 2488. For instances of trials by German military courts of members of the German armed forces, with executions in some cases for offences against Allied personnel, both military and civilian, during World War II, see de Zayas, *Wehrmacht War Crimes Bureau 1939–1945* (1989), 18–22.

[100] See, e.g., *Buhler Trial*, 1948, Polish Supreme National Tribunal, 14 *Law Reports of Trials of War Criminals*, 23. For post-1945 international developments and trials, see chs 18, 19.

[101] Schindler and Toman, 621, see below text to n. 195, *et seq.*

emblem recognisable at a distance,[102] carry their arms openly and conduct their operations in accordance with the laws and customs of war.

From the point of view of armed conflict on land, in addition to Hague Convention IV the most important of the 1907 Conventions are III (Opening of Hostilities),[103] V (Rights and Duties of Neutral Powers and Persons in War on Land),[104] and IX (Bombardment by Naval Forces)[105] to which must now be added some of the provisions of Protocol I, 1977.[106]

The Conventions of 1907 were intended to remain in force until a Third Peace Conference. The convening of this was prevented by the outbreak of World War I and no conference for the purpose of revising the Hague Conventions has been called since. However, the law of armed conflict has in fact been amended at various conferences called to deal with specific issues, such as the 1954 conference for the protection of cultural property in armed conflict,[107] conference on the prohibition of military or other hostile use of environmental modification techniques,[108] conference relating to the use of certain conventional weapons,[109] and the conference that led to the adoption of Protocol I in 1977.

By and large, the belligerents in both World Wars accepted the 1907 Conventions as governing their activities, and this was reiterated by the war crimes tribunals trying those accused of war crimes consequent upon both of those wars, as well as by prize courts[110] sitting during the course of hostilities.[111] Insofar as members of the British Empire and Commonwealth were concerned, some had not become individual parties to any of the Conventions, but those ratified by Great Britain in 1900 and 1909 were binding upon those countries by virtue of the British ratification.

The Declaration of London

Another instrument that seems to have been applied as expressing accepted law,

---

[102] However, the United Nations command during World War II insisted that such bodies as the French Forces of the Interior were to be treated as lawful combatants, and they did in fact wear distinctive signs.

[103] See ch. 4 below.

[104] See ch. 16 below.

[105] See ch. 8 below.

[106] See n. 101 above.

[107] Convention, Schindler and Toman, 745.

[108] Convention 1976, *ibid.*, 163.

[109] Convention 1980, *ibid.*, 179.

[110] Prize courts are special tribunals established by belligerents to adjudicate upon seizures of vessels and goods belonging to or trading with the enemy. Although national courts, they apply the international maritime law of war, as amended by any national statutes which may apply to them as national courts, see, however, *The Zamora* [1916] 2 A.C. 77.

[111] See, e.g., *The Möwe*, n. 93 above.

even though it never received a single ratification, is the Declaration of London of 1909 concerning the laws of naval warfare.[112] This Declaration was intended to assist the International Prize Court envisaged by Hague Convention XII of 1907[113] in reaching its decisions on the rights and duties of neutrals in naval warfare and the susceptibility of ships and cargoes to seizure as prize. Although the Declaration of London expressly stated that 'the Signatory Powers are agreed that the rules contained in the following Chapters [I, Blockade; II, Contraband; III, Unneutral Service; IV, Destruction of Neutral Prizes; V, Transfer to a Neutral Flag; VI, Enemy Character; VII, Convoy; VIII, Resistance to Search] correspond in substance with the generally recognised principles of international law', neither it nor the Convention received a single ratification. By and large, the rules laid down by the Declaration were observed during World War I[114] and in 1960 the Egyptian Prize Court citing the Declaration condemned a cargo from Israel on a Greek ship seeking to traverse the Suez Canal.[115] Other agreements of relevance in naval warfare were adopted at Washington in 1922 relating to the use of submarines and noxious gases,[116] at London in 1930 on the limitation and reduction of naval armaments,[117] but confirming the 1922 rule regarding submarine warfare and reaffirmed by the London Protocol of 1936.[118] Also, in 1937, in view of the activities of unidentified submarines in the Mediterranean during the Spanish Civil War an agreement concerning their activities was drawn up at Nyon.[119] The most recent statement relating to the law of armed conflict at sea is the *San Remo Manual*[120] drawn up by a committee of experts under the auspices of the International Institute of Humanitarian Law and the International Committee of the Red Cross. Although this is an unofficial statement, it is generally regarded as expressive of accepted customary law.

War in the air

At the time of the Hague Conferences it was not appreciated that aerial warfare might be of major significance. In fact, the only reference to this type of activity is in the Declaration concerning the launching of projectiles from balloons. However, the role played by aircraft during World War I made it clear that some rules

[112] Schindler and Toman, 843. See Kalshoven's 'Commentary' on this Declaration in Ronzitti, *The Law of Naval Warfare*, 257.
[113] *Ibid.*, 825.
[114] See, e.g., Colombos, *The Law of Prize*, 25–8; see also Kalshoven, 'commentary', 71; and, more generally, Levie, *The Code of International Armed Conflict*, under relevant headings.
[115] *The Astypalia* (1960) 31 I.L.R., 519.
[116] Schindler and Toman, 877.
[117] *Ibid.*, 881.
[118] *Ibid.*, 883.
[119] *Ibid.*, 887.
[120] *San Remo Manual on International Law Applicable to Armed Conflicts at Sea*, 1994.

were necessary to regulate conflict in this theatre of activity. As a result of the 1922 Washington Conference on the Limitation of Armaments, a Commission of Jurists convened at The Hague and drew up agreed Rules of Air Warfare.[121] These rules were never embodied into any international treaty and are therefore not legally binding. However, they carry 'the authority which the eminence of the jurists who prepared [them] naturally conferred upon [them and] undoubtedly [have] had influence upon the practice of belligerent and neutral Governments' since their formulation[122] and they are generally regarded 'as an authoritative attempt to clarify and formulate rules of law governing the use of aircraft in war'.[123] Of these draft rules, the latest compilation of *The Laws of Armed Conflicts* states[124] that 'to a great extent, they correspond to the customary rules and general principles underlying the conventions on the law of war on land and at sea'. More-over, in its decision on the use of the atomic bombs in Hiroshima and Nagasaki the District Court of Tokyo[125] said:

> The Draft Rules of Air Warfare cannot directly be called positive law, since they have not yet become effective as authoritative with regard to air warfare. However, international jurists regard the Draft Rules as authoritative with regard to air war-fare. Some countries regard the substance of the Rules as a standard of action by armed forces, and the fundamental provisions of the Draft Rules are consistently in conformity with international law regulations, and customs at that time. Therefore, we can safely say that the prohibition of indiscriminate aerial bombardment on an undefended city and the principle of military objective,[126] which are provided by the Draft Rules, are international customary law, also from the point that they are in common with the principle in land and sea warfare. Further, since the distinction of land, sea and air warfare is made by the place and purpose of warfare, *we think that there is also sufficient reason for argument that, regarding the aerial bombardment of a city on land, the laws and regulations respecting land warfare analogically apply since the aerial bombardment is made on land.*[127]

On the other hand, while the United States Department of the Air Force has stated that 'although the draft Hague Rules have some authority because eminent jurists prepared them, *they do not represent existing customary law as a total code*',[128] nevertheless the same publication frequently draws attention to the compatibility

---

[121] Schindler and Toman, 207.

[122] Spaight, *Air Power and War Rights*, 1947, 42–3.

[123] Oppenheim-Lauterpacht, *International Law*, vol. 2, 519; see also Schwarzenberger, *International Law*, vol. 2, *The Law of Armed Conflict*, 153; Levie, *The Code.*, vol. 1, 207–26.

[124] See n. 121 above.

[125] *Shimoda* v. *Japan* (1963) 8 Jap. Ann. Int'l Law, (1964), 212, 237–8; 32 I.L.R., 626, 631 (italics in original).

[126] It has been suggested that the reasoning in the judgment can be read as supporting or condemning the bombing of the two cities, see, Green, 'Nuclear weapons and the law of armed conflict', *Essays*, 1999, ch. IV, 131, 149.

[127] In this connection, see also Pr. I, 1977, Art. 49(3), note 129 below.

[128] A.F.P. 110–31 1976, para. 5-3(c).

of its own rules with these Rules. Despite such statements as appear in the *Shimoda* judgment or elsewhere, care must be taken not to assume that the Hague Rules constitute a binding code of aerial warfare law, although to the extent that they reproduce general principles underlying the law of armed conflict as such they are declaratory of the customary law concerning aerial warfare.[129] Support for this contention may be drawn from Protocol I, 1977, which states[130] that the rules relating to the general protection of the civilian population[131] 'apply to any land, air or sea warfare which may affect the civilian population, individual civilians or civilian objects on land. They further apply to all attacks from the sea or from the air against objectives on land but do not otherwise affect the rules of international law applicable in armed conflict at sea or in the air'.

Gas as a weapon

Despite the customary law ban on the use of poison and the 1899 Declaration forbidding 'the use of projectiles the sole object of which is the diffusion of asphyxiating or deleterious gases',[132] gas was used by both sides during World War I. In 1925, therefore, the Geneva Protocol for the Prohibition of the Use in War of Asphyxiating, Poisonous or Other Gases, and of Bacteriological Methods of Warfare was adopted.[133] This reiterated the earlier prohibition and extended it to cover bacteriological methods as well. A number of countries have contended that the Protocol does not extend to lachrymose agents, while others reserve the right to employ gas in suppressing, for example, riots in a prisoners-of-war camp. Others state that it will only apply as between them and belligerents which have also ratified the Protocol, while a number reserve the right to resort to the use of gas against a belligerent that has employed it against its forces or those of an ally. Despite these reservations, it is likely that the Protocol would now be regarded as declaratory of customary law, at least as a weapon of first use. The United States did not ratify the Protocol until 1975 and during World War II did not consider its use to be contrary to customary law. In fact, from 1944 onwards, plans were being drawn up to employ gas against Japanese cities[134] and especially to assist in any land invasion.[135] The atomic bombs followed by Japan's surrender rendered such plans unnecessary.

[129] For general discussion, see 'Aerial considerations in the law of armed conflict', Green, *Essays*, 1999, ch. XVI.

[130] Art. 49(3).

[131] Part IV, Section I, Arts 48–67.

[132] Schindler and Toman, 109.

[133] *Ibid.*, 115.

[134] Palmar and Allen, 'The most deadly plan', 124 *Naval Institute Proceedings*, Jan. 1998, 79.

[135] Admiral King to General Marshall, 14 June 1945 – 'Gas is the one single weapon hitherto unused which we can have readily available which assuredly can greatly decrease the cost in American lives and should materially shorten the war', *ibid.*, 81.

World War II

During World War I it became clear that the Law of Geneva as it existed at that time was inadequate as regards the treatment of those *hors de combat*. In 1929, therefore, the Geneva Conventions were redrafted in the form of Conventions for the Amelioration of Conditions of the Wounded and Sick in Armies in the Field and Relative to the Treatment of Prisoners of War.[136] There was not the same feeling of a need to amend the Hague Law since the members of the League of Nations considered that the Covenant[137] and proposals for disarmament might provide a substitute for war, and they found reassurance in the Pact of Paris,[138] considering that the renunciation of war as an instrument of national policy had sounded the death knell for future wars. But the outbreak of World War II indicated that neither the Covenant nor the Pact was effective in preventing war, while the conduct of hostilities, particularly with regard to civilians in occupied territory, emphasised that existing treaties were not as effective as had been hoped in introducing principles of humanitarianism into the law of armed conflict.

While the war had made the inadequacies of the Geneva Conventions clear, it was the generally accepted view, at least among the United Nations,[139] as well as the Tokyo Court trying the *Shimoda* case,[140] that the rules embodied in Hague Convention IV 'were recognised by all civilised nations, and were regarded as being declaratory of the laws and customs of war',[141] and as such applicable to all belligerents, whether parties to the Convention or not. Problems also arose with regard to the 1929 Geneva Prisoners of War Convention since neither Japan nor the Soviet Union was a party thereto, and the German authorities refused to afford to Soviet prisoners the minimum protection traditionally accorded to prisoners.[142] Admiral Canaris, then German Chief of Military Intelligence, adopted an approach[143] that was similar to that of the Nuremberg Judgment towards Hague Convention IV:

> The Geneva Convention for the treatment of prisoners of war is not binding in the relationship between Germany and the USSR. Therefore only the principles of general international law on the treatment of prisoners of war apply. Since the 18th century these have been established along the lines that war captivity is neither revenge nor punishment, but solely protective custody, the only purpose of which is to prevent the prisoners of war from further participation in the war. This principle was

---

[136] Schindler and Toman, 325, 339, resp.
[137] See ch. 1 above.
[138] See ch. 1 above.
[139] The name of the wartime alliance against the Axis.
[140] See n. 125 above.
[141] *Nuremberg Judgment*, see n. 95 above.
[142] Re the treatment of Soviet prisoners of war, see *Nuremberg Judgment*, 46–8, 91–2; 41 Am. J. Int'l Law (1947), 226–9; 282–3.
[143] *Ibid.*, 48; 229.

developed in accordance with the view held by all armies that it is contrary to military tradition to kill or injure helpless people.

Field Marshal Keitel, who had signed many of the orders relating to prisoners of war, replied[144] 'The objections arise from the military concept of chivalrous warfare. This is the destruction of an ideology. Therefore, I approve and back the measures.' This comment is fully in line with the views of Clausewitz and Admiral Lord Fisher as to the role of international law and the fallacy of considering humanitarian principles as relevant during war.[145] As to prisoners captured by Japan, the latter informed the International Committee of the Red Cross[146] soon after Pearl Harbour that:

> since the Japanese Government has not ratified the Convention relating to the treatment of prisoners of war, ... it is not in fact bound by the said Convention. Nevertheless, as far as possible, it intends to apply the Convention, *mutatis mutandis*, to prisoners falling into its hands, while at the same time respecting the customs of each nation and people in relation to the food and clothing of prisoners.

Despite this assurance, the ill-treatment of prisoners by the Japanese soon became a matter of notoriety.[147]

The Nuremberg Judgment and Principles

The next step in the development of the law of armed conflict was the promulgation of the London Charter of 1945[148] establishing the International Military Tribunal which sat at Nuremberg, with jurisdiction over crimes against peace, war crimes and crimes against humanity.[149] The innovation in this document was the establishment of an *ad hoc* international tribunal to try the accused as distinct from the usual trial by national courts, either of the country of which the accused was a national or that which held him captive. A more significant development from the point of view of enforcement of the law was the description of crimes against peace and humanity. Neither of these had formerly been defined as a crime under international law, although a number of authorities had expressed the opinion that the Pact of Paris, 1928, had made aggressive war criminal.[150] Where crimes against

---

[144] *Ibid.*, 91–2; 282.
[145] See comments in ch. 1 above.
[146] Durand, *History of the I.C.R.C.*, vol. 2, *From Sarajevo to Hiroshima*, 521.
[147] Levie, *Documents on Prisoners of War*, US Naval War Coll., 60 Intl Law Studies, (1979), Doc. 191, citing the *Tokyo Judgment*. See also, Daws, *Prisoners of the Japanese*, 1994: Tanaka, *Hidden Horrors: Japanese War Crimes in World War II*, 1996, and, as to civilians, Chang, *The Rape of Nanking*, 1997.
[148] Schindler and Toman, 911.
[149] See Art. 6 and ch. 18 below.
[150] See ch. 1 above.

humanity are concerned, the Tribunal interpreted its Charter so as, for the purposes of the *Judgment*, crimes against humanity were virtually equated with war crimes as generally understood[151] or as part of the conspiracy to wage aggressive war and as such a crime against peace.[152] In 1946 the General Assembly of the United Nations adopted a resolution Affirming the Principles of International Law recognised by the Charter of the Nuremberg Tribunal,[153] though it should be remembered that this is only a recommendation lacking any legal force, but possessing significant political authority. Nevertheless, there is a tendency among the members of the United Nations, as well as writers, to accept this resolution as declaratory of customary law, especially as the International Law Commission, acting in accordance with a further resolution,[154] drew up a statement of Principles of International Law recognised by the Charter and Judgment.[155] Principle I affirmed the personal liability of anyone committing a crime under international law; Principle II affirmed the view that the failure of national law to condemn a particular act did not remove personal liability for that act under international law; Principle III confirmed that a head of state could not plead his status as constituting an immunity from criminal suit; Principle IV denied the defence of superior orders provided a moral choice was in fact open to an accused;[156] Principle V confirmed an alleged war criminal's right to receive a fair trial; Principle VI confirmed the criminality of the acts defined in Article 6 of the London Charter; while Principle VII reaffirmed the Tribunal's finding that complicity in any of the acts thus defined was itself criminal. In its Draft Code on Crimes Against the Peace and Security of Mankind,[157] the Commission reiterated these Principles by stating that individuals, regardless of status or rank, carried personal criminal liability. The concept of crimes against humanity has been widened by the decisions of the *ad hoc* tribunals for the former Yugoslavia and Rwanda, so as to apply in non-international as well as international conflicts and regardless of any connection with crimes against peace or war crimes as that term has been generally understood.

The Genocide Convention

A further development in the law of armed conflict was effected by the adoption of the Genocide Convention, whereby the acts defined therein are made crimes

---

[151] See, e.g., Schwelb, 'Crimes against humanity', 23 Brit. Y.B. Int'l Law (1946), 178.
[152] *Nuremberg Judgment*, 65; 249.
[153] Res. 95(I), Schindler and Toman, 921.
[154] Res. 177(II), 1947.
[155] 1950, Schindler and Toman, 923.
[156] This wording differs from that in the London Charter, which provided (Art. 8) that compliance with an order did not absolve from responsibility, 'but may be considered in mitigation of punishment if the Tribunal determines that justice so requires' see ch. 18 below.
[157] 1991, 30 I.L.M., 1584.

under international law, 'whether committed in time of peace or in time of war'. In order to give effect to the Convention, ratifying countries normally need to amend their criminal law and some of them have been somewhat more 'humane' in the punishment provided than is envisaged by the Convention.[158] However, for those countries, for example Canada,[159] which have amended their criminal law to make war crimes punishable,[160] the punishment may be more severe than is provided by the criminalisation of genocide as such. Thus, in 1997 a German court sentenced Nicola Jorgić, a Bosnian Serb, resident in Germany, for having committed genocide against Muslims in Bosnia. In the *Tadić* case[161] the Trial Chamber of the War Crimes Tribunal for the former Yugoslavia held that 'genocide [is] itself a specific form of crime against humanity', raising the possibility that in future cases it may be necessary only to charge crimes against humanity with genocide as part of the *res gestae*.

The Geneva Conventions, 1949

Perhaps one of the most significant developments in the law of armed conflict since 1907 was the adoption in 1949[162] of four Conventions replacing the two Geneva Conventions of 1929: I – Wounded and Sick in the Field; II – Wounded, Sick and Shipwrecked at Sea; III – Prisoners of War; IV – Civilians. Of these, the Civilians Convention is completely new and is the consequence of the treatment suffered by civilian populations of occupied territories during World War II and represents the first attempt to protect the civilian population during conflict, although it is essentially concerned only with the protection of civilians in occupied territory and not the treatment of civilians in a belligerent's own territory, unless such civilians possess enemy nationality.[163]

All four Conventions are to apply to any international armed conflict, whether a declared war or not, and even if one of the parties does not recognise the existence of a state of war. They also apply if there is a partial or total occupation of another's

---

[158] 1948, Schindler and Toman, 231.

[159] Whereas the Convention talks of 'effective remedies,' the amendment to the Canadian Criminal Code, for example, only embraces 'killing members of the group' and 'deliberately inflicting on the group conditions of life calculated to bring about its physical destruction', and imposes a penalty of only five years which is subject to reduction on parole.

[160] See, e.g., Green, 'Canadian law, war crimes and crimes against humanity', 59 Brit. Y.B. Int'l Law, 1988, 217; Fenrick, 'The prosecution of war criminals in Canada', 12 Dalhousie L. J (1989), 256.

[161] *The Prosecutor* v. *Dusko Tadić* (*Sentencing Judgment*) Case No. IT-94-1-T, 14 July 1997, para. 8.

[162] Schindler and Toman, 373, 401, 423, 495, resp.

[163] After the Gulf War, 1991, it was made clear that Iraq would be responsible for the ill-treatment of Coalition diplomats or civilians held in Kuwait or Iraq.

territory, even if the occupation has met with no armed resistance. Also, unlike the 1907 Hague Conventions, the 1949 Geneva Conventions expressly reject the 'all-participation clause'[164] and provide for their application as between the parties, even though one of the belligerents is not a party to the particular Convention. If the latter abides by the Convention, belligerents which are parties are obliged to observe the provisions of the Convention with regard to such a belligerent.

Since the Conventions are to apply in any international armed conflict and regardless of the recognition of the existence of a state of war, as well as in the event of an unopposed occupation, the Conventions reject the use of the technical term 'war' in favour of 'armed conflict', an important factor in view of the fact that most of the conflicts which had occurred after 1945 did not amount to war as that term was normally understood. As a consequence, too, the term 'enemy' has given place to 'adverse party'.

Common Article 3

Traditionally, international law and the Conventions relating to armed conflict have had no relevance to internal conflicts. In 1949, however, a decision was made to extend a minimum of humanitarian protection to the parties involved in a non-international conflict. As a consequence, each of the Conventions contains a common Article 3, whereby in such a conflict:

> each Party ... shall be bound to apply, as a minimum ... (1) Persons taking no active part in the hostilities, including members of the armed forces who have laid down their arms and those placed *hors de combat* by sickness, wounds, detention, or any other cause, shall in all circumstances be treated humanely, without any adverse distinction founded on race, colour, religion or faith, sex, birth, wealth, or any other similar criteria. To this end the following acts are and shall remain prohibited at any time and in any place whatsoever with respect to [such] persons: (a) violence to life and person, in particular murder of all kinds, mutilation, cruel treatment and torture; (b) taking of hostages; (c) outrages upon personal dignity, in particular, humiliating and degrading treatment; (d) the passing of sentences and the carrying out of executions without previous judgment pronounced by a regularly constituted court,[165] affording all the judicial guarantees which are recognised as indispensable by civilised peoples. (2) The wounded and sick [and shipwrecked] shall be collected and cared for.

This common Article 3 goes on to provide that 'the application of the preceding provisions shall not affect the legal status of the Parties'. This means that the application of the provisions does not change the nature of the conflict into an

---

[164] See above, text to n. 93.

[165] This may be a court martial or a military war crimes court, provided the safeguards referred to are observed.

international armed conflict,[166] nor does it remove the possibility that any member of the forces of the parties involved may be tried for treason and treated as any convicted traitor,[167] even though such treatment is not in accord with the treatment provided for prisoners of war by Convention III.[168] In an international conflict, a belligerent is entitled to treat as traitors, after trial, any members of the adverse party's forces who may in fact be nationals of that belligerent, or personnel originally belonging to its armed forces who, after capture, have joined the forces of the captor.[169]

Grave breaches and war crimes

The Conventions make one further departure of major significance. For the first time they provide in treaty form and in clear terms an obligation upon states to punish what the Conventions describe as 'grave breaches',[170] even if those states are not parties to the conflict, the offenders and their victims not their nationals, and even though the offences were committed outside the territorial jurisdiction of the state concerned.[171] In other words, the Conventions have introduced the concept of universal jurisdiction in so far as grave breaches are concerned, and if the state in question is unwilling to try an offender within its territory it is obliged to hand him over for trial to any party to the Convention making out a *prima facie* case. In order to remove any doubt that might exist as to whether any breaches of the law of war not amounting to grave breaches are still to be treated as punishable, Protocol I provides that 'without prejudice to the application of the Conventions and of this Protocol, grave breaches of these instruments shall be regarded

[166] See, e.g., the conflict between South Africa and the South West Africa People's Organization prior to the establishment of Namibia. However, when Yugoslavia disintegrated in 1992 and some of the Republics declared their independence and acquired recognition, sometimes prematurely, by third states, there was a tendency to regard the conflicts between these 'independent' entities and the rump Yugoslavia as international conflicts.

[167] See, e.g., *State* v. *Sagarius* [1983] 1 S.A.L.R., 833 (S.W.A.), Eng. tr. Green, 'Terrorism and armed conflict: the plea and the verdict', 19 Israel Y.B. H.R. (1989), 55; for a decision re the armed wing of the African National Congress in South Africa, see *State* v. *Mogoerane* (1982) South Africa Lawyers for Human Rights, Bulletin no. 1 (Feb. 1983), 18. In such cases, persons captured by the armed forces tend to be treated as prisoners of war until the political organs have decided whether to proceed against them or not.

[168] Problems arise when, as in Vietnam, one of the parties to a conflict is a state foreign to the territory involved and hands captives to the authority it recognizes as government of the entire territory, even though part of that territory may in fact be governed by an authority opposed to the intervening state's local ally.

[169] This occurred in World War II with large numbers of Indian Army personnel captured by the Japanese, see Green, 'The Indian National Army Trials', 11 M.L.R. (1947), 290. See also Green, *Essays*, 1999, ch. XI, 'The Azad Hind Fauj'; *R.* v. *Casement* [1917] 1 K.B., 98.

[170] Convention I, Art. 50; II, Art. 51; III, Art. 130; IV, Art. 147; see ch. 18 below.

[171] I-49; II-50; III-129; IV-146; see chs 17, 18 below.

as war crimes'.[172] This also means that those offences not amounting to 'grave breaches' are still 'war crimes' and punishable as such.

World War II showed that in modern war it is not only public property belonging to the enemy or private property belonging to enemy personnel that is liable to seizure or destruction. Historic monuments, particularly those of a military character,[173] places of worship, museums and the like were frequently destroyed, while cultural property, such as works of art, antiques, and similar memorabilia, were often stolen by government or other senior officers, or were transported by an occupying authority to its home territory.[174] To deal with such problems in the future, the Convention for the Protection of Cultural Property in the Event of Armed Conflict was signed in 1954.[175] The Convention defines cultural property rather widely describing it as part of 'the cultural heritage of all mankind',[176] which has been specially marked in accordance with the terms of the Convention as immune from attack during armed conflict. Protocol I makes an intentional attack upon such objects a grave breach of the Protocol, provided the object concerned has not been used in support of the military effort.[177] Problems will arise when, for example, a museum or a religious or educational building has been used as a temporary resting area for troops as is alleged to have been the case after the retreat of the British forces from Dunkirk in 1940.

Humanitarian law and civilian protection

The next major development in the history of international law that attempts to control the conduct of armed conflict was the adoption by the International Conference on Human Rights, Tehran, of a Resolution calling for Respect for Human

[172] Art. 86(5).
[173] Often, too, a victor destroyed such monuments in former enemy territory under temporary occupation after the cessation of hostilities.
[174] In many cases, the original owner had difficulty in recovering such national cultural objects from a victor who had 'liberated' them from a defeated enemy, or from one to which they had been transferred to prevent their falling into enemy hands, see, e.g., Williams, 'The Polish art treasures in Canada, 1946–60', 15 Can. Y.B. Int'l Law (1977), 146; see also Greenfield, *The Return of Cultural Treasures*, 1996; Akimsha and Kozlov, *Beautiful Loot: The Soviet Plunder of Europe's Art Treasures*, 1995.
[175] Schindler and Toman, 745. By Hague Regulations, 1907, Art. 27 (*ibid.*, 84) during 'sieges and bombardments all necessary steps must be taken to spare, as far as possible, buildings dedicated to religion, art, science, or charitable purposes, historic monuments, hospitals ... provided they are not being used at the time for military purposes' and the besieged was required to mark such places and notify the attacker beforehand.
[176] There is no difficulty with such monuments as the Vatican, the Louvre, the Pyramids, the Taj Mahal or St. Paul's Cathedral, but some countries, e.g., The Netherlands and Switzerland, have interpreted this to apply to all national monuments.
[177] Art. 85.

Rights in Armed Conflicts.[178] While none of the resolutions adopted by the Conference possessed legal force, the General Assembly of the United Nations instructed the Secretary-General to refer them to such bodies as might be concerned with their implementation. The resolution drew attention to the fact that the Hague Conventions were only intended as a first step in the codification of the law of armed conflict; that the 1925 Geneva Protocol on gas warfare had not been universally accepted[179] and probably needed revising; that the 1949 Geneva Conventions were not sufficiently broad in scope to cover all modern armed conflicts; and that there was generally insufficient regard given to humanitarian considerations in such conflicts. The resolution also made a major departure in the traditional law of armed conflict by including a reference to the need to protect those who were engaged in 'struggles' against 'minority racist or colonial régimes', recommending that they should be treated as prisoners of war or political prisoners.

Some six months later the General Assembly adopted a resolution[180] confirming the Resolution of the 1965 Vienna Conference of the Red Cross[181] on the Protection of Civilian Populations against the Dangers of Indiscriminate Warfare, and agreeing that '(i) the right of parties to a conflict to adopt means of injuring the enemy is not unlimited; (ii) it is prohibited to launch attacks against the civilian population, as such; (iii) distinction must be made at all times between persons taking part in the hostilities and members of the civilian population to the effect that the latter be spared as much as possible'. The Secretary-General was invited to consult with the International Committee of the Red Cross to give effect to this call for observance of human rights in armed conflicts.

Before the International Committee was able to do anything substantial from this point of view, the Institute of International Law[182] adopted a Resolution at its Edinburgh meeting 1969[183] concerning the distinction between military and nonmilitary objectives and the problems associated with weapons of mass destruction. Perhaps the major significance of this resolution lies in the references to the sources of the international law of armed conflict, and particularly the affirmation of what its members considered to be rules of established law, both conventional and customary. It should be noted, however, that the United States 'does not accept the [Institute Edinburgh Resolutions] as an accurate statement of international law relating to armed conflict ... [but] we regard as declaratory of existing customary international law ... [the] general principles recognised

---

[178] 1968, Schindler and Toman, 261. This Conference was convened by the UN as part of the International Human Rights Year 1968 celebrations, marking the twentieth anniversary of the adoption of the Universal Declaration of Human Rights in 1948.

[179] At that time the US had not yet ratified the Protocol, and its FM-27, *The Law of Land Warfare* made it clear that the US was not bound by it in any way. The US ratified in 1975.

[180] Res. 2444 (XXIII) 1968, Schindler and Toman, 263.

[181] *Ibid.*, 251.

[182] See n. 80 above.

[183] Schindler and Toman, 265.

[and] unanimously adopted by the United Nations General Assembly'.[184] Never-theless, in view of the status of the Institute and the importance of *opinio juris* in the development of international law with its Resolutions often forming the basis of later legal instruments, and especially in view of the significance of its Oxford *Manual*[185] as a source of armed conflict law, its resolution should not be ignored:

Reaffirming the existing rules of international law whereby the recourse to force is prohibited in international relations.

Considering that, if an armed conflict occurs in spite of these rules, the protection of the civilian population is one of the essential obligations of the parties.

Having in mind the general principles of international law, the customary rules and the conventions and agreements which clearly restrict the extent to which the parties engaged in a conflict may harm the adversary,

Having also in mind that these rules, which are enforced by international and national courts, have been formally confirmed on several occasions by a large number of international organisations and especially by the United Nations Organisation,

Being of the opinion that these rules have kept their full validity notwithstanding the infringements suffered,

Having in mind that the consequences which the indiscriminate conduct of hostilities and particularly the use of nuclear, chemical and bacteriological weapons, may involve for civilians and for mankind as a whole,

Notes that the following rules form part of the principles to be observed in armed conflicts by any *de jure* or *de facto* government, or by any other authority responsible for the conduct of hostilities:

1 The obligation to respect the distinction between military objectives and non-military objectives as well as between persons participating in the hostilities and members of the civilian populations remains a fundamental principle of the international law in force.

2 There can be considered as military objectives only those which, by their very nature or purpose or use, make an effective contribution to military action, or exhibit a generally recognised military significance, such as that their total or partial destruction in the actual circumstances gives a substantial, specific and immediate military advantage to those who are in a position to destroy them.

3 Neither the civilian population nor any of the objects expressly protected by conventions or agreements can be considered as military objectives, nor yet

(a) under whatsoever circumstances the means indispensable for the survival of the civilian population,

(b) those objects which, by their nature or use, serve primarily humanitarian or peaceful purposes such as religious or cultural needs.

4 Existing international law prohibits all armed attacks on the civilian population as such, as well as on non-military objects, notably dwellings or other buildings sheltering the civilian population, so long as these are not used for military pur-

---

[184] Letter, 22 Sept. 1972, from General Counsel, Dept. of Defense, to Senator Edward Kennedy, Chairman, Subcommittee on Refugees of Committee on Judiciary, 67 Am. J. Int'l Law, 1973, 122.

[185] See n. 81 above.

poses to such an extent as to justify action against them under the rules regarding military objectives as set forth in the second paragraph hereof.[186]

5 The provisions of the preceding paragraphs do not affect the application of the existing rules of international law which prohibit the exposure of civilian populations and of non-military objects to the destructive effects of military means.

6 Existing international law prohibits, irrespective of the type of weapon used, any action whatsoever designed to terrorise the civilian population.

7 Existing international law prohibits the use of all weapons which, by their nature, affect indiscriminately both military objectives and non-military objects, or both armed forces and civilian populations. In particular, it prohibits the use of weapons the destructive effect of which is so great that it cannot be limited to specific military objectives or is otherwise uncontrollable (self-generating weapons), as well as of 'blind' weapons.[187]

8 Existing international law prohibits all attacks for whatsoever motive or by whatsoever means for the annihilation of any group, region or urban centre with no possible distinction between armed forces and civilian populations or between military and non-military objectives.[188]

Subsequently, in 1970, the General Assembly adopted a Resolution,[189] without opposition, affirming 'the basic principles for the protection of civilian populations in armed conflicts, without prejudice to their future elaboration within the framework of progressive development of the international law of armed conflict'. The first of these principles asserted that 'fundamental human rights, as accepted in international law and laid down in international instruments, continue to apply fully in situations of armed conflict'. This is something of a departure from previous understanding for it would normally be thought that both the Hague and Geneva Law constitute *lex specialis* which override the *lex generalis* to be found in human rights instruments and which might be considered as applicable in time of peace, though these instruments do recognise that most of their provisions, but not all, are derogable in time of emergency,[190] which would include an armed conflict. The remaining principles proclaimed by the Assembly are abstracted from the Declaration of Tehran and the Institute's Edinburgh Resolution. The adoption of the resolution without opposition, not even that of the United States, lends support to the view that the members of the United Nations accept the opinion of the Institute that the principles embodied in its resolution are in fact expressive of existing international law.

---

[186] There can be little doubt that a munitions factory as well as the barracks within its compound in which the workers reside is a military objective. It is questionable, however, whether their houses outside the factory would also qualify, even in the absence of any barracks.

[187] This is clearly directed against nuclear weapons. However, there is no specific treaty banning such weapons and it is controversial whether they are legal or not, see ch. 7 below.

[188] This would seem to be directed against the pattern and saturation bombing raids of World War II.

[189] Res. 2675 (XXV), Schindler and Toman, 267.

[190] See, e.g., Green, 'Derogation of human rights in emergency situations', 16 Can. Y.B. Int'l Law (1978), 92.

In 1972 at the urging of the General Assembly, a Convention was adopted on the Prohibition of the Development, Production and Stockpiling of Bacteriological (Biological) and Toxin Weapons and their Destruction.[191] Its preamble recalls the 1925 Geneva Protocol[192] and states the conviction of the parties 'of the importance and urgency of eliminating from the arsenals of States, through effective means, such dangerous weapons of mass destruction as those using chemical or bacteriological (biological) agents'. However, in view of the difficulty of getting agreement with regard to chemical weapons they expressed their recognition of the fact that an agreement on bacteriological and toxin weapons would constitute a valuable first step, and they pledged themselves never to develop, produce or stockpile such weapons and undertook to destroy their stocks. In January 1993, however, a United Nations Convention on the Prohibition of the Development, Production, Stockpiling and Use of Chemical Weapons and on Their Destruction was adopted and signed by 144 states.[193]

Geneva updated

Responding to the calls made upon it by the Tehran Conference and the United Nations, the International Committee of the Red Cross undertook a study of the possibility of bringing the 1949 Geneva Law up to date, and in 1974 the Swiss Government invited the representatives of 122 governments as well as of national liberation movements to meet at Geneva to consider draft proposals prepared by the Red Cross. However, it failed to invite the Republic of South Africa then engaged in conflict with the South West Africa People's Organisation, even though that Organisation attended as a national liberation movement. The Geneva Diplomatic Conference on the Reaffirmation and Development of International Humanitarian Law Applicable in Armed Conflicts ended in 1977 with the adoption of two Protocols additional to the Geneva Conventions of 1949.[194] Protocol I dealt with international armed conflicts, while Protocol II for the first time constituted an international agreement directed at the application of humanitarian principles in non-international armed conflicts. Prior to this, there had only been Article 3 common to all four 1949 Conventions.[195]

Apart from bringing the law up to date, Protocol I makes fundamental changes in the law as it had existed in international armed conflicts.[196] It recognises that struggles conducted by national liberation movements in the name of self-

---

[191] Schindler and Toman, 137.
[192] See above, n. 133.
[193] 32 I.L.M. 800
[194] Schindler and Toman, 621, 689, resp.
[195] See above, p. 42.
[196] See, e.g., Green, 'The new law of armed conflict', 15 Can. Y.B. Int'l Law (1977), 3; and for a detailed analysis of the Protocols, paragraph by paragraph, see Bothe, *et al.*, *New Rules for Victims of Armed Conflicts.*

determination are to be considered as international conflicts and subject to the international law of armed conflict;[197] it changes the definition of combatants in respect of those fighting on behalf of such movements though not wearing a recognised uniform; it extends the protection given to civilian and non-military objects, and also forbids action which is likely to have a long-term deleterious effect upon civilians; forbids action against certain establishments which are likely to release 'dangerous forces'; it extends the rights and privileges of medical and similar personnel and units; deals with protection of civilians; defines mercenaries and denies them combatant status; widens the concept of grave breaches to be found in the Geneva Conventions; and for the first time recognises civil defence as a matter requiring separate acknowledgement in the law of international conflict.[198]

The Protocol does not replace the Geneva Conventions of 1949, but reaffirms and develops them. Insofar, therefore, as it merely restates or rephrases the obligations in those Conventions it would be binding even for a state which had not ratified or acceded to it, but which is a party to the Conventions. Equally, any state refusing to ratify or accede to the Protocol will remain bound by the Conventions and by any principle embodied in the Protocol which is in fact merely a reaffirmation of what already exists in customary international law. If the Protocol is compared with the Edinburgh Resolution of the Institute, it becomes clear that many of the principles embodied in the Protocol are really expressions of what the Institute already considered to be established and accepted law. However, how much is new will be controversial because of the fact that there is no clear articulation of the rules considered to be already in existence and because of modern state practice, as well as the tardiness or refusal of many major military powers to ratify the Protocol. Moreover, the Protocol has made little difference to the situation regarding aerial warfare, although it does state that its restrictions relating to attacks apply to all attacks from the air against objectives on land but do not otherwise affect the rules of international law applicable in armed conflict in the air.

For the main part, Protocol II seeks to extend the humanitarian protection afforded by Article 3 common to the Geneva Conventions to those participating in a non-international conflict, defined with so high a threshold as virtually to be confined to a civil war situation in which both the government and the rebel forces are in control of part of the national territory.[199]

While there has been no effort made to draw up a convention prohibiting the use of nuclear or other non-conventional weapons, in 1980 a Convention was drawn up on Prohibitions or Restriction on the Use of Certain Conventional Weapons which may be Deemed to be Excessively Injurious or to Have Indiscriminate Effects.[200]

---

[197] See ch. 6 below.
[198] See ch. 14 below.
[199] See ch. 19 below.
[200] Schindler and Toman, 179; I-185; II-*ibid.*; III-190. See also, Fenrick, 'New developments in the law concerning the use of conventional weapons in armed conflict', 19 Can. Y.B. Int'l Law (1981), 229.

To this were annexed three Protocols. Protocol I prohibits the use of any weapons 'the primary effect of which is to injure by fragments which in the human body escape detection by X-rays', although no state is understood to have any such weaponry in its armoury nor is it foreseen that such weapons will be developed in the future. Protocol II deals with the use of mines, booby traps and other devices on land, but expressly excludes from its purview anti-ship mines at sea or in inland waterways. The main aim is to protect civilians from such weapons, while at the same time to prevent them from being used against troops in a perfidious fashion, such as in connection with protective emblems or, for example, attached to corpses. In 1996 this Protocol was amended[201] with the aim of the eventual banning of the manufacture, stockpiling or use of all anti-personnel mines.[202] Finally, Protocol III prohibits or restricts the use of incendiary weapons, understood as those in which fire is a primary rather than incidental or consequential means of warfare. Incendiaries have become of less significance with the increasing recourse to mechanised warfare as compared with trench warfare or even house-to-house fighting. As a result, the Protocol excludes from its strictures weapons which are primarily intended to have a penetrating or blast effect and 'used against military objectives, such as armoured vehicles, aircraft and installations or facilities'. It would appear, therefore, that in those circumstances when fire is likely to be most effective and the military victims thereof most severely injured it remains a legitimate weapon. Additionally, in 1995, a further Protocol (IV)[203] was added to the Convention dealing with blinding laser weapons, prohibiting the use of 'laser weapons specifically designed, as their sole combat function or as one of their combat functions, to cause permanent blindness to unenhanced vision, that is to the naked eye or to the eye with corrective eyesight devices … [However,] blinding as an incidental or collateral effect of the legitimate military employment of laser systems, *including laser systems used against optical equipment*, is not covered by the prohibition.

Generality of the law

The above discussion on the history and sources of the law of armed conflict has paid most attention to warfare on land because this is the region for which most agreements have been drawn up, although attention has been paid to both aerial and naval warfare where that has been considered necessary. However, it should be noted that the principles underlying the agreements on land warfare are applicable, to the extent practicable, to both aerial and naval warfare too. In addition to the international agreements mentioned, the law of armed conflict is still governed by those principles of international customary law which have developed virtually

---

[201] 35 I.L.M. 1209.
[202] The US refused to sign this treaty on the ground that all its mines were self-destructive and that, in any case, such mines were essential along the North–South Korean border.
[203] 35 I.L.M. 1217, italics added.

since feudal times, together with such considerations of humanity as may be considered as amounting to general principles of law recognised by civilised nations[204] and, as such, rules of international law in accordance with Article 38 of the Statute of the International Court of Justice. Further, there is nothing to prevent any state from laying down additional rules regulating the conduct of its own forces. Individual countries may also pass legislation as to the means by which jurisdiction for breaches of the law of armed conflict is to be exercised over its own forces[205] or with regard to captured members of the forces of the adverse party or, even, of a belligerent in a conflict in which the state concerned is not involved.[206] Moreover, it should not be forgotten that, as pointed out by the World Court in its *Nuclear Weapons* opinion,[207] the Martens Clause with its reference to 'the principles of the law of nations, as they result from the usages established among civilized peoples, from the laws of humanity and the dictates of the public conscience' is still in force.

[204] See, e.g., charges in the *Einsatzgruppen Case* (*US* v. *Ohlendorf*, 1947), Charge 10 of which alleged 'acts and conduct … which constitute violations of the general principles of criminal law as derived from the criminal law of all civilised nations', 4 Trials of War Criminals before the Nuremberg Military Tribunals under Control Council Law no. 10, 21.

[205] This is done by way of national military codes which are to be found in most countries, e.g., US, Code of Military Discipline; UK, Army Act and Queen's Regulations and Orders; Canada, National Defence Act and Queen's Regulations and Orders; Federal Republic of Germany, the Soldiers' Act and the Military Penal Code; France, Decrét no. 66, 1966; while in other countries, e.g., Israel, the position is adequately covered by the Penal Code.

[206] See, e.g., Canadian War Crimes Act, 1946 or amendments to the Criminal Code, 1985; see also nn. 159, 160 above.

[207] I.C.J. [1996] 226, 257, paras. 78–9.

3

International and non-international armed conflict

Classic position

Historically, international law is concerned only with the relations between states. As a result, the international law of armed conflict developed in relation to inter-state conflicts was not in any way concerned with conflicts occurring within the territory of any state or with a conflict between an imperial power and a colonial territory. In accordance with the principle of absolute sovereignty over domestic affairs, such non-international conflicts were considered to be within the domestic jurisdiction of the sovereign concerned, although on occasion, allied states were prepared to offer assistance to a sovereign in suppressing such a conflict,[1] while, as was clear at the time of the Spanish Civil War, third states might intervene on behalf of a rebel organisation. Moreover, on occasion the parties to such a conflict have behaved *inter se* as if they were involved in an international conflict, while third states, either because the scale of the conflict has gravely intensified or their own interests have been affected, have on occasion declared their neutrality and treated the conflict as if it were one of an international character. This was what happened at the time of the American Civil War when Britain invoked the Foreign Enlistment Act.[2] Traditionally, for an armed conflict to warrant regulation by the international law of armed conflict it was necessary for the situation to amount to a war, that is to say a contention between states[3] through the

---

[1] See, e.g., *Ford* v. *Surget* (1878), 97 US 594; *Thorington* v. *Smith* (1868), 75 US 1.

[2] See British Proclamation, 13 May 1861, 51 B.F.S.P. 165; and for a US decision re the Cuban revolution against Spain, *The Three Friends* (1897), 166 US 1.

[3] In 1991 and 1992, when civil wars in eastern Europe resulted in the breakdown of, e.g., Yugoslavia, the Security Council and the European Community treated a number of such civil conflicts as if they were international conflicts and sought to mediate between the parties. In some cases, 'peace-keeping' forces were sent to maintain the peace between the contesting parties. Similar actions were taken in regard to Cambodia and Afghanistan. In Bosnia, formerly part of Yugoslavia, the intervening states tended to operate more as 'peace-makers', even organising elections, under the auspices of NATO, and undertaking bombing attacks against Serbian forces and installations. In 1999, when the Yugoslav authorities refused to accept NATO's demands that it cease its 'ethnic cleansing' and other

medium of their armed forces, such forces being under a regular command, wearing uniform or such other identifiable marks as to make them recognisable at a distance, and conducting their hostilities in accordance with the international rules of armed conflict. Normally, when such a conflict develops between states[4] there is a severance of the relations between them, with the exception of those agreements that have been drawn up to regulate conduct during armed conflict. However, on some occasions the parties to a conflict do not intend a complete severance to take place and then some of their relations remain subject to the international law of peace, as was the situation between the United Kingdom and Egypt during the Suez operations of 1956, when the Prime Minister of Great Britain maintained that there was no war in existence, but only an 'armed conflict'.[5] Such a situation, when some inter-state activities remain subject to the law of peace and others to the law of armed conflict, has been described as a *status mixtus*,[6] and, since 1949, at least the Geneva Conventions[7] would operate. However, there is nothing to stop a third state in such circumstances from holding, for such purposes as insurance[8] or contract,[9] that an armed conflict amounting to 'war' does in fact exist. This, however, is dependent on national rather than international law, even though the effect may be to bring some of the law of armed conflict into play. During 1991, 1992 and 1993 both the European Community and the Security Council have tended to regard some civil conflicts arising from the efforts of part of a federation to break away from the established state as if they were international conflicts, as has been the case in Yugoslavia with the Security Council going so far as to set up an *ad hoc* tribunal to judge those accused of war crimes, genocide and crimes against humanity.[10]

The impact of Protocol I, 1977

While the full panoply of the international law of armed conflict does not apply to non-international conflicts, the situation has now been changed and to some

---

atrocities against dissidents in Kosovo province, NATO launched extensive bombing attacks against Serbia, which formed the major part of what remained of Yugoslavia.

[4] Re the legal effects of the outbreak of an armed conflict, see ch. 4 below.

[5] Parliamentary Debates, Commons, 1 Nov. 1956, vol. 558, col. 1645. See Green, 'Armed conflict, war and self-defence', 6 *Essays*, 1999, ch. III.

[6] See, e.g., Schwarzenberger, 'Jus Pacis ac Belli?', 37 Am. J. Int'l Law (1943), 460; Jessup, 'Should international law recognise an intermediate state between war and peace?', 8 Am. J. Int'l Law (1954), 98.

[7] Schindler and Toman, 373–594.

[8] See, e.g., *Schneiderman* v. *Metropolitan Casualty Co. of New York* (1961), 220 N.Y. Supp. 947.

[9] See, e.g., *Kawasaki Kisen Kabushiki Kaisha of Kobe* v. *Bantham SS Co.* [1939] 2 K.B., 44; *Navios Corp.* v. *The Ulysses II* (1958), 161 F. Supp. 832.

[10] A similar tribunal has been established in relation to crimes committed during the civil war in Rwanda. See below, chs 18, 19.

extent certain non-international conflicts have come under the aegis of international law since 1977 with the adoption of Article 1 (4) of Protocol I and Protocol II[11] additional to the 1949 Geneva Conventions, while Article 3 common to those Conventions already sought to impose minimal humanitarian considerations even in such conflicts. However, acts of violence committed by private individuals or groups which are regarded as acts of terrorism,[12] brigandage, or riots which are of a purely sporadic character[13] are outside the scope of such regulation and remain subject to national law or specific treaties relating to the suppression or punishment of terrorism.[14] Such acts occurring during an international armed conflict may amount to war crimes or grave breaches of the Geneva Conventions or Protocol I[15] and render those responsible liable to trial under the law of armed conflict.[16]

Since the adoption of the Charter of the United Nations it has sometimes been contended that armed conflict contrary to the provisions of the Charter cannot be lawful and that since military operations conducted under the auspices of the United Nations constitute enforcement or policing undertakings they cannot be considered as war in the technical sense. In practice, in both these situations the laws of armed conflict will apply and will do so on an equal basis as between both sides.[17] Moreover, since the purpose of the law of armed conflict is to a great extent directed to the preservation of the principles of humanitarianism, even the forces of a state alleged to be waging an illegal war will be protected by and required to observe that law.[18] This principle of equality as between the parties is spelled out in Article 1 common to the Geneva Conventions which are to be respected 'in all circumstances', while common Article 2 declared that they are to apply 'to any … armed conflict which may arise between two or more of the High Contracting Parties, even if the state of war is not recognised by one of them'. As if to remove any possible doubt, the preamble of Protocol I proclaims that the Conventions and Protocol 'must be fully applied in all circumstances to all persons who are protected by those instruments, without any adverse distinction based on the nature or origin of the armed conflict or on the causes espoused by or attributed to the Parties to the conflict'. It is clear, therefore, that for the parties to these instruments

[11] Schindler and Toman, 621, 628, 689.
[12] See, e.g., *Pan American World Airways Inc.* v. *Aetna Casualty and Surety Co.* (1974), 505 F. 2d 99; see also Green, 'Terrorism and armed conflict: the plea and the verdict', 19 Israel Y.B.H.R. (1989), 131.
[13] Pr. II. Art. 1(2).
[14] See, e.g., the Conventions re offences against aircraft, Tokyo, 1963, 704 U.N.T.S. 219, The Hague, 1970, 860 *ibid.*, 105, Montreal, 1971, 974 *ibid.*, 177; re internationally protected persons, 1973, 1035 *ibid.*, 167; re hostage-taking, 1979, 18 I.L.M. 1422.
[15] Schindler and Toman, 621.
[16] See below, ch. 18.
[17] See below, ch. 20.
[18] See, e.g., Lauterpacht, 'Rules of warfare in an unlawful war', in Lipsky, *Law and Politics in the World Community*, 89; US Dept. of the Air Force, Pamphlet A.F.P., 110–34, *Commander's Handbook on the Law of Armed Conflict*, para. 1-4(b).

there can be no question but that the law of armed conflict, at least as much of it as is embodied in these instruments, will apply even in an unlawful war or a 'police' operation undertaken by the United Nations.

The significance of customary law

As to non-parties to the Conventions,[19] in so far as they embody rules of customary law they will apply in any international armed conflict, as will all other rules of the customary law of armed conflict. To the extent that they go beyond this, it has become common when one of the belligerents is not a party to these instruments, for the latter to announce, either spontaneously or in response to such a statement made on behalf of the signatory, that it will abide by the terms of the Conventions. Such statements were made during the Korean War by the Supreme Commander of the United Nations Forces and by the North Korean Minister of Foreign Affairs. On occasion, the non-party may also inform the International Committee of the Red Cross of its intention to abide by the Conventions so long as the belligerent which is party thereto does the same. This was done by Japan on the outbreak of the Pacific war in 1941.[20] Such declarations are always made on a *mutatis mutandis* basis, acknowledging the fact that the law of war, particularly the Geneva Law embodying principles of humanitarianism, operates on a reciprocal basis, as is emphasised by Article 2 common to the Conventions, although this provision appears to run counter to the opening paragraph of the Conventions and Protocol I which state that the 'Parties undertake to respect and ensure respect for [these instruments] in all circumstances'.

While it may be desirable to secure respect for humanitarian principles regardless of any belligerent disregarding such principles, reality demands recognition of the fact that treaty obligations not amounting to customary law

[19] A state cannot be a party to Protocol I if it is not a party to the Conventions; however a national liberation movement may, by Art. 96(3), make a declaration of accession with regard to any conflict it is waging for self-determination. On 21 June 1989 the Permanent Observer of Palestine to the Geneva Office of the UN informed the Swiss Government, as depository of the Protocols, 'that the Executive Committee of the Palestine Liberation Organisation entrusted with the functions of the Government of the State of Palestine by decision of the Palestine National Council decided, on 4 May 1989, to adhere to the four Geneva Conventions … and the two Protocols additional thereto'. On 13 September, the Swiss Federal Council informed the states parties to the Conventions and Protocols that it was not in a position to decide whether the document contained an instrument of accession, 'due to the uncertainty within the international community as to the existence or non-existence of a State of Palestine' – and 'Palestine' is not included in the list of parties published by the ICRC. As to the status of 'Palestine', see, e.g., Green, 'Terrorism and armed conflict: the plea and the verdict', 19 Israel Y.B.H.R. 1989, 131, 149–50, 157–62, 165–6; Rubin, 'PLO violence and legitimate combatancy: a response to Professor Green', *ibid.*, 167.

[20] Durand, *History of the International Committee of the Red Cross,* vol. 2, *From Sarajevo to Hiroshima,* 521.

will only be observed on a reciprocal basis. However, should any of the parties to the conflict reject all the principles and rules of the law of armed conflict, this will not excuse the other parties from their obligations to observe the minimum requirements of the law even with regard to that party. But it has been suggested that in such circumstances, especially if the lawbreaker indulges in activities that threaten the:

> preservation of ultimate values of society, it is possible that should those values be imperilled by an aggressor intent upon dominating the world the nations thus threatened might consider themselves bound to assume the responsibility of exercising the supreme right of self-preservation in a manner which, while contrary to a specific prohibition of International Law, they alone deem to be decisive for the ultimate vindication of the law of nations. The use of the atomic weapon in a contingency of this nature[21] would still be contrary to the principle that the rules of International Law apply even in relation to an aggressor in an unlawful war ... Thus if during the Second World War it had become established beyond all reasonable doubt that Germany was engaged in a systematic plan of putting to death millions of civilians in occupied territory, the use of the atomic bomb might have been justifiable as a deterrent instrument of punishment.[22]

When a treaty governing the conduct of armed conflict so provides, the rules embodied therein may be suspended in accordance with the terms of that treaty. Otherwise, and especially if it reproduces rules of customary law, they may only be disregarded on the basis of reprisals,[23] although certain treaty rules are regarded as so fundamental from the point of view of humanitarianism that they may not be made the subject of reprisal action,[24] and this principle is also part of the Vienna Convention on Treaties, 1969,[25] which states that while treaties may be revoked for prior material breaches, this does not extend to provisions relating 'to the protection of the human person contained in treaties of a humanitarian character, in particular provisions prohibiting any form of reprisals against persons protected by such treaties'. In fact, Protocol I seeks to abolish acts of reprisal against any protected persons, together with certain installations, destruction of which may cause excessive and lasting damage to civilians or to the environment.[26]

---

[21] This assumes that use of the atomic/nuclear weapon is illegal, although this is controversial at the present time, see Green, 'Nuclear weapons and the law of armed conflict', 17 Denver J. Int'l Law and Policy (1988 Fall), 1. See also I.C.J. *Nuclear Weapons* opinion [1996] 226.

[22] Lauterpacht, *Oppenheim's International Law*, vol. 2, 351.

[23] Reprisals are acts of retaliation, normally illegal, in response to prior illegal acts by the adverse party, seeking to compel the latter to comply with the rules of armed conflict. See, e.g., Kalshoven, *Belligerent Reprisals*, 1971.

[24] E.g., Convention III, Prisoners of War, Art. 13 forbids such action against prisoners.

[25] 1155 U.N.T.S. 331, 8 I.L.M. 624. Art. 60(5).

[26] E.g., Arts 51(6), 55, *etc.* See Greenwood, 'The twilight of the law of belligerent reprisals', 20 Netherlands Y.B. Int'l L. (1989), 35.

Non-international conflicts

While the rules of armed conflict law do not apply in a non-international conflict, the state in whose territory such a conflict is taking place may declare its intention to apply to the forces confronting it the principles of that law. This normally occurs when the conflict has reached the stage of major hostilities transcending a mere rebellion or revolution. When such a statement has been made, the forces confronting the government frequently make a similar statement. However, such statements only affect the parties involved in the conflict and non-involved states remain free to deny to the parties any claim to exercise against them the normal rights attaching to the parties to an international conflict. They cannot therefore invoke against such non-involved states the principles regarding neutrality that would operate in an international armed conflict.[27] However, the parties involved may, while not entitled to exercise such rights, by their activities so adversely affect the rights and interests of non-parties, for example by seeking to inhibit supplies from reaching an opponent, that a non-party may become entitled to recognise the parties to the conflict as possessing belligerent rights.[28] During the Spanish Civil War such declarations were made by a number of states that were not officially involved, although some of these refused to recognise the right of either the government or the nationalist authorities to exercise the rights accruing to belligerents against merchant vessels seeking to trade with the adverse party concerned.[29]

When a state not involved in the conflict makes a declaration recognising the belligerency of anti-government forces, the government is entitled to treat such declaration as an unfriendly or hostile act,[30] even amounting to a *casus belli* (cause of war). If, however, the government has itself recognised the belligerency of its opponents, it has no right to protest similar action by any non-involved state.

The first attempt to extend any sort of international recognition to non-international conflicts so as to impose obligations upon the parties thereto, requiring them to observe legal regulations during the conflict, was made in the form of Article 3 common to the four Geneva Conventions of 1949. By this Article, protection is stipulated on a basis of complete non-discrimination for all persons *hors de combat*, civilians and non-combatants in any non-international conflict occurring in the territory of a party to the Conventions. The purpose is to ensure that such persons are treated humanely, and the Article introduces what may be considered as the basics of humane treatment as generally understood at present. It expressly forbids such acts as cruelty, murder, torture, unfair trial, and the like. Since the provisions of Article 3 bind 'each party to the conflict', they would

---

[27] See below, ch. 16.
[28] See above, nn. 1, 2.
[29] See the Nyon Agreement, 1937, Schindler and Toman, 887.
[30] See, e.g., Lauterpacht, *Recognition in International Law*, (1947), 94–5; Chen, *The International Law of Recognition*, (1951), 50–1, 85–6; Stowell, *Intervention in International Law*, (1921), 289; Whiteman, *Digest of International Law*, vol. 2, 514, 518–19.

appear to operate even in a state of insurgency, and this is the position taken by the British *Manual of Military Law*:[31] 'if insurgency in the form of armed conflict, even if not amounting to a civil war in which the belligerency of the insurgents has been recognised, breaks out in the territory of a party to the Conventions, the requirements of the common Article 3 must be observed by both the legitimate government and the insurgents'. During the civil war in Bosnia–Herzegovina, 1991–93, it would appear that neither side was prepared to recognise such an obligation, even though Yugoslavia was a party to the Geneva Conventions and had ratified both 1977 Protocols. However, since Article 3 provides that 'the application of [its] provision shall not affect the legal status of the Parties to the conflict', the governmental authority retains the right to try any insurgent it may capture for treason, subject to the judicial guarantees and requirements of humane treatment specified in the Article. This would imply that the provisions of Article 3 would operate even though the conditions specified in Protocol II, for example, that the opponents of the government must be in control of some part of the national territory, have not been satisfied. In Bosnia, after the break-up of the former Yugoslavia, the dissident Serbs did in fact control sufficient territory to constitute themselves as the Republika SRPSKA, with enough stability to be able to enter into international agreements, for example, the Agreement on the Military Aspects of the Peace Settlement[32] annexed to the Paris General Framework Agreement for Peace in Bosnia.[33]

New developments in regard to what may be called international third-party intervention in non-international conflicts and the law applicable thereto, resulted from the break-up of Yugoslavia and the civil war in Rwanda. In each case, the Security Council decided that the situation, involving as it did extensive atrocities against civilians, constituted a threat to international peace and security calling for action under Chapter VII of the Charter. As a result the Council established two *ad hoc* criminal tribunals. That for Yugoslavia[34] was granted jurisdiction over grave breaches of the 1949 Geneva Conventions, violations of the laws and customs of war, genocide and crimes against humanity, and in the *Tadić* case[35] the Appeals Chamber decided that the rules in common Article 3, as well as the basic rules of customary law, the Genocide Convention and the law concerning crimes against humanity were applicable in non-international as well as international conflicts. Since the conflict in Rwanda was entirely non-international in character,

[31] 1958, Part III, *The Law of Land Warfare*, para. 8.
[32] 1995, 35 I.L.M. 92.
[33] *Ibid.*, 89.
[34] SC Res. 827 1993, 32 I.L.M. 1203. See, e.g., Bassiouni and Manikas, *The Laws of the International Criminal Tribunal for the Former Yugoslavia*, 1996; Fenrick, 'The development of the law of armed conflict through the jurisprudence of the International Criminal Tribunal for the former Yugoslavia', in Schmitt and Green, *The Law of Armed Conflict into the Next Millennium*, 1998, 77.
[35] Case No. IT-94-I-T 7 (May 1997); IT-94-I-A (Jan. 1998).

the Tribunal's Statute[36] only conferred jurisdiction over genocide, crimes against humanity and violations of common Article 3. Since there was no 'alien' participation in that country, there was no reference to grave breaches or the law and customs of war.

Protocol II, 1977

The first and only international agreement exclusively regulating the conduct of the parties in a non-international conflict is Protocol II of 1977 additional to the Geneva Conventions of 1949.[37] This Protocol makes it clear that the law concerning non-international armed conflicts is distinct from that regulating an international armed conflict which is subject to the provisions of Protocol I. But the former distinction between an international and a non-international armed conflict has been blurred by Article 1 of Protocol I. This includes within the definition of an international armed conflict a number of conflicts, especially those aimed at the overthrow of an alien colonial regime, which prior to 1977 were regarded as non-international conflicts outside the scope of international law.

In accordance with paragraph 4 of Article 1 of the Protocol, an international armed conflict now includes:

> armed conflicts in which peoples are fighting against colonial domination and alien occupation and against racist regimes in the exercise of their right of self-determination, as enshrined in the Charter of the United Nations and the Declaration on Principles of International Law concerning Friendly Relations and Cooperation among States in accordance with the Charter of the United Nations.[38]

Unfortunately, there is no definition of 'people' or of 'self-determination' in the Charter, and the nearest the Declaration comes to providing any is the statement: 'The establishment of a sovereign and independent state, the free association or integration with an independent State or the emergence into any other political status freely determined by a people constitute modes of implementing the right of self-determination by that people.' The Declaration goes on to provide that peoples seeking self-determination are entitled to seek and receive support in accordance with the purposes and principles of the Charter, but such support must not harm the territorial integrity or political unity of sovereign and independent States which are 'conducting themselves in compliance with the principle of equal rights and self-determination of peoples … and thus possessed of a government representing the whole people belonging to the territory without distinction as to race, creed or colour'. This would mean that only those revolutions that are aimed at the overthrow of a government made up of a minority section of the population,

---

[36] SC Res. 955 1994, 33 I.L.M. 1598.
[37] Schindler and Toman, 689.
[38] Gen. Ass. Res. 2625 (XXV), 1970.

as was the case in South Africa, or which is a colonial territory seeking its independence, as was the case in Angola, [Southern] Rhodesia or Namibia, would qualify as true seekers for self-determination. On the other hand, the Declaration goes on to provide that 'every State shall refrain from any action aimed at the partial or total disruption of the national unity and territorial integrity of any other State or country'. This suggests that third states are not permitted to assist by force of arms a movement seeking self-determination, if this would entail the creation of a breakaway state. However, this in no way inhibited India from supporting the people of East Pakistan when they broke away from Pakistan to form the separate and independent state of Bangladesh. Nor has it prevented members of the European Community or the United Nations from recognising former Republics of the Soviet Union or of Yugoslavia as independent states and admitting some of them to membership in the United Nations. Although no state has extended recognition to the Republika SRPSKA. Nor has it inhibited NATO from bombing Serbia in 1999 in the name of humanitarianism on behalf of dissidents seeking independence for the Yugoslav province of Kosovo.

Aggression

Closely related to these provisions and the duty of states to support or stand aloof from a conflict aimed at securing self-determination is the resolution of the General Assembly renouncing aggression.[39] Aggression is defined as 'the use of armed force by a State against the sovereignty, territorial integrity or political independence of another State, or in any other manner inconsistent with the Charter of the United Nations', and among the acts condemned as falling within this concept are:

> the action of a State in allowing its territory, which it has placed at the disposal of another State, to be used by that other State for perpetrating an act of aggression against a third State. The sending by or on behalf of a State of armed bands, groups, irregulars or mercenaries, which carry out acts of armed force against another State of such gravity as to amount to the acts listed above, or its substantial involvement therein.

Since it is within a state's discretion as to what entity it recognises as a state, and as so many have already done in regard to 'Palestine' or parts of Yugoslavia or the former Soviet Union, it is clear that the support given to the military forces of such national liberation or other revolutionary groups would fall within this definition. However, the resolution goes on to provide that nothing:

> in this Definition … could in any way prejudice the right to self-determination, freedom and independence, as derived from the Charter, of peoples forcibly deprived of

[39] Gen. Ass. Res. 3314 (XXIX), 1974; see also the International Law Commission's Draft Code of Crimes Against the Peace and Security of Mankind, 1991 (30 I.L.M., 1585), Arts 15–18.

that right and referred to in the Declaration on Principles of International Law concerning Friendly Relations and Co-operation among States in accordance with the Charter of the United Nations, particularly peoples under colonial and racist regimes or other forms of alien domination; nor the right of these peoples to struggle to that end and to seek and receive support, in accordance with the principles of the Charter and in conformity with the above-mentioned Declaration.

This would suggest that the United Nations has reintroduced the concept of the just war[40] and any state regarding the supporter of such an infiltration movement as acting illegally might well find itself condemned as in breach of the Charter and itself treated as an aggressor. It should be pointed out, however, that a number of western states which supported the resolution declared their opposition to the saving paragraph just spelled out. Moreover, despite the fact that the majority of the population of Kosovo in what remains of Yugoslavia is Albanian, the world community, while supporting demands for greater freedom and condemning Serbian attempts to forcibly suppress the revolt, declined in any way to encourage Kosovo's demand for self-determination. However, when, in 1999, Yugoslavia refused NATO's demands that it cease its 'ethnic cleansing' of that province, as well as other atrocities by Serb troops against the Albanian population, NATO resorted to bombing attacks on Yugoslavia, even though this seemed to encourage Kosovar demands for independence. At the time NATO instituted its bombing campaign against Yugoslavia in 1999 there was no suggestion the KLA (Kosova Liberation Army) was a national liberation movement, even though its avowed aim was self-determination and independence. In fact, only a year earlier western powers were describing the KLA as gangs of terrorists.

Self-determination and national liberation

As has been mentioned, by virtue of Protocol I a conflict directed towards the achievement of self-determination and national liberation is now regarded as an international conflict. However, neither the Protocol nor the Declaration on Friendly Relations makes any provision for determining what movement is seeking self-determination and thus qualifies as a national liberation movement. Nor does either instrument offer any assistance in determining whether a country is self-governing or what constitutes a people.[41] The decision as to whether the con-

---

[40] See above, ch. 1.

[41] Perhaps the nearest one can get to a definition is by analogy from the definition of a 'community' to be found in the advisory opinion of the World Court in the *Greco-Bulgarian Communities* issue (1930), Ser. B 17 (2 Hudson, *World Court Reports*, 640): 'a group of persons living in a given country or locality, having a race, religion, language and traditions of their own and united by this identity of race, religion, language and traditions in a sentiment of solidarity, with a view to preserving their traditions, maintaining their form of worship, ensuring the instruction and upbringing of their children in accordance with the spirit and traditions of their race and rendering mutual assistance to each other', at 21 (653–4).

ditions specified in Article 1 (4) of the Protocol have been met would appear to be completely subjective and within each state's discretion. In practice, however, the United Nations and international conferences held under its auspices or associated with it in any way have adopted the practice of allowing regional organisations within the area in which there is alleged to be a national liberation movement seeking self-determination to make the decision, and then to accept it.[42]

For states which have ratified Protocol I, a decision recognising a national liberation movement's campaign as fulfilling the requirements of Article 1 (4) suffices to bring the armed conflict undertaken by that movement into the definition of an international armed conflict. This means that the members of the national liberation movement concerned become entitled to all the privileges of a legally recognised combatant.[43] Moreover, by virtue of Protocol I, they are endowed with a number of privileges which are not normally afforded to other regular forces engaged in an international conflict. Thus, in certain circumstances, they and members of resistance forces are permitted not to wear uniforms, do not have to carry their arms openly at all times, do not have to wear marks of identification visible at a distance, and so on.[44]

As with the Geneva Conventions, Article 4 of Protocol I provides that its application 'shall not affect the legal status of the Parties to the conflict'. Nevertheless, it does have this effect in that, if the conflict is one for self-determination and within the terms of Article 1 (4), the members of the national liberation movement involved acquire the status of combatants and cannot be regarded as committing any criminal offence *vis-à-vis* the entity against which they are conducting their operations. However, if the latter is not a party to Protocol I, and probably even if it is a party thereto but continues to maintain that the struggle is not one for self-determination, it may continue to treat the members of the national liberation movement involved as traitors and subject to the national criminal law.[45] The same is probably true of a state which has ratified Protocol I prior to becoming involved in a conflict with a national liberation movement operating in its territory.

A problem may arise when a third state which is a party to the Protocol decides to recognise the conflict as one for self-determination and assists the national lib-

---

[42] See, e.g., Final Act of the Diplomatic Conference on the Reaffirmation and Development of Humanitarian Law in Armed Conflicts which produced the two Protocols: 'National Liberation Movements recognised by the Regional Intergovernmental Organisation concerned and invited by the Conference to participate in its work – Palestine Liberation Organisation, Panafricanist Congress, South West African People's Organisation. It is understood that the signature by these movements is without prejudice to the position of participating States on the question of a precedent', Schindler and Toman, 619.

[43] See below, ch. 6.

[44] It should be borne in mind that on occasion members of the regular forces left behind in occupied territory or acting as advisers to resistance movements may also operate out of uniform. It is possible that such persons are protected in the same way, Bothe, *et al.*, 352–3.

[45] As to the position during WW II, see Green, *Essays*, 1999, ch. 11 below – 'Azad Hind Fauj'.

eration forces. This may mean that members of the forces of the state against which the struggle is being waged and which has not ratified the Protocol, may find themselves if captured charged with breaches of the Protocol in that they have, on the orders of their own government, not afforded the adverse party the rights of a belligerent, while their own government may regard the intervening third state as being in breach of the Charter of the United Nations and the resolution condemning aggression. Some Arab states have afforded bases and arms to the Palestine Liberation Organisation in its conflict with Israel which has not ratified the Protocol and maintains that the PLO despite its purported accession to the Protocol is a terrorist organisation.[46]

By Article 96 of the Protocol, a national liberation movement is entitled to make a declaration undertaking to apply the Protocol and the Conventions in any conflict in which it may be engaged. When such a declaration is received by the Swiss government as depositary of the Protocol it comes into immediate effect, conferring upon the movement concerned all the rights and liabilities of a High Contracting Party, rendering 'the Conventions and this Protocol ... equally binding upon all Parties to the conflict'. By Article 100 the Swiss government is required to inform all parties to the Conventions and Protocol of receipt of this undertaking, but it may well be that due to delays in communication a party to the Protocol which is in fact unaware of the undertaking having been made would be immediately obliged to extend its rights and obligations to the national liberation movement involved, although from a practical point of view knowledge is clearly essential. This provision implies that a party to the Protocol which refuses to recognise the movement as being involved in a struggle for self-determination, and thus from the point of view of other parties an international armed conflict, would be equally bound, unless it was able to issue a formal statement to the contrary. In practice, a government which intended not to treat a 'disturbance' within its territory as one directed to self-determination when all the indications suggest that it was such a struggle, would almost certainly make this intention clear at a very early stage in the conflict. Despite its obligations with regard to information concerning accessions, the Swiss government was unwilling to regard 'Palestine' as entitled to accede to the Conventions or Protocols.[47]

Defining a non-international conflict

In view of the fact that an international conflict is subject to the law of war, while this is not so with a non-international conflict, the issue of classification becomes of major significance,[48] particularly in so far as the law concerning 'atrocities' and

---

[46] See nn. 11, 18 above. See, however, Green, *loc.cit.*, at n. 19.
[47] See n. 18 above.
[48] See, e.g., Gray, 'Bosnia and Herzegovina: civil war or inter-state conflict? Characterization and consequences', 67 Brit. Y.B. Int'l Law 1996, 155.

other 'breaches' is concerned. The *ad hoc* tribunal for Yugoslavia, however, appears to treat both international and non-international conflicts as virtually subject to the same law, at least when the acts of those accused appear to be partly independently committed, that is to say under command of Bosnian or Croatian Serbs, and partly when the actors were under control of Serbia or Croatia.

However, since Protocol I governs international armed conflicts and Protocol II those of a non-international character, the definition is of major significance. Non-international conflicts are defined in Article I of Protocol II as:

> all armed conflicts which are not covered by Article I of Protocol I and which take place in the territory of a High Contracting Party between its armed forces and dissident armed forces or other organised armed groups which, under responsible command, exercise such control over a part of its territory as to enable them to carry out sustained and concerted military operations and to implement this Protocol. The Protocol shall not apply to situations of internal disturbances and tensions, such as riots, isolated and sporadic acts of violence and other acts of a similar nature, as not being armed conflicts

even though the armed forces of the territory concerned may have been called upon by the authorities to deal with such a situation.

With the provision that the dissident movement must be in control of part of the national territory, Protocol II lays down a requirement that is more rigid than that prescribed for Protocol I, for there is no necessity for a national liberation movement to be in control of any part of the national territory for its struggle to be recognised as an international armed conflict. However, the 'control' envisaged does not necessarily involve any actual administration in a governmental sense of a defined portion of the national territory. What Article I requires is such control as will enable dissident authorities 'to carry out sustained and concerted military operations and to implement this Protocol'.

It should be noted that, to date, no group which has been recognised as a national liberation movement has been in such control of any part of the national territory, although prior to the independence of Angola all three national liberation movements involved were operating exclusively in the national territory and competing for supremacy. The Palestine Liberation Organisation, whose establishment of a 'State of Palestine' has been recognised by a number of states, to some extent still operates from outside of Israel the Organisation – now Authority – would argue – and receive much support for this contention – that the territory now placed under its control is in fact no longer part of Israel. Similarly, until the release of Nelson Mandela and the legalisation of the African National Congress the dissident movements directed against South Africa had their bases outside the country, while the South West Africa People's Organisation, which attended the Geneva Conference on Humanitarian Law which drafted the Protocol, equally had not sufficient control over any part of south-west Africa/Namibia to satisfy the terms of Protocol II.

The definition of a non-international armed conflict in Protocol II has a threshold that is so high in fact, that it would exclude most revolutions and rebellions, and would probably not operate in a civil war until the rebels were well established and had set up some form of *de facto* government, as had been the case with the nationalist revolution in Spain. It is interesting to note that in none of the conflicts which occurred in the Soviet Union or Yugoslavia prior to or during the dissolution of those states was there any suggestion that the situation was governed by Protocol II, while the recognition accorded by some third states to Croatia, Slovenia and other Yugoslav Republics implied that those states considered an international conflict to be in progress. Although the Protocol does not apply in an insurrectionary situation, the parties involved in such a conflict would remain bound by the minimum conditions laid down in Article 3 common to the Geneva Conventions as well as any human rights agreements to which the government involved was a party, or to any human rights principles which had hardened into *jus cogens* or customary law which is the position under the Statutes of the *ad hoc* tribunals.

The technicality of the definitions in both Protocols I and II makes it difficult for service personnel to know whether an adverse party is to be treated as a band of rebels, a dissident group entitled to treatment in accordance with Protocol II, a national liberation movement seeking self-determination in accordance with Protocol I and entitled to be considered as parties to an international armed conflict, or a group of criminals indulging in violence. The armed personnel concerned must be guided by the decision of their government in this regard. While a member of the armed forces of a country which denies that its opponents are engaged in a struggle for self-determination covered by Protocol I might find himself charged with breaches of the Conventions, the Protocol or the laws and customs of war if captured, there are no penal clauses attached to Protocol II. However, since common Article 3, which applies to non-international conflicts, expressly forbids certain acts, it may be presumed that there is an implied right granted to those capturing offenders to try them for breaches of that Article, and this is confirmed by the Statutes of the two Tribunals. But in the absence of any specially created tribunal, enforcement of the Protocol would normally lie solely with the government authorities of the country concerned or the dissident authority into whose hands the alleged wrongdoer might fall.

Intervention and non-international conflicts

While it may be argued, in accordance with the definition of aggression adopted by the General Assembly, that there is an obligation to come to the assistance of a national liberation movement seeking self-determination, Protocol II stipulates that it must not 'be invoked for the purpose of affecting the sovereignty of a State or the responsibility of the government, by all legitimate means, to maintain or re-establish law and order in the State or to defend the national unity and territorial integrity of the State'.[49] While the Protocol seeks to restrict the freedom of action of those engaged in a non-international conflict, this article recognises the right of the government to take such measures as it deems necessary to suppress the dissidents. It is likely that the use of the term 'legitimate means' refers to already enacted processes as distinct from *ad hoc* measures introduced to deal with the situation, and that the government would be clearly entitled, as under Article 3 common to the Conventions, to treat dissidents as traitors and proceed against them in accordance with the criminal law. While *ad hoc* measures are probably excluded, we must not overlook the fact that such instruments as the European Convention on Human Rights[50] permit derogation from a number of the rights guaranteed in the event of war or a declared emergency.[51]

Since Protocol I renders conflicts conducted in the name of self-determination international in character, they are of concern to third states not directly involved. Protocol II, however, states[52] that nothing in the Protocol may be invoked to justify intervention of any kind, whether it be ideological or in response to human rights abuses, either in the conflict or in the affairs of the state in whose territory the conflict is taking place. It follows, therefore, that the parties to a non-international conflict cannot invoke the Declaration on Friendly Relations to secure assistance from a non-party to the conflict. While the Protocol precludes outside intervention, it must be acknowledged that to the extent that international law recognises the existence of the principle of humanitarian intervention, a state not party to the conflict may decide, on this ground, to come to the aid of the dissidents and assist them in overthrowing the established government or even establishing a new state. This was one of the grounds put forward by India when intervening in the operations in East Pakistan that resulted in the establishment of Bangladesh in 1971, followed by the latter's admission to the United Nations regardless of Pakistan's membership and its right to territorial integrity. Such a decision is, however, political and not legal. In 1992 the Security Council claimed the right, despite Article 2(7) of the Charter precluding intervention in domestic affairs, increasingly to condemn such abuses of human rights and the Council, together with the European Community and individual states, refused to recognise the states created out of the Soviet Union and Yugoslavia until they had given undertakings with regard to the recognition of human rights. In the case of Kosovo, however, Yugoslav actions against the dissidents were so extreme, involving 'ethnic cleansing' and other atrocities, that NATO demanded their cessation accompanied by a temporary NATO military occupation of the province. When Yugoslavia rejected these terms NATO commenced its bombing attacks.

---

[49] Art. 3(1).

[50] 1950, 213 U.N.T.S., 222.

[51] Art. 15. See, e.g., *Ireland* v. *UK* (1978), 58 I.L.R., 188; Green, 'Derogation of human rights in emergency situations', 16 Can Y.B. Int'l Law (1978), 92; Meron, *Human Rights in Internal Strife*, 23–6, 50–61, 135–6, 155–6.

[52] Art. 3(2).

As has been seen in both the former Yugoslavia and Rwanda, there is nothing to prevent the Security Council from deciding that even a non-international conflict constitutes a threat to international peace and security and authorising military intervention or the establishment of international criminal tribunals.

Educating the fighter in the field

With the adoption of Protocol II, it is no longer sufficient for members of the armed forces to be instructed solely in the law concerning international armed conflict. They should also be aware of their rights and obligations together with those of the dissidents in a non-international armed conflict. Protocol II does not require this, although it does provide that the Protocol should be disseminated as widely as possible.[53] As regards countries which have not accepted Protocol II, members of the armed forces engaged in a non-international conflict must conduct themselves in accordance with the minimum considerations of humanitarian law as set out in Article 3 common to the four Geneva Conventions.[54]

[53] Art. 19.
[54] See, generally, Green, *Essays*, 1999, ch. VI. 'The man in the field and the maxim *Ignorantia Juris Non Excusat*.'

4

Hostilities: their commencement, effects and termination

The problem of the *status mixtus*

Members of the armed forces are not concerned with the manner in which a conflict begins, nor whether it is legal or illegal. So far as they are concerned, the law of armed conflict comes into operation and they must abide by it from the moment that hostilities begin and they are required to participate therein.

Traditionally, international law was divided into the law of war and the law of peace, with no intermediate stage between.[1] When hostilities began, usually following a declaration of war,[2] and non-parties to the conflict were held by the belligerents to be subject to the duties of, and they claimed the rights pertaining to neutrals,[3] war was recognised and the law of war came into operation. Frequently, however, inter-state relations deteriorated to a point where neither peace nor war in the strict sense existed, and states observed for some purposes the law of peace, and for others the law of war.[4] Because of the increasing frequency of this *status mixtus*[5] it became popular to distinguish between armed conflict and war,[6] with the term 'war' being reserved for the state of affairs which satisfied the traditional concept, while any other condition of active hostilities came to be described as an armed conflict,[7] a term which is now in general use for all conflicts.

---

[1] '*Inter bellum et pacem nihil est medium*', Cicero, *Philippica* VII, cited with approval by Grotius, *De Jure Belli ac Pacis*, Bk III, XXI, I, 1; see also *Janson* v. *Driefontein Consolidated Mines Ltd*. [1902] A.C., 484, 498, per Ld. Macnaghten.

[2] Grotius, *De Jure Belli*, Bk III, chs III, V.

[3] See ch. 16 below.

[4] This was often the state of affairs between England and France during the Hundred Years' War.

[5] See, e.g., Schwarzenberger, 'Jus Pacis ac Belli?', 37 Am. J. Int'l Law (1943), 460; Jessup, 'Should international law recognize an intermediate status between war and peace?', 48 *ibid*. (1954), 98.

[6] See, e.g., statement by British Prime Minister at the time of the Suez conflict to the effect that the United Kingdom was not at war with Egypt, but only in a state of armed conflict. As a result neither the law of treason nor trading with the enemy applied, Hansard, H.C., 1 Nov., 1956, vol. 558, col. 1645.

[7] See, e.g., Green, 'Armed conflict, war and self-defence', *Essays*, 1999, ch. III.

As may be seen from the conflict between China and Japan beginning with the invasion of Manchuria in 1931 and the widening of hostilities thereafter, even before the outbreak of World War II there were conflicts in which the belligerents did not regard themselves as being at war in the traditional and legal sense of the term. Thus, diplomatic relations were maintained and countries not involved did not regard themselves as subject to the law of neutrality. It was not until 1941 after Pearl Harbor and the American declaration of war against Japan and Germany that China declared war and regarded herself as a belligerent in a war as that term was generally understood. Since 1945 the number of hostile relationships not amounting to 'war' has greatly increased and it was not until 1989 that Iran formally declared war against Iraq with which it had been engaged in hostilities since 1981. Other conflicts, such as the Korean operations under the auspices of the United Nations, have been described as 'police actions',[8] or have been treated as if they were civil wars in which an outside party might have become involved as in the case of Vietnam, or for the restoration of democracy as with the United States invasions of Grenada in 1983[9] or Panama in 1989.[10] Even the conflict between the United Kingdom and Argentina resulting from the invasion of the Falklands in 1982 was not regarded as a 'war'.[11] However, regardless of the legal definition of the hostilities, or of the attitude of those engaged in conflict, national courts have tended to accept the popular meaning of the word when called upon to interpret, for example, exception clauses in a contract[12] or insurance policy,[13] but such interpretation is only of significance for the purposes of national and not international law.

Recognising the need to introduce humanitarian principles in every armed conflict, regardless of its legal classification, the Geneva Conventions of 1949[14] all

---

[8] See, e.g., *Burns v. The King, Sydney Morning Herald*, 14, 15 Nov. 1950, 20 I.L.R., 596, discussed in Green, 'The nature of the "war" in Korea,' 4 I.L.Q. (1951), 462.

[9] See, e.g., Moore, *Law and the Grenada Mission*; American Bar Association, Section of International Law and Practice, *Report of the Committee on Grenada*, 1984.

[10] See, e.g., Nanda, Farer and D'Amato, 'US forces in Panama: defenders, aggressors or human rights activists?', 84 Am. J. Int'l Law (1990), 494; Watson and Tsouros, *Operation Just Cause: The US Intervention in Panama*, 'The use of armed force in international affairs: the case of Panama', Assoc. of the Bar of the City of New York, 1992.

[11] See, e.g., Green, 'The Falklands, the law and the war', 38 Y.B. World Affairs (1984), 9; 'The rule of law and the use of force – the Falklands and Grenada', 24 *Archiv des Völkerrechts* (1986), 173.

[12] See, e.g., *Kawasaki Kisen Kabushiki Kaisha of Kobe v. Bantham SS Co.* [1939] 2 K.B., 44, re Sino-Japanese hostilities; *Navios Corporation v. The Ulysses II* (1958) 161 F. Supp. 32, re Suez.

[13] See, e.g., *Wilkinson v. Equitable Life Insurance* (1956) 195 N.Y. Supp. 2d 1018, re Korea; *Jackson v. North America Insurance of Virginia* (1971) 183 S.E. 2d 160, re Vietnam; *Borysoglenski v. Continental Insurance Co.* (1974) 14 I.L.M., 78, re Mid-East. Insurance decisions depend on the terms of the policy in question, so that the decisions and interpretations may vary.

[14] Schindler and Toman, 373 *et seq.*

provide for their application in any international armed conflict whether amounting to war or not.[15] This became important during the Falklands conflict after the British Prime Minister had denied that captured Argentinian personnel were prisoners of war protected by the third Convention, a denial that was remedied within days.[16] Similarly, even though the United States held General Noriega on ordinary criminal charges after the Panama campaign, he was treated by the American authorities as a prisoner of war,[17] even though in 1992 he was found guilty of a number of drug-related offences contrary to the law of the United States. Since the decision whether to declare war or to treat hostilities as an armed conflict is a political decision made by governmental authorities, members of the forces must behave as if every conflict amounts to war and they must therefore abide by the law of war. In fact, it is becoming increasingly clear that the terms war and armed conflict are being used as if they were synonyms.

Are declarations of war necessary?

In accordance with international treaty law,[18] for an armed conflict to result in a state of affairs governed by international law and constituting a war in the legal sense of that term, the hostilities should be preceded by a reasoned declaration or an ultimatum with a fixed time limit, indicating that a formal declaration would issue if the conditions laid down in the ultimatum were not met.[19] There is, however, nothing in the Convention specifying any minimum time limit between expiry of the ultimatum and the declaration commencing hostilities.[20] As a result both the ultimatum and the declaration may be contemporaneous, so that compliance with the

---

[15] Art. 2: 'the present Convention shall apply to all cases of declared war and any other armed conflict which may arise between two or more of the High Contracting Parties, even if the state of war is not recognised by one of them'. The 1929 Geneva Conventions (Schindler and Toman, 325 *et seq.*) contained no such provision; it appears to have been assumed then that there would be general appreciation of when their provisions would apply.

[16] *The Times* (London), 17 Apr., 3 May 1982.

[17] *New York Times*, 3 Jan. 1990; see also discussion at Am. Soc. Int'l Law Conf., Washington, Mar. 1990. The status is also confirmed in a personal letter to the author from the Special Assistant for Law of War Matters, Office of the JAG, US Dept. of the Army, 21 Feb., 1990; a letter to this effect was also sent to General Noriega while in a US gaol. See Albert, *The Case Against The General*, 1993, 116 – 'The US has determined as a matter of policy that Noriega ... should be given the protections accorded prisoners of war under the Geneva Convention'. For a general discussion of his status during the trial see ch. 12.

[18] Hague Convention III, 1907, Schindler and Toman, 57.

[19] See UK telegram to Germany, 1 Sept., 1939, HMSO, Cmd 6106, no. 110, and Ultimatum of 3 Sept., *ibid.*, no. 118; these documents, together with similar statements by France, are reproduced in R.I.I.A., *Documents on International Affairs 1939*, vol. 1, 513 *et seq.* In 1991 hostilities were initiated against Iraq because it had failed to evacuate Kuwait by the date set in SC Res. 678 (29 I.L.M. 1565).

[20] The UK ultimatum to Germany expired after two hours.

Convention does not necessarily exclude the element of surprise.[21] In fact, the German declaration and commencement of active hostilities against Poland in 1939 were simultaneous.[22]

Since 1939 most armed conflicts have commenced without any ultimatum or declaration, although the victim of the attack or its allies have normally responded with a formal declaration. With the exception of the attack upon Poland, this was what happened in the case of each country attacked by Germany, and with the Japanese attack upon the United States. The Soviet declaration of war against Japan in 1945 followed the expiry of a Soviet ultimatum calling upon Japan to accept the unconditional surrender demanded by the allies of the Soviet Union.[23] When hostilities commence without a declaration, whether the armed conflict amounts to a war in the international legal sense of the term depends upon the reactions of the victim of the attack and also, to some extent, upon the attitude of non-parties to the conflict. When Iraq refused to comply with Security Council resolutions to withdraw from Kuwait the Council set a date by which such evacuation was to ensue, and authorised states which were 'cooperating with the Government of Kuwait ... to use all necessary means to uphold and implement ... all ... relevant resolutions and to restore international peace and security'.[24]

The effect of the United Nations Charter

Since the coming into force of the Pact of Paris, 1928,[25] in which the parties renounced war as an instrument of national policy, and the adoption of the Charter of the United Nations, 1945, obligating the members to settle their disputes in a peaceful manner, refraining 'in their international relations from the threat or use of force against the territorial integrity or political independence of any state',[26] other than by way of exercising their 'inherent right of individual or collective self-defence if an armed attack occurs',[27] it has become con-

---

[21] See comments of Tokyo International Military Tribunal for the Far East: 'It [the Convention] permits of a narrow construction and tempts the unprincipled to try to comply with the obligations thus narrowly construed while at the same time ensuring that their attacks shall come as a surprise', *Tokyo Judgment* (1948) 988–9.

[22] Cmd 6106 (1939), nos 106, 107, R.I.I.A., *Documents*, 508.

[23] 3 Whiteman, *Digest of International Law*, 485–6. Similarly, in 1999 NATO commenced its bombing campaign against Yugoslavia when the latter rejected its terms for the immediate cessation of Yugoslav measures against the Kosovo population and dissidents.

[24] SC Res. 678 (29 I.L.M. 1565).

[25] 94 L.N.T.S., 57; 4 Hudson, *International Legislation*, 2522.

[26] 9 Hudson, *ibid.*, 327, Art. 2(4).

[27] Art. 51: there is much debate whether action by way of anticipatory self-defence is still permitted, see Dinstein, *War, Aggression and Self-Defence*, 182, 185, 190–1, 244; see also his discussion of self-help 175, 204, 209, and, in relation to rescue of nationals, 226–30; on this latter point, see also Green, 'Rescue at Entebbe – legal aspects', 6 Israel Y.B.H.R. (1976), 12, and Ronzitti, *Rescue of Nationals Abroad and Intervention on Grounds of Humanity*.

troversial whether any declaration, even though made in accordance with the terms of Hague Convention III, would be legal unless it complied with the terms of these two treaties. Thus, the Charter recognises a resort to self-defence or action by way of a regional organisation, until such time as the operation is taken over or ordered to be terminated by the Security Council,[28] or, as in the case of Iraq's invasion of Kuwait, authorises action against the 'aggressor'. As with the situation under customary law, from the point of view of the armed forces and their obligation to conduct themselves in accordance with the law of armed conflict, it is irrelevant whether the conflict is in accordance with the obligations of Hague Convention III, the Pact of Paris or the Charter of the United Nations. This is a matter for national governments or the United Nations, with effects that are political and legal only in the sense that a condemnation of one of the belligerents as an aggressor may have legal consequence against that belligerent, but not against individual members of the armed forces concerned.

In so far as the United Nations is concerned, there is no provision specifically requiring the issue of an ultimatum before military, that is to say enforcement, action is taken in the name of the Organisation.[29] Such measures will be ordered by the Security Council against a member or a non-member[30] if the Council is of opinion that such measures are needed to preserve or restore peace. Moreover, such measures will only be resorted to subsequent to a refusal by the country against which they are directed to comply with the demands of the Security Council for a change in policy. This demand may be regarded as a type of ultimatum, and with the rejection of the demand the enforcement measures will be instituted without any declaration of war. The only occasion on which such action has been resorted to as yet was in response to the invasion of South Korea by North Korea in 1950,[31] although in the case of Iraq's invasion of Kuwait the Council authorised members to take such enforcement action without actually undertaking it in the name of the United Nations.[32] Members of the United Nations complying with a decision of the Security Council to this effect must ensure that their forces obey

---

[28] Arts 51, 53.

[29] Chapter VII. See, however, SC Res. 678 (1990) regarding Iraqi withdrawal from Kuwait.

[30] Art. 2(6) – while a non-member is not obligated by anything in the Charter, the United Nations imposes an obligation upon members to take against a non-member such action as may be necessary to ensure that the latter acts 'in accordance with [the] Principles [established in the Charter] so far as may be necessary for the maintenance of international peace and security'.

[31] See, e.g., Green, 'Korea and the United Nations', 4 World Affairs (NS) (1950), 414; Stone, *Legal Controls of International Conflict*, ch. 8.

[32] See text to n. 28 above. Some type of 'enforcement' was threatened against Bosnia in 1993 and later, on the bases of similar authorisation, NATO forces actually bombed targets in Serbia. Where Kosovo was concerned, NATO acted without any consultation with, or authorisation from, the Security Council.

the law of armed conflict against such an 'enemy' of the United Nations,[33] even though such 'enemy' is engaged in an illegal conflict.

Effects of the outbreak of hostilities

Whether there has been a declaration of war or not, it is still open to non-parties to the conflict to decide for themselves whether they will recognise this fact. However, if there has been a declaration and the declarant has informed third states of this, any such state refusing to accept the consequences of the situation may find itself treated as a non-neutral and itself become the object of hostile action. In such circumstances it is open to either the original declarant or the non-party affected to declare war. However, in the absence of such a deterioration in relations, in so far as the parties engaged in a conflict are concerned they are under an obligation to regard third states abstaining from assisting any of the belligerents as entitled to treatment in accordance with the law concerning neutral rights. In the 1991 operations against Iraq, however, the members of the Coalition seeking to enforce the terms of Security Council Resolution 678 insisted that other members of the United Nations, whether they regarded themselves as neutrals or not, comply with the sanctions being imposed against Iraq, although no action was taken against Jordan which did not fully comply with Security Council resolutions to this effect.

Normally, for the parties engaged in hostilities, the existence of the conflict results in the severance of all normal relations between them. If, however, they do not recognise the situation as amounting to war, normal relations may still subsist to the extent that this remains possible. Thus, during the Sino-Japanese conflict both parties maintained diplomatic relations with ambassadors present at the seat of government, while during the Suez operations postal communication was still possible between the United Kingdom and Egypt. It is clear that treaties of a political or trading character between the belligerents will cease to operate, at least for the duration of the hostilities, but other treaties, for example those relating to boundary demarcation, are not affected, although the conflict itself may in fact be aimed at redrawing such a boundary. If the belligerents are parties to a multilateral treaty, the outbreak of hostilities does not affect the continued subsistence of the treaty as among the non-belligerents, nor does it affect its continuance as between each belligerent and such third states, although it may be possible for any party to argue that circumstances have so changed as a result of the outbreak of hostilities that the treaty may cease to apply by virtue of the doctrine *rebus sic stantibus*.[34] If, however, the situation has not deteriorated to the extent of hostilities having commenced, the mere fact that diplomatic or consular relations have

---

[33] See ch. 3 above. See also *Conduct of the Persian Gulf War*, Final Report to Congress, Apr. 1992, App. O, the role of the law of war, 31 I.L.M., 615.

[34] Vienna Convention on the Law of Treaties, 1969, 1155 U.N.T.S., 331, 7 I.L.M. 770, Art. 62.

been severed, even though this may be a prelude to the outbreak of conflict, is not sufficient to affect the continued application of a treaty.[35]

While a treaty between a belligerent and a non-party remains in force it may well be that observance of the treaty by the non-belligerent results in an accusation of unneutral conduct by the belligerent not a party to the treaty in question. This would be the case, for example, if the treaty in question is one for the supply of war *matériel*.

Although political and economic treaties between the belligerents are terminated or suspended, this is not the case with regard to treaties of a humanitarian character, such as the Genocide Convention, 1948,[36] while treaties relating to armed conflict, such as the Geneva and Hague Conventions, come into operation immediately upon the outbreak of hostilities. While this is not specifically provided for in any of the Conventions, Article 3 of Protocol I, 1977,[37] expressly states that 'the Conventions and this Protocol shall apply from the beginning of any situation referred to in Article 1' of the Protocol, which itself refers back to Article 2 common to all four 1949 Geneva Conventions.[38] From that moment members of the armed forces of the combatants are required, in their conduct of hostilities and in relations with the armed forces of the adverse party, or civilians in any hostile territory which they may be occupying, to comply with the law of armed conflict. They should be guided by the realities of the situation, without being unduly concerned with the question whether the armed conflict in question amounts to war in the technical sense.[39] Thus, during the Burmese campaign in World War II members of the British Army were required to treat members of the Indian National Army[40] whom they captured as prisoners of war. It was a political decision of the Government of India that these persons were to be considered as traitors with some of them brought to trial.[41] Similarly, members of the South African Army were under orders to treat captured members of the South West Africa People's Organisation as prisoners of war, until such time as the South African authorities decided otherwise. Moreover, in accordance with the Geneva Convention on Prisoners of War, 1949,[42] captured personnel are entitled to be con-

---

[35] Art. 63.

[36] 78 U.N.T.S., 277.

[37] Schindler and Toman, 621.

[38] See n. 15 above.

[39] See, e.g., the Canadian attitude during the War of 1812: *The Brig Dart* (1812) Steward 301, in which the Court of Vice-Admiralty at Halifax held, 'if a war *de facto* subsists between Great Britain and any other country, without a regular declaration, the subjects of that country would be enemy aliens' – a status that exists only in war.

[40] Army raised by the Japanese from among captured members of the (British) Indian Army.

[41] See Green, 'The Indian National Army trials', 11 M.L.R. (1948), 47; 'The Azad Hind Fauj: The Indian National Army', Green, *Essays*, 1999, ch. XI.

[42] Schindler and Toman, 423, Art. 5.

sidered as prisoners of war until there has been a decision of a competent tribunal denying them that status.[43]

While war was formerly defined as an armed contest between state forces,[44] it may happen that countries may in fact be at war without any active hostilities being conducted between them. This was the situation in World War I when China declared war on the Central Powers in 1917, but was never involved in conflict. Prior to this China had protested at the breach of its neutrality committed by Japan when, in 1915, Japanese forces crossed Chinese territory in order to occupy the German-leased territory in China. China declared the area a 'war zone', an act which resulted in a protest by Germany alleging this to be a breach of China's neutrality.[45] Similarly, during World War II a number of Latin American countries declared war on the Axis Powers treating their nationals as enemies, but taking no part in hostilities. Moreover, a party to a conflict may be at war with some of the belligerents while remaining neutral with regard to others. This was the position of the United States during World War II in regard to Finland,[46] and while Thailand declared war on the United Kingdom and the United States, the latter country did not consider itself at war with Thailand since that country was completely occupied by Japan and not regarded as capable of acting in an independent manner.[47] The United Kingdom, however, considered itself to be at war with Thailand. The Soviet Union did not declare war against Japan until 8 August 1945, two days after the dropping of the atomic bomb on Hiroshima and a week before Japan's surrender.

Nationals in enemy territory

When an international conflict amounting to war exists, nationals of a combatant resident in the territory of the adverse party become liable to such restrictions upon their freedom as the latter imposes upon them, subject to any limitations arising from the customary or conventional law of armed conflict or any human

---

[43] See, e.g., *Public Prosecutor* v. *Koi* [1968] A.C., 829; see also *Osman Ben Haji Mohamed Ali* [1969] 1 A.C., 430, which may have been rendered obsolete by Protocol I, Art. 44. It should be borne in mind that in many common law jurisdictions the tribunal will be bound to accept an executive statement as to whether a war exists or not, see, e.g., *R.* v. *Bottrill, exp. Kuechenmeister* [1947] K.B. 1; *In re Hourigan* [1946] N.Z.L.R., 1. See also Canadian War Measures Act, R.S.C 1970, c. W-2, s. 2: 'The issue of a proclamation by Her Majesty, or under the authority of the Governor in Council shall be conclusive evidence that war . . . exists and has existed for any period therein stated until by the issue of a further proclamation it is declared that the war . . . no longer exists.'

[44] See, e.g., decision of German Federal Social Court in *Spanish Civil War Pension Entitlement Case* 80 I.L.R., (1978) 666.

[45] See Garner, *International Law and the World War*, vol. 2, 237–41.

[46] As a result, the US is not a party to the Peace Treaty with Finland, 1947, 4 U.N.T.S., 266.

[47] 10 Whiteman, 73.

rights conventions. Even if the conflict does not amount to war in the legal sense of that term, there is nothing in international law, other than human rights conventions, preventing a country imposing restrictions upon the freedom of residents possessing adverse party nationality. For countries which have ratified Geneva Convention IV relative to the Protection of Civilian Persons in Time of War, 1949,[48] civilians present in the territory of the adverse party are protected by the terms of that Convention immediately upon the outbreak of hostilities.[49] Relations between nationals of the combatant countries are governed by national legislation.[50]

It was formerly customary to allow enemy nationals to remain at liberty, although perhaps subject to restriction as to their movements, or to grant them days of grace in which to depart.[51] During World War II the United Kingdom, for example, interned or sent to overseas Commonwealth territories large numbers of enemy nationals. Now, for parties to the Civilians Convention they may only be interned or assigned to restricted places of residence if the 'security' of the power in whose hands they are makes it 'absolutely necessary'.[52] The Convention does not affect the right of any party to intern those of its nationals whom it may consider sympathetic to the adverse party, even though such persons may hold dual nationality or possess an ethnic relationship with the adverse party. This would mean that, subject to any constitutional or human rights conventional limitations, internments like those of locally born Japanese in Canada and the United States during World War II would still not be illegal according to the law of armed conflict. Subject to special legislative measures or principles based on common law,[53] the outbreak of hostilities has no effect on the continued operation of national law, which applies equally to nationals and enemy and neutral subjects alike.[54] This does not apply to those in enemy territory[55] or in enemy-occupied territory.[56]

While the outbreak of war involves the breaking off of diplomatic relations between the combatants, it has generally been recognised that the immunities of

[48] Schindler and Toman, 495.

[49] Arts 4, 6.

[50] E.g., Trading with the Enemy Act, 1939, 2 & 3 Geo. 6, c. 89.

[51] See, e.g., *R.* v. *Ahlers* [1915] 1 K.B., 616, and, by way of contrast, *Re Schaefer* (1918) 31 Can. C.C., 22.

[52] Arts 41, 42.

[53] Thus, subject to human rights conventions, enemy nationals are not able to take advantage of such prerogative writs as *habeas corpus*. It should be remembered, however, that many conventional human rights may be derogated from in time of emergency, including war, see, e.g., European Convention on Human Rights, 1950, 213 U.N.T.S., 222, Art. 15; see also Green, 'Derogation of human rights in emergency situations', 16 Can. Y.B. Int'l Law (1978), 92; Meron, *Human Rights and Humanitarian Norms as Customary Law*, 215–22.

[54] Hague Regulations, 1907, Schindler and Toman, 75, Art. 23(h).

[55] See, e.g., *Porter* v. *Freudenberg* [1915] 1 K.B. 857; *Daimler Co. Ltd.* v. *Continental Tyre and Rubber Co. Ltd.* [1916] 2 A.C., 307.

[56] Here the Civilians Convention governs.

the diplomats themselves are unaffected and exchanges have been arranged,[57] while the official residence is normally placed under the care of some other foreign envoy.[58] Today, the situation is governed by the Vienna Convention on Diplomatic Relations,[59] which provides that even in time of conflict the receiving state must allow diplomatic representatives to depart, providing transport facilities if necessary, while care must be taken to respect and protect mission premises, property and archives.[60] The general practice, when diplomatic relations are severed in this way, is for the belligerents to appoint agreed-upon diplomats of neutral states to act as Protecting Powers.[61]

The position of merchant vessels and aircraft

Just as it was formerly the practice to allow days of grace for enemy nationals to depart, so in accordance with Hague Convention VI, 1907,[62] the parties[63] agreed that it was 'desirable' to allow merchant ships of the adverse party present in their ports or harbours at the outbreak of hostilities to depart immediately or after a period of grace.[64] Those failing to depart within the time allowed were liable to seizure against the payment of compensation.[65] This attitude reflects the nineteenth-century view that war is nothing but an inter-state conflict affecting the armed forces of the state, and not directed against the civilian population or civilian property. With the development of the concept of total war[66] this attitude has become outdated, and modern practice as demonstrated during both world wars indicates that all vessels belonging to the adverse party or its nationals will be

---

[57] See, e.g., *Oppenheim, International Law*, vol. II, s. 98. In World War II, the Germans interned Sir Lancelot Oliphant, the British Ambassador to Belgium, while the UK refused to exchange diplomats with Japan until the latter agreed to include certain named civilians in the exchange.

[58] For the practice in 1914, see Garner, *International Law*, vol. 1, ss. 27–33, 39 n.

[59] 1961, 500 U.N.T.S., 95.

[60] Arts 44, 45.

[61] See n. 77 below.

[62] Schindler and Toman, 791.

[63] The US did not sign or accede to this Convention, since it considered this to be a rule of international customary law and in 1898 at the beginning of the Spanish–American War allowed periods of grace to Spanish merchant vessels, see Garner, *International Law*, vol. 1, 49–51. The UK did not share this view, *ibid.*, 151, and renounced the Convention in 1925. See de Guttry's *Commentary* on the Convention in Ronzitti, *The Law of Naval Warfare*, 102. See *Annotated Supplement to the [US], Commander's Handbook on the Law of Naval Operations*, 1997, NWP 1–14M/MCWP 5–2.1/COMDTPUB P.5800.1. para 8.2.2, n. 37.

[64] Art. 1.

[65] Art. 2. In 1917 the US requisitioned all ships, including neutral, over 2,500 tons, material, contracts, plans and specifications in US shipyards, see *Norwegian Shipowners' Claims* (1922) 1 R.I.A.A., 309.

[66] See Smith, *The Crisis in the Law of Nations*, 75–7.

seized on the outbreak of hostilities.[67] Since Protocol I, 1977, only extends protection to 'the civilian population, individual civilians or civilian objects on land' or to attacks from the sea against the land,[68] its provisions do not have any effect on the right of a belligerent to seize enemy or neutral merchant vessels in its ports at the outbreak of hostilities.

There are no clearly established rules relating to the conduct of aerial warfare[69] or to the obligations or rights of belligerents with reference to civil aircraft belonging to enemy nationals and present in the territory of the adverse party. The only 'rules' that exist are those adopted by a Commission of Jurists meeting at The Hague in 1923.[70] While these are completely unofficial and have never formed the basis of an internationally agreed document, they are generally considered to be expressive of what tends to be accepted as the customary law of aerial warfare.[71] Article 52 of these rules provides that 'enemy private aircraft are liable to capture in all circumstances' and this seems to be what happens in practice. Moreover, it is generally accepted that the basic rules[72] apply in aerial as in other fields of warfare, but Protocol I, 1977, introduces special provisions with regard to medical aircraft.[73]

Operation of the laws of armed conflict

Wars frequently begin with the crossing of an international border and the invasion of the territory of the adverse party. When this occurs, for parties to the Geneva Conventions of 1949 and Protocol I the laws of war as defined in those instruments come into immediate effect, even in the absence of a declaration. This means that the members of the armed forces of those parties are bound to respect their provisions, and if their country is a party to Geneva Convention IV regarding Civilians must treat civilians within any territory they occupy in accordance with the terms of that Convention, an obligation that was made very clear to Iraq on its occupation of Kuwait and in respect of Coalition nationals held hostage in Kuwait and Iraq. In fact the Convention extends beyond giving rights merely to civilians possessing the nationality of the occupied territory, for it grants protection to any persons in the hands of the adverse occupying party.[74] As to the Hague Conventions, these too become immediately applicable for the forces of parties

---

[67] For an assessment of the present significance of Convention VI, see de Guttry, *Commentary*, 108–9.

[68] Art. 49.

[69] See ch. 9 below.

[70] Schindler and Toman, 207.

[71] See, e.g., *ibid.*, 207; Oppenheim, ed. Lauterpacht, *International Law*, vol. II, 519; Green, *Essays*, 1999, ch. XVI, 'Aerial considerations in the law of armed conflict'.

[72] See ch. 21 below.

[73] Arts 24–31.

[74] Art. 4.

thereto, and to the extent that their provisions have hardened into customary law[75] they are applicable to all the parties to the conflict.

Although diplomatic relations between belligerents are normally broken once a conflict has commenced,[76] there remains a number of issues, not all of which are concerned with their inter-belligerent relations, which require them to remain in contact. It is customary, therefore, for them to agree upon the identity of neutral states whose diplomatic representatives will protect the interests of each belligerent and its nationals within the territory of the adverse party. In such circumstances, when operating in this way the diplomatic representative concerned is representing the belligerent on whose behalf he has been appointed and not of his own state, so that it is the international responsibility of the former that is engaged by his activities in this capacity.[77] Since the choice of the neutral diplomat to represent the interests of a belligerent is by agreement between the adverse parties, it may happen that occasionally both opponents will select the same national representative to act for each of them.[78] In his capacity as protector of the interests of a party to the conflict, the protecting diplomat should do nothing that might involve a breach of his own state's neutrality or his status as a protector.[79] At the same time, the diplomatic representatives of neutral states remain inviolable and, to the extent that military operations or security allow, have the right to carry on with their normal functions, and this is true even of those who are acting in a representative capacity for an adverse party. However, it may happen that, on a temporary basis at least, a belligerent may be entitled to restrict some of the normal privileges attaching to foreign diplomats, as occurred in the United Kingdom with regard to the security of diplomatic pouches just prior to D-day. Further, a neutral diplomat must be careful to ensure that he does nothing to jeopardise his neutral status.[80]

For states which ratify or accede to Protocol I, 1977, a legal obligation exists with regard to the designation of Protecting Powers from the beginning of a conflict with tasks more extensive than those traditionally attaching to a neutral diplomat nominated as representative of an adverse party. In accordance with the Protocol the Protecting Power is 'to secure the supervision and implementation of

[75] See, e.g., *Coenca Bros.* v. *Germany* (1927) 7 Rec. T.A.M. 683, 687–8; *Nuremberg Judgment* (1946) HMSO, Cmd 6964, 65; 41 Am. J. Int'l Law (1947), 172, 248–9.

[76] As has been indicated above, when the parties are not prepared to recognise the existence of 'war' between them, diplomatic relations may in fact continue.

[77] See, for a similar situation between allies, *Chevreau Claim* (1931), 2 R.I.A.A., 1113.

[78] From 1914 to 1917 the US played this role, Garner, *International Law*, vol. 1, s. 39, n. 3.

[79] During World War II, the Germans sometimes alleged that protecting diplomats were accepting mail from detainees for transmission to the governments of those detainees; see, e.g., Sir Lancelot Oliphant, *Ambassador in Bonds*.

[80] During World War I, the Swedish minister to Argentina transmitted cipher messages on behalf of the German envoy, thus violating Swedish neutrality; Oppenheim, in Lauterpacht (ed.), vol. 2, 748, n. 1.

the Conventions and of this Protocol', and if there is any delay in this matter the International Committee of the Red Cross 'shall' offer its services.[81]

One of the first things a party to a conflict is required to do upon outbreak of hostilities is establish an official information bureau for prisoners of war,[82] with sufficient equipment and staff to fulfil its functions properly. The bureau is to receive and collate all information about prisoners in the hands of the adverse party and pass such information through the Protecting Power[83] to the prisoner's home state so next of kin may be informed.

Termination of the conflict

The law of armed conflict operates and must be observed until the conflict ends, but, as with the commencement of hostilities, there is controversy as to the date of its end.[84] The most authoritative and clearest method of terminating an armed conflict is by means of a peace treaty.[85] However, since the terms of a treaty must be negotiated and depend upon the political desires of the parties to the negotiations, there may be a complete cessation of hostilities and a factual resumption of normal peaceful relations between the combatants. Thus, at the end of World War II, while it proved possible for peace treaties to be negotiated and signed with Bulgaria, Finland, Hungary, Romania and Italy, as well as with Japan, although not all belligerents became parties to the latter treaty, it proved impossible to negotiate a peace treaty affecting Germany, and many countries passed legislation or issued proclamations re-establishing peace.[86] Moreover, despite the absence of any peace treaty, both the Federal and Democratic German Republics established diplomatic relations with their former enemies and were admitted to the United Nations and became members of NATO or the Warsaw Pact respectively. When in 1990 discussions were being held regarding the reunification of Germany, these

[81] Art. 5, see ch. 13 below.

[82] Convention III (Prisoners of War), 1949, Schindler and Toman, 423, Art. 120, see ch. 10 below.

[83] See ch. 13 below.

[84] In *Bordier* v. *Lorilleux* (1960) 40 I.L.R., 434, the French Cour de Cassation held that, in the absence of a peace treaty with Germany, a contract to enter into force six months after signature of that treaty would in fact come into force six months after the date fixed by French legislation as the end of hostilities.

[85] On the 'significance of a peace treaty', see Dinstein, *War, Aggression and Self-Defence*, 1994, 35–8.

[86] For the United Kingdom, the formal state of war with Germany ended at 4 p.m. on 9 Jul. 1951, Supp. to *London Gazette* for 6 Jul. 1951, published 9 Jul. In Canada, by the War Measures Act (R.S.C 1970, c. W-2), s. 2, the re-establishment of peace requires a Proclamation by the Governor General in Council, and such a Proclamation was issued on 5 Jul. 1951, *Canada Gazette*, 25 Jul. 1951, p. 720. In the absence of such a proclamation the state of war legally continues, despite the absence of any active hostilities, see, e.g., *R.* v. *Bottrill, exp. Kuechenmeister* [1947] K.B. 41; *Re Hourigan* [1946] N.Z.L.R., 1. See, also Kunz, 'Judicial termination of the end of the War', 47 Columbia Law Rev. (1947).

were conducted between the two Germanies and also with the four principal European allies – France, the Soviet Union, the United Kingdom and the United States – and it soon became clear that there would be no peace treaty in the normal sense of that term between Germany and those countries which had been its enemies in World War II.[87] The absence of a peace treaty has no relevance to the conduct of the armed forces. Once the national states concerned have declared the armed conflict to be at an end the armed forces are bound by this decision and their relations towards former enemy subjects are governed by the law of peace, unless there is a military occupation of the adverse party's territory which is not governed by a specific bilateral treaty. In such a case, Geneva Convention IV[88] concerning civilians in occupied territory would continue to govern.

Active hostilities may cease in a variety of ways, and this cessation may be on a permanent or temporary basis, general or local or even for a specific purpose, such as the collection of the dead or wounded. The most complete indication of a cessation of hostilities is the announcement of complete and unconditional surrender by the adverse party.[89] When this occurs it is for the party to whom the surrender has been made to decide in its discretion whether to annex the territory of the surrendering party or to proceed to a peace treaty or some other *modus vivendi* regulating future relations. In the past, annexation was common, but in order to give the conqueror a legal title recognition of the annexation by third states is required. Although the Pact of Paris, 1928,[90] would appear to have rendered such recognition illegal, since the Pact banned war as an instrument of national policy, and although the League of Nations had adopted a policy of non-recognition in such cases,[91] the Italian conquest of Ethiopia was in fact recognised,[92] at least until Italy became an active belligerent in World War II. Today, it would seem that annexation after victory, at least over a member of the United Nations, would be contrary to the Charter,[93] and the Israeli annexation of Eastern Jerusalem and the Golan Heights has not been recognised.

Any acts of hostility carried out after such a surrender, or for that matter in breach of a suspension of hostilities while such suspension subsists, are war crimes rendering the offenders liable to trial.[94]

[87] For the text of the Treaty on the Final Settlement with respect to Germany, see 29 I.L.M., 1186.

[88] Schindler and Toman, 495.

[89] This was the manner in which hostilities with Germany and Japan were terminated at the end of World War II in 1945.

[90] 94 L.N.T.S., 57.

[91] See League Covenant, Art. 10, and Assembly Resolution, 11 Mar. 1932, Off. J., Ann. Supp. no. 100, 8.

[92] See, e.g., *Haile Selassie* v. *Cable & Wireless Ltd.* (no. 2) [1939] ch. 182.

[93] Art. 2(4). In 1990 the Security Council 'decide[d] that annexation of Kuwait by Iraq under any form and whatever pretext has no legal validity, and is considered null and void', Res. 662 (29 I.L.M., 1327).

[94] See, e.g., *In re Grumpelt*, (Scuttled U-Boats Case) (1945) UNWCC 1 *Trials of War Criminals* 55.

Significance of an armistice

As distinct from a peace treaty or an act of unconditional surrender, an armistice,[95] which may be local or general,[96] is a suspension of hostilities by agreement between the belligerents and does not terminate the conflict, but only brings active hostilities to an end in accordance with the terms of the agreement. If no time limit for the duration of the armistice is stipulated in the agreement, active hostilities may be resumed by either party, provided the adverse party is made aware of this fact.[97] To resume hostilities without such notice is only permissible as a matter of urgency, and as with any other serious breach of the armistice would give the adverse party the right to resume hostilities in the fullest sense immediately.[98]

If the armistice has been agreed between local commanders for a specific purpose, such as removal of the dead or exchange of the wounded, it is only valid for the purpose and for the forces specified in the agreement. In so far as other aspects or areas of the conflict are concerned, the armistice has no effect and the conflict continues as before. Moreover, such an armistice cannot include general or political agreements purporting to affect the conflict at large, and once the purpose for which the armistice had been agreed is satisfied the conflict resumes as before. In the case of such a local armistice or suspension of hostilities, the adverse party is entitled to assume that the local commander with whom the armistice is being arranged has the necessary authority to enter into such an arrangement, and no confirmation by higher authority is required. Should the local commander lack such authority, he would be amenable to disciplinary measures under his national law, but this would not affect the validity of the suspension of hostilities arranged between him and the adverse party.

As distinct from a local suspension of hostilities, the armistice may be partial, affecting named zones of operations, named forces, or entire arms thereof, particular geographic areas, or certain belligerents only. The local commander is competent to enter into such a partial armistice, which only requires governmental ratification if it so provides.[99] A general armistice ends all military operations between all the parties to the conflict in all areas and by all forces and constitutes a formal termination of the conflict in all regions contemporaneously, although this may be varied by the armistice[100] agreement itself. In practice,

---

[95] See Dinstein, *op.cit.*, 41–6.

[96] Hague Regulations (Schindler and Toman, 75), Art. 37. See also Dedijer, *On Military Conventions*, ch. 4; Bernard, 'L'armistice dans les guerres internationales'.

[97] *Ibid.*, Art. 36.

[98] See, e.g., *The Anna Maria* (1946) 13 Ann. Dig., 403: The French Conseil des Prises upheld seizure of Italian vessel after signature of the Italo-French Armistice of 1940 on the ground of Italian violation by virtue of Italian occupation of French territory in breach of the armistice agreement.

[99] See Oppenheim, vol. II, 7th ed., s. 235 (1) and (2).

[100] The Armistice with Italy, signed 3 Sept. 1943 (HMSO, Cmd 6693 (1945)), contained the conditions laid down by General Eisenhower 'acting by authority of the United Nations

therefore, all commands should be informed in good time of the coming into force of the armistice.[101] Should a breach of the armistice occur, or cessation of military operations not take place in a particular theatre at the time provided, because of the ignorance of its existence by those responsible for the act in question, this does not constitute a war crime. Any advantage gained thereby would have to be restored or an indemnity paid in respect thereof. While a general armistice terminates all active hostilities it does not bring about an end to the legal state of war, nor a return to the law of peace, so that occupied territory remains occupied. The purpose of such a general armistice is, normally, to terminate hostilities until a peace treaty is negotiated. Occasionally, however, the armistice may be of such a character in the generality of its terms and the length of its duration that, despite the absence of any proclamation terminating the 'war',[102] it becomes the equivalent of a peace agreement. This, for example, has often been maintained is the position between Israel and her Arab opponents consequent upon the armistice agreements of 1949.[103] As a result it has been suggested that the various resumptions of hostilities between Israel and its Arab opponents have constituted 'new war[s] and not the resumption of fighting in an on-going armed conflict'.[104] However, the legal situation in such circumstances is so confused that the same author has stated that a 'number of rounds of hostilities between Israel and the Arab countries … are incorrectly adverted to as "wars". Far from qualifying as separate wars, these were merely inconsecutive time-frames of combat, punctuated by extended cease-fires, in the course of a single on-going war'.[105]

Since a general armistice operates to bring the conflict to a conclusion, it requires ratification by the political authorities and is usually entered into after their prior agreement has been secured. If such agreement is absent, hostilities may be resumed after notice has been given to the adverse party. While the signing of such a general armistice means the complete cessation of all hostile acts, without affecting the continuance of the right to occupy enemy territory, it does not mean the establishment of peace, so that states not parties to the conflict are entitled to continue to claim the rights of neutrals.[106] Moreover, as a general armistice requires approval of the political authorities, such matters as the transfer of sovereignty over territory would need to be ratified in the subsequent peace treaty. In the absence of such a treaty, any purported annexation of territory of the

and in the interest of the United Nations' [wartime name of the anti-Axis alliance], and was accepted by General Badoglio as head of the Italian Government.

[101] See, e.g., the Armistice terminating World War I, 11 Nov. 1918.

[102] See above, n. 86.

[103] On these agreements, see, e.g., Rosenne, *Israel's Armistice Agreements with the Arab States*. Peace treaties have now been signed between Israel and Egypt and Israel and Jordan.

[104] Dinstein, 46.

[105] *Ibid.*, 56.

[106] See ch. 16 below.

adverse party would require recognition by third states which, since the adoption of the Charter of the United Nations, would probably not be granted.[107]

As has been indicated, a general armistice is intended to bring about a final end of the hostilities, but any serious breach of its terms may entitle the aggrieved party to denounce it and resume hostilities,[108] although this has not been the effect of the periodic resumption of active hostilities between Israel and its Arab opponents, the assumption being that the armistice agreements still subsist.[109]

[107] This is the position with the Israeli claim to sovereignty over the Golan Heights captured from Syria, as well as the proclamation claiming Jerusalem as the capital of Israel.

[108] The effect of an armistice upon inter-belligerent relations is considered in ch. 5 below.

[109] See, however, nn. 102 and 105 above.

5

Inter-belligerent relations

Enemies and adverse parties

Traditionally, the parties[1] to an armed conflict, commonly described as combatants or belligerents,[2] terms which are merely descriptive, possessing the same meaning and frequently used interchangeably, described each other as enemies, and this term was generally employed in all writings and international documents concerned with war. However, in the light of the various conflicts occurring after 1945, which were never regarded as amounting to war in the traditional legal sense of that term,[3] the Geneva Conventions of 1949,[4] seeking to extend the principles of humanitarian law to every conflict, introduced the term 'adverse party' in preference to 'enemy', although on occasion the two terms have been used interchangeably.[5] The 1977 Protocols[6] rarely use the term 'enemy', though it is still in ordinary parlance.

While normally the relations between belligerent powers are broken off with the commencement of hostilities, if the belligerents do not consider themselves to be at war in the traditional meaning of that term,[7] it is possible for them to continue to have limited relations as if they were at peace,[8] and may find themselves participating together at meetings of the General Assembly of the United Nations

---

[1] This refers to the political authorities and not to the individuals involved.

[2] Strictly, this term has a legal significance indicating a party to a conflict recognised by non-parties as sufficiently grave to allow the parties involved to exercise all the rights, known as belligerent rights, of parties at war. The term 'combatant' strictly applies only to those engaged actively in conflict and who are protected or bound by the law *in bello*.

[3] See ch. 1 above, n. 6.

[4] Schindler and Toman, 373 *et seq.*

[5] Convention I, Wounded and Sick, states, e.g., Art. 14, that 'the wounded and sick of a belligerent who fall into *enemy hands* shall be prisoners of war', while Art. 28 provides that medical personnel 'who fall into the hands of the *adverse party*' shall not be prisoners of war.

[6] *Ibid.*, 621: Protocol I, Art. 41 is entitled 'Safeguards of an *enemy hors de combat*,' though the Article itself only refers to persons 'in the power of an *adverse party*'.

[7] See above, ch. 4, nn. 6, 7.

[8] *Ibid.*, para. 1.

or in international multilateral conferences, as was the case with Iran and Iraq between 1980 and 1988. Moreover, the conflict itself may make it necessary for them to maintain certain contacts, for example negotiations for a cease-fire, although these contacts are normally organised through an acceptable neutral power or the countries which have been appointed Protecting Powers for the respective belligerents.[9] In addition, the facilities of the International Committee of the Red Cross, a body frequently employed in ensuring the mutual application of the Geneva Conventions which come into operation between the belligerents on the outbreak of hostilities, may be utilised for this purpose.[10] In addition, there is nothing to prevent the belligerents inter-acting through any other means of their choice, such as the United Nations or its Secretary-General,[11] or even directly through specially appointed intermediaries[12] or by radio.

It is traditional when a conflict occurs for the diplomats of the adverse parties to continue to be afforded every protection and for their immunities to be respected. Their right to depart is confirmed by the Vienna Convention on Diplomatic Relations.[13]

Belligerents and enemy nationals

The relations between a belligerent government and the adverse party's nationals[14] are regulated partly by international and partly by national law. Nationals of the adverse party are normally classified as combatants[15] and non-combatants, with the latter including some members of the armed forces – chaplains, medical personnel and those *hors de combat*[16] – and all civilians, that is to say, individuals

---

[9] See ch. 15 below.

[10] Pr. I, Art. 5(3).

[11] This was done in Cambodia, Afghanistan and Yugoslavia.

[12] This was the method used by Nelson after his victory at Copenhagen. He sent a letter under protection of a flag of truce to the Adjutant General of the Danish Fleet: 'The brave English to their brethren the brave Danes – I am now in possession of the batteries; and wishing to stop any further effusion of blood, I consent to a cessation of hostilities', *The Times* (London), 17 Apr. 1801. In 1992, the European Community sent a mediator to the various parties involved in the hostilities accompanying the dissolution of Yugoslavia.

[13] 500 U.N.T.S., 95, Art. 44. When Iraq occupied Kuwait in 1990, it denied diplomatic status to the diplomats of those states which refused to close their embassies in Kuwait and declined to allow them to leave, an action condemned by S.C. Res. 674 (29 I.L.M., 1561).

[14] In most countries the term 'national' is here understood in a wide sense to apply to all persons, regardless of formal nationality, normally resident in a territory of the adverse party, and includes the representatives of commercial undertakings operating from there.

[15] By Pr. I, Art. 43(2) 'Members of the armed forces of a Party to a conflict ... are combatants, that is to say, they have the right to participate directly in hostilities.' See ch. 6 below.

[16] This refers to prisoners of war, the wounded, sick and shipwrecked, as well as chaplains and medical personnel.

having no attachment, direct or indirect, to the armed forces.[17] Civilians in the adverse party's territory are treated broadly speaking in accordance with the provisions of the latter's national law, and while their freedom of movement may be restricted their treatment overall must be in accordance with Geneva Convention IV.[18] The mass internment policies pursued by many parties to the Second World War II would now seem to be improper, except as a matter of control and security necessary as a result of the war.[19] Far from sanctioning detention, the Convention provides[20] that 'all protected persons who may desire to leave the territory at the outset of, or during a conflict, shall be entitled to do so, unless their departure is contrary to the national interests of the State', a provision which would operate to prevent the departure of those likely to be of assistance to the adverse party in its war efforts. After it occupied Kuwait in 1990, Iraq originally refused to allow the departure of any national, even children, of the states which had condemned its aggression. Such a provision would also appear to throw into question policies such as those employed during World War II, involving the wholesale transfer to overseas territories of nationals of the adverse party regardless of their age or health or the likelihood of their acting in support of the adverse party of which they were nationals. The United Kingdom tended to intern locally or to send overseas almost all Germans resident there, including religious and political refugees, and often regardless of age, though appeal boards were later established. It is, however, probably still within the discretion of a belligerent to impose restrictions upon the movement, for example within the vicinity of strategic areas, of nationals belonging to the adverse party, even though they are not applied generally, subject to any provision in human rights agreements, provided that they continue to apply in war. However, the Iraqi decision in 1990 to detain thousands of nationals of countries engaged in an economic blockade against Iraq and concentrate them in 'vital' areas was a clear breach of international law. On the other hand, there is nothing to prevent the internment of local nationals who possess an ethnic or historic kinship with the adverse party, as was done to locally born Japanese by both Canada and the United States in World War II.[21]

International law is silent as to the relations between civilian nationals of the belligerent countries. These are, subject to any provisions in relevant human

[17] The international status of enemy nationals is now affected by the trend towards total war (see Smith, *The Crisis in the Law of Nations*, World War 75–7), intensification of air attacks, and the number of 'civilians' engaged in war industries. Insofar as camp followers attached to the Japanese Army in Burma during World War II were concerned, they were treated as detained civilians. The status of civilians in enemy hands is now governed by the relevant Geneva Convention of 1949 and Additional Protocol I, 1977 (see ch. 12 below).
[18] Schindler and Toman, 495, ch. 12 below.
[19] Art. 27.
[20] Art. 35.
[21] The decision by these states to compensate the nationals concerned was in accordance with national policy and did not arise from international law.

rights agreements, completely within the discretion of the belligerents, and are regulated by national law. This is particularly true of trading with the enemy, although in such conflicts as the hostilities in Korea or Suez, Great Britain, for example, permitted postal communication to continue, and even allowed British nationals to visit the territory of the adverse party without incurring any criminal liability.

Relations between belligerent forces

While, for the main part, the relations between the belligerent forces are confined to military matters, direct contact may sometimes be necessary, as for example to arrange for the collection of the dead or exchange of the wounded.[22] Normally, the relations between belligerent forces are confined to military matters only, but occasionally such relations, for example, the arrangement of a local truce or surrender, may involve political considerations. In view of modern radio and similar means of communication, such issues tend nowadays to be undertaken on an inter-governmental level, thus avoiding actual negotiations between belligerent commanders.[23]

Any agreement made by belligerent commanders must be scrupulously adhered to[24] and any breach of the conditions they contain would involve international responsibility if ordered by a government, and personal liability, which might in some circumstances amount to a war crime,[25] if committed by an individual on his own authority.[26] If it seems that the negotiations are likely to be long-drawn out, it may be convenient for the belligerents to agree to set up a neutralised area, which might even be protected by sentries provided by the belligerents, as was the case during the armistice negotiations at Panmunjom during the Korean War, 1952–53 and which persists to this day.[27]

---

[22] See Pr. I, Art. 33; Sick and Wounded Convention, 1949, Art. 15 resp.

[23] According to the US Dept. of the Army, *Law of Land Warfare*, REST-101, 1956, para. 58 'radio messages to the enemy and messages dropped by aircraft are becoming increasingly important as a prelude to conversations between representatives of the belligerent forces'. In July 1990 a telephone hotline was established between the director-generals of military operations of India and Pakistan to reduce the threat of confrontation between their forces along the Kashmir border, *The Times*, 12 July 1990.

[24] This is in accordance with the customary law principles of *pacta sunt servanda* and good faith (now embodied in Arts 26 and 31 of the Vienna Convention on Treaties, 1968, 1155 U.N.T.S. 331), and is based on the premise that the commanders concerned are acting within their competence. Insofar as truces and the like are concerned, this is confirmed by Hague Regulations, Art. 35.

[25] See ch. 18 below.

[26] This was already envisaged by Vattel, writing in 1758, although he is referring to truces: 'If any of the subjects, whether military men or private citizens, offend against the truce … the delinquents should be compelled to make ample compensation for the damage and severely punished', *Le Droit des Gens*, Bk III, ch. XVI, S. 241.

[27] HMSO, *Manual of Military Law*, Part III, *The Law of War on Land*, 1958, para. 388.

The terms of any agreement, whatever the nature of its substance, should be clear and precise and carefully explained to the troops affected by it. If this is not done, problems may arise as was evident from the British surrender in Singapore on 15 February, 1942.[28] To avoid the possibility of misunderstandings, such agreements should be reduced to writing whenever possible.

Parlementaires

When negotiations between commanders do take place they are normally conducted, at least to begin with, by intermediaries known as *parlementaires*. In the past, especially when adverse parties faced and were in sight of each other, the wish to negotiate by *parlementaires* was usually indicated by the raising of the white flag,[29] but any other method of communication may of course be employed and today such a desire to talk would almost certainly be indicated by radio or through the medium of the Protecting Power or some organisation like the International Committee of the Red Cross. Usually, *parlementaires* operate under a flag of truce and the section of the Hague Regulations[30] dealing with flags of truce is exclusively concerned with *parlementaires* and specifically states that a white flag is to be carried. The Regulations also provide that a *parlementaire* may be accompanied by a bugler or some other signaller as well as an interpreter, together with such other persons as may have been agreed by the belligerent commanders.

To show his good faith and his serious intentions, the belligerent wishing to dispatch a *parlementaire* should cease firing until a reply is received from the adverse party, and there is no obligation upon the adverse party to receive a *parlementaire*.[31] While the receiving commander may not fire upon the *parlementaire*, his flag or his party, the former does not have to cease combat, particularly if the *parlementaire* has been dispatched with an offer to surrender and to work out the requisite terms. Since the receiving belligerent may continue combat, the *parlementaire* should cross during a lull in the fighting or seek some other suitable

[28] Colonel Hunt, representing General Perceval, told the Indian personnel involved that they were being surrendered to the Japanese, whose orders were to be unquestioningly obeyed. He made no reference to their becoming prisoners of war. This made it easy for the Japanese to set up an Indian National Army under the command of 'General' Mohan Singh (Captain, 1/14 Punjab Regt), and to inform the surrendered Indian troops that in accordance with Perceval's statement they were to obey Singh unreservedly and fight for the independence of India, see Green, 'The Indian National Army trials', 11 M.L.R. (1948), 47; see also *Essays*, 1999, ch. XI.

[29] The raising of a white signal is a traditional indication of an intention to suspend hostilities, or to mark a person who is *hors de combat*. When employed by an individual soldier it normally signifies his desire to surrender; when raised in the vicinity of a group it indicates a desire to talk, often with a view to an honourable surrender.

[30] Arts 32–4.

[31] Art. 33.

moment for making his journey, or travel by a route that reduces the risk to himself or his party, all members of whom are covered by the white flag.

In the Falklands War, during the battle for Goose Green, the British Forces Area Commander informed his Argentine opposite number, on 29 May 1982, that he had 'sent a POW … under a White Flag of truce' calling upon him to surrender by a given time, acceptance being indicated by 'returning the POW under the White Flag'. Rejection of the summons to surrender would be indicated 'by returning the POW without his White Flag, although his neutrality will be respected'.

The *parlementaire* and his party are entitled to complete inviolability,[32] so long as they do nothing to abuse this protection,[33] or take advantage of their position.[34] While the receiving belligerent may of course take all steps necessary to protect the safety of his position or unit and prevent the *parlementaire* from taking advantage of his visit to secure information[35] and to detain him if he abuses his position by collecting information surreptitiously. However, it is not an abuse of his position for the *parlementaire* to report back anything he may have observed, so that he cannot be punished for this if captured subsequently.

To fire intentionally upon the white flag carried by a *parlementaire* or any other member of his party protected by that flag is a war crime,[36] and the sending authority may, as a retorsion,[37] declare that he will refuse to accept any *parlementaire* from the offending party. However, no offence is committed if the *parlementaire* or his party are injured accidentally, or even if the white flag he carries is fired upon inadvertently. If the journey is made by night, the flag may be illuminated by searchlight or other means. The receiving belligerent may prescribe the route to be taken by the *parlementaire,* may bind his eyes, limit the size of his party, or take other similar measures to preserve the security of his position and his force. Depending on agreement, the party may proceed on foot, by armoured vehicle or other means of transport. To avoid any mistakes or risk to themselves they should approach slowly and announce their arrival to the advance post of the adverse party in the latter's own language as soon as they are within hailing distance. After

[32] Hague Regulations, Art. 32.

[33] Abuse of a protective emblem amounts to perfidy and constitutes a war crime under the customary law of armed conflict. By Art. 37, para. 1(c) of Protocol I, 1977, 'the feigning of an intent to negotiate under a flag of truce' is specifically cited as an example of perfidy, and by Art. 85, para. 3(f) would amount to a grave breach of the Protocol (see ch. 18 below), if committed wilfully and causing a death or serious injury to body or health. It is equally perfidy for the *parlementaire* to use the white flag as cover for the collection of information.

[34] Hague Regulations, Art. 34.

[35] Art. 33.

[36] See ch. 18 below.

[37] A retorsion is an unfriendly but legal act taken in retaliation for a previous illegal or unfriendly act. Since there is no obligation to receive a *parlementaire* such a refusal is not an illegal act and would not justify resort to reprisal – an illegal act in response to an illegal act with the aim of securing termination of the prior illegal act.

making contact, the *parlementaire* must obey any order given him with respect to entering the lines and must withdraw if so instructed, when he must be given a reasonable time to comply. Should he fail to obey or linger unduly, he loses his inviolability and may be fired upon or made a prisoner of war. Any measure taken against the *parlementaire* or any member of his party must be conveyed to the sending belligerent without delay.

While the *parlementaire* is conducting his negotiations the conflict continues and both sides are entitled to reinforce or take such other action as they may consider necessary. Although reinforcements may be brought up while such negotiations are taking place, it is an abuse of the flag of truce amounting to perfidy to make use of a *parlementaire* and his flag of truce for the sole purpose of moving troops without interference by the adverse party,[38] and would constitute a war crime. When the *parlementaire* is approaching or being received,[39] the party sending him should cease fire.

As between himself and the receiving authority, the *parlementaire* should not discuss anything outside the task which he has undertaken and should take every precaution to avoid imparting any military information. Only he and his interpreter are entitled to enter the enemy lines. The other members of the party must obey any orders given them, but remain entitled to protection until the *parlementaire* rejoins them and they return to their own lines. The message carried by the *parlementaire* should be in writing whenever possible and the contents should be clear and unambiguous. Unless this is impossible, the *parlementaire* should be an officer and is entitled to all the courtesies of his rank. However, regardless of his rank, the *parlementaire* cannot demand to be taken to the adverse party's commanding officer unless this has been previously arranged. If requested, he must hand his message, or if it is verbal deliver it, to the officer receiving him, who whenever possible should be of equal or higher rank. If the message is verbal, the receiving officer is entitled to demand that it be reduced to writing, and the *parlementaire* is entitled to a receipt for any message written or verbal that he has delivered.

Like any agreement made between commanders, that made by a *parlementaire* must be carried out in good faith and breach thereof may render the individuals responsible liable for war crimes and if committed by a party to the conflict render that party liable to pay compensation.[40] If the breach is more than minor in character, the injured party has the right to treat the agreement as abrogated and to resume full hostilities.

---

[38] It is as much an act of perfidy, and so a war crime (see ch. 18 below), for the commander to send a *parlementaire* for this purpose as it is for the *parlementaire* to abuse his flag, or for the receiving belligerent to fire upon it.

[39] This only refers to the moment of contact and not while the *parlementaire* is within the adverse party's lines.

[40] Hague Convention IV, Art. 3.

Capitulation and surrender

If the agreement is in the nature of a capitulation,[41] which is a purely military agreement, its terms should be in accord with rules of military honour.[42] In the call for surrender at Goose Green, the Argentine forces were instructed to '[leave] the township, forming up in a military manner, removing your helmets and laying down weapons'. A capitulation is concerned with the surrender of troops, the place they are defending and their disposition thereafter. It should contain nothing touching on other issues. If the capitulation relates to the surrender of an inhabited place, it may contain stipulations concerning the treatment of the civilian population. Any such stipulations would be additional to those concerning the position of the civilian population in the hands of the adverse party as laid down in Geneva Convention IV, 1949[43] and should not be in conflict with such provisions.

Conditions in a capitulation should relate only to the immediate purpose of effecting the surrender and not contain terms which, for example, would forbid the surrendered personnel from carrying arms in the future, for this is a political and not a military issue. If the commander is so authorised by his government, a capitulation may include political terms, and, generally speaking, the adverse commander is entitled to assume that a commander offering a capitulation is entitled so to do, but he should endeavour to ascertain whether this is so. Liability for offering to surrender depends upon the surrendering officer's national law. In some cases, unless there is no longer any possibility of the commander, or for that matter an individual soldier, making a successful defence,[44] an act of surrender may be treated as criminal.[45]

[41] This is another term for surrender.

[42] Hague Regulations, Art. 35. This is the only article in the regulations dealing with capitulations, which are, therefore, for the main part subject to the rules of customary law. By the 'rules of military honour' there was formerly understood the right, e.g., to march out of a surrendered city with flags flying or bayonets fixed. This is no longer a common occurrence, although it may in fact be agreed upon by the parties concerned, particularly if the surrendering troops have fought valiantly and have been ultimately faced with the alternative of surrender or death. The term now tends to signify an obligation not to humiliate the forces involved, so that they should not, for example, be paraded through the streets to humiliate them before the local inhabitants as was sometimes done by the Japanese seeking to humiliate Caucasian prisoners before their colonial subjects. Nor should they be photographed in humiliating circumstances so that these pictures may be used by the captor's news media, as was done by Iraq to captured Coalition airmen during Operation Desert Storm after the invasion of Kuwait.

[43] See ch. 12 below.

[44] See, e.g., US Dept. of the Army, Pamphlet 27, 161–2, 1962, *International Law*, vol. II, 05-Code of Conduct for Members of the United States Armed Forces, II: 'I will never surrender of my own free will. If in command I will never surrender my men while they still have the means to resist.'

[45] See, e.g., National Defence Act, Canada, R.S.C., 1970, c. N-4; s. 63 'Every officer in command of a vessel, aircraft, defence establishment, unit or other element of the Canadian Forces who ... (c) when capable of making a successful defence, surrenders his vessel, defence establishment, *matériel*, unit or other element of the Canadian Forces to the

All personnel covered by a capitulation become prisoners of war and subject to the orders of the adverse party and are liable to punishment if these are disobeyed. The captor's freedom in giving such orders is limited by Geneva Convention III, 1949[46] Protocol I, 1977, the Hague Regulations and customary law. Sometimes the number involved in a surrender is so large that a captor finds it inconvenient to treat them in the normal way or confine them in a prisoner-of-war camp and may decide to leave them under the administrative control of their own commanders. The latter's powers are strictly limited to an administrative role and punitive rights remain with the captor, for by Article 6 of the Convention, no agreement may be made which could adversely affect the rights of the prisoners as provided in the Convention. This suggests that the incident affecting the relations between surrendering German troops and their Canadian captors in The Netherlands in 1945, when the German commander was allowed to exercise judicial control and the Canadian captors provided the weapons to give effect to the death penalty thus imposed,[47] would now probably constitute a war crime. This situation seems to have arisen because the Canadian commander considered the German personnel involved to be 'disarmed surrendered personnel' and as such not prisoners of war – although there is no such classification in the Convention or customary law.

Immediately upon capitulation all warlike activities on the part of those affected by the surrender must cease. A commander contemplating surrender is permitted to destroy any matériel, weapons or other objects under his control, subject to restrictions concerning civilian[48] or other protected[49] objects, in order to pre-

---

enemy … is guilty of an offence and on conviction, if he acted traitorously, shall suffer death, if he acted from cowardice is liable to suffer death or less punishment, and in any other case is liable to dismissal with disgrace from Her Majesty's service or to less punishment.' It is, of course, open to the court martial trying the officer to hold that the surrender was premature, in which case the accused would be dismissed with disgrace. S. 64: 'Every person who … (d) improperly abandons or delivers up any defence establishment, garrison, place, matériel, post or guard … is guilty of an offence and on conviction, if he acted traitorously, shall suffer death, and in any other case, if the act was committed in action, is liable to suffer death or less punishment or, if the offence was *committed otherwise than in action*, to imprisonment for life or less punishment.' This section applies to every member of the Canadian Forces regardless of rank, and the italicised phrase would cover a decision to surrender a city or post without any attempt to defend it.

[46] See ch. 10 below.

[47] See Commons Debates, Oct. 11 1966, col. 8511, Dec. 21, 1966, col. 11445. See also Levie, *Prisoners of War in International Armed Conflict* (US Naval War College, Studies in International Law, vol. 59), 336, n. 102 – the author seems to regard such a proceeding as a 'kangaroo court'. This incident formed the basis of the film *The Fifth Day of Peace*. See, however, *R. v. Perzenowski et al.* [1947] D.L.R., 705 (Alberta C.A.), and *R. v. Werner* [1947] 2 S.A.L.R., 828, when German prisoners were tried and executed for the murder of a fellow prisoner tried by a 'kangaroo' court set up by the prisoners themselves.

[48] See, e.g., Pr. I, Ch. III, Arts 52–6. Art, 52(1) states that 'civilian objects shall not be the object of attack or reprisals'. Art. 49(1) defines 'attacks' as 'acts of violence against the adversary whether in offence or defence'; it is thus clear that a surrendering authority destroying civilian objects would be in breach of these provisions.

[49] *Ibid.*, Art. 55.

vent them falling into the hands of the adverse party after the capitulation. Any such destruction must be completed before the capitulation is accepted, for any hostile acts committed thereafter would be a war crime.[50]

Passports and safe-conducts

On occasion a commander may make an arrangement with an individual or group of nationals belonging to the adverse party or to a neutral power. These are normally in the form of passports or safe-conducts.

A passport is a document issued by a commander permitting the holder to move unmolested within the territory occupied by his troops. It may be general or limited in character and for a limited or unlimited time. It should clearly specify the person to whom it has been issued and is non-transferable. It may also specify what goods may be carried by the holder and, unless expressly prohibited, such protected goods may be transferred to another, particularly when granted as a licence to trade or as a guarantee against seizure. Passports may be granted by a commander on his own authority or in accordance with his own military law. They may also be granted as the result of an agreement with the adverse party or with a neutral or the Protecting Power.[51] Only when granted by agreement in this way does the passport regime become subject to international law.

Safe-conducts may be issued by an individual commander to individuals or groups seeking to go to some place which can only be reached by passing through an area occupied by his troops, particularly when they are in contact with the adverse party, or to enable them to leave a besieged area or one about to be made the object of attack. Protocol I provides that the parties to the conflict:

> shall, to the maximum extent feasible, ... (a) endeavour to remove the civilian population, individual civilians and civilian objects under their control from the vicinity of military objectives ... [and] take the other necessary precautions to protect the civilian population, individual civilians and civilian objects under their control against the dangers resulting from military operations.[52]

After Iraq invaded Kuwait in 1990, it not only refused to allow foreign civilians to depart, but concentrated them in 'vital areas' to protect these from attack.

While a passport enables the holder to move freely within the area occupied by troops under the command of the issuing authority, a safe-conduct permits him to pass through such an area, even to enemy territory. They are frequently issued to the diplomatic representatives of neutral states accredited to the issuing authority's adverse party who need to travel through territory controlled by the issuing authority if they are to carry out their diplomatic duties. Invariably, such safe-

---

[50] See, e.g., *In re Grumpelt* (Scuttled U-Boats Case) (1946), 13 Ann. Dig., 309.
[51] See ch. 13 below.
[52] Art. 58(a).

conducts are issued or authorised by the political or senior military authorities concerned rather than by a subordinate commander.

Despite the distinction between passports and safe-conducts, nomenclature is not important in classifying the document. Sometimes the term 'pass' or 'permit' is used. The decisive factor is the purpose for which the instrument has been issued and not its label. Those carrying such permits are protected by them so long as the period for which they are valid subsists, provided they comply with any conditions set out and refrain from any act which may be construed as incompatible with the purpose for which the document was issued. They may be revoked at the discretion of the issuing commander, but in such a case the holder must be permitted to withdraw in safety. Revocation must not be used as an excuse for detention.

Safeguards

On occasion, it may be necessary to leave behind a party of soldiers as a protection for enemy or neutral persons or property when the main body of troops withdraws. Those so left are inviolable if they fall into the adverse party's hands and it is usual to allow them to return to their own lines as soon as military exigencies permit. Since such safeguards are only regulated by international law when they result from arrangements between the combatants, in the absence of such arrangements any failure to grant those remaining inviolability and treat them instead as prisoners of war does not amount to a breach of the law of armed conflict. A violation of an arranged safeguard is a violation of the law and punishable as a war crime.[53]

Cartels

Belligerents sometimes make arrangements permitting acts which would not normally be allowed between themselves, such as permitting the passage of correspondence, which would still probably be subject to censorship, or trade in certain commodities. Such arrangements are known as cartels, although in a narrow and technical sense this term is applied to arrangements for the transfer of prisoners of war or the sick and wounded.[54] Any cartel is voidable by either party if intentionally

---

[53] Para. 457 of the US Dept. of the Army Field Manual, *The Law of Land Warfare*, FM 27-10, 1956, provides 'The violation of a safeguard is a grave violation of the law of war [this is not identical with a grave breach as that term is used in the 1949 Geneva Conventions or Protocol I, 1977] and, if committed by a person subject to the Uniform Code of Military justice is punishable under Art. 102 thereof with death or such other punishment as a court-martial may direct.' A Canadian officer violating a safeguard would probably be accused of 'scandalous' or 'disgraceful' conduct contrary to the National Defence Act, ss. 82, 83.

[54] See British *Manual of Military Law*, n. 23 above, paras. 497, 250; US FM 27-10, para. 469.

violated in any material point by the other. In August 1941 the International Committee of the Red Cross secured permission from Germany for a Royal Air Force Blenheim bomber to fly with safety from Britain to Germany and home again to deliver an artificial leg to Wing Commander Bader then held as a prisoner of war at Colditz.[55]

Safety zones

It is also not uncommon for belligerents to make arrangements for particular areas to be placed outside the zone of operations, and this may be done on a temporary or permanent basis. They may be made directly between the belligerents or through the good offices of a neutral power or perhaps more commonly the Protecting Power.[56] They may be concerned with the establishment of safety zones where civilians may be concentrated,[57] neutralised zones,[58] undefended places[59] or open cities.[60] Since the adoption of Conventions I and IV it is recognised that during peace time a state may declare that in the event of armed conflict a particular area shall be a safety zone for the protection of the sick, aged, expectant mothers and children. On the outbreak of hostilities and during their course the combatants may agree to recognise that such zones are to be immune from attack and outside the area of activities.[61] After the commencement of the conflict, safety and hospital zones may be established in occupied territory as well. A neutralised zone may also be set up in the area of operations for the protection of the wounded and sick[62] or other persons *hors de combat* as well as non-combatants taking no part in the hostilities or any activities of a military character.[63] The agreement should clearly indicate the area of the zone, together with the period for which it

[55] *The Times* (London), 19 Dec. 1996.

[56] See ch. 13 below.

[57] Such zones were established under neutral arrangements during the Spanish Civil War in 1936, Castren, *The Present Law of War and Neutrality*, 176.

[58] See British *Manual*, para. 388.

[59] *Ibid.*, para. 290.

[60] See Castren, *The Present Law*, 203–4: 'A town which has been declared open or which is protected by an agreement, must be surrendered to the enemy without resistance so that the enemy will have no cause to batter or destroy it in other ways. A separate agreement must be made concerning the possible right of the enemy to use the town for his own military purposes and providing that he in his turn must surrender the town in the same way if the fortune of war should later turn.'

[61] Arts 23, 14 resp. Annex I to each Convention is a Draft Agreement Relating to Hospital and Safety Zones and Localities.

[62] See, e.g., the historical examples cited in Green, *Essays*, ch. vi, 'War law and the medical profession', 104–5.

[63] Civilians Convention, Art. 15. Even though the United Nations set up 'safety zones' in Srebrenica in Bosnia, the local Serbs attacked them and, on the withdrawal of the peacekeeping forces, killed many of those taking refuge therein.

has been neutralised. Agreements of this kind may be negotiated directly or through the medium of a neutral or the Protecting Power or with the assistance of the International Committee of the Red Cross, and may be entered into by a local commander or the local government authorities.

A neutralised zone may also be established when it is anticipated that negotiations concerning, for example, a surrender or the arranging of an armistice may be prolonged. The area in question would then be set aside for the purposes of such negotiations, as at Panmunjom in 1951 in connection with the arranging of a cease-fire in Korea.

Demilitarised zones

The parties to a conflict may also agree to treat a particular area as demilitarised. This is usually in accord with a pre-existing treaty wherein the parties have agreed not to fortify or station troops in the named area, seeking to ensure its immunity from any hostilities.[64] Article 60 of Protocol I permits the combatants to agree to treat any area as demilitarised, the agreement in question having to be express, written or oral and arranged either directly or through the medium of a neutral or Protecting Power, or any impartial humanitarian organisation such as the International Committee of the Red Cross. It may be made by reciprocal or concordant declarations and should specify the means of supervision. In such an area:

(a) all combatants as well as mobile weapons and mobile military equipment must have been evacuated; (b) no hostile use shall be made of fixed military installations or establishments;[65] (c) no acts of hostility shall be committed by the authorities or by the population;[66] and[67] (d) any activity linked to the military effort[68] must have ceased.[69]

The party in control of a demilitarised zone is responsible for marking it, especially on its perimeters, limits and highways, with such identification marks as have been agreed upon, but the fact that there is no agreement does not remove

[64] Oppenheim, *International Law* (7th ed. by Lauterpacht), 244, n. 1.

[65] The presence of a munitions factory would not make the place defended, but would deprive it of its immunity from attack. By Protocol I, Art. 51(5)(b), however, an attack is considered to be 'indiscriminate' and, therefore, forbidden, if it 'may be expected to cause incidental loss of civilian life, injury to civilians, damage to civilian objects, or a combination thereof, which would be excessive in relation to the concrete and direct military advantage anticipated'.

[66] Any such act, particularly by the authorities, will remove the immunity enjoyed by the zone, but an individual act of terrorism or assassination by a civilian inhabitant will not have this effect.

[67] The conditions are cumulative.

[68] The parties to the conflict must agree upon the interpretation of this condition.

[69] Protocol I, Art. 60(3).

the duty to mark.[70] Provided the parties agree, if the fighting approaches the zone, no party may use it for purposes related to military operations nor unilaterally revoke its status,[71] but if any party to the conflict commits a material breach of the conditions the other is released from its obligations and the zone loses its protected status. The loss of such status does not remove any normal protection provided by the customary and treaty law of armed conflict.[72] The fact that Red Cross, civil defence[73] or other protected persons or police forces retained for the security of the population or the maintenance of peace and order remain in the zone does not deprive it of its protected status.[74]

Undefended places

The law of armed conflict forbids attack by any means on undefended places,[75] most of which are behind the lines and it is desired to protect them from any attack. It was formerly the view that an undefended place should contain no fortified installation and it is still controversial whether a place defended by anti-aircraft guns intended to protect it against an illegal attack renders the place defended.[76] The better opinion would suggest that such a place is in fact defended, for it cannot be certain that this is the true reason for the emplacement of the guns.[77] This would also seem to be the case of a city shielded by forces holding a line in front of it, so that the approach of adverse forces would be impeded and its occupation without fighting impossible.

In accordance with customary law, the adverse party had to agree to treat a place as undefended, but now[78] the appropriate civil or military authorities of a party to the conflict may declare as undefended any inhabited place near or in a zone where the armed forces of the parties are in contact rendering it open for occupation by the adverse party. A declaration to this effect must be addressed to the adverse party, defining as precisely as possible the locality's limits. Receipt must be acknowledged and the recipient is obliged to treat the place as undefended

---

[70] Protocol I, Art. 60(5). The same conditions relate to undefended places, Art. 59(6).

[71] Art. 60(6).

[72] Art. 60(7).

[73] See ch. 14 below.

[74] Art. 60(4). This is also the case with undefended places, Art. 59(3).

[75] Hague Regs., Art. 25; see also Hague Convention IX, Art. 1, concerning naval bombardment, and Protocol I, Art. 59(1): 'It is prohibited … to attack, by any means whatsoever, non-defended localities'.

[76] For a discussion of the difference between a defended and an undefended city, see decision of Tokyo District Court in *Shimoda* v. *The State* (1963), 32 I.L.R., 626, 631–2.

[77] During the Gulf War the Iraqis often situated guns in the grounds of hospitals or mosques and these guns were legitimate targets, although every endeavour was made to avoid attacking them, see *Conduct of the Persian Gulf War*, Final report to Congress, 1992, App. O, 'The role of the law of war', O 12, 31 I.L.M. (1992), 615.

[78] Art. 59(2).

unless the conditions already referred to are unfulfilled or broken, in which case he shall immediately inform the declaring party of his intention to treat the place as having lost its protected status. Loss of such status does not remove any of the protection arising from the customary or treaty law of armed conflict.[79] There is nothing to prevent the parties from agreeing to treat as undefended a place which does not satisfy the Protocol requirements, nor are they precluded from introducing such conditions as they may agree upon.[80]

In practice today, reflecting the trend towards total war whereby the entire population of a belligerent country tends to be involved in some measure in the war effort,[81] it may be that no place behind the enemy lines and out of the immediate contact zone may qualify as open or undefended, especially as the adverse party could not be sure that the requisite conditions for the grant of such status could be met, and he would be unable to occupy it or take possession of any military resources that might exist. However, despite this, the International Committee of the Red Cross has, for example, been successful[82] in creating:

> neutralised zones and protected areas in various situations in which it was imperative to shield civilians from the effects of hostilities, such as Dhaka (Bangladesh) in 1971, in Nicosia (Cyprus) in 1974, in Saigon (Vietnam) and Phnom Penh (Cambodia) in 1975 and in the major cities of Nicaragua in 1979. [All such places intended] to provide temporary shelter from the immediate dangers of combat for people taking no part in hostilities … were placed under the protective emblem of the red cross … Admission to such areas is restricted to the people whom they are intended to protect and to the personnel entrusted with their administration, organisation and inspection; those who enter the areas must take no part in hostilities or military activities of any kind; and weapons and military supplies are forbidden inside their boundaries. [However, a] protected area cannot provide political asylum or exemption from capture or any security measures taken by the administration.

In addition to any other agreements that may be made between the commanders in the field, the Geneva Conventions and Protocol I contain provisions recognising that in the circumstances specified in these treaties agreements between belligerents may be desirable or necessary.[83] However, such agreements must not reduce in any way the rights granted to protected persons under those treaties.

---

[79] Art. 59(4), (7). It would still be protected by Arts 48–58. Hague Regs, Art. 25, would still be operative: 'The attack or bombardment, by whatever means, of towns, villages, dwellings, or buildings which are undefended is prohibited.'

[80] Pr. I, Art. 59(5), confirming the position under customary law.

[81] See Smith, *The Crisis*.

[82] ICRC Bulletin no. 175 (Aug. 1990), 1. In 1993 the UN proclaimed certain areas of Bosnia protected, but to no practical effect.

[83] Such agreements refer to hostilities, combatants, prisoners of war, civilians, the Protecting Power, the sick and wounded, etc.

6

Lawful combatants

Historical background

In ancient times as evidenced by the Laws of Manu, the Old Testament or the writings of Kautilya or San Tzu there was no attempt to identify those who were entitled to be treated as combatants. There was merely a description of what was regarded as proper conduct by those engaged in hostilities. During feudal times, when the law of arms was developing, there was equally no attempt at definition, although there was some differentiation of treatment as regards knights who were covered by the code of chivalry and subject to courts of honour[1] and the peasantry who tended to provide the foot soldiery and who were subject to their national military codes.[2] At the same time, identification depended on banners and colours.

While there was no attempt by the classical writers to define 'combatants', some of them provided definitions of 'soldiers'. Thus, Ayala[3] stated that 'those only are called soldiers who have had the oath put to them and have taken it and have been incorporated in the ranks. Sailors and oarsmen in the navy are soldiers. Further, not every one is admissible as a soldier and some persons are not compelled to become soldiers', and among those excluded were clerics, agriculturists and the disabled (*debilitati*). Gentili agreed:[4]

---

[1] See, e.g., Keen, *The Laws of War in the Late Middle Ages*; Contamine, *War in the Middle Ages*; see also Ward, *The Foundation and History of the Law of Nations*, vol. 2, ch. 14 'The influence of chivalry'. See, e.g. *Waldeshef* v. *Wawe* (1383) and *Hoo* v. *Bretvill* (1385) re-exchange of prisoners and payment of ransom, resp., see Squibb, *The High Court of Chivalry*, 1997, 17. At 166 Squibb states, 'Cases concerning prisoners of war were described as being determined according to the law of arms', *Tatesham* v. *Garenserres* (1351).

[2] See, e.g., Richard II's *Estatuz, ordenances et custumes à tenir en l'ost*, 1385, c. Twiss, *Black Book of the Admiralty*, vol. 1, 453–4; Hen. V, *Statutes and Ordinaunces to be keped in Time of Warr*, 1419, c. Contamine, *War in the Middle Ages*, 120; Fourqueveux, *La Discipline Militaire*; see also Laws and Ordinances of Warre; c. Clode, *Military Forces of the Crown*, vol. 1, App. VI.

[3] *De Jure et Officiis Bellicis et Disciplina Militarii*, Lib. III, cap. IV, ss. 3, 4 (tr. Carnegie, 1912, 184).

[4] *De Jure Belli*, Lib. II, cap. XVI (tr., Carnegie, 1933, 199).

To be considered as a soldier one ought to be written down as a soldier in the list. It is not sufficient for one's name merely to be on the list, unless he is actually listed as a soldier; for a scribe or some other attendant might be on the list, but yet would not necessarily be a soldier ... One is also a soldier who is not necessarily so called; in the fleet all the oarsmen and sailors are soldiers, and so also are the watch.

Vattel was among the earliest to emphasise the difference between the time before soldiering became a profession and the situation he knew:[5]

in former times, and especially in small States, as soon as war was declared every man became a soldier; the entire people took up arms and carried on the war. Soon a choice was made, and armies were formed of picked men, the rest of the people keeping to their ordinary occupations. At the present day, the custom of having regular armies prevails almost everywhere, and especially in the large States. The public authority raises soldiers, distributes them into different divisions under the command of general and other officers, and maintains them as long as it sees fit ... But [the sovereign] should choose only persons suited to bear arms ... Those alone are exempt who are incapable of bearing arms, or of enduring the hardships of war. On this ground, old men, children, and women are exempted. Although there may be found women as strong and brave as men,[6] that is not usual; and rules are necessarily general in character, and are based upon conditions which ordinarily prevail. Besides women are needed for other duties in society, and, in short, the mingling of the two sexes in armies would result in too many inconveniences. As far as possible, a good government should employ all the citizens and distribute duties and offices in such a way that the State, in all its affairs, may be most effectively served. Hence, when not under pressure of necessity, it should exempt from the army all those who are engaged in functions either useful or necessary to society. For this reason magistrates are ordinarily exempt.

But the same exemption does not apply to embrace all the clergy, for the:

law of the church which forbids ecclesiastics to shed blood is a convenient device for dispensing from the duty of fighting persons who are often ready to fan the flame of discord and to provoke bloody wars ... [Only those should be exempt] who are engaged in teaching religion, in governing the church, and in celebrating public worship.

However, this refusal to extend immunity to all clerics seems to have been rather unique to Vattel, for in practice not only were all clerics exempt from military service, but their presence on the battlefield frequently resulted in a temporary cessation of hostilities, just as conflict ceased on saints' days and religious holidays.[7]

---

[5] *Le Droit des Gens*, Liv. III, ch. II, ss. 9–10 (tr., Carnegie, 1916, 237–8).

[6] See, e.g., Newark, *Women Warlords*; Howes and Stevenson, eds, *Women and the Use of Military Force*; Jones, *Women Warriors: A History*, 1997. During the Gulf War 1991 women served in active units in both the American and British forces; some were killed in action and some were taken prisoner; see, e.g., Cornum, *She Went to War*, 1992.

[7] The last occasion on which this seems to have occurred was Christmas 1914, during World War I, when fraternisation across the lines took place and was immediately suppressed by the authorities on both sides.

Grotius does not even attempt to define who soldiers are, although the Carnegie translation of his *De Jure Belli*[8] includes in the Index an entry 'Combatants, definition of', and heads its version of his Book III, chapter XXI, s. x 'Who may be classed under the term combatants'. In fact, this section has nothing to do with classification, but informs us that safe-conducts granted to the army extend even to include senior officers. The term used by Grotius is *milites*, and the English translation of 1738 uses the term 'soldiers' and explains that this includes officers.[9]

It is only with the writers of the nineteenth century that either a clear definition of the rights of soldiers or the first usage of the term 'combatants' is found. Thus, von Martens states,[10] writing of 'Persons by whom Hostilities ought to be exercised',

> Soldiers, by the order of their commanders, and such other subjects as may obtain express permission for the purpose from their sovereign, may lawfully exercise hostilities, and are looked upon by the enemy as lawful enemies; but those, on the contrary who, not being so authorised, take upon them to attack the enemy, are treated by him as banditti; and even the state to which they belong ought to punish them as such.

Similarly, while there is no reference to combatants in the Lieber Code since this is directed to United States Armies in the Field,[11] Articles 18 and 19 refer to the position of non-combatants in relation to hastening a surrender or warning before bombardment.

According to Wheaton[12] non-combatants are 'all those not in military service … [but if they] make forcible resistance, or violate the mild rules of modern warfare, give military information to their friends, or obstruct the forces in possession, they are liable to be treated as combatants' – today they are more likely to be treated as unlawful combatants[13] and tried as war criminals.[14] Bluntschli does not use the terms 'combatants', although he does speak of 'non-combatants'. He states:[15]

> Sont ennemis, dans le sens propre et actif du mot, en première ligne, les chefs de l'état ennemi et ceux qui dirigent sa politique, et ensuite tous les personnes qui, prenant personnellement part à la lutte, font régulièrement partie de l'armée et sont placées sous les ordres d'une puissance ennemie.

---

[8] 1625 (tr., Carnegie, 1925, 287).

[9] At p. 721.

[10] *A Compendium of the Law of Nations*, 1788 Bk VIII, ch. III, s. 2 (tr., Cobbett, 1802, 287).

[11] General Orders No. 100, 1863 (Schindler and Toman, 3).

[12] *Elements of International Law* (1986), ed. Dana (1866), s. 346, n. 168 (ed., Carnegie, 936, 362).

[13] It is not strictly correct to describe them as 'unlawful combatants', since they are non-combatants unlawfully taking part in combat.

[14] See ch. 18 below.

[15] *Le Droit International Codifié*, tr. (Rivier, 1895, s. 569).

Finally, reference might be made to Hall who writes:[16]

> Of the non-combatant class little need be said … [T]he immunity from violence to which they are entitled is limited … in that though protected from direct injury, they are exposed to all the personal injuries indirectly resulting from military or naval operations directed against the armed forces of the state.

Although the next paragraph is headed 'Combatants', this word does not appear in the text, which merely states that 'the right to kill and wound armed enemies is subordinated to the condition that those enemies shall be able and willing to continue their resistance … A belligerent therefore may only kill those enemies whom he is permitted to attack while a combat is actually in progress'.

It is clear, therefore, that it matters little whether we use the term soldiers or combatants, so long as we mean thereby those who are embodied in a state's armed forces and are entitled to take part in conflict. Today, we employ simply the nomenclature of combatant, for the main part regarding the civilian population as non-combatants. However, it must always be remembered that prisoners of war,[17] the wounded, sick and shipwrecked[18] and others who are *hors de combat* are also entitled to be treated as combatants, although no longer active.[19]

The law today

It is one of the purposes of the law of armed conflict to ensure that a member of one class entitled to special status or treatment does not, save in exceptional circumstances, enjoy the rights of the other. That is to say, he cannot be a combatant and a non-combatant at the same time. However, by Article 51(3) of Protocol I, 1977,[20] a non-combatant, that is to say, civilian, who takes a direct part in hostilities loses his status as protected civilian under both the Protocol and the Civilians Convention, 1949,[21] only for so long as he acts in this manner, and he then becomes a legitimate object of attack, although, contrary to the views of Wheaton,[22] he does not while so participating become entitled to the rights pertaining to a combatant. Since non-combatants are not entitled to take part in combat, it would be improper for a commander to allow those under his control, such as medical or religious personnel attached to his command, to take a direct part in combat, although if unlawfully attacked they would be entitled to defend themselves and those within their care by the use of small arms.

---

[16] *A Treatise on International Law*, s. 128.
[17] See ch. 10 below.
[18] See ch. 11 below.
[19] For a recent discussion of this issue, see Rogers, *Law on the Battlefield*, 1996, 7–9.
[20] Schindler and Toman, 621.
[21] *Ibid.*, 495.
[22] See text to n. 13 above.

The first attempt to produce an internationally accepted definition of combatants was embodied in the Project of an International Declaration concerning the Laws and Customs of War adopted by the Brussels Conference of 15 European states convened by Alexander II of Russia in 1874.[23] Agreement was reached in determining 'who should be recognised as belligerents, combatants and non-combatants':

> Art. 9. The laws, rights and duties of war apply not only to armies, but also to militia and volunteer corps fulfilling the following conditions: 1. That they be commanded by a person responsible for his subordinates; 2. That they have a fixed distinctive emblem recognisable at a distance [so that they may be distinguished from the civilian population]; 3. That they carry arms openly; and 4. That they conduct their operations in accordance with the laws and customs of war [to a great extent these are spelled out in the Hague Regulations annexed to Hague Convention IV, 1907].[24] In countries where militia constitute the army, or form part of it, they are included under the denomination *army*.
>
> Art. 10. The population of a territory which has not been occupied, who, on the approach of the enemy, spontaneously take up arms to resist the invading troops without having had time to organise themselves in accordance with Article 9, shall be regarded as belligerents if they respect the laws and customs of war.

Such civilian bodies are known as *levées en masse*, but they do not include groups of the inhabitants of occupied territory who take up arms subsequent to the occupation in order to harass or engage the occupant. However, during World War II such forces were invariably described by the anti-Axis belligerents as legitimate forces entitled to treatment as combatants.

> Art. 11. The armed forces of the belligerent parties may consist of combatants and non-combatants [e.g., medical and religious personnel]. In case of capture by the enemy, both shall enjoy the rights of prisoners of war.

Today, however, by Protocol I, Art. 33, medical and religious personnel do not become prisoners of war, although entitled to treatment as such.

The Brussels definition was amended slightly in the *Oxford Manual on the Laws of War* published by the Institute of International Law in 1880.[25] Having stated that 'persons not forming part of a belligerent armed force should abstain from' acts of violence, the Manual defined an 'armed force' as including:

> 1. The army properly so called, including the militia; 2. The national guards, landsturm,[26] free corps, and other bodies which fulfil the three following conditions: (a)

---

[23] Schindler and Toman, 25.

[24] *Ibid.*, 63.

[25] *Ibid.,* 35, Art. 2.

[26] According to Rivier's note to Bluntschli, *Le Droit International*, s. 598, r. l, the landsturm comprises 'l'ensemble des hommes valides qui ne font partie ni de l'armée active, ni de la réserve, ni de la landwehr (armée territoriale), a le droit de prendre les armes pour défendre la patrie. Il est placé sous les ordres de son gouvernement et des autorités militaires. Les soldats du landsturm doivent donc être traités en ennemis au même titre que les

That they are under the direction of a responsible chief; (b) That they must have a uniform, or a fixed distinctive emblem recognisable at a distance, and worn by individuals composing such corps; (c) That they carry their arms openly 3. The crews of men-of-war and other military boats; 4. The inhabitants of non-occupied territory, who, on the approach of the enemy take up arms spontaneously and openly to resist the invading troops, even if they have not had time to organise themselves.

The *Manual* made it clear that 'every belligerent armed force is bound to conform to the laws of war'.

The Brussels and Oxford definitions formed the basis of the definition finally adopted at the Hague Peace Conferences of 1899 and 1907 and what appears in the Hague Regulations is the wording of Brussels, with but minor verbal changes. This definition remained unaltered until the adoption of Protocol I in 1977, which introduced changes rendered necessary by the experience gained as a result of armed conflicts taking place after the end of World War II.

While the civilians participating in a *levée en masse* are regarded as combatants, this is only true so long as they carry their arms openly and comply with the laws and customs of war. As combatants they are entitled to treatment in accordance with the Geneva Conventions of 1949 if wounded or if taken prisoner. A *levée en masse* may be raised with regard to any part of the national territory which has not been occupied by the adverse party. It follows, therefore, that if the inhabitants of a town under attack take up arms in its defence, they would be protected as constituting such a *levée*. If, however, the *levée* is raised in occupied territory, its members are not entitled to be treated as combatants, unless they are so organised as to constitute a resistance movement.

Distinct from civilians acting in this fashion are those who are employed in industries or other activities connected with the war effort, for while so engaged they may lose some of their immunities as civilians and become liable to attack. However, this does not mean that they therefore become combatants. Subject to arguments based on the theory that modern war is total affecting the whole population including civilians[27] – which runs counter to the distinction between combatants and civilians in both the Geneva Conventions of 1949 and the Protocols of 1977 – this would mean that though munition workers are legitimate targets while engaged in production within the factory, they are not liable to attack when in their homes.

As distinct from a *levée en masse*, civilians, whether in occupied territory or not, who take up arms on their own initiative and not under the control of the government or some other higher authority who may be responsible for their actions, do not

soldats de l'armée régulière, de l'élite, de la réserve ou de la landwehr, et ils peuvent être faits prisonniers. On doit leur appliquer les lois de la guerre et non les lois pénales'; see also *Cassell's German Dictionary*, 'General summons and levy of the people; last reserve comprising all men capable of bearing arms that are not included in the *Linie* [line regiments], the Reserve and the *Landwehr* – the second reserve, between the Reserve and the Landsturm'.

[27] See, e.g., Smith *The Crisis* (1947), 74–7.

receive any protection as combatants. They are regarded as marauders or bandits and may be tried as such if captured by the adverse party. This is, however, not the case if they are sufficiently well organised to be regarded as a resistance movement.

While the Hague Regulations define who is a combatant and entitled to treatment as a prisoner of war if captured, this definition must be read in the light of the 1949 Convention on prisoners of war[28] indicating those entitled to be treated as such. This definition is somewhat more extensive than that in the regulations:

A ... (1) Members of the armed forces of a Party to the conflict as well as members of militias or volunteer corps forming part of such armed forces.[29]

(2) Members of other militias and members of other volunteer corps, including those of organised resistance movements, belonging to a Party to the conflict and operating in or outside their own territory, even if this territory is occupied,[30] provided that such militias or volunteer corps, including such resistance movements [otherwise satisfy the conditions prescribed for combatants]. (3) Members of regular armed forces who profess allegiance to a government or an authority not recognised by the Detaining Power. (4)[31] Persons who accompany the armed forces without actually

---

[28] Schindler and Toman, 423, Art. 4 (see ch. 10 below).

[29] This will include members of the UK Territorial Army, the Canadian Reserve, the US Reserve, such volunteer bodies as American citizens recruited as the Ninety-seventh Bn. CEF in 1915, which never saw action as a unit, although individual members were absorbed into regular Canadian regiments; the 'Eagle Squadron' made up of neutral US personnel and attached to the RAF in both World Wars; the Lafayette Squadron of American volunteers enlisted in the French Foreign Legion in World War I and transferred to various French flying units – all while the US was still neutral; as well as ordinary units of the armed forces either made up of volunteers or conscripts, in addition to those on regular engagement. It also includes irregular units, not forming part of the established forces, specially recruited for the duration of a particular conflict, such as the Singapore Volunteer Corps raised in 1941. In addition, it covers members of foreign armed forces attached on temporary duty or neutral nationals serving as volunteers, e.g., US nationals serving with allied armies before Pearl Harbor. It would also include such units as the British Home Guard, but would not include boys' battalions or cadet forces. Prior to the adoption of Protocol I, it would also include mercenaries serving in a belligerent force. However, mercenaries as defined in Art. 47 of Protocol I are not entitled to prisoner-of-war status if captured (see below).

[30] This refers to such movements as the French Forces of the Interior and other partisan or guerrilla units organised during World War II, many of which were declared to be constituent parts of the forces of the United Nations – name of the alliance confronting the Axis powers. Members of regular forces serving with resistance movements retain their combatant status, although it may be advisable for them to remain in their normal uniform. As a result of Pr. I, Art. 1(4) members of national liberation movements are considered to be engaged in an international conflict and therefore enjoy combatant status, although, as will be seen below, they are not always required to satisfy the normal conditions attaching to other combatants.

[31] This applied to members of the North Korean forces captured by United Nations forces during the Korean War, and would apply to members of the Israel Defence Force captured by Syria. As to members of the North Vietnam forces captured by the United States forces during the Vietnam War, these were not always afforded such status and were often handed over to the South Vietnam authorities.

being members thereof, such as civilian members of military aircraft crews,[32] war correspondents,[33] supply contractors,[34] members of labour units,[35] or of services responsible for the welfare of the armed forces,[36] provided that they have received authorisation from the armed forces which they accompany [and carry some form of identification to prove this]. (5) ... [This refers to the status of maritime non-naval personnel and the crews of civil aircraft who, while not combatants nevertheless enjoy prisoner of war status if captured].

and the same is accorded to members of a *levée en masse*.

The impact of Protocol I

A new category of international armed conflict was created by Protocol 1. By Article 1, paragraph 4, 'international armed conflicts' shall include

armed conflicts in which peoples are fighting against colonial domination and alien occupation and against racist régimes in the exercise of their right of self-

[32] Civilians employed during World War II to ferry unarmed aircraft from the United States to air bases in the United Kingdom would be included.

[33] War correspondents are full-time newspaper or other media reporters in uniform, carrying identity cards indicating their status and attached to the armed forces. They must be distinguished from 'journalists engaged on dangerous professional missions in areas of armed conflict', whose status is regulated by Protocol I, Art. 79. Sixty-six journalists in seventeen countries were killed on duty in 1991, seventeen of them during the civil war in Yugoslavia, *The Times*, 18 Apr. 1992. It is improper for members of the armed forces out of uniform to carry cards identifying themselves as journalists rather than soldiers, as was done for a period by British personnel confronting the IRA in Northern Ireland in 1976: letter by Green to *The Times*, 1 March, 1976. They must also be distinguished from reporters and staff of newspapers published by the armed forces, such as the British *Blighty*, the Canadian *Maple Leaf*, or the American *Stars and Stripes*, who are all regular combatants.

[34] It has been suggested that such persons might be described as 'quasi-combatants'. However, as Rogers points out, *op.cit.*, 9, 'This is an extreme view. The idea that civilians should have quasi-combatant status depending on the job they do seems to take little account of the confusion that it would cause ... [T]he rules must be as simple and straightforward as possible. At least the present law is clear: combatants may be attacked directly; civilians who are in or near military objectives [including troops] run the risk of being killed as a side effect of attack on those objectives'.

[35] E.g., the Labour Corps attached to the British forces from 1917–1919, as well as the Auxiliary Military Pioneer Corps formed in October 1939 of a variety of nationalities, including Jewish and political refugees from Germany. This was deemed to be a corps for the purposes of the British Army Act and the Reserve Forces legislation and its personnel wore uniform and claimed combatant and prisoner of-war-status. Such groups as civilians captured while working for German *Organisation Todt* in France during World War II would also be included, see Levie, *Prisoners of War in International Armed Conflict*, 61.

[36] E.g., members of the UK Navy, Army and Air Force Institutes (NAAFI) or Entertainments National Service Establishment (ENSA), all of whom were in uniform. It would also include members of the American United Services Organisation (USO), as well as civilian ambulance drivers, such as members of the American Field Service of World War I and the Friends Field Service of World War II.

determination, as enshrined in the Charter of the United Nations[37] and the Declaration on Principles of International Law concerning Friendly Relations and Co-operation among States in accordance with the Charter of the United Nations.[38]

Since the personnel involved in such an exercise are considered to be engaged in an international armed conflict, they are entitled to combatant rights and duties and, if captured, are to be treated as prisoners of war. By Article 96 (3) of the Protocol the 'authority representing a people engaged against a High Contracting Party [in such a conflict] may undertake to apply the [Geneva] Conventions and the Protocol in relation to that conflict by means of a unilateral declaration addressed to the depositary', which is the Swiss Government.[39] Immediately thereon the Conventions and Protocol become applicable, so that the members of the force concerned receive combatant status, but this will not affect the position of an adverse party which has not ratified the Protocol.[40] The 'authority' responsible for waging such a conflict is generally known as a national liberation movement, but such a nomenclature is, in United Nations practice and the practice of international organisations associated with the United Nations, only granted to a movement recognised as such by the regional organisation in the geographic area in which the movement is operating.[41]

By Article 43 of the Protocol the armed forces of a party to a conflict comprise all organised armed forces,[42] groups and units which are under a command responsible to that party, even if the latter is represented by a government or authority not recognised by the adverse party. All such forces must be subject to an internal disciplinary system[43] providing for the enforcement of adherence to the rules of

[37] See Art. 1(2).

[38] Gen. Ass. Res. 2625 (XXV), 1970.

[39] In 1989, on receipt of such declaration on behalf of the PLO, the Swiss Government informed the parties that it could not decide whether this constituted a proper instrument of accession 'due to the uncertainty within the international community as to the existence or non-existence of a State of Palestine', ICRC, *Dissemination*, No. 13, May 1990, and 'Palestine' is not included in the published list of states parties. See also Green, 'Terrorism and armed conflict: the plea and the verdict', 19 Israel Y.B.H.R. (1989), 131, 149–50, 165–6.

[40] The provisions regarding a movement so engaged are among the basic reasons for the US refusal to ratify and the Israeli refusal to sign the Protocol.

[41] Thus the Palestine Liberation Organisation (PLO), Panafricanist Congress (PAC) and South West Africa People's Organisation (SWAPO) were invited to participate in the Geneva Conference which drafted the Protocols, being 'National Liberation Organisations recognised by the regional Intergovernmental Organisations concerned', Final Act 1977, Schindler and Toman, 619.

[42] The fact that a person is a member of the forces of a state establishes his right to be treated as a prisoner of war if captured. This principles was already recognised in Art. 3 of the Hague Regs.

[43] The system should be sufficient to indicate adherence to the law of armed conflict, with evidence of its ability to enforce its orders and punish breaches.

international law relating to armed conflict.[44] The requirements relating to organisation, responsibility and compliance with the law of armed conflict apply equally to national liberation movements and their forces. However, the requirement dating from the Brussels Declaration that combatants shall wear a fixed distinctive emblem identifiable from a distance has been relaxed as a result of Article 44 of the Protocol. In the light of the experience with resistance movements in World War II and conflicts since 1945, wherein the armed forces of national liberation movements or anti-colonial rebels are not professional soldiers but are frequently 'farmers by day and soldiers by night', it is now provided that:

> while all combatants are obliged to comply with the rules of international law applicable in armed conflict, violations of the rules shall not deprive a combatant of his right to be a combatant ... In order to promote the protection of the civilian population from the effects of hostilities,[45] combatants are obliged to distinguish themselves from the civilian population while they are engaged in an attack or in a military operation preparatory to an attack.[46] Recognising, however, that there are situations in armed conflicts where, owing to the nature of the hostilities[47] an armed combatant cannot so distinguish himself, he shall retain his status as a combatant, provided that, in such situations, he carries his arms openly (a) during each military engagement, and (b) during such time as he is visible to the adversary[48]

[44] The fact that there has not been compliance with the laws of armed conflict, especially if such compliance is sporadic or clearly the act of an individual soldier, does not deny the force or the movement its status as recognised combatants, although it might make the individual offender liable as a war criminal (see ch. 18 below). If there is consistent disregard as a matter of policy on the part of the force in question it may lose this status, thus removing from its members their normal rights and protection as combatants.

[45] Since a *levée en masse* is made up of members of the civilian population, they are only required to carry arms openly and respect the laws of war. They are not required to wear any specific distinguishing mark, though it may be to their advantage to do so.

[46] 'A combatant commits no offence and is subject to no sanction if he does not distinguish himself when engaged in such military operations as recruiting, training, general administration, law enforcement, aid to underground political authorities, collection of contributions and dissemination of propaganda. In view of the purpose of the rule, the term "military actions preparatory to an attack" should be construed broadly enough to include administrative and logistic activities preparatory to an attack. As such activities are more likely to be conducted in a civilian environment, the civilian population is in greater risk by failure to distinguish in such preparatory activities than in an ambush attack which is frequently conducted in a remote defile,' Bothe, 252.

[47] This is meant to indicate that the situation is indeed exceptional and could only arise in respect of resistance movements in occupied territory or a liberation movement engaged in hostilities against a colonial power. US *Operational Law Handbook*, JAG School Pub. JA 422, 1996, p. 18-6: '... regardless of how the conflict is characterized ... all enemy personnel should initially be accorded the protection of the GPW Convention, at least until their status may be determined ... When doubt exists as to whether captured enemy personnel warrant continued PW status, Art 5 Tribunals must be convened'.

[48] The provision must be interpreted in the light of present-day realities. Therefore, this would seem to include visibility by binoculars and with the aid of such instruments as infra-red equipment at night.

while he is engaged in a military deployment[49] preceding the launching of an attack.

These provisions suggest that there may well be occasions when there is reasonable doubt whether the person captured is a legitimate combatant entitled to claim treatment as a prisoner of war. The 1949 Prisoners of War Convention provided[50] that if there was any doubt as to the proper status of a captive he is to enjoy the protection of the Convention until his status had been determined by a 'competent tribunal',[51] the nature of that tribunal being determined by the captor. An administrative board as distinct from a court would suffice, although there is nothing to forbid such determination being made by a tribunal, civil[52] or military.[53] The situation has been changed by Article 45 of Protocol I to the benefit of the captive. Any person who has taken part in hostilities and is captured is now – for parties to the Protocol – presumed to be a prisoner of war. Should any doubt arise as to his entitlement, he shall continue to be treated as a prisoner until a 'competent tribunal' decides otherwise. Moreover, should it be alleged that a captive has committed some crime rendering him liable to trial by his captor, he has the right to assert his status as a prisoner of war and to have that claim determined by a judicial tribunal. While it is not specifically so provided, such determination should be made before any trial is instituted for the alleged offence, for if he is entitled to treatment as a prisoner of war his actions would have been those of a lawful combatant and not necessarily criminal.[54] He does, however, remain liable for any war crime he may have committed. He is also liable for any offence he may have committed before the conflict and when General Noriega surrendered to American forces after the invasion of Panama in 1989 he was, although initially treated as a common criminal, recognised as a prisoner of war and wore his uniform and decorations up to and during his trial for drug offences in 1992.[55]

In normal circumstances, that is to say other than those specially excepted from the general rule, the distinction between combatants and non-combatants is

---

[49] This would appear to cover any movement towards the place from which an attack is to be launched.

[50] Art. 6.

[51] According to the British *Manual*, this is intended to indicate 'a tribunal similar to a board of inquiry convened under Army Act 1955, s. 135', para. 132, n. 3. By the US FM 27-10 para. 71(c), (d). 'A "competent tribunal" of the US ... is a board of not less than three officers acting according to such procedures as may be prescribed for tribunals of this nature ... Persons who have been determined by a competent tribunal not to be entitled to prisoner-of-war status may not be executed ... or otherwise penalised without further proceedings to determine what acts they have committed and what penalty should be imposed therefore.'

[52] E.g., *Public Prosecutor* v. *Koi* [1968] A.C. 829; *Osman b.Haji Mohd. Ali* v. *Public Prosecutor* [1969] 1 A.C., 430.

[53] *Military Prosecutor* v. *Kassem* (1969, Israel) 42 I.L.R., 470.

[54] Thus the killing of a member of the enemy force would be criminal if committed by a civilian, but not usually if committed by a lawful combatant.

[55] See, e.g., re Noriega, Albert, *The Case Against the General*, 1993, ch. 12.

indicated by the uniform worn by a state's regular armed forces, but this does not mean that there is any need to indicate the arm of the service or the unit to which the individual concerned belongs. Since it is only required that he distinguish himself from the civilian population, any insignia or emblem clearly recognisable as such would suffice.[56] However, the fact that members of an armed force are not in uniform does not affect their status and rights as combatants and to be treated as such. This, however, is only the case if they remain subject to an internal disciplinary system which 'shall'[57] enforce compliance with the rules of international law applicable in armed conflict, and, as with other forces not required to distinguish themselves in the normal fashion, carry their arms openly during attack and while deploying preceding such attack. This means that infiltrators should, whether or not they shed any disguise they may be wearing for the purpose of the infiltration, carry their arms openly when launching or preparing to launch the attack for which they have effected the infiltration. Should they fail to do so they may find themselves treated as unlawful combatants. It should be noted that these requirements are cumulative, so that failure to satisfy any of them would result in loss of entitlement, but though the individual in question would not become a prisoner of war, 'he shall, nevertheless, be given protections equivalent in all respects to those accorded to prisoners of war by the Third Convention and this Protocol'.[58] This would mean that he is eligible to assert that he is a legitimate combatant entitled to appear before a 'competent tribunal' to have his claim settled. On the other hand, individual members of the armed forces acting separately from their units remain protected, even when employing methods of surprise or violent combat, provided they wear uniform when so doing.[59] If they are not in uniform, they are liable to be tried as spies.[60]

Should a party to a conflict incorporate paramilitary[61] or armed law enforcement agencies[62] into its armed forces it must inform other parties to the conflict of

[56] This is more likely to be the case with irregular than regular forces.

[57] Pr. I, Art. 44(3).

[58] E.g., the Special Auxiliary Force attached to Bishop Muzorewa's United African National Congress in Zimbabwe and which was embodied into the national army after independence; also, India's Border Security Force in Assam.

[59] This provision would protect commando or airborne personnel. During World War II Hitler issued a *Führerbefehl* that captured commandos were to be killed, even if in uniform and even if they tried to surrender, see *Falkenhorst* trial, 11 Trials of War Criminals 8. In 1945 the Allied Supreme Commander announced that such acts would be treated as war crimes, and this was confirmed by the International Military Tribunal in the *Nuremberg Judgment* 1946 (HMSO, Cmd 6964, (1946), 45, 91; 41 Am J. Int'l Law 225, 282).

[60] Pr. I, Art. 46.

[61] Pr. I, Art. 44(4).

[62] When the Pacific War commenced during World War II the Burma Frontier Force was serving as a police force under the authority of the Burma Frontier Force Act; after the fall of Burma to the Japanese the Burmese Government in exile in Simla, India, passed legislation making the Force part of the Burmese Army and subject to the Burma Army Act, see Green, 'The Indian National Army Trials', 11 M.L.R., 1948, 47, 49–50; see also *Essays*, 1999, ch. XI.

this fact,[63] so that such forces may be acknowledged as lawful combatants. At the same time, the party concerned must ensure that such incorporated personnel are made subject to proper military discipline and are governed by the same rules with regard to combat and satisfy the same requirements as to potential recognition as are the regular forces.

Mercenaries

Until the adoption of Protocol I no attempt was made to discriminate among the members of an armed force on the basis of their nationality or the motives which lead them to join that force, whether those motives are ideological or mercenary.[64] In view, however, of the number of mercenaries who enrolled in colonial armies or were prepared to serve for pay in campaigns directed against national liberation groups, widespread agitation among third world states resulted in the condemnation of such mercenary groups. Attempts were even made to classify such units as the Gurkha Regiments serving with the British or Indian Armies, as well as the French Foreign Legion and volunteers serving with the Israel Defence Force as mercenaries to be condemned. Both the Security Council and the General Assembly of the United Nations have adopted a series of resolutions relating to specific anti-colonial conflicts in Africa recommending[65] prohibition of the use of such personnel against national liberation movements. It should be borne in mind that General Assembly resolutions lack binding legal force and only amount to recommendations, while the resolutions of the Security Council are only obligatory if they are framed as decisions under Chapter VII of the Charter relating to action with respect to threats to the peace, breaches of the peace and acts of aggression. Even the outright condemnation of mercenaries by the General Assembly in 1969,[66] reaffirming the Declaration on Independence for Colonial Countries and Peoples,[67] which itself has no more binding effect than any other General Assembly Resolution,[68] stating that:

> the practice of using mercenaries against national liberation movements in the colonial territories constitutes a criminal act and calls upon all States to take the neces-

---

[63] Pr. I, Art. 43(3).

[64] Since the basis of the law of armed conflict is to humanise war, it must be applied on a basis of complete non-discrimination and the 1949 Conventions provide for this (see, e.g., Prisoners of War Convention Art. 16). General practice in the past tended to be in accord with this, though World War II practice did not always apply this principle.

[65] See, e.g., SC Res. 226 (1966), 241 (1967): Gen. Ass. Res. 2395 (XXIII), all relating to Portugal and Angola.

[66] Gen. Ass. Res. 2548 (XXIV).

[67] 1961, Res. 1514 (XV).

[68] Statement by Legal Dept., UN Secretariat defining status of a 'Declaration', Doc. E/CN.4/L610 (c. Schermers, 2 *International Institutional Law*, 500).

sary measures to prevent the recruitment, financing and training of mercenaries in their territory and to prohibit their nationals from serving as mercenaries,

was merely a *vœu* addressed to the members, leaving it to each to give effect to it or not as it pleased. None of these resolutions affected the legal status of mercenaries, although the government of Angola instituted criminal proceedings against captured mercenaries and executed some of them.[69]

For those states which have ratified Protocol I the position has changed. In accordance with Article 47 'a mercenary shall not have the right to be a combatant or a prisoner of war'. However, a mercenary is not devoid of all protection. Since he is not a combatant, he is presumably a civilian and would, therefore, remain protected under the IVth (Civilians) Convention to the extent that he is not considered an unlawful combatant and tried as such, but he would still be entitled to the minimum prerequisites concerning a fair trial and would also be entitled to the fundamental guarantees embodied in Article 75 of Protocol I, which extend to all 'persons who are in the power of a Party to the conflict and who do not benefit from more favourable treatment under the Conventions or under the Protocol'.

By Article 47: A mercenary is any person who: (a) is specially recruited locally or abroad in order to fight in an armed conflict; (b) does, in fact, take a direct part in the hostilities; (c) is motivated[70] to take part in the hostilities essentially by the desire for private gain and, in fact, is promised, by or on behalf of a Party to the conflict, material compensation substantially in excess of that promised or paid to combatants of similar ranks and functions in the armed forces of the Party;[71] (d) is neither a national of the Party to the conflict nor a resident of territory controlled by a Party to the conflict;[72] (e) is not a member of the armed forces of a Party to the conflict;[73] and (f) has not been sent by a State which is not a Party to the conflict on official duty as a member of its armed forces.[74]

These conditions are cumulative. If any one of them is not satisfied the person in question cannot be regarded as a mercenary. Moreover, it is to be presumed that if the forces to which the mercenary offers his service is a properly organised

[69] See, e.g., Green, 'The status of mercenaries in international law', *Essays*, 1999, ch. XV; Lockwood, 'Report on the trial of mercenaries', 7 Manitoba Law J. (1977), 183.

[70] This is the only occasion on which mental state and financial inducements, as distinct from function, have been used to determine status from the point of view of the law of armed conflict and runs contrary to the whole basis of non-discrimination.

[71] This would appear to leave open the possibility of employing a skilled alien at a high rate of pay if there is no person in the force of the employing state equally qualified.

[72] This would suggest that US citizens visiting or resident in England who joined the British forces before the US became a belligerent in World War I would, if the Protocol had been force, probably have had to defend themselves against charges of mercenarism if captured, see, however, n. 73.

[73] Embodiment in the armed forces of a person otherwise satisfying the definition would remove him from the category of mercenary.

[74] Whatever motives may have been responsible for the enrolment of, for example, Cubans for service in Africa, the fact that they were sent by their government 'on official duties as members of its armed forces' precludes them from being treated as mercenaries.

force, he will almost certainly be embodied into that force, thus taking him out of the mercenary classification.[75]

Despite the condemnation of the employment of mercenaries, a number of qualified military personnel from western countries joined the Croatians in the early days of the conflicts in the former Yugoslavia,[76] while 'former senior members of the United States forces, apparently with the acquiescence of the Department of Defense, joined the Bosnian forces officially as 'advisers' or to train local personnel.[77] In addition, it was disclosed in 1998 that, despite an arms embargo imposed by the United Nations against Sierra Leone, British mercenaries, with the knowledge of the local British diplomatic representative, were involved in supporting and reinstating the president overthrown in a *coup*. The British Government, in fact, suggested that while there may have been a formal breach of the embargo, it was for a legitimate purpose and the 'end justifies the means'.[78]

In accordance with the International Convention against the Recruitment, Use, Financing and Training of Mercenaries,[79] it is not necessary for the person recruited as a mercenary actually to take part in the conflict. Further, the definition has been extended to include 'anyone specially recruited locally or abroad for the purpose of participating in a concerted act of violence aimed at overthrowing a government or otherwise undermining the constitutional order ... or ... the territorial integrity of a State', provided he satisfies the other conditions defining a mercenary. Any person thus defined 'commits an offence for the purposes of this Convention'. Moreover, the parties to the Convention are bound not to recruit or use mercenaries in their operations. By Article 16, the Convention applies 'without prejudice to ... the law of armed conflict and international humanitarian law, including the provisions relating to the status of combatants or prisoner of war', so that a captured mercenary is still not considered as a legitimate combatant. In fact, when white mercenaries were employed by the Mobutu regime in Zaïre, the rebel leader who succeeded him indicated that any who were captured 'would be shot on the spot'.[80] The International Law Commission has now adopted a Draft Code of Crimes against the Peace and Security of Mankind[81] based on the provisions of the Protocol and the Mercenaries Convention. By Article 23 anyone who recruits, uses, finances or trains 'mercenaries for activities directed against

[75] It is interesting that neither Rogers, then Director of UK Army Legal Services, in his *Law on the Battlefield*, nor the contributors to the Australian Defence Studies Centre publication *The Force of Law: International law and the Land Commander*, ed. Smith, 1994, makes mention of the problem of mercenaries.

[76] *The Times* (London), 3 Oct. 1991; 7 Feb. 1992.

[77] *Baltimore Sun*, 12 Nov. 1997, which also states that 'President Clinton sanctioned the despatch of 180 "military advisers" ... All retired US Army personnel ...'.

[78] *The Times*, 12 May 1998.

[79] Gen. Ass. Res. 44/34, 1989, 29 I.L.M., 89. By December 1991 there were only sixteen signatories and four ratifications.

[80] *The Times*, 15 Feb. 1997.

[81] 1991, 30 I.L.M., 1584.

another State or for the purpose of opposing the legitimate exercise of the inalienable right of peoples to self-determination as recognised under international law' is guilty of a crime. However, the Statute of the International Criminal Court established by treaty in 1998 makes no reference to mercenarism as a crime.[82]

While, under the Protocol, mercenaries are not entitled to be treated as combatants and prisoners of war, there is nothing to prevent the adverse party from treating them as such. For those states becoming parties to the 1989 Convention this right would no longer exist, having been replaced by the obligation to amend their criminal law to treat mercenaries as criminals subject to trial or extradition.

Irregular forces

Irregular forces and resistance movements are only protected so long as they satisfy the normal requirements for recognition as combatants, in which case they are entitled if captured to be treated as prisoners of war. During World War II it was considered sufficient that the recognisable emblem to be worn should consist of a brassard identifying membership in such a force,[83] which brassard was attached to the clothing and not easily removable. In the case of countries which have ratified Protocol I, their irregular or resistance forces do not need so to identify themselves, although this would be a wise safeguard. They are only required to be under a proper command and carry their arms openly when attacking or deploying preparatory to an attack.[84] Since it is in the interest of the unit concerned, although there is no obligation upon a party to do so, a party to the conflict would be wise to inform the adverse party of the existence of such irregular units and the nature of their identification emblem. In giving such information, there is no need to specify strengths or locations.

The recognition of the existence of such irregular units or resistance movements does not extend to individuals or small unorganised groups, operating against the adverse party without authorisation,[85] and such individuals or groups are not recognised as combatants and enjoy no protection. This would not affect the status of such groups as the Long Range Desert Group or 'Popski's Private Army' which operated in North Africa during World War II, for although they appeared to be units completely detached from the main armed forces, they were in fact part of those forces and operating under the authority of the supreme commander.

---

[82] 37 I.L.M. 998 17 July 1998.

[83] See, e.g., the French Forces of the Interior acknowledging the supreme authority of General de Gaulle, who wore a brassard bearing the Croix de Lorraine. Similarly, the Dutch Royal Emergency Decree, 1944, gave the Netherlands Forces of the Interior the status of a part of the Dutch army. The German authorities were not always prepared to recognise such persons as combatants, but a series of war crimes trials arising out of their treatment confirmed their status as such.

[84] Pr. I, Arts 43, 44.

[85] This is in line with the English Articles of Warre, 1639, see n. 2 above.

In the event of a belligerent being confronted by the forces of a government or authority which the former does not recognise, such forces are granted protection by the Geneva Conventions, 1949.[86] Members of the armed forces must extend to these too the rights and protections afforded by the law of armed conflict.[87] It is not for the soldier in the field to determine his conduct in accordance with what he believes to be the political approach of his government. Thus, soldiers should be reminded that enemy personnel falling into their hands must be 'treated' as prisoners of war; it is not for them to decide upon the 'status' of such captives.[88] Equally, members of the armed forces of a country engaged in a war of aggression retain their status as combatants in every respect,[89] even though senior members of the supreme command or of the government may subsequently be tried for aggression.

Children

Countries vary as to the minimum age of enlistment. A number of states which owe their existence to anti-colonial struggles, as well as forces seeking to overthrow established regimes, frequently enlist children even below the age of twelve. Other countries will enlist 'boy soldiers' from a young age, but will often not allow them to engage in combat until they are more mature.[90] Giving effect to the Convention on the Rights of the Child,[91] by Article 77 of Protocol I, parties are to 'take all feasible measures in order that children who have not attained the age of fifteen years do not take a direct part in hostilities and, in particular, shall refrain from recruiting them … If, in exceptional cases, … children [under] fifteen years take a direct part in hostilities and fall into the power of an adverse Party, they shall continue to benefit from the special provisions of this Article, whether or not they are prisoners of war … The death penalty for an offence related to the armed conflict shall not be executed on persons who had not attained the age of eighteen

---

[86] Conventions I, II, Art. 13(3); III, Art. 4A(3).

[87] This follows from the customary law of armed conflict that belligerents operate on a basis of reciprocity.

[88] See US *Operational Law Handbook*, 18-6.

[89] The preamble to Protocol I expressly states that the Conventions and the Protocol 'must be fully applied in all circumstances to all persons who are protected by these instruments, without any distinction based on the nature or origin of the armed conflict or on causes espoused by or attributed to the Parties to the conflict.' Combatants, non-combatants and civilians attached to a state declared criminal or outlaw by the United Nations would remain protected by the Conventions and Protocol. See Lauterpacht, 'Rules of warfare in an unlawful war', in Lipsky, *Law and Politics in the World Community*, 89.

[90] In 1998 there were 945 aged 16 and 4,480 aged 17 in the British forces, but 'they were kept away from areas of conflict and did not serve on the front line until after their 18th birthday' *The Times*, 14 Jan. 1998.

[91] 1989, 28 I.L.M. 1448. See generally Kuper, *International Law Concerning Child Civilians in Armed Conflict*, 1997.

years at the time the offence was committed'. By the end of 1997 it was estimated that '250,000 children under the age of 18, some as young as 5, served in 33 armed conflicts around the world in 1995 and 1996'[92], and in October 1998 the United Nations' envoy for children and armed conflict reported[93] that there were now some '300,000 children under the age of 18 serving as combatants in government-armed forces or armed-opposition groups, in ongoing conflicts … Many more are being used for mine clearance, spying and suicide bombing … The development and proliferation of lightweight automatic weapons has made it possible for very young children to bear and use arms'.

Deserters and spies

Members of the armed forces of a party to a conflict who join the armed forces of an adverse party either by desertion or after capture, whether as members of the captor's force or of a force raised under the protection of the captor and described as a national liberation movement,[94] do not lose their original status.[95] Even if the captor maintains that they have become liable to his military law, they nevertheless remain entitled to their rights as prisoners of war, to the extent that the provisions of the military law in question detract from their rights as combatants.[96] If such persons are captured by members of their own forces, they are entitled to receive from the soldiers capturing them the same treatment as any other captive, even though their national authority may decide, in accordance with national law, that they are not to be treated as enemy combatants and prisoners of war, but as members of its own forces liable to trial for treason.[97] They may also be tried for treason after the termination of hostilities and their repatriation to their home country. Any attempt by the adverse party to compel any captive, even if he is a deserter or a defector, to serve in his armed forces amounts to a grave breach of

---

[92] *Washington Times*, 3 Dec. 1997. See, generally, Cohn and Goodwin-Gill, *Child Soldiers – The Role of Children in Armed Conflict*, 1994.

[93] *Globe and Mail* (Toronto) 23 Oct. 1998.

[94] See, e.g., The Irish Brigade raised by the Germans in World War I or the Indian National Army raised by the Japanese in World War II after the British surrender, particularly after the fall of Singapore.

[95] Conventions III (Prisoners of War), Art. 7: 'Prisoners of war may in no circumstances renounce in part or in entirety the rights secured to them by the present Convention.'

[96] In the *Gozawa* case (1945 – Sleeman, The *Gozawa Trial*, 1948) a British war crimes tribunal held that the defence plea that an Indian Army prisoner of war had become liable to Japanese military law by joining the Indian National Army was unacceptable, so that the deceased had remained a prisoner of war entitled to the rights of a combatant in enemy hands.

[97] Members of the Indian National Army who were captured by or surrendered to the British were tried by Indian military courts for waging war against the Crown contrary to the Indian Penal Code, see Green, n. 64 above, and 'The Azad Hind Fauj: The Indian National Army', in Green, *Essays*, 1999, ch. XI.

the Prisoners of War Convention.[98] However, many Russian soldiers captured by Afghan *mujahudin* during the Afghanistan hostilities were compelled to adopt Islam to avoid torture or execution.[99] There were also reports that Iraqi prisoners captured by Iran were 'brainwashed' into becoming 'fanatical supporters of Ayatullah Khomaini'.[100]

The gathering of information either in the area in which adverse armies are confronting each other or behind enemy lines is a recognised practice of warfare. However, a distinction must be made between those who gather such information in uniform and those who do so in plain clothes. This is clear from the language of Article 29 of the Hague Regulations:

> A person can only be considered a spy when, acting clandestinely or on false pretences, he obtains or endeavours to obtain information in the zone of operations of a belligerent, with the intention of communicating it to the enemy.
>
> Thus, soldiers not wearing a disguise who have penetrated into the zone of operations of the hostile army, for the purpose of obtaining information, are not considered spies.

Most countries regard espionage as a crime, but it is not contrary to the law of armed conflict. Any person, civilian or combatant, properly charged with espionage is entitled to a trial,[101] which may sentence him to death. If a military spy is captured after he has rejoined his unit he is entitled to all the rights of a combatant and incurs no liability for his previous act of espionage.[102]

The law with regard to the treatment of spies has been changed by Article 46 of Protocol I. This provides that a member of the armed forces who is captured while engaged in espionage is not entitled to the status of a prisoner of war, unless he is wearing uniform while so engaged. Moreover, if the member of the armed forces is a resident of occupied territory and, acting on behalf of his own party to the conflict, 'gathers or attempts to gather information of military value within that territory', he is not considered to be a spy unless he operates 'through an act of false pretences or deliberately in a clandestine manner'. Such a person does not lose his right to be treated as a prisoner of war, as is also the case with every member of the armed forces present in territory occupied by the adverse party, unless he is captured while actually engaged in espionage. If the member of the armed forces is not a resident of occupied territory and engages in espionage in that territory he retains his status as a combatant and his right, if captured, to be treated as a prisoner of war, and may only be treated as a spy if 'he is captured before he has rejoined the armed forces to which he belongs'. According to the United States *Operational Law Handbook* 'civilians who are not wearing a disguise and perform their missions openly after penetrating friendly [that is to say, United

---

[98] Art. 130.
[99] *The Times*, 16 May 1992.
[100] *The Globe and Mail* (Toronto), 2 Sept. 1988.
[101] Hague Regs, Art. 30.
[102] *Op.cit.*, p. 17-7.

States] lines [together with] persons living in occupied territory who report on friendly activities without lurking, and without acting clandestinely or under false pretenses' are not considered spies, although 'such individuals may be guilty of aiding the enemy'.[103]

Attached non-combatants

There are often a variety of personnel who accompany the armed forces and who may be in uniform but are not considered to be combatants.[104] The best-known of these groups are religious personnel[105] and medical staff. So long as these persons are in uniform and members of the armed forces they are under the protection of the law of armed conflict and, if captured, while they do not become prisoners of war, they are entitled to the same treatment as prisoners of war. If military exigencies permit, they should be allowed to return to their own lines, unless required, preferably, for the welfare and care of members of their own forces.

[103] *Ibid.*, Art. 31.

[104] During World War II the Japanese Army in Burma had a number of Korean and other non-Japanese conscripted prostitutes attached to their forces. They were under the control of Japanese women who seemed to be wearing a type of uniform, and these, when captured, were treated as if they were prisoners of war. See Green, 'Japan's "comfort women"', *The Times* (London), 17 Aug. 1993.

[105] Protocol I, Art. 8(d). During the Geneva Conference at which the Protocol was adopted it was felt that the term 'chaplain' had a particularly Christian connotation and was not wide enough for modern purposes. The formulation 'military or civilian persons ... who are exclusively engaged in the work of ministry' was considered more suitable. All such persons must be 'exclusively' so engaged, and the term would not include lay preachers (Bothe, *et al.*, 99). The personnel affected must also be 'attached' to the armed forces to which they minister.

7

Conduct of hostilities: land

The purpose of armed conflict is to defeat the adverse party. The law of armed conflict only permits such actions as are imperative for this purpose and forbids acts which go beyond this and cause injury to persons or damage to property not essential to achieving this end.[1] The law restricts both the means of waging war and the objects against which such means may be employed and the basic rules of armed conflict[2] apply equally to all theatres, whether on land, sea or in the air. For the main part the rules which have evolved in relation to warfare on land have been adopted, adapted or developed to the particular situations that arise in connection with maritime[3] or air[4] warfare.

The law of armed conflict has its origins in both customary and conventional law. The customary law has developed and the conventional law drafted in the light of military needs,[5] and, generally speaking, may only be disregarded in the light of military necessity when expressly permitted by the particular rule itself.[6]

[1] See Kalshoven, *Constraints on the Waging of War*, 1987, and Fleck, *et al.*, *The Handbook of Humanitarian Law in Armed Conflicts*, 1995.

[2] See ch. 21 below.

[3] See ch. 8 below.

[4] See ch. 9 below.

[5] Thus, the preamble to Hague Convention IV (Schindler and Toman, 69) expressly states: 'According to the views of the High Contracting Parties, these provisions [embodied in Regulations annexed thereto], the wording of which has been inspired by the desire to diminish the evils of war, *as far as military requirements permit*, are intended to serve as a general rule of conduct' (italics added).

[6] See de Mulinen, *Handbook of the Law of War for Armed Forces*, 1987, Part 4, Ch. D, para. 352 – '"Military necessity" means a principle which justifies those measures: (a) not forbidden by the law of war; and (b) required to secure the overpowering of the enemy. Military necessity is not an overriding principle allowing breaches of the law of war'; see also paras. 353–5. See also McCoubrey, 'The nature of the modern doctrine of military necessity', *Military Law and Law of War Rev.*, 1991, 240 – 'Military necessity is a doctrine within the laws of armed conflict which recognizes the potential impracticability of full compliance with legal norms in certain circumstances and, accordingly, may mitigate or expunge culpability for *prima facie* unlawful actions in appropriate cases in armed conflict. Its precise effects in any given case will rest upon the combination of issues of circum-

The mere plea of military necessity, *raison de guerre* or *Kriegsraeson*[7] is not sufficient to evade compliance with the laws of war. Otherwise, the concept of military necessity would reduce 'the entire body of the laws of war to a code of military convenience, having no further sanction than the sense of honour of the individual military commander or chief of staff and no practical effect where the contending forces were sufficiently equal to render the issue doubtful'.[8]

Basic rules[9]

The rules of armed conflict law, whether customary or conventional, are imperative and may only be disregarded when this is expressly permitted or by way of reprisals when such action is not expressly forbidden, as, for example, in Convention III, 1949,[10] or in a number of articles in Protocol I, 1977.[11] Reprisals are measures which are normally illegal, but are taken in response to a breach of the law by the adverse party, which breach continues after a demand for cessation and a warning that reprisals would be taken if the prior illegal act is not terminated. They are not retaliatory measures as this term is normally understood, but are intended to ensure the cessation of prior illegal actions and a return to legality by the adverse party.[12] They must be proportionate to, but need not be identical with the original illegal act,[13] and must terminate as soon as that illegality ends. A reprisal has been recently defined:[14]

> An act ... constitutes a reprisal when, firstly, both the actor and the addressee of the act are States or other entities enjoying a degree of international personality.[15]

stances, fact and degree and the strength of the claims of the norms concerned. The effect of the doctrine is limited to particular events and circumstances and does not have a general suspensory effect upon the law of armed conflict'; see also Fleck, *op.cit.*, paras. 130–2.

[7] As Oppenheim pointed out in the first edition of his *International Law*, vol. 2, s. 69, it was only a minority of mainly German writers even then who maintained that *Kriegsraeson geht vor Kriegsrecht* – necessity in war overrides the law of war. See for some modification of this view, *The German War Book*, Eng. tr. Morgan, 1915, 52–5).

[8] Fenwick, *International Law*, 655.

[9] See ch. 21 below.

[10] Schindler and Toman, 423, Art. 13: 'Measures of reprisal against prisoners of war are prohibited.'

[11] *Ibid.*, 621, Art. 20: 'Reprisals against the persons and objects protected by this Part [Wounded, Sick, Shipwrecked, Medical Transportation, Missing and Dead] are prohibited' Arts 51–6 [Civilian Population and Objects].

[12] The action taken against Iraq, 1990–91, after its invasion and annexation of Kuwait, sought termination of Iraq's illegal acts and a return to the *status quo ante*, but they were not reprisals since they were authorised as 'enforcement measures' by a series of S.C. Resolutions, see,e.g. Lauterpacht *et al.*, *The Kuwait Crisis: Basic Documents*.

[13] See, e.g., arbitral awarded by Huber re the *Naulilaa Incident* (Germany–Portugal, 928), 2 R.I.A.A., 1019, 1026–8.

[14] Kalshoven, *Belligerent Reprisals*, 33.

[15] From the point of view of armed conflict, this would include a national liberation

The act must be a retort to a previous act on the part of the addressee which has adversely affected or continues so to affect the interests of the actor and which the latter can reasonably consider a violation of international law. It must, moreover, amount to a violation either of the identical or of another norm of international law.

The *prima facie* unlawful act is not authorised by any previous authoritative community decision.[16] Neither is it an act of self-defence, as its aim is not directly to ward off the blow of the addressee's preceding act.

Its purpose is to coerce the addressee to change its policy and bring it into line with the requirements of international law, be it in respect of the past, the present or the future. This function of law enforcement qualifies the act as a sanction under international law.

The act, finally, must respect the conditions and limits laid down in international law for justifiable recourse to reprisals; that is, first of all, objectivity, subsidiarity, and proportionality.[17]

... [B]elligerent reprisals presuppose a state of *bellum*, or 'war'.

Perhaps the most basic rule of the law of armed conflict is that civilians and civilian objects must not be made the object of direct attack,[18] although incidental injuries[19] caused to such persons or objects in the course of a legitimate attack[20] must be proportionate to the purpose of the attack.[21] The 'attack' here referred to relates 'to the advantage anticipated from the specific military operation of which the attack is a part taken as a whole and not from isolated or particular parts of that operation'.[22]

Combatants are legitimate objects of attack, but only so long as they are capable of fighting, willing to fight or resist capture. Once incapable in this sense, and

movement or some other body recognised as a legitimate combatant (see ch. 6 above), or the United Nations if hostilities were conducted in its name under ch. VII of the Charter.

[16] See text to n. 12 above.

[17] In the Final Report to US Congress on Conduct of the Persian Gulf War, 1992, 31 I.L.M., 615, it states: '... [the principle of proportionality] prohibits military action in which the negative effects (such as collateral civilian casualties) clearly outweigh the military gain. This balancing may be done on a target-to-target basis, ... but also may be weighed in over-all terms against campaign objectives ... Some targets were specifically avoided because the value of destruction of each target was outweighed by the potential risk to nearby civilians or, in the case of certain archaeological and religious sites, to civilian objects', App. O, p. O 10, at 622, I.L.M.

[18] By Art. 23 of the Hague Regulations, 1907, attacks on undefended towns, cities, villages (see ch. 6 above) or dwellings are prohibited. See, now, Pr. I, Arts 48, 51. In so far as aerial bombardment of the land is concerned, the same principle is to be found in the unadopted Hague Rules of Air Warfare, 1923 (Schindler and Toman, 207), Arts 22, 24; on air warfare see ch. 9 below.

[19] Generally described as 'collateral damage'.

[20] Pr. I, Art. 49: '"Attacks" mean acts of violence against the adversary, whether in offence or in defence.'

[21] *Ibid.*, Art. 51, (5)(c). Indiscriminate attacks include those 'which may be expected to cause incidental loss of civilian life, injury to civilians, damage to civilian objects, or a combination thereof, which would be excessive in relation to the concrete and direct military advantage anticipated'. See also Art. 57.

[22] Bothe, *et al.*, 311.

so *hors de combat*, they are immune from attack, but may be taken prisoner. Military objectives are lawful objects of attack and are defined[23] as 'those objects which by their nature, location,[24] purpose or use make an effective contribution to military action and whose total or partial destruction, capture or neutralisation, in the circumstances ruling at the time [which will depend upon the discretion[25] of the commander of the forces involved], offers a definite military advantage' to the whole operation and not merely the particular attack contemplated. The commander must also exercise his discretion in determining whether the extent of incidental damage that his attack is likely to cause to civilians or civilian objects is so excessive or disproportionate to the military objective sought as to render his attack unlawful. If this be so, the attack should be abandoned,[26] for if carried through it would become 'indiscriminate' and a breach of law as laid down in Protocol I.[27] Certain objects are always immune from attack, being those 'normally dedicated to civilian purposes, such as a place of worship, a house or other dwelling or a school', and if there is any doubt whether such an establishment is being used for its proper purpose it is to be given the benefit of the doubt and remain immune from attack.[28] Such immunity would not extend to dwellings inhabited by munitions workers if established within the perimeter of the munitions works, nor to churches or schools used for the purpose of providing rest centres for troops after an engagement as, for example, after the British withdrawal from Dunkirk in 1940.

Illegal weaponry

Though the object of an armed conflict is to achieve victory over the adverse party with the least possible expenditure of men, resources and money, principles of humanity remain relevant. The means of delivering a lawful attack are 'not

---

[23] Pr. I, Art. 52(2).

[24] This would include an area of land, provided that particular area would be of direct use to the defending forces or those attacking, as well as any tract of land through which the adverse party is likely to move its forces, or an area the occupation of which would provide the occupant with the possibility of mounting a further attack.

[25] Pr. I, Art. 57 (2)(a)(iii).

[26] *Ibid.*, Art. 57(2)(b).

[27] *Ibid.*, Art. 51(5)(b), 51(4). Problems arose after Operation Desert Storm (the Gulf War, 1991) concerning the US bombing of the 'Amariyah shelter' in Baghdad. According to intelligence reports this was in a fact a command communication centre (US *Operational Law Handbook*, JA 422, 1996, p. 18-2), but it has been alleged that it was known to be a civilian air raid shelter and that there were some 1,500 civilian casualties, thus constituting a war crime on the basis of disproportionality, Clark, *The Fire This Time: US War Crimes in the Gulf*, 1994, 70–2. It should be borne in mind that at that time neither Iraq nor the US was a party to Protocol I, so customary law concerning legitimate objectives applied.

[28] Pr. I, Art. 52(3).

unlimited',[29] and 'it is prohibited to employ weapons, projectiles and material and methods of warfare of a nature to cause superfluous injury or unnecessary suffering'.[30] These terms are used in an objective and not subjective sense, so that the measurement is not that of the victim, but indicates there should be no resort to measures which entail suffering beyond that necessary for achieving the purpose of the attack.

This is merely the modern version of Sun Tzu's statement[31] that 'to capture the enemy is better than to destroy it ... To subdue the enemy without fighting is the acme of skill'. Or, as expressed by Clausewitz,[32] some two millennia later, 'to impose our will on the enemy is [the] object [of force] ... The [enemy's] fighting forces must be *destroyed: that is they must be put in such a condition that they no longer carry on the fight'*. This does not, however, mean that the enemy forces must be exterminated.

In conducting hostilities, the opposing forces should be guided by three basic principles: necessity, humanity and chivalry.[33] Necessity concerns those activities, subject to any restrictions imposed by law, such as the ban on the killing of prisoners, which are essential to achieve victory. The principle of humanity regulates the degree of permitted violence, forbidding action which is unnecessary or excessive for the achievement of victory, particularly with regard to the treatment of non-combatants. The principles of necessity and humanity are complementary, seeking to adjust the means essential to realise the purpose of the conflict with the minimisation of human suffering and physical destruction. The rules that have evolved to this end constitute international humanitarian law.[34]

The principle of chivalry derives from the concept of propriety in feudal times in the relations of the orders of knighthood.[35] It requires the exercise of fairness in both offence and defence, and a certain amount of mutual respect between the opposing forces, and modern instances may be seen in the conduct of the Emperor Franz Joseph in 1914[36] or, occasionally in aerial combat, particularly in World War I.[37] Chivalry also denounced recourse to dishonourable means of combat. Today,

---

[29] Hague Regs, Art. 22; Pr. I, Art. 35(1).

[30] Pr. I, Art. 35(2). Art. 23(e) of the Hague Regs merely forbids the use of 'arms, projectiles, or material calculated to cause unnecessary suffering'. See, e.g., Green, '"Unnecessary suffering", weapons control and the law of war', *Essays*, 1999, ch. IX; Fleck, *op.cit.*, para. 402

[31] Sixth century BC; *The Art of War*, (tr. Griffith, 1963, III), 'Offensive strategy', 77.

[32] *On War*, 1832, Howard and Paret, eds., (1976), 90 (italics in original).

[33] See, e.g., Rogers, *Law on the Battlefield*, 1996, 2; US *Operational Law Handbook*, p. 18-2; Smith, ed., *The Force of Law – International Law and the Land Commander* (Australian Defence Studies Centre), 1994, chs 6, 7.

[34] See Pictet, *Le Droit Humanitaire et la Protection des Victimes de Guerre, Development and Principles of International Humanitarian Law; Herczegh, Development of International Humanitarian Law; Delissen and Tanja, Humanitarian Law of Armed Conflict: Challenges Ahead*; Fleck, *op.cit., passim.*

[35] See, e.g., Keen, *Chivalry*, 1984, esp. chs 1, 2.

[36] Cited in letter from Maj. T. J. D. Holmes to *The Times* (London), 24 Jul. 1984.

[37] See, e.g., Spaight, *Air Power and War Rights*, (1947), 20–1, 109–18.

this would cover such acts of perfidy[38] as wrongful use of protected emblems or a flag of surrender[39] or the use of the flags or emblems of a neutral or of the adverse party while engaging in attack,[40] or the refusal of quarter.[41] In former times it went much further. Thus the crossbow and the arc were condemned as:

> weapons whereby men not of the knightly order could fell a knight.[42] ... Worse, they were weapons that enabled a man to strike without the risk of being struck ... [and] Paolo Vitelli while recognising and using the cannon put out the eyes and cut off the hands of captured arquebusiers because he held it unworthy that a gallant and ... noble knight[43] should be laid low by a common, despised foot soldier.[44]

A further limitation on weapons causing unnecessary suffering has been intro- duced by Protocol I. Article 35(3) formulates a new 'basic rule' regarding the methods and means of warfare. This has no origins in customary law, so that, *prima facie*, unless there are other reasons to indicate that a customary rule has developed,[45] 'it is prohibited to employ methods or means of warfare which are intended, or may be expected, to cause widespread, long-term and severe damage to the natural environment'. This is a confirmation of the 1977 Convention on the Prohibition of Military or any Other Hostile Use of Environmental Modification Techniques.[46] During the Gulf War, 1991, Iraq set fire to oilwells and oilfields in its own territory and in Kuwait causing damage to the Gulf, its livestock and the

---

[38] Pr. I, Art. 37.

[39] During the Falklands War, 'Jeremy Hands, an *Independent Television News* corre- spondent [reported] that at least one British soldier was killed at Goose Green when Argen- tine soldiers raised the white flag of surrender and then opened fire as troops came forward to take them prisoner', *Ottawa Citizen*, 3 Jun. 1982. For similar incident during the Gulf War, 1991, see *Conduct of the Persian Gulf War*, n. 17 above, 20–2.

[40] Pr. I, Art. 39.

[41] *Ibid.*, Art. 40.

[42] It was only between knights that the rules of chivalry were observed.

[43] See, e.g., treatment of captured French knights by John of Gaunt in 1370, Keen, *The Laws of War in the Middle Ages*, 1.

[44] Draper, 'The interaction of Christianity and chivalry in the historic development of the law of war', 5 Int'l Rev. Red Cross (1965), 3.19. See, for a modern example of this atti- tude, that of Kapitänleutnant (Ing) Lenz at the sinking of *The Peleus, In re Eck* (1945), 1 UNWCC, *Law Reports of Trials of War Criminals*, 1, 3, 7; Cameron, *The Peleus Trial*, 85–6, 116, 131.

[45] In its Report on State Responsibility (1979–II Y.B.I.L.C. 91), the International Law Commission adopted Art. 19(3)(d): '... an international crime may result from ... a seri- ous breach of an international obligation of essential importance for the safeguarding and preservation of the human environment', and in its Draft Code of Crimes Against the Peace and Security of Mankind, 1991 (30 I.L.M., 1584), Art. 22(2)(d), it declares that 'employing methods or means of warfare which are intended or may be expected to cause widespread, long-term and severe damage to the natural environment' constitutes an 'exceptionally serious war crime'; however, the Statute of the International Criminal Court agreed upon in 1998 does not include this 'crime'.

[46] 1108 U.N.T.S., 151, Schindler and Toman, 163 – by 31 Dec. 1991 this had been accepted by only fifty-five states.

water installations of some Gulf States. It was alleged that this constituted a breach of the Convention, but Iraq is not a party thereto and these acts were not making use of techniques modifying the environment, nor did they prove to be 'widespread, long-term and severe'.[47]

All the restrictions upon the means and methods of warfare and the weapons that may be used during conflict[48] are directed to protect both combatants and non-combatants from unnecessary suffering, to restrict the amount of damage likely to be long-term extending beyond the period of hostilities,[49] to safeguard the human rights of all those falling into enemy hands[50] and to facilitate the restoration of peace, for, as may be seen from the consequences of a civil or ideological conflict,[51] the more bitter the hatreds aroused by the hostilities and the methods by which they were conducted, the more difficult to agree upon the terms for a cessation of hostilities or the ultimate peace agreement.

Nuclear weapons

In the absence of any specific rule of international law relating to a particular weapon and restricting or controlling its use, the employment of weapons is subject to the general rules of the law of armed conflict, with the question of legality decided in accordance with those rules, particularly those concerning unnecessary suffering and proportionality. There are treaties regulating the use of particular weapons, but as yet there is no black letter law concerning the use of nuclear[52] and other unconventional weapons, though there are treaties directed against the testing or stockpiling of such weapons and the major nuclear powers have sought to prevent their proliferation. In fact, it has even been claimed that 'war to prevent

[47] See, e.g., McCarthy, 'Not quite a global disaster', *The Times* (London), 15 Jan. 1992; Nuttall, 'Pollution from Gulf War less than feared', *ibid.*, 20 Aug. 1992. See also Green, 'The environment and the law of conventional warfare', 29 Can. Y.B. Int'l Law (1991), 222; Zedalis, 'Burning of the Kuwaiti oilfields and the laws of war', 24 Vanderbilt J. Int'l Law (1991), 71.

[48] See, e.g., Green, 'What one may do in conflict – then and now', Delissen and Tanja, *Humanitarian Law*, 269.

[49] See Pr. I, Art. 55, 'Protection of the natural environment', which forbids practices which might 'cause such damage to the natural environment and thereby prejudice the health or survival of the population'; Art. 56, 'Protection of works and installations containing dangerous forces', namely, dams, dykes and nuclear electrical generating stations.

[50] See ch. 10 and 12 below.

[51] See, e.g., the Spanish Civil War, Cambodia (Kampuchea), Afghanistan, the former Soviet Union and the former Yugoslavia.

[52] See, e.g., Schwarzenberger, *The Legality of Nuclear Weapons*, Green, 'Nuclear weapons and the law of armed conflict', *Essays*, 1999, ch. IV; Singh and McWhinney, *Nuclear Weapons and Contemporary International Law*, Meyrowitz, 'Les armes nucléaires et le droit de la guerre', Delissen and Tanja, *Humanitarian Law*, 297. See also *Shimoda* v. *Japan* (Tokyo District Court, 1963) 8 Jap. Ann. Int'l Law (1964), 212, 235–42.

new nuclear powers from emerging would be reasonable in some circum-stances'.[53] In view of the uncontrollable effects of a nuclear explosion, the long-term nature of its radioactive fallout, and the ban on the use of poison or other deleterious gases,[54] it might be expected *prima facie* that these weapons would fall under the ban of those causing unnecessary suffering, adverse effects to the environment and casualties disproportionate to the military advantage likely to be gained. Moreover, in its advisory opinion on *Legality of the Threat or Use of Nuclear Weapons*,[55] the World Court, after reaffirming the current significance of the Martens Clause, stated 'In the view of the vast majority of States as well as writers there can be no doubt as to the applicability of humanitarian law to nuclear weapons. The Court shares that view'. It held unanimously that 'a threat or use of nuclear weapons should be compatible with the requirements of the international law applicable in armed conflict, particularly those of the principles and rules of international humanitarian law ...'.

In the light of the devastation caused at Hiroshima and Nagasaki, Lauterpacht contended that:[56]

> There is room for consideration whether the destruction and suffering – both imme-diate and consequential – entailed in the use of the atomic weapon are not such as to place it ... 'outside the principles of the law of nations as they result from the usages established among civilised peoples, from the laws of humanity and the dictates of public conscience'.[57] From that point of view the prohibition of the use of the atomic weapon would also apply to States ... which are not formally bound by the Geneva Protocol of 1925[58] or other conventional limitations on the use of force. However, ... there is still some controversy both as to the decisive relevance of considerations of humanity in warfare and the possibility of recourse to the atomic weapon against objectives in relation to which such considerations would not be relevant. For these reasons it is difficult to express a clear view as to whether an explicit prohibition of the use of the atomic weapon in warfare would be merely declaratory of existing principles of International Law. In any case, so long as the production of the [nuclear] bomb has not been prevented in practice by international agreement and supervision,[59] there must be envisaged the possibility of its being resorted to in con-tingencies not amounting to a breach of International Law. In the first instance, its use must be regarded as permissible as a reprisal for its actual prior use by the enemy

---

[53] Posen and Ross, 'Competing views for US grand strategy', 23 *Int'l Security* (Winter 1996/7), 5, 28, c. 'corporate security advocates'.

[54] Geneva Protocol for the Prohibition of the Use of Asphyxiating, Poisonous or Other Gases and of Bacteriological Methods of Warfare, 1925, 94 L.N.T.S., 65 (Schindler and Toman, 115).

[55] [1996] I.C.J. 226, 238, 266.

[56] Oppenheim's *International Law*, vol. 2, 350–1.

[57] Preamble to Hague Convention IV, 1907.

[58] See n. 54 above.

[59] See, e.g., Graefrath, 'Implementation measures and international law of arms con-trol', Delissen and Tanja, *Humanitarian Law*, 351. The World Court referred to this lacuna in the course of its Opinion.

The contemporary law of armed conflict

or his allies.[60] Secondly, recourse to the [nuclear] weapon may be justified against an enemy who violates rules of the law of war on a scale so vast as to put himself altogether outside the orbit of considerations of humanity and compassion.[61]

It may be questioned, however, whether any action by an adverse party, however extreme, could legally justify a response which would itself be 'outside the orbit of considerations of humanity and compassion'. This reservation underlies the warning:[62]

> True, the use of nuclear weapons may (with some right) be regarded as uncivilised, or as contrary to the interests of humanity. Such considerations are, however, only half of the argument, the other half being the military interest involved. Put another way, the principles and standards in question all rest on the basic idea of a balance between the interests of humanity and the military interest at stake, and in this equation it cannot be simply asserted that humanity preponderates in all cases: it will depend on the peculiarities of the concrete situation which side outweighs the other.

Thus, while the World Court held,[63] unanimously, that 'a threat or use of force by means of nuclear weapons that is contrary to Article 2, paragraph 4 of the United Nations Charter and that fails to meet all the requirements of Article 51 [relating to self-defence], is unlawful'. Nevertheless, it went on to hold, by the casting vote of the President, that 'in the current state of international law ... the Court cannot conclude definitively whether the threat or use of nuclear weapons would be lawful or unlawful in an extreme circumstance of self-defence, in which the very survival of a State would be at stake'. In this connection, it is interesting to note that at the end of 1997, that is to say after delivery of the Court's Opinion, President Clinton instructed the United States military to 'aim its nuclear forces to deter the use of nuclear arms against US forces or allies simply by threatening a devastating response, and drop any planning for a long nuclear war'.[64]

Even before the World Court had been called upon to deliver its Opinion on this matter, the legality of the use of such unconventional weapons had been judicially considered in relation to the bombing of Hiroshima and Nagasaki. The Tokyo District Court concluded[65] that both bombings constituted an 'illegal act', but the judgment is so worded that one may easily apply its reasoning to whatever

---

[60] It must be remembered that reprisals against civilians and civilian objects are, for those parties thereto, forbidden by Pr. I, Arts 51(6), 52(1), 53(c), 54(4), 55(2), 56(4).

[61] Lauterpacht gives as an example the German 'systematic plan of putting to death millions of civilians in occupied territory'. See, e.g., the account of Japanese behaviour when occupying Nanking, Chang, *The Rape of Nanking*, 1997. For a view strongly differing from Lauterpacht, see Cassese, *Violence and Law in the Modern Age*, 1988, ch. 1. See also ch. 3 on 'First Use'.

[62] See, however, Lauterpacht, *Rules of Warfare*, 89, 94–5.

[63] *Loc.cit.*, 266.

[64] *Washington Post*, 8 Dec. 1997.

[65] *Shimoda. v. Japan*, 8 Jap. Ann. Int'l Law (1964), 212; 32 I.L.R., 626.

purpose one chooses.[66] Both the British and American Manuals of Military Law, foretelling the *Nuclear* Opinion, dogmatically state that there is no rule of customary or conventional international law which forbids the use of the nuclear weapon, so that, if used, the overriding principles concerning proportionality and the like would be the standards by which its legality would be judged.[67]

From the language of Protocol I[68] it would appear that nuclear weapons fall within the provision prohibiting attacks endangering the civilian population and the ban on 'methods of warfare which are intended, or may be expected, to cause widespread, long-term and severe damage to the natural environment'. However, in introducing its draft, the International Committee of the Red Cross stated[69]

> Problems relating to atomic, bacteriological and chemical warfare are subjects of international agreements or negotiations by governments, and in submitting these draft Protocols the ICRC does not intend to broach these problems. It should be borne in mind that the Red Cross as a whole at several International Red Cross Conferences has clearly made known its condemnation of weapons of mass destruction and has urged governments to reach agreements for banning their use.

The United Kingdom, the United States and the Soviet Union, the three powers known to possess the largest arsenals of such weapons, expressed concurrence in these views,[70] which are reiterated in British and American statements made at the time of signature.[71] Since the nuclear powers have made their position clear in this manner, it matters little that the United Nations has adopted resolutions condemning nuclear weapons or that any number of non-nuclear states have condemned their use. It can hardly be said that there is any *opinio juris* to this effect and this seems to accord with the unanimous view of the World Court,[72] 'there exists an obligation to pursue in good faith and bring to a conclusion negotiations leading to nuclear disarmament in all its aspects under strict and effective international control'.

While there may be controversy as to the legality or otherwise or nuclear weapons used against cities constituting military objectives, in so far as there may exist smaller weapons of a tactical kind for use on the battlefield and the fallout and long-term effects of which may be controlled, it would appear that there is no doubt as to their legality, provided it could be maintained that the suffering caused

---

[66] *Ibid.*, 234 *et seq.*; 628 *et seq.* For discussion of this judgment, see Green, 'Nuclear weapons'.

[67] HMSO, *Manual of Military Law*, Part III, *The Law of War on Land* (1958), s. 113; US Dept. of the Army, FM 27–10, *The Law of Land Warfare*, 1956, s. 35; see also FM 27-161-2, *International Law*, vol. 2, (1962), 42–4.

[68] Arts 33, 51, 52, 57.

[69] Bothe, *et al.*, 188–9.

[70] *Ibid.*

[71] Schindler and Toman, 717–18. The British statement is also reproduced in Wortley, 'Observations of the revision of the 1949 Geneva 'Red Cross' Conventions,' 54 Brit. Y.B. Int'l Law (1983), 143.

[72] At 267.

to combatants was not disproportionate or unnecessary in view of the military end to be achieved. In its Opinion, the World Court has cast some doubt on this view. It stated[73] 'humanitarian law, at a very early stage, prohibited certain types of weapons either because of their indiscriminate effect on combatants and civilians or *because of the unnecessary suffering caused to combatants*, that is to say a harm greater than that unavoidable to achieve legitimate military objectives … '. It continued, ' … none of the States advocating the legality of the use of nuclear weapons under certain circumstances, including the "clean" use of smaller low-yield, tactical nuclear weapons, has indicated what, supposing such limited use were feasible, would be the precise circumstances justifying such use … This being so, the Court does not consider that it has a sufficient basis for a determination on the validity of this view'. It might be felt that the comments regarding 'unnecessary suffering caused to combatants' were sufficient to conclude that even such tactical weapons were probably illegal.[74]

Weapons in desuetude

Customary law has rendered the use of certain weapons, together with any substances likely to inflame a wound illegal, but this is rather the result of technological developments in weaponry or changes in the nature of warfare.[75] The *German War Book*[76] specifies chain shot, red-hot shot, pitch balls, etc., all of which, together with boiling oil, were useful during a siege, and goes on to condemn the employment of

> men and troops … who are without the knowledge of civilised warfare and by whom, therefore, the very cruelties and inhumanities forbidden by the usages of war are committed [and the employment of, for example, African colonial troops in] a European seat of war [is] undoubtedly to be regarded as a retrogression from civilised to barbarous warfare, since these troops had and could have no conception of European-Christian culture, of respect for property and for the honour of women.

Today, with the coming into independent statehood of almost all colonial territories and with their accession to the Geneva Conventions and participation in such conferences as that which drafted the 1977 Protocols, together with their anti-discrimination provisions – except against mercenaries[77] – such a comment would

---

[73] At 256, 262 (italics added).

[74] See, for comment on the Opinion, Matheson, 'The Opinions of the I.C.J. on the threat or use of nuclear weapons', 91 Am. J. Int'l Law, 1997, 417; Schmitt, 'The I.C.J. and the use of nuclear weapons,' 51, Naval War Coll. Rev. 1998 (spring issue) 91.

[75] Weapons like the mace or the battleaxe were useful against knights in armour, but are of no value in modern combat. See, e.g., Green, 'Acts and weapons forbidden *in bello*', in *Pax-Ius-Libertas*, Constantopoulos, *Festschrift* (1990), vol. I, 355.

[76] *The German War Book.*, 65–7.

[77] See ch. 6 above.

no longer be acceptable. Moreover, imperial powers like France and the United Kingdom have never hesitated in their modern wars in using troops of any ethnic or geographic origin, relying upon their training and discipline to ensure their compliance with the laws of war. The very idea of measuring the status of forces or of countries by the indefinable standard of 'civilization'[78] has given place to independence and condemnation based on conduct.

Treaties regulating weaponry

The first treaty, as distinct from any Church ban,[79] to declare a specific weapon illegal was the 1868 Declaration of St Petersburg.[80] This states that, the only true purpose of war being to weaken the enemy to a point at which he is prepared to surrender, there is no reason to cause aggravated suffering or disablement of the fighting forces, and any arms directed to this end would be contrary to the laws of humanity, 'the Contracting Parties engage mutually to renounce, in case of war among themselves, the employment by their military or naval troops of any projectile of a weight below 400 grammes [13½–14 ounces], which is either explosive or charged with fulminating or inflammable substances'.

The Declaration was adopted before the introduction of aircraft and has not since been extended to aerial combat.[81] In fact, the latest convention on incendiary weapons[82] expressly states that its prohibition does not extend to:

> Munitions designed to combine penetration, blast or fragmentation effects with an additional incendiary effect, such as armour-piercing projectiles, fragmentation shells, explosive bombs and similar combined-effects munitions in which the incendiary effect is not specifically designed to cause burn injury to persons, but to be used against military objectives, such as armoured vehicles, aircraft and installations or facilities.

From a practical point of view it may be difficult to apprehend how such a weapon used against a tank or an aircraft may be considered as not being specifically designed for use against the crew as well as the vehicle.

---

[78] See, e.g., *Walton* v. *Arab American Oil Co.* (1956), 253 F. 2d 541, 545, in which the Second Circuit Court refused to consider Saudi Arabia as 'uncivilized'.

[79] The Second Lateran Council, 1139, anathematised the use of the crossbow and the arc – at least against Christians, see Draper, 'The interaction of Christianity'.

[80] Schindler and Toman, 101.

[81] Spaight, *Air Power*, n. 37 above, states that the Declaration *does* apply to air warfare: 'The standard of international morality and the claims of humanity are not lower and less imperative in aerial than in other forms of warfare. Unless and until the restrictive rules applicable to the other arms are relaxed by international agreement for the purpose of air fighting, they must be binding upon air forces', 198 – he cites Fauchille-Bonfils and Rolland in support.

[82] Protocol on the Prohibition or Restrictions on the Use of Incendiary Weapons, 1980 (Schindler and Toman, 190).

The Declaration does not apply to the use of small arms ammunition. It was proposed because of the use of such explosive projectiles against ammunition wagons, and the fear of their use against troops.[83] The 1899 Hague Conference took the matter up, for the munitions factory at Dumdum, India, had produced a bullet with a lead nose which spread on impact,[84] and it had been suggested to the Russian Government to make use of an explosive bullet without a cap which would explode on contact with a soft target, such as the human body. This proposal was rejected by the Government and the 1899 Conference adopted Hague Declaration IV(3)[85] by which the parties agreed to 'abstain from the use of bullets which expand or flatten easily in the human body, such as bullets with a hard envelope which does not entirely cover the core or is pierced with incisions'.[86]

Declaration IV(2)[87] condemned 'the use of projectiles the sole object of which is the diffusion of asphyxiating or deleterious gases'. Seemingly, therefore, an explosive projectile releasing asphyxiating or other deleterious gases at the moment of explosion would not be unlawful under this Declaration. Closely related to the ban on such gases is that on the employment of 'poison or poisoned weapons',[88] which again would seem not to include weapons releasing poison gas as an incidental to their explosion.[89] The Regulations also give treaty form to the traditional chivalrous concept that weapons that causing unnecessary suffering should not be used,[90] now understood in an objective sense to refer to the military objective desired, rather than the subjective reaction of the victim. Further, a weapon which does in fact cause a wounded combatant unnecessary suffering, in the sense that it goes beyond merely rendering him *hors de combat*, is illegal.

[83] Schindler and Toman, 101; see, also Bordwell, *The Law of War*, 87–8.

[84] Spaight, *War Rights on Land*, (1911), comments (79) that this 'was designed for use against fanatical savages, such as Afridis and Fuzzi-Wuzzies, whose rushes the calibre Lee-Enfield bullet was found inadequate to check'.

[85] Schindler and Toman, 109.

[86] This has been extended to forbid such activities as 'notching' a bayonet or smearing it with, e.g., faeces to aggravate the wound. Today, it would seem that what is forbidden against an enemy is not necessarily illegal when used against one's own nationals. A number of police forces are using such weapons, maintaining that they 'do not pass through the body of a perpetrator ... do not easily ricochet, endangering bystanders ... The hollow-point bullets consistently penetrate a human body to depth that will cause rapid incapacitation ... These are not exploding bullets, these are not dum-dum bullets. These are a much safer ammunition ...' *Globe and Mail* (Toronto), 10 August 1995.

[87] Schindler and Toman, 105 (italics added).

[88] Hague Regs, 1899, 1907, Art. 23(a).

[89] It would include such weapons as poisoned arrows, or the punji stick – a sharpened stick covered with excrement and placed in a camouflaged hole – widely used in Vietnam, Bond, *The Rules of Internal Conflict*, 142. Such weapons would, in any case, probably inflict a wound sufficient to disable the victim, so that the poison or excrement would be superfluous. The punji stick would also offend the customary rule against secret weapons and the Protocol against booby traps, see below.

[90] Art. 23(e). For examples of 'Dirty tricks in ancient warfare', see Mayor, 10 *Quarterly J. of Mil. Hist.* 1997, 32.

While the use of such banned weapons would constitute a war crime,[91] any tribunal before which an individual was charged would have to consider whether the ordinary soldier to whom such weapons had been issued could reasonably[92] be expected to disobey, especially if he had no other ammunition with which to defend himself against the adverse party. In such circumstances, it is probable that only those responsible for issuing the weapons would carry liability.[93]

These agreements all include an 'all-participation clause' and are only valid in a conflict in which all belligerents have accepted the obligations imposed by them. This caused difficulty during World War I as Brazil, Bulgaria, Greece, Italy – one of the Principal Allied and Associated Powers – Montenegro, Servia and Turkey had not acceded to Hague Convention IV.[94] However, by the end of World War II, the rules and customs of war as embodied in that Convention and those in the 1929 Prisoners of War Convention[95] had come to be regarded as declaratory of customary law and so binding on all belligerents, regardless of whether they were parties or not.[96]

Gas, chemical and bacteriological weapons

Perhaps the most significant international agreement relating to a specific weapon is the 1925 Geneva Gas Protocol.[97] Article 119 of the Treaty of Versailles had already forbidden Germany, which had been the first belligerent to use gas in World War I, to manufacture or import such materials, while the 1922 Washington Treaty[98] sought to generalise the ban on the use of gas. This Treaty, however, never came into force. In the 1925 Protocol the parties affirm that: 'the use in war of asphyxiating, poisonous or other gases, and of all analogous liquids, materials or devices, has been justly condemned by the general opinion of the civilised world', and point out that this condemnation is to be found in 'Treaties to which the majority of Powers of the world are Parties', and:

> to the end that the prohibition shall be universally accepted as a part of International Law, binding alike the conscience and the practice of nations: Declare: That the

[91] See ch. 18 below.

[92] See, e.g., Green, 'Superior orders and the reasonable man', *Essays*, 1999, ch. VII.

[93] See, e.g., Parks, 'Command responsibility for war crimes', 62 Mil. Law Rev. (1973), 1; Green, 'Superior orders and command responsibility', 27 Can. Y.B. Int'l Law (1989), 167.

[94] See, however, re maritime warfare, *The Möwe* [1915] P., 1, 12; *The Blonde* [1922] 1 A.C., 313, 323–5.

[95] Schindler and Toman, 423.

[96] See, e.g., *Nuremberg Judgment* (1946) HMSO Cmd 6964 (1946), 64–5; 41 Am. J. Int'l Law (1947), 172, 248–9.

[97] Protocol for the Prohibition of the Use in War of Asphyxiating, Poisonous or Other Gases and of Bacteriological Methods of Warfare, 94 L.N.T.S., 65 (Schindler and Toman, 115).

[98] *Ibid.*, 877.

> High Contracting Parties, so far as they are not already Parties to Treaties prohibiting such, accept this prohibition, agree to extend this prohibition to the use of bacteriological methods of warfare and agree to be bound as between themselves according to the terms of this declaration.

The parties undertook 'to exert every effort to induce other States to accede' to the Protocol, but it was not until 1975 that the United States did so. Italy ratified the Protocol in 1928, but used gas during its war with Ethiopia, 1935–36;[99] Egypt deposited its ratification in 1928, but used gas against Yemen in 1967;[100] Iraq ratified in 1931 and reaffirmed its adherence to the Protocol and its condemnation of all forms of chemical warfare at the Paris Conference of the signatories to the Geneva Protocol,[101] but used it against Kurdish rebels in the same year[102] and against Iran during its war with that country. Moreover, a number of states made reservations to their instruments of accession either on the basis of reciprocity or against any adverse party first resorting to the use of such weapons.[103] In addition, many have maintained that the prohibition does not prevent the use of lachrymose agents, especially to maintain or restore discipline in internment or prisoner-of-war camps.[104] During the Gulf War, 1991, the United States Defense Department authorised the use of tear and other non-lethal riot control gases against Iraqi forces during search and rescue missions[105] After the termination of that war, United Nations inspectors discovered that Iraq had quantities of chemical weapons stockpiled and these were systematically destroyed under supervision of the inspectors.

In 1972 a Convention was adopted on the Prohibition of Development, Production and Stockpiling of Bacteriological (Biological) and Toxin Weapons and Their Destruction,[106] but, other than authorising any party to bring breaches to the attention of the Security Council, it contains no provision for action in the event of non-observance of its provisions, and is silent on use. However, if development, production and stockpiling are forbidden, it implies that use would be contrary to the 1925 Geneva Protocol and to customary and conventional law on unnecessary suffering and constitute a war crime. This lacuna in the 1972 Convention has been remedied by the 1993 Convention on the Prohibition of the Development, Production, Stockpiling and Use of Chemical Weapons and Their Destruction[107]

[99] 2 Walters, *A History of the League of Nations*, 677; see also speech by Haile Selassie to League Assembly, 2 Keith, *Speeches and Documents on International Relations 1918–1937*, 85–6.

[100] *The Times*, 14, 28 Jul., 20 Sept., 1967.

[101] Jan. 1989, 28 I.L.M., 1021.

[102] *The Times*, 16 Mar., 1989. It has also been alleged that Burma used germ warfare against Karen rebels, *The Times*, 15 Nov. 1994.

[103] Schindler and Toman, 121–7.

[104] E.g., US Executive Order 11850 on the Renunciation of Certain Uses in War of Chemical Herbicides and Riot Control Agents, 1975, 17 I.L.M., 794.

[105] *The Times* (London), 26 Jan. 1991.

[106] 1015 U.N.T.S. (1976) 164 (Schindler and Toman, 137).

[107] 32 I.L.M. 800.

whereby the parties have undertaken not to use chemical weapons[108] – even in response to a prior unlawful use by an adverse party – or engage in any military preparations to that end. In addition they are obligated not to use riot control agents as a method of warfare. However, this would not preclude using such agents to maintain order in, for example, a prisoner of war camp. Similarly, some countries, for example, the United States, maintain that it is not forbidden to use chemical herbicides to clear a field of fire or protect a defensive perimeter.

The agreements against gas and chemical warfare are also directed against the use of biological weapons, the use of which seem to have been known to the ancient Greeks.[109] The first recorded use of such weapons in modern times appears to have been in 1917[110] when the Germans sought to interfere with Allied horse- and reindeer-drawn supply lines across Norway – 'A piece of sugar containing anthrax bacilli [was] found in the luggage of Baron Karl von Rosen, when he was apprehended in Karasjok in January 1917, suspected of espionage and sabotage'. After the Gulf War, 1991, the Security Council established a commission of experts to supervise the chemical and bacteriological disarmament of Iraq and these experts found ample evidence that Iraq had been developing both.[111]

Environmental protection

Without specifying any particular weapon, in 1976 a Convention was adopted on the Prohibition of Military or Any Other Hostile use of Environmental Modification Techniques.[112] The Convention makes no reference to any sanction, but is affected by Protocol I. By Article 35(2) of the Protocol 'it is prohibited to employ methods or means of warfare which are intended, or may be expected, to cause widespread long-term and severe damage to the natural environment'. This is described as a 'basic rule' in the section of the Protocol devoted to methods and means of warfare. By Article 55:

[108] Art. 2 defines chemical weapons as '(a) Toxic chemicals and their precursors, except where intended for purposes not prohibited under this Convention, as long as the types and quantities are consistent with such purposes; (b) Munitions and devices, specifically designed to cause death or other harm through the toxic properties of those toxic chemicals specified in subparagraph (a), which would be released as a result of the employment of such weapons and devices; (c) Any equipment specifically designed for use directly in connection with the employment of munitions and devices specified in subparagraph (b)'.

[109] See Mayor, *loc.cit.*

[110] *New York Times*, 25 June 1998.

[111] *Washington Post*, 21 Nov. 1997.

[112] 108 U.N.T.S. (1977), 151 (Schindler and Toman, 163). See, e.g., Blix, 'Arms control treaties aimed at reducing the military impact on the environment', in Makarczyk, (ed.), *Essays in International Law in Honour of Judge Manfred Lachs* (1984), 703. See also Green, 'The environment and the law of conventional warfare', 29 Can. Y.B. Int'l Law 1991, 222, and for a variety of essays dealing with the environment in wartime, see Grunawalt, *et al., Protection of the Environment During Armed Conflict*, 1997.

Care shall be taken in warfare to protect the natural environment against widespread, long-term and severe damage. This protection includes a prohibition of the use of methods or means of warfare which are intended or may be expected to cause such damage to the natural environment and thereby to prejudice the health or survival of the population [and] attacks against the natural environment by way of reprisals are prohibited.

While there is no suggestion in the Protocol that breach of this prohibition would constitute a grave breach, it cannot be doubted that it would be a war crime,[113] and by the Statute of the International Criminal Court [114] war crimes include 'Internationally launching an attack in the knowledge that such attack will cause … widespread, longterm and severe damage to the environment which would be clearly excessive in relation to concrete and direct overall military advantage anticipated'. During and after the Gulf War accusations were made against Iraq that it had committed such environmental war crimes because of its destruction of oilfields and oil-wells, even though Iraq was not a party to the ENMOD Convention or Protocol I and there was no evidence to suggest that this destruction was directed against the environment,[115] even though the consequences may have been disproportionate to any military advantage that may have been gained. This is in line with the views expressed in the United States *Operational Law Handbook*:[116] 'The application of ENMOD is limited, as it only bans efforts to manipulate the environment with extremely advanced technology. The simple diversion of a river, destruction of a dam [but if this results in releasing "dangerous forces" it would be in breach of Article 56 of Protocol I and constitute a grave breach under Article 85], or even the release of millions of barrels of oil do not constitute "manipulation" as contemplated under the provisions of the ENMOD. Instead, the technology must alter the "natural processes, dynamics, composition or structure of the earth …"' Examples of this type of manipulation are (1) alteration of atmospheric conditions to alter weather patterns, (2) earthquake modification, and (3) ocean current modification (tidal waves etc,).

Mines, booby-traps and incendiaries

In 1980 a Convention on Prohibitions or Restrictions on the Use of Certain Weapons Which May be Deemed to be Excessively Injurious or to Have Indiscriminate Effects was adopted:[117]

---

[113] See ch. 18 below.

[114] 17 July 1998, 37 I.L.M. 998, Art. 8 (2) (b) (iv).

[115] See, e.g., literature cited n.47 above; see also *Conduct of the Persian Gulf War* at 636.

[116] *Op.cit.*, p. 5-7.

[117] Schindler and Toman, 179. See Fenrick, 'New developments in the law and concerning the use of conventional weapons in armed conflict', 19 Can. Y.B. Int'l Law (1981), 229.

Basing themselves on the principle of international law that the right of the parties to an armed conflict to choose the means or methods of warfare is not unlimited, and on the principle that prohibits the employment in armed conflicts of weapons, projectiles and material and methods of warfare of a nature to cause superfluous injury or unnecessary suffering, Also recalling that it is prohibited to employ methods or means of warfare which are intended, or may be expected, to cause widespread, long-term and severe damage to the natural environment,

Confirming their determination that in cases not covered by this Convention and its annexed Protocols, or by other international agreements, the civilian population and the combatants shall at all times remain under the protection and authority of the principles of international law derived from established custom, from the principles of humanity and from the dictates of public conscience.[118]

The parties adopted three Protocols.

Protocol I[119] prohibits the use of any weapon the primary effect of which is to injure the human body by fragments which escape detection by X-rays. So far as is known, there is no such weapon in use at present, which perhaps explains why it was easy to adopt this one-sentence Protocol.

Protocol II prohibits the use of mines, booby and other devices.[120] Mines in this Protocol only relate to those, however distributed, which are on land. A booby-trap is 'any device or material which is designed, constructed or adapted to kill or injure and which functions unexpectedly when a person disturbs or approaches an apparently harmless object or performs an apparently safe act'. Among the items which may not be attached to explosives and thus constitute forbidden booby-traps are protected emblems, like the Red Cross or Crescent or those indicating cultural objects; sick, wounded or dead persons;[121] burial sites; medical facilities; children's toys, clothing, educational material and the like; food or drink; kitchen utensils,[122] other than those in military locations; religious objects; historical or other objects constituting part of the cultural heritage of peoples; animals or their carcasses. It is also forbidden to set a booby-trap designed to cause superfluous injury or unnecessary suffering, into which category there would fall the punji stick common in the Vietnam war. Booby-traps directed against the military[123] or military objects are not forbidden, which suggests that it is legitimate to booby-trap a residence in a village which has been evacuated of civilians. Replica rocks reported to have been used by Iranian-backed Hezbollah fighters in southern Lebanon and made in Iran of glass fibre to disguise roadside

---

[118] This last phrase reproduces the Preamble to Hague Conv. IV.

[119] Schindler and Toman, 185.

[120] *Ibid.*

[121] In 1998 Muslim rebels in Algeria, having attacked a small village, booby-trapped the corpse of a seven-month old baby which exploded wounding the soldier removing the body for burial, *The Times*, 8 Oct. 1998.

[122] This is reminiscent of the protection afforded to household goods in feudal military codes.

[123] Since the *punji* stick (see n. 89) used in Vietnam caused superfluous injury it would probably fall within the ban.

bombs against occupying Israeli troops and filled with plastic explosive and ball-bearings capable of penetrating steel[124] would probably not be illegal if they are not likely to appeal to civilians.

Further restrictions on the use of mines and booby-traps were imposed when the Protocol was amended in 1996,[125] while a new treaty directed against anti-personnel mines was adopted in 1997. By the Convention[126] on the Prohibition of the Use, Stockpiling, Production and Transfer of Anti-personnel Mines the parties undertake 'never under any circumstances: (a) to use anti-personnel mines; (b) to develop, produce, otherwise acquire, stockpile, retain or transfer to anyone, directly or indirectly, anti-personnel mines; (c) to assist, encourage or induce, in any way, anyone to engage in any activity prohibited to a State Party under this Convention'. They also undertook 'to destroy or ensure the destruction of all anti-personnel mines'. The United States refused to sign this Treaty asserting that all its mines were self-destructive, contending, further, that such mines were essential to protect the northern border of South Korea. Regardless of the ban imposed by this treaty, as has been seen in the 1999 situation on the Kosovo–Albanian border, since mines are readily and cheaply manufactured they are likely to continue to be made and used by irregular forces or by forces not possessing more advanced weapons, while some military commanders might be inclined to use them to guard the perimeter of any established post, contending that the security of his personnel is his prime concern. Much of the agitation against mines has revolved round the number of civilian casualties that they have caused, most of which have occurred after the cessation of hostilities or the evacuation of an area, particularly as civilians are not likely to be in the area during active hostilities. Perhaps more realistic than a ban would be full enforcement of the requirement to map a minefield and to clear it once operations have terminated.

For those accepting the original Protocol or as amended in 1996, but rejecting the 1997 Treaty, they are obliged if laying or setting minefields or setting booby-traps to keep a register of their location and, immediately after the cessation of hostilities, 'take all necessary and appropriate measures, including the use of such records, to protect civilians from the effects of minefields, mines and booby-traps', to inform the Secretary-General of the United Nations and the adverse party of such locations and, 'whenever possible, by mutual agreement, provide for the release of information concerning the location of minefields, mines and booby-traps, particularly in agreements governing the cessation of hostilities'. Due to failure to keep such adequate records, numerous injuries were caused to civilians after cessation of hostilities particularly in Cambodia, and the Falklands. If United Nations forces are operating in the area, parties to the conflict are to remove or render harmless any mines or booby-traps there, take such measures as are necessary to protect such forces, and make available to its head

---

[124] *The Times*, 8 Nov. 1996.
[125] 35 I.L.M. 1209.
[126] 36 *ibid.* 1507.

all information in the party's possession concerning the location of minefields and booby-traps. After the Gulf War, military personnel acting under Security Council resolutions concerning the disarmament of Iraq suffered severe casualties during clearing operations since Iraq had not maintained proper records.

Protocol III[127] prohibits or restricts the use of incendiaries, weapons which are 'primarily designed to set fire to objects or to cause burn injury to persons through the action of flame, heat, or combination thereof, produced by a chemical reaction of a substance delivered on the target'. They may never be used directly against the civilian population or objects, or against forests or other plant cover, 'except when such natural elements are used to cover, conceal or camouflage combatants or other military objectives, or are themselves military objectives'. Presumably, a forest would be considered a military objective in jungle warfare or if it were likely to be used by retreating or advancing forces as a cover in the future.

As World War II showed, much incendiary damage results from aerial bombardment, and:

> it is further prohibited by the Protocol to make any military objective located within a concentration of civilians the object of attack by means of incendiary weapons other than air-delivered incendiary weapons, except when such military objective is clearly separated from the concentration of civilians and all feasible precautions are taken with a view to limiting the incendiary effects to the military objective and to avoiding, and in any event to minimising, incidental loss of civilian life, injury to civilians and damage to civilian objects.

This suggests that incendiary bombs may be used against a city containing a military objective if that objective is sufficiently distant from the civilians to enable it to be attacked without the risk of collateral damage. During the conflict in Bosnia, 1992, it was reported that Serb guerrillas were using incendiary weapons and napalm against Bosnian cities.[128] In 1994 United Nations observers reported that Serb bombers dropped napalm in United Nations-declared 'safe areas'.[129]

It is still permissible to use projectiles which may have incidental incendiary effects, including illuminants, tracers, smoke or signalling systems. Equally, while incendiary bombs are clearly forbidden if used against a city, explosive devices which may cause incidental fires, however extensive, are not within the prohibition. Similarly, 'munitions designed to combine penetration, blast or fragmentation effects with an additional incendiary effect, such as armour-piercing projectiles, fragmentation shells, explosive bombs and similar combined-effects munitions in which the incendiary effect is not specifically designed to cause burn injury to persons, but to be used against military objectives, such as armoured vehicles, aircraft and installations or factories' are not forbidden, even though their use makes inevitable the destruction by fire of the crews involved. Napalm, flame-throwers and the like fall within the ban, but in view of the mechanised

---

[127] Schindler and Toman, 190.
[128] *Globe and Mail* (Toronto), 9 Oct. 1992.
[129] *The Times*, 19 Nov. 1994.

nature of modern warfare the value of such weapons against troops in the field is somewhat reduced, though they may probably still be used, subject to the rules on unnecessary suffering and proportionality in clearing foxholes or house to house fighting.

Finally, in 1995 an additional Protocol (IV) on Blinding Laser Weapons[130] was adopted. By this 'it is prohibited to employ laser weapons specifically designed, as their sole function or as one of their combat functions, to cause permanent blindness to unenhanced vision, that is to the naked eye or to the eye with corrective eyesight devices ... [However, b]linding as an incidental or collateral effect of the legitimate military employment of laser systems, including laser systems used against optical equipment, is not covered by the prohibition ... '. Thus, the Protocol does not prohibit optical or electro-optical equipment or laser systems for such things as rangefinding, target designation or similar purposes.[131]

Poison and starvation

The ban on the use of poison goes back to ancient Greece[132] and the laws of Manu in the second century BC,[133] for these were considered to be secret and therefore treacherous weapons, foretelling the modern rule that weapons should be carried openly. By the time of the classical 'fathers' of international law, it was generally accepted that the use of poison or poisoned weapons was contrary to the law of nations, as was the poisoning of springs,[134] although Grotius considered that springs and other sources of drinking water might be legitimately polluted by other means.[135] Even if a notice has been affixed to the water source stating it has been poisoned, it would still be unlawful, for the notice may be rendered illegible by the weather, damaged by animals, or removed by third parties. More important, the use of poison is contrary to established customary law and is embodied in Hague Regulation 23(a), 1907. Although poisoning water sources is now forbidden, it remains lawful to divert, dam or dry them up. But if the purpose is directed

---

[130] 35 I.L.M. 1217.

[131] *Operational Law Handbook*, p. 18–5.

[132] Phillipson, *The International Law and Custom of Ancient Greece and Rome*, states (vol. 2, 221): 'It was considered injurious to cut off or poison the enemy's water supply, or to make use of poisoned weapons'; see also Homer's *Odyssey*, tr. Lattimore, 1965, Bk I, 11, 260–3; Mayor, *loc.cit.*

[133] Buhler, *The Laws of Manu*, Tit. VII, 90: 'when the king fights his foes in battle, let him not strike with weapons concealed, nor with barbed, poisoned, or the points of which are blazed with fire ... These are weapons of the wicked.'

[134] See, e.g., Gentili, *De Jure Belli*, (1612), Lib. II, cap. VI; Grotius, *De Jure Belli ac Pacis*, (1625), Lib. III, cap. IV, ss. xv, xvi; Vattel, *Le Droit des Gens*, 1758, Liv. III, ch. VIII, ss. 155–7. In 1997 the retreating Taliban forces in Afghanistan were reported to have poisoned village wells by throwing dead cows into them, *The Times*, 13 Aug. 1997.

[135] Grotius, *De Jure Belli.*, s. xxvii.

at the civilian population as such, action of this kind would be contrary to Article 54 of Protocol I concerned with the protection of objects indispensable to the survival of the civilian population.

It is forbidden to use starvation as a weapon against the civilian population,[136] but it is lawful to take steps necessary to deprive the adverse party of his food supplies. If a military occupant takes food away from the civilian population in order to deny them to the adverse party's forces or feed his own troops, compensation must be paid.[137] Such action should not be so extreme as to place the civilians at risk. If compensation is not paid at the time of this requisition, a receipt is to be given which is to be redeemed at the earliest opportunity.[138] Protocol I deals with the issue in a comprehensive fashion:

1. Starvation of civilians as a method of warfare is prohibited.

2. It is prohibited to attack, destroy, remove or render useless objects indispensable to the civilian population [and this applies to one's own civilian population as well as that of the adverse party], foodstuffs, crops,[139] livestock, drinking water installations and supplies and irrigation works, for the specific[140] purpose of denying them for their sustenance value[141] to the civilian population of the adverse Party,[142]

---

[136] Pr. I, Art. 54(1). Problems arose in 1990 in relation to the UN-imposed economic interdiction of Iraq under SC Res. 661, since the ban did not include 'supplies intended strictly for medical purposes, and, in humanitarian circumstances, foodstuffs' and the US, the leader among the interdicting powers, differed from, e.g., India in interpreting 'humanitarian circumstances'. It based its opposition on SC Res. 666 which established a supervisory committee to determine such circumstances, and required any such aid to be administered under UN auspices or by an internationally recognised relief agency: the US apparently did not consider the Indian Red Cross sufficiently independent, *The Times*, 19 Sept., *The Globe and Mail* (Toronto), 21 Sept. 1990. After the cessation of hostilities similar problems arose because of criticism by some of the former Coalition powers of the manner in which Iraq was carrying out the cease-fire conditions, even though there was much evidence to suggest that young children were dying as a result of the restrictions on imports. Differences to the same effect were still being expressed at the end of 1998.

[137] Hague Regs, Art. 46, forbids the confiscation of private property, which includes privately owned foodstuffs as distinct from those found in state storehouses.

[138] *Ibid.*, Art. 52.

[139] It would still be permitted to destroy, e.g., a field of wheat to deny cover to enemy forces.

[140] If, therefore, in the course of ordinary military operations such objects indispensable to the civilian population were destroyed, this would not be unlawful; the purpose must be to deny sustenance to the civilian population.

[141] It may be that, because of the possible starvation of the civilian population, permission may have to be granted for the passage of food supplies for that population. This was envisaged during the interdiction of Iraq, and became of major importance in Bosnia in 1993 and in Kosovo in 1998.

[142] Starvation of enemy forces is permissible; the reference to the adverse party must be construed as meaning a denial which would prevent that party from feeding the civilian population, such as might follow from requisitioning foodstuffs beyond a level necessary to deny them to the opposing forces.

whatever the motive, whether in order to starve out civilians, to cause them to move away, or for any other motive.[143]

Since 'wilful killing' and 'inhumane treatment' of protected persons, including prisoners of war and civilians, constitute grave breaches, the same would appear to be true of a policy of starvation.[144] Sustenance intended solely for the armed forces of the adverse party may be attacked or destroyed, as may materials required 'in direct support of military action', provided that action taken against such objects cannot 'be expected to leave the civilian population with such inadequate food or water as to cause its starvation or force its movement'.[145] Similarly a party defending 'its national territory against invasion [may derogate] from the[se] prohibitions ... within such territory under its own control where required by imperative military necessity'.[146] It may resort to a 'scorched earth' policy, regardless of the effect upon its own population, when evacuating or retreating from its own territory prior to its occupation by the enemy, but it may not resort to such a policy when seeking to expel the enemy or reoccupy its own territory.[147]

Forbidden practices

It is sometimes suggested during conflict that a named member of the adverse party's administration or senior command should be assassinated, but such acts directed against a specific individual, as distinct from enemy personnel in general, or against a named enemy commander would be contrary to customary law.[148]

---

[143] Since Iraq and many of the parties enforcing the interdiction had not ratified or acceded to Pr. I, it has been suggested (Greenwood, 'Supply decisions rest with councils', *The Times*, 13 Sept. 1990) that this provision would not apply *vis-à-vis* Iraq in 1990. However, it should be noted that by customary law civilians may not be made the object of 'attack'. Moreover, by Geneva Convention IV, 1949 (Civilians – Schindler and Toman, 95), Art. 23, 'Each High Contracting Party ... shall permit the free passage of all consignments of essential foodstuffs, clothing and tonics intended for children under 15, expectant mothers and maternity cases' – specifically mentioned by Iraq as suffering severely as a result of the interdiction – and passage of which was permitted by SC Res. 666, and which condition Iraq maintained was aggravated by Coalition policy after the cease-fire.

[144] See Fleck, *op.cit.*, 1209.

[145] Pr. I, Art. 54(3)(b).

[146] *Ibid.*, Art. 54(5).

[147] 'Canada, note on current law of armed conflict relevant to environment in conventional conflicts' (paper by JAG to Ottawa Conference of Experts, Jul. 1991, c. Rogers, *op.cit.*, 117). In the *Hostages Case* (1948), 8 *War Crimes Reports* 34, 69, General Rendulic was acquitted of the charge of having devastated enemy-held territory in Norway to deny it to advancing Soviet forces. This would probably not be legal for those ratifying the Protocol, Rogers, 107.

[148] Lieber Code (Schindler/Toman, 3), Art. 148; Hague Regs, Art. 23(b); *The German War Book*, 65; *British Manual*, para. 115; US FM27-lo, s.31; see also *The Army Lawyer*, US DA PAM 27-50-204, Dec. 1989, Parks, 'Memorandum on the law: executive order 12333 and assassination', 4 *et seq*. Schmitt, 'State-sponsored assassinations in interna-

Article 23(b) of the Hague Regulations 'does not, however, preclude attacks on individual soldiers or officers of the enemy whether in the zone of hostilities, occupied territory, or elsewhere'.[149] Equally, nothing prevents an attempt by members of the forces of one belligerent against an individual commander at his headquarters, behind the lines or outside the field of conflict, since he is regarded as a legitimate combatant in such circumstances.[150] If the attempt were made on neutral territory it would amount to a breach of neutrality.[151]

The assassination of the head of an enemy state[152] or the placing of a price on his head or that of a named enemy individual, as was done by the United States against Noriega during the Panama campaign, is equally forbidden. Problems might arise if the head of state is also commander-in-chief of the armed forces, particularly if he is in uniform for then he would be regarded as a legitimate target. In view of the role now being played by women in the armed forces, this is probably true even when the sovereign is female.

It is also prohibited to kill an enemy national or member of the armed forces by an act of treachery[153] and any person responsible for such killing would be liable for trial as a war criminal, so it would have been open to the authorities to try as war criminals those who, in civilian clothing, had assassinated Heydrich in 1942.[154] It would be treacherous to feign surrender or incapacitation by wounds or sickness and then attack those coming to accept the surrender[155] or render assistance and, in accordance with Protocol I, Article 37, such acts would be considered perfidy, since they invite 'the confidence of an adversary lead[ing] him to

---

tional and domestic law', 17 Yale J. Int'l Law 1992, 609. In 1998 it was reported that, under instruction from Churchill, during WW II the British military authorities had actually drawn up plans to assassinate Hitler, but they were never put into operation. See also Levie, 'Was the assassination of President Lincoln a war crime?' in Schmitt and Green, *Levie on the Law of War*, 1998, 437.

[149] Parks, 'Memorandum on the law', 6.

[150] E.g. the commando raid in Nov. 1941 against Field Marshal Rommel, 3 Churchill, *The Second World War*, 498; the Apr. 1943 US Air Force interception and destruction of the Japanese aircraft carrying Admiral Yamamoto, or the Oct. 1951, US Navy airstrike killing 500 senior Chinese and North Korean officers attending a military planning conference at Kapsan, N. Korea, Parks, 'Memorandum on the law', 5.

[151] See ch. 16 below.

[152] If a government learns that such an attempt is to be made, it should take all steps within its power to prevent it, *British Manual*, para. 115. When in 1806 the British government received an offer to assassinate Napoleon, they detained the man concerned and informed the French government, Rose, *Life of Napoleon*, vol. 2, 70. Equally, it is forbidden to put a price upon the head of a named individual belonging to the adverse party, as was done by the US against Noriega during the Panama campaign, 1989, *The Times*, 23 Dec. 1989. Similar action was taken against Gen. Aidid in Somalia in 1993, see Kelly, *Peace Operations* (Australian Govt. Publishing Service) 1997, 137, para. 904.

[153] Hague Regs, Art. 23(b).

[154] But it was not lawful for the Germans to destroy the Czech town of Lidice by way of reprisal.

[155] See n. 38 above.

believe that he is entitled to, or is obliged to accord, protection under the rules of international law applicable in armed conflict'. Although the terms 'treachery'[156] and 'perfidy' are used in both literature and conventions, the two are really synonymous and the more usual term in current usage is 'perfidy'. If the killing has been done under the apparent protection of an emblem like the red cross, the person responsible would be liable to trial for a grave breach under Protocol I.[157]

Stratagems and ruses

While perfidy is forbidden, stratagems and ruses are permitted.[158] These are measures taken to secure an advantage over the adverse party by seeking to mislead him, for example, as to the strength of the force opposing him, or to induce him to act recklessly. They infringe no rule of armed conflict law since they do not invite his confidence with respect to protection under that law. Neither the Hague Regulations nor Protocol I defines a stratagem or ruse, care must be taken to ensure that the act does not amount to bad faith, so that the adverse party must be aware during actual engagement that his opponent is who he purports to be, and is entitled to the status he claims.

In accordance with customary law it has been considered lawful to advance under the enemy flag or wearing enemy or even neutral uniform, so long as the correct insignia is worn during attack. Protocol I[159] prohibits the making 'use ... of the flags or military emblems, insignia or uniforms of neutral or other States not parties to the conflict [or those] ... of adverse Parties while engaging in attacks or in order to shield, favour, protect or impede military operations'.[160] The Article goes on to exclude from its scope any action considered lawful under general rules of international law appertaining to espionage, so that spies could still pass themselves off as members of the forces of the party against which they are operating. While such action would be legal, they could nevertheless be tried and executed as spies if captured. The Article expressly states that it does not 'affect the existing generally recognised rules of international law applicable ... to the use of flags in the conduct of naval warfare', so it would still be lawful to follow the practice

---

[156] This term should not be confused with 'war treason', often found in the literature. This may be defined as 'hostile acts committed inside the area controlled by the belligerent against whom the acts are directed by persons who do not possess the status of combatants', Greenspan, *The Modern Law of Land Warfare*, 330.

[157] Art. 85(1)(f); see ch. 18 below.

[158] Hague Regs, Art. 24; Pr. I, Art. 37(2). Rogers, the US *Operational Law Handbook* and the Australian *The Force of Law* are all silent on these.

[159] Art. 39.

[160] Since Art. 49 defines 'attack' as an act of violence, it implies that false marks could be worn during deployment. But the reference to shielding, favouring or protecting in Art. 39 would appear to extend to all manoeuvres preparatory to attack including deployment, thus abolishing any customary rule for those becoming parties to the Protocol.

of the Royal Navy in World War I and make use of 'Q-ships', vessels disguised as merchant ships or as belonging to the enemy until the moment of engagement, a practice also indulged in by the German Navy.[161]

Legitimate ruses in land warfare[162] include surprises; ambushes; feigned attacks or retreats; constructing works which it is not intended to use, including false airfields, munitions dumps, and the like, as was done in the United Kingdom prior to launching Operation Overlord in World War II;[163] transmitting false messages, so long as the wave lengths of, for example, medical aircraft, are not used for this purpose; allowing false information to fall into enemy hands, as was done with the floating off the Spanish coast of the 'man who never was' carrying false papers as to the second front landing zones; dressing a single unit in the uniforms of a variety of – or non-existing – units; removing identification marks from uniforms; giving false signals to induce the enemy to drop supplies, or enemy aircraft to land in hostile territory; pretending to communicate with non-existent units, and the like.[164] It was not an unlawful ruse during the Gulf War for Iraqi tanks to advance with their turrets reversed, even though this is occasionally taken as a sign of invitation to surrender: however, it is 'not a recognised indication of surrender *per se*'.[165] Feigning distress or making false claims of non-combatant status would amount to perfidy rather than be considered as legitimate ruses or stratagems.[166]

While it is lawful to employ false information to induce the adverse party to surrender by inducing him to believe, for example, that he is surrounded or about to be bombarded by batteries which do not exist, it is unlawful intentionally to lie to the enemy to suggest that an armistice has in fact been agreed upon.

Denial of quarter

Both Sun Tzu and Clausewitz pointed out that to achieve the ends for which war was undertaken it was unnecessary to kill all the enemy forces. However, in former times it was often the practice to deny quarter to the garrison of a fortress carried by assault, or to the garrison and citizens of a besieged city that had refused to surrender or continued to resist after it had become clear that resistance was pointless.[167] Nevertheless, the normal practice was not so extreme and this formed

---

[161] Colombos, *International Law of the Sea*, 497; see also *The Peacock* (1802) 4 C. Rob., 85, 187. For present position see, e.g., US *Annotated Supplement to Commander's Handbook on the Law of Naval Operations*, 1997, para. 12.5.1, and n. 13.

[162] *Ibid.*, 12.5.3.

[163] Churchill, *The Second World War*, 3:526.

[164] See, further, Bothe, *et al.*, 207.

[165] *Conduct of the Persian Gulf War*, p. O 21.

[166] *Annotated Supplement*, paras. 12.6, 12.7.

[167] See, e.g., Rothenberg, 'The age of Napoleon', in Howard, *The Laws of War*, 1994, 86, 92–4.

part of the basis for the ban on unnecessary suffering. In accordance with Hague Regulation 23(d) it is forbidden to declare that no quarter shall be given, while Protocol I, Article 40, extends the ban to cover a threat to deny quarter or conduct hostilities on the basis that it will not be afforded, as when a price is placed on an opponent's head.[168] Even today, subject to the ban on excessive injury to the civilian population, a refusal to surrender after it has become clear that resistance is pointless, may be met by a threat of complete destruction. In such circumstances, however, individual acts of surrender would still have to be honoured. Concomitant with the ban on denying quarter, is the prohibition to kill or wound an enemy after he has laid down his arms or is otherwise unable to defend himself and has surrendered unconditionally.[169] If having apparently offered to lay down his arms, he attempts to attack the person accepting his surrender he would be liable to trial as a war criminal.[170] It is questionable if a sniper who only offers to surrender after exhausting all his ammunition is entitled to be treated as others offering surrender.

Compulsory enlistment

It is not illegal to use propaganda to incite enemy civilians to rebel or enemy troops to mutiny or desert,[171] but it is forbidden to compel nationals of the adverse party to take part in warlike operations against their own state,[172] and by Article 51 of the Civilians Convention an Occupying Power[173] is forbidden to compel civilians belonging to the occupied territory to serve in the occupant's forces. This prohibition extends even to those who may have been serving in the occupant's forces before the outbreak of hostilities. If, however, such persons had given an oath of allegiance when enlisting they might find themselves charged under the criminal law if they refused to serve. If they continued to serve and were captured by their national forces, they would face a charge of treason.[174] If persons taken prisoner

[168] See n. 152 above, re Noriega and Aidid.

[169] Re prisoners of war, see ch. 10 below. See *Annotated Supplement*, para. 6.2.5, at p. 6-28.

[170] This would probably be considered perfidious.

[171] Leaflets were dropped over Japanese troops in Burma during World War II in the shape of the chrysanthemum (*kiri* – Japan's national emblem) leaf indicating that bombs would fall as heavily as the leaf, but out of season and calling on them to surrender; similar surrender leaflets were dropped during the Gulf War, *Conduct of the Persian Gulf War*, pp. O 18, O 30. In both, the leaflet was to serve as a safe-conduct for any enemy personnel in possession and offering to surrender. Similar leaflets were dropped over German forces in Europe, but after the German surrender in Amsterdam in 1945 the Canadian forces handed two deserters back to the German command and they were sentenced to death, see Levie, *Prisoners of War in International Armed Conflict*, 1979, 335, n. 102, and Canadian Broadcasting Corp. 'Fifth estate – Canada and German prisoners of war', 24 Mar. 1998.

[172] Hague Regs, Art. 23(h).

[173] See ch. 12 below.

[174] See Green, *Essays*, 1999, ch. XI 'The Azad Hind Fauj'.

are willing to serve in the captor's force, the captor should refuse such offers since by Article 7 of the Prisoners of War Convention there is an absolute ban on prisoners giving up their rights under the Convention, and such enlistment would have this result. In view of this there is a presumption that captured personnel retain their status as prisoners of war until their release or recovery by their own forces,[175] and any prisoner enlisting in this way would remain liable to his national criminal law.[176] To compel civilians or captured military personnel to serve in the captor's or occupant's forces constitutes a war crime. While it is unlawful to enlist prisoners in the captor's force, it is permissible to invite them to broadcast propaganda, or calls for rebellion or desertion. Any prisoner responding to this invitation retains his status as a prisoner of war, although he becomes liable to prosecution and punishment under his own criminal law.[177] The same treatment is afforded to any civilian who behaves in this way.[178] Members of the armed forces taken prisoner should not volunteer false statements, but it is not unlawful for them to give false information in response to questions by their captors.

Although it does not seem that many Soviet personnel were suborned by the *mujahudin* in Afghanistan during the conflict leading to that country's liberation, a number of them were induced to convert to Islam in order to avoid torture or execution.[179]

In an attempt to assist personnel who may be captured and subjected to pressure directed at their subornation, a number of countries have introduced special courses directed to this end. As happened in Korea and Vietnam, many American prisoners were 'for the most part ignorant of the law and were consequently unaware of the legal basis for their actions during the conflict.[180] Many prisoners succumbed to their captors' accusations that those acts constituted war crimes and confessed to such "crimes". Undoubtedly many of those confessions were exacted under physical and psychological torture. Nevertheless, many repatriated prisoners were left with feelings of guilt not only because they had "confessed" but also

---

[175] See, e.g., the *Gozawa* trial (1946) in which a Japanese accused of murdering an Indian prisoner was unable to prove that this prisoner of war by joining the Indian National Army had become subject to Japanese military law as a *heiho* (private) in the Japanese Army (Sleeman, *The Gozawa Trial* lxiii–lxv, 121, 195–8).

[176] During World War II and until 1949 there was nothing to prevent a captor from enlisting captured personnel into his own armed forces or into units specially organised or, as in the case of the Indian National Army (see Green, 'The Indian National Army trials', 11 M.L.R. (1948), 47), into a separate army organised for the purpose of liberating colonial territory belonging to the adverse party, but they would still be liable to the national criminal law if recaptured, see Green, *loc.cit.* and n. 174 above.

[177] E.g., *US* v. *Fleming* (1957) 23 C.M.R., 7, 20, 25, 12 F.2d 962, 976.

[178] See, e.g., *R.* v. *Steane* [1947] 1 K.B., 997, 1005–1006; *Gillars* v. *US* (1950) 182 F.2d 962, 76; *D'Aquino* v. *US* (Tokyo Rose) (1951) 192 F.2d, 338, 358; *Joyce* v. *D.P.P.* ('Lord Haw-Haw') [1946] A.C. 347.

[179] *The Times* (London), 26 May 1992.

[180] See, e.g., attempts directed against Dr. Cornum when captured by the Iraqis, Cornum, *She Went to War*, 1992.

because they harboured doubts as to the legality of their conduct, and that of their nation, during the conflict … [T]he chances of prisoners of war surviving their captivity would be enhanced if they could be certain in their own minds that they had not breached international law before capture'.[181] This emphasises the need to teach the law of armed conflict in peacetime rather than making use of a 'crash course' when hostilities begin.

Permitted practices

The law of armed conflict does not forbid acts of sabotage, so long as the object of the sabotage is a legitimate military objective. Saboteurs, generally, are persons operating behind the lines of the adverse party, including his home territory, to commit acts of destruction. If in uniform they are combatants and entitled to prisoner of war status if captured. Civilian saboteurs or military saboteurs not in uniform are not so protected,[182] and are liable to be treated on capture as spies. International law permits the employment of spies, but if captured they may be tried in accordance with the law of the captor and may be sentenced to death, but to punish them without a proper trial[183] is a war crime.[184]

A spy is one who collects information[185] clandestinely behind enemy lines while wearing civilian clothing.[186] Any person who collects information while in uniform retains his status as a combatant, is liable to be fired upon like any other member of the armed forces, and if captured is to be treated as a prisoner of war and not as a spy any more than one penetrating enemy lines to deliver dispatches to his own forces or messages to the enemy.[187] This is equally true of a civilian on a similar undertaking.

To avoid the risk of being treated as spies, members of the armed forces engaged in the collecting of information or sabotage in enemy or enemy-occupied territory should, whenever possible, wear uniform.[188] Members of the armed

[181] Hickling, 'Training to win – lawfully', in Smith *The Force of Law* (Australian Defence Studies Centre) 1994, 93, 96, citing American teaching practice; see now, Protocol I, Art. 82, 83 (1), 87 (2).

[182] See, e.g., *Ex p. Quirin* (1942) 317 US 1.

[183] Hague Regs, Art. 30.

[184] See *Re Rhode, Zeuss and Others* (1946) 13 Ann. Dig., 294 (Webb, *The Natzweiler Trial*).

[185] Hague Regs, Art. 24: 'measures necessary for obtaining information about the enemy and the country are considered permissible'.

[186] On the status of spies as combatants or otherwise, see ch. 6 above.

[187] Hague Regs, Art. 29.

[188] If forces personnel wear civilian clothing over or under their uniform to facilitate escape they run the risk of being treated as spies if captured, although it is not the general practice so to treat escaping prisoners who wear civilian clothing or even enemy uniform to assist in their escape. Moreover, by Prisoners of War Convention, Art. 6, captives claiming prisoner-of-war status are entitled to be treated as such until the contrary is proved, see ch. 6 above. On Prisoners of War generally, see ch. 10 below.

forces who have evaded capture while engaged in espionage cannot be charged as spies if subsequently captured, but must be treated as prisoners of war.[189] The same immunity attaches to a civilian spy who regains his national territory and subsequently falls into enemy hands. However, civilian residents of occupied territory committing espionage or sabotage there may be punished for such acts whenever they are captured, even if not captured while engaged in the act in question. This is not so in the case of members of national liberation movements engaged in a conflict seeking self-determination,[190] nor to members of properly organised guerrilla movements or of a *levée en masse* while engaged in those capacities.[191]

Persons assisting in the escape of saboteurs, spies or escaped prisoners of war are liable to trial in accordance with the law of the belligerent against whose interests they have been acting[192] or, if in occupied territory, in accordance with the law of the occupying authority. Such acts are not contrary to the law of armed conflict unless the person involved enjoys a protected status incompatible with such action.[193] They are always entitled to a fair trial.

The problem of aircrews

By Article 29 of the Hague Regulations 'persons sent in balloons for the purpose of carrying dispatches and, generally, of maintaining communications between the different parts of an army or a territory' are not to be treated as spies. This exemption is now extended to a person in an aircraft, although if captured in civilian clothing he may be charged with espionage and punished if this be proved. The crew of an aircraft carrying spies cannot be treated as such unless there is clear evidence that they have themselves been guilty of spying. This is also true of members of the armed forces travelling in military aircraft of their own country, even in civilian clothing. Members of the forces, including personnel from crashed aircraft, wearing civilian clothing to facilitate escape have the burden of proving they are not spies.

It is generally considered a rule of customary law that aircrew baling out of a damaged aircraft are *hors de combat* and immune from attack whether by enemy aircraft or from the ground.[194] Protocol I, Article 42, has made this part of treaty

---

[189] Hague Regs, Art. 31.

[190] Pr. I, Art. 1(4).

[191] See ch. 6 above.

[192] See, e.g., trial of Nurse Edith Cavell in World War I, Green, *Essays*.

[193] As appears to have been the case with Edith Cavell, although by assisting escapees she had abused her protected status.

[194] Hague Regulations on Air Warfare, 1923 (Schindler and Toman, 207; see, on aerial warfare, ch. 9 below), Art. 20. Though unadopted these are generally regarded as indicative of customary law (*ibid.*, see also Spaight, *Air*, n. 37 above, 420–43). In World War I and II there were many instances of such persons being fired upon by aircraft and from the ground.

law. Should such a person land in the territory of an adverse party he must be given an opportunity to surrender before being made the object of attack, unless it is apparent that he is engaged in a hostile act, such as destruction of his aircraft or sending a radio signal to indicate his location. If while descending he manoeuvres his parachute so as to land behind his own lines he may be fired upon, as he may if he succeeds in this, but if he is wounded he is protected by Geneva Convention III.[195]

The ban on shooting down those descending by parachute does not extend to the dropping of agents or parachute troops,[196] and airborne troops in civilian clothing or enemy uniform are not entitled to combatant status.[197] To protect aircrew in aircraft used by paratroops, the former should wear a uniform easily distinguishable from that worn by the latter, although in practice this may be difficult to determine by those on the ground.

The treatment of enemy property

Property taken from the adverse party, members of its forces or its nationals, provided it may be lawfully seized, belongs to the state and not to the individual captor. Property, other than personal effects, taken from those captured,[198] wounded or dead is known as booty. It is forbidden to steal from prisoners of war or the sick and wounded,[199] or to mutilate or steal from corpses.[200] Any property lawfully removed from them, such as weaponry or identity tags from corpses, belongs to the capturing authority and must be returned if of a personal character.[201]

Save in the case of absolute necessity,[202] it is forbidden to seize or destroy submarine cables connecting an occupied with a neutral territory, and should this occur they must be restored and compensation paid when peace is restored.[203] The

[195] Schindler and Toman, 373.

[196] Pr. I, Art. 42(3).

[197] In World War II it was alleged that German paratroops wore both Dutch and French uniforms, but Germany maintained that they had in fact worn a uniform distinct from that of other German forces and were so entitled to combatant status, Spaight, *op.cit.*, 104–5.

[198] They are entitled to retain their uniform and decorations as well as items, e.g., helmets, necessary for their personal defence. After Noriega had surrendered in Panama he was originally, wrongly, deprived of his uniform and decorations, but was subsequently permitted to wear them, and did so throughout his trial on drug charges, see Albert, *The Case Against the General*, 1993, ch. 12.

[199] See, e.g., Convention I (Wounded and Sick) 1949, Art. 15. After her capture, Dr. Cornum's wedding ring and necklace were taken and not returned, *op.cit.*, 45, 173–4.

[200] Thus, the taking of, e.g., ears for the purpose of a body count, as during the Vietnam war, is forbidden.

[201] See, e.g., Convention III (Prisoners of War), Art. 18.

[202] See, e.g., *Eastern Extension, Australasia and China Telegraph Co.* Claim (1923) 6 R.I.A.A., 112; *Cuba Submarine Telegraph Co.* (1923) *ibid.*, 118.

[203] Hague Regs, Art. 54.

British *Manual* suggests that this only applies to those portions of the cable which lie on land, when no compensation would be due, or in territorial waters and not beyond those limits.[204] Cables joining one part of enemy territory with another may be destroyed, although if they belong to private citizens compensation may be due. Cables joining the territories of two belligerents may be severed at the option of either, although intelligence requirements may militate against this.[205] With the developments in radio and satellite communication, this provision in the regulations may have fallen into desuetude.

Property belonging to the enemy authorities may be seized,[206] as may all means of transport and communication, subject to the provisions concerning submarine cables, including those used for the transmission of news even though belonging to private individuals, but these must be restored at the end of the conflict and compensation paid.[207] Occasionally, for propaganda purposes a belligerent may allow enemy news reporters to continue sending information, particularly that regarding damage done by the enemy, as was done by Iraq during the Gulf War 1991 and in 1999 during NATO's bombing of Yugoslavia. As to enemy property generally, this may not be seized or destroyed unless imperatively demanded by the necessities of war.[208] By Protocol I[209] attacks are 'limited strictly to military objectives ... those objects which by their nature, location, purpose or use make an effective contribution to military action and whose total or partial destruction, capture or neutralisation, in the circumstances ruling at the time, offers a definite military advantage'. Buildings, transports and other installations used exclusively for medical purposes must not be attacked.[210] Similar immunity attaches to buildings dedicated to religion, art, science or charitable purposes together with historic monuments,[211] so long as these are not being used for military purposes. Such places must be distinctively marked and the emblem used notified to the adverse party beforehand.[212] The definition of cultural property is spelled out in the Hague Convention for the Protection of Cultural Property in the Event of Armed Conflict:[213]

[204] *The British Manual.*, para. 597, n. 2.
[205] See Schwarzenberger, *International Law*, vol. 2, *The Law of Armed Conflict*, ch. 35.
[206] For the rights of an occupant, see ch. 15 below.
[207] Hague Regs, Art. 53. See, however, *N.V. De Bataafscht Petroleum Maatschappij* v. *The War Damage Commission* (Singapore Oil Stocks Case – 1955, Singapore) 23 I.L.R., 8, 10.
[208] Hague Regs, Art. 23(g).
[209] Pr. I, Art. 52(2).
[210] See ch. 11 below, re treatment of wounded and sick.
[211] Problems arise with regard to war and similar military monuments in occupied territory, particularly if that territory is in the hands of a victor. Since the Cultural Property Convention only protects items 'of great cultural importance to the cultural heritage of every people', war memorials do not fall within its purview.
[212] Hague Regs, Art. 27.
[213] 1954, Art. 1, 249 U.N.T.S. 215 (Schindler and Toman, 745). By the Protocol to the Convention (*ibid.*, 777), the export of such property from occupied territory is forbidden. Iraq ratified the Protocol in 1967 and Kuwait in 1970, so removal of such property from Kuwait to Iraq in 1990 was in breach of this Protocol.

(a) movable or immovable property of great cultural importance to the cultural heritage of every people,[214] such as monuments of architecture, art or history, whether religious or secular; archaeological sites;[215] groups of buildings which, as a whole, are of historic or artistic interest; works of art; manuscripts, books and other objects of artistic, historical or archaeological interest; as well as scientific collections and important collections of books or archives or of reproductions of [such] property;[216]

(b) buildings whose main and effective purpose[217] is to preserve or exhibit cultural property ... such as museums, large libraries and depositaries of archives, and refuges intended to shelter, in the event of armed conflict, the movable cultural property so defined ...;

(c) centres containing a large amount of cultural property as [so] defined ... to be known as 'centres containing monuments'.

The distinctive emblem introduced by the Convention consists of a shield comprising a royal blue square, one of the angles of which forms the point of the shield and of a royal blue triangle above the square, the space on either side being taken up by a white triangle, and this should be displayed singly or in triangular formation. All such cultural property is protected, regardless of origin or ownership and belligerents not parties to the Convention remain bound by Article 27 of the Hague Regulations.

Closely related to this Convention is that on Means of Prohibiting and Preventing the Illicit Import, Export and Transfer of Ownership of Cultural Property,[218] which includes within its prohibitions the sale in peacetime of such property seized during conflict.[219]

The protection extended by Protocol I to religious establishments is somewhat narrow, for it refers only to places of worship 'which constitute the cultural or spiritual heritage of peoples,'[220] suggesting that ordinary places of worship are

---

[214] Protection does not extend to every object regarded as of cultural significance or part of the national heritage by the country of location. It protects those items, such as the Colosseum, the Sphinx, the Taj Mahal, the *Mona Lisa*, Picasso's *Guernica*, the Chagall Windows at the Hadassah Hospital in Jerusalem, and the like, considered part of the cultural heritage of the entire world.

[215] For the Gulf War 1991, see US Report, *Conduct of the Persian Gulf War* above, p. O 14; 3 I.L.M., 615 at 626.

[216] Views as to the items concerned may be subjective. In many instances these items are of the type likely to be attractive to individual members of the forces and the subject of looting. This was the case after the Gulf War when British troops took the Gulf soccer gold cup back with them to England, where it was discovered in an antique shop and returned to Kuwait. Also views as to the items concerned may vary from period to period.

[217] The mere fact that a building houses such a treasure will not bring it within the definition.

[218] 1970, 10 I.L.M., 289.

[219] See *Autocephalus Greek Orthodox Church of Cyprus and Republic of Cyprus* v. *Goldberg and Feldman Fine Arts Inc.* (1990) 917 F.2d 278, re property seized by the unrecognised Turkish authorities in Cyprus.

[220] Art. 53.

protected only by the Hague Regulations, while the Protocol applies to such well-known religious establishments as the Vatican, St Paul's Cathedral, Dome of the Rock, Mecca and Medina. Any religious establishment used for military purposes loses its protection, as happened with the monastery at Monte Cassino in 1944; while in the Gulf War Coalition aircraft refrained from attacking military objectives in the vicinity of religious or other cultural establishments.[221]

Enemy-owned public property in the territory of a belligerent is subject to seizure, although diplomatic buildings are placed under protection pending return on the re-establishment of relations after the cessation of hostilities. Private property is often placed in sequestration in the hands of an administrator and is likely to be returned to its private owners at the end of hostilities.[222]

Precautions in attack[223]

The general rule regarding active warfare is established by Article 25 of the Hague Regulations forbidding any 'attack or bombardment by any means whatever, of towns, villages, dwellings or buildings which are undefended'.[224] This rule applies to any attack, whether in offence or defence, directed against the land or establishments thereon, whether from land, sea or air, a fact now clarified by Protocol I.[225] Legitimate military objectives[226] within a city in enemy territory, even though well behind the lines – including within its mainland – may be attacked since, such a city, though it may be technically undefended, cannot be occupied without opposition,[227] unless, in accordance with the rule concerning proportionality, the damage to civilians and civilian property would be so excessive, compared with the military purpose to be secured, measured by the overall objective, as to render the attack indiscriminate[228] and unlawful. Article 52 of Protocol I has shifted the emphasis from the concept of defence to that of military objective and all attacks should now be limited to military objectives. All objectives which are not military are considered civilian, and may not be made the object of direct attack or of reprisals. Injury caused to civilians or civilian objects incidental to a legitimate attack against a military objective does not render the attack illegal.[229]

---

[221] US Report, *Conduct of the Persian Gulf War*, p. O 14., at 626 of I.L.M.

[222] See Rogers, *op.cit.*, ch. 3; *Operational Law Handbook*, paras. 18-2, 18-3; Fleck, *op.cit.*, paras. 411, 457.

[223] See, e.g., *Oppenheim*, vol. 2, s. 102; see also Schwarzenberger, *International Law*, vol. 2, 84–9.

[224] For definition of 'undefended places', see ch. 6 above.

[225] Art. 49(30).

[226] See, however, comments by Tokyo court in *Shimoda* v. *Japan* (1963) 32 I.L.R. 626, 631–2.

[227] See text to n. 23 above. See also Fleck, *op.cit.*, paras. 441–9.

[228] See under 'Protection of civilians' below.

[229] As to the attack on the Al-Firdus/Al-Amariyah Bunker during the Gulf War, 14 Feb. 1991, when heavy civilian casualties ensued, see US Report, *Conduct of the Persian Gulf*

If the commander has any doubt in his mind whether an object normally dedicated to civilian purposes is being used to make an effective contribution to military action, he should give it the benefit of the doubt.[230] In practice, the commander will have to use his discretion, for the location and surrounding situation may make the object a military objective, as might be the case of a dwelling-house in the centre of a combat area or in the event of street and house-to-house fighting. Even in such circumstances, however, the rule of proportionality must be observed. To minimise unnecessary or excessive suffering, those who plan or decide upon an attack must do everything feasible, that is to say practicable or practically possible in the light of all the circumstances, including those of a military nature, to verify that the objectives about to be attacked are neither civilians nor civilian objects, nor specially protected, but are in fact military objectives, and that there is no other specific prohibition against their being attacked.[231] He must also take all feasible precautions in the light of the attack as a whole, and not merely of that part of it in which he is himself engaged, to avoid and minimise civilian losses.[232]

Should it become apparent that the object to be attacked is not a military objective, for example a locality abandoned by the adverse party, or is subject to special protection, the commander at the scene responsible for the proposed attack must ensure that it does not take place or is abandoned.[233] He must abandon or suspend the attack if it should become apparent[234] that it may cause civilian damage excessive to the military advantage anticipated.[235] As always, this relates to the military operations as a whole and not merely the particular operation in which the commander is involved. If a choice is possible among military objectives, the one attacked should be that likely to cause the least civilian damage.

In the light of the prevailing military situation, advance warning should be given of any attack which might affect the civilian population,[236] a requirement already included in the Hague Regulations,[237] except when surprise is of the essence. It is also to be found in Hague Convention IX regarding the bombardment of the land from the sea.[238] There is no similar rule regarding aerial bombardment, but before the use of the atomic bomb against Hiroshima in World War II the Japanese authorities were warned that named cities were likely to be heavily bombarded and that civilians should be evacuated. Similar warnings were

War, p. O 14, at 626 of I.L.M. See also, *Operational Law Handbook*, para. 18-2; Rogers, *op.cit.*, 45, 78.

[230] See Pr. I, Art. 52(3); Fleck, *op.cit.*, para. 446.
[231] Pr. I, Art. 57(2)(a)(i).
[232] Art. 57(2)(a)(ii).
[233] Art. 57(2)(b).
[234] This means that he must always make sure that his intelligence is up to date.
[235] Art. 57(2)(b).
[236] Art. 57(2)(c). See also Rogers, *op.cit.*, 48–51.
[237] Art. 26.
[238] Schindler and Toman, 811, Art. 6. See also *Annotated Supplement*, paras. 8.5, 8.6.1, 11.2.

occasionally given in the European theatre.[239] By Protocol I,[240] in the conduct of air or naval operations all 'reasonable precautions' must be taken to avoid loss of civilian lives and damage to civilian property, and this too may require advance warning. During the Falklands War, when the British commander in the Goose Green Area called on his Argentine opposite number to surrender, he warned him that, if this was refused by the stated time, 'in accordance with the terms of the Geneva Conventions and the laws of war, you shall be held responsible for the fate of any civilians in Goose Green and we, in accordance with the laws, give you prior notice of our intention'. Since the law of armed conflict now[241] seeks to protect the environment by the prohibition to use any means or methods of warfare which is intended or may be expected to cause widespread, long-term and[242] severe damage thereto, care must be taken to ensure that any such damage does not prejudice the health or survival of the population. If the damage can be confined to a small locality it would probably not be unlawful while, the damage caused must be lasting and not transient, though there is nothing in the law to indicate how this is determined. For parties to the ENMOD Convention the obligation is widened to prevent damage to any other state party and not merely, as in Protocol I, to the civilian population. Environmental modification[243] techniques are defined as any technique for changing, through the deliberate manipulation of natural processes, the dynamics, composition or structure of the earth, including its biota,[244] lithosphere,[245] hydrosphere[246] and atmosphere,[247] or outer space.

Dangerous installations

Though they may be military objectives, Protocol I, Article 56, prohibits any attack upon dams, dykes and nuclear electrical generating stations if the result would be to release dangerous forces and consequent severe losses among the

---

[239] See, e.g., Spaight, *Air Power*, 242–3. In 1945, the German commander of Munster was warned the city would be intensely bombarded if he did not surrender and on his refusal this threat was carried out. Warnings were also occasionally given by the UN command during the Korean war 1950–53, see Greenspan, *The Modern Law*, 340.

[240] Art. 57(4).

[241] Pr. I, Arts 35, 55.

[242] These conditions are cumulative.

[243] Blix, 'Arms control'. The term 'modification' indicates permanence or durability. See also definition from *Operational Law Handbook*, above.

[244] Animal and plant life, thus forbidding long-term defoliation and the like. It should be noted that when the United States ratified the 1925 Geneva Gas Protocol it reserved the right to use herbicides 'for control of vegetation within US bases and installations and around their immediate defensive perimeters', 14 I.L.M. 299.

[245] The earth's crust, thus forbidding artificial earthquakes.

[246] The earth's water surface, so as to forbid, e.g., deviation of the Gulf Stream.

[247] The gaseous envelope surrounding the earth, including within the prohibition any adverse modification of Van Allen's radiation belt.

civilian population. The two are cumulative and though dangerous forces might be released, an attack would be legitimate if, for example, it were away from an urban centre and would not affect the civilian population. 'Underlying the prohibition ... is a sort of "worst case" analysis, an assessment which deems the serious risk of releasing dangerous forces to constitute an unacceptably high risk of collateral damage. In view of the risk potential inherent in the respective installations, that assessment is doubtless correct. It is nearly inconceivable that massive risks to the civilian population could ever be outweighed by military considerations so as to justify an attack on such installations used for purely civilian purposes. The attack is accordingly strictly prohibited and cannot be justified by any claim of military necessity, except under the exception of paragraph 2 of Article 56.'[248] The list is exhaustive, so that any other installation would remain a legitimate object for attack even though such forces were released causing losses to the civilian population, so long as those losses were not excessive or unnecessary contrary to the rule on proportionality. Other military objectives in the vicinity of such dams, dykes or nuclear electrical generating stations are also immune if an attack might by way, for example, of blast, cause the release of dangerous forces from the named installations and consequent severe losses among the civilian population. States not party to the Protocol are not so bound and may attack such installations, subject to the rules concerning proportionality and unnecessary suffering, which may mean that their freedom is similarly limited. The protection afforded such an installation ceases if it is used for other than its normal function, and for all such installations and nearby military objectives 'only if they are used in regular, significant and direct support of military operations and if such attack is the only feasible way to terminate such support'.[249]

While belligerents must avoid locating military objectives near such protected works, they may erect emplacements necessary for their defence. The armament of these must be limited to weapons capable only of repelling hostile attacks against the protected works or installations.[250] In view of the difficulty of distinguishing between offensive and defensive weapons today, it is difficult to deter-

---

[248] Oeter, 'Methods and means of combat', in Fleck, *op.cit.*, 105, at 195, para. 4. See also *Annotated Supplement*, para. 8.5.1.7.

[249] Art. 56(2). This would mean that the 'dam-buster' raids during World War II directed against hydroelectric sources in the Ruhr used for the manufacture of munitions would have been legal even if the Pr. had been in force then (5 Churchill, *The Second World War* 63). Problems arise when, as with the Mohne Dam, large numbers of civilians live in the area. The principle of proportionality then applies. The situation is even more complex when the occupant of the installation has, in breach of the obligations towards civilians in occupied territory (Civilians Conv. Arts 40, 49, 51), brought numbers of displaced persons for employment as 'slave labour' in war industry and intermingled them with the local population. Then, a commander, regardless of any question of proportionality, will have to use his discretion. If the displaced persons were brought to secure immunity from attack for a legitimate military objective, it would be in breach of the law (Pr. I, Arts 51(7), 58(b)), and punishable as a war crime.

[250] Pr. I, Art. 56(5).

mine how it would be ascertained that this weaponry is only capable of repelling an unlawful hostile attack.

Confirming customary law, the Protocol[251] authorises parties to agree between themselves on any additional protection they may wish to provide for 'objects containing dangerous forces', thus including within the classification other installations. To facilitate identification the parties are urged to mark them with three bright orange circles arranged on the same axis, although failure to do so does not affect their immunity.[252] But how is an attacker to know, other than from his own intelligence activities, that an unmarked installation is in fact protected and immune from attack?

Even when these installations are attacked, civilians remain entitled to the protection accorded them under international law, including the precautionary measures envisaged by the Protocol. If the protection afforded the installations ceases, there is still an obligation to take all practical precautions to prevent the escape of dangerous forces, although it is difficult to see how the party launching the attack will, in practice, be able to prevent such consequences.

Finally, reprisals against such installations are forbidden.[253]

Protection of civilians[254]

In accordance with customary law, now given treaty recognition by Article 51 of Protocol I, direct attack against the civilian population and objects is forbidden and they are protected against dangers arising from military operations. While this does not save them from incidental – collateral – injury resulting from an offensive attack, it means that the defending force should, so far as possible, not locate military objectives in the vicinity of civilian habitations or objects, nor should the presence or movement of civilians be used to protect an area from military operations, or to shield military objectives from attack,[255] or to shield, favour or impede military operations undertaken by the attacker or defender.[256]

It is also forbidden to indulge in acts or threats of violence, including those made by radio or psychological warfare,[257] the primary purpose of which is to spread terror among the civilian population. Raids like the World War II attacks against Rotterdam, Coventry or Dresden, or the threat of such raids against Baghdad in 1990, are unlawful, but a warning to the civilian population to induce the

---

[251] Art. 56(6).

[252] Art. 56(7).

[253] Art. 56(4).

[254] See Gasser, 'Protection of the civilian population', in Fleck, *op.cit.*, ch. 5; *Operational Law Handbook*, ch. 13; Rogers, *op.cit.*, 7–14; *Annotated Supplement*, para. 11.3.

[255] Iraq's detention of foreign civilians in the vicinity of vital centres in 1990 to deter attack after its annexation of Kuwait is a clear breach of the law.

[256] Pr. I, Art. 51(7).

[257] This would not forbid such leaflets raids as those described in n. 171 above.

surrender of a town or its evacuation by civilians would probably not fall under the ban.[258] Neither civilians nor the civilian population may be made the object of reprisals.[259]

This means that their protection against indiscriminate attack remains obligatory, even if the adverse party violates these prohibitions, and this obligation extends to the precautionary measures that have to be taken when launching an attack whether in offence or defence.[260] Indiscriminate acts by whatever weapons or means and in whatever theatres are forbidden, although for the purposes of Protocol I any attack from the sea or air must be directed against targets on land. Article 51(4) of Protocol I defines indiscriminate as those not directed at a specific military objective or employing means or methods which cannot be so directed or whose effects cannot be limited as required by the Protocol concerning protection of the wounded and sick, civilians and civilian objects, as well as prohibitions relating to protected places and excessive non-military damage, and which are of a nature likely to strike military objectives and civilians or civilian objects without distinction.[261]

While Protocol I provides the first definition of indiscriminate attacks, customary law concerning the distinction between military and non-military objectives and the rule regarding proportionality are directed to this end. Article 51(5)(b) expressly refers to the proportionality rule by giving as an example an attack 'which may be expected to cause incidental loss of civilian life, injury to civilians, damage to civilian objects, or a combination thereof, which would be excessive in relation to the concrete and direct military advantage anticipated'.[262] This relates to command discretion in the light of all information, including the advantage to the overall military operation. To determine the specificity of an objective may require prior reconnaissance to ensure that it is in fact a military objective, and the attack must follow so soon afterwards that the attacking commander may be reasonably certain that what was observed to be a legitimate objective is likely to have remained so at the time of attack. If a number of clearly distinct and separate military objectives are located in an area containing a concentration of civilians or civilian objects, these may not be the subject of a single area attack, so that the area bombing attacks of World War II would now be illegal. This does not mean, however, that merely because a built-up area exists the larger area is no longer a military objective, but the civilian areas within it should be clearly defined, and the rule of proportionality should always be observed. It would follow that 'blind' weapons, such as the German V-1 and V-2 of World War

---

[258] Such as were directed against Hiroshima and other cities during World War II.

[259] Pr. I, Art. 51(6).

[260] See *Annotated Handbook*, para 9.1.2; Rogers, *op.cit.*, 19–24; Fleck, *op.cit.*, paras. 404, 455–6.

[261] Art. 51(8).

[262] See, e.g., Fenrick, 'The rule of proportionality and Protocol I in Conventional Warfare', 98 Mil.Law Rev. (1982), 91; see also Report to Congress, *Conduct of the Persian Gulf War*, App. O, O-10, at 622 of I.L.M.

II and the Scud missiles launched by Iraq against Israel and Saudi Arabia during the Gulf War, are illegal, although as seen earlier it is not certain if this would apply to nuclear weapons, even though their effects cannot be limited.

With the possible exception of nuclear weapons, any weapons, including those of a bacteriological, biological or chemical nature, whose effects are uncontrollable so as to expose civilians to risks which are excessive in relation to the military objective to be achieved are illegal. Similarly, delayed action weapons, such as time bombs, likely to affect civilians and combatants alike, should be fitted with a device rendering them safe after a reasonable time has elapsed.[263] If minefields are sown in areas where civilians are likely to be, they should be marked with warning signs, although the use of mines has now been regulated, as has the use of explosive devices attached to objects likely to appeal to civilians constituting booby traps.[264] For parties to the 1998 Treaty, the use of mines has been banned.

Violation by a belligerent of any of these rules does not entitle the adverse party to declare that he regards himself free of the obligation to conduct his hostilities in accordance with these rules, as was contended by Germany in World War II as justification for denying protection to Soviet personnel, especially political commissars, an order condemned as illegal by the Nuremberg Tribunal. However, particular rules may be dispensed with when a treaty so provides, or if a belligerent in adhering to a treaty has added a reservation that it will be bound only so long as the adverse party observes the treaty, as has been done by most of the parties to the 1925 Geneva Gas Protocol. However, as pointed out by the World Court,[265]

> it is the compatibility of a reservation with the object and purpose of the Convention that must furnish the criterion for the attitude of a State in making the reservation as well as for the appraisal which it must make, individually and from its own standpoint, of the admissibility of any reservation ... As no State can be bound by a reservation to which it has not consented, it necessarily follows that each State objecting to it will or will not ... consider the reserving State to be a party to the Convention.

Further, by the Vienna Convention on Treaties[266] a reservation 'incompatible with the object and purpose of the treaty' is invalid. Since the Hague and Geneva law on armed conflict are humanitarian in character, it may be argued that any reservation detracting from their humanitarian purposes would be equally invalid. Finally, rules may be temporarily dispensed with if such action is by way of legitimate reprisal.[267]

---

[263] This is an adaptation of a rule of naval warfare law which provides that unanchored contact mines must become harmless one hour after they cease to be under control of the minelayer, or immediately they break away from their anchors, while torpedoes which miss their mark must become harmless immediately, Hague Convention VIII, 1907, Schindler and Toman, 803.

[264] See text to n. 120 above.

[265] *Reservations to the Convention on Genocide* [1951] I.C.J. 15, 24, 26.

[266] 1969, 8 I.L.M., 679, Art. 19(c).

[267] See text to nn. 12–17 above.

8

Conduct of hostilities: maritime

The law of maritime warfare is based on the customary rules of warfare with regard to unnecessary suffering, indiscriminate attack, respect for those *hors de combat*, and to the extent that they are applicable to the maritime theatre those principles embodied in the Hague Regulations annexed to Hague Convention IV, 1907,[1] concerning the rules and customs of warfare on land which may be considered to be declaratory of customary rules relating to armed conflict in general. These principles are supplemented by such rules as are necessary by reason of the theatre in which the conflict is being waged.

Area of operations

The law of maritime warfare[2] relates to conflict between naval vessels – warships – at sea, the relations between belligerent warships and merchant ships belonging to the adverse party[3] and to neutrals,[4] the right of a warship to attack targets on land,[5] the limitations upon targeting at sea,[6] the right of belligerent warships in neutral territory,[7] and the rights of a combatant towards enemy or neutral shipping within its territory,[8] that is to say its ports, territorial sea, perhaps also, to a limited

---

[1] Schindler and Toman, 63.

[2] See *San Remo Manual on International Law Applicable to Armed Conflicts at Sea, 1995*; US *Annotated Supplement to the Commander's Handbook on the Law of Naval Operations*, 1997, Part II – The Law of Naval Warfare.

[3] *Annotated Supplement*, para. 8.2.2.

[4] Para. 7.10.

[5] Para. 8.5.

[6] Para. 8.1.

[7] Paras. 7.3.2, 7.3.2.1.

[8] Paras. 7.3.2, 7.3.2.1, 7.3.2.2.

extent, its exclusive economic zone, inland lakes and waterways,[9] and the air space above.[10]

Within these areas and in the vicinity of naval operations a belligerent is permitted to set restrictions upon the activities of neutral vessels and aircraft and may even forbid them entry. Any vessel or aircraft ignoring such instructions may be fired upon or captured. If their activities are likely to endanger his operations, a belligerent commander may control the communications of any neutral vessel or aircraft, but such control should not normally interfere with legitimate distress signals.

A belligerent may also establish exclusion zones,[11] normally covering vast sea areas and not necessarily connected with a zone of operations. Any vessel or aircraft entering such an exclusion zone lays itself open to attack on sight. Exclusion zones were established in both world wars as well as in the Falklands War. During World War II the German Navy operated a submarine sink-on-sight policy against any shipping in an operation or exclusion zone, but the Nuremberg Tribunal[12] held that such a policy directed against neutral merchant shipping was illegal, and implied that it was only lawful against belligerent merchant vessels when they were incorporated into the belligerent war effort – as in fact was the case with most belligerent merchant ships which carried supplies to and from belligerent states, for most of these travelled in convoy protected by naval vessels and many were armed with defensive weapons.

During the Falklands War controversy arose over the extent to which a warship belonging to one of the belligerents was a legitimate target when outside an immediate combat zone or a declared exclusion zone. The Argentine warship *General Belgrano* was sunk by a British submarine in such circumstances with heavy loss of life. The sinking was strongly criticised both in Britain and abroad. However, the captain of the *Belgrano* made it clear that in his view the sinking was legitimate and the criticism unjustified. He emphasised that a warship was a legitimate target and that he would have attacked and sunk any 'British ship wherever it was'.[13]

[9] See, e.g., *In re Craft Captured on Victoria Nyanza* [1919] P. 83. The same is true of vessels in navigable waters or ports, see *The Impero* (1946 – France) 13 Ann. Dig. 402. Wrecks may also be treated as prize, *see The Nordmeer* (1946 – France) *ibid.*, 401.

[10] For discussion of some of the problems relating to naval warfare today, see Ronzitti, 'The crisis of the traditional law regulating international armed conflict at Sea and the need for its revision', in Ronzitti, *The Law of Naval Warfare*, 1. For a statement as to the 'areas of naval warfare', see *San Remo Manual*, ss. 10–12, 14–37.

[11] Fenrick, 'The exclusion zone device in the law of naval warfare', 24 Can. Y.B.Int'l Law, 1986, 91; *San Remo Manual*, paras. 105–7; *Annotated Supplement*, para. 7.9.

[12] HMSO Cmd 6946 (1946), 108–12, 41 Am. J. Int'l Law (1947), 172, 303–8 – although both Admirals Dönitz and Raeder were found guilty of waging unrestricted submarine warfare against neutral shipping, they were not punished for this crime, since both England and the United States had pursued similar sink-at-sight policies.

[13] *The Times* (London), 1 May 1992.

The impact of UNCLOS

Problems have arisen since the adoption in 1982 of the United Nations Convention on the Law of the Sea.[14] Even before this came into force, there was a tendency to regard its general principles as declaratory of current practice. From the point of view of maritime warfare this was of major significance for the Convention has established sea areas not formerly recognised, and some states are claiming absolute sovereignty not only over their internal and territorial seas, but also over their continental shelves, international straits lying within their territorial limits, archipelagic waters and even over the exclusive economic zone. If these claims were conceded it would mean that the area in which belligerent maritime activities can be conducted would be radically reduced.[15]

In assessing its impact on the law of armed conflict at sea it should be borne in mind that the Convention was adopted in the knowledge of the existence of Hague Conventions XI and XIII, 1907[16] and Geneva Convention II, 1949,[17] while the Protocols of 1977 were adopted while the Conference was in progress. It is clear, therefore, that the draftsmen were aware that there was a law in existence relating to conflict at sea. Nevertheless the Convention is silent as regards the status of the seas in time of war.

The situation is complicated by the fact that the Convention grants rights of innocent;[18] or transit[19] passage to warships and submarines, although this concept of 'innocence' refers to the relations between the vessel and the littoral state and has nothing to do with the situation as it exists between belligerents who are unlikely ever to consider a warship or submarine belonging to an adverse party as innocent. Moreover Article 19 concerning innocent passage through the territorial sea makes it clear that this passage is to 'take place in conformity with this Convention *and with other rules of international law*,' which clearly includes those relating to armed conflict. Further, Article 88 provides that 'the high seas shall be reserved for peaceful purposes', implying that the seas shall not be used by a party in a fashion that would threaten the security of any other state. This interpretation is strengthened by the terms of Article 301, which appears as part of the General Provisions of the Convention: 'in exercising their rights and performing their duties under this Convention, States Parties shall refrain from any threat or use of force against the territorial integrity or political independence of any state, or in any other manner inconsistent with the principles of international law embodied in the Charter of the United Nations', which is a clear reference to Article 2(4) of the Charter.

---

[14] 21 I.L.M., 1261.

[15] Most maritime powers tend to protest these extensive claims.

[16] Relative to Restrictions on the Right of Capture, and Concerning the Rights and Duties of Neutrals, resp.

[17] Concerning the Wounded, Sick and Shipwrecked.

[18] *San Remo Manual*, paras. 31–3; *Annotated Supplement*, paras. 2.3.2.1–2.3.2.4.

[19] *San Remo Manual*, paras. 28–30; *Annotated Supplement*, paras. 2.3.3, 2.3.4.

It cannot be denied that the territorial integrity and political independence of an adverse party are endangered once a conflict has commenced, but this does not mean that during the conflict the belligerents are unable to exercise their normal rights under the law of armed conflict. It should also be borne in mind that the provisions of the Charter are directed against a breach of the peace, that is to say relate to the *jus ad bellum*, and not the law that applies during the conflict, the *jus in bello*.

If it is suggested that UNCLOS constitutes *lex generalis* it must be pointed out that it cannot invalidate any rights arising under *lex specialis* such as the law of armed conflict, unless there is incontrovertible evidence in the text that it was intended to override such *lex specialis*. To the extent that UNCLOS may itself be considered as *lex specialis* it clearly cannot invalidate any principle of another *lex specialis*, especially when so much of the latter arises from custom and therefore is not affected by any application of the principle that later potentially inconsistent law invalidates any earlier principles. It is also significant that when the World Court considered the *Military and Paramilitary Activities [of the United States] in and against Nicaragua*,[20] neither the majority, nor Judges Schwebel or Jennings in their dissents referred to UNCLOS, though they mentioned Hague Convention VIII on the laying of mines.

The fact that new classifications of sea areas have been introduced by the Convention and have become accepted into international law does not mean that the traditional rights and duties of belligerents or neutrals have been automatically amended or terminated. To suggest otherwise is reminiscent of the rejected contention that the development of new weapons, be they the crossbow, tanks, aircraft or others, means that their use is unregulated. It merely means that, to the extent possible, the existing law is – as has tended to be the case with air warfare[21] – extended and adapted to cover these developments. Equally, therefore, the extension of the territorial sea from three to twelve miles or the 'analogisation' of archipelagic waters to the territorial sea should not form the basis for granting to belligerents or neutrals, however powerful or weak they may be, the right to ignore traditional rights and duties in those waters.

Finally, the Convention is only relevant to the extent that it affirms for every state that, as the preamble puts it, 'matters not regulated by this Convention continue to be governed by the rules and principles of general international law', which include the laws of armed conflict.

Prize and contraband

The customary law of maritime warfare developed primarily in relation to the right of warships to seize[22] enemy or neutral vessels trading with the adversary and

---

[20] [1986] I.C.J. 14, 112, 379–80, 536, resp.
[21] See ch. 9 below.
[22] *San Remo Manual*, paras. 135–40; *Annotated Supplement*, para. 8.2.2.

to seek their condemnation as prize, while at the same time recognising the right of a neutral to continue to trade and exercise its other rights under international law.[23]

Prize is a technical term applicable to those ships or goods which may legitimately be seized and condemned to the use of the captor because they are intended for or may be used on behalf of the adverse party's war effort. Any ship or goods seized on this ground must be brought before a prize court for condemnation. A prize court is created by national law as a national court, but the law that it applies is for the main part international law.[24]

When deciding whether a ship was trading with an enemy port[25] or whether its cargo was intended for an adverse party, prize courts developed the doctrines of continuous voyage and ultimate destination.[26] This enables them to look behind the apparent destination indicated in the ship's papers to ascertain the true destination of the ship or its cargo. Prior to World War I, it was generally accepted that while enemy merchant ships and their cargo were liable to capture or condemnation as prize, neutrally owned goods other than military *matériel* or goods classified as contraband remained exempt.

Contraband[27] is the term applied to goods considered as being useful to the enemy and carriage of which would render the vessel carrying such goods amenable to condemnation as prize. Contraband was regarded as absolute if the articles in issue were, like munitions, clearly intended for military use. Articles like food or heating fuels which could be used for either civilian or military purposes constituted conditional contraband, the decision as to actual use being made by the prize court in the light of the evidence before it.[28]

Belligerents would normally issue lists indicating to neutrals those goods which were considered by them to be absolute or conditional contraband, but by the end of World War I the distinction had virtually disappeared,[29] although even today there are still some goods, particularly medical supplies, including those intended for the wounded and sick, which are regarded as non-contraband.[30] In

---

[23] See ch. 16 below.

[24] See, e.g., *Le Caux* v. *Eden* (1781) 2 Dougl., 594, 602; see also *The Zamora* 2 [1916] A.C. 7. In its *Oxford Manual of Naval War*, 1913, (Ronzitti, The Law of Naval Warfare, 277) the Institute of International Law stated: 'The legality and the regularity of the capture of enemy vessels and of the seizure of goods must be established before a prize court', Art. 110.

[25] The captain of a warship is entitled to assume a hostile destination if the ship's papers indicate a call at any enemy port at any stage of the voyage.

[26] See, e.g., *The Kim* [1915] P., 215. *Annotated Supplement*, para. 7.4.1.1.

[27] See *San Remo Manual*, paras. 147–50; *Annotated Supplement*, para. 7.4.1.

[28] See, e.g., *The Cysne* (1930) 2 R.I.A.A., 1052 – ship carried materials which could be either trench supports or pit-props; since the vessel was going to Newport, in the South Wales coalmining district, the tribunal held that the German destruction of the vessel was illegal.

[29] See, e.g., *The Hakan* [1918] A.C., 148, 151.

[30] After Iraq's invasion of Kuwait in 1990 and after the termination of the Gulf War 1991 the Security Council permitted the supply of some foodstuffs and humanitarian supplies to be sent to Iraq.

addition, belligerents may agree to treat any particular goods as free, that is to say, non-contraband.

Combatant status

As in both land and air warfare, so in maritime warfare only properly authorised combatants are permitted to participate in warlike activities. Only ships, military aircraft and personnel forming part of the armed forces of a belligerent are legitimate combatants. To constitute a warship, the vessel must belong to the:

> armed forces of a State bearing the external marks [pennant and ensign] distinguishing such ships of its nationality, under the command of an officer duly commissioned by the government of the State and whose name appears in the appropriate service list or its equivalent, and manned by a crew which is under regular armed forces discipline.[31]

A military aircraft must similarly belong to the state under military command and with a military crew. It must also exhibit the national rondel. Prior to going into action, it is permitted to display false signs, so long as the correct national sign is exhibited before engaging.

Hague Convention VII[32] permits the conversion of a merchant ship into a warship, so long as it is placed under the authority, control and responsibility of the flag state and is commanded by a commissioned officer whose name appears on the navy list, while the crew must be subject to military discipline. The vessel must carry the proper identification marks and abide by the laws and customs of war. In addition, the flag state should announce its conversion in its list of warships. Many maritime states place their entire merchant fleets under military command immediately on the outbreak of hostilities. It is the general view that once a merchant ship has been converted in this way it cannot be reconverted, thus preventing it from claiming, at its pleasure, the status of a warship or a merchant vessel. However, this does not prevent the use of 'Q-ships', which appear to be neutral or merchant vessels but which are armed and will engage the enemy. Prior to such engagement, they must display evidence of their status as warships.[33]

While merchant ships may be converted into warships, private vessels may not be issued with certificates, letters of marque, permitting them to act as privateers, entitling them to carry on hostilities at sea, including the capture of enemy

---

[31] United Nations Convention on the Law of the Sea (UNCLOS) 1982, Art. 29, 21 I.L.M. 1261 (reproducing, with minor verbal alterations, Convention on the High Seas, 1958, Art.8(2), 450 U.N.T.S. 11).

[32] Schindler and Toman, 797. The US is not a party to the Convention, but its definition of 'warships' is wide enough to include such converted merchant ships, *Annotated Supplement*, 2.1.1. For comments on the present significance of the Convention, see Venturini in Ronzitti, *The Law of Naval Warfare*, 120.

[33] *San Remo Manual*, para. 111.2; *Annotated Supplement*, para. 12.3.1.

merchant ships. This practice was forbidden by the Declarations of Paris, 1856,[34] and this ban has now become part of customary law.

If a merchant vessel is or anticipates that it is likely to be unlawfully attacked, it is permitted to defend itself and take preventive and even offensive action,[35] and many merchant ships belonging to belligerents frequently carry defensive weapons. However, if so armed they run the risk of being treated as unlawful combatants.[36] If a vessel other than a commissioned warship or embodied auxiliary takes offensive action against a warship, other than by way of legitimate defence against an unlawful attack, or against a neutral vessel, its crew may be treated as pirates[37] or war criminals.[38] Since merchant ships sailing under protection of a convoy are considered as taking part in hostilities they are entitled to take offensive action against an enemy ship or aircraft attacking the convoy.[39]

Merchant ships in enemy ports

By Hague Convention VI[40] enemy merchant ships in ports of the adverse party at the outbreak of hostilities were allowed to depart and were granted a period of grace for this purpose. If unable to leave before this period elapsed, they could be interned but not confiscated and were to be restored at the end of hostilities. The same rule applied for merchant ships on the high seas at the time of the commencement of hostilities, provided they were unaware of this, a situation unlikely to occur today in view of radio communication.

Prior to World War II, the Convention was renounced by France and the United Kingdom, while the United States was not a party. During that conflict such vessels were seized and their seizure referred to a prize court for adjudication.[41] In view of the tendency to embody merchant ships into the war effort at the beginning of hostilities, the Convention may be considered to have fallen into desuetude and periods of grace are no longer granted.[42]

---

[34] Schindler and Toman, 787; for comment thereon, see Fujita in Ronzitti, *The Law of Naval Warfare*, 66.

[35] The German execution of Captain Fryatt of the British merchant marine in 1915 for having attempted to ram a U-boat when called upon to surrender at a time and in an area where merchant vessels were being unlawfully attacked by U-boats was a war crime, Garner, *International law and the World War*, vol. 1, 407–13. *San Remo Manual*, para. 69.

[36] See ch. 6 above.

[37] Piracy is an offence under both customary and treaty law and comprises acts of violence or depredation for private gain by one vessel against another on or over the high seas.

[38] See ch. 18 below.

[39] *San Remo Manual*, para. 120.3.

[40] Re the Status of Enemy Merchant Ships at the Outbreak of Hostilities, Schindler and Toman, 791.

[41] See, e.g., *The Pomona* [1943] P., 124.

[42] For comments on the Convention, see de Guttry, in Ronzitti, *The Law of Naval Warfare*, 102.

The role of warships

The most important function of warships is offensive against the warships, surface or submarine, of the adverse party. Warships may attack enemy military aircraft provided they are flying over the territorial sea of the adverse party or the high seas. They are also used against the merchant shipping of the adverse party in order to damage the trading activities of the latter or to prevent it receiving munitions and other war *matériel*. All such activities must be conducted outside neutral jurisdiction.

As in other theatres, attacks may only be directed against military objectives. All military vessels, whether surface or submarine, are legitimate targets, but they may only be attacked by lawful weapons and subject to the normal restrictions on unnecessary suffering. Since there is no treaty definition of a military objective for the purpose of maritime warfare, due consideration must be accorded to the environmental peculiarities of that theatre.[43] If warships are used to attack military objectives on land, due precautions must be taken to ensure that no unnecessary damage is done to civilians or civilian objects.[44] At the same time, due attention must be paid to the principle of proportionality.[45] Intelligence is, therefore, important in determining the location of military objectives particularly when employing long-range or, for example, cruise or other self-homing missiles.

Warships in neutral waters[46]

While it is forbidden for belligerents to take hostile action within neutral waters, belligerent warships are normally permitted to remain there for not more than twenty-four hours, although even so short a period may be denied by the neutral, provided this denial is applied to all belligerents equally. The time restriction does not apply to vessels devoted to medical, humanitarian or scientific purposes, and it may be extended for other vessels if the neutral regards this as necessary because of stress of weather. If a belligerent warship stays beyond the time permitted it must be interned together with its officers and crew. Unless local legislation or treaty provides otherwise, no more than three warships belonging to any one belligerent may be in a neutral port at any one time, and if warships of adverse parties are present together, at least twenty-four hours must elapse between the departure of enemy vessels, the order of departure depending on that of arrival. An enemy warship must not leave a neutral port until twenty-four hours after departure of an adversary's merchant ships.

A belligerent warship is permitted to hover outside neutral waters to await and

---

[43] *San Remo Manual*, para. 11; *Annotated Supplement*, para. 8.1.3.
[44] Pr. I, Art. 49(30). See also *Annotated Supplement*, para. 8.5.
[45] *San Remo Manual*, para. 46.5; *Annotated Supplement*, para. 8.1.2.1.
[46] *San Remo Manual*, paras. 19–22; *Annotated Supplement*, para. 7.3.2.

attack any enemy warship leaving those waters, but this is no ground for an extension of an adverse party's warship to stay in such waters. Equally, if a belligerent warship has been rendered unseaworthy in any way, it may use a neutral port and its facilities to restore its seaworthiness, but it must not aid its fighting ability in any way. The neutral state has the right to decide what repairs are necessary for this purpose.[47]

A prize may be brought into neutral waters or port because of unseaworthiness, stress of weather or want of fuel or provisions, and the mere passage of a prize through neutral waters does not infringe the neutrality of the coastal state.[48] On the other hand, an auxiliary carrying seamen rescued from attacked merchant vessels of the adverse party must not be brought into such waters to evade interception and recovery by an adverse party's warship, and if a neutral fails or is unable to protect its waters in such circumstances a belligerent is entitled to enter those waters and free the seamen concerned.[49]

Many of the provisions relating to the use of neutral waters and ports and the concomitant rights and duties of neutral powers are found in Hague Convention XIII.[50] Great Britain is not a party to this, but France, Germany, Japan and the United States are, though each added reservations. For the main part, the provisions of the Convention are now regarded as customary law,[51] but its definition of 'neutral waters' must, now be read in the light of the 1982 UNCLOS as regards passage through archipelagic waters and international straits.[52]

Seizure, capture and condemnation

Enemy merchant vessels are legitimate objects of seizure with a view to capture[53] and condemnation, so long as they are outside neutral jurisdiction. *Prima facie*, the flag determines nationality,[54] but the carrying of a neutral flag does not necessarily mean that the vessel is in fact neutral, for it may be owned or controlled by

[47] In December 1939, the Uruguayan authorities refused the request of the German pocket battleship *Graf Spee* that it be allowed to stay fifteen days to effect repairs in these circumstances and was granted three days. Rather than face engagement by the British warships waiting, the *Graf Spee* was scuttled, 1 Churchill, *The Second World War*, 407–15. See also O'Connell, *The Influence of the Law on Sea Power*, 27–39.

[48] *San Remo Manual*, para. 168.7; *Annotated Supplement*, para. 7.3.2.3.

[49] In 1940 the German auxiliary *Altmark* entered Norwegian waters carrying a number of British prisoners originally captured by the *Graf Spee*. The British warship *Cossack* was outside these waters and when Norway failed to take action to free the prisoners and expel the *Altmark*, the *Cossack* entered Norwegian waters, boarded the *Altmark* and freed the prisoners, see Waldock, 'The release of the *Altmark*'s prisoners', 24 Brit. Y.B. Int'l Law (1947), 216. See also O'Connell, *The Influence of the Law*, 40–4.

[50] Schindler and Toman, 951.

[51] See Dietrich in Ronzitti, *The Law of Naval Warfare*, 212, 215.

[52] Arts 46 *et seq.* and 34 *et seq.*, resp; re impact of UNCLOS see above.

[53] *San Remo Manual*, paras. 135–8, 146–9; *Annotated Supplement*, para. 8.2.2

[54] UNCLOS Art. 91(1).

an enemy state, national or corporation. If this is the case, or if a belligerent commander reasonably believes this to be so, it may be seized and the issue of nationality determined by a prize court. Any ship flying an enemy flag is considered to possess enemy character.[55]

On encountering enemy merchant ships or a neutral vessel which he suspects may be liable to seizure, a belligerent commander may instruct it to heave-to and submit to visit and search.[56] If after the visit he has grounds for seizing the vessel, he must divert[57] it to the nearest prize court to adjudicate upon the legality of the seizure and to authorise condemnation of the vessel or its cargo if these prove to be of enemy character. The seized vessel may be escorted by its captor, or a prize crew may be put on board. The prize crew may request the crew of the seized ship for assistance in navigating, but the latter are under no obligation to do so. In the case of distress, the capturing captain may ask a neutral port to allow him to bring his prize in, and if such permission is granted both the prize and its captor are immune from the local jurisdiction, but must depart as soon as the cause for distress has been terminated.[58]

If circumstances preclude the possibility of diversion, an enemy prize may be destroyed[59] by its captor. Before destruction, however, the belligerent officer must take all possible steps to secure the safety of the passengers and crew together with all the ship's papers and documents, and this rule applies whether the attacking vessel is a warship or a submarine.[60] Whether the vessel's boats constitute a safe place for this purpose will depend on the prevailing conditions[61] These rules:

> must be interpreted in the light of current technology, including satellite communications, over-the-horizon weapons, and antiship missile systems. Accordingly enemy merchant vessels may be attacked and destroyed by surface warships [or submarines], either with or without prior warning, in any of the following circumstances: 1. Actively resisting visit and search or capture 2. Refusing to stop upon being duly summoned to do so 3. Sailing under convoy of enemy warships, or enemy military aircraft 4. If armed 5. If incorporated into, or assisting in any way, the intelligence system of the enemy's armed forces 6. If acting in any capacity as a naval or military auxiliary to an enemy's armed forces 7. If integrated into the enemy's war-fighting/war-sustaining[62] effort and compliance with the rules of the 1936 London Protocol would, under the circumstances of the specific encounter,

---

[55] *San Remo Manual*, paras. 112–17.
[56] *Annotated Supplement*, para. 7.6.
[57] *San Remo Manual*, paras. 119, 138.
[58] *San Remo Manual*, paras. 186.8–186.9; *Annotated Supplement*, para. 7.3.2.3.
[59] *Annotated Supplement*, para. 8.2.2.2.
[60] *San Remo Manual*, para. 151.1.
[61] Declaration and Protocol of London, 1930, 1936 resp., Schindler and Toman, 881, 883. For comment on their present significance, see Nwogugu in Ronzitti, *The Law of Naval Warfare*, 353.
[62] It is controversial whether a belligerent may consider as war-sustaining activity the carrying by a neutral of, for example, during the Iran–Iraq War, oil from one belligerent for sale abroad the income being used for, perhaps, the purchase of war *matériel*.

subject the surface warship to imminent danger or would otherwise preclude mission accomplishment.[63]

Any destruction should be reported without delay to higher authorities.

Sometimes the delay involved in diverting a ship to port for adjudication may result in such deterioration of the cargo that it will not survive diversion. A prize court may then make its adjudication in the absence of the cargo on the basis of evidence presented to it. Similarly if the vessel is in such poor condition that it is likely to sink before reaching the port of diversion, the captor may destroy it and seek a determination from the prize court that it was a legitimate prize, but if the seizure or destruction proves unjustified, compensation is due.

If a neutral vessel stopped for inspection is found not to be suspect in any way,[64] the warship carrying out the search should issue a certificate to this effect,[65] which may be presented to a warship belonging to the same belligerent or an ally to secure immunity from further search. This certificate is sometimes described as a 'navicert', and should not be confused with one issued to the neutral vessel after search by a consular officer of the state whose warship subsequently confronts it. There is no obligation to recognise the validity of a 'navicert' issued by the adverse party.

Neutral merchant vessels are liable to capture[66] if they attempt to avoid determination of their identity; attempt to break a blockade;[67] transmit information in the interest of the enemy; violate regulations imposed by a belligerent in the immediate area of naval operations or seek to enter or refuse to leave an exclusion zone; or if, as a result of visit and search, it is found that they carry personnel in the military or public[68] service of the enemy, lack or present irregular papers or seek to destroy or conceal their papers, or are operating under enemy control,[69] orders, charter or direction.

Neutral vessels sailing under belligerent convoy[70] are regarded as having so assimilated themselves to that belligerent's cause as to render themselves liable to immediate destruction. They may also be attacked and destroyed for taking part in hostilities on behalf of the adverse party, including the transport of troops, and for active resistance to visit and search, including refusal to stop when ordered.

If an enemy merchant ship is captured, the crew, though not members of the

[63] *Annotated Supplement*, para. 8.2.2.2.
[64] If the warship suspects that the vessel's papers are false as to, e.g., destination, cargo or ownership, it may seize it for verification by a prize court.
[65] *San Remo Manual*, paras. 122–4; *Annotated Supplement*, para. 7.4.2.
[66] *San Remo Manual*, para. 146; *Annotated Supplement*, para. 7.10.
[67] See below.
[68] If these persons are diplomats, it should not affect the status of the vessel and they should be released, see *The Trent* (1861–62) 7 Moore, *Digest of International Law*, 1906, s. 265, p. 768 *et seq.*; and the *Vereker* incident, 1939, Colombos, *International Law of the Sea*, 710.
[69] See, e.g., *The Rebecca* (1811) 2 Acton, 116, *per* Lord Stowell.
[70] *San Remo Manual*, para. 120.3; *Annotated Supplement*, para. 7.5.2, n. 113.

forces, become prisoners of war under Convention III, 1949,[71] so long as they do not benefit from more favourable treatment under other provisions of international law. Neutral nationals in the crew do not become prisoners so long as they promise, while hostilities last, not to undertake any action connected with the war.[72]

In practice, the extent to which the relative rights of naval belligerents and neutrals are observed varies according to the strength of the powers concerned. This may be seen from the position of the United States in both World Wars depending on whether it was a neutral or a belligerent. In a limited war,[73] especially when major powers are not directly involved in hostilities among themselves,[74] the rights of neutrals tend to receive general recognition. This is largely because disregard of such rights might be treated by the neutrals as a *casus belli* (cause of war) and change a limited into a more general conflict.

Restrictions on the right of capture

Not all enemy vessels are liable to capture.[75] By Hague Convention XI[76] the postal correspondence of neutrals or belligerents, whether official or private, is inviolable and if the ship is detained, the correspondence should be forwarded without delay. Today, however, public mail from or to an enemy destination would probably be treated as contraband, while the private mail would be subjected to censorship. This immunity does not extend to mail coming from or destined for a blockaded port.

Small boats used in local trade, which is a question of fact in each case, as well as coastal, but not deep-sea fishing vessels, together with their equipment and cargo, are exempt from capture so long as they take no part in hostilities. This means that they lose their immunity if used for collecting or reporting information, even if they do so on their own initiative. Problems arise if they belong to a belligerent which is a coastal state and the bulk of its industry is carried on by way of such vessels, especially if these are fitted with radio equipment.[77] If it is

[71] Art. 4 A(5).

[72] Convention XI, Arts 5 and 6.

[73] Hostilities may be limited in geographic area as in the Falklands, although the remarks of the captain of the *Belgrano*, see n. 13 above, should not be ignored. They may also be limited as to the parties involved.

[74] This is true even though, as in Korea, major powers may be taking an active part, but are not prepared to assert their belligerent rights. It also applies when, as in Vietnam, one or more major powers are involved on behalf of one of the belligerents, while the other is receiving aid from or is representative of the interests of another major power, or the latter is using the belligerent as a surrogate. During that war, the US in 1972 announced the laying of mines in North Vietnamese territorial waters to prevent all vessels from entering or leaving. The mines only became active after three days, so that neutral vessels had time to depart safely. The Soviet Union and other allies of North Vietnam accepted this action.

[75] *San Remo Manual*, para. 136–7; *Annotated Supplement*, para. 8.2.3.

[76] Schindler and Toman, 819.

[77] This was a problem during the Vietnam War.

believed that this equipment is used for imparting information useful to their state, they may be seized pending adjudication.

The Convention also extends immunity to vessels engaged in religious, scientific or philanthropic missions. With scientific vessels doubts may arise because of the sophisticated nature of their radio or other equipment and such doubts may justify seizure pending adjudication. During World War I the Hong Kong Prize Court denied that a vessel requisitioned by the Germans, at the outbreak of war with Japan, to transport women and children to China was on a philanthropic mission.[78] But a vessel so engaged is entitled to the same treatment as any other merchant ship engaged in non-hostile activities. Moreover, vessels may be exempted by agreement between combatants and such cartel ships may be used for exchanging prisoners, transporting enemy civilians or carrying supplies for interned civilians.[79] Since 1899[80] hospital ships are exempt from capture and this exemption is confirmed in Convention X, 1907,[81] Convention II 1949,[82] and Protocol I 1977, Article 22. Hospital ships must fly a large red cross or red crescent[83] flag from the mainmast, be painted white and exhibit large red crosses or crescents on the hull and horizontal surfaces and display their national flag. If the hospital ship belongs to a neutral it must display its own flag and the flag of the belligerent to which it is attached.

A belligerent warship is entitled to search any hospital ship and can refuse it assistance, order it to follow a particular course or not to use its radio,[84] or place a commissioner on board to see that its orders are followed. Enemy wounded and sick may be removed from a hospital ship, provided they are fit to be moved and the warship has adequate facilities for their proper medical treatment.[85]

If hostilities take place on board a vessel, although this is not now common, all sick-bays must be respected or spared as far as possible and may not be diverted from their purpose so long as they are required for the care of the wounded and

---

[78] *The Paklat* [1915] 1 B. & C.P.C., 515.

[79] In 1944 and 1945 the US and Japan agreed to allow the *Awa Maru* to carry supplies for allied civilians interned in Japan. She was sunk by a US submarine unaware of the arrangement and the US accepted liability and agreed to discipline the submarine commander, see Voge, 'Too much accuracy', 76 Naval Academy Proceedings (1950), 257; Speer, 'Let pass safely the *Awa Maru*', l00 *ibid*. (1974), 69.

[80] Hague Convention III for the Adaptation to Maritime Warfare of the Principles of the Geneva Convention of 22 August 1864 [for the Amelioration of the Condition of the Wounded of Armies in the Field], Schindler and Toman, 289.

[81] *Ibid.*, 313.

[82] *Ibid.*, 401.

[83] The red crescent may be used in place of the red cross.

[84] Geneva Convention II, 1949 forbids hospital ships from using coded radio messages. However, the *San Remo Manual*, para. 171, states 'In order to fulfil most effectively their humanitarian mission, hospital ships should be permitted to use cryptographic equipment. The equipment shall not be used in any circumstances to transmit intelligence data nor in any other way to acquire any military advantage'. See also *Annotated Supplement*, para. 8.2.3, n. 67.

[85] Geneva Conv. II, Arts 31, 14.

sick. However, provided proper arrangements for their care are made by a commander into whose hands they have fallen, the sick-bay may be used for other purposes in case of urgent military necessity.

It is forbidden to attack shipwrecked personnel[86] or to refuse quarter to any enemy who has surrendered in good faith.[87] It is equally forbidden to attack vessels which have clearly indicated an intention to surrender, normally done by hauling down the flag, hoisting a white flag, stopping engines and responding to the attacker's signals, by the crew taking to lifeboats or, in the case of a submarine, by surfacing. At night, stopping the vessel and switching on navigation, masthead and deck lights also serves this purpose and if the attack continues those responsible would be guilty of a violation of the customary laws of sea warfare.[88] Moreover, so far as military interests permit. after the engagement all steps should be taken to look for and pick up the shipwrecked, sick and wounded and recover the dead.[89] A warship engaged in this task is not entitled to fly the red cross while doing so, but special arrangements may be made to enable it to do so without fear of attack.[90]

The above statement applies equally to surface and submarine vessels. While the former may sometimes be able to take survivors on board, this will rarely be the case with a submarine. In any case, it is unlikely that a submarine will be able safely to stay in the vicinity to offer such assistance. Instead of attacking a vessel, provided military exigencies permit, a submarine may order it to stay in place until a surface vessel or an aircraft is able to escort it into port.

Attacks on land targets

There are also restrictions concerning the use of warships against land targets. Since only military objectives may be attacked, the ordinary rules relating to the

---

[86] Conv. II, Arts 12, 13. See *Llandovery Castle* (1921), Cameron, *The Peleus Trial*, 1948, App. X, also *Re Eck (The Peleus) ibid.*, abbr. 13 Ann. Dig. 248.

[87] This follows from Hague Regs, Art 23(c) which is now considered to be part of customary law, and is expressed in modern treaty form in Pr. I, Art 40.

[88] See *In re Ruchteschell* (1947), UNWCC, 9 *War Crimes Reports*, 82, 89–90.

[89] Conv. II, Art. 18.

[90] In Sept. 1941, U-156 sank the *Laconia*, a troopship with 1,800 prisoners of war on board. On learning this, the U-boat captain radioed for help in rescue operations, provided he himself was not attacked. Dönitz ordered other U-boats to co-operate and Vichy warships were sent to assist, as were two Royal Navy ships. A US bomber saw U-156 flying a white flag with a red cross and towing two lifeboats. After leaving the area, the aircraft contacted base and was told that there were no friendly submarines in the area and he should attack. U-156 was then bombed and Dönitz ordered abandonment of the operation. He then issued the *Laconia* Order to all submarines forbidding the rescue of shipwrecked personnel, unless 'their statements would be of importance for your boat ... Rescue runs counter to the rudimentary demands of warfare for the destruction of enemy ships and crews'. The order is reprinted in Tucker, *The Law of War and Neutrality at Sea*, 72.

protection of civilians and civilian objects apply. However, by Hague Convention IX[91] special provision was made in the event of a warship seeking to bombard installations on land. While proper precautions had to be taken to ensure the protection of civilians, even undefended places could, in certain circumstances, be attacked provided notice was given in advance.

To all intents and purposes, Convention IX is now of little more than historic interest. By Protocol I, Article 49, the provisions of the Protocol relating to the general protection of the civilian population against the effects of hostilities 'apply to all attacks from the sea ... against objectives on land [and are additional] to other rules of international law relating to the protection of civilians and civilian objects on land, at sea or in the air against the effects of hostilities'. As a result it would appear that Protocol I actually merges the law relating to bombardment by naval and land forces, so that both are bound by the same restrictions with regard to the protection of civilians and civilian objects. as well as protected places and cultural objects.

Should bombardment from the sea take place, so long as he takes all reasonable precautions to protect such persons and objects, and observes the principle of proportionality, a naval commander will not be responsible for incidental collateral damage that may be caused. When military exigencies permit, he should still give notice before bombarding any place in which civilians or protected objects are located.

Mines and torpedoes

Mines[92] and torpedoes[93] are lawful means of maritime warfare, but the method of their use is controlled. By Hague Convention VIII[94] unanchored contact mines may only be used if they become harmless within one hour of the minelayer losing control of them, or as soon as they break loose from their moorings. If anchored contact mines are used they must become harmless as soon as they break loose from their moorings. Torpedoes, whether used by surface or submarine vessels, must become harmless on missing their target.

Automatic contact mines must not be laid off the coast or ports of the enemy if the sole purpose is to intercept commercial shipping and, when so employed, 'every possible precaution must be taken for the security of peaceful shipping [and belligerents are bound] should they cease to be under surveillance to notify the danger zones as soon as military exigencies permit by a notice addressed to ship owners, which must also be communicated to Governments through the

[91] Schindler and Toman, 811. See comment on present significance of the Convention, Robertson in Ronzitti, *The Law of Naval Warfare* 161.
[92] *San Remo Manual*, paras. 80–92; *Annotated Supplement*, para. 9.2.
[93] *San Remo Manual*, para. 79; *Annotated Supplement*, para. 9.4.
[94] Relative to the Laying of Contact Mines, Schindler and Toman, 803.

diplomatic channel'.[95] Belligerents must do their utmost to render anchored contact mines harmless within a limited time.[96] Neutrals may lay automatic contact mines off their ports and coasts to prevent unlawful access by belligerents, but they must abide by the same rules as belligerents and issue notices indicating where such mines have been laid.

At the end of hostilities parties which have laid automatic contact mines must remove them. They must inform the adverse party of any laid in the latter's waters and remove any laid in their own.[97]

Convention VIII is the only treaty dealing with naval mines and torpedoes and to some extent the weaponry with which it deals has been outdated by technological developments. However, in the Nicaragua *Military and Paramilitary Activities case*[98] the World Court made it clear that the Convention is still relevant and that its 'principles of humanitarian law' govern the laying of mines in both war and peace.

Today mines may be armed and/or detonated by contact, acoustic or magnetic signature, sensitivity to changes in water pressure caused by passing vessels and may be laid by ships or aircraft or even by subsurface platforms. They may also be *armed*, that is, placed with all safety devices withdrawn, or *armed* following placement, to detonate when preset mechanisms are satisfied, or *controlled*, having no destructive capability until activated by some arming order.[99] Modern torpedoes may be controlled by radio and even redirected to another target.

Ruses and stratagems

Warships, whether surface or submarine, may use ruses and stratagems.[100] They may sail under false flags, both enemy and neutral,[101] but before going into action whether at sea or if about to attack a land target they must strike any false colours and raise their own battle colours.[102] It would be perfidy for them to use the red

[95] Conv. VIII, Art. 3.

[96] Mines laid by the US off Haiphong Harbour in 1977 during the Vietnam War were set to neutralise in six months.

[97] It was because of Albania's failure to remove mines or notify foreign shipping of their presence in the Corfu Channel that she was held liable for the loss of two British warships, *Corfu Channel* case [1948] I.C.J., 124.

[98] [1986] I.C.J., 14, 111–12.

[99] *Annotated Supplement*, s. 9, 2.1.

[100] For a general discussion of ruses and stratagems, see text to n. 159 *et seq.*, ch. 7 above. *San Remo Manual*, para. 110; *Annotated Supplement*, para. 12.1.

[101] Pr. I forbids the use of enemy and limits the use of neutral emblems, but specifically states that this does not affect the generally recognised rules of international law concerning the use of flags in naval warfare.

[102] In 1914 the German cruiser *Emden* rigged a dummy fourth smoke stack and flew the Japanese flag to enable it to enter the port of Penang. It then replaced this flag with the German ensign and torpedoed the Russian cruiser *Zhemshug* then lying at anchor there, Oppenheim, vol. 2, 7th Lauterpacht, ed., 510.

cross or crescent or any other protected emblem in this way.[103] Warships may disguise themselves as merchant ships by, for example, flying a commercial ensign or altering their superstructure, so long as they show their true colours before going into action.[104]

Blockade[105]

International law allows a belligerent to take measures to cut the adverse party off from intercourse with the rest of the world. If the adverse party is a coastal state access to and from its ports may be enforced by mining[106] those ports or interdicting access to them, this interdiction being enforced by warships or with the assistance of aircraft. The blockade may be maintained from a distance so long as it is effective and on a basis of complete equality so as to prevent access by all. It may be enforced by an aircraft ordering a vessel seeking to break the blockade to halt until an enforcement vessel arrives. The fact that an occasional vessel successfully runs the blockade does not mean that it has been rendered illegal or ineffective. A mere paper blockade, however, that is to say one which has been proclaimed but cannot be enforced, is illegal. To permit a neutral ship in distress to enter a blockaded port does not mean that the blockade has been raised or applied discriminately.

Blockade runners and those attempting to breach the blockade are liable to capture, and an attempt begins from the moment the vessel or aircraft begins its voyage for this purpose. The doctrine of ultimate destination applies, so that it is immaterial that there is an intermediate neutral stopping-place or that the cargo is to be trans-shipped through the blockaded port. If the neutral port serves as a transit point for the blockaded area there is a presumption of attempted breach. The liability of a blockade runner only terminates with the conclusion of its voyage or flight, and if it succeeds in leaving the blockaded area it remains liable to capture until it returns to its home base.

Since blockade is a belligerent operation it is only legal during armed conflict, nor should it affect neutral ports unless the neutral has been guilty of unneutral conduct.[107] Occasionally, as during the Cuban missile crisis, 1962, a state which is not officially at war with another may seek to interdict the shipping of third states

---

[103] Geneva Conv. II, Art. 44 restricts the use of this emblem to hospital ships and Art. 45 imposes an obligation upon parties to take the measures necessary to prevent and repress any abuses.

[104] 'Q' boats of this kind were used frequently in World War I.

[105] *San Remo Manual*, paras. 93–104; *Annotated Supplement*, para. 7.7; see also Levie, *Mine Warfare at Sea*, 1992.

[106] While Conv. VIII, Art. 2 forbids the laying of mines 'with the sole object of intercepting commercial shipping', the blockading state can always maintain that the mines have been sown to prevent egress by adverse party warships.

[107] See ch. 15 below.

178

from entering the ports and harbours of its opponent. Such an interdiction is frequently described as 'pacific blockade' and would seem to be inconsistent with the obligations in Article 2(3) and (4) of the United Nations Charter. However, if such action is authorised by the Security Council of the United Nations. as was done after Iraq's invasion of Kuwait, 1990–91, the interdiction would be legal.

While a blockade is intended to prevent ingress and egress by the shipping and aircraft of all nations, if its purpose is to deprive the enemy population of foodstuffs, so as to starve them in the hope that this will cause them to apply pressure on their government to seek peace, it would now appear to be illegal. Article 54(1) of Protocol I prohibiting starvation of the civilian population as a method of warfare is part of the Protocol concerning the general protection of the civilian population against the effects of hostilities, which, by Article 49(3), applies to all 'attacks' including those from the sea against the land, and an 'attack' means any act of violence against the adversary whether in offence or defence.[108] Violent action applied to frustrate an enemy blockade would amount to an 'attack' in this sense. However, since Article 54(2) only condemns destruction or removal of objects indispensable to the sustenance of the civilian population and makes no reference to prevention of such objects reaching that population, and since any blockade runner would probably be carrying a mixed cargo of foodstuffs and other materials, inhibition of entry would be for purposes wider than starvation of the civilian population.

A legal blockade can only be instituted by a belligerent government, but the commander of a blockading fleet may act as his government's agent for this purpose. The blockade should be established by means of a declaration directed to the governments of all states, neutral, allied and enemy and to the local coastal or port authorities. It should specify the date of commencement, its geographic limits and the period during which neutral vessels will be permitted to depart. Knowledge of the blockade is essential, so that a neutral vessel attempting to enter or making for a blockaded port able to prove that it lacked such knowledge would be exempt from seizure.

The conditions regulating the establishment of a blockade were laid down in the Declaration of London, 1909,[109] This remains unratified, but its provisions are regarded as declaratory of customary law,[110] and when the United States mined the waters and ports of North Vietnam with the intention of denying them to all shipping, the relevant proclamation was in accord with these principles, even though there was no 'war' in the technical sense of that term.[111]

During both world wars the belligerents sought to interdict all commerce with their enemy and resorted to a variety of measures, including sink-at-sight policies,

---

[108] Art. 49 (1). See also *San Remo Manual*, pp. 176–8.

[109] Arts 1–21, Schindler and Toman, 845. For comments on the present significance of the Declaration, see Kalshoven in Ronzitti, *The Law of Naval Warfare* 257, 259–62, 274.

[110] See, e.g., *Annotated Supplement*, ss. 7.7.2, 7.7.3, 7.7.4.

[111] *Ibid.*, s. 7.7.5.

which did not conform to the regulations concerning blockade. Instead they asserted their right to institute 'long-distance blockades', stopping vessels believed to be heading to an enemy coast wherever they encountered them, justifying this policy on their right of reprisal against illegal acts by the adverse party. Recent technological developments in weaponry and delivery systems have rendered the inshore blockade of less significance and difficult to maintain other than in a local or limited conflict,[112] as was the case during the Gulf War.

As has been pointed out, much of the law concerning maritime warfare, particularly as regards the actions of belligerents towards merchant shipping, stems from the provisions of the Hague Conventions. Each of these contains an 'all-participation' clause providing that it only takes effect if all the belligerents in a particular conflict are parties to the Convention in question. In practice, the tendency has been that if a majority of the belligerents have accepted the Convention, and the non-parties are smaller states either only nominally involved in the hostilities or non-naval powers, the Convention will be applied.[113] In fact, practice illustrates that for the main part the provisions in these Conventions are declaratory and codificatory of customary law and are to be applied in naval warfare. Naval personnel ignoring or breaching these rules or those of a general character arising from customary or treaty law relating to protected persons, objects or places are liable to be tried as war criminals.[114]

---

[112] *Ibid.*

[113] See, e.g., *The Möwe* [1915] P. 1; *The Blonde* [1922] 1 A.C., 313.

[114] The most common offences would be unlawful attacks on hospital (see, e.g., *The Llandovery Castle* (1921) Cmd 450, Cameron; *The Peleus Trial*, 1948, App. X) and other protected vessels or abandonment of or attacks against shipwrecked personnel (see, e.g., *The Peleus Trial ibid.*; an abbreviated report appears in 13 Ann. Dig. 248). As pointed out above, since both sides in World War II conducted unrestricted submarine warfare against merchant shipping, the Nuremberg Tribunal refused to punish Dönitz or Raeder for having issued unlawful orders to this effect.

9

Conduct of hostilities:
air

There is very little treaty law directly concerned with aerial conflict, although such treaties as the Geneva Conventions regarding international humanitarian law are applicable in this theatre as on land and at sea. Moreover, the principles embodied in Hague Convention IV on land warfare are considered to be expressive of general principles and, to the extent that this is practical, they apply to aerial warfare too.[1] The Hague Rules of Air Warfare adopted by a Commission of Jurists in 1923[2] have never been embodied into a treaty, or officially declared to constitute a statement of the law. However, it is generally agreed that they do in fact constitute rules of customary law relating to air warfare.[3] In addition, Protocol I, 1977, for the first time establishes a number of rules directly applicable to air warfare, insofar as aircraft are operating against targets on land;[4] concerning the protection of the civilian population[5] or persons parachuting from aircraft in distress;[6] and providing for the protection and activities of medical aircraft.[7]

Military aircraft defined

It was not until 1899 that any attempt was made to define or consider problems

---

[1] See, e.g., *Coenca Bros* v. *Germany* (1927) 7 M.A.T. 683, when the Greco-German Mixed Arbitral Tribunal held the Convention IV rules regarding bombardment applicable to air warfare. For a discussion of air warfare at sea, see *Annotated Supplement*, para. 8.4.

[2] Schindler and Toman, 207.

[3] See, e.g., *ibid.*; Spaight, *Air Power and War Rights*, (1947), 42–3; *Oppenheim*, vol. 2, 519. See, however, Johnson, who contends that the code in the Hague Rules 'has no claim to rank as a statement of international law apart from its own intrinsic merits and the reputation of its authors', *Rights in Air Space*, 39. For a modern American view of the law, see Parks, 'Air war and the law of war', 32 Air Force Law Rev., 1990, 1. See also Green, *Essays,* 1999, ch. XVI.

[4] Art. 49 (3).

[5] Art. 49 (4).

[6] Art. 41.

[7] Arts 24–30.

relating to aerial warfare and Hague Declaration IV, as renewed in 1907 (Declaration XIV),[8] soon became inadequate. This merely bound the parties to prohibit 'the discharge of projectiles and explosives from balloons, or by other new methods of a similar nature.' Clearly aeroplanes fall into this latter classification, but there is no generally recognised international definition of what constitutes an aircraft. While the Chicago Convention, 1944,[9] distinguishes between civil and state aircraft it provides no definition of 'aircraft' as such. Annex 7, however, refers to 'all machines which can derive support in the atmosphere from the reactions of the air'. This would include:

> (a) machines heavier than air (such as aeroplanes, seaplanes or helicopters), as well as those that are not mechanically driven (such as gliders or even kites) and (b) machines lighter than air (such as captive or free balloons).

But, by confining the term 'aircraft' to machines which fly *because* they can derive support from the reactions of the air, the above definition excludes machines which are able to fly in the air independently of any support derived from the reactions of the air, such as missiles, rockets or earth satellites although this type of machine is included in the legal definition of aircraft in many countries and other municipal legislation would include spacecraft too.[10] From the point of view of aerial warfare the definition in the United States Federal Aviation Act[11] is probably the most comprehensive and acceptable: 'any contrivance now known or hereafter invented, used, or designed for navigation of or flight in air'.[12]

Although the Convention lists 'state aircraft' as those used in 'military, customs and police services', for the purposes of the law of air warfare only 'military aircraft' should be considered, with postal and police aircraft normally regarded as 'civil'. 'Military aircraft' are defined in the United States *Annotated Supplement to the Commander's Handbook on the Law of Naval Operations*[13] 'to include all aircraft operated by commissioned units of the armed forces of a nation bearing the military markings [which should be distinct from that of other state aircraft] of that nation, commanded by a member of the armed forces, and manned by a crew subject to regular armed forces discipline … Military aircraft are "state aircraft" within the meaning of the … Chicago Convention', which include 'military', 'customs' and 'police' service.

[8] Schindler and Toman, 201.
[9] Convention on International Civil Aviation, 15 U.N.T.S., 295.
[10] Cheng, *The Law of International Air Transport,* 111.
[11] 49 USC s. 1301(5), 1970.
[12] See n. 10 above for other definitions.
[13] 1997, paras. 2.2.1, 2.2.2.

The status and rights of aircraft

Because of their potential offensive character, military aircraft may not enter the air space of a third state without prior consent, unless proceeding expeditiously through the air space over water where the rights of innocent transit passage or archipelagic sea lanes passage exist.[14] Should they enter without permission they must obey all reasonable orders of the territorial state to land, turn back or pursue a named flight path. The territorial state must not expose the overflying aircraft to unnecessary danger, but if it disobeys the orders given and the reason for its flight cannot be ascertained it may be forced down or, if necessary, attacked and destroyed,[15] but the territorial sovereign should 'take into consideration the elementary obligations of humanity, and not use a degree of force in excess of what is commensurate with the reality and the gravity of the threat'.[16] However, in view of the difficulty in ascertaining the innocence of the flight by a foreign military aircraft, it may be difficult to comply with this obligation.[17]

Military aircraft have the right to fly over international waters and to use such flight for surveillance or photographing another state's territory even including its military installations. Satellites are also used for this purpose, apparently without interference. However, as a result of state practice customary law recognises the right of a state to declare air defence identification zones over the high seas adjacent to its coasts and territorial sea. Any aircraft on a course to enter such zone may be called upon to identify itself and even denied entry, unless it can prove that it is only passing through the zone and has no intention of entering the local air space.[18] Military aircraft intruding into the local air space and which refuse to obey the orders of the local state may be pursued out of territorial air space and any air defence identification zone that may have been proclaimed, so long as the pursuing aircraft remains in contact and the intruding aircraft does not enter the air space of another state, unless it is during conflict and that air space is being used as sanctuary by aircraft belonging to the adverse party.

[14] UNCLOS 21 I.L.M. 1261, UNCLOS Arts 37–54.

[15] See, e.g., Lissitzyn, 'The treatment of aerial intruders in recent practice in international law', 47 Am. J. Int'l Law (1953), 559.

[16] Whiteman, *Digest of International Law*, 328, citing Memorial of Government of Israel, Jun. 1958, I.C.J. *Pleadings, Aerial Incident of 27 July 1955*, 46. As to the Soviet destruction of KAL flight 007 in 1993 and the subsequent amendment of the Chicago Convention, see Cheng, 'The destruction of KAL flight KE007, and article 3 *bis* of the Chicago Convention' in Van Gravesade and Van der Veen Vonk, *Air Worthy*, 1985, 49.

[17] See Brownlie, *International Law and the Use of Force by States* (1963), 373. During the Iran–Iraq War, when the US and other navies were protecting oil tankers passing through the Gulf, the *USS Vincennes* destroyed an Iranian civilian aircraft while on a recognised flight path, due to a mistaken belief that it was a military aircraft about to attack. In 1989 Iran referred the issue to the World Court, but by the end of 1998 the matter had not yet been heard.

[18] American Law Institute, Restatement of the Law, *The Foreign Relations Law of the United States*, 1987, s. 521, Reporters' Note 2; see also Note, 'Air defense identification zones: creeping jurisdiction in the airspace', 18 Virginia J. Int'l Law (1978), 485.

The role of aircraft in war

Since they are lawful combatants[19] and entitled to the rights as well as subject to the duties of such, military aircraft must be clearly identifiable by the national rondel which should be reported to the adverse party. Any aircraft not so marked and taking part in combat does so illegally and its crew members may be treated as war criminals,[20] even if they and their passengers are members of the forces, and are in uniform. Members of the crew of a military aircraft are entitled to prisoner-of-war status if captured and should, whenever possible, wear an identifiable uniform or flight suit. Civilian crew members of a military aircraft are also entitled to prisoner-of-war status if captured.[21] If it is intended to use civilian aircraft for combat purposes, they must be embodied into the air force and correctly marked.

Military aircraft may be used for such purposes as direct support of land or sea forces, to interdict activities by the adverse party, for reconnaissance, as transports for airborne troops, for bringing up reinforcements of men or supplies, as a strategic strike force, to bombard enemy forces to induce their surrender, for anti-naval activities or to enforce a blockade.[22] If they are being used to establish or enforce a long-distance blockade their activity must be effective in preventing contact with the blockaded territory, and this may be effected by capture[23] or, if this is not possible, by destruction of an alleged blockade-runner. If the sinking has been unlawful, the responsible belligerent may be required to pay damages. Before and during the Gulf War, 1991, aircraft played a major part in enforcing the trade interdiction imposed upon Iraq.

In addition to their employment against legitimate military objectives on land, while paying due attention to the principle of proportionality as regards collateral damage, '[m]ilitary aircraft may employ conventional weapons systems to attack warships and military aircraft, including naval and military auxiliaries, anywhere beyond neutral territory. Enemy merchant vessels and civil aircraft may be attacked and destroyed by military aircraft only under the following circumstances: 1. When persistently refusing to comply with directions from intercepting aircraft; 2. When under convoy of enemy warships or military aircraft; 3. When armed [other than for purposes of self-defence against unlawful attack]; 4. When incorporated into or assisting in any way the enemy's military intelligence system; 5. When acting in any capacity as a naval military auxiliary to an enemy's armed forces; 6. When otherwise integrated into the enemy's war-fighting or war-sustaining effort.'[24]

---

[19] See ch. 6 above.

[20] See ch. 18 below.

[21] Geneva Conv. III, 1949, Art. 4(A)(4): 'Prisoners of war are ... Persons who accompany the armed forces without actually being members thereof, such as civilian members of military aircraft crews.'

[22] See, on blockade, ch. 8 above.

[23] This may be done by remaining in the vicinity of the offending vessel until such time as a surface vessel takes over.

[24] *Annotated Supplement*, para. 8.4.

Basic rules for aerial warfare were promulgated by the League of Nations in 1938,[25] but these were almost completely ignored during World War II. Similar rules are now to be found in Protocol I[26] and the intentional bombing of civilians and civilian objects is illegal; objectives aimed at from the air must be military objectives and identifiable as such,[27] and any attack on a military objective must be conducted in such a way that civilian populations in the vicinity are not bombed through negligence, but incidental collateral civilian damage does not render the attack illegal, provided it is not excessive[28] in relation to the concrete and direct military advantage anticipated for the operation to which the aerial attack is necessary. An attack 'which treats as a single military objective a number of clearly separated and distinct military objectives located in a city, town, village or other area containing a similar concentration of civilians or civilian objects' is illegal as indiscriminate.[29] During the Gulf War every endeavour was made to observe these rules,[30] although mistakes did occur, as they occasionally did, despite the use of laser-directed, 'smart' bombs, during the 1999 NATO bombing of Yugoslavia.[31]

Belligerent military aircraft may engage legitimate targets of the adverse party wherever these may be found, though they may not do so over neutral territory, land or sea. Operations in international air space must be conducted with due consideration for the rights of non-parties to the conflict. Belligerents may, however, establish air combat zones over the territory and territorial sea of all adverse parties, provided that notice of their existence is given. Any aircraft entering such zones are subject to damage from military hostilities. However, belligerents may not deny access to international air space by neutrals and must permit neutral aircraft passage through such air space even though the neutral aircraft may be bound for enemy territory. Under authority of the Security Council all aircraft may be banned from flying to or from a state subject to United Nations sanctions as was the case with the 'no-fly zones' in Iraq after Desert Storm. Similarly, during the air attacks against Yugoslavia, NATO, usually with the consent of the state affected, declared large areas of Balkan airspace closed to all aircraft other than those operationally engaged. Belligerent aircraft may not enter neutral air space even in pursuit of enemy aircraft, unless it is known that the neutral air space in question is a sanctuary for such aircraft, in which case the neutrality of the state

[25] Schindler and Toman, 221.

[26] Part IV Civilian Population, Section I General Protection against Effects of Hostilities, Arts 48–60, esp. Art. 49(3) and (4).

[27] This implies that commanders must make their decision in the light of all the knowledge available to them in the particular circumstances, Art. 57(2)(a)(ii).

[28] Pr. I, Art. 51(5)(b).6.

[29] Art. 51(5)(a).

[30] US Dept. of Defense, *Conduct of the Persian Gulf war*, Final Report to Congress, App. O, *The Role of the Law of War*, p. O 9 *et seq.*; this Appendix is reprinted in 31 I.L.M.; 615 at 21 *et seq.*

[31] As to the destruction of the Al-Firdus bunker, see *ibid.*, O 14, 626 of I.L.M.

becomes questionable. Belligerent aircraft flying over neutral territory innocently should be ordered to leave and should they fail to do so they may be attacked from the ground or the air in defence of the state's neutrality. If damage is caused to the neutral state as a result of such intrusion the intruder may become liable.[32] During the Gulf War, 1991, Iran protested at intrusions into its air space by Coalition aircraft, even though it may be questioned whether, as a member of the United Nations, Iran was not obligated to co-operate in every way with the Coalition against Iraq. Coalition authorities apologised for such intrusions and any damage caused.[33] The neutral state is under a duty to protect its neutrality against such intrusions and failure to do so may result in violations of its air space by aircraft of the opposing belligerent. The decision as to such 'violation' is political and should not be made by an aircraft's commander. Military aircraft brought down by a neutral state or which land in neutral territory should be detained by the neutral until the end of the conflict and then returned to their home state. Personnel on board such aircraft should be interned until the cessation of hostilities.[34] During the Gulf War a number of Iraqi civil and military aircraft took refuge in Iran. As regards Coalition aircraft during that war, Iran was informed[35] that in accordance with Security Council Resolution 678[36] it was expected to return downed aircraft and crew rather than intern them, and the Coalition claimed the right to enter both Iranian and Jordanian air space to rescue any downed aviators.

Methods of combat

A belligerent aircraft may make use of such ruses as camouflage so long as its national marks are identifiable during combat, as well as false radio signals including those of the adverse party, but not those reserved for medical channels. It must not commit perfidy. Like any other combatant it must properly identify itself as a legitimate belligerent before engaging in combat and must not at any time make use of the markings of medical or United Nations aircraft; but captured enemy aircraft may be used so long as their identification marks are changed. It is lawful to pretend to be a friendly aircraft and to use false or enemy rondels, so long as the proper markings are displayed before engaging.

Older or slower aircraft may be used as decoys to entice the enemy into action with more sophisticated aircraft. It is also permissible to stage false aerial combats to seek to induce an enemy plane into action in aid of a supposed comrade. Fires or flares may be used to lead the enemy to believe that a major raid is taking place on a particular place so as to divert its intercepter aircraft from the raiding force,

---

[32] See *Coenca Bros.* v. *Germany* (1927) 7 M.A.T. 683.

[33] See Report, n. 30 above, p. O 30, at 639–40 of I.L.M.

[34] See Hague Conv. V, 1907, Schindler and Toman, 941. Art. ll and Geneva Conv. III, Art. 4(B)(2).

[35] *Conduct of the Persian Gulf War*, p. O 30, at 639 of I.L.M.

[36] 29 I.L.M., 1565.

and it is lawful for a raiding force to set out on one course and switch to another target for the same reason.

While such ruses are lawful, it would not be lawful to feign distress by wrongful use of internationally recognised protective signs like the red cross or crescent or one suggesting that the aircraft is on a scientific mission; nor is it permissible to feign surrender. It is, however, lawful to feign distress in order to enable escape or even to entice an enemy to break off an attack, but it would be perfidy to use a protected sign or signal for this purpose. It is also unlawful to suggest to enemy aircraft that an armistice has been agreed when this is not so.

Although it is forbidden to refuse quarter or to kill an enemy who is wounded or seeks to surrender, it must be recognised that this prohibition is sometimes difficult to observe in aerial combat and the ramming of one aircraft by another is permitted. If enemy crew are clearly offering to surrender that offer must be respected. Aircrew who have parachuted into the sea or whose aircraft crashes into the sea are regarded as shipwrecked and are entitled to be treated in accordance with all the provisions of the second 1949 Geneva Convention,[37] and this is so even if they should be in a raft or similar craft. It is permitted to attack members of the adverse party attempting to rescue crashed aircrew, unless they are protected as medical personnel attempting to rescue a wounded airman.[38] If a non-protected vessel has picked up injured aircrew, the presence of the latter does not confer immunity upon that vessel. Disabled aircraft are frequently pursued to destruction to prevent them returning to their own bases where they may be refitted and their crews enabled to serve in further combat. However, while in the past it was controversial whether aircrew baling out of a disabled aircraft could be attacked during parachute descent,[39] this practice is now forbidden by Protocol I. By Article 42 any airman who successfully bales out into enemy territory must be given an opportunity to surrender, 'unless it is apparent that he is engaging in a hostile act', such as trying to use his radio or destroy his aircraft or its equipment. An airman from a disabled aircraft who does not surrender when called upon to

[37] Schindler and Toman, 401; see ch. 11 below.

[38] During World War II, Great Britain objected to German rescue vessels being marked with a red cross and refused to recognise their immunity, on the ground that this was not a legitimate medical activity, and that the vessels involved were not medical craft. It did, however, accept the use of and grant immunity to floating casualty stations marked with the red cross. By Art. 27 of Geneva Conv. II small craft employed by the state or recognised lifeboat institutions for coastal rescue work are protected, so far as operations permit. However, Dr. Cornum, while *prima facie* protected as a medical officer, probably lost this status when engaged in a search and rescue operation during Desert Storm while a member of the crew of a Special Operations Pathfinder helicopter; she was treated by the Iriqis as a prisoner of war, Cornum, *She Went to War*, 1992.

[39] See Spaight, *Air Power*, 155–63. There were occasions, especially in World War I, when parachuting airmen were protected by their opponent who occasionally would summon rescue craft. For examples of chivalry in aerial warfare, particularly in World War I, see Spaight, *Air Power*, 110–27; see also Meijering, *Signed With Their Honour*, for a contrary view, see letter by Derek Robinson to *The Times*, 1 Jun. 1987.

do so may be attacked. He may be captured by non-combatants, but may not be subjected to violent assault by them. This does not exclude such lawful violence as may be used by a police officer or other non-combatant in effecting an arrest. It is controversial whether a crew member parachuting from an aircraft in distress is entitled to protection if it appears that he is seeking to manoeuvre his parachute to ensure that he lands in friendly territory,[40] and if he does so land he may be attacked unless he is wounded.

The protection afforded to crew abandoning an aircraft in distress does not extend to airborne troops. These are combatants being transported by air to enable them to enter into combat and may be attacked during their descent. In order to protect those entitled to protection, airborne troops should wear a uniform distinct from that worn by air force personnel.

During World War II unarmed transport aircraft flown by unarmed civilian personnel were often used, particularly to bring aircraft from production areas in North America to the United Kingdom. They were also often used as troop transports. Such aircraft are legitimate targets and may be attacked.

Protected aircraft

Medical aircraft, correctly identified and exclusively used as such, are immune from attack.[41] The parties to a conflict may, by agreement, confer immunity from attack upon specific aircraft,[42] such as cartel aircraft transporting the wounded or exchanging prisoners[43] so long as they take no part in hostilities and scrupulously observe the conditions laid down in the agreement.

Civil aircraft in flight should not be attacked.[44] They are presumed to be carrying civilians who may not be made the object of direct attack.[45] If there is any doubt as to the status of a civil aircraft it should be called upon to clarify this and if it fails to do so or is engaged in carrying troops or other non-civil activity it

[40] See, for debate at Geneva re adoption of Art. 42., Bothe, *et al.*, 226–31.

[41] See ch. ll below.

[42] In 1941, during World War II, arrangements were made for an RAF aircraft to fly into enemy-held territory to drop an artificial leg for Wing-Commander Douglas Bader who had been shot down and captured.

[43] 'White aircraft', that is aircraft which are painted white, may be used for transporting *parlementaires* (see ch. 5, above); in August 1945 such an aircraft was used to bring Japanese representatives to the Ryukyus to discuss surrender terms, Spaight, *Air Power*, 134.

[44] Although some were attacked during World War II, 'international air traffic ... suffered but little, on the whole, as a result of belligerent action', Spaight, *Air Power*, 404. In view of the increase in air traffic since 1945, it is probable that in any future conflict the number of civilian aircraft subjected to attack would be vastly increased, although if such an aircraft is in a restricted area it should not be attacked unless an attempt has been made to ascertain its status and this attempt has failed.

[45] Pr. I, Art. 49 protects civilians on land from aerial attack. Since civilians are non-combatants they are protected by customary law from direct attack in any theatre.

may be attacked. Civil aircraft should avoid entering areas which have been declared restricted flight areas or combat zones by the belligerents, since this increases their risk of being attacked and exposes its civilian passengers to improper risk. If in the vicinity of a combat area or the enemy coast, it runs the risk of being attacked before its status can be determined. It should, therefore, avoid such areas whenever possible. If it enters such an area without prior permission, fails to identify itself when called upon, or fails to obey an order to land or to leave the area it is likely to be assumed that it is not on a civilian journey and to be attacked.

Civilian aircraft which have been embodied into a belligerent's air force or are being ferried from the manufacturer to a belligerent for this purpose may be attacked. The crew of such aircraft, together with civilian crew members of a military aircraft become prisoners of war if captured. If a civilian aircraft has been lawfully attacked its crew members become prisoners of war, but if the attack is unlawful they and civilian passengers should be freed or held in accordance with the Geneva Civilians Convention.[46]

Civil aircraft on the ground may only be attacked in accordance with the normal rules regarding military objectives. However, since they may be used for transporting troops or supplies, their status will often depend upon the prevailing military situation. Moreover, airfields are subject to attack and incidental damage caused to civil aircraft on the ground does not render the attack unlawful. In any such attack due attention must be paid to the obligation to prevent damage to civilians or civilian objects and to respect the principle of proportionality.

All the normal rules with regard to the protection and survival of the civilian population, the ban on terror bombing of towns and other civilian habitations,[47] restrictions on the use of weapons, protection of the environment and dangerous installations, respect for cultural objects and other protected places, and for the wounded, sick and shipwrecked apply in aerial warfare as they do in warfare on land and sea.[48] Vessels which are correctly marked for relief or medical services must not be attacked. While there is no direct provision protecting vessels engaged in picking up survivors at sea, Article 18 of Geneva Convention II imposes an obligation to 'take all possible measures to search for and collect the shipwrecked, wounded and sick', and this can only be effectively accomplished if the vessels involved are protected from aerial attack.[49] Belligerents may make arrangements to provide immunity for such vessels.[50]

---

[46] Conv. IV, Schindler and Toman, 495; see ch. 12 below.

[47] Raids on civilian refugees like those which took place during the German attacks on France in World War II are clearly illegal.

[48] See chs 7, 8 above.

[49] See, e.g., the *Laconia* incident, ch. 8, n. 90 above.

[50] See, e.g., re such an arrangement, the *Awa Maru* incident, ch. 8, n. 49 above.

Legitimate targets

Enemy warships may be attacked from the air wherever they are encountered out-side neutral waters, and inside those waters if the adverse party is abusing their neutrality and the local state is unable or unwilling to assert its authority and ful-fil its obligations as a neutral.[51] Before launching such an attack the neutral should, if military exigencies permit, be called upon to expel the offender. Enemy war-ships, including submarines, may be captured from the air;[52] there is no need for them to be submitted to prize proceedings and ownership is transferred to the cap-tor state immediately upon capture. Any warship or crew member offering to sur-render must have that offer accepted.

Adapting the rules applicable in naval warfare,[53] enemy merchant ships may only be attacked from the air if they actively resist visit and search, refuse to stop after being duly summoned to do so, if they are sailing under convoy of enemy warships or military aircraft, if they are armed and the aircraft has reasonable grounds to believe that this armament is for offensive purposes, if they are being used for intelligence purposes by the adverse party,[54] integrated into the enemy intelligence service, or if they are serving as auxiliaries to the enemy's forces.[55]

Neutral warships and merchant ships are immune from aerial attack so long as they do nothing to assimilate themselves to a belligerent. A neutral vessel trying to run a legal blockade[56] may be attacked, as may one sailing in convoy protected by aircraft or ships of the adverse party.

When attacking enemy or neutral merchant ships, the attacking aircraft must apply the general rules relating to humanity and proportionality. It should also respect the rules regarding survivors, and no attack should ever be directed against those who are in the sea or have taken to lifeboats.

Aircraft may be used to attack troops or ground targets when all the precautions required in regard to attacks on land must be observed and by Protocol I, Article 49, the protection of Part IV of the Protocol relating to protection of the civilian population is extended to all air attacks directed against the land. This means that

[51] See ch. 16 below.
[52] In August 1941 the German submarine U-570 was damaged by depth charges dropped from the air, surfaced and surrendered. Air patrols were maintained until a naval vessel arrived and took the U-boat in tow, Spaight, *Air Power*, 133. In June 1943 the island of Pamtellaria surrendered to aircraft and in March 1945 German forces in the Saar salient sur-rendered to allied aircraft, 132. In June 1945 a fleet of thirty enemy vessels, including a hos-pital ship, surrendered off Trieste and were escorted into the port of Grado, *ibid.*, 134.
[53] See ch. 8 above.
[54] The German ship *Ophelia*, though marked and certified as a hospital ship, was con-demned as prize, because of the signalling equipment on board and evidence that she had been sending coded messages, [1915] P. 129, [1916], A.C., 206.
[55] Thus, the *Altmark* could have been attacked from the air when sailing through Nor-wegian waters, see ch. 8, n. 49 above. See also list reproduced above from *Annotated Supplement*.
[56] See ch. 8 above.

attacks may only be directed against military objectives and must not be indiscriminate, and, to the extent that it is feasible,[57] in accordance with the principle of proportionality and the rule against unnecessary suffering care must be taken to avoid excessive damage to civilians and civilian objects.

It is generally accepted that military objectives include military bases and training establishments, military personnel and transports, lines of communication used for military purposes, petroleum and other fuel storage and distribution areas, ports, airfields, military aircraft, warships, weapons, munitions, buildings and objects providing administrative and logistic support for military operations and other things used in military operations, areas of land that would be of direct use to attacking or defending forces, as well as economic targets that indirectly but effectively support enemy operations.[58] Civilian vessels, aircraft, vehicles and buildings are also legitimate targets if they contain combatant personnel or military equipment or supplies or are otherwise associated with combat activity incompatible with their civilian status. In such cases collateral civilian damage must not be excessive and attacking aircraft must have received reliable intelligence information.

In accordance with those parts of the Hague Regulations which are considered to be part of customary law, aerial attack or bombardment of an undefended place is prohibited,[59] and before commencing any such attack the party responsible for ordering it should, unless circumstances do not permit, give effective advance warning of attacks which may affect the civilian population.[60] Those involved in attacks should take all measures necessary to spare buildings dedicated to religion, art, science, historic monuments and the like, provided they are not being used for military purposes.[61] During the Gulf War Coalition aircraft were under instructions to avoid such establishments and on occasion attacks were called off when it was ascertained that they might be endangered.[62] Care must also be taken to spare hospitals and other places where the wounded and sick are being cared for.[63]

Aerial attacks which would treat as a single military objective a number of clearly separated and distinct military objectives, such as a variety of munitions factories or main line railway stations used for the movement of troops, located in

---

[57] That is to say, practicable or practically possible taking into account all existing circumstances, including those of a military character.

[58] After the American Civil War the British–American Claims Commission held that it was lawful for federal forces to seize and destroy cotton, since its sale provided funds for almost all Confederate arms and ammunition, *Cotton Claims* (1871) 4 Moore, *International Arbitrations*, 1894, 3679.

[59] Art. 25; see also Pr. I, Art. 59. See discussion by Tokyo court in *Shimoda* v. *Japan*.

[60] Art. 26; see also Pr. I, Art. 57(2)(c) and (4). During World War II such warnings were occasionally given in both Europe and the Far East.

[61] Art. 27; see also Pr. I, Arts 52, 53 and the 1954 Convention on the Protection of Cultural Property in the Event of Armed Conflict, Schindler and Toman, 777.

[62] *Conduct of the Persian Gulf War*, pp. O 12, O 14, at 624, 626 of I.L.M.

[63] Art. 27; see also Geneva Convs. I and II, ch. 11 below.

an area containing a concentration of civilians or civilian objects are illegal. This means that area bombing in such a place would be unlawful, although it is still permitted to bomb two or more legitimate military objectives in such a place, even during the same aerial attack. This is a new rule introduced by Protocol I,[64] and any country which has not become a party would still be at liberty to attack such separate objectives as if they were a single objective, so long as the incidental damage cause to civilians is not disproportionate to the military advantage expected to be gained from the attack. An aerial attack which cannot be directed against a specific military objective and which is likely therefore to affect both military objectives and civilians or civilian objects without distinction is forbidden. 'Blind' weapons like the V-1 and V-2 missiles of World War II, or the 'Scuds' used by Iraq in the Gulf War are illegal, as would be saturation bombing or the use of weapons of mass destruction and fire bombs which cannot be controlled.[65] As to the use of nuclear weapons, the World Court has held that the use or threat thereof, even those of a tactical nature, would be contrary to the principles of international humanitarian law, but was unable to declare that their use was unlawful in all circumstances, leaving open the issue of self-defence against actual destruction of the state.[66]

Aerial attacks may not be launched against objects indispensable to the survival of the civilian population, if the purpose is to deny the means of sustenance. Food stores, water installations, crops, livestock, agricultural areas and the like may not be attacked if they are necessary to sustain the population, but it is permissible to destroy an agricultural area to deny its military use, as, for example, a military staging area, by the adverse party. It is also permissible to destroy from the air such stores if their sole use is to sustain the armed forces of the adverse party. It is also forbidden to attack from the air dams, dykes and nuclear electrical generating stations, even though they may be military objectives, if the result would be to release dangerous forces and consequent severe losses among the civilian population. Military objectives near such installations must not be attacked if this would cause consequential release of dangerous forces from such installations.[67] If the release of the dangerous forces is not likely to affect the civilian population such installations and objectives may be attacked.

Aerial attacks which are intended or may be expected to cause long-term, widespread *and* severe damage to the environment are forbidden. States which are parties to the Environment Modification Treaty[68] have undertaken not to engage in military use of environmental modification techniques having widespread, long-lasting *or* severe effects as a means of injuring a party to the Treaty.[69]

---

[64] Art. 51(5)(a).
[65] On incendiary weapons see below.
[66] See various references in Table of Cases and Index.
[67] Pr. I, Art. 56. Such damage may result from blast.
[68] 1977, Schindler and Toman, 163.
[69] It is forbidden, for example, to alter the Van Allen radiation belt.

If it appears during an aerial attack that the military advantage to be gained may be equally obtained from attacking one of two objectives, that which is likely to cause less civilian damage should be decided upon.[70] If it transpires, as a result, for example, of later intelligence information, that the objective of an aerial attack is not or has ceased to be a military objective, or is subject to special protection, or the attack is likely to cause civilian damage excessive to the overall military advantage anticipated and not merely from the particular raid, the attack should be cancelled or suspended by those possessing authority to take such action. This is a new limitation introduced by Protocol I,[71] but since it is based on the principle of proportionality it would apply to restrict the attacks of aircraft belonging to non-parties as well.

Insofar as protected places, such as medical and cultural installations and those likely to release dangerous forces, or civil defence establishments[72] are to be marked for purposes of identification, these should also be identifiable at night. Since illumination of such places may act as a guide to attacking aircraft, commanders may be unwilling to illuminate them. If, therefore, night bombing is to take place, proper daylight reconnaissance or other proper identification procedures should have been undertaken to indicate where such protected places are located to ensure their safety.

Forbidden weapons

The general rules regarding the use of weapons forbidding those which cause unnecessary suffering apply in air warfare. As in other fields of warlike activity, it should be remembered that, while they may cause long-lasting, severe and widespread damage and extensive casualties among the civilian population, as has been seen there is no law which forbids the use of nuclear weapons as such. Their use is restricted in accordance with the customary rules concerning unnecessary damage and proportionality.

As to the use of incendiaries by aircraft, the rules laid down in Protocol III of the Conventional Weapons Convention[73] apply. Incendiaries may not be used against civilians or civilian objects,[74] nor against military objectives located within 'concentrations of civilians'. They may however be used against military objectives in urban conurbations if the objective is not located within such a concentration.[75] The ban on incendiaries only applies to munitions which have flame as an incidental effect of their use. The Protocol expressly states that the prohibition against attack-

---

[70] Pr. I, Art. 57(3).
[71] Art. 57(2)(b).
[72] See ch. 14 below.
[73] See ch. 7, n. 127 above.
[74] This rule adds nothing to the existing law, since customary law forbids attacks directed against civilians.
[75] E.g. tanks located in a large park.

ing a military objective located within a concentration of civilians, other than by 'air-delivered incendiary weapons', does not apply to 'air-delivered incendiary weapons', 'except when [the] military objective is clearly separated from the concentration of civilians and all feasible precautions are taken with a view to limiting the incendiary effects to the military objective' and to avoiding or minimising incidental civilian losses. This permits incendiary attacks from the air if the civilians are protected in bunkers or shelters or are otherwise insulated from the effects of the attack either by space or a natural feature such as a hill. It also implies that there is an obligation upon the local defender to provide such protection for civilians as would 'separate' them from military objectives likely to be attacked.

Finally, incendiaries may not be used against forests or other plant cover unless these are used to conceal combatants or other military objectives, or are themselves military objectives, in the circumstances ruling at the time. This means that they may be attacked by fire to clear a field of fire or facilitate an advance or retreat.

Protocol III contains no provision forbidding the use of incendiaries against combatants, but if their use is intended to cause unnecessary suffering they would be banned under customary law. If combatants are in trenches or other protective locations or in houses during street fighting, incendiaries may be employed against them, so long as precautions are taken to protect the civilian population, and so long as the incendiaries, for example, white phosphorous rounds, are used as marking and not as normal rounds.[76]

Protocol II of the Conventional Weapons Convention[77] regulates the use of mines and booby-traps. The indiscriminate laying of mines, whether by air or otherwise, is expressly forbidden. Remotely delivered mines, such as those sown by aircraft, may only be used in areas which are or which contain military objectives, and only if their location can be accurately recorded or they are fitted with an effective neutralising mechanism which will operate either automatically or by remote control, when 'it is anticipated that the mine will no longer serve the military purpose for which it was placed in position'. Provided circumstances permit, advance warning is to be given of the delivery or dropping of such mines if they may affect the civilian population. For those states which are parties to the 1997 Mines Treaty, any use of anti-personnel mines is illegal.[78]

New problems relating to use of the air space are now becoming common in view of the manner in which computers may be available to intercept and neutralise computerised signals and mechanisms, including those affecting aircraft, land weapons, warships and the like. Such possibilities are being described as 'information warfare' or 'cyberwar'.[79]

---

[76] US, *Operational Law Handbook*, JA 422, 1996, p. 18-5.

[77] See ch. 7, n. 104 above.

[78] 36 I.L.M. 1507.

[79] See, e.g., Greenberg *et al.*, *Information War and International Law*, 1998; Libecki, *What is Information Warfare?* 1995; 'Authorities struggle to write the rule of cyberwar', *Washington Post*, 8 Jul. 1998.

Basic rule

At all times, regardless of any breaches of the law of armed conflict that may have been committed by the adverse party, reprisals by way of aerial attack against the civilian population or civilian objects are forbidden. Not only are these condemned by Protocol I,[80] but they would be in breach of the customary rule forbidding attacks directed against the civilian population.

In the absence of any specific rule relating to air warfare as such, the general rules governing land warfare and the selection of targets are equally applicable to aerial attacks directed against enemy personnel and ground or sea targets.

[80] Arts 51(6), 52(1), 57(5).

10

Prisoners of war

The basic rule

In classical and to some extent feudal times a member of the enemy forces captured in battle was considered to be in the power and at the disposal of his individual captor, who could kill or enslave him,[1] free him[2] or hold him for ransom.[3] This is no longer the case, and captured personnel are now the responsibility of the power by whose forces they have been captured[4] and their rights and status regulated in accordance with the 1949 Convention relative to the treatment of prisoners of war.[5] World War II was governed by the 1929 Convention,[6] to which, neither Japan nor the Soviet Union was a party, but, as was pointed out in the Nuremberg Judgment,[7] these rules were generally regarded as part of the customary law of armed conflict, so that its basic principles are binding even upon a state which has not become a party. In fact, by Article I[8] 'the High Contracting Parties undertake to respect ... the Convention in all circumstances', so parties are bound even though the enemy is not a party and this is confirmed in Article 2, at least to the extent that the non-party 'accepts and applies' the Convention as was done by Japan in 1941,[9] though in practice Japanese conduct was often contrary to the 1929

[1] See, e.g., 2 Phillipson, *The International Law and Custom of Ancient Greece and Rome*, 251.

[2] *Ibid.*, 256–7.

[3] See, e.g., Keen, *The Laws of War in the Late Middle Ages*, ch. 10.

[4] Hague Regs, Art. 3, confirmed by Geneva Conv. III, Art. 12. For general accounts of the law concerning prisoners of war, see Rosas, *The Legal Status of Prisoners of War*, Levie, *Prisoners of War in International Armed Conflict*, also his *Documents on Prisoners of War*.

[5] Schindler and Toman, 423.

[6] *Ibid.*

[7] The Judgment cited with approval the statement of Admiral Canaris to this effect in relation to the treatment of Soviet prisoners, the Soviet Union not then being a party to the 1929 Geneva Prisoners of War Conv (Schindler and Toman, 325), HMSO Cmd 6964 (1946) 8, 41 Am. J. Int'l Law (1947), 172, 228–9.

[8] This article is common to all four 1949 Conventions.

[9] In its note to the ICRC, after pointing out that it was not a party to the Conv., Japan stated 'as far as possible it intended to apply the Convention, *mutatis mutandis*, to all persons falling into its hands, while at the same time respecting the customs of each nation and

Convention's provisions.[10] None of the parties to the Korean conflict had ratified or acceded to the Convention; however, they 'agreed to be bound by its "humanitarian principles"[11] and the United Nations Command issued a number of regulations concerning the treatment of captured personnel in accordance with the Convention.[12] As regards the Vietnam War, the National Liberation Front informed the ICRC that 'it was not bound by the international treaties to which others beside itself subscribed … [T]he NLF, however, affirmed that the prisoners it held were humanely treated and that, above all, enemy wounded were collected and cared for'.[13] Since 1945 the majority of conflicts have not been acknowledged as wars in the formal sense of that term,[14] but by Article 2 the 1949 Convention is to apply in all cases of international armed conflict, whether a declared war or not even if one of the parties denies that there is a state of war. The application of the Convention, therefore, depends on the state of fact rather than any formal legal definition.

From the point of view of members of the armed forces this means that they must consider themselves bound by the laws of war with regard to the treatment of captured personnel whenever a conflict arises in which they are confronted by an adverse party. It also means that the Convention protects members of the forces of an aggressor. The Convention also applies when members of the forces are committed to a limited operation against foreign forces. It should therefore have been fully applicable in 1992–3 in the operations between the parts of the former Yugoslav state, even though there was evidence that none of those involved appeared prepared to respect the Convention, even while describing some of the captives as prisoners of war.[15]

Who are prisoners of war?

Not all those falling into the hands of a belligerent become prisoners of war or are entitled to prisoner of war status. Enemy civilians, for example, when taken into custody or interned do not fall into this category, and if captured are entitled to treatment in accordance with Geneva Convention IV, 1949,[16] unless they have

people in relation to the food and clothing of prisoners', Durand, *History of the ICRC*, vol. 2, *From Sarajevo to Hiroshima*, 521.

[10] See, e.g., Daws, *Prisoners of the Japanese*, 1994; Tanaka, *Hidden Horrors: Japanese War Crimes in World War II*, 1996.

[11] Levie, *Prisoners of War in International Armed Conflict*, 1978, 30, n.114.

[12] These are to be found in Levie, *Documents on Prisoners of War*, 1998.

[13] Levie, 'Maltreatment of prisoners of war in Vietnam', 2 Falk, *The Vietnam War and International Law*, 361, 362; Schmitt and Green, *Levie on the Law of War*, 1998, 95.

[14] See ch. 1 above.

[15] See, e.g., *The Times*, 7 Aug. 1992. It was not clear in 1999 whether the Yugoslav authorities would in fact treat captured US pesonnel, part of the NATO forces, as prisoners of war, despite demands that they be so regarded.

[16] Convention Relative to the Treatment of Civilians in Time of War, Schindler and Toman, 495, see ch. 12 below.

taken part in hostile activities when they may be regarded as unlawful combatants and treated accordingly.[17] A civilian head of state who is Commander-in-Chief of his nation's forces becomes a prisoner of war if he falls into enemy hands.[18] However, this may not be true if the civilian head holds that status in only a very formal sense, as is the Queen of England or the President of the United States, although the status of the latter is not as clear as is that of the former. Neutral nationals captured by a belligerent must be released as soon as operations permit, unless they have been guilty of unneutral activities,[19] or are volunteer members of the adverse party's forces.

Diplomatic representatives of the adverse party must not be made prisoners of war, but allowed to return to their own country and this is true whether the diplomat is accredited to the country by whose force he has been captured,[20] or if he is found in occupied territory, and this is normally done on a reciprocal basis.[21] After the occupation of Kuwait by Iraq in 1990 diplomats of countries supporting the United Nations resolutions condemning Iraq and intending to take military action against it were detained by the Iraqi authorities and in some cases located in potential military objectives, clear breaches of both customary and conventional law. Neutral diplomats, including military and other service attachés accompanying the forces of the adverse party in the field may not be taken prisoner, so long as they have a certificate of identity and have taken no part in the hostilities. They may, however, be ordered to leave the conflict area.

When there is doubt as to the status of a captive he is to be treated as if he were a prisoner of war[22] until such time as his status has been determined by a properly constituted tribunal,[23] which need not, however, be a court. If he is not held as a prisoner-of-war and is to be tried by the captor for an offence arising out of the hostilities, he is entitled to assert his entitlement to prisoner of war status before a judicial tribunal. This adjudication should, whenever possible, be made before his trial and unless, in the interest of the security of the holding state, the adjudication is held in camera, representatives of the Protecting Power[24] must be informed of the proceedings and are entitled to attend.[25]

[17] On lawful combatants, see ch. 6 above.
[18] The position of Leopold III of Belgium in World War II was anomalous. As commander-in-chief he surrendered his forces to the Germans, but this surrender was repudiated by the Belgian government in exile and, despite his internment by the Germans throughout the war, he was compelled to abdicate after Belgium's liberation.
[19] See ch. 16 below.
[20] In World War II, Sir Lancelot Oliphant, British Ambassador to Belgium, was captured and held by the occupying German forces, see his *Ambassador in Bonds*.
[21] In World War II the UK delayed the repatriation of their diplomats in Japan and the return of Japanese diplomats until certain named civilian journalists were included in the exchange arrangement.
[22] Conv. Art. 5.
[23] See, e.g., *Public Prosecutor* v. *Koi* [1968] A.C., 829, arising out of Indonesia's confrontation with Malaysia.
[24] See ch. 13 below.
[25] Pr. I. Art. 45.

A member of the forces who is captured while engaged in espionage out of uniform is not entitled to prisoner-of-war status and may be dealt with like any other spy.[26] If such person is resident in occupied territory and attempts to gather military information he is not to be regarded as a spy unless he does so by 'false pretences or deliberately in a clandestine manner', and he remains entitled to prisoner-of-war status even though captured while so engaged. A member of the forces who is not so resident and has engaged in espionage in occupied territory does not lose his prisoner entitlement and may not be treated as a spy unless captured before rejoining his own forces.[27]

In accordance with Article 16 of the Convention, subject to distinctions necessitated by sex[28] or by rank,[29] all prisoners are to be treated equally, without any adverse distinction based on race, nationality,[30] religious belief or political opinions,[31] or any other distinction founded on similar criteria, such as language, colour, social or professional status or the like.

The reference to nationality makes it clear that aliens serving in a belligerent force who are captured are entitled to the same treatment as prisoners of war as nationals of that belligerent. However, while the Protocol has widened the category of those entitled to treatment as prisoners of war, there is one group of 'fighters' which is expressly excluded and if captured denied combatant and prisoner-of-war status. Article 47 expressly condemns mercenaries[32] in this fashion, and this regardless of whether they are in the uniform of the state whose forces they have joined unless properly embodied as members of that force. However, it is probable that one who is alleged to be a mercenary has the right to question that status and assert that he is in fact entitled to prisoner of war status in the same fashion as any other captive. Moreover, there seems little doubt that even mercenaries are entitled to the minimum guarantees embodied in Article 75 of the Protocol[33] with regard to the treatment of persons in the power of a party to the conflict.

Treatment of prisoners of war

Responsibility for the treatment of prisoners of war rests upon the detaining power, although they may be transferred to the custody of another party to the

---

[26] See ch. 6 above, nn. 101 *et seq.*

[27] Pr. I, Art. 46.

[28] Art. 14.

[29] Arts 43–5.

[30] The Germans in World War II did, however, treat Soviet prisoners differently from any others, Nuremberg Judgment, 46–8, 226–9, resp.

[31] There was no such provision in the 1929 Prisoners of War Conv., but this did not sanction the treatment by Germany of Soviet political commissars, *Nuremberg Judgment*, 6, 226 resp.

[32] See ch. 6 above, nn. 70 *et seq.*

[33] See discussion re mercenaries at Geneva in Bothe, *et al.*, 269–72.

Convention[34] and even, in some circumstances, to a neutral power.[35] This suggests that they cannot be held by a joint command such as the Coalition during the Gulf War nor by NATO, nor even by the United Nations. Thus in Korea they were the responsibility of the power in whose camp they were held. If United Nations forces were directly involved in hostilities under a United Nations command it would be possible for the Security Council to set up camps under United Nations command and subject to inspection by the ICRC. Should a holding power fail to carry out its responsibilities it would be liable to pay compensation,[36] while the individuals responsible for or ordering ill-treatment as a result of the holding power's failure to exercise proper responsibility would be liable for war crimes.[37] This means prisoners of war must be treated humanely and protected at all times, particularly against any acts of violence[38] or intimidation, as well as against insults and public curiosity.[39] During the Gulf War 1991 there were complaints when the Iraqis subjected Coalition air force prisoners, who, it seemed, had been physically assaulted[40] to worldwide television exposure, and also when Iraqi prisoners were shown in a cowed posture while held by Coalition forces.

Prisoners of war are entitled to respect for their persons and honour and must be allowed to exercise the rights attaching to their civil capacity to the extent that the captivity permits.[41] 'Person' is a synonym for 'personality' and relates to both the moral and the physical person. The moral aspect of the concept covers their right to religious and intellectual freedom[42] and protection against acts, other than the mere fact of captivity, which might demoralise them. Article 14, together with Article 75(2) of Protocol I provides protection against physical violence or torture. Moreover, they must not be exposed to conditions likely to affect their health, due attention being paid to the climate, and must not be exposed to the dangers of the zone of operations and should be provided with air raid shelters.[43] The

---

[34] Art. 12.

[35] Arts 109–11.

[36] Hague Conv. IV, Art. 3 – after the Gulf War the conditions imposed by the Security Council upon Iraq, Res. 687, 692 (30 I.L.M., 847, 864) included an obligation to compensate all foreign nationals for any direct injury resulting from the invasion of Kuwait.

[37] See *In re Heyer* n. 38 below and ch. 18 below.

[38] See, e.g., *In re Heyer* – the Essen Lynching Case (1945) 1 War Crimes Reports, 88 – captured British airmen were murdered by a German civilian mob while being taken by a military escort for interrogation.

[39] During World War II the Japanese sometimes exposed Caucasian prisoners to public gaze in an attempt to induce ridicule on the part of bystanders.

[40] For a personal account of their treatment by two RAF officers, see Peters and Nichol, *Tornado Down*. See also Cornum, *She Went to War*, 1992. Her account differs from that of other females captured during this conflict; see n. 61 below.

[41] Conv., Art. 14.1.

[42] Conv., Arts 34, 38. This means that they should have access to chaplains and spiritual advisers as well as educational and sporting facilities. During World War II 'universities' existed in some prisoner-of-war camps in Europe and the Far East.

[43] Conv., Arts 22, 23.

location of their camps, which are to be clearly marked 'PW' or 'PG' (*prisonniers de guerre*), is to be given to the adverse party through the medium of the Protecting Power and should not be sited near military objectives. The practice sometimes resorted to in World War I of siting camps near such an objective as a reprisal for an alleged illegal action[44] is now unlawful since reprisals against prisoners of war are forbidden.[45] They are to be provided with proper shelter and food as well as proper medical treatment and should on no account be subjected to any medical or scientific treatment or experimentation which is not required by their own state of health.[46] This latter prohibition is so comprehensive that it cannot even be waived by a prisoner giving consent, other than for a blood transfusion or skin graft, 'provided that [consent is] given voluntarily and without any coercion[47] or inducement, and then only for therapeutic purposes, under conditions consistent with generally accepted medical standards and controls designed for the benefit of both the donor and the recipient'. It is possible that in exceptional circumstances, such as a kidney transplant from one sibling to another, this may be permitted if the surgery is performed by a medical officer of the same force as that of the two patients or under the supervision of the Red Cross.

The protection of the civil capacity of the prisoners includes their right to wear national insignia, uniform, badges of rank and decorations.[48] Officers are to be treated with due regard to their rank and age and are entitled to be attended by orderlies who speak the same language.[49] A prisoner's right to make a will or power of attorney or similar legal arrangement must be respected, as well as the right to transfer accounts. The Power of Origin should inform the Detaining Power of the necessary legal requirements and at the request of the prisoner, and

---

[44] See Spaight, *Air Power*, 376–84. After the invasion of Kuwait, 1990, Iraq placed foreign civilians and diplomats in similarly exposed positions to protect objectives considered likely to be attacked from the air.

[45] Conv., Art. 13, reproducing Conv. II, 1929, Art. 2. For a rather extreme example during the Carlist wars, see *The Times*, 14 Apr. 1875, and for incidents during World War II, e.g., Dieppe, Sark, the German 'Commando Order', and killing of German prisoners of war by Free French Forces of Interior, see Kalshoven, *Belligerent Reprisals*, 178–200.

[46] Conv., Art. 13, Pr. I, Art. 11; see, e.g., re World War I for reference to experiments on Italian prisoners of war obituary of Prof. Albert von Szent György, *The Times*, 27 Oct. 1986; for World War II, see, e.g., *In re Brandt* (doctors' trial) (1947) 1 T.W.C., 1, 2 T.W.C., 171; 14 Ann. Dig. 296. See also re Japanese experiments, Morimura Seichi, *The Devil's Feast*; Williams and Wallace, *Unit 731*, 1989; and statement by Prof. Tanaka Yuki re tests on Chinese prisoners of war to assess effects of ingesting liquid mustard gas, *Edmonton Journal* 18 Sept. 1988, citing article in Bulletin of Atomic Scientists; see also his *Hidden Horrors*, pp. 148–50, and Williams and Wallace, *Unit 731*.

[47] During the Yugoslav campaign against dissidents in Kosovo, which led to the 1999 NATO bombing campaign, there were allegations that Serb forces were taking blood from Kosovo males, against their wishes, who were too young or too weak for forced labour, *The Times*, 17 Apr. 1999.

[48] Conv., Art. 40. General Noriega of Panama was so dressed even during his trial in the United States on drug charges see Albert, *The Case Against the General*, 1993, ch. 12.

[49] Conv., Art. 44.

in any case immediately after death, any will should be transmitted to the Protecting Power with a certified copy to the Central Agency. Personal rights, such as those of a parent or to contract marriage, are excluded, although a detaining power may permit this when both a male and female prisoner are held.[50]

Should a prisoner die a proper certificate shall issue and if the death has been caused by a sentry or some other person an official inquiry must be held and the Protecting Power informed. If the report indicates any personal guilt, prosecution of the person responsible must follow.[51] Any prisoner who dies must be buried honourably and, if possible, according to his own religious rites and in an individual grave. Cremation is permitted at the request of the deceased, in accordance with his religious beliefs or for reasons of hygiene. The grave should be properly marked and information recorded with the Graves Registration Service maintained by the Detaining Power. Whenever possible dead prisoners should be buried with their own nationals.

Prisoners, other than officers, may be compelled to work, but no prisoner is to be employed on work of a humiliating kind whereby he might be made a laughing stock to those around him, either fellow prisoners or civilians among whom he might work,[52] nor should he be employed on work of a dangerous character[53] or in support of the Detaining Power's war effort.[54] The removal of mines or similar devices is considered to be dangerous[55] When the job requires skill, training should be provided. 'A fair working rate of pay' is required, which shall be no less

[50] During World War II, arrangements were sometimes made, by endowing a false nationality upon a building, to enable a female prisoner to give birth to a child in her own 'country' – information imparted by Max Habicht, ICRC representative, based on his own experience.

[51] Arts 120, 121. For such an investigation by British authorities into the death of an Argentine officer prisoner of war after the Falklands hostilities, see *The Times*, 29 Apr., 13 May, 2 Jul. 1982. See also *ibid.*, 12 Apr. 1983 for report of killing by a British sergeant of an Argentine prisoner of war who had been badly burned in an explosion and was shot to put him out of his misery: 'The facts [were] explained to Argentine officers who accepted them and did not pursue them further.'

[52] By, e.g., being made to do work which is normally only done by women.

[53] By Arts 53–6, the duration of work should not be excessive and there should be proper rest periods, with one 24-hour period off per week, preferably that normal in their own country, or Sunday. If injured at work they shall receive due care and attention and receive a certificate to present to their home authorities to claim compensation. Fitness to work shall be checked periodically and medical authorities may recommend exemption. Prisoners employed privately, e.g., on farms, shall receive treatment not inferior to that prescribed in the Convention, with the camp authorities remaining responsible for their care, maintenance, treatment and payment, and the prisoners retaining their right of access to the prisoners' representative (see n. 97 below).

[54] See, e.g., *In re Milch* (1947) 2 T.W.C., 353, 773; 14 Ann. Dig. 299. Since nearly all activities in modern war contribute in some way to the war effort, the 1949 Conv., unlike the Hague Regs and the 1929 Conv. (Art. 31), rather than forbidding kinds of work lists the kind that may be ordered. The list is only exemplary and not exhaustive (Art. 50).

[55] Art. 52.

than 'one-fourth of one Swiss franc for a full working day'[56] and arrangements must be made to safeguard any money taken from a prisoner at the time of his capture, and they are to be paid monthly advances with proper accounts kept.

Prisoners must be allowed to retain all their personal property, except vehicles, arms, and other military equipment and documents. However, protective equipment must be left in their possession, as must clothing and articles used for feeding, even though the property of their government, together with articles of sentimental value.[57] If they lack identity cards or papers, these should be provided.[58] Money may only be taken from them by order of an officer, with details as to amount and ownership properly registered and a receipt given. Sums paid in the Detaining Power's currency or changed into such currency must also be properly accounted for. But money belonging to the government, for example in the hands of the paymaster for payment to the troops, is legitimate booty and becomes the property of the government of the captors. This is also the case with all property, other than personal, taken from prisoners. None of it belongs to the individual captor.[59]

Female prisoners must be treated with due regard to their sex and must in no case be treated less favourably than male prisoners. Their sex must be taken into consideration in the allocation of labour and the provision of sanitary and sleeping facilities. If undergoing disciplinary or judicial punishment, this must be no more severe than would be imposed upon a member of the Detaining Power's forces, male or female, for the same offence, and if held for disciplinary punishment they must be kept in separate quarters from men and under the guard of women.[60] While all prisoners must be protected from violence, by Protocol I, Article 76, all women in the hands of a Detaining Power must be specially protected against rape and other sexual assaults. After the Gulf War, 1991, it was disclosed that women members of the Coalition forces taken prisoner by Iraqi forces had in fact been sexually assaulted.[61]

The rights granted to prisoners of war under the Convention are absolute and cannot be renounced by them,[62] so that if a captive volunteers to join the captor's forces any disciplinary treatment to which he may become subject by so doing does not detract from his rights as a prisoner of war.[63] While the belligerents may

---

[56] Art. 62.

[57] Thus, they must not be deprived of family photographs and the like, nor should attempts be made to persuade them to surrender these by bartering for other objects which might be of value to them. 'Souvenir hunting' is forbidden.

[58] Conv., Art. 18.

[59] This is a provision of customary law and was already embodied in the Lieber Code, see ch. 1 above.

[60] Arts 14, 49, 25, 29, 88, 97, resp.

[61] See 'Crossing the front line' by Kate Muir, *The Times* (Life and Times Section) 12 Jun. 1992.

[62] Art. 7.

[63] See, e.g., Sleeman, *The Gozawa Trial* (Indian prisoner of war joining the Indian National Army).

make various agreements affecting prisoners of war and their treatment, 'no special agreement [so made] shall adversely affect the situation of prisoners of war, as defined by the present Convention, nor restrict the rights which it confers upon them'.[64]

Duties of the Detaining Power

Broadly speaking the duties of the Detaining Power are the concomitant of the rights of prisoners of war. In addition, however, there are duties directly imposed upon them and controlling their freedom of action. The Convention specifically provides that prisoners of war are in the hands of the enemy Power and, irrespective of any individual responsibilities that may exist for the individual captor, it is 'the detaining Power [which] is responsible for the treatment given them'.[65]

Immediately upon capture, the Detaining Power must establish an information bureau for prisoners which shall be informed and maintain all records concerning them. Similar bureaux must be established in any neutral or non-belligerent country receiving within its territory persons entitled to be treated as prisoners of war and these bureaux must co-operate with the Central Prisoners of War Information Agency set up in a neutral country or by the ICRC.[66] This agency shall collect all information that can be obtained through official and private channels and shall pass it as soon as possible to the prisoners' country of origin or the country to whose forces they belong. The bureau is also responsible for replying to enquiries concerning prisoners of war and collecting valuables and documents useful to next of kin, left by prisoners who have been repatriated or released, escaped or died.

In accordance with Articles 70 to 74 of the Convention, immediately upon capture and upon transfer from one place of detention to another, prisoners shall be allowed to send a card, which must be forwarded without delay, to their families and to the Central Agency giving information of their capture, address and state of health. They must also be allowed to send and receive not less than two letters and four cards monthly and in exceptional circumstances even telegrams. The language of such correspondence should be in the prisoner's language, although the Detaining Power may permit use of another. They shall also be allowed to receive parcels of clothing, food, medical supplies, religious and educational material, books, examination papers, musical instruments and the like, as well as collective relief parcels in accordance with special agreements made between the parties or in accordance with rules annexed to the Convention, and distribution of which shall be under the control of the Protecting Power or the ICRC. All relief shipments are free of customs, other duties, and postal charges, but correspondence to

[64] Art. 6.
[65] Art. 12.
[66] Conv., Arts 122, 123.

and from prisoners is subject to censorship, although this must not be used to delay transmission.

The Detaining Power must inform prisoners and, through the Protecting Power,[67] the powers on whom they depend of the measures taken by the Detaining Power to fulfil its obligations under the Convention and a copy of the Convention in a language that the prisoners understand must be posted in every camp.[68]

The Convention is to be applied in co-operation with and under the scrutiny of the Protecting Power whose duty it is to safeguard the interests of the parties to the conflict. To fulfil this task the latter may, with the consent of the parties affected, nominate delegates even from neutral countries. The parties to the conflict must co-operate with the Protecting Power which must take account of the Detaining Power's security when fulfilling its task. In addition to the Protecting Power, the ICRC or some other humanitarian organisation may, subject to the consent of the parties, undertake activities for the protection and relief of the prisoners.[69] By Article 126 of the Convention, delegates or representatives of Protecting Powers and the ICRC must be allowed to visit all places where prisoners of war may be, including places of detention and labour, and may interview prisoners and prisoners' representatives without witnesses, either personally or through interpreters. With the consent of the Detaining Power and the Power of Origin such visiting delegations may include compatriots of the prisoners being visited.

For the Detaining Power the greatest value to be derived from a prisoner is intelligence about the adverse party. Every prisoner of war may be interrogated but he is only required to give his name, rank, date of birth and serial number and for this purpose he should be in possession of an identity card, which may not be taken from him. If he is unable to give this information because of physical or mental illness, he must be handed to the medical service for treatment and care, and efforts made to establish his identity. Should he refuse to supply such information, he may forfeit privileges due to his rank or status. No form of coercion may be applied to a prisoner in an attempt to secure any other information and all questioning must be done in a language that he understands.[70] Any torture, physical or mental, or outrage upon his personal dignity to secure such information or for any other reason[71] would amount to a war crime.[72]

Captors must not kill prisoners of war for any reason, even if they are unable to provide the necessary facilities or personnel to guard them or to restrict their

---

[67] See ch. 13 below.

[68] Arts 69, 41.

[69] Arts 8, 9. The role, appointment and training of the Protecting Power and its representatives has been affected by Pr. I, see ch. 13 below.

[70] Art. 17.

[71] Pr. I, Art. 75 – Fundamental Guarantees.

[72] See ch. 18 below.

movements,[73] or because they will have to be fed thus reducing the supplies available to the captors,[74] nor because they may gain their liberty in the event of an early success by their own forces. Self-preservation or military necessity on the part of the captor can never provide an excuse for the murder of prisoners.[75] This admits of no exception, so that it extends to commandos,[76] airborne troops, guerrillas, and the like, although circumstances in a particular operational situation may permit measures of supervision and even restraint,[77] and captured escapers may be specially confined so long as this does not affect their health or detract from any of the protection afforded by the Convention.[78] Weapons may not be used against prisoners of war, even those attempting to escape,[79] except as an extreme measure and after proper warning has been given.[80]

As already indicated, prisoner-of-war camps must not be situated near the combat zone or military objectives, and prisoners must be evacuated from danger areas as soon as possible. The only exception is in respect of those who, because of wounds or sickness, would run greater risk by being moved. They shall not be exposed to undue risk during evacuation, which must be conducted in conditions at least similar to those for the forces of the Detaining Power during changes of station, and during the evacuation they must be provided with adequate food, clothing and medical attention and proper lists must be maintained of those affected.[81]

The camps for prisoners of war must be on land and those captured at sea must

---

[73] In such circumstances the captor may have to release them, but he is entitled to remove their arms and other military equipment. If the area in which they are to be released is, e.g., a jungle with wild beasts, they should be allowed to retain such weapons as will enable them to preserve their lives. They should also be supplied with the means of sustenance. By Pr. I, Art. 41(3), if captured in 'unusual conditions', e.g. while on a long-range patrol, and cannot be easily evacuated, they must be released and all 'feasible', i.e., practicable, precautions taken for their safety, even if this means leaving them with some of their weapons.

[74] If they are to be released for this reason, they must be supplied with sufficient provisions for their immediate needs.

[75] See, e.g., US, Dept of the Army, 'The Geneva Conventions and Hague Convention IV of 1907', ASubjScd 27–1, 8 Oct. 1970, and 'Lesson plan' annexed thereto; see summary in Green, 'Aftermath of Vietnam: war law and the soldier', 4 Falk, *The Vietnam War and International Law*, 147, 169–71.

[76] The German 'Commando Order' of World War II was a clear war crime.

[77] Thus the tying of the hands or legs of prisoners to prevent escape during, e.g., a commando raid, is permissible, but the permanent shackling of prisoners, particularly in a prison camp, is not.

[78] Art. 92.

[79] Recaptured prisoners must on no account be put to death, simply because of their flight, as happened in 1944 to a number of RAF, Dominion and Allied Air Force personnel who escaped from Stalag Luft III and were recaptured, see *Stalag Luft III* case (1947), 11 War Crimes Reports 31; 13 Ann. Dig., 292. Recaptured personnel are only liable to disciplinary punishment, and if captured after a successful escape, i.e., after rejoining his forces, they cannot be punished for the original escape.

[80] Art. 42.

[81] Arts 19, 20.

be transferred to land as soon as possible. The camps must be in healthy areas, with proper facilities for guaranteeing hygiene and health. So long as these guarantees are met the prisoners may be housed in tents. Only prisoners sentenced for criminal offences may be detained in penitentiaries. The captor may restrict the movements of his prisoners to a fenced area or order them to remain within a defined area. They may not be held in close confinement, other than by way of disciplinary or penal measures in accordance with the Convention,[82] or because such confinement is necessary for their health or safety.[83]

Officers should be housed separately,[84] and prisoners should be gathered in camps according to nationality, language and customs.[85] They should not, other than with their own consent, be separated from the forces with whom they were serving at the time of capture.[86] They may be released on parole,[87] provided their national law permits this, although an individual prisoner may give his parole even though it my lay him open to criminal charges on his return home.[88] No prisoner may be compelled to give his parole.[89]

Since the Detaining Power is responsible for the care and health of prisoners, they are to receive medical and spiritual attention, if possible from doctors or chaplains of their own forces or of their own nationality.[90] Medical officers and chaplains who are detained are not prisoners of war, although they must be treated at least as well as prisoners, and are to receive all facilities necessary for the medical care and religious ministration of the prisoners and should be employed primarily in attending to the needs of their own personnel.[91] Prisoners who are medically qualified but not attached to their force's medical branch may be required by the Detaining Power to exercise medical functions on behalf of their own prisoners. They remain prisoners, but must be treated as other medical personnel and are exempt from any other work.[92] It is not an offence against their national law for such persons also to attend to the needs of the adverse party.

[82] Arts 82–98.

[83] Art. 21.

[84] Art. 44.

[85] Difficulties may arise in this connection in view of Pr. I, Art. 85(4)(c), which makes 'practices of *apartheid* ... based on racial discrimination' a grave breach (see ch. 18 below). In so far as this provision relates to cooking or food generally, Conv., Art. 26 provides that they shall, as far as possible, be associated with preparation of their food.

[86] Conv., Art. 22.

[87] Parole is an undertaking not to escape and, once given, must be scrupulously observed. It is often granted to those whose health necessitates less stringent confinement than is normally the case with prisoners of war.

[88] On the outbreak of hostilities, parties to the conflict are required to exchange information as to their laws concerning parole. Some countries, e.g., Canada, make it an offence for a prisoner of war to fail 'to rejoin H.M.'s service when able to do so' (National Defence Act, R.S.C., N-4). If he is free of restriction, as he would be on parole, he would be able to attempt to rejoin the forces.

[89] Art. 21.

[90] Arts 30–7.

[91] Arts 30, 33, 35; see also ch. 11 below.

[92] Art. 32.

Prisoner-of-war camps must be under the command of a responsible commissioned officer[93] of the Detaining Power who, regardless of his rank, is entitled to a salute from all prisoners regardless of their rank. Other officers of the Detaining Power are entitled to receive from prisoners the same respect they would afford officers in their own forces. The camp commandant must be in possession of a copy of the Convention and ensure that its provisions are known to all members of his staff and guard,[94] and he is responsible for its application.[95] The copy of the Convention made available for the prisoners must be posted where all may read it and any prisoner who does not understand that copy may request one in his own language, and any prisoner who cannot have access to where it is posted is also entitled to a personal copy. Similarly, any regulations, orders or other notices for the attention of prisoners, or addressed to prisoners individually, must be in a language they understand.[96]

Prisoners have the right to address complaints to the military authority detaining them or to the representative of the Protecting Power or of the ICRC. This may be done either individually or through a prisoners' representative.[97] When officers and other ranks are detained in the same camp, the senior officer prisoner shall be recognised as the prisoners' representative and is responsible for representing them whenever this is necessary. When no officer is present, the prisoners shall elect one of their own as the prisoners' representative, who must be acceptable to the Detaining Power.[98] If the latter rejects the elected representative, he must inform the Protecting Power of his reasons. If prisoner officers are attached to a labour camp for administrative purposes they may be elected as prisoners' representative. In an officers' camp, the senior officer is the representative. Prisoners' representatives may be assisted by elected representatives, chosen from the officers or other ranks by themselves. Where camps hold prisoners of various nationalities, each national group must be permitted to elect its own representative. Neither a complaining prisoner, nor the representative passing the complaint, may be punished for frivolous or unfounded complaints.[99] Apart from acting as an intermediary with the Detaining Power, the prisoners' representative is concerned with the physical, spiritual and intellectual well-being of the prisoners, and in supervising the organisation of mutual assistance and collective relief.

Subject to the limitations already referred to,[100] prisoners of war who are physically fit may be made to work by the Detaining Power, taking into account their

[93] Art. 39. This is intended to prevent a recurrence of the World War II situation when some German camps were under command of SS or Gestapo officers, while some Japanese camps were commanded by non-commissioned officers.

[94] By Art. 127 parties must disseminate its text as widely as possible and include its study in their programmes of military instruction. This obligation is reiterated in Pr. I, Art. 83.

[95] Conv., Art. 39.

[96] Art. 41.

[97] Arts 78–9.

[98] Art. 79.

[99] Art. 78.

[100] See nn. 52–4 above.

age, sex and physical aptitude, especially with a view to maintaining their physical and mental health. Non-commissioned officers may only be engaged in supervisory work unless they ask for other employment, while officers may only be employed at their own request.[101]

Prisoners' representatives are not responsible for any offences committed by prisoners.[102] They shall not be required to perform any other work if this would interfere with their activities as representative.[103]

The law controlling prisoners of war

As among themselves, and subject to their obligation to comply with the disciplinary regulations of the Detaining Power, which may make them subject to its own Code of Service Discipline, prisoners remain subject to their own system of military law and such regulations as may be issued by the prisoners' representative and his assistants. Since the 1949 Convention forbids any agreements which detract from the rights of prisoners and the delegation of any disciplinary powers to any prisoner,[104] the arrangements sometimes made at the end of World War II whereby large numbers of prisoners were left under the administrative direction military discipline and law of their own officers[105] rather than held in prisoner of war camps would now be unlawful. The Canadian suggestion that as 'unarmed surrendered enemy personnel' they were no longer prisoners of war lacks any support in law. Breaches of a prisoner's national law or of the representative's regulations should be punished by his own military authority on his repatriation.

Prisoners of war are subject to the laws, regulations and orders of the Detaining Power, but must not be punished for any act which would not have been punishable if committed by a member of that Power's own forces. They are subject to the same courts and procedure as those forces,[106] but this does not prevent them from being punished for offences against camp discipline. Proceedings may be judicial, conducted by ordinary criminal courts or court martial, or disciplinary,

---

[101] Art. 49.

[102] Art. 80.

[103] Art. 81.

[104] Arts 6, 96. During World War II trials were held by prisoners of their own personnel accused, e.g., of collaborating with the Detaining Power and executing them after such proceedings. In such cases, the Detaining Power often tried the prisoners responsible for murder and executed them, see, e.g., *R. v. Werner* [1947] 2 S.A.L.R., 828, 14 Ann. Dig. 205; *R. v. Perzenowski* [1947] 1 D.L.R., 705, 13 *ibid.* 300.

[105] As a result of such an arrangement the Commander of German 30 Corps was able to authorise the trial and execution, with weapons supplied by his captors, of two of his men after surrender of his forces to Canadian 1st Army in 1945, see, e.g., Levie, *Prisoners of War in International Armed Conflict*, (1978), 336, n. 102; see, also, Canada, *Commons Debates*, 1 Oct. 1966, 8510 and 21 Dec. 1966, 11445–6; C. B. C. *Fifth Estate – Canada and German Ps.W.*, 24 Mar. 1998.

[106] Art. 82.

tried by a non-judicial body such as the camp commandant. They may only be tried by a civil tribunal if the detaining Power's forces may be so tried for the offence involved,[107] and provided the tribunal offers the essential guarantees of independence and impartiality generally recognised as compatible with the rule of law.[108] Prisoners may be tried for offences, e.g., war crimes, committed before capture, and, it would seem, for offences committed previously against the captor's law.[109] Even if convicted, so long as they remain prisoners of war, they retain the benefits of the Convention.[110] They should not, therefore, be handed by their captor to another state which might have some claim against them.[111] In so far as the Security Council may establish *ad hoc* tribunals for the trial of alleged war criminals, holding powers may be under an obligation to transfer persons for trial by the tribunals. For those countries recognising the jurisdiction of the proposed International Criminal Court a right to effect such transfer is introduced.[112]

No prisoner may be punished more than once for the same offence or on the same charge.[113] This does not, however, prevent his home state from trying him upon repatriation even though he has already been tried by the camp commandant while a prisoner.

Penalties imposed must be the same as those provided for members of the Detaining Power's own forces guilty of the same offences, and women prisoners must be treated no more harshly than women members of those forces, nor than their male comrades.[114] In fixing the penalty, the Detaining Power must remember that the prisoner does not owe him allegiance and is not voluntarily within his power, so that the penalty may be less than the minimum that would be imposed on a member of the holding force. Prisoners who have completed their sentence must be treated as any other prisoner of war. Collective or corporal punishment,

---

[107] In some countries, e.g., Canada, such offences as murder, rape or manslaughter committed by a member of the Canadian forces in Canada cannot be tried by service tribunals and prisoners of war committing such offences would be tried by a civil court, see *R. v. Perzenowski.*

[108] Arts 84, 105, and Pr. I, Art. 75 (fundamental guarantees).

[109] Thus, the US tried General Noriega after his capture in Panama for drug offences against the United States.

[110] Art. 85. The Soviet Union and its allies made a reservation against this Article, maintaining their right to treat convicted war criminals in accordance with their own laws for such offences, even though these might be inconsistent with the provisions of the Convention. Some western powers refused to recognise the validity of this reservation. Persons guilty of espionage are probably not protected by this Article, since they are not war criminals and customary law removes from them the status of combatant so that they are not considered prisoners of war. The same is true of mercenaries. Both groups, however, would still be protected by Pr. I, Art. 75 concerning fundamental guarantees.

[111] See, e.g., the instance during the Falklands War when the UK proposed to hand over Captain Astiz for interrogation by Sweden and France, *The Times*, 13, 14 May 1982.

[112] See, ch. 18 below.

[113] Conv., Art. 86, Pr. I, Art. 75(4)(h).

[114] Conv., Art. 88, Pr. I, Art. 75.

imprisonment without daylight, deprivation of clothing or sustenance, cruelty and torture are all forbidden.[115]

Disciplinary punishment is limited to a fine of not more than 50 per cent of advances and working pay which might be earned during a maximum of thirty days, discontinuance of privileges above the minimum stipulated in the Convention, fatigue duties to a maximum of two hours daily, although officers may not be sentenced to such duties. Confinement may also be imposed. In no case may a disciplinary punishment be brutal, inhuman or dangerous to health.[116] The maximum period of any punishment is thirty days, regardless of the number of charges, but if separate disciplinary hearings are held and the duration of any one punishment exceeds ten days at least three days must elapse between punishments. Any period of confinement awaiting a hearing is deducted from the award.

Prisoners charged with disciplinary offences may only be held in confinement if members of the forces of the Detaining Power would be so held and the confinement must not exceed fourteen days and, without prejudice to the competence of the courts and superior military authorities, disciplinary punishment may only be awarded by the camp commandant or his delegate.[117] The accused must be informed of the charges, given an opportunity to defend himself, call witnesses and, if necessary, have the services of a competent interpreter. The decision must be announced to the accused and the prisoners' representative, and while serving a disciplinary punishment he continues to enjoy the benefits of the Convention, including postal, parcel and medical rights. He must not be confined in a penitentiary and only in proper sanitary conditions with facilities for keeping himself clean, with women detained separately from men and supervised by women.[118]

While a prisoner of war may be tried by the Detaining Power for acts committed prior to captivity, he remains protected by the Convention,[119] even if the charges arise from war crimes so long as he remains a prisoner of war. He may not be subjected to any pressure to make him plead guilty and must be allowed to present his defence, so he cannot be tried *in absentia*,[120] and he may be represented by qualified counsel or advocate, though instead of counsel he may choose to be assisted by a prisoner comrade, and if he fails to select counsel the Protecting Power may select one for him. It would seem that the practice in World War II of

[115] Conv., Art. 87.

[116] Conv., Art. 89.

[117] While such power cannot be delegated to any prisoner, administrative punishments like deprivation of games participation or 'sending to coventry' may be imposed by a prisoner's representative or a prisoner non-commissioned officer so long as this does not derogate from rights conferred by the Convention.

[118] Conv., Arts 95–8. There is no similar provision for men to be supervised by men. Since, by Art. 87, they must not be confined in places without daylight, the World War II practice of confinement in a 'hole' is now clearly illegal, as would be prolonged kneeling in the sun or between or over sharp projectiles.

[119] Conv, Art. 85.

[120] See, e.g., *In re Rhode* (1946), Webb, *The Natzweiler Trial*; see Pr. I, Art. 75 (3) and (4).

appointing a defending officer who might not be professionally legally qualified[121] would now be unlawful, though he could agree to be defended by such.

Whenever it is intended to institute judicial proceedings against a prisoner of war, the Protecting Power must be given at least three weeks notice of the date of trial. The prisoners' representative must also be informed, and if neither is so told the trial must be postponed. The Protecting Power's representative is entitled to be present at the trial, unless it is decided to hold it in camera. The Protecting Power must be told of any such decision and while the prisoner cannot be tried *in absentia*, he may be sentenced while absent, but must be told of the sentence in a language he understands. The Protecting Power and the prisoners' representative must be informed of any judgment and sentence, together with details as to the right of appeal, which shall be the same as that available to members of the Detaining Power's forces.[122] Where no local right of appeal exists, the prisoner must depend on a petition of clemency put forward by himself, his counsel, the Protecting Power or the prisoners' representative.

Prisoners of war must be told of any orders, rules or regulations prevailing in the camp,[123] and the Protecting Power must be told as soon as possible of those offences which are subject to the death penalty so that the Power of Origin may be informed, and no other offence shall be made subject to that penalty without concurrence of the Power of Origin. Before pronouncing any death penalty the court should be told that the prisoner owes no allegiance to the Detaining Power. No death sentence may be carried out until six months after the Protecting Power has been informed, and this period must be observed even though the Detaining Power's national law requires that a death sentence be carried out immediately after the final appellate process has been exhausted.[124]

End of captivity

Unless he has given his parole, a prisoner of war commits no offence against international law by attempting to escape. An escape is considered successful if he has rejoined his own forces or those of an ally; left the territory of the Detaining Power or of an ally of that Power; or has joined a ship flying his national or an allied flag. If he reaches neutral territory his position is dependent on Hague Convention V regarding the rights and duties of neutrals.[125] A prisoner who has made good his escape and is subsequently recaptured is not liable to punishment in respect of the escape, and it would seem that an escapee who has been picked up in the territorial

[121] See, e.g., Green, 'The Problems of a wartime international lawyer', 2 Pace Y.B. Int'l Law (1989) 93.
[122] Conv., Arts 103–7.
[123] Conv., Art. 41.
[124] Arts 100, 101.
[125] See ch. 16 below; see also Conv., Arts 110, 111.

waters of the Detaining Power by a vessel of his own or an allied Power should be considered to have successfully escaped,[126] since he left the Detaining Power's territory, and should not therefore be punished for that escape.

All prisoners of war are to be released and repatriated immediately upon cessation of active hostilities and although this is obligatory and no prisoner of war may agree to a diminution of his rights,[127] a practice has grown up since the Korean War of not repatriating prisoners who are unwilling to return home. After World War II criticism was levelled at the United Kingdom for having compulsorily repatriated Cossack prisoners of war to the Soviet Union and anti-Communist prisoners to Yugoslavia.[128] Despite the obligation to release and repatriate immediately upon cessation of hostilities, Iran delayed repatriation of 496 Iraqi prisoners until 1997, nine years after the end of the Iran–Iraq war, with Iraq contending that Iran continued to hold a further 18,000.[129] Parties are to repatriate, regardless of rank or number, all seriously wounded or sick prisoners when fit to travel and, when possible, agreements should be made between the parties and with the co-operation of neutrals for the detention of such persons in neutral territory pending such repatriation, but no sick or wounded person should be repatriated against his wishes during hostilities.[130] Arrangements should also be made for the retention in neutral territory of able-bodied prisoners of war who have undergone a long period of imprisonment.[131]

Offences against prisoners

Parties to the conflict shall take such measures as are necessary to suppress and punish all breaches of the Convention and all such breaches amount to war crimes and are punishable as such.[132] Some breaches are considered so serious as to be specifically defined in the Convention as 'grave breaches'.[133] Every person

---

[126] Art. 91.

[127] Conv., Arts 118, 7.

[128] See, e.g., Tolstoy, *The Minister and the Massacres*, 1986; Grigg, 'Mac and the massacres: good intent but a bad decision', *The Times*, 23 Aug. 1986.

[129] *Washington Times*, 30 Nov. 1997.

[130] Art. 109. Prisoners eligible for repatriation in this way cannot be denied repatriation on the ground of disciplinary punishment (Art. 115), and no prisoner so repatriated may be employed on active military service (Art. 117).

[131] Arts 118, 119.

[132] See ch. 18 below.

[133] Art. 130: wilful killing, torture or inhuman treatment, including biological experiments, wilfully causing great suffering or serious injury to body or health, compelling a prisoner of war to serve in the forces of the adverse party, or wilfully depriving him of the right to a fair and regular trial. Pr. I, Art. 85 adds an intentional attack directed against prisoners of war, unjustifiable delay in repatriation, or subjecting them to practices of *apartheid* or other inhuman and degrading practices involving outrages upon personal dignity based on racial discrimination.

responsible for such offences or having ordered or knowingly failed to prevent such acts by those under his command[134] is, regardless of nationality,[135] liable to trial by any party to the Convention, thus making grave breaches, which are in fact war crimes, subject to universal jurisdiction so that those accused may be tried in any country into whose hands they fall, including neutrals. Moreover, they may be handed over for trial by any party to the Convention making out a *prima facie* case,[136] including a neutral whose nationals may have been made prisoners of war and subjected to treatment in breach of the Convention. When the Security Council has established tribunals for the trial of war criminals, those accused of such offences against prisoners of war may be handed over in accordance with the terms of the constituent instrument, and such transfer may also be effected by parties to the proposed International Criminal Court.

Non-international conflicts

The Geneva Convention on Prisoners of War only applies in international conflicts. However, by Article 3 of the Convention, the parties to such a conflict are obligated 'to apply, as a minimum, the following provisions: (1) persons … including members of armed forces who have laid down their arms and those placed *hors de combat* by sickness, wounds, detention, or any other cause, shall in all circumstances be treated humanely …'. The parties, or any one of them, may of course decide to treat any captured personnel in accordance with the Convention. Problems, however, arise when the conflict is not recognised as being subject in any way to the Convention, an attitude which Israel adopts to 'terrorists' acting in the name of the Hezbollah. However, even in these relations Israel demands that its personnel be treated according to the law of armed conflict and tends to treat many of those captured by it as if they were prisoners of war. In 1998, however, it was reported that Israel was delaying the release and 'repatriation' of ten Lebanese citizens, held without trial, including eight members of Hezbollah, retaining them as hostages against the return of missing or captured Israeli servicemen. The detainees in question were said by security forces to have been 'kidnapped during military operations in southern Lebanon,' where Israel has maintained a presence since the War for Peace in the Galilee.' They had

---

[134] See *Re Yamashita* (1945) 4 *War Crimes Reports*, 1, and (1946) 327 US 1, and *Re Meyer* (1945), reported as *Abbaye Ardenne* case, 4 *ibid.* 97 – a fuller report is to be found in Green, *Essays*, 1999, 292. See also Parks, 'Command responsibility for war crimes', 6 Mil. Law Rev. (1973), 1; Green, 'Superior orders and command responsibility', 27 Can. Y.B. Int'l Law (1989), 167 and 'War crimes, crimes against humanity and command responsibility', in *Essays*, 1999, ch. VIII..

[135] This authorises the trial for war crimes of one's own forces (see, e.g., for some examples, de Zayas, *The Wehrmacht War Crimes Bureau, 1939–1945*, (1989), those of an ally, of the enemy or his allies, as well as any neutral national.

[136] Art. 129.

applied for their release and the Supreme Court held that 'Israel may hold in custody people, citizens of another country, that the State believes may be of use during negotiations over the missing and the captured.' It was conceded that this infringed human rights, but that Israel's 'vital interests' took precedence.[137]

[137] *The Times*, 5 Mar. 1998.

11

The wounded, sick and shipwrecked

Common approach

Traditionally the international law of armed conflict has distinguished between land and sea warfare dealing with the wounded and sick in these theatres as two separate categories. In 1864 the first Convention for the Amelioration of the Conditions of the Wounded and Sick in Armies in the Field was adopted,[1] to be followed four years later by a further Convention[2] comprising Additional Articles so as to include maritime warfare, and making provision for care of the shipwrecked. Though this never came into force, the parties involved in the Franco–German War, 1870–71, and the Spanish–American War, 1889, agreed to abide by its provisions. At the 1899 Hague Conference a Convention was adopted[3] for the Adaptation to Maritime Warfare of the Principles of the Geneva Convention of 1864 and in 1906 this latter was brought up to date. At the 1907 Hague Conference, Convention X provided for the Adaptation to Maritime Warfare of the Principles of the Geneva Convention.[4] The 1929 Geneva Conference again amended the Convention on the Wounded and Sick in Armies in the Field,[5] but left the Convention on maritime warfare as adopted in 1907.

The practice of distinguishing between those wounded or sick in land and sea warfare resulted in the adoption of two distinct Conventions at Geneva in 1949,[6] but Protocol I, 1977, deals with the wounded, sick and shipwrecked collectively. To a great extent the terms of the various Conventions overlap and are best considered together, especially as they are largely repetitive, with much of each being concerned with the identification of protected persons and establishments. The

[1] Schindler and Toman 279. For earlier instances of efforts to protect the wounded and sick, see Green, *Essays*, 1999, ch. XIV ('war law and the medical profession'); Boissier, *History of the International Committee of the Red Cross*, vol. 1, *From Solferino to Tsushima*, Part II, ch. 1.
[2] *Ibid.*, 285.
[3] *Ibid.*, 289.
[4] *Ibid.*, 301, 313 resp.
[5] *Ibid.*, 323.
[6] *Ibid.*, 373, 401 resp.

basic difference lies in the problem of the shipwrecked. This term applies to any shipwreck whether at sea or in any other waters, and whether by act of nature or enemy action, and whether from a vessel or an aircraft, provided the individual in question refrains from any hostile act. This status continues during rescue and until another status, such as that of prisoner of war or combatant, is acquired.[7] There is no treaty definition of the sick or wounded, these terms being left to common sense and general usage.

The interplay of the two Conventions is clear from Article 4 of the Maritime Convention which provides that in the event of hostilities between land and sea forces it shall only apply to forces on board ship, while forces who are put ashore, which would include a landing party of marines, immediately become subject to the provisions of the Land Convention.

Subject to the few obligations applying before actual capture, the responsibilities of a belligerent towards the wounded, sick and shipwrecked only arise when a member of the adverse party's forces falls into his hands, when the provisions of the Prisoners of War Convention come into operation[8] and the various provisions for recording the details of those captured or dead apply. It is, however, open to the parties to the conflict to make special arrangements concerning the wounded, sick and shipwrecked, other than those relating to prisoners of war generally, provided they do not adversely affect the position of such persons, medical personnel or chaplains, and, as with all prisoners of war, protected persons are forbidden to renounce any of their rights.[9]

Parties to a conflict must, without delay, take all possible measures to search for and collect those wounded, sick or shipwrecked. In land warfare this obligation exists at all times, but at sea only after an engagement. Parties must protect them from pillage and ill-treatment, ensure their adequate care, search for the dead and prevent their being despoiled. This may be impossible in the case of a submarine, but by the London Naval Treaty, 1930, and confirmed in 1936,[10] a submarine must not attack or destroy a merchant vessel unless the crew and passengers have first been placed in safety.[11] Even a warship may have difficulty in fulfilling

---

[7] Pr. I, Art. 8(b).

[8] See ch. 10 above. It is not intended in this chapter to repeat what appears there. See Art. 14 of the Land and 16 of the Maritime Convention.

[9] Both Convs, Arts 6, 7.

[10] See text to n. 61, ch. 8 above.

[11] See, e.g., Moger, '"Inhuman" submarine commander sacrificed civilians', *The Times*, 7 May 1988, re destruction in 1944 by HMS *Sturdy* of an Indonesian coastal vessel, which had been shelled and boarded. The crew took to the boats, leaving fifty women and children on board. Despite knowing this, Lt. Anderson ordered destruction of the vessel: 'Owing to the nature of the cargo (oil) and the use of this type of vessel to the enemy, I disregarded the humanitarian side of the question. Having no means at my disposal of saving the lives of the remaining passengers, I placed demolition charges which exploded four minutes later.' In the same waters, Lt. Cmdr. Young had destroyed eleven ships 'without killing or wounding a single soul'. See, by way of contrast, the sinking of the British hospital ship *Dover Castle* by U-67 in World War I. The ship was travelling in convoy and the U-boat allowed 2½ hours to elapse between firing the first torpedo which damaged the ship

this task because of danger of air or submarine attack, when the commander must use his discretion.[12]

Protection and care

As with other prisoners of war, the Conventions relating to the care of the wounded, sick and shipwrecked are under the scrutiny of the Protecting Power[13] and do not detract from the general humanitarian activities of the ICRC.

Should wounded, sick or shipwrecked persons fall into the hands of a neutral power, the latter must apply the provisions of the Conventions by analogy.[14]

Wounded, sick and shipwrecked members of the armed forces and others entitled to be treated as combatants[15] are to be protected and respected; treated humanely and cared for by the Detaining Power without any adverse discrimination; attempts upon their lives and violence against their person shall be prohibited; they shall not be murdered nor subjected to any biological or medical experiments;[16] nor exposed to conditions which might result in contagion or infection and only urgent medical requirements justify priority in treatment among them, although women must be treated with all consideration due to their sex.[17]

Medical personnel, military or civilian, cannot be required to afford preferential treatment to any wounded or sick person save on medical grounds, nor compelled to carry out any act incompatible with their humanitarian mission or medical ethics, nor punished for carrying out their activities in accordance with those ethics, regardless of nationality or status of the person treated. They are protected against providing information to any party to the conflict, either their own or the enemy, regarding any person who may have been under their care, if such information might prove harmful to the patient or his family. In the case of their own party, the immunity is limited by any provision in national law, which may therefore make the withholding of such information criminal. The right to withhold information does not apply to concealment of communicable diseases, where notification of such is compulsory. Similarly, civilians or aid societies assisting the Detaining Power in caring or searching for the wounded and sick are protected from harm, prosecution, conviction or punishment for humanitarian acts they may perform on behalf of those persons.[18]

and the second which sank it, by when an escort vessel had taken off the crew and all the wounded and sick – for report of the war crime trial at Leipzig, 1922, acquitting the U-boat captain, see 16 Am. J. Int'l Law, 704.

[12] During World War II the German pocket battleship *Graf Spee* rescued a number of survivors from vessels which it had sunk.

[13] See ch. 13 below.

[14] Land Art. 4, Maritime Art. 5.

[15] See ch. 6 above.

[16] See, e.g., Green, 'Human rights and medical experimentation', 13 Israel Y.B.H.R. (1983), 252.

[17] Both Convs, Art. 12.

[18] Pr. I, Arts 15–17.

For parties to Protocol I, the obligations owed to the wounded, sick and ship-wrecked have been spelled out more clearly than in the Conventions and by Article 8 the terms are defined to include civilians, so, unlike the Conventions, its relevant provisions apply to both civilians and military. This becomes clear in the light of Articles 10 and 11(1) which affirm that regardless of the party to which they belong, and whether they are combatants or civilians, they are to be protected and respected without discrimination, and the physical and mental health of all persons detained or otherwise deprived of their liberty in connection with the conflict must not be endangered by any act or omission of the Detaining Power. This language is so wide that it clearly includes nationals of the Detaining Power detained by that power for any reason relating to the conflict, even including those held under emergency powers. The Protocol reiterates that they must not be subjected to any medical procedure inconsistent with generally accepted medical standards which would apply in similar cases to nationals of the Detaining Party remaining at liberty. This means that they must not, even with their consent,[19] be subjected to physical mutilations, medical or scientific experiments,[20] or the removal of tissue for transplantation except where justified by medical needs and the standards outlined above.[21] However, blood for transfusion or skin for grafting may be taken, provided this is done solely for therapeutic purposes and given voluntarily without any coercion or inducement, and in conditions consistent with standards and controls designed for the benefit of both donor[22] and recipient, and in accordance with generally accepted medical standards. This precludes taking blood or skin for purely experimental purposes. Records must be maintained of all donations of blood or skin, and of all medical procedures undertaken, and these must be available for inspection by the Protecting Power.

Any detainee may refuse any surgical operation, but should he do so every endeavour must be made to secure his written and signed statement to this effect.[23] A necessary surgical amputation does not amount to mutilation and, while experiments are forbidden, if the treatment is new and the only way to save

---

[19] Art. 11(2).

[20] This provision is a response to practices during World War II and condemned as war crimes, see, e.g., *In re Brandt* (the doctors' trial, 1947) 14 Ann. Dig. 286, and Appleman, *Military Tribunals and International Crimes*, esp. 146–8, where the tribunal's comments on 'experiments' which would satisfy 'moral, ethical and legal concepts' are reproduced.

[21] See ch. 10 above, n. 46, and text thereto.

[22] After the hostilities with Pakistan, Bangladesh alleged that Bangladeshi prisoners of war had been subjected to excessive transfusions on behalf of Pakistani wounded to an extent inimical to their own health and welfare. During the Yugoslav campaign against dissidents in Kosovo, which led to the NATO bombing campaign in 1999, there were allegations that the Serbs were taking blood from young Kosovan males (too young for forced labour) against their wishes, and using it for Serb wounded personnel, *The Times*, 17 Apr. 1999.

[23] Art. 11(5).

the patient's life it would not be forbidden if in accordance with applicable medical standards.[24]

If a belligerent is compelled to abandon the wounded and sick during warfare on land he must, as far as military considerations permit, leave medical personnel and equipment to care for them. Their presence does not exempt the Detaining Power from providing any additional assistance that may be required.[25] Once the services of these persons can be safely dispensed with they should be repatriated. Any wilful act or omission seriously endangering the physical or mental health or integrity of any person in the power of a belligerent, other than that on which he depends,[26] or which violates any of these provisions is a grave breach of the Protocol,[27] and if committed by a non-party to the Protocol would amount to a war crime or a grave breach of the Prisoners of War or, if a party to it, the Civilians Conventions. Reprisals against the wounded, sick or shipwrecked, or against medical personnel, buildings and equipment are absolutely forbidden.[28]

Removal of the wounded, sick and shipwrecked

In a land engagement, agreements may be made between opposing commanders for the exchange, removal and transport of the wounded in the field. Whenever possible, similar arrangements should be made for removal of the wounded and sick by land or sea from any besieged or encircled area and for the passage of medical personnel or chaplains proceeding to such an area.[29]

Belligerent warships have the right to demand the handing over of any wounded, sick or shipwrecked persons, whether carried on hospital ships or other vessels, including private or neutral, provided they are fit enough to be transferred and the warship involved has sufficient facilities for their proper care and treatment. If they have been taken on board a neutral vessel or military aircraft or landed at a neutral port, care should be taken to ensure that they take no further part in combat. If they are in enemy hands they are prisoners of war, but the captor may convey them to a port of its own or a neutral port or even the captives' own territory. In the latter case they must take no further part in hostilities.[30]

---

[24] Bothe 114, citing the World Medical Association's Helsinki Declaration: 'In the treatment of the sick person the doctor must be free to use a new therapeutic measure, if in his judgment it offers hope of saving life, reestablishing health, or alleviating suffering … The doctor can combine clinical research with professional care, the objective being the acquisition of medical knowledge, only to the extent that clinical research is justified by its therapeutic value for the patient.'

[25] Conv., Art. 12.

[26] This excludes from protection nationals of the Detaining Power, despite the provision in Art. 11(l) of Pr. I that the protection of that Art. extends to them.

[27] Art. 11(4).

[28] Land Art. 45; Maritime Art. 47; Pr. I, Art. 20.

[29] Land Art. 15; Maritime Art. 18 resp.

[30] Maritime Arts 14–17.

Civilian assistance

During land warfare appeals may be made to the charity and humanity of local inhabitants and relief societies to assist in the collection and care of the wounded and sick, and such inhabitants and societies, even in occupied or invaded territory, are permitted to act in this way spontaneously, and may not be molested or prosecuted for having done so, regardless of the nationality of the persons assisted. The immunity only extends to medical care or nursing and does not permit civilians to conceal the wounded or sick to assist them to escape, nor is it compatible with the status of medical personnel to assist an escapee, even one of the same nationality.[31] The activities of civilians or relief societies in this regard do not relieve the Detaining or Occupying Power of any of its own obligations to ensure that the wounded and sick receive proper medical attention,[32] nor is its power to interrogate them restricted in any way.

At sea, there being no inhabitants to whom such appeals may be made, a belligerent may appeal to captains and masters of neutral vessels to fulfil this task, which they may also undertake spontaneously. They may not be captured because of such transport, but this does not exempt them from liability for any unneutral act they may commit.[33]

Medical personnel, establishments and units

Medical personnel are those, military or civilian, assigned exclusively to medical purposes, or to the administration of medical transports, and the assignment may be permanent or temporary. In addition to doctors, dentists, nurses, medical orderlies, hospital administrators and the like, attached to the forces or military and civilian establishments, medical personnel include members of national Red Cross, Red Crescent[34] and other voluntary aid societies recognised and authorised by a party to the conflict,[35] medical personnel attached to civil defence units,[36] and any made available for humanitarian purposes by a neutral state, a recognised and authorised aid society of such a state, or an impartial humanitarian organisation

---

[31] See the case of Nurse Edith Cavell, shot by the Germans in 1917. Although condemned as an outrage (2 Garner, *International Law and the World War* (97–105), it must be remembered that she did abuse her immunity as a nursing sister.

[32] Land Art. 18; Pr. I Art. 17.

[33] Maritime Art. 21.

[34] With the overthrow of the Shah and establishment of the Islamic Republic of Iran there is no longer any country using the Red Lion and Sun.

[35] The Magen David Odom, Red Shield of David, used by Israel is not a recognised emblem, but some countries, e.g., Germany and the United States, consider it on equal terms with other protected emblems, and in conflicts between Israel and its enemies it normally receives recognition. UN forces in the Middle East treat it as a protected emblem.

[36] See ch. 14 below.

similar to the international Catholic organisation Caritas.[37] Even for belligerents not parties to the Protocol this definition, which reflects practice, would apply.

The Conventions and Protocol I treat chaplains and religious personnel together with medical personnel and neither group become prisoners of war if captured, although they are entitled to all the rights and privileges under the Prisoners of War Convention.[38] Article 8 of the Protocol defines religious personnel as military or civilian chaplains or others[39] exclusively engaged in the work of their ministry and attached to the armed forces, medical units or transports, including hospital ships, and civil defence organisations of a party to the conflict. The person in question must be engaged 'exclusively' in this work, so a lay preacher, since he is not so engaged, would not be among the 'religious personnel' protected in this way.

Medical establishments[40] on land,[41] hospital ships,[42] including those belonging to national Red Cross and other relief societies, as well as private individuals or neutrals, and medical aircraft[43] are to be respected and protected at all times and must not be made the object of attack,[44] but this immunity ceases if they are used for purposes hostile to the adverse party and outside their humanitarian purpose.[45]

Medical units are establishments, both military and civilian, organised for medical purposes, that is to say the search for, collection, transportation, diagnosis or treatment, including first-aid treatment, of the wounded, sick or shipwrecked, or for the prevention of disease. They may be fixed or mobile, permanent and assigned exclusively for medical purposes for an indeterminate period, or temporary for a fixed and limited period. Medical transports are any means of transportation, military or civilian, assigned exclusively to medical transportation and under control of a competent authority of a party to the conflict. Once a merchant vessel has been transferred to hospital purposes it cannot be transferred to any other use for the duration of the hostilities. Neither Convention

[37] Pr. I, Arts 8, 9.

[38] See ch. 10 above.

[39] At the drafting conference it became clear that there were differences of opinion among the delegates as to who could rightly claim to be considered a 'minister of religion', hence the wording.

[40] E.g., hospitals, blood transfusion centres, preventive medical centres, medical depots and their medical or pharmaceutical stores.

[41] Land Conv., Art. 19, Pr. I Art. 12(1).

[42] Maritime Arts 22, 24, 25.

[43] Land Art. 36, Pr. I Art. 24; see text to n. 61 below.

[44] The Leipzig war crimes trials were concerned with, among others, the sinking of the hospital ships *Dover Castle* and *Llandovery Castle*, and during the Falklands War there was a threat by Argentina to deny immunity to *HMS Canberra*, but this did not materialise, *The Times*, 24, 31 May 1982.

[45] Land Art. 21, Maritime Art. 34; see also *The Ophelia* [1915] P. 129. The ICRC questioned Britain's use of fighting hospital ships, such as the Royal Fleet Auxiliary *Argus*, during the Gulf War. *Argus* was not designated a neutral hospital ship and retained a number of defensive weapon systems, *The Times*, 10 Apr. 1992.

forbids the emergency use, other than of a merchant ship, of a transport not normally used for medical purposes, so long as it is properly marked and exclusively used for this purpose while so marked.[46] This indicates, for example, that an aircraft transporting troops on its outward journey should not be used, even if properly marked, to evacuate wounded and sick on its homeward journey. Since the transport must be under a competent authority it seems that civilians voluntarily searching for and collecting and removing the wounded would only be able to use transports which are under such control if they are to be protected. The rights granted by the Conventions apply equally to temporary and permanent medical personnel, units and transports.

All medical personnel, units and transports must be clearly marked with the protective emblem of the red cross,[47] crescent[48] or shield of David,[49] each on a white background. Personnel should wear on their left arm a water-resistant armband so marked and issued and stamped by the military authority to which they are attached, and should carry an official identity card. Members of the armed forces who are specially trained as orderlies or stretcher bearers must wear a similar armband when employed on medical duties. Fixed and mobile units must fly a flag carrying this emblem and if belonging to a neutral state the national flag as well as that of the belligerent to which the unit is attached. It is a matter of discretion whether the national flag is flown by land installations. A medical installation which has been captured should only fly the red emblem.[50] Parties should endeavour to make the protective emblem clearly visible to enemy land, sea and air forces.

Hospital ships

The identity of military hospital ships, those built or equipped by the parties to the conflict specially and solely to assist, treat and transport the sick, wounded or shipwrecked must be notified to the adverse party at least ten days before they are so employed.[51] They, hospital ships used by national Red Cross Societies, recognised relief societies or private persons, including neutrals, must be painted white,

---

[46] Land Art. 21, Maritime Art. 34. During the Falklands War controversy arose over the use of the *Queen Elizabeth* as a troop transport on its outward journey and a hospital ship on its return.

[47] This reversion of the Swiss flag was adopted to acknowledge the role of Henri Dunant the Swiss founder of the movement.

[48] Although the red cross, as an equal arm cross, is not a Christian cross, the Ottoman Empire and Islamic countries have refused to use this and use the crescent in its place.

[49] As already indicated, this is not an emblem recognised in the Conventions or the Protocol, but is used by Israel and in practice receives protection.

[50] Because of the proliferation of emblems – prior to the Islamic revolution Iran used the Red Sun and Lion – there is strong pressure to select one emblem which would be used by all.

[51] See n. 45 above.

with large dark red crosses[52] on the hull and horizontal surfaces so they may be seen from the sea and air. Lifeboats belonging to hospital ships must be similarly marked, and coastal lifeboats operating from occupied territory may be permitted to fly their national flag if prior notice has been given to all parties to the conflict.

Hospital ships must fly the protected emblem from the mainmast together with the national flag, and neutral hospital ships must also fly the flag of the belligerent to which they are attached. With the latter's consent, all these vessels may take steps to ensure that their identification marks can be seen at night or during poor visibility. Hospital ships which are detained by an adverse party may only fly the protected emblem, but those in a port captured by an adverse party must be allowed to depart and do not rank as warships with regard to their stay in a neutral port.[53]

The sick-bay on a warship should be separated from the rest of the ship and if fighting takes place on board it should be respected and spared.[54] The sick-bay and its equipment are subject to the law of war, but may not be used for any other purpose so long as they are needed for the sick and wounded, although if military necessity demands a captor may divert them from their normal use provided he makes proper provision for care of the sick and wounded.[55]

Hospital ships and other craft employed on medical duties are subject to visit and search; their services may be rejected; they may be directed to follow a particular course; their radios and other means of communication[56] may be controlled and they may not use any secret code, there is strong support for allowing them to use cryptographic equipment,[57] and, if the gravity of the circumstances require, they may be detained for up to seven days. Neutral observers may be put on board to ensure that the provisions of the Convention are observed.[58]

Protection ceases if they commit any hostile act against the adverse party, so long as they are given due warning and time to correct these activities. Their immunity is not affected because the crews are armed to maintain order to protect themselves or their patients; by the presence of arms taken from the wounded or shipwrecked and not yet transferred to the proper holding service; by the presence of civilian wounded or shipwrecked; nor by transporting medical equipment or personnel intended for medical purposes in excess of their normal requirements.[59]

[52] Islamic states and Israel will use their own emblem.

[53] Maritime Arts 22–33.

[54] In modern warfare the possibility of combat on board a warship is somewhat remote. However, in World War II HMS *Cossack* did send an armed boarding party to rescue British prisoners on board the *Altmark*.

[55] Maritime Art. 28.

[56] If these are used for hostile purposes their immunity is lost and they may be condemned as prize, see *The Ophelia* [1915] P., 129.

[57] *San Remo Manual*, para. 171.

[58] Art. 31.

[59] Arts 34, 35.

Medical aircraft

The Conventions define medical aircraft as those exclusively employed in the transport of the sick and wounded or medical personnel and equipment, and this definition is widened by Protocol I to mean 'any medical transports by air'.[60] They must be clearly marked with the protective emblem on their lower, upper and lateral surfaces, together with their national rondels and any other distinctive sign agreed upon by the parties.[61] They must not be used to gain any military advantage nor to collect or transmit intelligence or carry equipment for this purpose. They may only carry the wounded, sick and shipwrecked and personnel involved in their treatment or transport. The only armament permitted to them are the weapons taken from their patients or light individual weapons carried by their personnel for the protection of themselves or those in their care. This means that these weapons may only be used to defend themselves from attack when the aircraft is on the ground.

Medical aircraft may fly over land areas controlled by their own or friendly powers and over sea areas not under enemy control. However, if they are likely to fly within range of enemy surface-to-air weapon systems the adverse party should be made aware of this. They may only fly over enemy territory with his consent and if they fly in parts of the contact zone,[62] or over areas the control of which is doubtful, they do so at their own risk, although once recognised as medical aircraft they must be respected.

If prior agreement has been obtained from the adverse party, medical aircraft remain protected when flying over land or sea under that party's control. If it lacks such agreement or deviates from its terms for any reason, including navigational errors or emergencies, it must take immediate steps to identify itself. Once recognised, the adverse party may order it to land or take other steps to safeguard its interests, and must allow time for compliance before attacking. While flying over enemy territory, even with agreement, medical aircraft may not be used to search for the wounded or shipwrecked, unless this has been expressly permitted by the agreement.

A medical aircraft must obey any order to land and permit inspection, as it must if it has landed for any reason on land or water. Wounded and sick on board may be removed to enable inspection to proceed only if this will not adversely affect their welfare. Whatever may have been the reason for landing, if inspection finds it is a medical aircraft, has not violated any restrictions affecting such aircraft, and is not in breach of any prior agreement, it and any occupant belonging to its home or a neutral country must be permitted to leave.[63] If these circumstances are not

[60] Land Art. 36; Maritime Art. 39, Pr. I Art. 8.

[61] Land Art. 36, Maritime Art. 39. By Art. 36 of Annex I to Pr. I flashing blue light of specific intensity is also available for identifying medical aircraft.

[62] Any area of land where forward elements of opposing forces are in contact, especially if exposed to direct fire from the ground, Pr. I. Art. 26(2).

[63] Pr. I, Art. 30(2), (3).

satisfied it may be seized, but if it has been assigned exclusively for medical purposes the captor may only use it for such purposes. For parties not bound by Protocol I, the Conventions provide that if it makes an involuntary landing because of emergency in enemy or enemy-occupied territory, the sick, wounded and crew become prisoners of war, but the medical personnel must be treated as other medical personnel captured by the adverse party.[64]

In accordance with the Conventions, unless there are restrictions imposed by a neutral in this respect, and which must operate equally against all belligerents, medical aircraft may fly over neutral territory, land thereon and use it as a port of call. They must give prior notice of their passage and land if so ordered. When flying on routes, at heights and times agreed between the parties to the conflict and the neutral concerned, they are immune from attack. Unless otherwise agreed by the neutral and the parties, wounded, sick and shipwrecked disembarked in neutral territory must be detained and prevented from taking any further part in hostilities. For parties to Protocol I flights by medical aircraft over neutral territory are subject to similar regulations as for flights over enemy territory, so that prior agreement is necessary, the aircraft may be ordered to land and is subject to inspection, and if found not to be a medical aircraft it should be detained together with those on board. Any expenses involved in treatment or internment are borne by the home state.[65]

Special protection

Parties to Convention I on land warfare may, in peace or after hostilities have begun, establish in their own or occupied territory hospital zones or localities to protect the wounded and sick from war risks, and during hostilities parties to the conflict may enter into agreements for the recognition of such zones and localities.[66] There is of course nothing to prevent a party establishing such a zone in peace time and informing other parties to the Convention of this.

Medical and religious personnel whose detention is no longer necessary for the ministration of the wounded and sick should be allowed to return to their own party, without discrimination on racial, religious or political grounds in selecting those for return, although consideration should be given to the length of their detention and the state of their health. Members of recognised aid societies from neutral countries should not be detained but returned to their own country, or the country of the force to which they were attached; pending release they are under control of the Detaining Power, but should be employed in assisting personnel of that force.

By Article 109 of the Prisoners of War Convention a Detaining Power is

[64] Land Art. 36, Maritime Art. 39.
[65] Art. 31.
[66] See Green, *Essays*, 1999, p. 341.

obliged, regardless of rank and number, to repatriate seriously wounded and sick prisoners, after having cared for them until they are well enough to make the journey, and arrangements may be made for them to be held in neutral territory.[67] No sick or wounded prisoner may be repatriated against his will while hostilities continue.

The Conventions impose certain obligations upon the Detaining Power with regard to the burial and reporting of dead persons belonging to the adverse party and more specific regulations are introduced by Protocol I concerning the search for the missing and reporting on the disposal of the remains of those who die. As soon as possible and immediately upon the end of hostilities each party must search for those reported missing by the adverse party. The requests and all information likely to assist in tracing or identifying them, such as the names of their units or the place at which they were last known to have been in action, must be submitted through the Protecting Power or the Central Tracing Agency of the ICRC or the national societies. To facilitate the finding of missing persons, parties to the conflict must try to reach agreements to allow teams to search for, identify and recover the dead from battlefield areas. They may attach to these teams representatives of the adverse party when the search takes place in areas controlled by that party. When carrying out these tasks, team members must be respected and protected. The remains of all who have died as a result of hostilities, under occupation or while detained in relation thereto must be respected, with their grave stones properly marked and maintained.[68] Protocol I provides for agreement between the parties to the conflict concerning maintenance and visits to grave sites, as well as for repatriation of the remains, and with regard to exhumation procedures by indicating what must be done if there are no such agreements.[69] In 1991, 1992 and 1998, arrangements were made between the United States and Vietnam for teams to visit Vietnam to seek out survivors or remains and arrange for their repatriation.

Use of the emblem

During conflict the red cross, crescent or shield of David may only be used to identify medical personnel, units, installations, ships or aircraft. Wrongful use in order to secure a protection to which the user is not entitled or to induce in the adverse party a belief that he is so entitled constitutes perfidy and is a war crime.

In time of peace use of the emblem is restricted to personnel, units and installations which would be protected by the 1949 Conventions in the event of hostilities.

[67] Art. 110 indicates who should be repatriated and who transferred to neutral territory.

[68] During the conflict in Bosnia there were many instances of wounded or sick personnel being murdered and their bodies mutilated or buried in unmarked mass graves. When it was possible to identify those responsible, indictments were issued by the *ad hoc* tribunal charged with trying war criminals in the former Yugoslavia.

[69] Art. 34.

It may however be used by representatives of the ICRC and by national societies in accordance with local legislation. Parties to the Conventions have undertaken to take steps to prevent any wrongful use of the emblem.[70] It may also, 'as an exceptional measure, in conformity with national legislation and with the express permission [of the National Red Cross Society] be used to identify vehicles used as ambulances and to mark the position of aid stations exclusively assigned to ... giving free treatment to the wounded or sick'.[71]

[70] In 1991 the Canadian New Democratic Party was ordered to cease using the Red Cross as a postmark on propaganda material concerning the Canadian medicare system.
[71] Convention I, Art. 44.

12

Civilians

Classical position

One of the oldest rules of the law of war provides for the protection of the civilian non-combatant population and forbids making civilians the direct object of attack.[1] This rule appears in the Hague Regulations ban on the bombardment of undefended places, the requirement that an attacking officer should warn the authorities before commencing a bombardment, and the ban on the pillage of a town even if taken by assault.[2]

Before and during World War II there were no special provisions in the law of armed conflict concerning the treatment of the civilian population in territory controlled by a belligerent,[3] other than isolated provisions in the Hague Regulations[4] concerning the duties of an occupant although atrocities against the civilian population of the adverse party would amount to war crimes.[5]

The impact of World War II

As a result of the treatment of civilians in occupied territory during World War II action was taken in 1949 to spell out the rights of an occupant and of the occupied in the form of Geneva Convention IV relative to the treatment of civilians in time of war,[6] and these provisions were expanded by Protocol I, 1977.[7]

---

[1] See ch. 2 above.

[2] Arts 25, 26, 28.

[3] See, however, *In re Kramer* (the Belsen trial, 1945) 2 *War Crimes Reports* 1, 13 Ann. Dig., 267; Phillips, *The Belsen Trial* 1949; *In re Hoess* (the Auschwitz trial, 1947) 7 *ibid.*, 11, 3 *ibid.*, 269.

[4] Arts 44–7, 50, 2.

[5] See, e.g., *In re Klein* (1945) 1 *War Crimes Reports*, 46, 14 Ann. Dig., 253; Kintner, *The Hadamar Trial*, 1949; *In re Kramer*, *In re Ahlbrecht (no.2)*, (1948–9) 16 Ann. Dig; 396; *In re Haruzo* (Changi Jail trial 1946) Sleeman and Silkin, *The Double Tenth Trial*, 1951; see also ch. 18 below.

[6] Schindler and Toman, 495.

[7] *Ibid.*, 621.

Those protected

The Convention only applies to civilians in the hands of or under the physical control of an adverse party or an occupying power. Those in their own territory are, for the main part, only protected by the general rules limiting warlike acts and methods of combat. However, Part two of the Convention dealing with General Protection of Populations against Certain Consequences of War is of general application covering 'the whole of the civilian populations of the countries in conflict'. This Part of the Convention reproduces or adapts much of the wounded and sick Conventions extending them to civilians, with particular regard to the rights of pregnant women, children under fifteen and the immunity of hospitals and their personnel. Although these provisions are to operate without any adverse distinction based on race, nationality, religion or political opinion, the Convention does not protect those definitely suspected of or engaged in activities prejudicial to the security of the state, nor, in occupied territory, those detained as spies or saboteurs or against whom there is strong suspicion of activity hostile to the occupant's security. If absolute military security requires, these persons may be deemed to have lost any rights of communication with the exterior granted by the Convention.[8] However, as soon as the security of the belligerent or the occupant permits they should restore to those concerned the full rights and protection of the Convention.[9]

As to nationals of non-parties to the Convention, under the Hague Law it was generally the case that if any party to the conflict was not a party to the particular Convention it would not apply. In so far as humanitarian law is concerned, it is now generally the case that a Convention will apply as between the parties, while the nationals of a non-party will remain protected by the basic minima of the rule of law. The situation is now changed. While the Convention does not protect the nationals of a non-party, if the latter accepts and applies the Convention its nationals fall within its purview.[10]

In addition, Part IV of Protocol I is concerned with the civilian population as such, laying down as a basic rule[11] that 'in order to ensure respect for and protection of the civilian population and civilian objects, the Parties to the conflict shall at all times distinguish between the civilian population and combatants and between civilian objects and military objectives and accordingly shall direct their operations only against military objectives'.[12] The Protocol also contains a number of articles providing for the general protection of civilians, civilian objects and the civilian population as such against the dangers resulting from military operations,[13] with further provisions for relief of the civilian population,[14] for the

[8] See Arts 106–16.
[9] Art. 5.
[10] Art. 2.
[11] Art. 48.
[12] Arts 51–60.
[13] Arts 68–71.
[14] Arts 72–8.

treatment of persons in the power of a party to the conflict, including refugees and stateless persons, those detained in connection with the conflict who might include their own nationals, as well as women and children.[15]

In a non-international conflict civilians are protected by Article 3 of the Convention which is common to all the 1949 Conventions and applies to civilians as well as those *hors de combat*. This embodies the minimum principles of humanitarian law, forbidding violence to life and person, particularly murder, mutilation, cruelty and torture; hostage-taking;[16] outrages on personal dignity, especially humiliating and degrading treatment; and sentencing or executing without a proper trial conducted according to generally accepted principles of justice. These provisions are minimal and the Article goes on to state that sick and wounded are to be collected and cared for, with humanitarian organisations like the ICRC authorised to offer their services. The parties to the conflict are also encouraged to reach agreements to extend other parts of the Convention to the conflict. However, since the legal status of the parties is not affected by the Article, it is open to the legal government to treat its opponents as traitors so long as these minimum conditions are observed. Protocol II of 1977 relating to humanitarian law in non-international conflicts is equally significant regarding civilian protection.[17]

Application of the Convention

The Convention comes into operation immediately upon the outbreak of hostilities or the commencement of an occupation.[18] It ceases in the territory of parties to the conflict on the general close of military operations and any restrictive measures taken against protected persons should be cancelled as soon as possible. If such measures affect property they are to be cancelled in accordance with the law of the detaining Power.[19] Persons detained on security grounds must be released then at latest, unless the sentence imposed by a proper trial has not yet expired. In occupied territory, however, the Convention continues for a year beyond the end

[15] In the civil wars being waged in parts of the former Soviet Union in 1992, there were many reports of members of the local government forces or of the government of Russia being taken hostage and held under threats of death, *The Times*, 29 Sept. 1992.

[16] See, e.g., activities of the ICRC during the conflicts in Nicaragua, El Salvador, Cambodia, Somalia, Afghanistan, as well as the former Yugoslavia where UN peacekeepers were also taken hostage.

[17] Schindler and Toman, 689; see ch. 19 below. The reason Art. 3 and Pr. II are mentioned here is because of their significance for the protection of civilians.

[18] After Iraq invaded Kuwait in 1990, the Security Council condemned its violations of international humanitarian law, 'reaffirming that the Fourth Geneva Convention applies to Kuwait and that as a High Contracting Party to the Convention Iraq is bound to comply fully with all its terms and in particular is liable under the Convention in respect of grave breaches committed by it, as are individuals who commit or order the commission of grave breaches', Res. 674, 21 I.L.M., 1561; Lauterpacht, *et al.*, *The Kuwait Crisis: Basic Documents*, 95. See also ch. 18 below.

[19] Art. 46.

of hostilities, but if the Occupying Power still exercises governmental powers[20] the articles of the Convention relating to its general provisions; the status and treatment of protected persons; conduct concerning, for example, inviolability of rights, deportation, labour and protection of workers and supervision of the Convention remain operative.[21]

The Convention only applies to those, other than persons protected by Conventions I, II and III who, during conflict or occupation of territory, find themselves in the hands of a party to the conflict or an Occupying Power[22] of which they are not nationals, as well as nationals covered by the general protection sections. Neutrals and nationals of a co-belligerent are not protected so long as their home state maintains diplomatic representation in the state in whose hands they are.[23]

Major problems arose in the former Yugoslavia as to whether detained Bosnian civilians held, for example, by Bosnian Serbs, were detained by an occupying power and so within the protection of Convention IV. Thus, the majority of the Trial Chamber in the *Tadić* case, the President dissenting,[24] held 'The central question is whether at all relevant times the victims of the accused were in the hands of "a Party to the conflict or Occupying Power of which they are not nationals"'. Implicit in this expression is a threefold requirement. The first and second requirements are that the victims be 'in the hands of [a] Party to the conflict or Occupying Power'. The third is that the civilian victims not be nationals of that 'Party or Occupying Power ... [T]he Republika Srpska [established by the Bosnian Serbs] was a party to the conflict ... While the victims ... were in the hands of armed forces and authorities of the Republika Srpska', the expression 'in the hands of' is not restricted to situations in which the individual civilian is physically in the hands of a Party or Occupying Power.

> [T]hose persons ... in territory effectively occupied by a party to the conflict can be considered to be in the hands of that party ... [T]he exact date when the victims ... fell into the hands of the opposing forces is highly relevant to the assessment of their status under international law ... The armed forces of the Republika Srpska and the

---

[20] This applies to Israel's conduct within occupied territory taken from an Arab state. However, Israel has annexed Eastern Jerusalem and the Syrian Golan Heights, and maintains that the other territories never 'belonged' to any Arab state and are thus not 'occupied' but 'administered' and, as such, not subject to the Convention. Israeli tribunals often refer to the Convention treating many of its articles as customary law. See, e.g., Cohen, *Human Rights in the Israeli-Occupied Territories, 1967–1982*, esp. ch. 3; see also Playfair, ed., *International Law and the Administration of Occupied Territories*. See also Shamgar, 'The observance of international law in the administered territories', 1 Israel Y.B.H.R. 1971, 262.

[21] Arts 1–12, 27, 29–34, 47, 49, 51, 52, 53, 59, 61–77, 143.

[22] See ch. 15 below.

[23] Art. 4.

[24] *Prosecutor* v. *Dusko Tadić* (1997) 36 I.L.M. 908, paras. 578–9, 584. See also Gray, 'Bosnia and Herzegovina: civil war or inter-state conflict? Characterization and consequences', 67 Brit. Y.B. Int'l Law 1996, 155.

Republika Srpska as a whole, were, at least from 19 May 1992 [when the majority considered active support from the Yugoslav Republic ended] onwards, legal entities distinct from the VJ [Yugoslav Army] and the Government of the Federal Republic of Yugoslavia. However, as a rule of customary international law, the acts of persons, groups or organizations may be imputed to a State where they act as *de facto* organs or agents of that State ... [T]he acts of the armed forces of the Republika Srpska, though nationals of the Republic of Bosnia and Herzegovina, after 19 May 1992 ... may be imputed to the Republic of Yugoslavia if those forces were acting as a *de facto* organ or agent of that State for that purpose or more generally.

Having examined the relationship existing between the Republika Srpska and Yugoslavia and the armed forces of both, and acknowledging their common aim of securing a Greater Serbia, the majority concluded[25] that the

relationship ... cannot be said to be anything more than a general level of coordination consonant with their relationship as allied forces of the Serbian war effort ... After 19 May 1992 the armed forces of the Republika Srpska could not be considered as *de facto* organs or agents of the Government of the Federal Republic of Yugoslavia ... For that reason, each of the victims ... enjoy the protection of the prohibitions contained in Common Article 3 [of each of the Geneva Conventions], applicable as it is to all armed conflicts, rather than the protection of the more specific grave breaches regime applicable to civilians in the hands of a party to an armed conflict of which they are not nationals.

Therefore, Convention IV does not apply to them, though it may apply to those who, before or after that date, found themselves in the hands of the Yugoslav forces, whether in Bosnia or elsewhere. It should be pointed out that in her dissent, Presiding Judge McDonald considered[26] the conflict under consideration to be an international conflict and the Republika Srpska a puppet or offshoot of Yugoslavia, so that the civilians were not being victimised by co-nationals, but by a force representing an occupying power.

It must be borne in mind that a different Trial Chamber differently constituted might come to an opposite decision. This may well be the case if the accused is a Bosnian Croat since the relationship between the Bosnian Croats and Croatia seems to be even closer than that between the Republika Srpska and Yugoslavia, with Croatia providing some $30 million a month to the Bosnian Croat Army (Croat Defence Council) which is integrated with the Croatian Army 'in combat, administratively, financially and logistically', and with the Bosnian Croats apparently carrying Croatian passports, using Croatian currency and voting in Croatian elections.[27] In fact, the Appeals Chamber held in *Erdemović* that in so far as the Bosnian Croats were concerned, they were engaged in an international conflict.[28]

[25] Paras. 604, 607.
[26] 36 I.L.M. 970.
[27] *New York Times*, 20 Sept., 1977.
[28] Case IT-96-22-A, 7 Oct. 1997; see also Green, '*Erdemovic´* – *Tadić* – *Dokmanović*: jurisdiction and early practice of the Yugoslav War Crimes Tribunal', 27 Israel Y.B.H.R. 1997, 313.

In the event of doubt as to a person's status, he is to be considered as a civilian. The presence within the civilian population, defined as comprising all those who are civilians, of individuals not falling within the definition does not deprive the population of its civilian character.[29] This provision has become of major significance since the recognition of a war of national liberation as an international conflict,[30] for now persons not in uniform and apparently civilians and so not easily recognisable as combatants may in fact be lawful combatants and not civilians committing unlawful belligerent acts.[31]

Parties to the conflict may enter agreements altering the rights of civilians, but none of these may in any way detract from the Convention rights granted to protected persons, nor may the latter surrender or waive any of the rights granted them by the Convention.[32]

The Convention is to be applied under the scrutiny and with the co-operation of the Protecting Power, who may appoint for this purpose members of its diplomatic or consular staff,[33] its own or neutral nationals. Every appointee must be approved by the Power with which he is to carry out his duties. This representation does not limit the Convention right of the ICRC or any other international humanitarian organisation from carrying out its tasks, with the consent of the parties to the conflict.[34]

Free passage must be provided for consignments of medical and hospital stores, together with objects necessary for religious worship, as well as essential foodstuffs, clothing and tonics for children under fifteen, expectant mothers and maternity cases. This obligation does not inhibit the right to blockade an area inhabited by such persons[35] and the presence of civilians must not be used to secure immunity from attack for a legitimate military objective.[36]

The rights of protected persons

As with other protected persons, civilians in enemy hands, whether in national or occupied territory, are entitled to respect for their persons, honour, family rights,

[29] Pr. I, Art. 50(3).

[30] *Ibid.*, Art. 1(4). See ch. 6 above.

[31] *Ibid.*, Art. 44(3).

[32] Arts 7, 8.

[33] For a similar case in World War I, although in this case it was the consul of an Occupying Power acting on behalf of an ally, see *Chevreau Claim* (1931) 2 R.I.A.A., 1115.

[34] Arts 9, 10.

[35] After Iraq's invasion of Kuwait and during and after the Gulf War, the Security Council Resolutions imposing economic sanctions against Iraq permitted the import of foodstuffs necessary for women and children, Res. 661, 666, 686 (29 I.L.M., 1330, 30 *ibid.*, 847).

[36] After invading Kuwait in 1990 Iraq concentrated foreign nationals, including diplomats, in places which it thought might be subject to attack by Coalition forces and was condemned by the Security Council for so doing, Res. 664, 674 (29 *ibid.*, 1328, 1561).

religious convictions and practices, manners and customs. This does not mean that practices contrary to the public policy or morality of the holding party must be allowed to continue.[37] They must be humanely treated and protected from violence, threats,[38] insults and public curiosity. Women must be protected against sexual attacks and, subject to considerations based on sex, all must be treated with the same consideration without any adverse discrimination.[39] The Convention makes no specific reference to preservation of life, but this is inherent especially as murder and mutilation are forbidden,[40] and such acts would amount to war crimes.[41] The protection against indecent acts, including forced prostitution,[42] is extended to all regardless of sex.

None of these rights prevents a party from taking measures necessary for its security, including restrictions on the freedom of movement of protected persons. However, the holding power is responsible for the care of protected persons and liable to the country of origin for any injury suffered by its nationals while in that power's control. This responsibility remains regardless of the liability of any individual injuring a protected person contrary to the Convention provisions, as well as for any such action by its agents,[43] such as the administrators of a detention camp.

Subject to what has been said above, protected persons whether in detention or not must be given every opportunity to communicate with the Protecting Power, the ICRC and the National Red Cross or similar Society of the country where they are, as well as any other organisation able to help them, and the holding authority must provide all necessary facilities to enable this and permit visits by representatives of these organisations.

Protected persons must not be coerced physically or morally in any way and especially not to secure information from them or from third persons aware of such coercion. They must not be subjected to corporal punishment or brutality, killing or any medical treatment or experiment not needed for their own treatment.[44] Similarly, their property is protected against pillage by way of wanton

---

[37] Prior to the Gulf War, but after the invasion of Kuwait, problems arose when Coalition forces in, e.g., Saudi Arabia wished to celebrate Xmas 1990; they did so at sea rather than at base.

[38] The various SC resolutions following the invasion of Kuwait all condemned such acts and called for compensation by Iraq to the civilians affected.

[39] Art. 27.

[40] Art. 32.

[41] See ch. 18 below.

[42] In 1992 there was public acknowledgement that, during World War II, Japan had compelled a number of Chinese and Korean women to become 'comfort women' for Japanese forces, and Japan has offered some, perhaps inadequate, compensation.

[43] See the SC resolutions cited re Iraq.

[44] For the position during World War II, see *In re Brandt* (the doctors' trial, 1947) 14 Ann. Dig., 296 – for comments by the tribunal concerning lawful experiments, see Appleman, *Military Tribunals and International Crimes*, 1954, 142 *et seq.* In 1999 there were allegations that Serb forces were illegally taking blood from young Kosovan male civilians to treat their own wounded, *The Times*, 17 Apr. 1999.

destruction, spoliation or looting, whether committed by an individual or public authority. Reprisals against them or their property are forbidden[45] and they must not be taken hostage and made answerable with their freedom or life for the carrying out of the holding power's orders and the security of his armed forces or his property, or against acts of destruction by military or civilian personnel. To take them hostage is a grave breach of the Convention.[46]

By Article 75 of Protocol I, which, unlike the Conventions, applies to all including nationals, everyone in the power of a party to the conflict not enjoying more favourable treatment under the Conventions or the Protocol itself must be treated humanely, enjoying at least the conditions listed in the Article, without any adverse distinction based on colour, race, sex, language, religion or belief, political or other opinion, national or social origin, wealth, birth or other status, or any other similar criteria. These considerations might be important if adversaries possess conflicting social, political or economic ideologies. To the extent that this does not conflict with local concepts of public policy, morality or decency, their religious practices, as well as their person, honour and dignity must also be respected.

Any person arrested, detained or interned in connection with the conflict must be told promptly of the reasons why in a language that he understands. Unless detained for a penal offence, he must be released as soon as possible and no later than when the reasons for the detention cease to exist. No sentence may be passed without a proper trial by a properly constituted judicial tribunal applying recognised principles of regular judicial procedure, which are those normally regarded by western states as conforming with their concept of due process.[47] A protected person may only be punished for acts that he himself has committed and collective punishments directed or threatened against a community are forbidden,[48] as are acts of terrorism, intimidation and reprisal.[49]

All held in this way are protected by the fundamental guarantees in Protocol I, Article 75, until their final release, repatriation or re-establishment, even after the

---

[45] This is a departure from customary law introduced by the Conv., Art. 33.

[46] Art. 147; for World War II see *In re List* (the Hostages trial 1948) 9 *War Crimes Reports*, 34. See also *Priebke* case, *The Times*, 4 Apr. 1996 ('Former SS captain defends massacre of Rome captives') *New York Times*, 9 Aug. 1986 ('A Nazi's flawed trial').

[47] Pr. I, Art. 75 (3) and (4). Art. 75(4) lists some of the requirements if a trial is to be considered a proper judicial proceeding. States not acceding to Pr. I remain bound by the Conv., Arts 66–76, and should continue to organise judicial proceedings according to the requirements of a fair trial and the rule of law.

[48] This prohibition is wider than that in Hague Regs. Art. 50 which only forbids collective penalties for acts by individuals for which the population as a whole cannot be regarded as jointly and severally responsible. It is now clear that even a fine imposed on the community at large because of an act by one of its members would be a breach of both the Conv. and the Pr., as would destruction of houses in a village of which the offender is an inhabitant, a practice resorted to by Israel in the 'occupied' territories.

[49] Conv., Art. 33; see also Pr. I, Arts 51–6. For World War II, see *In re Kesselring* (Ardeatine Caves trial, 1947) 8 *War Crimes Reports*, 9.

end of the conflict. Women whose liberty has been restricted must be kept separate from men and under the supervision of women, although families should, whenever possible, be kept together as family units. Male prisoners apparently do not have to be supervised by men, even though during World War II male inmates of German concentration camps were sometimes sexually assaulted by female attendants.

The prosecution and trial of any protected person[50] charged with war crimes or crimes against humanity[51] must accord with the rules of international law and if he is not entitled to more favourable treatment under the Conventions or Protocol he must be granted the guarantees embodied in Article 75 even if the charges against him amount to grave breaches.

The position of aliens

Any alien civilians, including enemies, in the territory of a party or in occupied territory[52] at the beginning of, or during a conflict, are entitled to leave and return to their home state[53] unless the national interests of the adverse party prevent this. Frequently, men of military age are not allowed to leave and during World War II, particularly during the early days and during the period when invasion was feared, most German nationals in Great Britain including refugees and male juveniles were detained,[54] many of them being sent to detention camps overseas. In the United States and Canada large numbers of Japanese, including those locally born, were interned and their property frequently confiscated. If departure is forbidden, those affected are entitled to have their position reconsidered by an appropriate court or specially established administrative board, and the Protecting Power must normally be informed of the names of those refused permission to leave, together with the reasons. Parties may, of course, enter into agreements for the repatriation of nationals and in 1943 1,500 Canadian and American civilians were exchanged for an equal number of Japanese. Any alien who has been confined may request repatriation when his confinement ends, and until then he must be treated humanely.[55]

In principle, non-repatriated aliens remaining at liberty should be treated according to the regulations concerning the treatment of aliens in peace time. They are also entitled to receive any individual or collective relief extended to them; the

---

[50] Since the provision in Art. 75 concerns the treatment of 'persons in the power of a party to the conflict' this right (para. 7) extends to nationals.

[51] See ch. 18 below.

[52] Conv., Art. 48.

[53] In World War I a period of grace was granted to permit such return and in *R.* v. *Ahlers* [1915] 1 K.B., 616 the German consul at Sunderland, a British subject, was acquitted of treason for helping German nationals to return home after the outbreak of hostilities.

[54] See, e.g., Chappell, *Island of Barbed Wire*.

[55] Conv., Arts 35–7.

same medical attention as provided for the Detaining Power's population; to practise their religion; if living in a dangerous area they must be allowed to leave in
the same way as local nationals; and children under fifteen, pregnant women, and
the mothers of children under seven must receive the same benefits as nationals of
the Detaining Power.[56] Subject to security considerations, they are entitled to seek
paid employment on the same terms as local nationals, and if unable to support
themselves must receive support from the Detaining Power for themselves and
their dependents. They are subject to the same terms regarding compulsory labour
as locals, but if of enemy nationality they may only be compelled to do work necessary to feed, clothe, shelter, transport and maintain the health of human beings
so long as it is not directed to military operations. Protected persons engaged in
compulsory labour are entitled to the same conditions as to hours, safety, protective clothing, compensation and the like as locals. They may not be compelled to
serve in the Occupying Power's armed or auxiliary forces, nor subjected to pressure or propaganda to secure their voluntary enlistment.[57]

The status of persons in occupied territory must not be adversely affected by
any changes in the law enacted by the Occupying Power and their full civil capacity must be preserved,[58] even if they are interned. Should the Occupying Power
have changed the local law so as to affect the status or rights of local inhabitants,
the returning sovereign on resuming power after the occupation ends may find it
necessary to recognise some of these measures, for example, those affecting the
procedure for registering or performing marriages.[59] Protected persons may not be
deprived of any of their Convention rights by changes in the law, nor as a result
of any purported annexation of the territory.[60] No annexation may be recognised
so long as hostilities, whether with the national authorities or his allies, continue,
as was made clear in the series of resolutions adopted by the Security Council
after Iraq's purported annexation of Kuwait in 1990.[61] Annexation will only have
legal effect if confirmed in a peace treaty or if recognised by third states.[62] If
changes in the law have been effected because the former law was considered
inconsistent with accepted international standards concerning, for example,
human rights, and are intended to remedy the position of the local population in
this regard, such changes would probably not be considered contrary to the obligations of the occupant under the Convention. This has been Israel's contention in
amending some laws previously operative relating to the rights of women in the
occupied territories.

---

[56] Art. 38. By Pr. I, Art. 76(2) pregnant women and mothers of dependent children must
have their cases reconsidered with the utmost priority.
   [57] Arts 39, 40, 51.
   [58] Conv., Art. 80.
   [59] See, e.g., Das, 'Japanese occupation', *Malayan Law Journal* (1959).
   [60] Art. 47.
   [61] See, e.g., Lauterpacht, *et al., The Invasion of Kuwait: Basic Documents.*
   [62] Thus, Israel's annexation of the Golan Heights from Syria and of Eastern Jerusalem
has not been recognised.

Control measures

If the Detaining Power considers special measures of control necessary, it may only make use of assigned residence or internment. Such measures may be resorted to only if security makes them absolutely essential and an appellate procedure must be available.[63] Any non-repatriated person has the right to request through the Protecting Power that he be placed in voluntary internment, because he fears, for example, the antagonism of the local population. Control measures of this kind must end when hostilities cease or as soon as possible thereafter.

Individual or mass transfers of protected persons from occupied territory are forbidden, except when necessary for their safety or for imperative military reasons. Evacuation must not involve displacement of protected persons outside the occupied territory, except when material reasons make it impossible to avoid this[64] and they must be returned to their homes as soon as military conditions permit. The Occupying Power must not deport or transfer its own nationals into occupied territory.[65] Israel has been strongly criticised for expelling Arab inhabitants from occupied areas and establishing Israeli settlements there, although it contends that the Convention does not apply, the area being 'administered' rather than 'occupied', and that most of those expelled were terrorists or active sympathisers. In 1992 Serbia was accused of war crimes and crimes against humanity because of its assistance to Serb guerrillas pursuing a policy of 'ethnic cleansing', particularly against Muslims, in parts of Bosnia. However, a Detaining Power may transfer protected persons to another party to the Convention if satisfied that the latter will abide by the Convention, and if this is not complied with it may request their retransfer which must be complied with. But no protected person may be transferred to any country where he fears persecution for religious or political belief. This provision does not affect any liability to extradite a protected person against whom criminal charges have been brought in accordance with an extradition treaty entered into before the commencement of hostilities. Other than a transfer effected by way of extradition, no transfer may interfere with a protected person's right to repatriation to his own state or return to his country of residence once hostilities have ended.[66]

Persons who have fled from their home state and are in fact refugees should not automatically be subjected to restrictive measures merely because of their enemy nationality.[67] This would prevent any repetition of the position during World War II when some countries treated refugees from Nazi Germany as if they were still

---

[63] Arts 42, 44.

[64] In Bosnia in 1992 and 1993 and in Kosovo in 1999 it was often necessary for relief agencies to remove civilians, especially Muslims, from areas threatened with 'ethnic cleansing' by the Serbs, especially when their lives were endangered, even though this raised allegations that the agencies were in fact supporting 'ethnic cleansing'.

[65] Conv., Art. 49.

[66] Art. 43.

[67] Art. 44.

loyal to that country and interned them with other German nationals, although many were later released after administrative hearings. Further provision for the safety of refugees has been made by Protocol I,[68] so that stateless persons or refugees under international agreements recognised by the parties concerned or even under the legislation of the state of residence or refuge are likewise considered protected persons and must not be automatically restricted. This provision does not apply to persons who may have been born locally to such refugees or stateless persons and possess the nationality of the party to the conflict in whose power they are and which retains the right to intern them as nationals.

The position of children

Children under fifteen must be specially cared for, particularly when orphaned or separated from their families as a result of a conflict. Proper provision must be made for their education and religious care, and to the extent possible this should be entrusted to persons of similar cultural background. Every effort should be made to bring dispersed families together[69] or to keep them in contact, but correspondence among them may be restricted to personal matters only. Humanitarian agencies should be encouraged in their efforts to achieve family reunions.[70] If children are arrested or otherwise detained for reasons connected with the conflict, they must be kept separate from adult detainees, unless they are held in family units.

An Occupying Power is responsible for maintaining the functioning of local organisations concerned with child welfare and must facilitate identification and registration of children. If the local organisations are inadequate, the Occupant must take all possible steps to guarantee their care, welfare, education, language and religion. He must do nothing to alter their personal status or to enrol them in organisations established by him and any intentional action directed at the destruction of their cultural characteristics may amount to genocide. Care must also be taken to protect children from indecent assault.

Only children who are nationals of the party may be evacuated to a foreign country, other than temporarily for medical reasons, or when in occupied territory because their safety demands this.[71] In such cases, written consent must be obtained from their parents, legal guardians or, where these are absent, the person recognised as legally responsible for their care. Evacuation must be supervised by

---

[68] Art. 73.

[69] In 1992 during hostilities in Bosnia relief agencies, including the ICRC, were compelled to participate in the separation of families, evacuating children and occasionally women to 'safe' areas because of the 'blockade' imposed by Serb guerrillas.

[70] Conv., Arts 24–6, Pr. I, Art. 74. For a comprehensive survey of the position of children, see Kuper, *Law Concerning Child Civilians in Armed Conflict*, 1997.

[71] See, however, the position of children in Bosnia in 1992 and 1993, when children in threatened as well as occupied territory were affected.

the Protecting Power, although in Bosnia the ICRC, as well as United Nations peace-keepers were involved, and the evacuation must be carried out with the agreement of the evacuating and receiving powers and the state of the children's nationality.

Children under fifteen should not be recruited into the armed forces and every effort should be made to prevent their taking part in the conflict. During the Iran–Iraq war and some civil wars in Africa, children's battalions were raised. If children between fifteen and eighteen are recruited, priority should be given to the oldest. If any children who have taken part in hostilities are captured they continue, even if treated as prisoners of war,[72] to enjoy the special protection granted to children.[73] If a child commits an offence connected to the conflict, even a war crime, he must not be executed unless he was eighteen or over at the time of the act in question.[74]

Punishment of civilians

When civilians are detained they are subject to the laws in force in the country in which they are held, provided these accord with the minimum set out in the Convention or internationally recognised human rights standards. If laws are enacted which treat non-detainees differently, detainees may only be subjected to disciplinary penalties. If charged with criminal offences they must be given a fair trial and proper opportunities to defend themselves. When imposing punishment it must be remembered that non-national civilians owe no allegiance to the Detaining Power, which nevertheless retains the right to punish offences against its security.

When a detainee escapes and is recaptured he is only liable to disciplinary punishment, even if he is a repeating escaper. In such cases, however, he may be subjected to special surveillance. The escape is not an aggravating factor with regard to any offence committed during or connected with the escape.[75]

The penal laws of occupied territory remain in force and may only be amended if they endanger the occupant or are inconsistent with the provisions of the Civilians Convention. Amendments may be made to give effect to the Convention, to protect the security of the occupant, members of his forces and their property, their establishments and lines of communication. However, an occupant cannot be expected to retain in force such penal laws as Nazi racial legislation or laws contrary to his concept of public morality. The penal laws of occupied territory remain subject to the jurisdiction of the local judges and courts, and if they only

[72] See ch. 10 above.

[73] Pr. I, Art. 77. See Cohn and Goodwin-Gill, *The Role of Children in Armed Conflict*, 1994.

[74] This opens up the possibility of older persons getting a juvenile to commit such acts. This, however, would not mean that the former would escape liability.

[75] Arts 120, 121. The provisions regarding escapers and their punishment are similar to those for prisoners of war.

enforce those laws and non-policy laws of the occupant they should not be treated as treasonable by the returning sovereign.[76] Any new penal legislation must be brought to the knowledge of those affected before it can be enforced. It must be in their own language and not retroactive, with any punishment proportionate to the offence.[77] Any act committed before the occupation and lawful under local law cannot be made punishable even if it was contrary to the occupant's security or his law. This would protect those, even refugee nationals of the occupant, making statements that were contrary to the latter's interest before the occupation commenced. This protection does not, however, extend to acts which are in breach of the law of war. Refugee nationals of the occupant are not protected if the act alleged against them was extraditable by the law of the occupied state during peace time.[78]

A protected person sentenced to death after properly constituted judicial proceedings is entitled to appeal or petition for pardon or reprieve. No death sentence may be carried out for at least six months after notice has been given to the Protecting Power, although this period may be reduced in the event of a grave emergency threatening the security of the occupying forces, provided the Protecting Power is told of the reduction and the reasons for it.[79] Problems concerning the period before execution may arise where the law of the occupant requires execution immediately after dismissal of the final appeal on the ground that delay constitutes inhumane punishment.

Criticism always arises when women are executed for offences connected with the conflict, whether the accusations relate to espionage or assisting persons to escape.[80] If they do not reprieve expectant mothers, most nations retaining the death penalty postpone execution until after the child has been born. Now, by Protocol I[81] parties to the conflict are obliged to the maximum extent feasible to avoid sentencing to death pregnant women or mothers having dependent children,[82] and if such a sentence has been pronounced it must not be carried out. This protection only relates to offences committed in relation to the conflict. It does not affect any sentence for other criminal offences.

In addition to the provisions in the Convention and Protocol regarding the protection of civilians, the rules concerning the conduct of hostilities provide for the protection of civilian property and objects,[83] as well as for the protection of such property in occupied territory.[84]

---

[76] Some of the problems in this connection concerning Malaya after World War II are considered in Das, 'Japanese occupation.' See n. 59 above.

[77] Conv., Arts 64, 65.

[78] Art. 70.

[79] Art. 75.

[80] See for examples, 2 Garner, *International Law and the World War*, 97–104.

[81] Art. 76(3).

[82] By failing to indicate the age limit, it is possible for a child of almost any age to be dependent for physical or psychological reasons.

[83] See chs 7, 8, 9 above.

[84] See ch. 15 below.

Journalists

The law of armed conflict recognises the position of war correspondents properly identifiable and attached to a belligerent's forces.[85] Increasingly in modern conflicts there are instances of individuals not accredited as war correspondents undertaking journalistic activities, sometimes because, as in the Gulf War, they are regular journalists and have remained behind in occupied territory or because they have undertaken individual commissions to report to some news media on specific engagements. Many of these persons have been killed, often intentionally, as appears to have been the case in Vietnam and Bosnia, and measures have been taken to secure their protection.

By Article 79 of Protocol I journalists engaged on dangerous professional missions in areas of armed conflict and carrying proper identity cards[86] are to be treated as civilians. They are protected under the Convention and Protocol so long as they take no action adversely affecting their status as civilians, as would be the case if, for example, they are given transport facilities by the forces in the area and assist them in beating off an attack[87] or dealing with a sniper.

[85] See n. 33, ch. 6 above.

[86] See, e.g., letter by Green, 'Journalists in battle areas', *The Times*, 1 Mar. 1976, re undercover military personnel carrying such documents in Northern Ireland.

[87] See, e.g., Fisk, 'Times correspondent riding shotgun with Soviet Army', in Afghanistan, *The Times*, 21 Jan. 1980.

13

The Protecting Power

Background

In peace time when diplomatic relations are broken off between two countries or when one is not represented in the territory of the other, the normal practice is for each or the unrepresented one to nominate a third state acceptable to the recipient to represent its interests and protect its nationals in the recipient's territory.[1] Occasionally, both states may request the same third state to fulfil this function.

While it is not unknown for states conducting hostilities to assert that they are not at war in the traditional sense of that term[2] and to maintain diplomats at each other's capital,[3] it is usual on the outbreak of hostilities for the belligerents to break off all diplomatic relations and withdraw their diplomats.[4] In such circumstances protecting powers are named to represent the interests of the belligerents in each other's territory, and here too the same power may represent both conflicting states.[5] In addition to the regular tasks of a protecting power, during war they also assume the duty of supervising the application of the various Geneva Conventions. If the diplomat of a third state is appointed to this task, he remains the representative of his own state, while anything he does on behalf of the protected state is the responsibility of the latter.[6] He should try to avoid any action that may embarrass the neutrality of his own state.

[1] For an example of one belligerent requesting an ally to represent it in occupied territory, see *Chevreau Claim* (1913) 2 R.I.A.A., 115.

[2] See ch. 1 and 2 above.

[3] This was the position between China and Japan from 1931 to 1941, and during the NATO bombing of Yugoslavia in 1999.

[4] See ch. 4 above.

[5] 'Until the breaking off of diplomatic relations with Germany in February 1917, the representatives of the United States took charge of the interests of four of the Allied powers in Germany (Great Britain, Japan, Servia and Romania) and of five in Austria Hungary (Great Britain, France, Italy, Japan and Romania). They also looked after the interests of Germany and Austria–Hungary in all the countries with which they were at war except Italy, Japan and Portugal', 1 Garner, *International Law and the World War*, 53, n.3.

[6] See *Chevreau Claim*.

The impact of Geneva

While practice recognised the importance of protecting powers,[7] it was not until the Prisoners of War Convention, 1929,[8] that there were any treaty provisions concerning them, although there had been earlier recognition of the role of humanitarian organisations like the ICRC. That Convention made provision for protecting powers to visit prisoner-of-war centres, contact the prisoners and offer good offices to the contesting parties on the application of the Convention.

Each of the 1949 Conventions contains specific articles relating to the powers and functions of the Protecting Power, while Protocol I, 1977, has greatly improved the machinery for the appointment of a Protecting Power and increased its functions. Each Convention is to be applied[9] with the co-operation and under the scrutiny of the Protecting Power whose duty it is to safeguard the interests of the parties to the conflict. To effect this, the Protecting Power may appoint members of its diplomatic or consular service, or from among its own or neutral nationals, provided each nominee is acceptable to the belligerent with which he is to carry out his duties. The recipient is obliged to offer every assistance to the representative concerned, who must take care not to exceed his mission under the Convention.[10] He must respect the security of the party with which he is serving, who, when overwhelming military necessity demands, may restrict his activities on a temporary and exceptional basis. If territory is occupied no agreement made by the parties concerned may derogate from the Convention role of the Protecting Power, but if the territory is annexed as the result of a peace treaty the Protecting Power's functions come to an end.

Protocol I has introduced a procedure[11] to prevent delays in the assumption of activities by the Protecting Power and there is now a duty upon parties to apply the protecting system from the beginning of hostilities. If no Protecting Power has been nominated or accepted, the ICRC or some similar organisation is authorised to offer its good offices to help the parties agree on the selection by asking each party to submit names and then seeking agreement. If no agreement is possible the ICRC or other organisation concerned may offer to act as a substitute. Since 1967, in fact, the ICRC has undertaken the functions of a Protecting Power in the Israeli-occupied territories, with the exception of East Jerusalem, which Israel claims to have annexed.[12]

So that representatives of a Protecting Party may enter upon their task immediately a conflict begins, the Protocol requires parties to it, even in peace time, to try to train persons who may be able to assume these functions if necessary, and

---

[7] See Garner, *International Law*, for examples before World War I.

[8] Schindler and Toman, 325.

[9] Conv. I, II, III, Art. 8, Conv. IV, Art. 9.

[10] During World War II there were instances of a Protecting Power passing messages from detained personnel to their government.

[11] Art. 5

[12] See Cohen, *Human Rights*, 55.

the ICRC is to be informed of the identity of any trained persons so that parties to a conflict may be told of any specialists available. Should the Protecting Power consider it advisable in the interests of protected persons, especially if there is a dispute concerning the application of a Convention, it may offer its good offices to assist in solving the dispute and may suggest a meeting in neutral territory, together with a representative of the ICRC, or a neutral power. The parties to the conflict must accept any proposal of this kind.[13]

The fact that a state has agreed to represent the diplomatic interests of a party to the conflict or that diplomatic relations are preserved between them does not mean that a Protecting Power, which may be either of the above, need not be appointed to fulfil the duties required by the Conventions.

Prisoners of war

Information concerning protected persons in the hands of an adverse party is transmitted to the state on whom they depend through the Protecting Power and the Central Prisoners of War or Central Information Agency.[14] Wounded and sick who are held as prisoners of war are entitled to all the protective activities of the Protecting Power which relate to prisoners, and the Protecting Power is responsible for informing the home state of the location of camps and may also offer its good offices in arranging safety zones for hospitals. If the captor transfers prisoners to another party to the Convention, the Protecting Power may, should it discover that the latter is not fulfilling its obligations under the Convention, request the transferring power to secure their return.

Among the tasks of the Protecting Power's representative concerning prisoners of war is to check that the conditions of the places in which they are detained conform to the Convention requirements[15] regarding health, warmth, safety and the like. He must also be informed of the location of any labour detachments dependent on a prisoner-of-war camp and is entitled to visit these too. At the same time, he is entitled to communicate with and receive communications from prisoners on a private basis, interviewing them without any representative of the Detaining Power present. Such communications must relate to the conditions in the camp or the prisoner's comments concerning his treatment and the application of the Convention. He may also receive communications on an unrestricted basis from prisoners' representatives,[16] including periodic reports on camp conditions.[17]

The Detaining Power must report to the Protecting Power any action taken

[13] Conv. I, II, III, Art. 11, Conv. IV Art. 12.
[14] For prisoners of war and the wounded it is the Central Prisoners of War Information Agency for civilians the Central Information Agency.
[15] A similar right exists under the Civilians Convention.
[16] See n. 96, ch. 10 above.
[17] Conv. III, Art. 78.

against prisoners. If it wishes to limit the number of letters or cards prisoners may send or receive it must inform the Protecting Power which must be satisfied that this is in the interest of the prisoners as, for example, when lack of translators for censorship would result in an undue backlog. Similarly, only the Protecting Power may propose limitations upon the receipt of relief parcels and these proposals must be in the interests of the prisoners, but a relief organisation may propose limitations based on transport difficulties concerning its own relief packages. Even if the parties to the conflict agree, the right of the Protecting Power to supervise the distribution of collective relief parcels cannot be limited. If military operations prevent the Detaining Power from conveying correspondence or relief parcels, this task may be undertaken by the Protecting Power.[18]

The Protecting Power is the intermediary for informing the home state of prisoners of the arrangements made by the Detaining Power to give effect to its obligations under the Convention concerning the prisoners' rights to communicate with the exterior, meaning the world outside the camp and authorities other than the Detaining Power. The Protecting Power is also the medium for informing the home state of rates of pay prisoners receive and is entitled to inspect prisoners' accounts. It also informs that state of the standing of such accounts when prisoners are repatriated, and of any claim that a prisoner is entitled to compensation for injury suffered while working as a prisoner of war.

While the Protecting Power must not pass unauthorised materials to and from prisoners, it is available for the transmission of legal documents, such as wills, to and from the home state.

It is the task of the Protecting Power to ensure that any prisoner charged with an offence receives a fair trial. It must be informed of all offences which carry the death penalty, and no death sentence may be carried out until six months after it has been told of its imposition. It must be notified of any judicial proceedings against a prisoner of war and when necessary is responsible for finding a defending advocate or counsel. Unless the trial is held in camera, the representative of the Protecting Power is entitled to attend, and any judgment or sentence must be brought to his notice.

The Protecting Power must be informed if any prisoner suffers serious injury or dies other than by natural causes and must be given a copy of the report of the official inquiry held in connection therewith.

Apart from any special rights granted or duties imposed upon the Protecting Power, its representatives are entitled to take whatever steps they consider necessary to carry out their duties concerning supervision of the Convention in the interests of prisoners of war and are free to choose which places they will visit,[19] the frequency of those visits, which may only be restricted because of over-

---

[18] In 1992 and 1993 during the fighting in Bosnia–Herzegovina this task was carried out by the ICRC and UN relief representatives.

[19] In 1992 and 1993 they were often prevented from visiting particular camps in Serb-held areas of Bosnia. In 1998, similar interference was experienced in Kosovo.

whelming military necessity,[20] and if the parties agree co-nationals of the prisoners may be included in the visiting groups.

Civilians

In accordance with the Civilians Convention the Protecting Power has a role to play in protecting civilians, especially those in occupied territory. In most cases this Power will be the same as that chosen to represent a belligerent's diplomatic interests for the representatives of that power will be present in the occupied territory. The Protecting Power's main function is to co-operate in the administration and supervision of the Convention and offer its good offices in the event of a dispute between the parties as to its interpretation or application. Should civilians be detained or interned the Protecting Power has similar rights of visit as in the case of prisoners of war.

The passage of medical and hospital supplies, as well as articles intended for religious purposes, and of essential foodstuffs, clothing and tonics for children under fifteen, for expectant mothers and maternity cases may be made subject to the supervision of the Protecting Power.[21] This relates to the civilian population of any party to the Convention – enemy, allied, associated or neutral – and wherever that population may be.

If children under fifteen are orphaned or separated from their families and it becomes necessary to evacuate them to a neutral country, the evacuation and their reception shall be under the supervision of the Protecting Power.[22] In 1992 this issue became of serious concern during the fighting in Bosnia. In accordance with Article 49 of the Civilians Convention mass forcible transfers or deportations of civilians from occupied territories are forbidden. However, in Serb-occupied areas of Bosnia a policy of 'ethnic purification' was being pursued and the ICRC was compelled to organise evacuations in order to save the children affected from possible death by starvation or massacre. Similar arrangements had to be made at later stages of the conflict in the former Yugoslavia, as well as in Kosovo.

The Protecting Power must be told of any persons transferred or evacuated from occupied territory or denied the right of repatriation together with the reasons, as well as of any persons placed in internment or assigned residence, and of those who have been released together with the decisions of any hearing boards. Any protected person who wishes to be placed in voluntary internment makes his application through the Protecting Power.[23]

---

[20] In Bosnia it was alleged that visits were delayed by the Serbs to give them time to clean up camps in which it was alleged conditions were below the required standards.

[21] In the case of Iraq after the invasion of Kuwait and the end of the Gulf War, such supplies were made subject to a United Nations supervisory commission.

[22] Conv. IV, Art. 24; see also Pr. I, Art. 78.

[23] See ch. 12 above.

If any protected person loses his means of livelihood and becomes unable to support himself or his dependants, the Protecting Power may make the necessary relief allowances. Similarly, if a contract or regulation affects the rights of any worker, whether a volunteer or not, he may apply to the Protecting Power for intervention on his behalf. That Power has an unrestricted right to inspect the food and medical supplies in occupied territory, except when imperative military necessity makes restrictions inevitable.

If relief supplies are passing through the territory of one party to the conflict to territory occupied by the adverse party, the Protecting Power must satisfy the country of transit that these supplies will be used solely for the benefit of the population of the occupied territory and not by the Occupying Power. The distribution of relief consignments is supervised by the Protecting Power, and if the Occupying Power wishes to divert them from their intended purpose it must satisfy the Protecting Power of the absolute necessity of this in the interest of the population of the occupied territory.[24]

Detention and trial

An Occupying Power's right to amend the penal law in occupied territory is restricted and on no account may it introduce discriminatory legislation similar to the Nazi race laws.[25] If it wishes to try a protected person for an offence carrying the death penalty or imprisonment for two years or more, no trial may be instituted before the Protecting Power has been informed. If the accused fails to appoint defence counsel, the Protecting Power may choose one. It has the right to attend any trial, whatever the nature of the penalty, unless it has been informed that as an exceptional measure in the interests of the Occupying Power's security the trial is being held in camera. It must also be informed of the location of any prison in which a protected person is held; all records of proceedings must be available for its inspection and no appellate period is to be computed until after it has been informed of the sentence. It is also to be told if it is intended to reduce the six months that must elapse between imposition and execution of any death sentence.

As with prisoners of war, the Protecting Power has the right to visit any detained protected person both before and after sentence and to interview him in the absence of any witnesses. Visits to labour detachments dependent on a place of internment must also be allowed. The duration and frequency of visits may be restricted only as a temporary and exceptional measure for imperative military reasons.

The Protecting Power may make financial allowances to internees and act as intermediary for conveying allowances from the home state. Statements of account relating to detained personnel must be made available on request. It also

---

[24] Arts 59–61.
[25] See ch. 15 below.

has general supervisory rights regarding the Convention's provisions on relations with the exterior, such as those dealing with correspondence, relief parcels or legal documents. In addition it has the right to receive any complaints about the conditions of detention from individual internees or the Internee Committee set up in places of internment,[26] and this Committee may send periodic reports to the Protecting Power on the conditions and treatment there. If any interned protected person is subjected to disciplinary punishment the record of such punishment must be open to inspection by the representative of the Protecting Power.

Apart from any specific rights stemming from the Convention, Protecting Powers enjoy a general supervisory competence regarding the obligations of the Detaining Power and the rights of protected persons, including the right to visit and interview any protected person, and to inspect any quarters in which they may be detained or confined.

Cultural property

Apart from functions derived from the Civilians Convention, the Protecting Power must also co-operate in supervising execution of the Hague Convention for the Protection of Cultural Property in the Event of Armed Conflict.[27] The Protecting Power is to appoint a representative to deal with such property, and he may order the removal of the protective emblem from any interim refuge established for this property should he consider that proper. Even states not parties to the Convention are obliged by the Hague Regulations[28] to respect buildings dedicated to religion, art, science, charitable purposes and historic monuments.

If a dispute arises between the parties to the conflict concerning the protection of cultural property, the Protecting Powers are to offer their good offices in the interests of that property. To this end they may propose meetings of their representatives with those of the parties, and these may be attended by neutral nationals or a representative of the Director-General of the United Nations Educational, Scientific and Cultural Organisation who is to maintain a Register of Cultural Property under Special Protection.

The role of humanitarian organisations

The parties to the conflict may agree that the responsibilities of a Protecting Power should be granted to an impartial humanitarian organisation like the ICRC. If wounded and sick or medical and religious personnel do not or no longer enjoy the protection of a Protecting Power the Detaining Power may ask a neutral or

[26] Art. 102 deals with the election of Internee Committees, and 104 with communications between the Committee and the Protecting Power.
[27] 1954, Schindler and Toman, 745, and Pr. thereto, 777.
[28] Art. 27.

such an organisation to assume protection responsibility for these persons. If there is no third power available or willing to undertake this task, an offer to do so by such an organisation must be accepted.

The presence of a Protecting Power does not interfere with or limit in any way the activities of the ICRC or National Red Cross Societies,[29] or of any other international or national humanitarian organisation in accordance with the terms of the Conventions or the Protocol. If there is no Protecting Power or if the one appointed is unable to act for any reason, the ICRC or other impartial humanitarian organisation may always offer itself as a substitute. This offer is made to both parties to the conflict and is subject to their consent.[30]

[29] The same is true of the Red Crescent or Red Shield of David Societies.

[30] For some discussion of the role of humanitarian nongovernmental organisations during conflict, see Hampson, 'Nongovernmental organizations in situations of conflict: the negotiation of change', Schmitt and Green, *The Law of Armed Conflict into the Next Millennium*, 1998, 233; Nanda, 'Nongovernmental organizations and international humanitarian law', *ibid.*, 337.

14

Civil defence

Every community has, in the event of disaster, and this includes war, organised efforts to assist those injured or adversely affected by the disaster. During armed conflict this responsibility has often fallen on voluntary organisations like the National Red Cross Society, the St John's Ambulance Brigade or the Salvation Army. Some countries have organised governmental movements to operate in these circumstances, some on an *ad hoc* basis and some by way of permanent organisation.

During World War II, because of the intensive bombing attacks experienced by the civilian population, some, like the United Kingdom, set up trained units to work in the field of civil defence, assisting those injured or rendered homeless because of air raids. Others already had organised corps of civil defence workers able to operate in any emergency, manmade or natural. There was, however, no special recognition of the existence of this service nor any need to protect its personnel in the event of armed conflict. The nearest one came to finding any recognition of such a service is in Article 63 of the Civilians Convention, 1949,[1] requiring an Occupying Power to allow National Red Cross Societies and other humanitarian organisations to continue to function, as well as 'special organisations of a non-military character, which already exist or which may be established for the purpose of ensuring the living conditions of the civilian population by the maintenance of essential public utility services, by the distribution of relief and by the organisation of rescues'.

Protocol I

A major change was effected with the adoption of Protocol I[2] in 1977. Chapter VI is concerned solely with civil defence, defined as 'the performance of humanitarian

[1] Schindler and Toman, 495.
[2] *Ibid.*, 621.

tasks intended to protect the civilian population against the dangers, and to help it to recover from the immediate effects, of hostilities or disasters and also to provide the conditions necessary for its survival'. The tasks envisaged are:

> warning; evacuation; management of shelters; management of blackout measures; rescue; medical services, including first aid and religious assistance; fire-fighting; detection and marking of danger areas; decontamination and similar protective measures; provision of emergency accommodation and supplies; emergency assistance in the restoration and maintenance of order in distressed areas; emergency repair of indispensable public utilities; emergency disposal of the dead; assistance in the preservation of objects essential for survival; complementary activities necessary to carry out [these] tasks, including, but not limited to, planning and organisation.

Civil defence organisations are those establishments and units organised or authorised by the competent authorities to carry out these tasks, and civil defence personnel are persons assigned exclusively to this function, including administrators, medical and religious personnel. Since civil defence activities are limited to civilian interests it would seem that if their personnel were involved in fighting a fire at a military installation they would lose any protection otherwise attaching to them. These organisations and their personnel are to be respected and protected and are entitled to carry out their tasks subject to 'imperative military necessity',[3] and this protection extends to civilian volunteers, not members of any civil defence organisation, responding to an appeal by the authorities to assist in these activities, provided they do so under the control of those authorities.

Civil defence buildings and *matériel* are immune from attack, in the same way as any other non-military objectives, and this same exception extends to shelters provided for civilian protection.[4] However, such shelters should not be located near to military objectives nor used to secure immunity for such objectives. Articles intended for civil defence may only be destroyed or diverted by the party to which they belong, and if they are in occupied territory this may not be done by the Occupying Power if it would result in harm to the civilian population. However, if these objects are required for the security of that population the Occupying Power may divert or even requisition them for so long as the necessity persists. This power does not extend to shelters provided for or needed by the civilian population.

An Occupying Power must grant civil defence organisations all facilities required to carry out their tasks and they cannot be compelled to do anything

---

[3] Art. 62(1). It is difficult to appreciate why the word 'imperative' is used, for 'military necessity' is only recognised for disregarding protective provisions in the Conventions and Protocol when this is absolutely necessary.

[4] During the Gulf War 1991, controversy arose because of the destruction by bombing of Al-Firdus/Al-'Amariyah Bunker in which a number of Iraqi civilians had taken shelter. It was maintained by the Coalition authorities that this was a legitimate military objective part of which was being used by civilians, whose presence was unknown to the Coalition, US Defense Dept., Report to Congress, *Conduct of the Persian Gulf War*, App. O, 'The role of the law of war', 31 I.L.M. (1992), 615, 626.

which would interfere with those activities. Nor may that Power make any change in their organisation or personnel if that might interfere with the efficient performance of their duties, and these organisations cannot be required to give any priority to the Occupant's nationals or interests. Equally, the Occupying Power is forbidden from making any attempt to coerce or induce civilian civil defence organisations to operate in any way inimical to the interests of the civilian population.

Civilian civil defence personnel may carry light individual weapons for their own protection or to preserve order, but not weapons like fragmentation grenades or those intended for non-human targets. When operating in areas where land fighting may be expected they may only carry handguns and, provided they can establish their identity as civil defence operatives, the carrying of such weapons does not affect their protected status. They may be disarmed for security reasons.

Any neutral nationals performing civil defence tasks in the territory of a party to the conflict, with that party's consent, are entitled to the same protection as all other civil defence personnel. Their participation must be notified to the adverse party and does not amount to interference in the conflict or a breach of neutrality.[5] Should they offer such assistance in occupied territory, it may only be rejected if the Occupying Power is able to fulfil these tasks from its own resources.

As is the case with other protected personnel or organisations, the protection enjoyed by civil defence personnel ends if they operate outside their proper tasks or in a fashion inimical to the adverse party. They must, however, be given an opportunity to cease the unauthorised activity.

The fact that civil defence activities are being carried out under the direction of or in cooperation with the armed forces or military personnel attached to civil defence units, or on behalf of military victims, especially those *hors de combat*, is not sufficient to amount to acts inimical to the adverse party and affecting the immunity of the personnel involved, provided these acts are incidental to normal civil defence operations.

To ensure their proper protection, civil defence personnel should carry the authorised identity card, while establishments and *matériel* should display the internationally prescribed civil defence emblem[6] of an equilateral blue triangle on an orange background in a manner recognisable by the adverse party, and the parties may agree to any additional emblem that they select. National authorities must repress unauthorised use of the emblem, but may permit its use by civil defence establishments in peace time.

When medical or religious personnel are attached to civil defence units they are protected by the provisions relating to the special civil defence emblem as well as those concerning use of the Red Cross emblem.[7]

[5] See ch. 16 below.
[6] Chapters I and V of Annex I of the Protocol provide details regarding the use and exhibition of the emblem and of the identity card.
[7] Art. 66(9).

Military personnel and civil defence

When, as in the former Soviet Union, the civil defence organisation is part of the defence establishment, or members of the armed forces are assigned to civil defence organisations, they enjoy the protection afforded such organisations so long as their assignment is permanent and they only fulfil civil defence duties for the duration of the conflict. They must be clearly identifiable from other members of the armed forces and must display the emblem and carry civil defence identity cards, and may only carry light individual weapons for self-defence or maintaining order.

Military personnel assigned to civil defence duties may only perform these duties within their own national territory and must not commit any act outside those duties which might be inimical to the adverse party. Once assigned to civil defence duties they may not be retransferred to active service and later on revert to civil defence activities, and, since they retain their military status, if captured they become prisoners of war.[8] In occupied territory they may be employed in civil defence work only in the interest of the territory's civilian population, and if the work is dangerous only if they volunteer.

Military buildings or major items of equipment or transport assigned to civil defence purposes must be clearly marked with the distinctive emblem. If captured military *matériel* is assigned on a permanent basis and exclusively used for this purpose it must not be diverted from its civil defence function so long as so required, unless for imperative military necessity, and only if alternative arrangements for civil defence have been made.

If the parties to the conflict are not parties to the Protocol they are not bound by any treaty regulations concerning the activities or rights pertaining to civil defence. The only obligations upon such a belligerent are those concerning the protection of civilians and civilian objects generally.[9]

[8] See ch. 10 above.
[9] See ch. 7 above.

15

Rights and duties of the Occupying Power

The basic rules

In former times there was a tendency for a belligerent occupying enemy territory to annex that territory and treat it as part of his own. However, in the nineteenth century it was recognised that frequently such occupation might be only temporary and that the territory would revert to its former sovereign. In his Code,[1] Professor Lieber had already outlined limited regulations for the conduct of an occupant,[2] which were supplemented by the general rules with regard to the treatment of civilians.

In the Regulations Respecting the Laws and Customs of War on Land appended to the 1899 and 1907 Hague Conventions on land warfare,[3] Section Three is concerned with 'Military Authority over Hostile Territory' making it clear that the territory concerned must be under the actual occupation and authority of the occupant who must insure, as far as possible, the maintenance of public order through the medium of the laws already in force.[4] The Regulations also prescribe the rules of conduct and the limitations imposed upon the occupant on behalf of the inhabitants of the territory in question,[5] including the obligation to respect their lives.[6] Further limitations upon the activities of an occupant were introduced by the Civilians Convention 1949 and Protocol I, 1977,[7] but these documents have not abrogated the Hague Regulations, so that the powers of an occupant are now defined by customary law and these three instruments.

[1] Instructions for the Governance of Armies of the United States in the Field, General Orders no. 100 by President Lincoln, 24 Apr. 1863.

[2] Arts 1, 2, 6, 7.

[3] Schindler and Toman, 69.

[4] See, however, Rowson, 'The abolition of Nazi and Fascist anti-Jewish legislation by British military administrations of the Second World War', 1 Jewish Y.B. Int'l Law (1948), 61.

[5] See, e.g., Graber, *Development of the Law of Belligerent Occupation 1863–1914*.

[6] See, e.g., *JK* v. *Public Prosecutor* (Netherlands, 1981) 87 I.L.R., 93, holding that the killing of a civilian by a member of the occupying forces was a breach of Art. 46 of the Hague Regs and therefore a war crime, see ch. 18 below.

[7] Schindler and Toman, 495, 621 resp.

Occupation does not create any change in the status of the territory, which can only be effected by a peace treaty or by annexation followed by recognition. The former sovereign remains sovereign and there is no change in the nationality of the inhabitants. Their allegiance does not change and the Occupying Power may not compel them to swear an oath of allegiance to himself, nor compel them to serve in his armed or auxiliary forces,[8] or impart information concerning the forces or defences of their own state.[9] While they may work for him, their liability under the original law remains and they may therefore find themselves charged with treason when the occupation ceases and the former sovereign regains control.

Occasionally territory may be under the temporary occupation of an ally. This might occur, for example, when the original sovereign of a country which has been completely overrun and occupied and then liberated from enemy occupation has not reassumed authority.[10] This is particularly the case when the lawful local administrative system has been virtually destroyed by the occupant, and in many cases the liberating authority will have reached agreement with the former sovereign specifying the nature of regime which is to assume power. At the end of World War II, for example, some of the United Nations[11] which had been involved in the liberation of Europe had established 'civil affairs' departments to carry out this task. On occasion a belligerent may reconquer some of its own territory and place it under military occupation and administration until civil authority has been restored. Occupation of this kind is subject to national and not international law, unless there are enemy nationals present in which case international regulations with regard to the treatment of civilians in adverse hands[12] may also be relevant.

The nature of belligerent occupation

Territory is occupied only when it is actually under the control and administration of an occupant and extends only to those areas in which he is actually able to exercise such control. A mere declaration that territory is occupied or its temporary occupation by a raiding party, or even defeat of the lawful sovereign's forces does not amount to occupation. However the occupant must make it clear that the occupation has been established and indicate the penalties for disobeying any laws and regulations he may promulgate. It must be clear that in the affected territory there is no longer any semblance of authority other than that imposed or tolerated by the

[8] Conv., Art. 51.

[9] Hague Regs., Art. 44; see also Civilians Conv., Art. 31,

[10] See, e.g., Donnison, *British Military Administration in the Far East, 1943–1946, ibid. Civil Affairs and Military Government North-east Europe 1944–1946*, Holborn, *American Military Government*, Rennell of Rodd, Lord, *British Military Administration in Africa 1941–1947*.

[11] Name of the alliance against the Axis powers.

[12] See ch. 12 above.

occupant, that the local forces are no longer effective in the area, that the population is to all intents and purposes disarmed, and that it is the occupying authority which is effectively maintaining law and order with troops available or easily secured to assist in this task if needed.

For an occupation to be effective the legitimate authority must be unable to exercise its functions publicly, but the presence of isolated areas in which that authority is still functioning does not affect the reality of the occupation if those areas are effectively cut off from the rest of the occupied territory.

Even if the occupying authority declares the occupation to be civil and not military in character it remains subject to the law of armed conflict. When, however, hostilities have ceased and one of the parties has surrendered unconditionally, or all former governmental institutions have disappeared, the basis of the occupation may change with the Occupying Power establishing his own system of law, regardless of the law of armed conflict, as was the case with Germany after 1945 and before the establishment of local German governments.[13]

If, after establishing his occupation, the Occupying Power continues his advance and only leaves token forces behind, so long as they are available to uphold the occupant's authority effectively, the territory remains occupied. But if he evacuates or retreats from the territory and the legitimate government is able to reassert its authority the occupation ceases. Its existence is not affected because citizens commit acts of sabotage or rebel or that guerrilla forces make successful raids, unless these activities result in the overthrow of the occupying authorities.

Relations with the population

If the occupation ceases for any reason, the relations between the former occupant and the inhabitants again become subject to the normal rules of armed conflict concerning contacts between a belligerent and enemy civilians. Reoccupation of the territory constitutes a new occupation and not a continuation of the former.

Today, the relations between the Occupying Power and the population are regulated primarily by the terms of the Civilians Convention, which come into force from the time the area is actually placed under the occupant's authority. They cease one year after the end of hostilities, it being thought in 1949 that twelve months was ample time for an occupation to be wound up. However, certain articles of the Convention remain binding so long as the Occupying Power continues to exercise governmental authority.[14] If the occupied territory is annexed at the end of the conflict and that annexation is recognised the occupant is freed from these limitations and may extend his own law to what is now his territory.

When an occupation is established all the responsibilities of the local authorities end, although the Occupying Power may allow or request them to continue to

---

[13] See, e.g., Friedmann, *The Allied Military Government of Germany*.
[14] See text to n. 19, ch. 12 above.

function and it depends on the law of the lawful sovereign whether they may legally do so. The Occupying Power may not alter the status of public officials or judges nor apply coercion, sanctions or any discrimination against them should they, on grounds of conscience, refuse to continue in office.[15] After World War II some restored governments tried public officials, who had co-operated, for treason, though often this was because they went beyond what the national law provided, or actively assisted the occupant in enforcing his policies.

As administrator of the occupied territory the Occupying Power is responsible for the maintenance of public order and safety.[16] Political laws like those concerning elections, and constitutional safeguards such as *habeas corpus*, cease to apply, as do laws constituting a threat to the security of the occupation, such as those relating to recruitment or the bearing of arms. However, the Occupying Power's competence to amend either the local civil or penal law is not unlimited, and he should not introduce any regulation that suspends, extinguishes or renders unenforceable the legal rights of enemy subjects.

Where the local system does not measure up to current standards of the rule of law the Occupying Power may make the amendments necessary to remedy this. He may, therefore, remove from the penal code any punishments that are 'unreasonable, cruel or inhumane' together with any discriminatory racial legislation. In view of the modern approach to human rights, the Israeli action in conferring the vote in mayoral elections on women who had not formerly enjoyed this right in territory which had come under its administration, would probably also be acceptable.

The Occupying Power may only extend his own law to the territory if it is annexed and the transfer of sovereignty recognised. If he introduces his own or unlawfully amends the local law, the lawful sovereign is under no obligation to recognise the effects of such amendments when the occupation ceases. However, when this has an adverse effect on the local population, as would be the case when the changes affect regulations concerning marriage or the law of banking or contract, the restored sovereign will frequently enact legislation confirming the effect of these changes.[17]

It is open to the Occupying Power to stop circulation of the local currency and issue his own, and the two may be in use at the same time. But he may not debase or devalue the former currency so as to injure the economic life of the occupied territory or enhance his own at that territory's expense. The local economy may only be required to bear the expense of the occupation and only to the extent that this can be reasonably expected of it.[18]

Problems may arise, as happened in Bosnia after the collapse of the former Yugoslavia, when it is not clear whether the occupant is in fact an alien power or an agent of such a power, for the protection provided by the Convention only

[15] Conv., Art. 54.
[16] Hague Regs, Art. 43.
[17] See, e.g., Das, 'Japanese occupation', Malayan Law Journal (1959).
[18] Hague Regs, Arts 48, 49.

extends to those 'in the hands of a Party to the conflict or an Occupying Power'.[19] Should the Convention not apply in such a case, because the conflict is non-international rather than international, the civilian population remains under the protection of Common Article 3 of the four Geneva Conventions.

The limitations preventing undue amendment of the laws do not extend to the news media and they may be suspended or subjected to censorship. If they are permitted to operate the local staff may be called upon to co-operate but are under no obligation to comply. Both public and private means of transport are subject to such regulations as the occupant may introduce and if he seizes any that is privately owned it must be restored and compensation paid when peace is made and the same is true for any organ of the press that may have been seized.[20]

Obligations of the occupying power

The Occupying Power must take all necessary steps to give effect to the provisions of the Civilians Convention concerning persons in occupied territory and to provide penal sanctions in respect of any grave breaches and suppress all other acts contrary to that instrument.[21] It is also obliged to ensure that family honour and rights, together with the dignity and lives of those in occupied territory are respected.[22] The religious convictions and practices of the population must be respected, subject to the needs of public morality, and religious ministers must be allowed to give spiritual assistance to their communities.

An occupant is forbidden from confiscating private property or that of municipalities and institutions, whether state owned or not, dedicated to religion, charity, education and the arts and sciences. Any seizure or wilful damage to such property is forbidden and must be made subject to legal proceedings.[23] Steps must also be taken to prevent pillage and any destruction of real or personal property, even if belonging to the state or any other public authority, is forbidden unless rendered absolutely necessary by military necessity.[24]

Since the Occupying Power is only an administrator and usufructuary of public buildings, real estate, forests and agricultural estates belonging to the adverse party, he must safeguard the capital of these properties and administer them in the same way as a usufructuary[25] and is therefore liable for any waste or destruction resulting from that use. If military operations render this absolutely necessary real

[19] See extract from *Tadić* case, ch. 12 above.
[20] Hague Regs, Art. 53.
[21] Art. 146; see also ch. 18 below.
[22] Hague Regs, Art. 46; Conv., Art. 27.
[23] Hague Regs, Art. 56 – the German depredations in occupied Europe in World War II were in breach of this provision and also constituted pillage. See, now, Convention for the Protection of Cultural Property in the Event of Armed Conflict, 1954, Schindler and Toman, 45, and Pr. I, Art. 53.
[24] See Hague Regs, Arts 46, 47; Conv., Arts 56, 33, 53.
[25] Hague Regs, Art. 55.

property may be destroyed, while agricultural areas for the production of food-stuffs and crops, together with other objects indispensable for the sustenance of the civilian population may only be converted to military use if the population is left with sufficient food and water to prevent starvation or the need to move from the area.[26]

Actions against the population

Protected persons may only be punished for acts for which they are personally responsible and the population may only be subjected to a pecuniary or other penalty for acts which its members may be regarded as jointly and severally liable.[27] No reprisal may be taken against the population nor hostages taken from among them.[28] In fact, taking hostages amounts to a grave breach of the Convention.[29]

The occupant may continue to collect taxes, but this should be in line with the current assessment rules and he should bear the same administrative costs as the former government. Any additional taxes levied by the occupant must be for the needs of the army or administration of the territory. No other monetary contribution may be collected except under written authorisation from the commander in chief and should be in accordance with current assessment rules with a receipt provided.[30] Requisitions, whether in kind or services, must be for the needs of the army and in proportion to the resources of the country.

If labour is requisitioned it must be within the occupied territory and only involve the population in work for the needs of the army of occupation, public utility services or the welfare of the population. It must not involve them in any work which would mean their participating in military operations, nor may they be compelled to help secure places where they are involved in compulsory labour. Every endeavour must be made to keep workers in their place of employment, and they must receive a fair wage and the local legislation on conditions of labour should be respected.[31]

The Occupying Power is permitted to requisition food and medical supplies for the occupation forces and administration personnel only so long as the needs of the civilian population have been taken into account and fair payment made. If

---

[26] Conv., Art. 53, Pr. I, Art. 54. In 1992 the Serb authorities in occupied Bosnia cut off water and electricity supplies to Sarajevo and instituted a virtual blockade of relief supplies of food going in under UN auspices.

[27] Hague Regs, Art. 50; Conv., Art. 33.

[28] Conv., Art. 33 and Pr. I, Art. 51(6); Conv., Art. 34.

[29] Hostages were frequently taken during World War II, see *In re List* (hostages trial 1948) 9 *War Crimes Reports* 34.

[30] Hague Regs, Arts 49–51.

[31] Conv., Art. 51. This provision is a direct consequence of the German policy of forced labour in the occupied territories of Europe in World War II. By Hague Reg. 52 if a monetary wage is not paid, a receipt for labour must be provided.

local resources are insufficient for the needs of the population, the Occupying Power must bring in such supplies as are needed. He may requisition civilian hospitals temporarily to care for the military wounded and sick, but only if proper arrangements are made on behalf of the population. He must also make sure that there is adequate clothing, bedding, shelter and other supplies essential for the population's survival, together with facilities for their religious worship and, if necessary, he must co-operate with relief organisations, allowing free passage of medical and hospital stores and articles for worship, as well as essential foodstuffs, clothing and tonics for children under fifteen, expectant mothers and maternity cases. While he may require these to be distributed under the supervision of the Protecting Power, this does not relieve him of his own responsibilities in this respect.[32]

In so far as children are concerned, the Occupying Power must take care that those under fifteen separated from their parents or orphaned are not left to their own devices, and that proper steps are taken to look after their education and religious welfare making its own arrangements for this if necessary, while preserving their nationality, language and religion. It should co-operate with all institutions concerned with their care and facilitate their identification and registration of their parentage.[33]

The Occupying Power must enable persons in occupied territory to exchange personal information with family members whether present in the occupied territory or not. It must also facilitate enquiries by families which have been dispersed as a result of the conflict and support relief organisations working in this field.

Amendments to the local law

As has been indicated, the Occupying Power only enjoys a limited right to amend the local law. He may however introduce penal legislation to enable him to carry out his obligations under the Convention and maintain orderly government or for the security of the occupation, including his lines of communication. Such legislation must be published in a language that the population understands. It must not be retroactive and an offender may only be tried in accordance with provisions which are consistent with the general principles of law and which were valid before the enactment If these laws are disregarded the accused may be handed over to a properly constituted non-political military tribunal sitting in the occupied territory.

If the offence is only intended to harm the Occupying Power and does not involve an attempt on the life, limb or property of his forces or administration, nor

---

[32] Conv., Arts 55–9, 23, Pr. I, Art. 69(1).
[33] Conv., Arts 24, 50; see also Pr. I, Arts 77, 78, which refer to the care of children generally in time of conflict. See Kuper, *International Law Concerning Child Civilians in Armed Conflict*, 1997.

a grave collective danger, it is only punishable by internment or simple imprisonment, and when assessing sentence the tribunal must remember that local inhabitants owe no allegiance to the occupant, and any punishment must be
proportionate to the offence.

The death penalty may be imposed for espionage or serious acts of sabotage or
any intentional offence resulting in the death of any person, whether a member of
the occupying authority or a local inhabitant, provided that this penalty was
embodied in the law before the territory was occupied. No person may be executed if he was under eighteen at the time of the offence.[34] Since the act must cause
death it would appear that the death penalty may not be imposed for persistent
attacks, short of death, against the occupying forces. It would also seem that if the
death penalty did not already exist, the occupying authority cannot introduce it
even for acts against his forces resulting in death, even if the lawful government
abolished the penalty in anticipation of the occupation. If the methods of killing
employed by the population amount to combatant acts, those concerned would
lose their protected status and become triable for war crimes.

If there are nationals of the occupant present in the occupied territory as
refugees, no punitive action may be taken against them except for offences committed after the outbreak of hostilities or for common-law non-political offences
committed before the outbreak provided they were extraditable under the law of
the occupied state. Similarly, save for breaches of the laws and customs of war
which would result, for example, from internment and treatment of inhabitants of
the occupied territory before the occupation began,[35] protected persons may not
be arrested or punished for crimes committed or opinions expressed[36] before or
during any temporary interruption of the occupation. Protected persons who had
committed common crimes like murder and were awaiting trial may be tried by
such national tribunals as continue to function.[37]

Protected persons are entitled to a properly conducted regular trial during
which they enjoy all the rights consistent with the rule of law, as well as the right
of appeal or petition. If the sentence is likely to be death or imprisonment of two
years or more the Protecting Power[38] must be informed and, unless the trial is
exceptionally held in camera in the interests of the Occupying Power's security,
his representative must be permitted to attend. No death sentence may be carried
out unless six months have elapsed since the Protecting Power has been told of its
confirmation.[39]

Protected persons convicted by the Occupying Power must be detained within

---

[34] These provisions are to be found in Conv., Arts 64–8.

[35] Thus the Security Council condemned as war crimes the internment prior to the outbreak of the Gulf War of civilians possessing Kuwaiti or Coalition nationality.

[36] This will protect them from trial for any statements they may have made in opposition or criticism of the adverse party while not in occupation.

[37] Conv., Art. 70.

[38] See ch. 13 above.

[39] Conv., Arts 71–5.

the occupied territory and may not be conveyed elsewhere.[40] They should be held separately from other detainees and their food and hygiene must be sufficient to maintain their health and at least equal to those in the prisons in the occupied territory. They should be provided with medical and religious or spiritual assistance. Women should be detained in separate quarters under the care of women and proper attention should be given to the care of minors. They must be allowed to receive visits from representatives of the Protecting Power and the ICRC as well as one relief parcel monthly.

The Occupying Power may restrict the freedom of movement in parts of the territory and if he finds it necessary for security reasons to take safety measures against the population, these must be restricted to internment or assigned residence and in accordance with the procedure in the Convention[41] and there must be a right of appeal. He may not apply any measures causing adverse discrimination among the population,[42] nor reduce in any way the rights guaranteed by the Convention or make any agreement with the local authorities or national government of the territory which would have this effect.[43]

The local laws continue to operate in respect of a person committing offences while detained, but if the act with which he is charged is not actionable if committed by one not a detainee he may only be subjected to disciplinary punishment, which is normally meted out by the commandant or his representative and may only consist of a fine not exceeding 50 per cent of the wages which he would otherwise receive for thirty days work, discontinuance of privileges, fatigues not exceeding two hours a day or confinement, and in no case may a single punishment exceed thirty days. Escape is subject to disciplinary proceedings and even if repeated may not constitute an aggravating factor when assessing any punishment in relation to an offence committed during the escape.

When the occupation comes to an end, the Occupying Power must transfer to the returning authorities all persons accused or convicted during the occupation together with the relevant documentation.

Restrictions on the occupying power

Articles 27 to 34 of the Civilians Convention comprise provisions concerning the treatment of civilians in the territories of parties to the conflict including occupied territories. These concern their general protection against indignities or violence of any kind and against adverse discrimination, while preserving the right of the occupant to protect his own security. They forbid the use of civilians as shields for military objectives or their subjection to coercion or to being taken hostage, or to corporal punishment or torture.

[40] Israel has often expelled Arab dissidents from the 'administered' territories.
[41] Art. 78.
[42] Conv., Art. 13, Pr. I, Art. 75(1).
[43] Conv., Arts 7, 8, 47.

In addition to these general provisions, Articles 47 to 78 are concerned with conditions in occupied territories. Here we find the regulations concerning inviolability of rights, repatriation, deportation, labour, the courts, food, medical and religious supplies, relief, the care of children, and the provisions respecting penal legislation.

Non-nationals of the former sovereign must be allowed to leave, while, regardless of motive, the Occupying Power is forbidden from resorting to individual or mass transfers or deportations,[44] except for their own security and no protected person may be detained in a dangerous area unless it is in the interest of the general population or for imperative military reasons.[45] On occasion, it may be more dangerous to allow the civilian population to leave an area because of the nature of the military operations[46] or because their presence on the roads might hinder troop movements. At the same time the Occupying Power is forbidden to move parts of its own population, other than those required for the purpose of administration, into the occupied territories, with the intention of annexing or colonising the area.[47]

The Occupying Power is forbidden from compelling protected persons to enlist in its armed forces or using any pressure to persuade them to volunteer,[48] and this prohibition relates to enlistment for use in any theatre or against any belligerent, not necessarily their own state. To compel such enlistment is a grave breach of the Convention, while any volunteer may find himself liable for treason under his own legal system.[49]

While the occupant may compel those over the age of eighteen to work, this

---

[44] Israel has been criticised for deporting individual Arabs from the administered territories; see, e.g., Falk and Western, 'The relevance of international law to Israel and Palestinian rights in the West Bank and Gaza', in Playfair, (ed.), *International Law and the Administration of Occupied Territories* 125 at 127–8. This work contains a number of papers relating to problems concerning the Israeli-occupied territories. In Dec. 1992 Israel expelled some four hundred Palestinians accusing them of being members of Hamas, a fundamentalist Islamic movement and supporters of terrorism. Lebanon refused to admit them and they have remained camped out in 'no-man's-land' between Israel and Lebanon. It was only after protests by the Security Council and the ICRC that the latter was permitted by Israel to visit them and provide them with supplies: press reports, Dec. 1992, Jan. 1993. See Dinstein, 'The Israeli Supreme Court and the law of belligerent occupation: deportations', 23 Israel Y.B.H.R. 1993, 1.

[45] In 1992 and 1993 the Serbs in occupied parts of Bosnia were indulging in policies of 'ethnic cleansing' especially of Muslims, although in the village of Hrtkovci the victims have been Croats, *The Times*, 29 Aug. 1992 and the ICRC found it necessary to assist in the 'ethnic cleansing' policies to save the lives of those affected, particularly children. This was also the case in Kosovo in 1999.

[46] In 1992 and 1993 it was often more dangerous for civilians to attempt to leave cities in Bosnia which were under heavy fire than for them to remain.

[47] Art. 49. Both Israel and the Serbs in Bosnia have been criticised on this ground.

[48] See, for example, the Japanese use of Indian prisoners during World War II, see Green, 'The Azad Hind Fauj: The Indian National Army', in *Essays*, 1999, ch. XI.

[49] See, e.g., Green, 'The problems of a wartime international lawyer', 2 Pace Y.B. Int'l Law (1989), 483.

may only be for the needs of the army of occupation, for public service or welfare of the population and must not involve any contribution to military operations, nor may they be compelled to assist against attacks by, for example, guerrillas, saboteurs or infiltrators, directed at places of compulsory labour. At the same time, the Occupying Power may not seek to stimulate unemployment to induce the population to work for him. Even when they are engaged in compulsory labour, the Occupying Power must permit access to the services of the Protecting Power. On no account may the Occupying Power requisition labour in sufficient numbers to constitute mobilisation in an organisation of a military or semi-military nature. This ensures preservation of the protected status of the population and prevents their subjection to the military law applicable to the forces of the occupant.

Regulations regarding detention

When the Occupying Power establishes detention centres for detained members of the local population they must be under command of a responsible officer from the regular military forces or civil administrative service of the Occupying Power, who must be in possession of a copy of the Convention and with a staff instructed in its provisions. These centres must be located away from danger or unhygienic areas and separate from prisoner-of-war camps. Accommodation and hygiene, religious practices, canteens and protective measures including air raid shelters, together with proper provision with regard to clothing, water and food with due attention paid to any dietary requirements, must be in accordance with the provisions of the Convention. Every detention centre must be provided with proper medical facilities and the services of medical staff of the same nationality as the detainees when possible, and with proper facilities for maternity, contagious and mental cases. In addition, there must be proper opportunities for intellectual and physical activities and proper arrangements made for their personal property and financial resources.[50]

Internees shall have the right to elect a committee to represent them in relations with the Occupying Power and may present complaints concerning the conditions of their internment either directly, through the Internment Committee or through the Protecting Power. The Occupying Power is obliged to inform the power to which internees owe allegiance as well as the Protecting Power of measures taken to execute the relevant provisions of the Convention. In addition internees must be allowed visitors, especially near relatives, regularly and frequently. They must also, if possible, be allowed to visit their homes. particularly in the event of death or serious illness of relatives.

Regardless of any specific obligations imposed on the Occupying Power, he is obliged to ensure that all rights guaranteed to those within occupied territory in accordance with customary law, the Hague Regulations, the Civilians Convention

---

[50] Conv., Arts 83–98.

or Protocol I are fully complied with, as well as any rights requiring the co-operation or supervision of the Protecting Power. He must make sure that protected persons and their property are not subjected to any form of adverse discrimination and that all rights are fully respected, with breaches prevented or punished.

Any party to the conflict alleging a breach of the Convention or expressing discontent with its mode of application may request an inquiry and once the complaint is substantiated steps must be taken to end it.

16

Rights and duties of neutrals

Basic rules

Even in major conflicts involving a number of countries, including the most powerful, there are always some which remain outside the conflict and seek to assert their right as neutrals not to be interfered with by the belligerents. The extent to which they are successful often depends on the relative power of the belligerents and those claiming to be outside the conflict. The international law of armed conflict grants rights and imposes duties upon these non-participants which are known as neutrals, and the relevant legal regime as neutrality.[1]

So long as the activities of these non-participants do not interfere with the legitimate activities of the belligerents or benefit one at the expense of the other, neutrals are entitled to have their territory and doings respected and unaffected because of the conflict.

Occasionally it is conceded that in certain circumstances a neutral may offer assistance to one of the belligerents on the basis of benevolent neutrality. This situation usually arises because the belligerent in question is the victim of aggression and is based on the provisions of the Kellogg–Briand Pact, the Pact of Paris,[2] which condemned recourse to war as an instrument of national policy, with the Pact-breaker renouncing the benefits of the Pact. This was interpreted by the International Law Association in 1934[3] as entitling parties to come to the assistance of a victim of aggression without committing any breach of the Pact or any rule of international law or becoming parties to the conflict. The adverse party may nevertheless treat such aid as a *casus belli*.

Aid to the victim of belligerency might also flow as a result of a treaty of mutual assistance, although in such a case the state offering the aid will often

---

[1] See e.g., US *Annotated Supplement to the Commander's Handbook on the Law of Naval Operations*, 1997, ch. 7 and *San Remo Manual on International Law Applicable to Armed Conflicts at Sea*, 1995, index references.

[2] Treaty for the Renunciation of War, 1928, 94 L.N.T.S., 57, 4 Hudson, *International Legislation*, 2522.

[3] Budapest Articles of Interpretation, *Report of the 38th Conference*, 66. These articles are reprinted in Harvard Research in International Law, 33 Am. J. Int'l Law Supp., (1939), Part III, 'Rights and duties of states in case of aggression', 819, 825, n.1.

declare itself an ally of the victim. In the light of the almost universal membership of the United Nations, the Charter may be considered a multilateral treaty of mutual assistance, particularly in the light of Article 2(4) and (5)[4] and Chapter VII concerning 'action with respect to threats to the peace, breaches of the peace and acts of aggression'. Moreover, since Article 25 obligates all Members 'to accept and carry out the decisions of the Security Council in accordance with the present Charter', any member which has been condemned by the Council for breach of the Charter and subjected to any type of enforcement measure is precluded from maintaining that other members assisting the victim of its aggression are in breach of their neutrality. During the Gulf War, while recognising that mere sympathy for Iraq might not be inconsistent with membership of the United Nations, the Coalition authorities opposing Iraq contended that all members of the United Nations, whether actively supporting the Coalition or not, were obliged to pursue a policy, active or quiescent, of aid for Kuwait, while doing nothing that might support Iraq. However, Jordan continued to supply Iraq, while others, particularly Iran and India, tended to pursue policies of traditional neutrality.[5]

So that third states may know when the duties of neutrality are expected from them, belligerents should notify non-parties to the conflict that a state of war exists, although if it is clear that this is a matter of public notoriety and they do in fact know of this state of affairs they cannot defend what would otherwise be un-neutral conduct on the lack of notification.[6] Regardless of notification, the rights and duties of neutrality come into effect with the outbreak of hostilities and it is usual, if no declaration of war has been announced or notification thereof made, for third states to issue declarations proclaiming their neutrality. Nevertheless, if the belligerents deny that a state of war exists, as did the United Kingdom at the time of the Suez conflict in 1956, they cannot complain if third states refuse to observe the rules of neutrality.

Frequently, as has been seen in the discussion concerning protecting powers,[7] a neutral power is appointed to represent the interests of one belligerent in the territory of the adverse party or for some of its nationals to be appointed to the Fact Finding Commission called for in Protocol I in relation to the investigation of alleged breaches of the law of armed conflict.[8] In neither case can a belligerent suggest that such action is in breach of the obligations of neutrality.

---

[4] '(4) All Members shall refrain in their international relations from the threat or use of force against the territorial integrity or political independence of any state, or in any other manner inconsistent with the Purposes of the United Nations. (5) All Members shall give the United Nations every assistance in any action it takes in accordance with the present Charter, and shall refrain from giving assistance to any state against which the United Nations is taking preventive or enforcement action.'

[5] See US Dept. of Defense, Final Report to Congress, App. O, *Conduct of the Persian Gulf War*, Apr. 1992, 'Conduct of Neutral Nations', 0-28-31, 31 I.L.M., 615, 637–40.

[6] Hague Convention III, 1907, relative to the Opening of Hostilities, Schindler and Toman, 57, Art. 2.

[7] See ch. 13 above.

[8] Art. 90; see ch. 17 below.

The rights of belligerents

A belligerent is, generally speaking, under the duty to respect neutral territory, including the territorial sea and air space,[9] together with any exclusion zone that the neutral may be strong enough to enforce, as well as the neutral's right to continue to maintain intercourse with other states, even the adverse party. At the same time it has the right to demand that, in addition to its obligation to behave towards all belligerents with impartiality, the neutral recognise the validity of any blockade which has been established as well as any rules concerning contraband.[10] With regard to the latter it should be noted that modern practice tends to list all goods intended for an adverse party as contraband, thus virtually cutting off all neutral trade with the enemy. After the invasion of Kuwait and during and after the Gulf War, the Security Council permitted essential foodstuffs and other humanitarian necessities to go to Iraq, despite the continuance of the general trade embargo.

For the main part, the rules concerning the rights and duties of neutrals in land warfare are to be found in Hague Convention V, 1907,[11] which has been ratified by most major powers and, although Italy, the United Kingdom and members of the Commonwealth among others, are not parties, it is considered to be largely declaratory of customary law.[12]

Belligerents may not violate neutral territory by, for example, overflight,[13] moving troops or military *matériel* or conducting hostilities across it. If, however, forces of a belligerent enter neutral territory and the neutral authority is unable or unwilling to expel or intern them, the adverse party is entitled to undertake their hot pursuit and attack them there,[14] and may seek compensation from the neutral for this breach of neutrality. The right of hot pursuit extends into neutral waters if these are being used for the transport of troops or to evade combat and the neutral fails to prevent such abuse.[15] The mere presence of such forces does not justify hot pursuit; there must be some failure by the neutral respecting the preservation of

---

[9] During the Gulf War Austria and Switzerland, a non-member of the UN, allowed overflights, while India did not, *Conduct of the Persian Gulf War*, pp. 0-30–32, I.L.M., 640.

[10] See text to nn. 27–30, ch. 8 above.

[11] Schindler and Toman, 941.

[12] *Ibid.*; see also Schwarzenberger, 2 *International Law*, 'The Law of Armed Conflict', (1968), 549.

[13] See n. 9 above.

[14] During its campaign against 'terrorists' in South West Africa before the establishment of Namibia, South Africa frequently pursued fleeing 'freedom fighters' into neighbouring countries. Similarly, Turkey has pursued on land and by bombing rebel Kurds taking refuge in Iraq. In the same way, Israel entered southern Lebanon and established bases there to protect its northern settlements neither country regarded this as constituting 'war' between them, nor did Lebanon claim any compensation in respect of a breach of its 'neutrality'.

[15] Thus when in 1940 the *Altmark*, with British prisoners on board, used Norwegian waters to evade interception and Norway failed to expel or seize it, HMS *Cossack* pursued it into those waters, boarded it and released the prisoners, see Waldock, 'The release of the *Altmark*'s prisoners', 24 Brit. Y.B. Int'l Law (1947), 216; for the correspondence between the two governments, see HMSO, Cmd 8012 (1950).

its neutrality. If belligerent aircraft land on neutral territory they must be interned and returned to the flag state at the end of hostilities. Iran interned Iraqi military aircraft evading capture by Coalition forces during the Gulf War and delayed their return after hostilities ceased.

Provided the neutral power gives its consent, it is not a breach of neutrality for belligerent medical aircraft to fly over or land on neutral territory.[16] If the neutral orders such aircraft to land or alight on water or imposes any restrictions concerning passage, which must be applied impartially to all belligerents, they must be strictly complied with. Any medical aircraft belonging to a belligerent entering neutral air space without consent must identify itself as soon as possible and obey any order to land, and if the neutral recognises it as medical it must give an order to land with adequate time for compliance before attacking[17]

The rights and duties of neutrals

A neutral has the right to permit belligerent troops to take refuge in his territory, but must intern them and prevent them from taking any further part in the conflict.[18] Unless there is an agreement providing otherwise, the neutral is responsible for feeding, clothing and maintaining these persons, but is entitled to reimbursement when peace is concluded. If the neutral is a party to the Prisoners of War Convention their treatment, if interned, must at least equal that required for prisoners of war.[19] The neutral is also permitted to allow officers to remain at liberty, provided they give their parole not to leave its territory. If these forces bring prisoners of war with them, they must be released, although a place of residence may be assigned them, as it must for escaping prisoners of war.[20] Any wounded or sick taken on board a neutral hospital ship or aircraft must also be prevented from taking any further part in hostilities.

Without breaching its neutrality in any way a neutral may permit medical transports carrying wounded and sick to cross its territory, but must make sure that there are no fighting personnel or war *matériel* in the convoy. If wounded personnel are left in neutral territory, the neutral is under an obligation to see that they take no further part in military operations,[21] and any personnel so left must be treated in accordance with the 1949 Conventions III and IV, and if the neutral is a party to Protocol I the relevant provisions will also apply.[22] The belligerents may

---

[16] See text to n. 43, ch. 11 above.

[17] For the general rules concerning military aircraft and the treatment of those on board, see ch. 11 above.

[18] Conv., V, Art. 11.

[19] Prisoners of War Conv., Art. 4(B)(2), see ch. 10 above.

[20] Conv., V, Art. 13. During World War II many escaped prisoners of war managed to use neutral territory as the means of returning to their own forces.

[21] Conv., Art. 14.

[22] See ch. 11 above.

agree with a designated neutral that it receive and intern serious sick or wounded prisoners until hostilities cease, and if it has received any prisoners of war in its territory the neutral must establish an Information Bureau similar to those set up in belligerent territory.

Neutral humanitarian organisations, and especially national Red Cross or Crescent societies may offer their services to a belligerent and if these are accepted the adverse party must be informed and the Society comes under the control of the belligerent to which it is attached. This is equally the case with neutral hospital ships.[23]

Enlistment and private trading

Neutrals may not allow belligerents to establish recruiting offices within their territory, although if the Security Council authorises the enrolment of volunteers against an aggressor they may be required to permit this. Nor may they permit the organisation of bodies of men intending to go to belligerent territory to enlist there, but it is not a breach of neutrality if individuals or small unorganised groups cross neutral territory with the intention of enlisting, even if the neutral knows that this is the intention. It is not a breach of neutrality for a neutral to allow its nationals to enlist in a belligerent's forces so long as this permission applies equally among all belligerents, but this does not extend to persons on its active service lists and if any are serving with the forces of a country that becomes belligerent they must be recalled. However, if a neutral state has seconded regular members of its armed forces as advisers, it may allow them to remain contending that this in no way affects its neutrality. It is, however, open to the adverse party to consider this a breach of neutrality or even treat it as a *casus belli*. Some countries make it a crime by way of foreign enlistment legislation for nationals to enlist against a state with which their own nation is in friendly relations,[24] but this does not apply if such enlistment is in response to a decision by the Security Council, even though such enlistment would be on behalf of one belligerent and its allies only.

A neutral does not have to forbid the supply of war *matériel* by resident individuals or companies, nor is it required to stop the passage of such goods across its territory unless there has been a Security Council decision forbidding such activity. It is under no obligation to forbid the use of privately owned communication equipment on behalf of belligerents,[25] but if it limits the freedom of its nationals to provide such facilities this restriction must operate against all belligerents. However, it became clear during World War II that prior to its entry into the war the United States was prepared to allow both private and state action on

[23] Land Conv., Art. 27, Maritime Art. 25.
[24] See, e.g., Green, *Essays*, 1999, ch. XI, 'The status of mercenaries in international law'.
[25] Conv., Arts 7, 8.

behalf of the United Kingdom and its allies and against the Axis powers. This was based on the benevolent neutrality it operated against the aggressors. Regardless of this, a neutral is required 'to employ the means at its disposal' to prevent the fitting out or arming of any vessel 'which it has reason to believe' is intended for use in hostile operations against a state with which it is at peace.[26]

Subject to any regulations imposed by their government, neutral nationals may continue trading with either or both belligerents,[27] but the articles involved are liable to seizure as prize.[28] Neutral nationals in unoccupied enemy territory, other than on a temporary or transient basis, are likely to be treated as if they were enemy and companies owned by them in or operating from that territory will normally be considered as enemy for the purpose of trading with the enemy legislation.[29] Mail originating in belligerent countries and intended for neutral recipients or going from neutral territory to addressees in belligerent or occupied territory is subject to censorship. Similarly, if a belligerent considers it necessary for his security, the correspondence or other rights of neutral diplomats in his territory may be subject to restrictions.[30] Whether in neutral or belligerent territory, it is a breach of neutrality for a neutral diplomat to convey military intelligence on behalf of a belligerent,[31] or pass messages to a detained diplomat's government.

Neutral nationals

Neutral nationals in the territory of a belligerent enjoy no rights beyond those granted to protected persons under the Civilians Convention,[32] provided they are

[26] Conv., XIII, 1907, concerning the Rights and Duties of Neutral Powers in Naval War, Art. 8, Schindler and Toman, 951. This is an application of the principle of 'due diligence' established in the Three Rules of Washington agreed in 1871 by the United Kingdom and the United States in connection with the *Alabama* incident 1862: 'The due diligence referred to ... ought to be exercised in exact proportion to the risk to which either of the belligerents may be exposed from a failure to fulfil the obligations of neutrality on their part', 1 Moore, *International Arbitrations*, 1898, 653, 654.

[27] Many members of the United Nations make it a criminal offence to trade with a country which the organisation has placed under boycott.

[28] See ch. 8 above, text to n. 22 *et seq.*

[29] See, e.g., *The Odessa* [1916] A.C., 145; *Daimler Co. Ltd.* v. *Continental Tyre & Rubber Co. (G.B.) Ltd.* [1916] 2 A.C., 307; *Government of Pakistan* v. *R.S.N. Co. Ltd.* (1965, Pakistan High Court) 40 I.L.R., 472.

[30] This happened in Great Britain just prior to D-Day, 1944. Postal restrictions were also imposed on some of the allies at that time.

[31] In World War I Baron Lowen, Swedish minister to Argentina, conveyed cipher messages on behalf of Count Luxburg, the German envoy, thus violating Swedish neutrality, 12 Am. J. Int'l Law (1918), 135. The immunity of diplomatic correspondence in Article 30 of the Vienna Convention on Diplomats, 1961, 500 U.N.T.S., 95 does not extend to any 'action relating to any professional or commercial activity exercised by the diplomatic agent outside his official functions', Art. 31(1)(c), and see Art. 3 re proper functions of a diplomat.

[32] See ch. 12 above.

nationals of a state party to that instrument. If, however, their home state maintains normal diplomatic representation in that territory they remain under diplomatic protection. If they are resident in occupied territory they have the right to leave unless this would be contrary to the interests of the occupant.[33]

If a neutral national commits hostile acts against or in favour of a belligerent he loses his neutral status. If he enlists in the armed forces of a belligerent he enjoys the rights of any other member of the forces. Subject to the provision in Protocol I concerning mercenaries,[34] if captured he must not be treated any more severely than a national of the adverse party. However, according to Convention V, a neutral national does not lose his neutral status by furnishing supplies or loans to a belligerent, so long as he is not resident in that belligerent's territory and the supplies do not originate there, nor if the services relate to police or civil administration.[35]

Neutral nationals resident in or visiting belligerent territory may be tried for war crimes or grave breaches of the Geneva Conventions and Protocol I in the same way as any other offender.[36] If a *prima facie* case of war crimes is made out against a person present in neutral territory, the neutral power concerned is under an obligation either to try him or hand him over for trial to the power presenting such evidence.[37] Since jurisdiction over war crimes is universal,[38] many countries have enacted legislation to confer jurisdiction over them regardless of the nationality of the offender or victim or location of the offence.[39] If the neutral concerned is not a party to any of these instruments it should try the offender itself or, if the offence is a common crime covered by an extradition treaty, make him available for extradition proceedings.

Aircraft belonging to neutral powers or companies are entitled to continue with their normal operations, but they fly into belligerent air space or combat areas at their own risk.[40]

Neutrals and maritime warfare

The rules of neutrality in maritime warfare are spelled out in Hague Convention XIII, 1907,[41] and are for the main part merely an application of the general rules amended where necessary to suit the needs of this particular theatre of war.[42]

[33] Conv., Arts 4, 48 resp.
[34] Art. 47.
[35] Arts 17, 18.
[36] See ch. 18 below.
[37] Land Conv., Art. 49, Maritime 50; Prisoners of War 129, Civilians 146.
[38] See, e.g., American Law Institute, Restatement of the Law Third, *The Foreign Relations Law of the United States*, vol. 1, 1987, s. 404.
[39] See, e.g., Green, 'Canadian law, war crimes and Crimes against humanity', 59 Brit. Y.B. Int'l Law (1988), 217.
[40] See ch. 9 for the law concerning war in the air.
[41] Schindler and Toman, 951.
[42] On maritime warfare see ch. 8 above and the *Annotated Supplement*.

Subject to any rights arising from hot pursuit,[43] any hostile act, such as seizure of an enemy vessel within neutral waters, is a breach of neutrality and forbidden.[44] Neutral powers must not permit the establishment of prize courts within their territory and are under an obligation to exercise their sovereign rights in preservation of their neutrality and, for example, release any prize wrongfully seized in the territorial sea or brought there.[45] A prize may be brought into the territorial sea because of stress of weather, unseaworthiness or lack of fuel or supplies, but must leave immediately these defects are remedied. If it fails to do so, it must be released and the prize crew interned. Likewise, the mere passage of a belligerent warship through neutral territorial waters does not affect the littoral state's neutrality, nor is it affected if local pilots are employed to help it make its passage. This does not mean that the warship may use those waters as a refuge to evade attack from pursuing vessels of the adverse party.

Although passage through neutral waters is permitted, neither the ports nor the waters may be used as a base for warlike operations, and no belligerent communications installation may be established there to communicate with belligerent forces at sea, on land or in the air. Neutral powers may not supply any warships or war *matériel* to any belligerent.[46] It does not have to forbid its nationals from so doing, although if it believes that a vessel is being fitted out in its ports to take part in hostile operations it must prevent this.[47]

Neutrals may impose such restrictions as they please upon the use by belligerents of their ports, roadsteads or territorial sea, so long as these restrictions apply on a non-discriminatory basis towards all belligerents. Normally, a belligerent warship may use these facilities for up to twenty-four hours, but if its presence is because of weather or damage it may stay until the weather improves or the vessel has been made seaworthy, but this does not mean that repairs may be undertaken to restore its battle worthiness. It may revictual to peacetime standards and refuel to the extent necessary to enable it to reach its nearest home port. Only three vessels belonging to a single belligerent may be present at the same time, and at least twenty-four hours must elapse between the departures of vessels belonging to opposing parties, and these depart in the sequence of their arrival.

If a belligerent warship disregards a neutral's order to depart, the neutral may take all steps it considers necessary to render the vessel incapable of going to sea for the duration of the hostilities. The captain must permit such action and the officers and crew must be interned or allowed to remain on board under such

[43] See the case of the *Altmark*, n. 15 above.

[44] See, e.g., *The Vrow Anna Catherina* (1803) 5 C. Rob. 15, 165 E.R., 681, 1 *Cases on the Law of the Sea*, 26.

[45] See, e.g., *The Appam* (1917) 243 US 124. In 1939 the American vessel SS *City of Flint* was captured by a German cruiser and taken into Soviet and subsequently Norwegian neutral waters, where the vessel was released and the prize crew interned, see 3 Hyde, *International law Chiefly as Interpreted and Applied in the United States*, 2277–82.

[46] During World War II the United States, while neutral, supplied the United Kingdom with 'over-age' destroyers on a lend-lease basis.

[47] See the reference to the *Alabama*, n. 26 above.

restrictions as the neutral power considers necessary, receiving treatment in accordance with the Prisoners of War Convention. If the crew is removed from the vessel, sufficient members must be left on board to ensure the safety of the vessel.

Since hospital ships belonging to a belligerent are not classified as warships they are not subject to the same restrictions with regard to their use of neutral ports.

Neutral–belligerent relations

Any steps taken by a neutral to preserve its neutrality, whether in relation to land or sea operations, are legal and cannot be taken by any belligerent as hostile. In both World Wars it became clear that in assessing the legality of a neutral's acts in preserving its neutrality, particularly in maritime matters, much depended on the relative power of the neutral and the belligerents. Thus, while the United States remained neutral it strongly supported neutral rights, but after it became a belligerent its stance shifted.

Should a neutral commit or allow severe and persistent breaches of its neutrality to go unanswered, a belligerent affected by those breaches may consider them sufficient to justify a declaration of war against the neutral. Where the breaches are of less consequence[48] the more usual procedure is to demand compliance with the law or seek damages.

[48] See, e.g., Report to Congress, *Conduct of the Persian Gulf War*, 0–31 (I.L.M., 640): 'The claim of neutral status by Iran and Jordan, or any of the traditional neutral nations, did not adversely affect the conduct of the Coalition's ability to carry out military operations against Iraq.'

17

Prevention of breaches and supervision of conduct

The difficulties

Like other branches of international law, the law of armed conflict has no permanent means to secure its observance.[1] Although there is as yet no permanent tribunal dealing with war crimes, and thus enforcing the law of armed conflict, the *ad hoc* tribunal established for the former Yugoslavia has jurisdiction over such offences as well as genocide, grave breaches of the Geneva Conventions and crimes against humanity. The tribunal established for Rwanda, dealing as it does only with offences committed during a non-international conflict, possesses jurisdiction over breaches of Common Article 3, genocide and crimes against humanity. When the International Criminal Court comes into operation it will have jurisdiction over genocide, crimes against humanity, war crimes and aggression.[2]

Allegations by one state of breaches of the law of war by another may lead to reprisals, to the extent that these are still permissible; or, subject to the special rules concerning its jurisdiction, limited as it is to disputes between states, be submitted for adjudication by the International Court of Justice which can, at the most, only call for cessation of the wrongdoing if it still subsists, the payment of damages and a statement of apology. In addition, a state which is party to one of the treaties relevant to the law of armed conflict may bring an action claiming breach of treaty or, of it assesses the breach to be serious enough, denounce the treaty, although it must be borne in mind that denunciation of the Geneva Conventions and Protocol I requires one year's notice and cannot in any case become effective during a current conflict.[3] Moreover, to the extent that these instruments are declaratory of customary international law, denunciation would not free the party resorting to it from any commitment which amounts to customary law.

Once a conflict has begun, and during its continuance, observation of the law

---

[1] See, e.g., Wolfrum, 'Enforcement of international humanitarian law', in Fleck, *et al.,* *The Handbook of Humanitarian Law in Armed Conflicts*, 1995, ch. 12; Roberts, 'Implementation of the laws of war in late-twentieth-century conflicts', Schmitt and Green, *The Law of Armed Conflict into the Next Millennium*, ch. XIV.

[2] These tribunals will be considered more fully in chapter 18 below.

[3] Conv. I, Art. 63, II Art. 62, III Art. 142, IV Art. 158, Pr. I Art. 99.

of armed conflict, apart from the threat to try war criminals,[4] resorting to reprisals, although the potential for this is now much reduced, or by using any of the means provided in the relevant treaties, depends on the effect of publicity to secure the support of public opinion, particularly in neutral countries. There is, however, the danger that such publicity tends to exaggerate or even misrepresent the situation, becoming little more than propaganda.[5] In addition, the complaining state may seek the support of a neutral country or recognised international humanitarian organisation like the ICRC to use its good offices to intervene. Apart from these means the only specific treaty provision that directly dealt with this issue was Article 3 of Hague Convention IV, 1907,[6] to the effect that 'A belligerent party which violates the provisions of the [annexed] Regulations shall, if the case demands, be liable to pay compensation. It shall be responsible for all acts committed by persons forming part of its armed forces',[7] but the sole reference to personal liability is Article 41 of the Regulations and this refers to breaches of an armistice by an individual.

In a number of countries many of the breaches of the law of war would amount to offences under national criminal law and be punishable as such. However, not every system of law grants jurisdiction to its courts when the offender or his victim is an alien and the offence has been committed abroad. However, since war crimes are breaches of customary international law, which all states are interested in upholding, jurisdiction over them is universal[8] and international law would permit the trial if the local system accepts this responsibility,[9] and many states have amended their criminal law to give effect to this.[10] In so far as members of a state's own forces are concerned, there is no need to have recourse to the universal jurisdiction granted by international law, nor is it usually necessary in any trial for breaches of the law of armed conflict even to describe the offence as a war crime or a violation of international law, although the local legislation may in fact use

---

[4] Such threats in the Security Council resolutions concerning Iraq's conduct after the invasion of Kuwait, or similar threats by the European Community with regard to events in Bosnia do not seem to have carried much practical weight, although the *ad hoc* tribunal for Yugoslavia has made some progress in this direction even if it has not secured the persons of those alleged to be the major offenders.

[5] Thus, after Iraq's invasion of Kuwait there was much publicity concerning despoliation of Kuwaiti hospitals resulting in numerous baby deaths. Subsequently, it was shown that this was pure propaganda having little relation to reality.

[6] Schindler and Toman, 63. This provision was not in the 1899 text.

[7] For an account of some of the relevant international decisions to this effect, see Green, *Essays*, 1999, ch. V – 'The international judicial process and the law of armed conflict'.

[8] See, e.g., American Law Institute, Restatement of the Law, *Foreign Relations Law of the United States*, vol. 1 (1987), s, 404.

[9] For a classic example of the problem, though not relating to the law of armed conflict, see *R. v. Keyn (The Franconia)* (1876) 2 Ex. D. 63 and the consequent enactment of the British Territorial Waters Jurisdiction Act, 1878, 41 & 42 Vict. c. 73.

[10] See, e.g., the law in Australia, Canada and the UK; see also Green, 'Canadian law, war crimes and crimes against humanity', 59 Brit. Y.B. Int'l Law (1988), 217. See, e.g., *R. v. Sawoniuk* (1997), *The Times*, 2 Apr. 1999.

such terms. Most members of these forces are nationals and subject to the national criminal law, while all of them, regardless of nationality, are subject to military law, whether this be, for example, the Army Act in the United Kingdom, the National Defence Act in Canada or the Uniform Code of Military Justice in the United States. Each of these creates jurisdiction for military courts in respect of offences committed by military personnel.

Dissemination

While most countries adhere to the principle that ignorance of the law is no defence and this principle extends to members of the military,[11] this is only true to the extent that the law is knowable to those whose conduct it purports to govern. So that this shall be true of the law of armed conflict, the various Conventions[12] impose an obligation upon the parties to disseminate the contents of these instruments among their armed forces and as widely as possible among the civilian population.

. The method of dissemination is left to the various states concerned and is normally carried out by means of instruction courses or commentaries upon particular Conventions, as in both the United States and Canada, or by manuals devoted to the law of armed conflict.[13] These manuals are often bulky in nature and are certainly not readily available to privates and junior non-commissioned officers. Unfortunately, too, in many active service units there is frequently an attitude among senior officers that humanitarian law is of less significance than knowledge of fighting methods, and inadequate time is frequently only grudgingly given to its dissemination.

Legal advisers

Some armed forces have trained legal officers attached to the higher echelons and these should be competent to conduct the necessary courses or to indicate to the command what the law is as it affects a particular operation and whether the proposed action is lawful, and in the Gulf War 1991 'Decisions were impacted by legal

[11] See, e.g., Green, *Essays*, 1999, ch. VI, 'The man in the field and the maxim *Ignorantia Juris Non Excusat'*.

[12] Hague IV, Art. 1; 1949 – Land Art. 47, Maritime Art. 48, Prisoners of War Art. 127, Civilians Art. 144, Pr. I Art. 83.

[13] See, e.g., Part III of the British Manual of Military Law, *The Law of War on Land*; US Dept. of the Army Field Manual, FM27-10, *The Law of Land Warfare*, US Dept. of the Navy, *Annotated Supplement to Commander's Handbook on the Law of Naval Operations*, 1997, US Dept. of the Air Force, AFP 110-31, *International Law – The Conduct of Armed Conflict and Air Operations*; Canada, National Defence, Maritime Command, MAOP 331, *Handbook on the Law of Naval Operations*. See also JAG's School, US Army, *Operational Law Handbook*, 1996.

considerations at every level, the law of war proved invaluable in the decision-making process'.[14] Parties to Protocol I are obliged[15] to ensure that such advisers are available. However, it does not indicate the level of command to which they are to be attached, merely providing that they will, 'when necessary', be available to advise 'military commanders at the appropriate level', and also to advise on the instruction that ought to be given to the troops. Strictly, this advice only relates to the application and interpretation of the Geneva Conventions and the Protocol, but it means that an officer to whose unit such advisers are attached will not be able to plead ignorance of the law if charged with offences against the law of armed conflict even those parts of it which may be considered customary or which is based on the Hague Conventions.[16]

The task of a commander

Article 1 of the Hague Regulations clearly establishes that for a force to enjoy the rights and protection of the law of war, it must conduct its operations in accordance with the laws and customs of war, and Protocol I confirms this by providing that the armed forces 'shall be subject to an internal disciplinary system which, *inter alia*, shall enforce compliance with the rules of international law applicable in armed conflict'.[17]

The commanding officer must ensure that the forces under his command comply with the laws and customs of war and is personally liable for illegal acts committed by those under his command if he knew or should have known that such acts were likely to be committed. It is therefore part of his duties as a commander to make those under him aware of their obligations.[18] He is presumed to have the necessary knowledge to carry liability if the illegal acts are committed within sight or hearing of his office, or if one of his officers or non-commissioned officers is present when the act is committed, or if his men had previously committed illegal acts.[19] He is equally liable if he is so reckless in maintaining his command that he is unaware of the doings of his troops.[20] These obligations of the commander

---

[14] Gen. Colin Powell, Chairman, US Joint Chiefs of Staff, commenting on the Role of Law in the Dept. of Defense Report to Congress, on *Conduct of the Persian Gulf War*, App., p. 0-1, 31 I.L.M., 615.

[15] Art. 82.

[16] See, e.g., Green, *Essays*, 1985, ch. 4, 'The role of legal advisers in the armed forces'; Draper, 'The role of legal advisers in armed services', 18 Int'l Rev. of Red X (1978), 6.

[17] Art. 43(1).

[18] Pr. I, Arts 86 and 87, deal with a commander's failure in this respect. See, e.g., Green, *Essays*, 1985, ch. 10, 'War crimes, extradition and command responsibility'; Parks, 'Command responsibility for war crimes', 62 Mil.Law Rev. (1973), 1.

[19] See, e.g., *In re Meyer* (1945, the *Abbaye Ardenne* case) 4 War Crimes Reports, 97; more extensive extracts from the Judge Advocate's summing-up based on the unpublished transcript may be found in Green, *Essays*, 1985, 226–7, 269–71.

[20] See *In re Yamashita* (1946) 4 *ibid.* 1; see also Parks, 'Command responsibility', 103.

confirm the position under customary law and he would be liable even if his state is not a party to the Protocol which contains the specific provisions outlined above.[21]

Perhaps it is worth drawing attention here, in relation to a commander's responsibility, the comment by Sun Tzu: 'If the regulations are not clear and orders not thoroughly explained, it is the commander's fault'![22] It should also be borne in mind that, to a great extent, the comments of the Nuremberg Tribunal with regard to war crimes and crimes against humanity are general in character, based on examination of the facts relating to German actions in the field towards prisoners of war and civilians in occupied territory and to a lesser extent in Germany itself. It is only when delivering judgment against individuals that issues relating to command responsibility become relevant.

State liability and restrictions on its actions

As has already been mentioned, the only liability imposed on the state by Hague Convention IV is that of paying compensation in respect of breaches. Under the Geneva Conventions no party is able to absolve itself from liability, criminal or otherwise, for any grave breach[23] of those Conventions.[24] Should there be persistent or series breaches of its obligations by a belligerent, the adverse party may consider it necessary to take immediate measures in an attempt to induce the law-breaking state to stop these illegalities and behave according to law. This is especially so if a protest at the behaviour has proved ineffective. Formerly, this would have meant that the victim would have resorted to measures of reprisal, that is to say temporary illegal action proportionate to the original illegality, which reprisal would terminate with the adverse party's return to legality.[25] Today, however, the scope for reprisal action is severely limited, since the Conventions and Protocol have forbidden any such action against protected persons or objects.[26]

Until the end of World War II it was also common for a belligerent to take hostages, especially from the civilian population in occupied territory, with the threat that they would be killed or exposed to danger from the military operations

---

[21] Both Meyer and Yamashita were tried before the adoption of Pr. I. See, generally, Green, *Essays*, 1999, ch. VIII – 'War crimes, crimes against humanity and command responsibility'.

[22] *The Art of War*, 6th century BC, Griffith tr., 1983, 58.

[23] See ch. 18 below.

[24] Land Art. 51 Maritime 52, Prisoners of War 131, Civilians 148.

[25] For a discussion of reprisals by a war crimes tribunal see *In re List* (1948 – the hostages trial) 15 Ann. Dig., 632, 644–7.

[26] Land Art. 46, Maritime 47, Prisoners of War 13, Civilians 33, Pr. I, 20 (wounded, sick, shipwrecked and medical personnel), 51(6) (civilians), 52(1) (civilian objects), 53 (cultural objects and places of worship), 54(4) (objects indispensable for sustenance of civilian population), 55(2) (natural environment) and 56(4) (works and installations containing dangerous forces).

of their own side, unless the adverse party behaved in accordance with the law of war or the civilians in that territory ceased from attacks on the occupant's forces or property. Occasionally, hostages were also taken as a preventive measure to forestall military actions by the adverse party,[27] including those of a lawful character directed against military objectives, as was done by Iraq in 1990 after its invasion of Kuwait. Such prophylactic reprisals may consist of concentrating protected persons in dangerous areas, or carrying prisoners of war on munitions trains or prisoners of war or healthy detained enemy civilians on hospital ships when it is alleged that such ships have been wrongly attacked in the past. Now, the taking as hostage of any person in the power of a party to the conflict is forbidden.[28] In addition to taking reprisals against or hostages from among civilians, up to and including World War II Occupying Powers[29] sometimes imposed or threatened collective fines or punishments on the inhabitants in an effort to deter them from taking action against the occupation. Such measures were forbidden by the Hague Regulations and any collective penalty is now forbidden by both the Civilians Convention and Protocol I.[30]

If there is prima facie evidence that an individual member of a belligerent's forces captured by the adverse party has committed a breach of the law of armed conflict the captor may try him and publicise that fact, hoping thereby that his comrades will not behave in a similar fashion. During World War II the governments of the United Nations[31] announced their intention to try Germans guilty of war crimes and warned of the dire consequences which would follow if such breaches continued.[32] In the light of reports concerning the commission of breaches of the law of occupation or of armed conflict following the invasion of Kuwait and in the course of the Gulf War, as well as during the hostilities in Bosnia, both the Security Council and the European Community announced their intention to gather evidence of such breaches and bring the offenders to trial for war crimes. While there has been no trial in relation to the Gulf War, the Security Council has established an *ad hoc* tribunal to try offences committed during the various conflicts in the former Yugoslavia, and a similar tribunal has been established with jurisdiction over offences committed during the civil war in Rwanda,

---

[27] See, e.g., *In re List* (1948 – the hostages trial), comments as to when hostages might be taken lawfully appear at 641–4.

[28] Pr. I, Art. 75(2)(c); see also Civilians Conv., Art. 34.

[29] See ch. 15 above.

[30] Hague Art. 50, Conv. 33, Pr. I 75(2)(d). Israel has been taking such action in occupied Arab territory, but has argued that since this territory did not belong to any recognised state before its occupation by Israel it is not 'occupied' and so not affected by the Convention. Israel has also not acceded to the Protocol. See works by Cohen and Playfair, ch. 12 above, n. 20.

[31] This was the title of the alliance against the Axis Powers.

[32] See, e.g., London Declaration 1942, and the Moscow Declaration, 1943; see also UNWCC, *History of the United Nations War Crimes Commission* 105–8. In 1999, similar threats were made by NATO regarding those responsible for criminal activities against inhabitants of Kosovo.

and both have heard a number of cases.[33] Moreover, in 1998 it was agreed to establish a permanent International Criminal Court which will possess jurisdiction over those accused of offences against the law of armed conflict, as well as those accused of aggression.[34]

Third-party action

If a belligerent persistently commits serious breaches of the laws and customs of war as established by treaty, it is open to any neutral co-signatory of that treaty to act on its own initiative in lodging a protest. If the treaty in question provides for judicial settlement, or the parties be otherwise amenable to the jurisdiction of the World Court, the matter in issue may be referred to that tribunal. Should the breaches be of customary rules, any dispute between the protesting neutral and the offending belligerent may also be submitted for judicial determination.

Protocol I introduced a new method of seeking to avoid breaches of the law or dealing with them when they occur. First, in an attempt to prevent the development of unlawful weapons, Article 36 obliges parties when developing, acquiring or adopting any new means or method of warfare 'to determine whether its employment would, in some or all circumstances, be prohibited by [the] Protocol or any other rule of international law applicable to the High Contracting Parties'. Unfortunately, the Protocol does not indicate how this determination is to be made or what action is to be taken if it proves positive. Presumably, it is assumed that in such a case the party concerned will act in good faith and not complete the development or acquisition of such weapons, or use them if already in their possession. In this instance the Protocol goes beyond merely supplementing the Geneva Conventions, for it forbids the development or acquisition of *any* means or method which contravenes *a rule of international law*, which obviously includes the Hague Law and customary law. Hence any new means or method which would involve unnecessary suffering[35] over and beyond that required for the immediate purpose of the conflict is forbidden.

Should a Protecting Power be in office, it may offer its services as an intermediary to settle any dispute between the belligerents affecting the application or interpretation of the Conventions. It may act on its own initiative or at the request of the belligerent alleging that it has been injured contrary to the law, and

---

[33] See, e.g., McDonald, 'The changing nature of the laws of war', 156 Mil.Law Rev. 1998, 30; Fenrick, 'The development of the law of armed conflict through the jurisprudence of the international criminal tribunal for the former Yugoslavia', Schmitt and Green, *The Law of Armed Conflict into the Next Millennium*, 1998, 77; see also Roberts, 'Implementation of the laws of war in late twentieth-century conflicts, *ibid.*, 337.

[34] See ch. 18 below.

[35] See, e.g., Green, '"Unnecessary suffering", weapons control and the law of war' in *Essays*, 1999, ch. VIII; Greenwood, 'The law of weaponry at the start of the new millennium', Schmitt and Green, *Millennium*, 185.

the parties to the conflict are obliged to execute any recommendation made by the representative of the Protecting Power in consultation with the representatives of the belligerents.[36] Similarly, if the Protecting Power or an international humanitarian organisation like the ICRC has been given any supervisory or visiting powers,[37] the representative of that Power or organisation is entitled, again on his own initiative, to draw the holding power's attention to any matter which the representative considers a breach of the law of armed conflict.

Fact-Finding Commission

The greatest innovation effected by the Protocol in relation to supervision of its execution is the establishment of a permanent International Fact-Finding Commission[38] which came into existence in 1992. It is competent to enquire into any allegation that a grave breach or other serious violation of the Conventions or Protocol has occurred, and to use its good offices to assist in helping to restore respect for those instruments. The Protocol provides details concerning the election of its members and the way it should operate. It can only institute an enquiry with regard to the conduct of parties to the Protocol expressly accepting its competence either on a permanent or an *ad hoc* basis. If the alleged violation does not relate to a provision of the Conventions or Protocol, the Commission can only function at the request of a complaining belligerent and with the consent of the belligerent against whom the complaint has been made.

The Fact-Finding Commission is additional to, and does not replace or affect in any way, Convention or Protocol provisions concerning an enquiry established at the request of a belligerent in agreement with the adverse party to examine any alleged violation.[39] If the enquiry finds the allegation proved and that a violation has occurred, the parties are obliged to end it.

Deterrence-producing compliance

Apart from the procedures established in relation to prevention and supervision of breaches of the law, the surest guarantee of observance is compliance by a belligerent, for breaches are almost certain to provoke breaches, even though reprisals or other retaliatory measures, such as the taking of hostages, are forbidden. In addition, from the point of view of the officer issuing orders and of the

[36] Land, Maritime and Prisoners of War Art. ll, Civilians Art. 12.
[37] See ch. 10 re prisoners of war and ch. 12 re civilians.
[38] Art. 90. See Kussbach, 'The International Humanitarian Fact-Finding Commission', 43 I.C.L.Q. 1994, 185.
[39] Land Art. 52, Maritime 53, Prisoners of War 132, Civilians 149, Pr. I 90(2)(e).

ordinary soldier in the field the knowledge that he may be called upon to answer for his breaches of the law before a war crimes tribunal[40] also acts as a deterrent and encourages compliance.

[40] See ch. 18 below.

18

War crimes and grave breaches

Historical background

War crimes are violations of the laws and customs of the law of armed conflict and are punishable whether committed by combatants or civilians, including the nationals of neutral states.[1] Occasionally, the term has been used to include acts like espionage[2] or war treason[3] committed within a belligerent's lines and intended to harm him and aid the adverse party. However, such acts are only offences against the law of the particular belligerent, and since they are not forbidden by international law do not constitute war crimes in the proper sense of that term.

The concept of war crimes, with trials and condemnation of those committing them is not new. In ancient Greece, 'treacherous stratagems of every description were condemned as being contrary to civilised warfare', while in Rome

> the *ius belli* imposed restrictions on barbarism, and condemned all acts of treachery
> ... [Livy] tells us there were laws of war as well as peace, and the Romans had learnt
> to put these into practice not less justly than bravely ... The Romans [says Cicero]
> refuse to countenance a criminal attempt made on the life of even a foreign aggressor ... Breach of faith, even when pledged to the enemy under compulsion was ever
> considered by the Romans grossly criminal and impious.[4]

---

[1] For a collection of essays on different problems relating to the current law concerning war crimes, see Dinstein and Tabory, *War Crimes in International Law*, 1996; for general comment, see US *Annotated Supplement to the Commander's Handbook on the Law of Naval Operations*, 1997, para. 6.2.5; Rogers, *Law on the Battlefield*, 1996, ch. 7.

[2] See, e.g., case of Jokoko and Jokki during Russo-Japanese War, 1904, 2 Oppenheim, *International Law*, (1st ed.), 269.

[3] See, e.g., *The German War Book*, tr. Morgan 1915, 121–3, and for comments thereon, Holland, *The Laws of War on Land*, 49, Spaight, *War Rights on Land*, 333–5; see also 2 Oppenheim, *International Law.*, 7th (Lauterpacht) ed., 425, 575–6.

[4] 2 Phillipson, *The International Law and Custom of Ancient Greece and Rome*, 221, 231–2.

In both the *Mahabharata*[5] and the Laws of Manu[6] there is condemnation of illegal weapons or methods of fighting. Likewise, the Code of Bushido[7] prescribes that 'every soldier must report to the commander about prisoners of war ... He shall be guilty of manslaughter if he kills them with his own hands. Prisoners of war shall not be executed wantonly regardless of whether they laid down their arms or fought to the last arrow'.

Monotheistic views

In the Old Testament there are many limitations upon what may be done during war.[8] Perhaps the clearest indication of the ancient Judaic approach is to be found in Elisha's reply to the king's query whether he should slay his prisoners:[9] 'Thou shalt not smite them: wouldest thou smite those whom thou hast taken captive with thy sword and with thy bow? Set bread and water before them that they may eat and drink and go to their master. And he prepared great provision for them: and when they had eaten and drunk, he sent them away and they went to their master.'

'Islam's rules of war are based on mercy, clemency and compassion and draw their binding rules from divine Authority, ... [enjoining] the faithful, fighting in the path of God against those waging war against them never to transgress, let alone exceed, the limits of justice and equity and fall into the ways of tyranny and oppression.'[10] Christianity, too, forbade the use of certain weapons and methods of combat, with both the Second Lateran Council[11] and the *Corpus juris canonici*[12] enforcing their prohibition under threat of anathema.

In feudal times many kings proclaimed Articles of Warre condemning acts against non-combatants, often making them subject to the death penalty.[13] By the time of Agincourt, 1415, the 'law of arms' was so well established that Henry V's

[5] Epic Sanskrit poem based on Hindu ideals and composed probably between 200 BC and AD 200, c. Armour, 'Customs and warfare in ancient India', 8 *Grotius Transactions* (1922), 1, 74, 81.

[6] 2nd Century BC, see Bühler, *The Laws of Manu*, 230, Tit. VII, 90.

[7] Sixteenth century, c. Samio Adachi, 'The Asian concept', in UNESCO, *International Dimensions of Humanitarian Law*, 13, 17.

[8] See, e.g., *Exodus*, XXIII, 29, *Deuteronomy*, XX, 10–18, 1 *Judges*, 28–32, *Proverbs*, XXV, 21; more generally see, Roberts, 'Judaic sources and views on the laws of war', 37 Naval Law Rev. (1988), 221; Green, 'The Judaic contribution to human rights', 28 Can. Y.B. Int'l Law (1990), 3.

[9] 2 Kings, VI, 22–3.

[10] Sultan, 'The Islamic concept', UNESCO, *International Dimensions*, 29, 32.

[11] 1139, Draper, 'The interaction of Christianity and chivalry in the historical development of the law of war', 3 Int'l Rev. Red X (1965), 3, 19.

[12] 1500, Decretal V, c. Belli, *De Re Militari et Bello Tractatus* 1563, Pars VII, cap. 29 (Carnegie tr., 186).

[13] See e.g. Proclamation of Richard II of England, 1385, Winthrop, *Military Law and Precedents*, App. II.

conduct towards French prisoners was soundly condemned[14] and becomes part of Shakespeare's play of that name.[15]

Similar codes were promulgated in Europe[16] and during the Middle Ages 'constituaient – et constitue encore – le meilleur frein pratique pour imposer aux armées le respect d'un *modus legitimus* de mener les guerres'.[17] By the Hundred Years War a code of behaviour was so well established, at least among the orders of knighthood, that, at the siege of Limoges in 1370, captured French knights could appeal to John of Gaunt, stating 'we are yours; you have vanquished us. Act therefore to the law of arms', and they were treated as prisoners.[18] Courts of chivalry were established with power to hear cases in which it was alleged that this 'law of armes' had been disregarded or blatantly broken, and these courts frequently sentenced accused knights to dishonour or death.[19]

What has been described as the first recorded trial of a war criminal by an international tribunal is that of Peter of Hagenbach for crimes against 'the laws of man and of God' by a court of representatives of the Hanseatic cities at Breisach in 1474 and who was condemned for 'having trampled under foot the laws of God and of man'.[20]

Of the classical 'fathers' of international law, reference need only be made to Gentili:[21]

> In war ... victory is sought in no prescribed fashion ... but an enemy should be dealt with according to law ... In dealing with a just and lawful enemy we have the whole fetial law and many other laws in common ... It is the manner of the killing which is forbidden. Necessity does not oblige us to violate the rights of our adversaries ... [but] the laws of war are not observed towards one who does not himself observe them ... He is foolish who connects with the laws of war the unlawful acts committed in time of war. In this connection I make no allowance for retaliation ... At some time the enemy will have to render account to God, and he will render it to the rest of the world, if there is no magistrate here to check and punish the injustice of the victor. He will render an account to those sovereigns who wish to observe honourable causes for war and to maintain the common law of nations and of nature.

[14] See, e.g., Holinshed's *Chronicles*, and Vattel, *Le droit des Gens*, Liv. III, ch. VIII, s. 51 (Carnegie tr., 285–6).

[15] Fluellen's comment, Act IV, Scene 7, l. 1, and Gower's reply, ll. 5–10. For a fuller account of the law of war applicable in the fifteenth century, see Meron, *Henry's Wars and Shakespeare's Laws*, 1993.

[16] See, e.g., Gardot, 'Le droit de la guerre dans l'œuvre des capitaines français du XVIe siècle', 72 *Hague Recueil* (1948), 297, 452–3, 467–73.

[17] de Taube, 'L'apport de Byzance au développement de droit occidental', 67 *Hague Recueil* (1939), 67.

[18] Keen, *The Laws of War in the Late Middle Ages* (1965), 1.

[19] *Ibid.* chs 2, 3; see also Contamine, *War in the Middle Ages* (Eng. tr., 1984), 289–92. See also Squibb, *The High Court of Chivalry*, 1997, ch. XII, 'The law of arms'.

[20] See Schwarzenberger, *International Law*, vol. 2, *The Law of Armed Conflict*, ch. 39.

[21] *De Jure Belli*, 1612, Lib. II, Cap. III, VI, XXIII, XXI (Carnegie tr., 142, 143, 146, 159, 272, 257).

Modern developments

From the time of the 'classical' fathers until the end of the nineteenth century there is little to comment upon with regard to the law concerning war crimes until the promulgation by President Lincoln of the Lieber Code in 1863.[22] This detailed a number of actions which would be criminal if committed by United States personnel, some being regarded as so grave as to warrant immediate death even without trial.[23] The Code even asserted the right of an American tribunal to try any person who 'intentionally inflicts additional wounds on an enemy already wholly disabled, or kills such an enemy, or who orders or encourages soldiers to do so, [and he] shall suffer death, if duly convicted, whether he belongs to the Army of the United States, or is an enemy captured after having committed his misdeed'.[24]

The significance of the Lieber Code became clear shortly after it was proclaimed, when Wirz, the commandant of the Confederate prisoner-of-war camp at Andersonville, was put on trial and sentenced to death for a series of atrocities committed against Unionist prisoners in his charge, many of which would now be described as crimes against humanity as well as the law of war.[25]

Within a very short while the Code became the model for a series of codes in Europe[26] and served as an example for the Brussels Project of an International Declaration concerning the Laws and Customs of War and for the *Oxford Manual of the Laws of War on Land* drawn up by the Institute of International Law.[27] Both of these stipulate that belligerents do not have an unrestricted right as to the means of warfare and indicate both permitted and forbidden modes of conduct. In so far as the development of the law concerning war crimes is concerned, Part III of the *Oxford Manual* is significant: 'Penal Sanction. If any of the foregoing rules be violated, the offending parties should be punished, after a judicial hearing, by the belligerent in whose hands they are, Therefore Art. 84. Offenders against the law of war are liable to the punishment specified in the penal law.'

The European states were not prepared to go this far and embody the requirement in any treaty. When the Hague Conference met in 1899 and 1907 and adopted the Convention with respect to the Laws and Customs of War on Land,[28] the most they were prepared to concede was that a 'belligerent party which violates the provisions of the Regulations [annexed to the Convention] shall, if the case demands, be liable to pay compensation. It shall be responsible for all acts committed by

---

[22] Instructions for the Government of Armies of the United States in the Field, General Orders no. 100, 24 April 1863, Schindler and Toman, 3. See Doty, 'The United States and the development of the laws of land warfare', 156 Mil. Law Rev. 1998, 224.

[23] See Art. 44 condemning 'wanton violence' against persons and property in invaded territory.

[24] Art. 71.

[25] (1865) H.R. Exec. Doc. no. 23, 40th Cong., 2d Sess., 1867–8, vol. 8.

[26] See Holland, *The Laws of War on Land*, 72–3.

[27] 1874, 1880, Schindler and Toman, 27, 35 resp.

[28] 1899 II, 1907 IV, *ibid.*, 63.

persons forming part of its forces'. The only reference to individual liability relates to that borne by a private person who intentionally breaks the terms of an armistice.[29]

The two world wars

The silence concerning personal liability in the Hague Convention did not mean that a belligerent could not proceed against an individual alleged to have committed a breach of the customary law of war, whether his own national or not and whether a combatant or a civilian. That this was so became clear during World War I. The Commission of Fifteen established to consider responsibility for the outbreak of the war[30] recommended that:

> on the whole case, both the acts which brought about the war and those which accompanied its inception, particularly the violations of the neutrality of Belgium and Luxembourg, it would be right for the Peace Conference, in a matter so unprecedented, to adopt special measures, and even to create a special organ in order to deal as they deserve with the authors of such acts. *It is desirable that for the future penal sanctions should be provided for such grave outrages against the elementary principles of international law.*

In the light of this, the Treaty of Versailles 'arraigned' the former Emperor of Germany for:

> a supreme offence against international morality and the sanctity of treaties ... [for trial by] a special tribunal ... assuring him the guarantees essential to the right of defence ... In its decision the tribunal will be guided by the *highest motives of international policy, with a view to vindicating the solemn undertakings and the validity of international morality.*[31]

The United States was opposed to trying a head of state, while Holland, where the Kaiser had taken refuge, refused to extradite him, and he never came to trial. The Treaty made no reference to any rule of law by which the tribunal was to be guided. 'Motives of international policy' are clearly political, while what constitutes 'international morality' tends to be determined subjectively. The Principal Allied and Associated Powers also sought the trial 'before military tribunals [of] persons accused of having committed acts in violation of the laws and customs of war',[32] and required Germany to hand over any persons so accused. Germany refused but itself tried some accused before its own courts.[33] While only a few

[29] Conv., Art. 3, Regs, Art. 41.

[30] *Violations of the Laws and Customs of War*, Carnegie Endowment of Int'l Peace, Division of Int'l Law, Pamphlet no. 3, 1919, ch. IV(a), italics added.

[31] 1919 (112 B.F.S.P. 1; 13 Am. J. Int'l Law (1919)), Supp.; 2 Israel, *Major Peace Treaties of Modern History 1648–1967*, 1265, Art. 227, italics added.

[32] Art. 228.

[33] See, e.g., Mullins, *The Leipzig Trials*.

such trials were held and the sentences were relatively mild, the *Reichsgericht* did lay down principles regarding the defence of superior orders which have formed the basis for the law as it stands today.[34] Occasionally, national courts also tried captured enemy personnel for offences against the law of war.[35]

It was not until World War II that the issue of war crimes again became significant. It was known that the Germans had ill-treated and in many cases executed captured Allied personnel belonging to both regular and resistance forces, as well as civilians, particularly Jews, in occupied countries. Similar persecutions had taken place against political opponents, Jehovah's Witnesses, gypsies, homosexuals, and many of the medically and mentally unfit among the German population. Allied statesmen made it clear that at the end of the war those responsible for committing or ordering such acts, regardless of their status, would be brought to trial.[36] Accordingly, an agreement was drawn up in 1945 for the establishment of an International Military Tribunal to try for crimes against peace, war crimes[37] and crimes against humanity those 'major' war criminals whose offences were not geographically limited to a single location,[38] and the principles established by that instrument and the Judgment of the Nuremberg Tribunal[39] are now accepted as declaratory of the law on the subject.[40] A similar tribunal was established in Tokyo to try Japanese war criminals. Since its judgment was to a great extent, in so far as statements of law were concerned, merely a reaffirmation of what was decided earlier at Nuremberg, there is no need to consider it separately.

As if to remedy the failure to try the Kaiser in 1919, the London Charter, and as a result the Nuremberg Judgment, made a major departure from what had formerly been recognised as customary law. Traditionally, a head of state has always been considered immune from prosecution in any foreign country. By the Charter[41] it was laid down that in no circumstances could the status of an accused be pleaded as a ground for immunity before a war crimes tribunal nor even be taken into account by way of mitigation and, while the United States has tried General Noriega and the Federal German Republic decided to try Herr Honnecker,[42] the

[34] See text to n. 106 below *et seq.*

[35] See, e.g., 2 Garner, *International Law and the World War*, 477, n. 3.

[36] See, e.g., Moscow Declaration 1943, UNWCC, *History of the United Nations War Crimes Commission*, 107.

[37] See, e.g., Dinstein, 'The distinction between war crimes and crimes against peace', Dinstein and Tabory, *op.cit.*, 1.

[38] The London Charter, Schindler and Toman, 911. A similar tribunal was established in Tokyo to try major Japanese war criminals.

[39] HMSO, Cmd 6964 (1946); 41 Am. J. Int'l Law (1947), 172.

[40] 'Principles of international law recognised in the Charter of the Nuremberg Tribunal and in the judgment of the tribunal', Schindler and Toman, 923, and affirmed by Gen. Ass. Res. 177(II) 1950.

[41] Art. 7.

[42] See Green, 'Die Bundesrepublik Deutschland und die Ausübung der Strafsgerichtlicher Sicht', *Humanitäres Völkerrecht* (1992), 1, 32; 'The German Federal Republic and the exercise of criminal jurisdiction', 43 University of Toronto Law J. (1993), 207. In fact, the German court discharged Honnecker and all charges were withdrawn because

principle of immunity still stands. Both these principles are included in the Statutes of the *ad hoc* criminal tribunals for the former Yugoslavia and Rwanda, as well as that of the International Criminal Court.[43] Similarly, the principle established at Leipzig and reiterated in the London Charter[44] regarding the inability to plead superior orders as a ground for acquittal has now received treaty recognition.

The effect of the Geneva Conventions and Protocol I

Certain offences against the provisions of the Geneva Conventions and Protocol I are specifically mentioned and are described by these instruments as 'grave breaches'.[45] Even though so described they are still war crimes,[46] but they may carry heavier punishment than other breaches of the law of war which it would seem are not regarded as being so serious, though some of these too may be punished by death. For those offences described as grave breaches, the parties are obliged to 'afford one another the greatest measure of assistance in connection with criminal proceedings'.[47]

Neither the Conventions nor the Protocol has in any way limited the operation of the pre-existing law, both customary and conventional, with regard to the trial and rights of enemy, allied or neutral personnel charged with war crimes. In fact any state into whose hands an alleged war criminal may fall is entitled to institute criminal proceedings. This includes a neutral in the conflict during which the offence was alleged to have occurred. Since 1945 it has generally been agreed that if a holding state is unwilling to institute its own proceedings, it may hand the offender over to any claimant presenting prima facie evidence that the accused committed the act alleged. If the offence amounts to a grave breach, there is now by virtue of the Conventions and the Protocol an obligation to this effect.[48] Members of a belligerent's own forces remain liable to trial under national law, which may consider some offences as amounting to war crimes in the traditional sense of that term, although the tendency is to lodge charges using the nomenclature in the relevant criminal code[49] while judges and counsel may refer to 'war crimes'.[50]

of his fatal cancer condition: he was allowed to leave Germany and join his family in Chile, *The Times*, 3 Jan. 1993.

[43] See below – Developments since 1977.

[44] Art. 8.

[45] Land Art. 50, Maritime 51, Prisoners of War 130, Civilians 147, Pr. I, 11, 85.

[46] Pr., 1977, Art. 85 (5) – 'Without prejudice to the application of the Conventions and of this Protocol, grave breaches of these instruments shall be regarded as war crimes'.

[47] Pr. I, Art. 88(1).

[48] Land Art. 49, Maritime 50, Prisoners of War 129, Civilians 147, Pr. I, 11, 88, 89.

[49] This appears to have been the case in Ethiopia after the overthrow of the Mengetsu regime, *Globe and Mail* (Toronto) 21 Oct. 1998.

[50] See, e.g. *US* v. *Calley* (1969/71/73) 46 C.M.R. 1131, 48 C.M.R. 19, 1 M.L.R. 2488; *R.* v. *Finta* (1994) 112 D.L.R. (4th) 513.

There is, of course, nothing to prevent a national legislature from widening the concept of war crimes. If such extension goes beyond what is traditionally under-stood in international law, the new definition would only be applicable against the state's own nationals. This is particularly true with regard to some national defin-itions of 'genocide' which do not coincide with the definition in the Genocide Convention.[51]

The treatment of war criminals

While international law permits national tribunals to try war criminals, these tri-bunals are established under national law in accordance with the jurisdictional limits and procedure established by that law, although the definition of war crimes is normally that prescribed by international law. Where national legislation has introduced such jurisdiction for its courts, as in Australia, Canada and the United Kingdom, the international law definition prevails, at least in so far as aliens are concerned.[52] Protocol I, however, makes it clear that persons accused of war crimes must 'be submitted for the purpose of prosecution and trial in accordance with the applicable rules of international law' and, unless they are entitled to more favourable treatment under the Conventions or Protocol, must be granted the fun-damental guarantees contained in Article 75,[53] whether or not the charge consti-tutes a grave breach.

One of the most important safeguards enjoyed by the accused is the ban on any trial unless the alleged war crime was an offence at the time of its commission.[54] Article 99 of the Prisoners of War Convention states that when committed it must have been criminal by international law or the law of the Detaining Power. If crim-inal only under the latter it must have been committed after capture, for otherwise it would infringe the ban on retroactive legislation since an alien offender is not normally subject to his captor's law. Provided these conditions are met, the pun-ishment must not exceed that applicable at the time the offence was committed.[55] In addition, any military prisoner held by an adverse party and charged with war crimes is considered a prisoner of war and entitled to treatment as such, until it is proved that he is not entitled to such status.[56] If an act, apparently permitted to a combatant, has in fact been committed by one found to be a non-combatant this determination is conclusive in deciding whether the doer may be charged or not.

---

[51] Schindler and Toman, 231. The statement in the text is an application of the ruling by Sir Wm. Scott in *The Le Louis* (1817).

[52] See, for a conflict between statutory and international definitions in the case of piracy *jure gentium, The Le Louis* (1817) 2 Dods, 210, 165 E.R., 1464.

[53] Broadly speaking these constitute the basic requirements of a fair trial and the rule of law as understood in democratic societies.

[54] See, however, position under Canadian law, *R.* v. *Finta, loc.cit.*, 588–90.

[55] International Covenant on Civil and Political Rights, 1966, 999 U.N.T.S., 171, Art. 15.

[56] See text to n. 27, ch. 10 above

A prisoner of war charged with war crimes can only be validly sentenced by the same courts and according to the same procedure as apply to members of the Detaining Power's forces and in accordance with the relevant provisions of the Prisoners of War Convention and the Protocol. This suggests that the practice of many countries after World War II of setting up *ad hoc* military tribunals to conduct such trials would not be permitted. There is, however, nothing to prevent a group of powers to which an adverse party has surrendered entering an agreement to set up an international tribunal for this purpose as was done at Nuremberg and Tokyo after the surrender of Germany and Japan. Such an agreement would constitute an amendment to the Convention in so far as the participating powers are concerned. Whether it is considered a breach of Article 6, precluding any agreement detracting from the rights granted by the Convention, would depend upon the acceptance or acquiescence by the remaining parties to the Convention.

After the conclusion of the Gulf War and in reaction to the evidence of war crimes during the hostilities in Bosnia, there were many suggestions that such an international tribunal should be established to try the alleged offenders. Since these suggestions came after the hostilities were over in the one case and from non-parties to the conflict in the other, it would not constitute a breach of the Convention since the persons affected are not in the hands of any adverse party and are therefore not prisoners of war. There is nothing to prevent the Security Council establishing an *ad hoc* tribunal in relation to a specific conflict and such tribunal would be bound by its constituent instrument which might in fact differ from the provisions in the Convention. A tribunal of this kind was in fact established by the Council for the trial of those accused of offences committed in the conflicts raging in the former Yugoslavia after 1991.[57] Similarly, the trials of civilians, neutral nationals who are not members of enemy forces, and members of allied forces are not subject to the same restrictions concerning trial, since none of these are prisoners of war, nor need they be tried by the same tribunal and procedure as required for the trial of the trying power's forces. However, by the Civilians Convention[58] a civilian tried for grave breaches by any country other than his own is entitled to the safeguards of proper trial and defence at least as favourable as those in the Prisoners of War Convention.[59]

The provisions for trial by the same courts as the holding power's forces appear to prevent further application of the customary practice that allowed the tribunal trying those accused of war crimes to include officers from forces other than those establishing the tribunal, if those forces claim to be particularly affected or interested in the particular trial. This would be the case if, for example, the accused belonged to an ally, if the victims were nationals of the state of such force, or the offence had been committed on its territory.[60] It would seem that this would now

[57] See, ch. 19 below.
[58] Art. 146.
[59] Arts 105–8.
[60] See, e.g., *In re Eck* (the *Peleus* trial – 1945) 1 *War Crimes Reports* l, Cameron, *The Peleus Trial*, 1948.

only be permissible if members of the trying power could, in similar circumstances, appear before a military tribunal including such foreign officers. Perhaps difficulties could be avoided if the foreign personnel were seconded temporarily to the holding power's force.

While members of one's own forces would be tried in accordance with their own law, there are some war crimes not likely to be committed by them. It is unlikely, for example, that they would scuttle enemy vessels after the cessation of hostilities which constitutes a hostile act outside of conflict.[61] It would seem, however, that even enemy personnel could now only be tried for such an offence if the Detaining Power's legislation provided for trials of members of its own forces in similar circumstances. The legislation need not use the same terminology as international law and, in the instance cited, it would suffice to try one's own forces for intentional damage to property, or other provisions of the criminal law.[62]

War crimes defined

It is now common to use the definition section of the London Charter[63] establishing the Nuremberg Tribunal as a convenient guide to what are generally known as war crimes:

> violations of the laws or customs of war. Such violations shall include, but not be limited to, murder, ill-treatment or deportation to slave labour or for any other purpose of civilian population of or in occupied territory, murder or ill-treatment of prisoners of war or persons on the seas, killing of hostages, plunder of public or private property, wanton destruction of cities, towns or villages, or devastation not justified by military necessity.

This list is only exemplary and not exhaustive, so that other breaches of the customary law of war, such as disregarding an offer of surrender or executing a spy without trial, still amount to war crimes.

Because of the offences committed against civilians, particularly in occupied territory, the Charter introduced a new nomenclature, describing some of these as crimes against humanity:[64]

> murder, extermination, deportation, and other inhumane acts committed against any civilian population, before or during the war, or persecutions on political, racial or religious grounds in execution of or in connection with any crime within the

[61] See, e.g., *In re Grumpelt* (the Scuttled U-Boats Case 1946), 1 *War Crimes Reports*, 55.
[62] This was the position in the United States when trying Lt. Calley for his offences at My Lai.
[63] *The London Charter*, Art. 6(b). The definition in Art. 8 of the Statute of the International Criminal Court is somewhat wider, spelling out in addition all the possible offences listed in the Conventions and Protocol I. See also essays by Levie and Draper in Dinstein and Tabory, *op.cit.*
[64] Art. 6(c). See Dinstein, 'Crimes against humanity', in Makarczyk, *Theory of International Law at the Threshold of the 21st Century*, 1997, 891.

jurisdiction of the Tribunal, whether or not in violation of the domestic law of the
country where perpetrated.

These offences, which in most cases would have amounted to war crimes anyway,
were made amenable to trial by the same tribunals as enjoyed jurisdiction over
war crimes as previously defined.

It was important to emphasise that local legality was irrelevant since many of
the offences committed by German forces in occupied Europe or Germany proper
were often in compliance with German legislation or that enacted by 'puppet'
administrations. This provision made the defence of 'prior legality' impossible in
such circumstances, and is fully consistent with the general rule that municipal
law cannot be pleaded as an excuse for disregarding international law, at least
before an international tribunal or one called upon to apply international law.

The Tribunal was also authorised[65] to try crimes against peace:

> planning, preparation, initiation or waging of a war of aggression, or a war in viola-
> tion of international treaties, agreements or assurances, or participation in a common
> plan or conspiracy for the accomplishment of any of the foregoing.

Since this is essentially a political crime only likely to be committed by a head of
state, his government and the senior officers of the high command, and not by personnel in the field or occupied territory, it is not one for which an occupying military authority is likely to initiate proceedings.

The scope of crimes against humanity was limited somewhat by the reference
to the need for them to have been committed 'in execution of or in connection
with' other offences within the Tribunal's jurisdiction. Thus, the persecution of
German Jews in Germany could only be considered as falling within this rubric
once it was shown that this related to the planning or waging of aggressive war,[66]
and it has been suggested that, to a great extent, this reduced the concept to the
equivalent of war crimes or crimes against peace.[67]

Action against grave breaches

Many of the crimes described in the London Charter as war crimes or crimes
against humanity are synonymous with those named as grave breaches in the
Geneva Conventions and Protocol I. Parties to the Conventions are obliged to
enact the legislation necessary to provide effective sanctions for those committing
or ordering any act which would be a grave breach under the Conventions. They
must also take the measures necessary to suppress violations not amounting to

---

[65] Art. 6(a).
[66] *Judgment*, 60–5, 243–7 resp.
[67] Schwelb, 'Crimes against humanity', 23 Brit. Y.B. Int'l Law (1946), 178, 205. Dinstein, 'The distinction beween war crimes and crimes against peace', Dinstein and Tabory,
op.cit., 1.

grave breaches.[68] Apart from requiring the parties to repress such breaches and suppress all others, Protocol I imposes a duty to take all measures necessary in the case of failure by those having responsibility in this regard, and obliges the parties to assist one another to this end, including cooperation in extradition,[69] as well as with the United Nations in regard to serious infractions.[70]

If the party concerned does not institute proceedings, it may, subject to its own law, transfer an accused to any party making out a *prima facie* case. Since the procedure is subject to local extradition legislation the argument may be made that the crimes were committed in accordance with governmental instruction and are therefore political and exempt from extradition. However, most jurisdictions define the political offence as one directed against a government and not in accordance with its instructions.[71]

Whenever a person accused of a grave breach is brought to trial, he is entitled, as a minimum, to all the safeguards of a proper trial and defence provided for by the Conventions.[72] Both the Prisoners of War Convention and the Protocol spell out what are considered to be the minima of a fair trial, with the Civilians Convention making it clear that civilians in occupied territory are protected, in this respect, by the provisions relating to prisoners of war.[73]

Grave breaches defined

According to the Geneva Conventions relating to the treatment of the wounded and sick on land or at sea,[74] grave breaches are:

> wilful killing, torture or inhuman treatment, including biological experiments, wilfully causing great suffering or serious injury to body or health [such as may arise from inadequate living conditions], and extensive destruction and appropriation of property not justified by military necessity and carried out unlawfully and wantonly.

To compel a prisoner of war to serve in the forces of an adverse party or to deny him his rights to a fair trial also constitute grave breaches.[75] The Civilians Convention confirms that similar acts against civilians are grave breaches and adds to

---

[68] Land Art. 49, Maritime 50, Prisoners of War 129, Civilians 146.

[69] In accordance with its Statute, the *ad hoc* tribunal for Yugoslavia is given primacy over national tribunals and a state holding an indicted accused is under an obligation to transfer him.

[70] Arts 86, 88, 89. Such co-operation was called for by the Security Council in gathering evidence concerning the commission of breaches in the Gulf War and during the hostilities in Bosnia.

[71] See, e.g., *Ex p. Schumann* (Ghana Court of Appeal) [1966] G.L.R., 703, 39 I.L.R., 433.

[72] Land Art. 49, Maritime 50, Prisoners of War 129, Civilians 146, Pr. I 75(7).

[73] Conv., Art. 105, Pr. I 75, Civilians 146.

[74] Arts 50 and 51 resp.

[75] Prisoners of War Conv., Art. 130.

the list 'unlawful deportation or transfer or confinement of a protected person [and the] taking of hostages'.[76]

Protocol I extends the definition of grave breaches in regard to anyone protected by the Protocol, that is to say to combatants and prisoners of war, any persons who have taken part in hostilities and to refugees and stateless persons, as well as the wounded, sick and shipwrecked, medical and religious personnel, medical units and transports under the control of the adverse party.[77]

A number of medical practices are added by the Protocol to the list of grave breaches,[78] so as to include any wilful act or omission seriously endangering the physical or mental health or integrity of any person in the power of a party other than that on which he depends, if it is not required by the state of his health and is not consistent with generally accepted medical standards as applicable to the detaining power's own nationals whose liberty is not restricted in any way. It would also be a grave breach to submit a detained person, even if consent is secured, to any physical mutilation, medical or scientific experiment, or removal of tissue or organs unless this treatment is warranted by the medical needs of that person. Blood transfusions and skin transplants, if given voluntarily, are not forbidden if taken for therapeutic purposes and in conditions consistent with the highest medical standards. It should be noted, however, that the prohibition is directed to the detaining power and its agents, leaving open the possibility that a private medical practitioner in occupied territory could carry out such activities without it amounting to a grave breach,[79] even though it might in fact amount to a war crime.

Protocol I, Article 85(3) provides a list of acts which constitute grave breaches if committed wilfully, in breach of the Protocol, and causing death or serious injury to body or health:

> making the civilian population or individual civilians the object of attack;
> launching an indiscriminate attack affecting the civilian population or civilian objects in the knowledge that such attack will cause excessive loss of life, injury to civilians or
> damage to civilian objects;
> launching an attack against works or installations containing dangerous forces in the knowledge that such attack will cause excessive loss of life, injury to civilians or damage to civilian objects;
> making non-defended localities and demilitarised zones the object of attack;
> making a person the object of attack knowing he is *hors de combat;*

---

[76] Art. 147.
[77] Arts 44, 45, 73, 85(2).
[78] Art. 11.
[79] Bothe, *et al.*, 112. One of the allegations made against Yugoslav forces in 1999 related to the unlawful taking of blood from Kosovan youths, *The Times*, 17 Apr. 1999.

perfidious use of the distinctive emblem of the red cross, crescent or lion and sun,[80] or other protected signs recognised by the Conventions or Protocol.[81]

In addition to this list, the Protocol provides[82] that certain other acts are grave breaches if committed wilfully and in violation of the Conventions or Protocol:

transfer by the Occupying Power of parts of its own civilian population into occupied territory or deportation or transfer of all or parts of the population of that territory within or out of the territory [although this is permitted on a temporary basis to permit the entry of administrators of the territory or if it is necessary for the security of the civilian population[83] or imperative military reasons]; unjustifiable delay in repatriating prisoners of war or civilians;[84] practices of *apartheid*[85] and other inhuman and degrading practices involving outrages upon personal dignity, based on racial discrimination;[86] making the clearly-recognised historic monuments, works of art or places of worship which constitute the cultural or spiritual heritage of peoples and to which special protection has been accorded by agreement,[87] the object of attack causing as a result extensive destruction thereof, where there is no evidence of prior use of such objects in support of the adverse party's military effort, and when such places are not located in the immediate proximity of military objectives;

[80] The lion and sun was formerly used by Iran, but has disappeared since the Islamic revolution. Any perfidious use of the red shield of David would be considered a grave breach by Israel and those powers which recognise this emblem *de facto*. Albanian refugees from Kosovo claimed in 1998 that they were being attacked by Serb helicopters marked with a red cross, *Long Island Newsday*, 22 Jun. 1998.

[81] For detailed discussion of each of the items mentioned, see the relevant entry in the index.

[82] Art. 85(4).

[83] The policy of 'ethnic cleansing' carried out in 1992 and 1993 by the Serbs against the Muslim population of Bosnia is clearly in breach of this provision, and has resulted in Yugoslavia's expulsion from the UN. However, the evacuation of some Muslims by the ICRC to prevent their being massacred cannot be considered a breach.

[84] It has been suggested that this may have been included as a grave breach 'somewhat lightly and perhaps overzealously', Tomuschat, 'Crimes against the peace and security of mankind and the recalcitrant third state', Dinstein and Tabory, *op.cit.*, 41, 47.

[85] The 1973 Convention on Suppression and Punishment of the Crime of Apartheid, 1015 U.N.T.S., 243, to which the majority of major western powers have not acceded, declares *apartheid* to be a crime against humanity. This crime 'shall include similar policies and practices of racial segregation and discrimination as practised in southern Africa ... for the purpose of establishing and maintaining domination by one racial group of persons over any other racial group of persons and systematically oppressing them'. While, with the ending of white rule in South Africa *apartheid* is no longer a policy of that country it is, however, included in the Statute of the International Criminal Court as a crime against humanity.

[86] See the Convention on the Elimination of All Forms of Racial Discrimination, (1965), 60 U.N.T.S. 195.

[87] See, e.g., Hague Convention for the Protection of Cultural Property in the Event of Armed Conflict, 1954, Schindler and Toman, 745. Agreements may also be specially entered into by the belligerents.

depriving any person protected by the Conventions or the Protocol of a fair and regular trial.

Environmental war crimes

A new type of offence against the law of armed conflict was introduced by the Convention on the Prohibition of Military or Any Other Hostile Use of Environmental Modification Techniques.[88] The parties undertook not to engage in any military or other hostile use of environmental modification techniques 'having widespread, long lasting or severe effects' as the means of destroying, damaging or injuring any other state party. 'Environmental modification techniques' means 'any technique for changing – through the deliberate manipulation of natural processes – the dynamics, composition or structure of the Earth, including its biota,[89] lithosphere,[90] hydrosphere[91] and atmosphere,[92] or of outer space.'

To these offences Protocol I added a prohibition on the use of any means of warfare intended or expected to cause 'widespread, long-term and severe damage' to the natural environment. It also enjoined parties to a conflict to protect the natural environment against such damage, especially prohibiting any means or method intended or expected to cause such damage and so prejudice the health or survival of the population. Reprisals against the natural environment are specifically forbidden.[93] It is noticeable that whereas the ENMOD Convention provides that the effects of the damage are alternative, the Protocol makes them cumulative.

Allegations of environmental war crimes were made during and after the Gulf War as a result of Iraq's destruction of oilwells and pipelines in Kuwait and Iraq, causing quantities of deleterious material to enter the Gulf damaging lower water purification installations and destroying wild life, as well as polluting the air and the ground. However, it could not be shown that Iraq had undertaken this destruction with the intention of modifying the environment and, therefore, could not be charged with environmental war crimes.[94]

The introduction of the concept of environmental war crimes does not affect the right to attack legitimate targets the destruction of which might have adverse environmental effects. It is therefore not illegal to destroy an enemy tanker or nuclear-powered vessel, including submarines or warships, simply because

[88] 1977, Schindler and Toman, 163.
[89] Part of earth's crust, waters and atmosphere where living organisms can subsist.
[90] Earth's crust, so inducing artificial earthquakes is forbidden.
[91] Water on or surrounding earth's surface, including the oceans and water in the atmosphere, so diverting the Gulf Stream is forbidden.
[92] Gaseous envelope surrounding the earth.
[93] Arts 35, 55.
[94] See, e.g., US Dept. of Defense Report to Congress, 'Conduct of the Persian Gulf War, App. O, 'The role of the law of war', 31 I.L.M., 612, 636–7. See also Green, 'The environment and the law of conventional warfare', 29 Can. Y.B. Int'l Law (1991), 222.

destruction would result in damage to the environment or even have widespread, long-term and serious adverse effects upon the civilian population.[95]

Customary law offences

Offences against the laws and customs of war, in addition to those described as grave breaches by the Conventions and Protocol, remain war crimes and punishable as such. The Hague Regulations, while not providing for personal liability other than for private breach of an armistice, declares certain acts to be 'especially forbidden'.[96] The Regulations are, for the most part, now recognised as customary law, while many of the acts listed are now grave breaches within the terms of the Conventions and Protocol. Those which have not been so described, would constitute war crimes as traditionally understood: the use of poison or poisoned weapons, as well as any forbidden weapon, such as Dum-Dum bullets; treacherous killing of any individual belonging to the adverse nation or army; killing or wounding an enemy who, having laid down his arms or no longer having a means of defence has surrendered at discretion, and by the Protocol it is forbidden to attack an airman who has abandoned his aircraft while in course of his descent, and it is a grave breach to attack any enemy who is *hors de combat*; declaring that no quarter will be given – while the Protocol expressly forbids this, it does not make it a grave breach; employing arms or any weapon calculated to cause unnecessary suffering, that is to say anything beyond that required to place an enemy *hors de combat*, so that weapons aggravating an injury, such as would be caused by a notched bayonet or one smeared with deleterious material are forbidden; improper use of a flag of truce, the national flag or military insignia or uniform of the adverse party, or the distinctive emblems of the Geneva Conventions, to which may be added by virtue of the Protocol similar insignia of a neutral – though ruses are not forbidden – or of the United Nations, but none of these prohibitions affects the generally recognised existing rules concerning espionage or the use of flags in naval combat; destroying or seizing enemy property, unless imperatively demanded by the necessities of war – the Protocol forbids making civilian objects the object of attack, while an indiscriminate attack affecting civilian objects would be a grave breach; declaring abolished, suspended or inadmissible in a court of law the rights of action of enemy nationals, moreover the Civilians Convention forbids any change in the institutions of government in occupied territory; compelling enemy nationals to take part in hostilities against their own country, even if they were members of the particular belligerent's forces

---

[95] For a collection of essays examining various aspects of the law of war and the environment, see Grunawalt, *Protection of the Environment During Armed Conflict*, 1996.

[96] Art. 23.

before the commencement of hostilities[97] – it is now a grave breach to compel any protected person to serve in the forces of a hostile power.

It is a war crime to violate the terms of an armistice or surrender by any individual, civilian or military, acting on his own initiative, as distinct from obeying an order of a party to the armistice. The adverse party is entitled to demand punishment of such an offender or to try him as a war criminal if captured.[98] It is not, however, a breach of an armistice if an individual member of the forces, not knowing of the armistice, continues to fight, as happened with many Japanese in isolated Pacific islands after the surrender of Japan. In accordance with Hague Regulation 40 any serious breach of an armistice by the adverse party entitles the injured belligerent to denounce the armistice. In the ongoing conflict between Israel and her Arab enemies, there have been many such breaches, but there has been no denunciation of the armistice agreements. In fact, it has been suggested that the various 'rounds of hostilities between Israel and the Arab countries [in breach of armistice agreements] do not qualify as separate wars, [being] merely inconsecutive time-frames of combat, punctuated by extended cease-fires, in the course of a single on-going war,'[99] as such no war crimes are committed.

The Hague Regulations also forbid pillage and punishment of a spy without trial[100] and such acts are war crimes. Customary law also recognises other acts as constituting war crimes, including mutilation or other maltreatment of dead bodies, and this includes such practices as taking ears as proof of a body count; looting or gathering trophies, an offence confirmed *a contrario* by the Prisoners of War Convention which indicates the property a prisoner may keep; using privileged buildings, such as schools, churches or cultural establishments as resting places for the forces or to secure immunity for non-privileged objects or persons; attacking protected places or an unarmed merchant vessel not sailing in convoy[101] or a properly marked hospital ship or aircraft; failing to provide for the security of the crew of a merchant vessel before attacking it or firing upon shipwrecked personnel;[102] hostile activities by non-combatants; using asphyxi-

---

[97] During both world wars problems arose with persons, including those called up in accordance with conscription legislation, who possessed the nationality of the adverse party as well as that of their own. United Kingdom practice was to secure their agreement that they had no objection to serving in conditions where they might oppose their own relatives. In France, during World War I, in some cases citizens of Alsace captured while serving in the German forces were subjected to treason trials.

[98] See, e.g., *In re Grumpelt* (the Scuttled U-Boats Case, 1946) 1 *War Crimes Reports*, 55.

[99] Dinstein, *War, Aggression and Self-Defence*, 1994, 56.

[100] See, e.g., *In re Rhode* (1946) 5 *War Crimes Reports* 54; Webb, *The Natzweiler Trial*.

[101] See ch. 8 above.

[102] See, e.g., *In re Eck*, (1945) 1 *War Crimes Reports* 1; Cameron, *The Peleus Trial*.

ating, poisonous and other gases[103] or bacteriological methods of warfare;[104] genocide.[105]

The fact that a particular act has not been listed as a war crime or a grave breach does not preclude its being treated as a war crime if it is in breach of any rule of the customary or treaty law of armed conflict. The whole issue will be changed when the International Criminal Court begins to function.[106]

Command responsibility

Every individual, regardless of rank or governmental status, is personally liable for any war crime or grave breach that he might commit.[107]

A commander, that is to say, anyone in a position of command whatever his rank might be, including a Head of State or the lowest non-commissioned officer, who issues an order to commit a war crime or a grave breach is equally guilty of the offence with the subordinate actually committing it. He is also liable if, knowing or having information from which he should have concluded that a subordinate was going to commit such a crime, he failed to prevent it.[108] and if, being aware of such commission, fails to initiate disciplinary or penal action.[109]

Any commander failing to exercise proper control over his forces with the result that they commit war crimes, even if he remains unaware of this when he should have known, is also liable for war crimes.[110] This is because a commander is responsible for the behaviour of his troops and ensuring that they behave in accordance with the law of armed conflict[111] He is also liable if the offences occur within sight or hearing of his office, in the presence of one of his officers or non-

---

[103] See the Geneva Protocol, 1925; Schindler and Toman, 115.

[104] *Ibid.*; see also, Convention on Prohibition of Development, Production and Stockpiling of Bacteriological (Biological) and Toxin Weapons and Their Destruction, 1972, *ibid.*, 137.

[105] See Genocide Convention, 1948, *ibid.*, 231. See also *Eichmann* v. *The Attorney-General of the Government of Israel* (1962) 36 I.L.R., 277.

[106] See below, this chapter – Developments since 1977.

[107] See, e.g., Green, 'Superior orders and command responsibility', 27 Can. Y.B. Int'l Law 1989, 167; 'Command responsibility in international humanitarian law', 5 Transnational law and contemporary problems', 1995, 319; 'War crimes, crimes against humanity and command responsibility', *Essays*, 1999, ch. VIII.

[108] Pr. Arts 86, 87. See also Green and Parks, *loc.cit.* n. 18, ch. 17 above.

[109] See *Koster* v. *United States* (1982) 685 F.2d, 407, 410, 414; see also for far-ranging comments on command and state responsibility, *Final Report of the Commission of Inquiry into the Events at the Refugee Camps in Beirut*, 7 Feb. 1983, 22 I.L.M. 473; Green, 'War crimes, extradition and command responsibility', 14 Israel Y.B.H.R. 1984, 17, 39–53; Burnett, 'Command responsibility and a case study of the criminal responsibility of Israeli military commanders at Shatila and Sabra', 107 Mil.Law Rev. 1985, 71.

[110] See *Re Yamashita* (1945–6) 4 *War Crimes Reports*, 1, 327 US 1.

[111] See Hague Regs, Art. 1, Pr. I, Arts 43, 87; see also text to nn. 17 *et seq*, ch. 17 above.

commissioned officers, or if members of his unit have committed war crimes previously.[112]

A useful statement as to the current law concerning command responsibility is to be found in *Dishonoured Legacy: The Lessons of the Somalia Affair*.[113] 'The term "responsibility" is not synonymous with accountability. One who is authorised to act or who exercises authority is "responsible". However, responsible officials are also held to account. A person exercising supervisory authority is responsible, and hence accountable, for the manner in which that authority has been exercised. A person who delegates authority is also responsible, and hence accountable, not for the form of direct supervision that a supervisor is expected to exercise but, rather, for control over the delegate and, ultimately, for the actual acts performed by the delegate. The act of delegation to another does not relieve the responsible official of the duty to account. While one can delegate the authority to act, one cannot thereby delegate one's assigned responsibility in relation to the proper performance of such acts. Where a superior delegates the authority to act to a subordinate, the superior remains responsible: first, for the acts performed by the delegate; second, for the appropriateness of the choice of delegate; third, with regard to the propriety of the delegation; and, finally, for the control of the acts of the subordinate. Even if the superior official is successful in demonstrating appropriate, prudent, diligent personal behaviour, the superior remains responsible for the errors and misdeeds of the subordinate. However, in such circumstances, when assessing the appropriate response to the actions of the superior whose subordinate or delegate has erred or has been guilty of misconduct, the authorities may be justified in selecting a penalty or sanction of lower order or no penalty or sanction whatsoever. It is the responsibility of those who exercise supervisory authority, or who have delegated the authority to act to others, to know what is transpiring within the area of their assigned authority. Even if subordinates whose duty it is to inform their superior of all relevant facts, circumstances, and developments fail to fulfil their obligations, this cannot absolve their superior of responsibility for what has transpired.'

Defences: necessity

Whenever a conference has been entrusted with the task of drafting rules relating to the conduct of armed conflict, the various national delegations have been assisted by military experts, so that the rules reflect what those experts believe to be tolerable and compatible with the needs of military necessity. This is evident from the preamble to Hague Convention IV: 'According to the views of the

[112] See, e.g., *In re Meyer* (1945 – the *Abbaye Ardenne* case) 4 *War Crimes Rep.* 97; for more extensive extracts from the Judge Advocate's summing-up, see Green, *Essays*, 1985, 226–7, 269–71.

[113] Report of the Commission of Inquiry into the Deployment of Canadian Forces to Somalia, Executive Summary, 1997, ES-14-15.

High Contracting Parties, these provisions, the wording of which has been inspired by the desire to diminish the evils of war, *as far as military requirements permit*.[114]

A person charged with war crimes or grave breaches is, therefore, unable to plead military necessity by way of defence,[115] unless the act in question relates to a breach of a treaty provision stipulating that military advantage may be taken into consideration.[116]

The fact that military necessity does not constitute a defence does not mean that an accused is unable to plead that he acted under duress as, for example, that he was in immediate and real fear for his life.[117] This does not, however, permit him to plead that he was threatened with subsequent disciplinary or penal action if he failed to obey an order to commit the act in question, although in such circumstances the threat may be taken into consideration in mitigation of punishment. Similarly he cannot plead that he committed a war crime on account of personal necessity relating to his own life or comfort, such as that he deprived a protected person of food to preserve his own life. This, too, however, may be considered a mitigating circumstance.

Defences: superior orders

It is almost inevitable in any war crimes trial that the accused will plead that he was only carrying out the order of a superior,[118] often one known to be dead or not in captivity. Formerly, particularly when armies were made up of professional volunteers, it was considered that a soldier must implicitly and without question carry out every order given him, so that he could never be personally liable for a war

---

[114] Italics added. For different uses of the term 'military necessity', see de Mulinen, *Handbook of the Law of War for the Armed Forces*, 1987, paras. 352–5.

[115] See, e.g., *In re Lewinski (called von Manstein)* (1949) 16 Ann. Dig., 509, 511–13.

[116] See, e.g., Regs. Art. 23, Pr. I, Art. 51 (5)(b). It should be noted that each of the four Conventions provides that 'the High Contracting Parties undertake to respect and to ensure respect for the present Convention in *all* circumstances' (italics added).

[117] See, e.g., *In re Holzer* (1946) cited at 5 *War Crimes Reports*, 16 and 21: 'The case of a person setting up as a defence that he was compelled to commit a crime is one of every day. There is no doubt on the authorities that compulsion is a defence when the crime is not of a heinous character. But the killing of an innocent person can never be justified.' See also *Erdemović* case in which it was held that even a threat to his life will not provide a defence when the charges relate to mass murder, *Prosecutor* v. *Drazen Erdemović*, Trial Chamber Sentencing Judgment, 5 Mar. 1998, (37 I.L.M. 1182, 1193) para. 17: 'duress does not afford a complete defence to a soldier charged with a crime against humanity and/or a war crime involving the killing of innocent human beings. It may be taken into account only by way of mitigation'. See, e.g., Green, '*Drazen Erdemović*: The International Criminal Tribunal for the former Yugoslavia in action', 10 Leiden J. Int'l Law 1997, 363, 369.

[118] See, e.g., Dinstein, *The Defence of 'Obedience to Superior Orders' in International Law*, Green, *Superior Orders in National and International Law*, Keijzer, *Military Obedience*; Osiel, *Obeying Orders*, 1998.

305

crime he had been ordered to commit.[119] Today, however, especially since con-scription has resulted in the enlistment of persons from every walk of life and every level of intelligence, he is no longer regarded as an unthinking automaton and is only required to obey lawful orders. As a result he cannot lawfully be pun-ished for refusing to obey an unlawful order. Moreover, since the Protocol requires commanders to ensure that those under their command are made aware of their responsibilities under the Conventions and Protocol, together with the presence of legal advisers to advise on the instruction to be given,[120] it is now pos-sible to presume that a soldier is aware of his obligations and he may legitimately question the order that he has been given.[121]

Already in the South African (Boer) War the defence was narrowly defined. In *R. v. Smith*,[122] Solomon J. declared:

> it is monstrous to suppose that a soldier would be protected when the order is *grossly illegal*. [But that he is] responsible if he obeys an order not strictly legal ... is an extreme proposition which the Court cannot accept ... [E]specially in war immedi-ate obedience ... is required ... I think it is a safe rule to lay down that if a soldier *honestly believes* he is doing his duty in obeying ... and the orders are *not so mani-festly illegal*; that he ... ought to have known they were unlawful, [he] will be pro-tected by the orders.

The judgment normally regarded as the leading authority on the issue of superior orders as a defence, prior to the Nuremberg Trial, was *The Llandovery Castle* decided by the German *Reichsgericht* at Leipzig in 1921.[123] This arose out of the sinking of a hospital ship and subsequent firing on its boats. The court pointed out that:

> The firing on the boats was an offence against the law of nations ... Any violation of the law of nations in warfare is ... a punishable offence, so far as, in general, a penalty is attached to the deed. The killing of enemies in war is in accordance with the law of the State that makes war . . only in so far as such killing is in accordance with the conditions and limitations imposed by the Law of Nations. The fact that this deed is a violation of International Law *must be well known to the doer*, apart from

---

[119] See, e.g., Oppenheim, *International Law*, vol. II, 1st through 5th eds. S. 253.

[120] Pr. I, Arts 87, 82.

[121] See, e.g. 'Lesson plan' annexed to US Dept. of the Army, ASubjScd 27–1, 8 Oct. 1970, 'The Geneva Conventions of 1949 and Hague Convention IV of 1907', and discussion thereof in Green, 'Aftermath of Vietnam: war law and the soldier', 4 Falk, *The Vietnam War and International Law*, 147, 169–72. See also US JAG School *Operational Law Handbook*, JA 422, 1996, p. 18 ff.: 'Troops who receive unclear orders must insist on clar-ification. Normally, the superior issuing the unclear directive will make it clear, when queried, that it was not his intent to commit a war crime. If the superior insists that his ille-gal order be obeyed, however, the soldier has an affirmative obligation to disobey the order and report the incident to the next superior CDR, military police, CID, nearest JA, or local inspector general'. See also Rogers, *Law on the Battlefield*, 1996, 143–8.

[122] (1900) 17 SC, 561 (Cape of Good Hope), italics added. See also Green 'Superior orders and the reasonable man', *Essays*, 1999, ch. VII.

[123] HMSO, Cmd, 1422, (1921), Cameron, *The Peleus Trial*, App. IX (italics added).

acts of carelessness, in which careless ignorance is a sufficient excuse. In examining the essence of this knowledge, the ambiguity of many of the rules of International Law, as well as the actual circumstances of the case, must be borne in mind, because in wartime decisions of great importance have frequently to be made on very insufficient material. This consideration, however, cannot be applied to the case at present before the Court. The rule of International Law which is here involved is *simple and universally known*. No possible doubt can exist with regard to the question of its applicability.

Despite this judgment, the pre-World War II military law manuals of both the United Kingdom and the United States, as well as *Oppenheim*, persisted in stating that superior orders constituted a valid defence. However, after the outbreak of the war and the increasing knowledge of German breaches of the law, the statements were amended to bring them into line with the *Llandovery Castle* decision, recognising that only lawful orders were to be obeyed, although an unlawful order might be considered by way of mitigation so long as the act was not one 'which violate[d] both unchallenged rules of warfare and outrage[d] the general sentiment of humanity'.[124]

By the London Charter[125] the defendants were expressly deprived of the possibility of pleading superior orders as a defence, although mitigation remained open to the tribunal. In its Judgment, the tribunal affirmed[126] that this was:

in conformity with the law of nations. That a soldier was ordered to kill or torture in violation of the International Law of war has never been recognised as a defence to acts of brutality, though, as the Charter here provides, the order may be urged in mitigation of punishment. The true test, which is found in varying degrees in the criminal law of most nations, is not the existence of the order, but whether moral choice was in fact possible ... [I]ndividuals have international duties which transcend the national obligations of obedience imposed by the individual State. He who violates the laws of war cannot obtain immunity while acting in pursuance of the authority of the State if the State in authorising action moves outside its competence under international law ... There is nothing in mitigation. Superior orders, even to a soldier, cannot be considered in mitigation where crimes have been committed consciously, ruthlessly and without military excuse or justification ... Participation in such crimes as these has never been required of any soldier and [they] cannot now shield [themselves] behind a mythical requirement of soldierly obedience at all costs as [their] excuse for commission of these crimes.

Confirmation of Nuremberg

In 1946 the General Assembly adopted Resolution 95(I)[127] affirming the Principles

[124] Oppenheim, *International Law* s. 253, 1940 ed.
[125] *The London Charter*, Art. 8.
[126] *Nuremberg Judgment*, 42, 92, 118; 221, 283, 316, resp.
[127] Schindler and Toman, 921.

of International Law Recognised by the Charter of the Nuremberg Tribunal, but without detailing what these Principles are. This lacuna was remedied in 1950 with the adoption by the International Law Commission of Principles of International Law Recognised in the Charter of the Nuremberg Tribunal and the Judgment of the Tribunal.[128] Principles III and IV confirm that status, whether as Head of State or not, does not confer immunity and that superior orders are not a defence 'provided a moral choice was in fact possible to' the accused, while Principle II made it clear that it was not open to him to plead that the act charged was legal under national law.

In addition, the Commission reiterated that the offences of which the Tribunal had been seized were in fact crimes at international law. It also stated as Principle I that any person committing a crime under international law is personally responsible and subject to punishment, but – Principle V – that he is in every case entitled to a fair trial on the facts and the law.

The present position

Although Protocol I contains specific provisions concerning the responsibility of the commander, it says nothing about the defence of superior orders.[129] However, it is now clear that an act done in compliance with an unlawful order which is obviously, palpably or manifestly unlawful to a reasonable soldier,[130] which is a question of law, in the circumstances prevailing at the time of the order, is not a defence and cannot be pleaded in mitigation. Since most war crimes are also crimes according to national law the test of reasonableness would coincide with what a person of ordinary sense and understanding would automatically know to be illegal. As to those crimes which are not of such a character and may be considered to be military in nature, the members of the tribunal, who should have military experience, would be expected to apply their military understanding in assessing the prevailing circumstances, while paying due attention to the age, intelligence and service experience of the person accused.[131]

If the order involves commission of an act which is unlawful, but not manifestly so, the fact that it is in obedience to an order may be taken into consideration for the purpose of mitigating the punishment. This is in accordance with the view of the Nuremberg Tribunal and was the policy adopted by the war crimes courts set up after World War II.[132]

---

[128] *Ibid.*, 923.

[129] See, however, for an account of the debate on this topic, Levie, *Protection of War Victims, Supplement*, 1985.

[130] See, e.g., Green, *loc.cit.*, n. 122 above.

[131] As was done in the *Erdemović* case.

[132] See, e.g., summing-up by Judge Advocate in the Canadian cases *Re Jung and Schumacher* (1946) ref. 5200-1TD 2257P (JAG/LRO) 18 Jan. 1973, and *In re Holzer* (1946), Public Archives of Canada, Record Group 25 F-3, vol.1000, 345, 349 – this material was made available through the good offices of the Deputy Judge Advocate General, N.D.H.Q., Canada.

Treatment of the accused

Non-national military personnel accused of war crimes, other than *in absentia*, are of course prisoners of war.[133] As such, they are entitled until their conviction to be treated in the same way as other prisoners of war. Their trial must take place before the same tribunals and in accordance with the same rules and procedure as apply in trials of members of the holding power's armed forces charged with similar offences.[134] This suggests that, since the adoption of the 1949 Convention, persons charged with war crimes may not be tried before the type of tribunal that was established in so many countries after World War II. While they are protected by the Convention's provisions in this matter, should these fall short of guarantees provided in human rights agreements remaining in force between belligerents despite the conflict, they must be supplemented accordingly.

Any civilian charged with war crimes while in the power of a state of which he is not a national is entitled to all the safeguards of a proper trial and defence, and these must not be less than those provided for prisoners of war by the Prisoners of War Convention. Further, they must always be presented for prosecution and trial in accordance with the applicable rules of international law and, if they do not enjoy as protected persons more favourable treatment under the Conventions and Protocol, they are to be granted the fundamental guarantees embodied in Article 75 of the Protocol.

Since, as has been pointed out, members of one's own forces are subject to their national criminal and military law, when they are charged with offences amounting to war crimes or grave breaches, whether so described or not, there is no need to have recourse to the provisions of international law to ground jurisdiction,[135] or to determine the conditions under which a trial may be held.

Customary law permits the imposition of the death penalty for those convicted of war crimes. However, since prisoners of war are to be afforded the same treatment and punishment as members of the holding power's forces for similar offences, if the holding power has abolished the death penalty it cannot be imposed upon an accused war criminal. Since civilians are entitled to the same procedural protection as prisoners of war, they too would be protected from imposition of this penalty. The situation would be different if the holding power's legislation provided for this penalty for members of its own forces similarly charged. The death penalty cannot be imposed by either of the *ad hoc* tribunals, nor by the International Criminal Court.

---

[133] See ch. 10 above.

[134] Prisoners of War Conv. Arts 102, 105–6.

[135] This was the case with a number of members of the US forces in Korea and Vietnam, of which we need only cite *US* v. *Calley* (1969/71/73) CM 426402, 46 C.M.R., 1131, 48 C.M.R., 9, 1 M.L.R., 2488.

Developments since 1977

From the moment Iraq invaded Kuwait it became clear that the government of that country was ordering the commission of a variety of war crimes and grave breaches directed against the civilian population of Kuwait as well as against foreign residents, travellers[136] and diplomats, many of whom were held as hostages and housed in potential military objectives. In addition, during the Gulf War Iraqi forces committed a variety of war crimes against Coalition prisoners of war, both male and female,[137] as well as against Kuwaiti private property.

Kuwait was invaded on 2 August 1990 and as early as the next day the United States commenced gathering information concerning the commission of war crimes by Iraq, and by October both the United States and the United Kingdom were issuing warnings concerning the liability of those responsible. In the preamble to its Resolution 674 of 29 October[138] the Security Council reaffirmed Iraq's liability 'under the [Civilians] Convention in respect of the grave breaches committed by it, as [well as of] individuals who commit or order the commission of grave breaches', while in the substance of the Resolution states were invited 'to collate substantiated information in their possession or submitted to them on the grave breaches by Iraq ... and to make this information available to the Security Council'. While the resolution makes no provision for the arrest or trial of offenders, it cannot be doubted that this was the ultimate intention, for otherwise there seems little point in collating such information. However, by the end of 1999 no attempt had been made to secure any of those allegedly responsible or to establish a tribunal with jurisdiction to try them if seized.

During the hostilities in Bosnia in 1992 there were similar condemnations by the European Community and the United Nations of the atrocities being perpetrated in that country with warnings that, in due course, those responsible would be brought to trial. In July 1992[139] the Security Council repeated its demand for compliance with the obligations under international humanitarian law, and particularly the 1949 Geneva Conventions. It further stated that those committing or ordering the commission of grave breaches of the Conventions are 'individually responsible in respect of such breaches'. Then, in October[140] it reaffirmed the earlier Resolutions, expressed increased concern at the continuing reports of widespread violations of international law including the practice of 'ethnic cleansing', and instructed the Secretary General to appoint a Commission of Experts to investigate and collect information concerning alleged crimes in the territory of the former Yugoslavia, and to make recommendations as to further action to be taken to deal with these alleged crimes. This was an interesting development since, while

---

[136] The passengers on board a British airliner that had stopped for refuelling were detained and held as hostages.

[137] See, e.g, *The Times*, 12 Jun. 1992. See also Peters and Nichol, *Tornado Down*, 1992.

[138] 29 I.L.M., 1561.

[139] SC Res., 764, 31 I.L.M., 1465.

[140] Res. 780, *ibid.*, 1467.

there were international conflicts between Bosnia and Serbia, Bosnia and Croatia and Serbia and Croatia, for the main part, most of the allegations arose from activities by one group of Bosnians against another so that there was no international armed conflict in progress and Protocol II concerning the law in non-international armed conflicts makes no reference to the Conventions, breaches of the Protocol or the law of war, and makes no provision for punishment. To the extent that any such atrocities were committed by, for example, Serbian Serbs, especially if this was due to negligence in failing to prevent or complicity by the Serb government, then it might be possible to argue that the laws of international armed conflict would apply to them. In the same way, if the activities of Bosnian Serbs or Bosnian Croats could be imputed to Serbia or Croatia respectively, then the offences would have been considered as occurring during an international conflict. However, in so far as the 'atrocities' were committed during hostilities between Bosnian Serbs and Bosnia or Bosnian Croats and Bosnia, they would have been perpetrated during a non-international conflict.[141]

Since there is no international criminal tribunal before which the accused might be brought, and there will be none until the International Criminal Court is actually set up, it must be presumed that, in the case of Iraqi criminals, members of the Coalition would make use of their own procedures if they managed to secure the person of anyone accused. In the case of the conflicts in the former Yugoslavia, which includes Kosovo, the situation is somewhat different. While it may have been possible for non-involved states to maintain that since war crimes and crimes against humanity are subject to universal jurisdiction they were enabled to prosecute any persons present in their territory accused of such offences, especially if they amounted to grave breaches under the Geneva Conventions, acting in accordance with what might appear to be an extensive interpretation of Chapter VII of the Charter of the United Nations,[142] the Security Council established[143] an *ad hoc* International Tribunal for the Prosecution of Persons Responsible for Serious Violations of International Humanitarian Law Committed in the Territory of the Former Yugoslavia since 1991.[144] The tribunal possesses competence to hear allegations concerning grave breaches, violations of the laws and customs of war, genocide and crimes against humanity. In this connection it might be pointed out that in its Sentencing Judgment the Trial Chamber in *Tadić*[145] held that genocide is 'itself a specific crime against humanity'. This raises the question whether there is any longer a need to charge accused persons with 'genocide' as a separate crime rather than cit-

[141] See ch. 12 above and 19 below.
[142] 'Action with respect to threats to the peace, breaches of the peace, and acts of aggression'; see e.g., Green, '*Erdemović – Tadić – Dokmanović*: jurisdiction and early practice of the Yugoslav War Crimes Tribunal 27 Israel Y.B.H.R. 313 (1997).
[143] For discussion of the Security Council's competence in this matter, see *Prosecutor v. Tadić* (1995) 35 I.L.M. 32, paras. 30–40.
[144] Res. 808, 1993 – The Statute of the tribunal is to be found in 32 I.L.M. 1192.
[145] Case no. IT-94-1-T, 14 Jul. 1997, para. 8.

ing it as an example and as such part of the *res gestae* constituting 'crimes against humanity'.

In accordance with what has now become established practice, the Statute postulates individual criminal responsibility, rejecting impunity based on status, affirming command responsibility and limiting the plea of superior orders to a claim of mitigating circumstances. Perhaps more significant, however, is the affirmation of the principle *non bis in idem* and the recognition of concurrent jurisdiction, while conferring primacy to the tribunal over national courts. This has resulted in, for example, Germany transferring an indicted accused to the tribunal.

Apart from the significant development relating to the tribunal and its view that genocide is but an example of crimes against humanity, there is a further point of importance. Bosnia has become a member of the United Nations and, taking advantage of Yugoslavia's ratification of the Genocide Convention, to which it had given notice of its succession, it initiated in March 1993 proceedings before the International Court of Justice alleging genocide by Yugoslavia (Serbia–Montenegro – all that remains of the former Republic of Yugoslavia) and seeking provisional measures under Article 41 of the Court's Statute. In April the Court delivered judgment.[146] It did not, however, find Yugoslavia guilty of the allegations brought against it.

Nevertheless it ordered Yugoslavia to 'immediately ... take all measures within its power to prevent commission of the crime of genocide ... [and] in particular ensure that any military, paramilitary or irregular armed units which may be directed or supported by it, as well as any organisations and persons which may be subject to its control, direction or influence, do not commit any acts of genocide, of conspiracy to commit genocide, of direct and public incitement to commit genocide, or of complicity in genocide, whether directed against the Muslim population of Bosnia and Herzegovina or against any other national, ethnical, racial or religious group'.

As the *ad hoc* tribunal proceeds to deliver a series of judgments establishing a *jurisprudence constante* relating to genocide, grave or other breaches of the Geneva Conventions, international humanitarian law or the law of war, it will be possible to argue that a new regime in this matter has been established, and that it is no longer necessary to cite the Nuremberg Judgment as the basis of the law. This is important, since it may be argued that while the International Law Commission and General Assembly have both affirmed the principles of international law embodied in the Nuremberg Charter and Judgement, it must not be forgotten that this Tribunal was established for the limited purpose of trying the major war criminals of the European Axis during a conflict that was clearly international in character. While it is true that the tribunal has been established on an *ad hoc* basis and only for events occurring in the former Yugoslavia, nevertheless its competence

---

[146] Case Concerning Application of the Convention on the Prevention and Punishment of Genocide, *Bosnia–Herzegovina* v. *Yugoslavia (Serbia and Montenegro)* (1993) I.C.J. 3. In 1996 the Court dismissed a series of preliminary objections and upheld its jurisdiction to proceed to the merits of the case [1996] I.C.J. 595.

is somewhat broader than that of Nuremberg, and it has the added advantage of having been constituted by decision of the Security Council concurred in by all the members of the United Nations. It, therefore, does not suffer from any allegations that it is creating new law or is an example of 'victors' justice'.

In 1998 a treaty was adopted establishing an International Criminal Court.[147] Although the Court has been established independently of the United Nations, it is to be a permanent tribunal brought into relationship with the world organisation. Its jurisdiction depends on a case being referred to it by a State party or 'by the Security Council acting under Chapter VII of the Charter', and the Council, acting under Chapter VII is given the power by making a Chapter VII decision to defer any hearing for a period of twelve months and this decision may be repeated.[148] Unlike the *ad hoc* tribunal which has primacy over national tribunals, this Court is to be 'complementary' thereto, so that it will have to deny jurisdiction if 'the case is being investigated by a State which has jurisdiction over it, unless the State is unwilling to carry out the investigation or prosecution.' However, recognising a situation which may well result from a revolution, *coup d'état* or devastating war, 'in determining inability in a particular case, the Court shall consider whether, due to a total or substantial collapse or unavailability of its national judicial system, the State is unable to obtain the accused or the necessary evidence and testimony or otherwise unable to carry out its proceedings.[149]

At one time it was thought that an International Criminal Court would possess jurisdiction over offences detailed in the various drafts of the International Law Commission. However, the new Court is clearly intended to deal only with 'the most serious crimes of concern to the international community as a whole', namely, genocide, crimes against humanity, war crimes and aggression.[150] Interestingly enough, although the Nuremberg Tribunal,[151] giving effect to its Charter, considered aggression to be the 'supreme international crime … in that it contains within itself the accumulated evil of the whole', and regardless of the Statement of Principles drawn up by the International Law Commission[152] or the General Assembly's Resolution defining aggression,[153] the draftsmen of the treaty were unable to agree as to what would constitute this offence. Genocide is defined as in the Convention. The definition of crimes against humanity is fairly detailed, indicating how far the international community has departed from the Nuremberg concept, 'when committed as part of widespread or systematic attack [thus excluding acts taken on an individual basis however extensive they may be] directed against any civilian population, with knowledge of the attack: (a) murder; (b) extermination; (c) enslavement; (d) deportation or forcible transfer of

[147] 37 I.L.M. 999.
[148] Arts 13, 16.
[149] Art. 17 (1) (a), 17 (3).
[150] Art. 5.
[151] HMSO, Cmd 6964 (1946) 13; 41 Am. J. Int'l Law (1947) 172, 186.
[152] 1950, Schindler and Toman, 923.
[153] 1974, Res. 3314 (XXIX).

population; (e) imprisonment or other severe deprivation of physical liberty in violation of fundamental rules of international law; (f) torture; (g) rape, sexual slavery, enforced prostitution, forced pregnancy, enforced sterilisation, or any other form of sexual violence of comparable gravity; (h) persecution against any identifiable group or collectivity on political, racial, national, ethnic, cultural, religious, gender [understood as applying to both sexes], or other grounds that are universally recognized as impermissible under international law ... [the requirement of universality would permit continuance of the type of discrimination against women practiced by the Taliban in Afghanistan]; (i) enforced disappearance of persons; (j) the crime of apartheid'. Then there seems to be a 'catch-all' – '(k) other inhumane acts of a similar character intentionally causing great suffering, or serious injury to body or to mental or physical health'. There follows a series of definitions, e.g., 'enslavement means the exercise of any ... of the powers attaching to the right of ownership ... including the exercise of such powers in the course of trafficking in persons, in particular women and children; deportation or forcible transfer means forced displacement ... by expulsion or other coercive acts from the area in which they are lawfully present, without grounds permitted under international law; torture ... shall not include pain or suffering arising only from, inherent in or incidental to, lawful sanctions'[154] – which seems to provide an extremely extensive area for many practices, such as amputation or stoning, which are regarded by a number of, at least, western powers as clearly falling within the concept of torture.

In so far as an international conflict is concerned, the Court possesses jurisdiction over 'war crimes in particular when committed as part of a plan or policy or as part of a large-scale commission of such crimes' and these are listed as grave breaches of the Convention, together with twenty-six other offences described as 'other serious violations of the laws and customs applicable in international armed conflict, within the established framework of international law'.[155] Since the principle of individual responsibility is postulated and jurisdiction exists over the person committing the offence, as well as anyone cooperating in or ordering its commission, the reference to 'plans, policy or large-scale commission' cannot be presumed to exclude jurisdiction over an individual committing a single breach of the law.

In accordance with normal practice the Court is bound to observe the principle *non bis in idem*, the non-retroactivity of its jurisdiction which does not apply to offences committed before it comes into existence – and sixty ratifications are required – there is no period of limitation and the principle of command responsibility, together with a denial of impunity based on status is emphasised. Article 33 makes up for the lacuna in Protocol I and spells out the nature of superior orders and prescription of law:

[154] Art. 7.
[155] The relation of the jurisdiction to non-international conflicts will be considered in ch. 19 below.

1 The fact that a crime within the jurisdiction of the Court has been committed by
   a person pursuant to an order of a Government or of a superior, whether military
   or civilian, shall not relieve that person of criminal responsibility unless:
   (a) The person was under a legal obligation to obey orders of the Government or
       the superior in question;
   (b) The person did not know the order was unlawful; and
   (c) The order was not manifestly unlawful.
2 For the purposes of this article, orders to commit genocide or crimes against
   humanity are manifestly unlawful.

The conditions are cumulative and in accordance with accepted customary law.
However, the article is silent on mitigation, although by Article 78 'in determining the sentence, the Court shall, in accordance with the Rules of Procedure and
Evidence [yet to be drawn up], take into account such factors as the gravity of the
crime and the individual circumstances of the convicted person', when presumably mitigation becomes possible.

While aggression is within the jurisdiction and much emphasis is given to war
crimes, the Court will have jurisdiction over genocide and crimes against humanity even when committed in time of peace.

The United States has made clear its opposition to the Statute, largely because
of the fear that attempts may be made to try American personnel and there exists
a basic conviction that, taking into consideration the number of peace-keeping and
other operations in which American forces may be involved, there is too much
risk that political considerations will become significant in seeking to ground
jurisdiction. However, as pointed out, if the United States were to initiate or indicate an intention to initiate proceedings against Americans in American courts the
Court would lack jurisdiction. Equally important is the fact that only nationals of
parties to the Statute may serve as judges or become members of the Prosecution
and American absence constitutes a major gap. However, until the Court becomes
functional it remains to be seen to what extent it will make a valuable contribution to the enforcement of the law of armed conflict and serve as a strong deterrent against future breaches.

The fact that the Statute of the International Criminal Court lists a series of
offences that constitute crimes against humanity; that the *Tadić* court has
described genocide as being such a crime; and that most people – and law depends
for its acceptance and compliance on public approval – would almost certainly
regard the more serious war crimes, that is to say those directed against human
beings, bearing in mind that the statutory definition is aimed at the protection of
civilians, as crimes against humanity, raises the important question whether it is
not time to abandon both war crimes and genocide as specific concepts, leaving
us to deal solely with crimes against humanity. Even when military personnel are
the victims, certainly in a non-international conflict, when the law of war and the
idea of grave breaches do not apply, leaving only common Article 3 as operative,
the same approach suggests itself.

This proposal goes beyond the definitions to be found in the Statute. This postulates that crimes against humanity should be 'part of a widespread or systematic attack' directed against civilians, and talks of war crimes, 'in particular when committed as a part of a plan or policy or as part of a large-scale commission of such crimes', and amounting to either grave breaches of the Conventions or 'serious violations of the laws and customs applicable in international armed conflicts'. However, if a soldier were on his own initiative to pursue a line of behaviour which involved the killing of every 'enemy' child he came across or the torture and murder of every wounded member of the adverse forces, such conduct would in the eyes of the public clearly amount to crimes against humanity and be condemned as such.

Moreover, adoption of the suggested policy would remove the complex and serious issue of characterisation as between international and non-international conflicts. War crimes are breaches of the conventional or customary law of war, which only applies in interstate conflicts. As has been seen, and will be considered further,[156] in non-international conflicts only common Article 3 is relevant, and there is no indication of how breaches are to be dealt with, although crimes against humanity are perhaps more common in non-international than international conflicts, particularly when religion, race or ideology is in issue. By resorting solely to crimes against humanity, it would no longer be necessary to proceed under one system of law when faced with atrocities in international and another for similar conduct in non-international conflicts. It is time, and this is particularly so when the conflict may be partly international and partly non-international contemporaneously, to apply a system of law which is common, based on the nature of the offence rather than on the nature of the conflict or the status of the offender.

[156] See ch. 19 below.

19

The law and non-international conflicts

The traditional view

One of the longest established principles of international law is that which recognises that states have no right to intervene in the internal or domestic affairs of another state. This principle receives conventional recognition in Article 2(7) of the Charter of the United Nations which declares that nothing in the Charter enables the Organisation to intervene in matters essentially in the internal affairs of any state unless there is a threat to the peace, a breach of the peace or an act of aggression, in which case the United Nations is entitled to have recourse to enforcement measures in accordance with Chapter VII of the Charter.

A non-international conflict is one in which the governmental authorities of a state are opposed by groups within that state seeking to overthrow those authorities by force of arms. In accordance with the fundamental principle of customary international law concerning the independence of a sovereign authority, this type of conflict has traditionally been regarded as falling outside the ambit of international law. If a third state considers its interests or those of its nationals are likely to be seriously affected by the intensity of the conflict it may proclaim its neutrality. Likewise, the parties involved may consider that the conflict has reached a stage of intensity when it is to their advantage to regulate their relations in accordance with the law of war and so declare their recognition of a state of belligerency[1] involving respect for the law of armed conflict by themselves and by third states as neutrals. It is only in such circumstances that customary international law concerned itself with this type of conflict. A declaration of belligerency is usually issued when each party to the conflict possesses a responsible authority exercising governmental functions within the territory under its control and shows willingness to abide by the law of armed conflict, including recognition of the rights of neutrals.

---

[1] During the American Civil War the state of belligerency was considered to exist as a result of the Presidential proclamation of blockade, accompanied by the British proclamation of neutrality, see, e.g, *The Prize Cases* (1863), 67 US 635. As to the position during the Spanish Civil War, 1936–39, see, e.g., Chen, *The International Law of Recognition*, 346–50; Lauterpacht, *Recognition in International Law*, 250–2; Padelford, *International Law and Diplomacy in the Spanish Civil Strife*.

Regardless of the normal position under customary law, states may declare that a particular non-international conflict has reached a stage that warrants treating the conflict, in whole or in part, according to the normal laws of war. An agreement of this kind only binds its parties, and does not necessarily affect the relations of the combatants as between themselves. As a result of attacks during the Spanish Civil War on merchant vessels in the Mediterranean by unidentified submarines, generally understood to be attached to the Franco forces, a number of European powers signed the Nyon Agreement[2] undertaking to counter-attack any submarine attacking a vessel in a manner contrary to that permitted by international law. This was extended later[3] to apply to air and surface attacks on merchant vessels if the attack was 'accompanied by a violation of the humanitarian principles embodied in the rules of international law with regard to warfare at sea'.[4]

Article 3 common to the 1949 Conventions

After the end of World War II a number of conflicts were being waged as a result of desires for independence by various groups in colonial territories, and because of the ideological character of the conflict many of them were accompanied by extreme cruelty. As a result it was decided in 1949 to include in each of the Geneva Conventions a provision introducing the minimum standards of humanity that it was hoped would be observed in future non-international conflicts.

While Article 2 of each Convention states that it applies in any declared war or armed conflict between two or more parties to the Convention, even if the state of war is not recognised by one of them, Article 3 does not attempt to define what is meant by a non-international conflict. It makes clear, however, that the introduction of these minimum rules does not affect the legal status of the parties. As a result, the legal government is still entitled to treat captured opponents in accordance with the national law of treason, as was done by, for example, the United Kingdom in regard to members of the Indian Army who had joined the Japanese after the surrender of Singapore.[5] However, as became clear in 1999, when Yugoslavia resorted to extreme measures amounting to atrocities in seeking to suppress the dissidents in Kosovo, some states, in this case NATO, may, in the name of humanitarianism, seek by means of military force to compel the authoritis to terminate such behaviour. Other than this common Article 3, the 1949 Conventions have no relevance to a non-international conflict, so that persons captured are not entitled to treatment as prisoners of war, and civilian supporters within the territory of either party cannot claim protection in accordance with the

---

[2] 1937, Schindler and Toman, 887.

[3] *Ibid.*, 889.

[4] See ch. 8 above; see also Ronzitti, *The Law of Naval Warfare*, commentary to ch. 16A by Goldie, 489.

[5] See, e.g., Green, 'The Indian National Army trials', 11 Mod. Law Rev. (1948), 47; 'The Azad Hind Fauj: The Indian National Army', *Essays*, 1999, ch. XI.

Civilians Convention. In practice, it is advisable for the ordinary man in the field to treat captured members of the opposing force as if they were prisoners of war, leaving the decision as to their proper status and treatment to governmental authorities.[6]

Common Article 3 lists the following as the minimum conditions to be applied by parties involved in a non-international conflict:

1 persons taking no active part in the hostilities, including members of armed forces [whether government or rebel] who have laid down their arms and those placed *hors de combat* by sickness, wounds, detention [including those it is intended to try for treason, prior to such trial], or any other cause, shall in all circumstances be treated humanely, without any adverse distinction based on race, colour, religion or faith [so that the 'ethnic cleansing' policies pursued in the territories of the former Yugoslavia after the collapse of the state in 1991 were clearly in breach of this], sex, birth or wealth, or any other similar criteria.

To this end the following are at any time and in any place prohibited with regard to such persons:

(a) violence to life and person, in particular murder of all kinds, cruel treatment and torture;

(b) taking of hostages;

(c) outrages upon personal dignity, in particular, humiliating and degrading treatment;

(d) the passing of sentences and the carrying out of executions without previous judgment pronounced by a regularly constituted court affording all the judicial guarantees which are recognised as indispensable by civilised peoples [– since no country is prepared to accept that it is not 'civilised', a rudimentary trial according to normal local practice would appear to satisfy the wording of the provision, even though there might be general condemnation that the proceedings fell below acceptable standards].

2 The wounded and sick shall be cared for.

Despite this last injunction, there have been cases in non-international conflicts, particularly in Latin America, where medical personnel attending the wounded among the anti-government forces have been harassed and even prosecuted.[7]

The intent of the Conventions is that Article 3 should apply to both sides equally, regardless of whether the revolutionary authorities have made any declaration of intent to comply. It might seem that non-compliance would result in charges of war crimes, but since there is no 'war' such trials would normally be in accordance with national criminal legislation,[8] and in fact this position has not been changed by the adoption of Protocol II in 1977. However, during the hostili-

---

[6] This was the practice during World War II with regard to members of the Indian Army who had joined the Japanese-sponsored Indian National Army and were recaptured by the British, and also the practice officially followed by South Africa in its operations against SWAPO, the South West African People's Organisation.

[7] Perhaps the worst example of this was the treatment meted out to the English Dr Shelagh Cassidy.

[8] See, e.g., *Pius Nwaoga* v. *The State* (1972 – Nigeria) 52 I.L.R., 494.

ties in Bosnia in l992, at a time when the authorities in Bosnia had not been recognised as a state, the members of the European Community indicated their intention in due course to bring those in breach of the law of armed conflict to trial as war criminals. In fact, these accusations ultimately led to the expulsion of Yugoslavia from the United Nations. Moreover, the United States announced that it was collecting evidence with a view to those responsible for such activities being ultimately brought to trial, and the Security Council declaring a threat to the peace to exist established, in accordance with Chapter VII of the Charter, an *ad hoc* tribunal for the trial of those accused of serious violations of international humanitarian law. Similar statements were made by NATO regarding activities in Kosovo, but the Yugoslave authorities refused to allow the chief prosecutor of the tribunal to enter the province to collect evidence. A further tribunal was established in respect of similar activities during the civil war in Rwanda.[9]

Article 3 also provides that the ICRC or some other impartial humanitarian organisation may offer its services to the parties in a non-international conflict, and to emphasise the humanitarian intent of the Article it calls on the parties to 'endeavour' to reach agreement among themselves to bring other articles of the Convention into operation. This may result in introducing grave breach clauses and thus authorise trials for war crimes.

There is no provision in Article 3 concerning breaches or enforcement. Further, Article 85 of Protocol I does not include this Article as one the non-compliance with which would amount to a grave breach. However, since the Conventions are binding, and have been held by the Yugoslav tribunal to amount to customary law[10] and since common Article 3 forbids a variety of activities, it may be presumed that it is the intention to ensure that its provisions are in fact observed. It may be possible to argue, therefore, that breach of any of the provisions of this Article, all of which are humanitarian in character, are enforceable in the same manner as are other breaches, even though they do not qualify as grave.

Protocol II

Apart from common Article 3, the first major attempt to introduce international legal control of non-international conflicts by way of a statement of black-letter law is Protocol II, l977,[11] relating to the protection of victims of non-international conflicts. Since the Protocol is a newly created convention, and there has not been time for it to harden into customary law, it creates treaty law only for those states which ratify or accede to it. Not all the major powers, perhaps because they are unlikely to be directly involved in a non-international conflict, have taken this step, while there is little evidence that even those states which have done so are in

[9] 32 I.L.M. 1192; 33 I.L.M. 1598, resp.
[10] *Prosecutor* v. *Dusko Tadić* (1997) 36 I.L.M. 908, para. 577.
[11] Schindler and Toman, 689.

fact complying with its provisions, although in many instances the ICRC is carrying out its functions. Equally, the Palestine Liberation Organisation, certainly before it secured control of any part of the formerly Israeli-administered territories, was outside the scope of the Protocol's operation, even if Israel had become a party thereto. The same is true of both Hamas and the Hezbollah movements.

According to the Protocol a non-international conflict is one, not an international conflict in the sense of Article 1 of Protocol I which includes non-international conflicts conducted in the name of self-determination, occurring in the territory of a party to the Protocol between its armed forces and dissident armed forces or other organised groups. Depending on the gravity of the situation, a military rebellion or attempted coup might fall within the Protocol II definition. These rebellious forces must satisfy the other requirements concerning territory and command, so as to exclude small scattered groups acting independently or lacking a central command even if their resistance to the authorities prove effective. The dissident forces must be under responsible command able to maintain discipline and ensure compliance with the Protocol. More important perhaps, they must also be able to exercise such control over a part of the national territory as to enable them to carry out sustained and concerted military operations and implement the Protocol, which should be respected on a reciprocal basis.

It is noticeable that there is no provision with regard to control of territory in Protocol I, so that a movement claiming to be engaged in a campaign for self-determination and as such conducting an international armed conflict may operate entirely from bases outside the national territory. This is not the case with non-international conflicts governed by Protocol II. In these the dissidents must be in actual control of part of the national territory, so that the threshold for the Protocol to operate is somewhat similar to that which prevailed during the Spanish Civil War when the Nationalist forces acquired recognition as a *de facto* administration with legal immunities similar to those enjoyed by the legitimate government.[12] If the dissident forces are constantly on the move and lack any fixed location from which to exercise control the Protocol will not operate. Guerrilla or partisan activities against the administration, however effective, would therefore not be protected by the Protocol, though they would be covered by common Article 3. Equally, terrorist groups like the German Red Army Faction, even though they describe themselves as national liberation movements protected by Protocol I,[13] or a revolutionary group seeking to overthrow its government and claiming to fall within the scope of Protocol II, would not be protected by that Protocol.

Even though regular governmental armed forces might be involved in the operations, as is the case with campaigns against drug 'barons' in some Latin American countries, if the 'campaigns' in question are mere internal tensions and disturbances, such as riots, strikes, demonstrations,[14] isolated acts of violence and

[12] See, e.g., *The Arantzazu Mendi* [1939] A.C., 256.
[13] See, e.g., *Public Prosecutor* v. *Folkerts* (1977) 74 I.L.R. 695.
[14] The use of the National Guard by the US against, e.g., demonstrating students is not limited by the terms of the Protocol.

other acts of a similar nature, the Protocol does not come into play.[15] This follows from the need for organisation and some semblance of permanent dissidence.

The Protocol in operation

In accord with current understanding of human rights,[16] Protocol II applies without distinction founded on race, colour, sex, language, religion or other opinion, national or social origin, wealth, birth or other status or on any other similar criteria. This provision is similar to that in Protocol I concerning international conflicts, but is even more necessary since so many non-international conflicts are in fact ideological, racial or religious in character.

Reflecting the principle of non-intervention in internal matters, the Protocol specifically states that its provisions may not be invoked to affect the sovereignty of the state or the right of a government to make use of all legitimate means to maintain or re-establish law and order within the state or defend its national unity and territorial integrity. This precludes a claim by any third state that a state's right to suppress a revolt is limited by the Protocol, while the guarantee of territorial integrity is only a reaffirmation of the customary law rule that premature recognition of the independence of part of a state is a wrong against that state.[17] Moreover, although the Protocol would appear to grant rights to parties against one of their fellows in breach of its terms, this does not authorise any direct or indirect intervention in the conflict or internal or external affairs of the state concerned,[18] thus precluding assistance to either party. However, this is not the case if the United Nations condones a premature recognition by admitting the breakaway state as a member as it did in the case of Bangladesh when it broke away from Pakistan in 1971, and with some of the states created from the breakdown of the Soviet Union in 1991, or with the collapse of the former Yugoslavia the same year.

Similarly, despite the provisions of Article 2(7) of the Charter and the terms of the Protocol, to which the majority of the members of the United Nations have become parties, the Security Council has acquiesced in the creation of 'no go' areas for Iraqi aircraft in the north and south of that state as protection for Kurdish and Muslim minorities. Likewise, some Muslim states have supplied the Muslim minority in Bosnia with arms to defend itself against the Serbs and have threatened open intervention on their behalf. In so far as Bosnia is concerned, while the *soi-disant* Bosnian-Serb group fighting the Bosnian government has set up an administration known as Republika SRPSKA which is unrecognised, the various international agencies operating under United Nations authority have dealt with

---

[15] Art. 1(2).

[16] See, e.g., Meron, *Human Rights in Internal Strife: Their International Protection; Human Rights and Humanitarian Norms as Customary Law*, 71–4.

[17] See, e.g., Chen, *The International Law of Recognition* 50–1, 85–6; Lauterpacht, *Recognition in International Law*, 282–4.

[18] Art. 3.

that body as if it were a legitimate state organ and actively intervened in an election held by it. Again, after the Security Council had condemned the [rump] Yugoslavia's military repression in Kosovo, a part of Serbia/Montenegro, which is all that is left of Yugoslavia, first the United Nations and subsequently NATO took an active role in seeking to restore peace and stability, while the latter, without consulting the United Nations, even went so far as to bomb Yugoslav sites and bases and threaten still more extensive intervention.

These actions are based on the contention that the activities of the state authority in each instance is so inconsistent with civilised standards and the generally accepted principles of human rights as to amount to a rejection of all humanitarian considerations,[19] entitling any non-party to the conflict, regardless of the terms of Protocol II, to take action in the name of humanitarian intervention, even though such action clearly amounts to intervention in the internal affairs of the country affected. Of course, when such intervention is undertaken by the Security Council or under its authority, there can be no suggestion that it might be improper.

Protection under Protocol II

All persons not participating in the conflict or who have ceased from doing so having been rendered *hors de combat* because of injury, surrender or detention are entitled to be treated humanely and to receive respect for their person, religious practices, honour and convictions without adverse distinction, although it must be acknowledged that in a non-international conflict political, ethnic or even religious convictions may be basic to the ideology of each party, and it is in these spheres that breaches are most likely to occur.

Reflecting the customary rule prevailing in international conflicts against the denial of quarter, Article 4 prohibits any order against survivors, although it has been claimed that in Bosnia and Kosovo in both of which mass graves have actually been discovered and the bodies evidencing brutal treatment have been disinterred, there have been numerous instances of the general massacre of persons detained. Since the Protocol contains no provisions for enforcement or punishment of breaches, it must be presumed that this provision is merely a reiteration of the customary rule with breaches punishable as such by the law of the country in which they have occurred. With the establishment of the *ad hoc* tribunals and the International Criminal Court the situation has been changed.[20]

Despite the silence on enforcement, Article 4 contains a statement of fundamental guarantees prohibiting at any time and anywhere:

[19] See, e.g., Meron, *Human Rights*.
[20] See, below, under 'Giving the Protocol substance'.

(a) violence to the life, health and physical and mental well-being of persons, in particular murder as well as cruel treatment such as torture, mutilation or any form of corporal punishment [the Protocol is silent as to the situation when national law permits amputation of limbs or corporal punishment in non-emergency situations];

(b) collective punishment [which may, however, be permitted by national law];

(c) taking of hostages [this is now generally regarded as contrary to the customary law of human rights and most legal systems have legislation making it criminal];

(d) acts of terrorism [this term is not defined by the Protocol and is here used in a non-technical sense equivalent to the prohibition in Art. 13(2) of acts 'the primary purpose of which is to spread terror among the civilian population', which they may do even if directed against an individual or a small group and which clearly include some of the acts of the Serb guerrillas in support of their policy of 'ethnic cleansing' in Bosnia in 1992 as well as the measures taken against the Albanian population of Kosovo during 1998 and 1999];

(e) outrages upon personal dignity, in particular humiliating and degrading treatment [this would include the type of treatment accorded to Jews in Germany before the outbreak of World War II], rape, enforced prostitution and any form of indecent assault [which would almost certainly be crimes under the national law];

(f) pillage [though under a different name this, too, would be criminal under the local law];

(g) threats to commit any of the foregoing.

The protection of children

While children are often separated from their parents or other family members during international conflicts, this is likely to be even more common in a non-international conflict. When this is so, they are to receive the aid and protection they need, including an education making provision for their religious and moral care. Whenever possible efforts should be made to reunite them with their families and if their safety requires removal from the area in which they are, as has often been the case in the former Yugoslavia, this should be done whenever possible with the consent of their parents or guardians and they should be accompanied by persons responsible for their safety and well-being. This evacuation has often been under the protection of the ICRC or military units sent to the area as United Nations peace-keepers.

Children under fifteen should not be enlisted or allowed to participate in the hostilities, although a number in fact do so,[21] but they nevertheless remain protected by the Protocol. No death penalty may be imposed upon a person under eighteen, regardless of the offence committed.[22]

---

[21] See, e.g., 1998 report by UN envoy for children and armed conflict, *Globe and Mail*, (Toronto) 23 Oct. 1998.

[22] Arts 4, 6(4) resp.

Protection of civilians

In non-international armed conflicts, as in those of an international character, civilians are to be protected against the dangers arising from the conflict. Neither the civilian population nor individual civilians may be made the object of attack. In the Bosnian conflict, however, the Muslim population, in particular, seems to have been made the object of direct attack by Serb guerrillas. Acts and threats of violence the primary purpose of which is to terrorise the civilian population are forbidden.[23]

The starvation of civilians as a method of combat is forbidden. If therefore the governmental forces were compelled to withdraw they may not take with them stocks of food for their own supporters, if this would endanger the survival of civilians remaining in the evacuated areas. It is equally forbidden to attack, destroy, remove or render unusable objects indispensable to civilian survival, such as foodstuffs, agricultural areas, drinking-water installations, irrigation works and the like, nor may a threat to do anything that would have this effect be used as a measure of pressure against the civilian population which supports the rebels. In many of the non-international conflicts and civil wars raging during 1992 such actions were in fact taken by either the government or its opponents and frequently relief organisations seeking to bring aid to the civilian population were subjected to attacks, or had their supplies stolen. In the former Yugoslavia houses and entire villages have been destroyed with the sole intention of making it impossible for their residents to return even though agreements have been drawn up to permit such return.

Reflecting the new dangers inherent in modern technological developments, works or installations containing dangerous forces, that is to say dams, dykes and nuclear electrical generating stations, must not be attacked, even if they are military objectives, if this might result in the release of dangerous forces and severe losses among the civilian population.[24] This list is exhaustive so that it would not be a breach of the Protocol to destroy a nuclear, chemical or bacteriological installation regardless of the effects upon the civilian population. The Protocol does not define what it means by 'military objective', but since it was drafted at the same Conference and subsequent to Protocol I, it is perhaps safe to assume that the definition in that instrument, Article 52(2), applies here.

Since non-international conflicts are so often ideological and full of hatred for the way of life of the opposing force, it is likely that objects reflecting the beliefs or history of the opponents will be a prime target. It has been alleged that the Serb guerrillas in Bosnia intentionally attack mosques and the anti-Croatian forces did the same to the historic areas of Dubrovnik. Since Protocol II had been ratified by Yugoslavia before it collapsed it is arguable that the successor entities are equally bound, in which case they would be in breach of Protocol II which forbids hostile

---

[23] Pr. II, Art. 13; see also the fundamental guarantees listed in Art. 4.
[24] Art. 15.

acts against historic monuments, works of art or places of worship forming part of the cultural heritage of peoples or to use them in support of the military effort. Unlike the similar provision in Protocol I, Protocol II does not forbid the taking of reprisals against these objects. The Protocol does not indicate whether it is forbidden to remove such works to prevent them falling into the hands of the opposing party, as was done by the Chinese Nationalists when they withdrew from the mainland to Taiwan. However, transfer of such works to a friendly administration abroad to prevent them falling into the hands of successful revolutionaries would be unlawful since the Protocol's purpose is to reduce or control the antagonisms that arise in non-international conflicts and preserve the fabric of the state for the future, and such removal would impede peaceful reconstruction and reconciliation.

Treatment of civilians

One of the principal aims of Protocol II is to ensure that in the event of a non-international conflict, both sides should conduct themselves and their forces in a manner consistent with the minimum requirements of the ordinary law of armed conflict, at least as regards the treatment of civilians, the wounded and prisoners, with attacks limited to military objectives and precautions taken to avoid unnecessary or excessive injury to these persons.

By Article 17 of Protocol II it is forbidden to displace the civilian population for reasons connected with the conflict, unless their security or imperative military reasons so demand. Should such removal prove necessary, it is incumbent upon the authorities responsible to provide, if possible, for their shelter, health, hygiene, safety and nutrition. Similarly civilians must not be compelled to leave their own territory for reasons connected with the conflict, as was done by Serb irregulars in Bosnia and by regular troops in the province of Kosovo by way of 'ethnic cleansing'. This prohibition also means that a defending or retreating authority should not remove the population merely because it fears that it may join its opponents.

As may be seen in almost any non-international armed conflict or one which does not reach the gravity of those covered by Protocol II, acts occur on both sides which, if committed during an international armed conflict would be considered war crimes. However, since such conflicts do not amount to international conflicts they are not within the purview of the law on this matter.[25] In fact, Protocol II is silent on the issue of breaches and their consequences. This means that both the governmental and the rebel authority should treat this type of act in accordance with the national criminal law. In the light of the atrocities committed in the former Yugoslavia in both the international and non-international conflicts taking place in that territory, as well as in the civil war in Rwanda, the Security Council authorised the establishment of *ad hoc* criminal tribunals to try those accused of

---

[25] See ch. 18 above.

offences against international humanitarian law, which was considered to be applicable in both types of conflict.

The treatment of prisoners and detainees

In non-international armed conflicts it is perhaps more necessary to make provision for the protection of those who fall into the hands of their opponents than is the case in an international conflict when ideologies and emotions are not normally so important. The Protocol seeks to provide for the proper treatment and care of all those in the hands of an opponent or whose liberty has been subjected to any restriction.

Article 5 provides that all such persons, including the wounded and sick are to be treated humanely receiving such medical care as their condition requires with no distinction made other than on medical grounds, so that the fact that they have fought on the other side must in no way lead to their being treated less well than their condition demands. All must receive food and water and enjoy the same safeguards concerning health, hygiene, protection against the climate and the dangers of the conflict as the local civilian population whose liberty is not restricted in any way, and if made to work enjoy the benefit of working conditions and safeguards similar to those of the local population. They must be allowed to practise their religion and receive spiritual assistance from those performing religious functions.

All persons whose liberty is restricted in connection with the conflict must be allowed to receive individual and collective relief, and local relief organisations, such as the Red Cross or Crescent, may offer to perform their traditional functions on their behalf. If the civilian population suffers unduly because of lack of supplies essential for survival, relief actions of a humanitarian and impartial nature shall be carried out with the consent of the High Contracting Party concerned, so long as these activities are conducted without discrimination. While the Protocol[26] does not indicate who is to undertake these activities, it may be presumed that it is the organisations already indicated. During the various conflicts in Eastern Europe, Africa and in the Far East in the 1990s these activities were usually discharged by the Red Cross or Crescent. Since there is specific reference to the consent of only the High Contracting Party, it would appear that those in the hands of revolutionaries are not entitled to similar assistance, although in Somalia, the former Yugoslavia and Rwanda various aid societies have sought to provide assistance to both sides.

The authority responsible for the detention or internment is under an obligation, unless family members are detained together, to hold men and women separately, with women under the direct supervision of members of their own sex. There is no similar provision regarding male detainees. All persons detained in

---

[26] Art. 18.

any way are entitled to send and receive letters and cards, subject to any numerical restrictions imposed by the detaining authority.

All detainees and internees, including prisoners belonging to the opposing forces, are to receive the benefit of medical examination and their physical and mental health and integrity shall not be endangered by any unjustified act or omission. They may only receive such medical attention as their condition requires and as is consistent with the generally accepted medical standards applicable in similar cases among those not detained or interned. While the Protocol does not contain any provision forbidding medical experiments against detained person, the above restriction relevant to treatment would clearly prohibit such activities.

To protect those held from the dangers of the conflict, places of detention or internment should not be located close to any combat zone and if the place in question becomes particularly exposed to danger the persons held there should be evacuated under conditions of safety. However, since the movement of forces in a non-international conflict is likely to be more fluid than in an international conflict, these places are likely to become exposed to danger more frequently and it may well be unduly onerous to satisfy this requirement.

When those who have been detained or interned are released the holding authority is obliged to take such steps as are necessary to ensure their security, which may well be gravely endangered if they are released among those loyal to that authority.[27]

Penalties

As regards the trial and punishment of those charged with criminal offences related to the conflict, no sentence shall be passed or sentence executed except pursuant to a conviction pronounced by a court offering the essential guarantees of independence and impartiality. There is nothing in the Protocol to preclude trial by regular military tribunals or those specially created for the purpose so long as they offer these essential guarantees. As a minimum:

> the accused shall be informed of the particulars of the offence charged against him and afforded all necessary rights and means of defence;
> no one shall be convicted other than on the basis of individual responsibility, which accords with the fundamental guarantee against collective punishments;
> in accordance with the principle against retroactivity of criminal law, no one shall be guilty of an offence for an act or omission which was not an offence when committed, nor may punishment be heavier than was applicable at that time, although if the penalty has been lowered he is entitled to such alleviation, and this is so even if not so provided in the national law;
> every accused is to be presumed innocent until proved guilty according to national law, and this provision applies equally to both inquisitorial and accusatorial systems;
> the accused has the right to be tried in his presence, which seems to exclude the

[27] These provisions for the care of detainees are to be found in Art. 5.

328

possibility of a hearing proceeding in the absence of an accused disrupting the proceedings, even if the national law provides for such a procedure;
no accused may be compelled to testify against himself or confess his guilt;
every person must be informed on conviction of all judicial and other remedies as
well as appellate procedures open to him.[28]

If the national system provides for the death penalty for the offence charged, it
must not, regardless of the offence, be pronounced upon any accused under eighteen when the offence was committed, nor shall it be carried out on pregnant
women or the mothers of young children, that is to say those women in charge
of children still young enough to depend on their mother for care, in line with
the intention of preventing the creation of infant orphans too young to fend for
themselves.

When hostilities come to an end, as part of the effort to facilitate a return to
peaceful conditions, the authority in power, whether the original government or
successful rebels, is to endeavour to grant the most extensive amnesty to those
who have participated in the conflict or been deprived of their liberty for reasons
connected with the conflict. This would apparently include those convicted of
treason, but not of common crimes, including assassination.[29] These provisions
were intended to prevent proceedings instituted merely by way of vengeance and
to assist in the rehabilitation of the country after the cessation of hostilities. In
Rwanda, however, the successful Tutsi administration has announced its intention
of trying some thousands of supporters of the overthrown Hutu regime as persons
guilty of crimes against humanity or genocide – and this in addition to any appear-
ing before the *ad hoc* tribunal.

Care of the wounded and sick

Whenever circumstances permit and after any engagement, all possible steps are
to be taken, without delay, to search for and collect the wounded, sick and shipwrecked, and the civilian population may on its own initiative offer to collect and
care for such victims. These persons must be protected from pillage or ill-treatment, and especially from attack by civilian supporters of their captors. They must
also be afforded adequate humane and medical care. Steps must be taken to search
for the dead and provide for their decent disposition, and corpses must be protected from despoliation, so that the type of treatment meted out to the body of
Mussolini in 1945 would now be forbidden during a non-international conflict in
the territory of a party to Protocol II.

Conforming to general medical practice, medical personnel may not be

[28] These provisions are to be found in Art. 6.
[29] In September 1992, as part of the endeavour to create conditions in South Africa con-
ducive to peaceful constitutional developments, the government, in agreement with the
African National Congress, granted amnesty to those accused of murders or acts of terrorism committed in the black struggle, as well as of an assassin belonging to the white forces.

required to give priority to any person except for strictly medical reasons, and medical and religious personnel are to be respected and protected at all times. They must receive all available assistance to enable them to carry out their medical duties, and may not be compelled to do anything which would conflict with their humanitarian mission.[30] They, together with their transports, shall display the distinctive emblem of the red cross or crescent, which is to be respected and not used improperly. There is no provision in the Protocol indicating the penalty if the emblem is improperly used, so that any punitive action rests with the competent authority. The requirement of consent from this authority is to prevent any improper display of the emblem, although, once their offer has been accepted, it may be displayed by civilians who have been authorised to collect and care for the wounded and the dead.

The respect to be accorded to medical transports and the immunity from attack that they enjoy shall only cease if they commit hostile acts outside their proper humanitarian function, and even then only after a warning has been given, with a time-limit when appropriate, and only if the warning and time-limit have been ignored.[31] In Bosnia there were numerous instances of attacks on such transports, many of which appeared to have been intentional, and even though the emblem had been properly displayed. In 1998 in Kosovo, it was alleged by parts of the Albanian population that helicopters exhibiting the emblem had in fact been used to attack them.

In accordance with the Protocol,[32] medical aid must be dispensed without distinction to all requiring it, whether supporting the government or in opposition to it, and no person may be punished for carrying out medical activities compatible with medical ethics. As a result, no medical person may be compelled to perform acts contrary to, or refrain from acts required by medical ethics or any rules embodied in the Protocol relating to the care of the sick, wounded or shipwrecked. This provides a further protection against medical personnel in a non-international conflict resorting to medical experiments upon those entrusted to their care.

In accordance with Article 10, the professional obligations of medical personnel regarding information concerning those in their care must, subject to national law, be respected and, again subject to national law, no person engaged in caring for the wounded or sick may be penalised for refusing or failing to give information concerning his patients. This Article appears to be self-destructive. By introducing the requirement of compliance with national law, a doctor may be required to give information to governmental authorities of all cases he attends involving gun wounds or even to provide information concerning the whereabouts of those considered by the government to be guilty of acts directed against the security of the state.

[30] Art. 9.
[31] Art. 11.
[32] Art. 10.

Giving the Protocol substance

The only statement with regard to educating the public of its rights or the government forces of their duties in the event of a non-international conflict is the single provision that it shall be disseminated 'as widely as possible'.[33] In many cases this may be little more than a pious hope, for countries prone to revolution are not likely to educate their civilian populations as to the rights they enjoy when seeking to overthrow the government.

There is no provision in the Protocol enabling a revolutionary authority to accede thereto, but if the governmental authority has already taken this step it is effective for all the inhabitants of the state. In the event of a non-international conflict affecting such a state, the Protocol will apply automatically. While there is no provision for enforcement or punishment of breaches, activities in defiance of the Protocol constitute breaches of the treaty, but they would not by this mere fact give any other signatory any legal standing to bring an action in respect thereof, since other signatories would not have suffered any damage by virtue of the breach in question. However, it should be noted that there is a growing tendency among states generally, and through the medium of international organisations, including the United Nations, to condemn such activities if they amount to extreme breaches of humanitarian law and threaten some measure of humanitarian intervention or recourse to prosecution of offenders for war crimes or crimes against humanity.[34] In so far as Kosovo is concerned, NATO resorted to bombing Yugoslavia with threats of ground operations should the bombing fail to stop the Yugoslav actions. In view of the reports of atrocities in both the former Yugoslavia and Rwanda, the Security Council acting under Chapter VII, holding that the situation in each constituted a threat to the peace, established Commissions of Inquiry to investigate the facts. As a result of the reports of these Commissions, *ad hoc* tribunals were established to try those accused of crimes against humanity. Complex problems regarding characterisation of the conflict were present in Yugoslavia since the situation was mixed with international and non-international conflicts taking place at one and the same time. This is not the place to discuss the competence of the tribunal as regards the former, nor the more interesting problem as to the competence of the Council to establish such tribunals.[35]

The Yugoslav tribunal was granted jurisdiction[36] over grave breaches of the 1949 Conventions, violations of the laws and customs of war, genocide and crimes against humanity. In so far as international conflicts are concerned, all four heads of jurisdiction are relevant. However, for non-international conflicts, there would be no problem concerning genocide as this is a crime even if committed in peacetime. As to crimes against humanity, as was pointed out in the Report of the

[33] Art. 19.

[34] See, e.g., *The Times*, 24 Sept. 1992.

[35] See, e.g., Green, '*Erdemović – Tadić – Dokmanović*; jurisdiction and early practice of the Yugoslav War Crimes Tribunal' 27 Israel Y.B.H.R. 313 (1997).

[36] The Statute is reprinted at 32 I.L.M. 1192.

Rwanda Commission,[37] the concept of crimes against humanity has developed far beyond what it was at the time of the Nuremberg Judgment, to cover 'gross violations of fundamental rules of humanitarian law and human rights law committed by persons demonstrably linked to a party to the conflict, as part of an official policy based on discrimination against an identifiable group of persons irrespective of war and the nationality of the victim', so that policies of 'ethnic cleansing', mass rape and the like being applied in the former Yugoslavia should, if not amounting to genocide, clearly constitute crimes against humanity. Moreover, Article 5 of the Statute[38] specifically states that the Tribunal has power 'to prosecute persons responsible for [such] crimes when committed in armed conflict, whether international or internal in character, and directed against any civilian population ...' and the *Erdemović* court has held[39]

> crimes against humanity are serious acts of violence which harm human beings by striking what is most essential to them: their life, liberty, physical welfare, health, and dignity. They are inhumane acts that by their extent and gravity go beyond the limits tolerable to the international community, which must perforce demand their punishment. But crimes against humanity also transcend the individual because when the individual is assaulted, humanity comes under attack and is negated. It is therefore the concept of humanity as victim which essentially characterises crimes against humanity,

and it is during non-international conflicts that the most horrendous acts going 'beyond the limits tolerable to the international community' are likely to be committed.

In a non-international conflict, the sole relevance of the Conventions is common Article 3, and since Yugoslavia had ratified the Conventions this would apply. Likewise, Yugoslavia's ratification of Protocol II would operate by continuity in the case of Serbia/Macedonia and succession for Croatia and Bosnia. In the *Erdemović* case, the indictment covered both crimes against humanity and violations of the laws or customs of war. On his pleading guilty to the former, the Tribunal dismissed the charges regarding the latter.[40] This lends support to the contention that once a charge of crimes against humanity is lodged, there is no real reason to bring any other since such a charge may be regarded as 'wholesale' in the character embracing within itself all other breaches of the law of armed conflict, and since the *Tadić* tribunal has held that genocide is itself a crime against humanity[41] there is no need to charge that offence separately and this is true whether the conflict concerned is international or non-international.

In the first case to come before it, the Tribunal held[42]

---

[37] UN DOC/S/1994/1125, paras. 114–17.
[38] The Statute of the Tribunal is to be found in 32 I.L.M. 1192.
[39] Para. 28.
[40] See Green, '*Drazen Erdemović*: The International Criminal Tribunal for the former Yugoslavia in action', 10 Leiden J. Int'l Law 1997, 363.
[41] Case No., IT-94-1-T, 14 Jul 1997, para. 8.
[42] *The Prosecutor* v. *Dusko Tadić*, 2 Oct. 1995, 35 I.L.M. 31, para. 70.

an armed conflict exists whenever there is a resort to armed force between States or protracted armed violence between governmental authorities and organized armed groups or between such groups within a State. International humanitarian law applies from the initiation of … armed conflicts and extends beyond the cessation of hostilities until a general conclusion of peace is reached; or, in the case of internal conflicts, a peaceful settlement is achieved. Until that moment, international humanitarian law continues to apply in the territory of the warring States or, in the case of internal conflicts, the whole territory under the control of a party, whether or not actual combat takes place there.

Perhaps one of the most interesting and significant holdings of the *Tadić* court[43] relates to the applicability of the laws or customs of war to a non-international conflict:

term 'laws and customs of war' should not be limited to international conflicts. Laws or customs of war include prohibitions of acts committed both in international and internal armed conflicts. Indeed, common Article 3 is clear evidence that customary international law limits the conduct of hostilities in internal armed conflicts. However, unlike contracting parties to treaties, the International Tribunal is not called upon to apply conventional law but instead is mandated to apply customary international law. Therefore, the element of internationality forms no jurisdictional criterion even if the Hague Convention [IV in which the term first appears] was originally envisaged by the Contracting Parties to apply to international conflicts. Violations of the laws or customs of war are commonly referred to as 'war crimes'. They can be defined as crimes committed by any person in violation of recognized obligations under rules derived from conventional or customary law applicable to the parties.

… [H]istorically laws or customs of war have not been limited to the nature of the conflict they regulate. [Thus, t]he Lieber Code[44] … was drafted to regulate the conduct of the United States armed forces during the American Civil War … The Trial Chamber finds that it has subject-matter jurisdiction under Article 3 [of its Statute concerning violations of the laws or customs of war] because [such] violations are a part of customary international law over which it has competence regardless of whether the conflict is international or national … Common Article 3 imposes obligations that are within the subject-matter of Article 3 of the Statute because those obligations are a part of customary international law … [T]he acts proscribed by common Article 3 constitute criminal offences under international law. The fact that [this] Article is part of customary international law was definitively decided by the International Court of Justice in the *Nicaragua* case[45] in which the Court, applying customary international law, determined that the rules contained in common Article 3 constitute a 'minimum yardstick' applicable in both international and non-international conflicts, thus finding that these provisions are part of customary international law.

[43] *Prosecutor* v. *Dusko Tadić*, IT-94-1-T, 10 Aug. 1995, paras. 60–74.
[44] Schindler and Toman, 3.
[45] *Military and Paramilitary Activities* (Nicaragua–US – Merits) [1986] I.C.J. 4.

Equally important, though not an issue that need be pursued in detail here, the *Tadić* tribunal held that, in the circumstances of the case, the Bosnian-Serb forces were sufficiently distinct from the Yugoslav-Serb authorities and forces to be considered a separate group of dissident Bosnians so that any persons held by them would be of the same nationality as themselves, that is to say Bosnians, and therefore could not be considered as protected persons under Convention IV (Civilians) since the persons detained could not be regarded as 'in the hands of a Party to the conflict or Occupying Power of which they are not nationals.'[46] On the other hand, there is much evidence to suggest that the Croatian-Bosnians are sufficiently close to the Croatian authorities and forces to be regarded as part or surrogates thereof so that, presumably, a contrary decision might be reached should they be holding Bosnian nationals.[47]

There need not be much discussion of the situation in Rwanda since the tribunal for that conflict was granted jurisdiction only over genocide, crimes against humanity and violations of common Article 3 of the Geneva Conventions. Even if the Tribunal's Statute had not specifically granted such jurisdiction over these offences committed in a particular non-international conflict, thus giving the Tribunal no option but to apply its constituent instrument, there can be no question that the offences specified would constitute crimes which are in any case amenable to the ordinary rules of international humanitarian law applicable in both international and non-international conflicts.

When the International Criminal Court agreed upon in 1998[48] begins its work the situation will be simplified. This tribunal is to exercise jurisdiction over genocide, crimes against humanity, war crimes and aggression. While aggression envisages state action and therefore results in an international conflict and war crimes are defined, in the first instance, as grave breaches or 'other serious violations of the laws and customs applicable in international armed conflicts', both genocide and crimes against humanity may be committed in both types of conflict. Moreover, the definition of crimes against humanity is limited to offences against civilians, suggesting that, even in a non-international conflict, it is not possible for military personnel to be victims of such offences. Since the definition of war crimes, though primarily concerned with international conflicts, does extend to 'serious violations of Article 3 common to the four Geneva Conventions', an apparent jurisdictional lacuna has been filled. The Court is also granted jurisdiction over 'other serious violations of the laws and customs applicable in armed conflicts not of an international character, within the established framework of international law'. While there is no reference to the 'laws or customs of war', a list is provided of the acts envisaged, and while these again seem primarily those in which civilians would be victims, these do include 'killing or wounding treacherously a combatant adversary; declaring that no quarter will be given; subjecting

[46] Trial Chamber Opinion and Judgment, 7 May 1997, 36 I.L.M. 908.
[47] See Green, '*Erdemović – Tadić – Dokmanović*' loc.cit.
[48] 37 I.L.M. 999.

persons who are in the power of another party to the conflict to 'physical mutilation' or any medical or scientific experimentation not in the interest of the victim, that is to say offences which, with the exception of the last mentioned, are almost exclusively directed against military personnel. Further, it is possible to argue that the laws and customs applicable in armed conflict falling 'within the established framework of international law' will include such principles as are laid down for non-international conflicts by the Yugoslav and Rwanda tribunals and will be indicative of what laws and customs fall 'within the established framework of international law' relevant to non-international conflicts.

In the light of the practice of the two *ad hoc* tribunals together with whatever is produced by the International Criminal Court there may develop a clear and well-established system expounding the law governing both international and non-international conflicts, perhaps even to the extent of supporting the contention that both should be governed by the same penal system.

20

United Nations operations

United Nations forces

The overriding purpose of the United Nations is the preservation of peace. With this in view it seeks to limit the right of any state to resort to war. Article 2(4) includes among the Principles of the Organisation that 'all members shall refrain in their international relations from the threat or use of force against the territorial integrity or political independence of any state, or in any other manner inconsistent with the Purposes of the United Nations'. This is little more than a reiteration of the ban on force as an instrument of national policy in the Kellogg–Briand Pact.[1] It must, however, be read in conjunction with Chapter VII of the Charter which states that 'the Security Council shall determine the existence of any threat to the peace, breach of the peace, or act of aggression and shall make recommendations, or decide what measures shall be taken ... to maintain or restore international peace and security'. Articles 41 and 42 indicate that these include measures short of force, such as the severance of diplomatic or economic relations, or even 'such action by air, sea, or land forces as may be necessary ... [and this] may include demonstrations, blockade, and other operations by air, sea, or land forces of Members of the United Nations'. Further, by Article 43 it was envisaged that the Council would enter into agreements with members for the latter to have available the necessary forces. So far, however, no such agreements have been entered, other than on an *ad hoc* basis in specific cases, although in 1992 the Secretary-General emphasised, in the light of the Gulf War and other developments, the importance of trying to put life into this commitment and called upon members to earmark troops to be available on call by the United Nations whenever needed,[2] although this has not yet been effected in any real fashion on an organised basis. When states have agreed to second forces to the United Nations either for enforcement or peace-keeping activities, they do so in accordance with agreements which specify the administrative, financial and disciplinary arrangements that are to apply,[3] although supreme authority rests with the

[1] 1928, 94 L.N.T.S., 57; 4 Hudson, *International Legislation.*
[2] *The Times*, 22 Sept. 1992.
[3] See, however, proposal by UN Sec. Gen. re 'Model agreement between the UN and

Secretary-General.[4] When raising such a force, the Secretary-General will require undertakings from the states providing contingents that their forces are under a responsible commander able to exercise disciplinary authority and jurisdiction over offences committed by members of his unit.

Although Chapter VII may have envisaged inter-state conflicts as being those threatening international peace, the troubles in the former Yugoslavia, a well as the atrocities committed during the civil war in Rwanda led the Council to decide that both of these constituted threats to the peace and, acting in accordance with its powers under Chapter VII, it established *ad hoc* tribunals for the trial of those accused of crimes against international humanitarian law.[5]

Since there is no special law relating to enforcement or other military measures taken in the name of the United Nations, all such operations are governed by the ordinary rules concerning armed conflict. At its Zagreb Conference in 1971 the Institute of International Law spelled out the Conditions of Application of Humanitarian Rules of Armed Hostilities in which United Nations Forces May be Engaged.[6] Having stated in Article 1 that the term 'United Nations Forces' applies to 'all armed units under the control of the United Nations', it continued

2. The humanitarian rules of the law of armed conflict apply to the United Nations as of right and they must be complied with in every circumstance by United Nations Forces which are engaged in hostilities.

   The rules referred to … include in particular

   (a) the rules pertaining to the conduct of hostilities in general and especially those prohibiting the use or some uses of certain weapons, those concerning the means of injuring the other party, and those relating to the distinction between military and non-military objectives;

   (b) the rules contained in the Geneva Conventions of … 1949;

   (c) the rules which aim at protecting civilian persons and property.

3 A. If United Nations Forces are set up through individual recruitments, the United Nations shall issue regulations defining the rights and duties of the members of such Forces.

   In the event of these Forces becoming involved in hostilities, these regulations shall name the international authorities, which, in regard to said Forces, shall be vested with the regulatory executive and judicial powers to secure effective compliance with the humanitarian rules of armed conflict.[7]

   B. If United Nations Forces are composed of national contingents with regard to which the United Nations has not issued any regulations such as those mentioned in the preceding paragraph, effective compliance with the humanitarian rules of armed conflict must be secured through agreements concluded

Member States contributing personnel and equipment to UN peace-keeping operations', Gen. Ass. Doc. A/46/185, 23 May 1991; see also e.g., Higgins, *United Nations Peace-Keeping*, Cassese (ed.), *United Nations Peace-Keeping*. The Model Agreement may be found in Kelly, *Peace Operations*, 1997, 63.

[4] For a sketch of the chain of command see, UN, *The Blue Helmets*, 323–8.

[5] See ch. 18, 19 above.

[6] Schindler and Toman, 903.

[7] In 1998 after disclosure of the role of British mercenaries in Sierra Leone it was

between the organization and the several States which contribute contingents.

These agreements shall at least confer upon the United Nations the right to receive all information pertaining to, and the right to supervise at any time and at any place, the effective compliance with the humanitarian rules of armed conflict by each contingent.

These agreements shall at least confer upon the United Nations the right to receive all information pertaining to, and the right to supervise at any time and at any place, the effective compliance with the humanitarian rules of armed conflict by each contingent.

Since each contingent remains under its own national command and law there may well be conflicts as to the proper role of its members in, for example, protecting the local civil population by force of arms, because of varying provisions in United Nations and national rules of engagement.[8]

If the forces operate under a unified command described as the United Nations Command, as was the case in Korea, the same rules apply as in any allied operation. Because the United Nations is not a state and therefore not a party to the Geneva Conventions, any central prison camp or centre for the holding of detained civilians would have to be under the nominal control of an officer of one of the national contingents making up the force, and it would be the responsibility of the state concerned and that of the forces making any capture to ensure that the provisions of the Conventions are fully complied with. However, during the Korean hostilities, the United Nations Command 'made the decision to consider itself to be the Detaining Power for all prisoners of war captured by the troops of the various national elements which had been made available to the UNC; and there being no national laws available to regulate the conduct and punishment of prisoners of war, it was necessary to promulgate a set of 'Rules' to govern the disciplinary and penal problems which were inevitable'.[9]

As to the general application of the Geneva Conventions, bearing in mind that the United Nations is not a party thereto and so cannot take advantage of the rights nor be burdened by the obligations thereunder, it should be noted that Article 38 of the Vienna Convention on Treaties[10] stipulates that nothing in the articles relating to third parties 'precludes a rule set forth in a treaty from becoming binding upon a third State as a customary rule of international law, recognized as such'. It was clearly established at Nuremberg that the Hague Conventions together with

suggested that peace-keeping and even peace-enforcing duties should be contracted out to such groups. However, the problem of supervision and liability would then be even more complex, see *The Times* (London) 5, 12 May 1998; see also statement by David Shearer, former UN adviser in Liberia and Rwanda, at conference of International Institute for Strategic Studies, London, 30 Mar. 1998, reported in *European Stars and Stripes*, 31 Mar. 1998.

[8] See, e.g., McCoubrey and White, 'The laws of armed conflict and UN forces', in *The Blue Helmets: Legal Regulation of UN Military Operations*, 1996, 159.

[9] Levie, *Documents on Prisoners of War*, US Naval War College, International Law Studies, 60 (1979), 564.

[10] 1969, 8 I.L.M. 679.

the 1929 Geneva Convention had hardened into customary law. The 1949 Conventions are part of the same system and, therefore, the system established thereby has achieved the same level. Moreover the *ad hoc* tribunal for Yugoslavia held in the *Tadić case* that the Conventions were in fact now part of customary law.[11]

It is possible for members of the United Nations to agree, either in advance or when a situation arises, to treat the United Nations Force as an independent force with its own command structure able and obliged to observe the laws of armed conflict. It would be necessary for the state against which operations are being undertaken to accept such a force as independent from the constituent national contingents, and this is a political and not a legal decision.

Should the members of the United Nations agree to allow the organisation to raise its own force as a standing force, with its own chain of command and administrative system, enrolment by individual volunteers would be in accordance with the terms of service drawn up by the United Nations. This task would probably be undertaken by the Military Staff Committee provided for in Article 47 of the Charter.

It is also open to the parties to the Geneva Conventions to agree that the United Nations be allowed to make a declaration of adherence to the Conventions. This, however, would amount, for those parties agreeing, to an amendment as between themselves of the terms relating to accession to the Conventions. Should the United Nations itself be a party to the conflict, as it would if a United Nations Force was operating, it is open to the Organisation and the other party to the conflict to agree that the Conventions should apply.[12] In view of the functions allotted to the International Committee of the Red Cross by the Conventions, the consent of that body would also be required, and it is the practice that the Sec. Gen. inform the ICRC that UN forces will apply the principles of the Conventions 'as scrupulously as possible'.[13] Should there be no agreement to bring the Conventions into operation, the United Nations Force would be obliged in its relations with the adverse party to apply the terms of Article 3 common to the four Conventions, since these represent the minimal of international humanitarian law, and constitute customary law. The fact that the party or parties confronting United Nations Forces do not comply with the provisions of the customary or conventional international law of armed conflict, does not excuse the United Nations Force from compliance. What has been said here of the obligation of a UN force to comply with international humanitarian law applies equally to any coalition forces acting in accordance with a Security Council decision as well as to any force operating in the name of some other international governmental organisation like NATO.

[11] See ch. 19 above.

[12] When the Korean conflict began none of the parties involved had yet become bound by the Conventions. Statements were, however, made on behalf of the UN Command and the Korean and Chinese authorities that they would abide by the terms of those Conventions. However, the UN Command and various national contingents complained that the Chinese and North Korean authorities did not treat prisoners in accordance with their undertakings.

[13] See, e.g., letter from U Thant to ICRC, Int'l Rev. Red X, Jan. 1962.

The rights of member states

The only freedom of action left to members in matters of this kind is to be found in Article 51 which emphasises that 'nothing in the Charter shall impair the inherent right of individual or collective self-defence if an armed attack occurs against a member, until the Security Council has taken the measures necessary to maintain international peace and security'. This leaves open the question whether anticipatory or preventive self-defence is still permitted as use of the term 'inherent' seems to imply. It should be noted that this provision relates to the *jus ad bellum*, the right to resort to war, and has nothing to do with the *jus in bello*, what may be done during a war undertaken by way of self-defence. From a practical point of view it cannot imply an obligation upon a victim of aggression resorting to self-defence that, unless ordered to do so by the Security Council, it must terminate its activities once the immediate threat has been terminated.

In accordance with Article 51 collective self-defence is equally permitted, thus enabling a coalition or group of states to act under this rubric when any state is attacked, as happened when Kuwait was attacked in 1990, provided the Security Council does not decide that this action is not justified by way of collective self-defence or takes over the operation on its own account. Further Article 52 envisages the existence of regional arrangements for dealing with the maintenance of international peace and Article 53 provides that the Council shall make use of such arrangements for this purpose when suitable, but no such arrangement may itself undertake enforcement measures without Council authorisation, although in 1998 both the United States and NATO decided to act alone in defence of the Albanian population in Kosovo, even though there was some debate whether the various Security Council resolutions calling for cessation of repressive activities by the Yugoslav authorities did in fact authorise action by force. In fact, NATO declined to consult the Security Council to evade a Russian or Chinese veto.

Since all members of the United Nations are obliged to abide by the terms of the Charter and since by Article 25 they have undertaken 'to accept and carry out the decisions of the Security Council', the question arises whether, if the Council authorises such action or undertakes it in its own name, a member of the United Nations may any longer claim to be neutral in such circumstances,[14] as was done by Iran during the Gulf War, or to assist or support a member against whom the action is being taken, as was done by Jordan at that time. It would appear that such action is inconsistent with the obligations of membership, although in the two instances cited neither the United Nations nor the Coalition powers took any active measures to bring the two countries into line.

While the decisions of the Security Council are legally binding upon all members, it must be borne in mind that the Council is made up of the representatives of the member states who act in accordance with instructions received from their governments. This means that the decisions reached are in fact based on political

[14] See, e.g., von Grünigen, 'Neutrality and peace-keeping', in Cassese, 125.

grounds, even though each member may make this decision in the light of its interpretation of the legal meaning of the Charter and its application to the issue that
has arisen.

Enforcement measures

While the United Nations will only authorise action in accordance with the terms
of the Charter against a state which is or is threatening to become an aggressor,
the law of armed conflict will apply equally to both sides if the Council decides
that enforcement measures must be undertaken. The normal rules of both the
Hague and Geneva law, together with any rules of relevant customary or treaty-
created law will apply on a reciprocal basis, so that the aggressor is equally protected and bound as those taking action against him.[15]

On only one occasion has the United Nations undertaken enforcement measures in its own name in accordance with a decision of the Security Council condemning a state, which was a non-member not recognised by the majority of
members, for an act of aggression against another. This was in 1950 when North
Korea invaded the South and the Council, there being no agreements of the type
envisaged by Article 43, called upon members to provide forces placed under a
unified United Nations command, the commander having been nominated by the
President of the United States who subsequently, without consulting the United
Nations, dismissed him for insubordination.

Unlike its actions in relation to the invasion of South Korea, when Iraq invaded
Kuwait in 1990 the Council did not raise a United Nations force. Instead, it passed
a series of Resolutions[16] condemning the invasion and calling upon Iraq to withdraw. When Iraq failed to comply, the Council, without stating that any armed
conflict existed between the United Nations or its members and Iraq called for
economic sanctions amounting to a blockade[17] of that state. In accordance with
this resolution[18] a number of states directed their naval forces to interdict trade
with Iraq, intercepting 'neutral' vessels, firing across the bows when necessary,
and diverting them with their cargoes. As to the existence of a conflict, this began
as between Kuwait and Iraq from the moment of the invasion which was met with
limited resistance. It may perhaps be argued that the countries enforcing the naval
interdiction were acting jointly with Kuwait in collective self-defence and were
thus entitled, particularly in view of the Security Council Resolution, to take

---

[15] See, e.g., Lauterpacht, 'Rules of warfare in an unlawful war', in Lipsky, 89.

[16] See, e.g., 13 I.L.M., 1990, 1323–36, 1561–5; see also Green, 'The "Gulf" War, and
the UN and the law of armed conflict', 28 Archiv des Völkerrechts (1991), 369; Greenwood, 'New world order or old? The invasion of Kuwait and the rule of law', 55 Mod. Law
Rev. (1992), 53; Centre de Droit International, Brussels, 'Entre les lignes: la Guerre du
Golfe et le droit international', 1991.

[17] See ch. 8 above, text to n. 103 *et seq.*

[18] Res. 661, 1325.

action which was normally only permissible during a war. Subsequently, when these measures were found to be inadequate, the Council passed a further resolution,[19] setting an ultimate date[20] by which Iraq was to evacuate Kuwait, failing which 'member States co-operating with Kuwait [were authorised] ... *to use all necessary means to uphold and implement*' all the resolutions that had been adopted in this matter. Consequently when the date in this ultimatum expired, those nations comprising the Coalition commenced military action by way of enforcement of the various Security Council resolutions.

Regardless of statements in the press and occasionally by politicians, the operations against Iraq were not truly United Nations enforcement measures. Rather they were measures authorised by the Security Council and undertaken by a group of members exercising the discretion given them in the various resolutions, all of which called for the withdrawal of Iraq from Kuwait. During these military operations, in spite of the fact that Iraq was an aggressor and the measures taken could be regarded as punitive, the Coalition authorities made every endeavour to ensure that the law of armed conflict, including Protocol I which had not come into force for Iraq or its major opponents, was fully observed even though Iraq and its forces ignored its restrictions in a variety of ways.[21]

Unlike the operations undertaken in Korea, the military personnel engaged in action against Iraq remained members of their own national forces under their own commanders although under the supreme strategic command of an officer belonging to the United States armed forces. They wore no insignia to identify them with the United Nations and the command was under no obligation to pay heed to United Nations directives. In the case of the former Yugoslavia, national contingents of peace-keepers were deployed in accordance with Security Council resolutions, but their rules of engagement were limited to self-defence and defence of their equipment, which resulted in criticism when they failed to protect civilians under threat, even when those civilians were held in United Nations 'safe areas', areas which were attacked by Serb-Bosnians who in fact went so far as to hold United Nations peace-keepers hostage. At a later stage these United Nations forces were replaced by military units raised by NATO contingents whose rules of engagement were somewhat wider than had been those of their predecessors.

Since the United Nations is not a state it cannot become a party to the Geneva Conventions. Nevertheless, states seconding forces for United Nations purposes are parties and the forces concerned remain protected in every way under the Conventions and the customary rules of armed conflict. Therefore, whether they wear blue berets and United Nations emblems or not they remain protected by the law of armed conflict and are entitled, if captured, to treatment as prisoners of war.[22]

[19] Res. 678, 1565 (italics added).
[20] As to the nature of an ultimatum, see ch. 4 above, text to n. 19 *et seq.*
[21] See, e.g., US Dept. of Defense Report *Conduct of the Persian Gulf War*, App. O – *The role of the law of war*, 31 I.L.M., 1992, 615. For an account of the treatment received by British SAS personnel, see *The Times*, 17 Oct. 1991.
[22] See ch. 10 above.

Moreover, since the Conventions are now considered to amount to customary law, United Nations forces would in any case be protected, although until the International Criminal Court is operating enforcement would rest with national tribunals.

Peace-keeping operations

It should be noted that by using the term 'enforcement measures' or even 'armed conflict' rather than 'war' for incidents in which military action is taken in the name of the United Nations, there need be no debate whether the United Nations, not being a state, is able to engage in war and enjoy the rights of a belligerent. Moreover, by using terms of this kind the United Nations enjoys freedom to authorise action in a variety of situations likely to endanger the maintenance of international security, including, as has been seen in the former Yugoslavia and Rwanda, non-international conflicts.

The most usual situation in which forces under the control of the United Nations operate, that is to say, do so in the name of the Organisation consequent upon a resolution of the Security Council authorising the Secretary-General to raise such a force, is one in which the members of the Council consider that deployment of personnel in the name of the Organisation may help to preserve the peace. Such troops, wearing the blue berets and armbands of United Nations forces, constitute an interposition or peace-keeping force, and are frequently stationed between rival forces creating a *cordon sanitaire* between the antagonists. United Nations emblems may only be worn by authority of the Organisation and by Protocol I[23] their improper use to secure a protected status is an act of perfidy and punishable as such.

Forces raised in this fashion have frequently been employed to serve after a civil war has terminated as in Cambodia, after major military operations have taken place as in the Middle East, or to separate rival national groups in a divided country as in Cyprus or in Bosnia, even when active operations are still in progress. Their role is strictly speaking non-military, it being hoped that their presence between the rival forces or in the vicinity will inhibit those forces from resorting to further hostile action, and they are under rules of engagement which limit the use of their weapons to self-defence if they or their stores are attacked, but not permitting their use merely because there is a revival of hostilities between the opposing forces. In the former Yugoslavia, when it became clear that peace-keeping in the traditional sense was not likely to prove successful, the peace-keepers were replaced by 'peace-makers', ultimately operating under NATO rather than the United Nations directly, and these forces were on occasion supported by aerial bombardment of Serb installations. In Kosovo, NATO acted without United Nations authorisation.

United Nations forces may also be used to supervise an election or administer a

---

[23] Art. 37(1)(d).

territory pending a plebiscite or referendum as to its future. Increasingly, the United Nations has undertaken humanitarian action to assist groups that are victims of civil wars or other internal disturbances and has called upon member states to provide military personnel to protect the activities of relief organisations, and to secure the safety of airports or seaports and keep them open so that relief supplies may be brought in. Although they are not normally permitted to take offensive action, in 1992 they were authorised to take action to protect the supplies being brought in for these humanitarian purposes. In September 1992 the Secretary-General announced that peace-keeping troops in Bosnia–Herzegovina 'would follow normal peace-keeping rules of engagement [and] would thus be authorised to use force in self-defence ... It is to be noted that in this context self-defence is deemed to include situations in which armed persons attempt by force to prevent UN troops from carrying out their mandate'. He also stated that the force would only protect those convoys it was asked to by the United Nations High Commissioner for Refugees and would escort freed prisoners of war to safety if asked to do so by the Red Cross.[24] However, for the main part the forces concerned did not construe their rules of engagement as permitting them to use force to protect local civilians. In many cases such restrictions were the result of national rules of engagement, regardless of the rules issued by the Secretary-General.

It is likely that this definition of self-defence will become generally accepted for United Nations forces in all circumstances, so that if the force carrying out these duties is attacked, any actions taken by way of self-defence must be limited by humanitarian considerations and the force employed proportionate to the objective sought, namely, suppression of the activity necessitating this response.[25]

If infiltrators, such as thieves, marauders or others, penetrate the lines or camps of a United Nations Peace-keeping Force, they should, until they can be returned to their own authorities, be held in conditions at least as satisfactory as those for prisoners of war. This would be in accord with the Model Agreement prepared by the Secretary-General in May 1991,[26] by which:

> The United Nations peace-keeping operations shall observe and respect the principles and spirit of the general international conventions applicable to the conduct of military operations. The international conventions referred to above include the four Geneva Conventions of 1949 and their Additional Protocols of 1977 and the UNESCO Convention on the Protection of Cultural Property in the event of armed conflict.[27] The Participating State shall therefore ensure that the members of its national contingent serving with the United Nations peace-keeping operation be fully acquainted with the principles and spirit of these Conventions.

This suggests that the members of a peace-keeping force do not need the same intensive training in regard to these instruments as they stipulate for members of

---

[24] *The Times*, 16 Sept. 1992.
[25] See, e.g., White, *The United Nations and the Maintenance of International Peace*.
[26] *The Times*, 22 Sept. 1992.
[27] 1954, Schindler and Toman, 745.

the forces who may be engaged in actual combat. Problems arose in Somalia when members of the Canadian peace-keeping contingent ill-treated Somali civilian detainees, involving unlawful killing, because of bad training, inadequate command control and lack of knowledge of the law of armed conflict.[28]

Should United Nations forces be deployed, in areas where civil wars or non-international conflicts as defined in Protocol II are in progress, even though the parties may not have been observing the terms of that Protocol, the role, function, rights and obligations of the United Nations personnel are the same as they are in any peace-keeping operation.

UN peace-keepers as prisoners

When undertaking peace-keeping operations United Nations Forces are not usually present in any hostile capacity and, normally, other than when acting in self-defence, do not engage in any sort of armed conflict. Their main task apart from the humanitarian aspects, is to prevent conflict not only as it affects themselves, but primarily as it affects the parties they are seeking to separate and keep apart. As a result, it might be assumed the Geneva Conventions and the Hague law cannot govern their activities or protect them in any way.

Since, however, the Civilians Convention of 1949 operates to protect any non-combatant in the hands of a party to a conflict,[29] it is probable that members of a United Nations Peace-keeping Force falling into the hands of such a party would be protected by this Convention. A difficulty arises in the case of members of such a Force who are members of the armed forces of the countries providing contingents and who are captured in uniform even though they also wear United Nations insignia. It seems incongruous to regard such persons as civilians and this means that, until such time as arrangements are made for their liberation, they would probably be entitled to treatment similar to that afforded prisoners of war.[30] Moreover, since United Nations Forces are considered to be operating in accordance with the rules of international humanitarian law and these are expected to operate reciprocally it is most likely that both the United Nations and the state which has provided them will maintain that they are protected by the Prisoners of War Convention if captured, although in Somalia and Rwanda a number were slaughtered and in Bosnia a number taken hostage.

In addition to any special agreement made for the protection of members of a United Nations Peace-keeping Force, they are entitled to the privileges and immunities provided in the 1946 Convention on the Privileges and Immunities of the

---

[28] See *Dishonoured Legacy: The Lessons of the Somalia Affair*, Report of the Commission of Inquiry into the Deployment of Canadian Forces to Somalia, 1997.

[29] See ch. 12 above. When, in 1999, Serb forces captured three US personnel on the Kosovan–Albanian border, the US, having first demanded their release, insisted that they be treated as prisoners of war.

[30] See ch. 10 above.

United Nations.[31] This protects them from arrest or seizure of their baggage, but makes no reference to their position if called upon to play an active role in any conflict. This is because at that time it was not envisaged that they would be called on to play this type of role.

The guiding principle

The guiding principle for all persons engaged in actions on behalf of the United Nations whether as part of a permanent or temporary United Nations Force, and whether engaged in peace-keeping or peace-enforcement operations, is that they operate at all times in accordance with the principles of international humanitarian law and, when necessary, with the law of armed conflict, as embodied in convention or customary law. Moreover, no measures of an enforcement nature had been taken by then, to ensure protection of United Nations proclaimed 'safety zones', but when those established in Bosnia were attacked by Serb dissident forces the United Nations peace-keepers proved unable – or unwilling – to protect them. Whenever they are engaged in peace-keeping operations, they must operate on a basis of absolute non-discrimination among the parties to any conflict which they have been sent to regulate. In 1993, however, allegations were made that the United Nations was not maintaining a truly level playing field in either Bosnia or Somalia.

---

[31] 1 U.N.T.S., 15.

21

Basic rules of the law of armed conflict

General applicability of the law

In the light of the preceding chapters it is possible to draw attention to what may be regarded as the basic rules and principles underlying the law of armed conflict on land, at sea or in the air. These rules and principles are applicable regardless of the legality or justness of the conflict, and even if operations are undertaken by way of punitive or police action in the name of the United Nations. Confirmation of this is to be found in the introductory chapter of the United States Department of the Air Force Commander's Handbook on the Law of Armed Conflict issued in the name of the Judge Advocate General:[1]

> The law of armed conflict applies equally to both sides in all international wars or armed conflicts.[2] This is true even if one side is guilty of waging an illegal or aggressive war. The side that is acting in self-defense against illegal aggression does not, because of that fact, gain any right to violate the laws of armed conflict.[3] Even forces acting under the sanction of the United Nations ... are required to follow the law of armed conflict in dealing with the enemy. The military personnel of a nation may not be punished simply for fighting in an armed conflict. This is so even if the side they serve is clearly an aggressor and has been condemned for this by the United Nations ... Because, as a practical matter, all nations claim that their wars are wars of self-defense courts ... [are] unwilling to punish officials for waging aggressive war if they were not at the policy-making level of government.

[1] US Dept. of the Air Force, Pamphlet A.F.P. 110–34, 1980, para. 1–4(b) (1–3).

[2] It should be borne in mind that by Pr. I, 1(4) (Schindler and Toman, 621), wars of national liberation are considered to be international armed conflicts governed by the laws of armed conflict.

[3] Any other rule would mean that the aggressor denied the protection of the law would disregard the law as to the adverse party. As a result, the conflict would be conducted without any consideration for restraint based on humanitarian or other principles. These principles should therefore apply even if one of the combatants disregards them. The preamble to Protocol I makes it clear that the application of the Conventions and the Protocol is unaffected by 'the causes espoused by or attributed to' the parties.

The Hague and Geneva Law

The main purpose of both the Hague and the Geneva Law is to minimise the horrors of the conflict to the extent consistent with the economic and efficient use of armed force, while not inhibiting the military activities of the parties in their endeavour to achieve victory with minimum cost to themselves. To this end, military necessity and *raison de guerre* or *Kriegsraison* must be balanced against overriding principles of a humanitarian character. This means that in no case may the force used exceed at any time the necessities of the situation or be directed towards any other object than the desired coercion of the enemy. In other words, no more force or greater violence should be used to carry out an operation than is absolutely necessary in the particular circumstances, if the application of such force would cause injury to non-combatants or civilians. The demands of military necessity are limited by legal and moral, as well as military or political considerations and it should be remembered that the laws of war have been drawn up with knowledge of the needs and the realities of armed conflict, so that such considerations cannot justify any disregard of the law. Thus during World War II political considerations meant that Britain did not protest at the fact that the Irish Free State remained illuminated at night serving to assist enemy raiders in their approach to the English coast, nor did the passage of iron ore across Sweden to Germany lead Britain to deny the continued neutral status of Sweden. Again, during both the Korean and Vietnamese operations, political considerations imposed restrictions upon the geographic freedom of operations that were considered militarily desirable by the United Nations and United States commands respectively. Similarly, during the Gulf War – Desert Storm – Coalition operations were frequently limited by the need to protect historical and religious sites.

Humanitarianism

The humanitarian principles that operate during armed conflict are to be found in customs originally based on rules of chivalry as between the feudal orders of knighthood, developed at a time when armed service was considered as an honourable profession among gentlemen knights. To these must be added principles of ethics and humanity, as well as those postulated in treaties entered into for this purpose. To a great extent these humanitarian principles are now to be found in Article 3 common to the four Geneva Conventions of 1949[4] and, broadly speaking, they amount to the basic and minimum conditions underlying the rule of law as understood in modern society. Common Article 3 provides that the principles therein contained shall be applied 'without any adverse distinction founded on race, colour, religion or faith, sex, birth, or any other similar criteria', which would include nationality or political ideology and the provisions of this Article

[4] Schindler and Toman, 373 *et seq.*

operate in non-international conflicts, while the rest of the Conventions together with the provisions of the Hague Law govern those of an international character. This principle of non-discrimination is repeated in Protocol I, 1977, which spells out the equality principle in more detail than it appears in common Article 3. Article 75 provides that:

> persons who are in the power of a Party to the conflict and who do not benefit from more favourable treatment under the Conventions or under this Protocol shall be treated humanely in all circumstances and shall enjoy, as a minimum the protection provided by this Article [which lays down 'fundamental guarantees'] without any adverse distinction based upon race, colour, sex, language, religion or belief, political or other opinion, national or social origin, wealth, birth or other status, or any other similar criteria. Each Party shall respect the person, honour, conviction and religious practices of all such persons.

Since this provision refers to 'persons who are in the power of a Party' it is clear that even persons who are nationals of the Power concerned now receive some measure of protection.[5]

Although the Hague Law regulating the actual conduct of war depends on reciprocity with the Hague Conventions operating, at least formally, only as between parties, the basic principles of humanitarian law are so fundamental that they apply in any conflict even though not all the parties to the conflict are parties to any particular Hague, Geneva or other humanitarian convention. Whether the Hague and Geneva Conventions are regarded as codificatory of customary or creative of new law, they are not and do not purport to be exhaustive. Moreover, to the extent that a particular treaty does not reproduce or clearly contradict what was formerly accepted as a rule of customary law, that law continues to exist and must be obeyed. This rule is to be found in the preamble to the regulations annexed to Hague Convention IV[6] as well as Article I, paragraph 2, of Protocol I, and is frequently referred to as the Martens Clause preserving to the extent necessary those 'principles of international law [which are] derived from established custom, the principles of humanity and the dictates of the public conscience'. Moreover, the tribunal for the former Yugoslavia has held that the principles of humanitarian law to be found in the Conventions have hardened into customary law applicable in all conflicts.

Restrictions on means and methods

Since the aim of any armed conflict is to achieve victory at the minimum of cost, and not the destruction of the adverse party as such, the means of conducting the conflict are not unrestricted and must not involve means likely to cause unnecessary suffering, that is to say, suffering or injury over and above that required to

[5] See, e.g., Bothe, *et al.*, 455–7.
[6] Schindler and Toman, 63, 70.

disable an enemy combatant or secure the objective of an operation.[7] While it is true that one of the aims of the parties in a non-international conflict is frequently the destruction of individual persons adhering to the opposing party, particularly government dignitaries, in international conflicts it is usually considered improper to seek, for example, the assassination of any individual leader of the adverse party,[8] although he may be made the object of an ambush[9] and, if captured and circumstances warrant, he may be tried for war crimes.

Acts of a warlike nature must be directed only against military objects and objectives, 'those objects which by their nature, location, purpose or use make an effective contribution to military action and whose total or partial destruction, capture or neutralisation, in the circumstances ruling at the time,[10] offers a definite military advantage'.[11] As a consequence, civilians are exempt from being made the object of attack, although it is not a breach of the law of armed conflict if civilians suffer injury incidental to an attack upon a lawful military objective. Attacks which fail to distinguish between military and civilian personnel or military objectives and civilian objects are forbidden as indiscriminate. It is for this reason that military personnel are required to distinguish themselves from the civilian population, while a home state must mark by the recognised emblems those places which are civilian in character and granted immunity, such as religious or cultural institutions, and to the extent that it is practical the home state should ensure that civilians and civilian objects are kept away from military objectives.

Identification and proportionality

The principle of identification, that is to say, the definition whether an objective is legitimate or not depends upon the contribution an attack upon that object will make to ultimate victory or the success of the operation of which the attack is part. If there is any doubt whether an object normally devoted to civilian use, such as a church, school or museum, is being used for its proper purpose or being put to military use, they must be given the benefit of the doubt and not subjected to attack. In deciding whether an objective is or is not a legitimate object of attack,

[7] Bothe, *et al.*, 195–7.
[8] This principle was already embodied in the Lieber Code (Schindler and Toman, 3), Art. 148, and is reiterated in US Army Dept. Field Manual F-27, *The Law of Land Warfare*, 1956, para. 31; see also HMSO, *Manual of Military Law*, Part III, *The Law of War on Land*, para. 115. However, it should be noted that during the US invasion of Panama, 1989, the President of the US placed a one-million dollar 'bounty' on General Noriega, *The Times* (London) 23 Dec. 1989; also re Gen. Aidid in Somalia in 1993.
[9] As was the case with Admiral Yamamoto shot down over the Solomons in April 1943, Toland, *The Rising Sun*, 441–4.
[10] See, e.g., *Mitchell* v. *Harmony* (1851) 54 US, 115.
[11] Pr. I, Art. 52(2).

the principle of proportionality[12] is of importance. This principle is well established in the customary law of armed conflict and seeks to achieve some measure of reasonable connection between related matters. The very fact that the various conventions pertaining to the law of armed conflict are obligatory and are drawn up in the knowledge that they are to operate during conflict indicates that the draftsmen are aware of the needs of military necessity vis-à-vis the limitations imposed. Although the decision as to proportionality tends to be subjective, it must be made in good faith, and may in fact come to be measured and held excessive in a subsequent war crimes trial. In deciding whether the principle of proportionality is being respected, the standard of measurement is always the contribution to the military purpose of the particular action or the operation as a whole, as compared with other consequences of that action, such as the effect upon civilians or civilian objects. It involves weighing the interests arising from the success of the operation on the one hand, against the possible harmful effects upon protected persons or objects on the other. There must be an acceptable relation between the legitimate destructive effect and undesirable collateral effects. The tendency in Protocol I is to state, for example, that the effect upon civilians shall not be 'excessive', a term which appears to be synonymous with 'disproportionate'.[13] But there is no definition as to what is 'excessive', so that the decision must be made in accordance with reasonable military assessments and expectations, taking into account potential collateral damage caused to civilians, civilian objects and other protected persons or installations. However, while whatever is 'disproportionate' may be considered as 'excessive', it is not necessarily the case that what is 'excessive' is always 'disproportionate'. Thus, during the Falklands War, 1982, while many critics considered the number of casualties resulting from the sinking of the Argentine cruiser *Belgrano* to have been 'excessive', its sinking was not considered by the British War Cabinet to have been 'disproportionate' to the end achieved.[14]

The principle of proportionality is best known in its relation to a recourse to reprisals, formerly regarded as the last resort of a belligerent subjected to persistent breaches of the law of armed conflict by the adverse party. Reprisals are otherwise illegal measures taken in response to prior illegal measures of the adverse party and which are intended to cause the adverse party to cease its illegal activities and comply with the law. They are not measures taken simply by way of retaliation.[15] While reprisals do not have to correspond in character to the illegal

---

[12] See, e.g., Fenrick, 'The rule of proportionality and Protocol I in conventional warfare', 1; see also Bothe, *et al.*, 309.

[13] Bothe, *et al.*, 195–7.

[14] See *The Times* (London), 10, 18, 20 Sept., 6 Dec. 1984.

[15] However, in *The Zamora* [1916] 2 A.C., 77 the Judicial Committee of the Privy Council held that an 'Order [in Council] authorising reprisals will be conclusive ... as showing that a case for reprisals exists' at 97. Difficulties may arise since English and French are equally authentic as texts of relevant conventions, since *répraisalle* is used in French for both 'reprisal' and 'retaliation'.

acts which have led to their being undertaken, they must be proportionate to that act.[16]

Permitted and forbidden activities

Certain types of reprisals are forbidden. Thus prisoners of war may never be made the object of reprisals, even if the original illegal act was directed against prisoners in the wrongdoer's hands. Protocol I forbids attacks by way of reprisal against civilians or the civilian population. It is also forbidden to use civilians to ensure immunity for a military objective. Thus, civilians may not be used as a screen for an attack, nor may they be brought into the vicinity of a military objective so as to ensure protection from an attack for that objective. Prophylactic reprisals[17] are likewise forbidden.

Attacks lacking any direct military purpose are forbidden, even though their indirect or ultimate purpose may be to terminate the conflict. Thus, acts of terror

---

[16] The leading case on the definition of reprisals is the Portuguese–German arbitration of 1928. In deciding upon the *Naulilaa Claim* the arbitrators said 'The most recent doctrine, especially German doctrine [it was German action which was claimed to have been a reprisal], defines reprisals as ... acts of self help by the injured State, acts in retaliation for acts contrary to international law on the part of the offending State, which have remained unredressed after a demand for amends ... They are limited by considerations of humanity and the rules of good faith applicable in the relations between States. They are illegal unless they are based upon a previous act contrary to international law. They seek to impose on the offending State reparation for the offence, the return to legality and the avoidance of new offences. This definition does not require that the reprisals should be proportionate to the offence. On this point, authors, unanimous until a few years ago, begin to be divided in their opinions. The majority regard a certain proportion between the offence and the reprisals as a necessary condition for the legitimacy of the latter. Other authors, among the most modern, no longer require this condition. In so far as international law in the making as a result of the experiences of the last war is concerned, it certainly tends to restrict the notion of legitimate reprisals and to prohibit any excess ... Germany admitted the need for proportion between the reprisals and the offence. Even if it is admitted that international law only requires relative approximation of the reprisals to the offence, reprisals out of all proportion to the act that inspired them ought certainly to be considered excessive and illegal', 2 R.I.A.A., 1019, 1025–6, 1028 (our tr.). The German action was held to have been disproportionate.

[17] The example usually cited is the placing of prominent local persons on the locomotives of trains passing through occupied territory to prevent attacks on the lines of communication, see, e.g., Fauchille, *Traité de Droit International Public*, vol. II, s. 1143; see also Greenspan, *The Modern Law of Land Warfare*, 417. It was also common in the past to situate prisoners of war and civil detainee camps in the vicinity of military objectives to protect the latter from attack, but such practices are now illegal. During the run-up to the Gulf War, Iraq used Coalition nationals as a way to secure immunity for potential military objectives, while in Kosovo it was alleged that Serb forces used ethnic Albanian Kosovans as protective screens for those forces.

directed against the civilian population of the adverse party with the purpose of compelling that party to terminate its military activities are forbidden. In fact, Protocol I expressly forbids such acts. However, acts, such as intensive bombing raids which involve high civilian casualties, are probably not illegal if the main purpose is to minimise the casualties which the bombing nation would suffer if the hostilities were to continue, particularly if the adverse party has been given warning of the likelihood of such raids to enable him to evacuate civilians from the threatened areas.

Since the law of armed conflict rests upon a judicious balance between military operational needs and humanitarianism, and since the purpose of the Geneva Law is the preservation of humanitarianism accompanied by respect for civilians and the long-term interests of the parties to the conflict by reducing the possibility of sentiments of *revanchisme*, application of humanitarian principles does not override the needs of practical realism. Idealism and a belief in humanitarianism must not result in an automatic rejection of military needs or careless accusations of war crimes or crimes against humanity. However, the assessment of military needs must always be made in good faith.

Equally, since the law of armed conflict is based on non-discrimination and the absolute character of humanitarian law, with the rights and obligations of all parties the same, it follows that the rights of a state in defence are the same as those of the state in offence. In accordance with customary international law a state defending its territory retained the freedom to take such measures within its territory as it deemed necessary, including, for example, a 'scorched earth' policy or denial of foodstuffs to its own citizens in order to sustain the armed forces. This was true even though such measures might be denied to the adverse party by convention. Today, however, a defending state must recognise the continuing relevance of the law concerning human rights and restrictions upon activities which 'may be expected to cause such damage to the natural environment [as might] prejudice the health or survival of the population'.[18] Protocol I recognises that in defence of the national territory against invasion, the ban on attacking, removing or destroying objects essential to the survival of the civilian population will not operate within territory under the control of the defending state when 'required by imperative military necessity'.[19] But the same power to take destructive action affecting civilians is not permitted in any part of the national territory which is in the occupation of the adverse party, and an occupying power is forbidden from acting in this way in the process of retreating from such occupied territory.[20] A further limitation which operates equally as regards both national and enemy territory relates to installations which contain dangerous forces. According to Protocol

[18] Pr. I, Art. 55(1).
[19] Pr. I, Art. 54(5).
[20] Bothe, *et al.*, 342.

I these are dams, dykes and nuclear electrical generating stations. These may not be attacked even if they are military objectives, 'if such attack may cause the release of dangerous forces and consequent severe losses among the civilian population'.[21] The immunity from attack only ceases when the installation is used for other than its normal purpose in direct support of military operations and no other means to terminate such support exists. Moreover, such installations may not be made the object of reprisals and, so as to protect the civilian population as much as possible, if they are attacked 'all practical precautions shall be taken to avoid the release of dangerous forces'. The prohibition is general and relates to both enemy territory and national territory occupied by the adverse party. Although the Protocol does not expressly contain a provision regarding occupied territory in this matter, since an attack is 'an act of violence against the adversary, whether in offence or defence',[22] this is clearly the case. While such installations may not be attacked once they have come under the control of the adverse party, they may be disabled to prevent their falling into his hands, provided that proper precautions are taken to prevent the release of dangerous forces.

For those countries which have not ratified Protocol I, their right to devastate their own territory whether under their own control or that of the adverse party remains, regardless of the effect this may have upon the civilian population, subject to treaty provisions respecting the human rights of persons within that territory. Moreover, even if it were the case that customary law now forbids actions in conflicts of the kind here outlined, it would be open to a state taking such measures against its own territory in the hands of the adverse party to contend that such action was in conformity with customary law with regard to the inherent right of self-defence which extends to the preservation of the territorial integrity of the state. However, it has been suggested that the right to take measures during an armed conflict may be limited by virtue of Article 51 of the Charter of the United Nations which only recognises the right of self-defence for the purpose of frustrating an armed attack, the argument being that action taken even during conflict must be limited to that required for self-defence alone.[23] Regardless of whether non-international conflicts are subject to the Hague or Geneva regimes, other than by way of common Article 3 to the Geneva Conventions, it is now well established that even in such conflicts basic rules of a humanitarian character operate and breaches of them may render the offenders liable to criminal prosecution.

The International Committee of the Red Cross has published three statements on the basic rules of the law of armed conflict:

[21] Pr. I, Art. 56(1).
[22] Pr. I, Art. 49.
[23] See, e.g., Greenwood, 'The concept of war in modern international law', 36 I.C.L.Q. 987, 283; 'Self-defence and the conduct of international armed conflict', in Dinstein, *International Law at a Time of Perplexity*, 273.

Basic rules of the law of armed conflict

I The Soldier's Rules[24]

1 Be a disciplined soldier. Disobedience of the laws of war dishonours your army and yourself and causes unnecessary suffering; far from weakening the enemy's will to fight, it often strengthens it.
2 Fight only enemy combatants and attack only military objectives.
3 Destroy no more than your mission requires.
4 Do not fight enemies who are 'out of combat' [hors de combat] or surrender. Disarm them and hand them over to your superior.
5 Collect and care for the wounded and sick, be they friend or foe.
6 Treat all civilians and all enemies in your power with humanity.
7 Prisoners of war must be treated humanely and are bound to give only information about their identity. No physical or mental torture of prisoners of war is permitted.
8 Do not take hostages.
9 Abstain from all acts of vengeance.
10 Respect all persons and objects bearing the emblem of the red cross, red crescent, red lion and sun,[25] the white flag of truce or emblems designating cultural property.
11 Respect other people's property. Looting is prohibited.
12 Endeavour to prevent any breach of the above rules. Report any violation to your superior. Any breach of the law of war is punishable.

II Fundamental Rules of International Humanitarian Law Applicable to Armed Conflicts[26]

1 Persons *hors de combat* and those who do not take a direct part in hostilities are entitled to respect for their lives and moral and physical integrity. They shall in all circumstances be protected and treated humanely without any adverse distinctions.
2 It is forbidden to kill or injure an enemy who surrenders or is *hors de combat*.
3 The wounded and sick shall be collected and cared for by the party to the conflict which has them in its power. Protection also covers medical personnel, establishments, transports and equipment. The emblem of the red cross or the red crescent is the sign of such protection and must be protected.
4 Captured combatants and civilians under the authority of an adverse party are entitled to respect for their lives, dignity, personal rights and convictions. They shall be protected against all acts of violence and reprisals. They shall have the right to correspond with their families and receive relief.
5 Everyone shall be entitled to benefit from fundamental judicial guarantees. No one shall be responsible for an act he has not committed. No one shall be subjected to physical and mental torture, corporal punishment or cruel or degrading treatment.
6 Parties to a conflict and members of their armed forces do not have an unlimited choice of methods and means of warfare. It is prohibited to employ weapons or

[24] Int'l Rev. Red X, (Jan.–Feb. 1978).
[25] The red lion and sun was formerly the emblem used by Iran, but since the Islamic revolution Iran uses the red crescent. The red shield of David is used by Israel and, though not officially recognised, does receive respect in practice.
[26] Schindler and Toman, 734.

methods of warfare of a nature to cause unnecessary losses or excessive suffering.

7 Parties to a conflict shall at all times distinguish between the civilian population and combatants in order to spare civilian population and property. Neither the civilian population as such nor civilian persons shall be the object of attack. Attacks shall be directed only against military objectives.

III Non-International Armed Conflicts
A General Rules[27]

1 The obligation to distinguish between combatants and civilians is a general rule applicable in non-international armed conflicts. It prohibits indiscriminate attacks.

2 The prohibition of attacks against the civilian population as such or against individual civilians is a general rule applicable in non-international conflicts. Acts of violence intended primarily to spread terror among the civilian population are also prohibited.

3 The prohibition of superfluous injury or unnecessary suffering is a general rule applicable in non-international conflicts. It prohibits, in particular, the use of means of warfare which uselessly aggravate the sufferings of disabled men or render their death inevitable.

4 The prohibition to kill, injure or capture an adversary by resort to perfidy is a general rule applicable in non-international armed conflicts; in a non-international armed conflict, acts inviting the confidence of an adversary to lead him to believe that he is entitled to, or is obliged to accord protection under the rules of international law applicable in non-international armed conflicts, with intent to betray that confidence, shall constitute perfidy.

5 The obligation to respect and protect medical and religious personnel and medical units and transports in the conduct of military operations is a general rule applicable in non-international armed conflicts.

6 The general rule prohibiting attacks against the civilian population implies, as a corollary, the prohibition of attacks on dwellings and other installations which are used only by the civilian population.

7 The general rule prohibiting attacks upon the civilian population implies, as a corollary, the prohibition to attack, destroy, remove or render useless objects indispensable to the survival of the civilian population.

8 The general rule to distinguish between combatants and civilians and the prohibition of attacks against the civilian population as such or against individual civilians implies, in order to be effective, that all feasible precautions have to be taken to avoid injury, loss or damage to the civilian population.

B Prohibitions and Restrictions on the Use of Certain Weapons

1 The customary rule prohibiting the use of chemical weapons, such as those containing asphyxiating or vesicant agents, and the use of bacteriological (bacterial) weapons is applicable in non-international armed conflicts.

2 The customary rule prohibiting bullets which expand or flatten easily in the

---

[27] Int'l Rev. Red X, 278, (Sept.–Oct. 1989), 404. Though published by the ICRC, these rules are in a Declaration adopted at the 14th Round Table on humanitarian law organised by the International Institute of Humanitarian Law, San Remo, in 1989.

human body, such as Dum-Dum bullets, is applicable in non-international armed conflicts.

3 The customary rule prohibiting the use of poison as a means of warfare is applicable in non-international armed conflicts.

4 In application of the general rules listed in section A above, especially those on the distinction between combatants and civilians and on the immunity of the civilian population, mines, booby-traps and other devices within the meaning of Protocol II to the 1980 Convention on conventional weapons may not be directed against the civilian population as such or against individual civilians, nor used indiscriminately.

The prohibition of booby-traps listed in Article 6 of the Protocol extends to their use in non-international armed conflicts, in application of the general rules on the distinction between combatants and civilians, the immunity of the civilian population, the prohibition of superfluous injury or unnecessary suffering, and the prohibition of perfidy.

To ensure the protection of the civilian population referred to in the previous paragraphs, precaution must be taken to protect it from attacks in the form of mines, booby-traps and other devices.

5 In application of the general rules listed in section A above, especially those on the distinction between combatants and civilians and on the immunity of the civilian population, incendiary weapons may not be directed against the civilian population as such, against individual civilians or civilian objects, nor used indiscriminately.

IV A somewhat similar statement is to be found in the United States
Operational Law Handbook
Soldiers' Rules

1 Soldiers do not harm captured enemy soldiers or civilian detainees; noncombatant civilians; medical personnel or chaplains; enemy soldiers 'out of combat'.
2 Soldiers collect and care for enemy wounded and sick.
3 Soldiers respect the medical symbol and do not attack medical facilities or medical vehicles.
4 Soldiers respect protected places.
5 Soldiers do not engage in treacherous acts.
6 Soldiers allow their enemy to surrender.
7 Soldiers do not steal from their enemy or from civilians.
8 Soldiers do not cause unnecessary suffering.
9 Soldiers report violations of the Law of War.
10 Soldiers obey orders and the Law of War.

Bibliography

Adachi, Samio, The Asian Concept, in UNESCO, *International Dimensions of Humanitarian Law*, Dordrecht, Martinus Nijhoff, 1988.

Akehurst, M., The hierarchy of the sources of international law, 47 *British Yearbook of International Law* (1947–75).

Albert, C. S., *The Case Against the General*, New York, Scribners, 1993.

Akimsha, K. and Koslov, G., *Beautiful Loot*, New York, Random House, 1995.

American Bar Association, *Report of the Committee on Grenada*, New York, 1984. (Restatement), St Paul, American Law Institute, 1987.

Anna Comnena, *The Alexiad*, Eng. tr Sewter E.R.A., Harmondsworth, Penguin, 1969.

Anon., Air defence identification zones: creeping jurisdiction in the air space, 18 *Virginia Journal of International Law* (1978).

Appleman, J. A., *Military Tribunals and International Crimes*, Indianapolis, Bobbs-Merrill, 1954.

Armour, W. S., Customs of warfare in ancient India, 7 *Transactions of the Grotius Society* (1922).

Ayala, B., *De Jure et Officiis Bellicis et Disciplina Militari*, [1582], Eng. tr. Bate, J. P., Washington, Carnegie Institution, 1912.

Bar of the City of New York, *The Use of Armed Force in International Affairs: the Case of Panama*, New York, 1992.

Bassiouni, M. C. and Manikus, P., *The Law of the International Criminal Court for the Former Yugoslavia*, Irvington-on-Hudson, Transnational, 1996.

Baxter, R., The first modern codification of the law of armed conflict, 25 *International Review of the Red Cross* (1963).

Belli, P., *De Re Militari et Bello Tractatus*, [1663], Eng. tr. Nutting, H. C., Oxford, Clarendon Press, 1936.

Bernard, R., *L'Armistice dans les Guerres Internationales*, Geneva, University of Geneva thesis, 1947.

Blix, H., Arms control treaties aimed at reducing the military impact on the environment, in Makarczyk, J. (ed), *Essays in International Law in Honour of Judge Manfred Lachs*, The Hague, Martinus Nijhoff, 1984.

Bluntschli, J. K., *Le Droit International Codifié*, tr. Lardy, M. C., Paris, Guillaumin, 1895.

Boissier, P., *History of the International Committee of the Red Cross*, vol. I, 'From Solferino to Tsushima', Geneva, Henry Dunant Institute, 1985.

Bond, J. H., *The Rules of International Conflict and the Law of War*, Princeton, Princeton University Press, 1974.

Bordwell, P., *The Law of War between Belligerents*, Chicago, Callaghan & Co., 1908.

Bothe, M., Partsch, K. and Solf, W., *New Rules for Victims of Armed Conflicts*, The Hague, Martinus Nijhoff, 1988.

British Manual of Military Law, Part III, *The Law of Land Warfare* London, HMSO, 1985.

Brown, G. D., P. W. Parole: ancient concept, modern utility, 156 *Military Law Review*, 1998.

Brownlie, I., *International Law and the Use of Force by States*, Oxford, Clarendon Press, 1963.

Burnett, W. D., Command responsibility: a case study of the criminal responsibility of Israeli, military commanders at Shatila and Sabra, 107 *Military Law Review*, 1985.

Butler and Maccoby, *The Development of International Law*, London, Longmans, Green, 1928.

Cameron, J., *The Peleus Trial*, Edinburgh, Hodge, 1945.

Canada Dept of National Defence, *Handbook of the Law of Naval Operation*, Ottawa, Maritime Command, MAOP 331, 1991.

Carnahan, B. M., Lincoln, Lieber and the laws of war, 92 *American Journal of International Law*, 1998.

Carnegie Endowment, *Violations of the Laws and Customs of War*, Washington, Division of International Law, 1991.

Cassese, A., *United Nations Peace-Keeping: Legal Essays*, Alphen aan den Rijn, Sijthoff & Noordhoff, 1978.

Cassese, A., *Violence and Law in the Modern Age*, Princeton: Princeton University Press, 1988.

Castren, E., *The Present Law of War and Neutrality*, Helsinki, Annales Academiae Scientiarum Fennicae, 1954.

Centre de Droit International, *Entre les Lignes: La Guerre du Golfe et le Droit International*, Brussels, 1991.

Chang, I., *The Rape of Nanking*, New York, Basic Books, 1997.

Chen, T. C., *The International Law of Recognition*, London, Stevens, 1951.

Cheng, B., *The Law of International Air Transport*, London, Stevens, 1962.

Chappell, C., *Island of Barbed Wire*, London, Robert Hale, 1984.

Churchill, W. S., *The Second World War*, London, Cassell, 1948–54.

Cicero, M. T., *Phillipics*, tr. Ker, W. C. A., Cambridge, Harvard University Press, 1926.

Clarke, R., *The Fire This Time: US War Crimes in the Gulf*, New York: Thunders Mouth Press, 1994.

Clausewitz, K. von, *On War*, [1832], Eng. tr. Howard, M. and Paret, P. Harmondsworth, Penguin, 1976.

Clode, C. M., *Military Forces of the Crown*, London, John Murray, 1869.

Coates, A. J., *The Ethics of War*, Manchester, Manchester University Press, 1997.

Cohen, E. R., *Human Rights in the Israeli-Occupied Territories*, Manchester, Manchester University Press, 1985.

Cohn, I. and Goodwin, G., *The Rights of the Child: The Role of Children in Armed Conflict*, Oxford: Oxford University Press, 1994.

Colombos, C. J., *The Law of Prize*, London, Longmans, Green, 1949.

Colombos, C. J., *International Law of the Sea*, New York, McKay, 1967.

Cornum, R., *She Went to War*, Novato, Presidio Press, 1992.

D'Amato, A., *The Concept of Custom in International Law*, Ithaca, Cornell University Press, 1971.

Das, S. K., Japanese occupation and *Ex Post Facto* legislation in Malaya, Singapore, Malayan Law Journal (1959).

Daws, G., *Prisoners of the Japanese*, London, Robson Books, 1994.

Dedijer, V., *On Military Conventions*, Lund, Gleerup, 1961.

Delissen, A. G. M. and Tanja, G. J., *Humanitarian Law of Armed Conflict: Challenges Ahead*, Dordrecht, Martinus Nijhoff, 1991.

de Mulinen, F., *Handbook of the Law of War for Armed Forces*, Geneva, ICRC, 1987.

Dinstein, Y., *The Defence of 'Obedience to Superior Orders' in International Law*, Leyden, Sijthoff, 1965.

Dinstein, Y., *International Law at a Time of Perplexity*, Dordrecht, Martinus Nijhoff, 1989.

Dinstein, Y., The Israeli Supreme Court and the law of belligerent occupation: deportations, 23 *Israel Yearbook on Human Rights*, 1993.

Dinstein, Y., *War, Aggression and Self-Defence*, Cambridge, Grotius Publications, 1994.

Dinstein, Y. and Tabory, M., *War Crimes in International Law*, The Hague, Martinus Nijhoff, 1996.

Dinstein, Y., 'Crimes against humanity', in Makarczyk, J., *Theory of International Law at the Threshold of the 21st Century*, The Hague: Martinus Nijhoff, 1997.

Dinstein, Y., 'The distinction between war crimes and crimes against peace', in Dinstein/Tabory.

Donnison, F. S. V., *British Military Administration in the Far East 1943–1946*, London, Oxford University Press, 1956.

Donnison, F. S. V., *Civil Affairs and Military Government North-East Europe 1944–1946*, London, Oxford University Press, 1961.

Doty, G. R., The US and the development of the laws of land warfare, 156 *Military Law Review* (1998).

Draper, G. I. A. D., The role of legal advisers in armed services, 18 *International Review of the Red Cross* (1976).

Draper, G. I. A. D., The interaction of Christianity and chivalry in the historical development of the law of war, 5 *International Review of the Red Cross* (1985).

Durand, A., *History of the ICRC, vol. 2. From Sarajevo to Hiroshima*, Geneva, Henry Dunant Institute, 1978.

Erasmus, *Bellum*, [1545], Eng. tr. Vershbow, C. Z., Barre, Mass., The Imprint Society, 1972.

Falk, R. (ed.), *The Vietnam War and International Law*, Princeton, University Press, 1976.

Fauchille, P., *Traité de Droit International Public*, vol. 2, Paris, Rousseau, 1921.

Fenrick, W. J., The prosecution of war criminals in Canada, 12 *Dalhousie Law Journal* (1968).

Fenrick, W. J., The rule of proportionality and Protocol I in conventional warfare, 98 *Military Law Review* (1982).

Fenrick, W. J., New developments in the law concerning the use of conventional weapons in armed conflict, 19 *Canadian Yearbook of International Law* (1981).

Fenrick, W. J., The exclusive zone device in the law of naval warfare, 24 *Canadian Yearbook of International Law* (1986).

Fenrick, W. J., 'The development of the law of armed conflict through the jurisprudence of the International Criminal Tribunal for the Former Yugoslavia', in Schmitt/Green, *Millennium*, 1998.

Fenwick, C. J., *International Law*, New York, Appleton-Century-Crofts, 1965.

Ferencz, B., *Defining International Aggression*, Dobbs Ferry, Oceana, 1979.

Fleck, D. (ed.), *Handbook of Humanitarian Law in Armed Conflict*, Oxford, Oxford University Press, 1995.

Friedmann, W., *Allied Military Government of Germany*, London, Stevens, 1947.

Gardot, A., Le Droit de la Guerre dans l'Œuvre des Capitaines Français du XVIe Siècle, 72 *Hague Recueil* (1948).

Garner, J. W., *International Law and the World War*, London, Longmans, Green, 1920.

Gentili, A., *De Jure Belli* [1612], Carnegie, tr. Rolfe, J. C., Oxford, Clarendon Press, 1933.

German War Book, 1902, Eng. tr. Morgan, J. H., London, John Murray, 1915.

Glueck, S., The Nuremberg trial and aggressive war, 59 *Harvard Law Review* (1946).

Goldie, L. F. E., 'Commentary on the 1937 Nyon Agreement', in Ronzitti, N. (ed.), *The Law of Naval Warfare*, Dordrecht, Martinus Nijhoff, 1988.

Graber, D. A., *Development of the Law of Belligerent Occupation 1863–1914*, New York, Columbia University Press, 1949.

Graefrath, B., 'Implementation measures and international law of arms control', in Delissen, A. J. M. and Tanja, G. J. (eds), *Humanitarian Law of Armed Conflict: Challenges Ahead*, Dordrecht, Martinus Nijhoff, 1991.

Gray, C., Bosnia and Herzegovina: civil war or inter-state conflict? 67 *British Yearbook of International Law* (1996).

Green, L. C., The Indian National Army trials, 11 *Modern Law Review* (1947).

Green, L. C., The nature of the war in Korea, 4 *International Law Quarterly* (1951).

Green, L. C., Armed conflict, war and self-defence, in *Essays on the Modern Law of War*, 1999.

Green, L. C., Korea and the United Nations, 4 *World Affairs* (NS) (1959).

Green, L. C., Superior orders and the reasonable man, in *Essays on the Modern Law of War*, 1999.

Green, L. C., Aftermath of Vietnam: war law and the soldier, in 4 Falk, R. (ed.), *The Vietnam War and International Law*, Princeton, Princeton University Press, 1976.

Green, L. C., Journalists in battle areas, *The Times* (London), 1 Mar. 1976.

Green, L. C., Rescue at Entebbe: legal aspects, 6 *Israel Yearbook on Human Rights* (1976).

Green, L. C., *Superior Orders in National and International Law*, Leyden, Sijthoff, 1976.

Green, L. C., The new law of armed conflict, 15 *Canadian Yearbook of International Law* (1977).

Green, L. C., Derogation of human rights in emergency situations, 16 *Canadian Yearbook of International Law* (1978).

Green, L. C., Human rights and medical experimentation, 13 *Israel Yearbook on Human Rights* (1983).

Green, L. C., The Falklands, the law and the war, 38 *Yearbook of World Affairs* (1984).

Green, L. C., *Essays on the Modern Law of War*, Dobbs Ferry, Transnational, 1985/1999.

Green, L. C., The rule of law and the use of force: The Falklands and Grenada, 24 *Archiv des Völkerrechts* (1986)

Green, L. C., Canadian law, war crimes and crimes against humanity, 59 *British Yearbook of International Law* (1988).

Green, L. C., International criminal law and the protection of human rights, in Cheng, B. and Brown, E. (eds), *Contemporary Problems of International Law*, London, Stevens, 1988.

Green, L. C., Nuclear weapons and the law of armed conflict, in *Essays on the Modern Law of War*, 1999.

Green, L. C., The problems of a wartime international lawyer, 2 *Pace Yearbook of International Law* (1989).

Green, L. C., Superior orders and command responsibility, 27 *Canadian Yearbook of International Law* (1989).

Green, L. C., Terrorism and armed conflict: the plea and verdict, 19 *Israel Yearbook on Human Rights* (1989).

Green, L. C., Acts and weapons forbidden *in bello*, in *Pax-Ius-Libertas*, Thessaloniki, Aristotelea Universitas, 1990.

Green, L. C., The Judaic contribution to human rights, 28 *Canadian Yearbook of International Law* (1990).

Green, L. C., The environment and the law of conventional warfare, 29 *Canadian Yearbook of International Law* (1991).

Green, L. C., The Gulf 'War', the UN and the law of armed conflict, 28 *Archiv des Völkerrechts* (1991).

Green, L. C., What one may do in conflict: then and now, in Delissen, A. J. M. and Tanja, G. J. (eds), *Humanitarian Law of Armed Conflict: Challenges Ahead*, Dordrecht, Martinus Nijhoff, 1991.

Green, L. C., Die Bundesrepublik Deutschland und die Ausübung der Strafsgerichtlicher Sicht, 1 *Humanitäres Völkerrecht* (1992).

Green, L. C., The German Federal Republic and the exercise of criminal jurisdiction, 43 *University of Toronto Law Journal* (1993).

Green, L. C., The Azad Hind Fauj: the Indian National Army, in *Essays on the Modern Law of War*, 1999.

Green, L. C., *Drazen Erdemović*: The International Criminal Tribunal for the Former Yugoslavia in action, 10 *Leiden Journal of Internal Law* (1997).

Green, L. C., *Erdemović – Tadić – Dokmanović*: Jurisdiction and Early Practice of the Yugoslav War Crimes Tribunal, 27 *Israel Yearbook on Human Rights*, (1997).

Green, L. C., The law of war in historical perspective, in Schmitt, M. *The Law of Military Operations* Newport, Naval War College, 1998.

Green, L. C. What is – why is there – the law of war, in Schmitt/Green, *Millennium*.

Green, L. C., and Dickason, O. P., *The Law of Nations and the New World*, Edmonton, Alberta University Press, 1989.

Greenberg, L. *et al., Information Warfare and International Law*, Washington, National Defense University, 1998.

Greenfield, J., *The Return of Cultural Treasures*, Cambridge, Cambridge University Press, 1990.

Greenspan, M., *The Modern Law of Land Warfare*, Berkeley, University of California Press, 1959.

Greenwood, C. J., New world order or old? The invasion of Kuwait and the rule of law, 55 *Modern Law Review* (1922).

Greenwood, C. J., Self-defence and the conduct of international armed conflict, in Dinstein, Y. (ed.), *International Law at a Time of Perplexity*, Dordrecht, Nijhoff, 1989.

Greenwood, C. J., The concept of war in modern international law, 36 *International & Comparative Law Quarterly* (1987).

Greenwood, C. J., The twilight of the law of belligerent reprisals, 20 *Netherlands Yearbook of International Law* (1989).

Greenwood, C. J., 'The law of weaponry at the start of the new millennium', in Schmitt/Green, *Millennium*.

Grotius, H., *De Jure Belli ac Pacis*, [1625], Amsterdam; Eng., tr., London [1738]; Carnegie tr. Kelsey, F. W., Oxford, Clarendon Press 1925.

Grunawalt, R. J. ed., *Protection of the Environment during Armed Conflict*, Newport, Naval War College, 1997.

Grüningen, M. von, Neutrality and peacekeeping, in Cassese, A., (ed.), *United Nations Peace-Keeping*, Alphen aan den Rijn, Sijthoff & Noordhoff, 1978.

Guttry, A. de, Commentary on the 1904 Hague Convention, in Ronzitti, N. (ed.), *The Law of Naval Warfare*, Dordrecht, Martinus Nijhoff, 1988.

Hackworth, G. H., *A Digest of International Law*, Washington, Government Printing House, 1940–44.

Hall, W. E., *A Treatise on International Law*, Oxford, Clarendon Press, 1895.

Hampson, F., 'NGOs in situations of conflict: the negotiation of change', in Schmitt/Green, *Millennium*.

Herezegh, G., *Development of International Humanitarian Law*, Budapest, Akadémia Kiado, 1984.

Higgins, R., *United Nations Peace-Keeping*, London, Oxford University Press, 1969–70.

Holborn, H., *American Military Government*, Washington, Infantry Journal Press, 1947.

Holland, T. E., *Letters on War and Neutrality*, London, Longmans, Green, 1909.

Holland, T. E., *The Laws of War on Land*, Oxford, Clarendon Press, 1908.

Homer, *The Odyssey*, Lattimore (ed.), New York, Harper & Row, 1965.

Howes, R. and Stevenson, M., *Women and the Use of Military Force*, Boulder, Lynne Rienner, 1993.

Hyde, C. C., *International Law Chiefly as Interpreted and Applied in the United States*, Boston, Little, Brown, 1947.

ICRC, Fundamental Rules for Non-International Conflict, *International Review of the Red Cross* (Sept.–Oct. 1988).

ICRC, *The Soldier's Rules, International Review of the Red Cross* (Jan.–Feb 1978).

Israel, F. L., *Major Peace Treaties of Modern History, 1648–1967*, New York, Chelsea House and McGraw-Hill, 1967.

Jessup. P. C., Should international law recognise an intermediate state between war and peace? 48 *American Journal of International Law* (1954).

Johnson, D. H. N., *Rights in Air Space*, Manchester, Manchester University Press, 1965.

Jones, D. E., *Women Warriors*, Washington, Brasseys, 1997.

Josephus, F., *Antiquities of the Jews*, tr. Marcus, R., Cambridge, Harvard University Press, 1934.

Josephus, F., *Contra Apion*. Fr. tr. Blum, L., Paris, Les Belles Lettres, 1930.

Kaijzer, N., *Military Obedience*, Alphen aan den Rijn, Sitjhoff & Noordhoff, 1978.

Kalshoven, F., *Belligerent Reprisals*, Leyden, Sijthoff, 1971.

Kalshoven, F., *Constraints on the Waging of War*, Geneva, ICRC, 1987.

Kalshoven, F., Commentary on the Declaration of London, in Ronzitti (ed.), *The Law of Naval Warfare*, Dordrecht, Martinus Nijhoff, 1988.

Keen, M. H., *The Laws of War in the Late Middle Ages*, London, Routledge, 1965.

Keith, A. B., *Speeches and Documents on International Relations 1918–1937*, London, Oxford University Press, 1938.

Kelly, M. J., *Peace Operations*, Canberra, Australian Government Publishing Service, 1997.

Khadduri, M., *The Islamic Law of Nations*, Baltimore, Johns Hopkins University Press, 1966.

Kintner, E. W., *The Hadamar Trial*, Edinburgh, Hodge, 1949.

Kuper, J., *International Law Concerning Child Civilians in Armed Conflict*, Oxford, Oxford University Press, 1997.

Kussbach, E., The International Humanitarian Fact-Finding Commission, 43 *International and Comparative Law Quarterly* (1994).

Lauterpacht, E., Greenwood, C. J., Weller, M. and Bethlehem, D., *The Kuwait Crisis: Basic Documents*, Cambridge, Grotius Publications, 1991.

Lauterpacht, H., *Recognition in International Law*, Cambridge, Cambridge University Press, 1947.

Lauterpacht, H., *Oppenheim's International Law*, 7th ed., vol. 2, London, Longmans, Green, 1952.

Lauterpacht, H., Rules of warfare in an unlawful war, in Lipsky, G. A. (ed.), *Law and Politics in the World Community*, Berkeley, University of California Press, 1953.

Legnano, G., da, *De Bello, De Represaliis et De Duello* [1447], Eng., tr. Brierly, J. L., Oxford, Oxford University Press, 1917.

Levie, H., Maltreatment of prisoners of war in Vietnam, in 2 Falk, R. (ed.), *The Vietnam War and International Law*, Princeton, Princeton University Press, 1969.

Levie, H., *Documents on Prisoners of War*, Newport, US Naval War College, 1979.

Levie, H., *Prisoners of War in International Armed Conflict*, Newport, US Naval War College, 1979.

Levie, H., *The Code of International Armed Conflict*, Dobbs Ferry, Oceana, 1985.

Levie, H., *Minewarfare at Sea*, Leyden, Martinus Nijboff, 1992.

Levie, H., 'Was the assassination of President Lincoln a war crime?' in Schmitt/Green, *Levie on the Law of War*, Newport, Naval War College, 1998.

Lieber, F., *Political Ethics*, Boston, Little, Brown, 1938–39.

Lipsky, (ed.) *Law and Politics in the World Community*, Berkeley, University of California Press 1953.

Lissitzyn, O. J., The treatment of aerial intruders in recent practice in international law, 47 *American Journal of International Law* (1953).

Lockwood, G. H., Report on the trial of mercenaries, 7 *Manitoba Law Journal* (1983).

Machiavelli, N., *Thoughts of a Statesman*, tr. Gilbert, A., Raleigh, Duke University Press, 1989.

Martens, G. F. von, *A Compendium of the Law of Nations*, [1788], tr. Cobbett, W., London, Cobbett and Morgan, 1802.

Matheson, M. J., The Opinions of the World Court on the threat or use of nuclear weapons, 91 *American Journal of International Law* (1997).

Mayor, A., Dirty tricks in ancient warfare, 10 *Quarterly Journal of Military History* (1997).

Meijering, P. H., *Signed With Their Honour*, New York, Paragon House 1987.

Meron, T., *Human Rights in International Strife: Their International Protection*, Cambridge, Grotius Publications, 1987.

Meron, T., *Human Rights and Humanitarian Norms as Customary Law*, Oxford, Clarendon Press, 1989.

Meron, T., *Henry's Wars and Shakespeare's Laws*, 1993.

Meyrowitz, H., 'Les armes nucléaires et le droit de la guerre', in Delissen, A. J. M. and Tanja, G. J. (eds), *Humanitarian Law of Armed Conflict: Challenges Ahead*, Dordrecht, Martinus Nijhoff, 1991.

Moore, J. B., *Digest of International Law*, Washington, Government Printing Office, 1906.

Moore, J. B., *International Arbitrations to which the United States is a Party*, Washington, Government Printing Office, 1848.

Moore, J. N., *Law and the Grenada Mission*, Charlotteville, University of Virginia Law School, Center for Law and National Security, 1984.

Morimura Seiichi, *The Devil's Feast*, Tokyo, 1982.

Mullins, C., *The Leipzig Trials*, London, Witherby, 1921.

Nanda, V., NGOs and international humanitarian law, in Schmitt/Green, *Millennium*.

Nanda, V., Farer, T., and D'Amato, A., US Forces in Panama: defenders, aggressors or human rights activists? 84 *American Journal of International Law* (1990).

Newark, T., *Women Warlords*, London, Blandford, 1989.

Nwogugu, E. I., 'Commentary on the 1936 London Procès-Verbal', in Ronzitti, N. (ed.), *The Law of Naval Warfare*, Dordrecht, Martinus Nijhoff, 1988.

O'Connell, D. P., *The Influence of the Law on Sea Power*, Manchester, Manchester University Press 1975.

Oliphant, Sir Lancelot, *Ambassador in Bonds*, London, Putnam, 1947.

Oppenheim, L, *International Law*, vol. 2, War and Neutrality, 1st ed., London, Longmans, Green, 1906.

Oppenheim, L., *International Law*, vol. 2, 7th ed. by Lauterpacht, H., London, Longmans, Green, 1952.

Osiel, M. J. *Obeying Orders*, Iowa City, Iowa University Press, 1998.

Padelford, N. J., *International Law and Diplomacy in the Spanish Civil Strife*, New York, Macmillan, 1939.

Palmer, N. and Allen, T. B., The most deadly man, 124 *Naval Institute Proceedings* (1998).

Parks, W. H., Command responsibility for war crimes, 62 *Military Law Review* 1973.

Parks, W. H., Memorandum on the law: executive order 112333 and assassination, *The Army Lawyer*, US DA PAM 27–50–204, 1989.

Peters, J. and Nichol, J., *Tornado Down*, London, Michael Joseph, 1992.

Phillips, R., *The Belsen Trial*, Edinburgh, Hodge, 1949.

Phillipson, C., *The International Law and Custom of Ancient Greece and Rome*, London, Macmillan, 1911.

Pictet, J., *Le Droit Humanitaire et la Protection des Victimes de Guerre*, Leiden, Sijthoff, 1973.

Pictet, J., *Development and Principles of International Humanitarian Law*, Dordrecht, Martinus Nijhoff, 1985.

Playfair, E., *International Law and the Administration of Occupied Territories*, Oxford, Clarendon Press, 1992.

Rennell of Rodd, Lord, *British Military Administration in Africa 1941–1947*, London, HMSO, 1948.

Roberts, A., 'Implementation of the laws of war in late twentieth-century conflicts', in Schmitt/Green, *Millennium*.

Roberts, G. B., Judaic sources of and views on the laws of war, 37 *Naval Law Review* (1988).

Robertson, H. B., Commentary on Hague Convention IX 1907, in Ronzitti, N. (ed.), *The Law of Naval Warfare*, Dordrecht, Martinus Nijhoff, 1988.

Rogers, A. P. V., *Law on the Battlefield*, Manchester, Manchester University Press, 1996.

Ronzitti, N., *Rescue of Nationals Abroad and Intervention on Grounds of Humanity*, Dordrecht, Martinus Nijhoff, 1985.

Ronzitti, N. (ed.), *The Law of Naval Warfare*, Dordrecht, Martinus Nijhoff, 1988.

Rosas, A., *The Legal Status of Prisoners of War*, Helsinki, Suomalainen Tiedeakatemia, 1976.

Rose, J. H., *The Life of Napoleon*, London, G. Bell, 1924.

Rosenne, S., *Israel's Armistice Agreements with the Arab States*, Tel Aviv, Blumstein, 1951.

Rowson, S. W. D. (also known as Rosenne, S.), The abolition of Nazi and Fascist anti-Jewish legislation by British military administrations of the Second World War, 1 *Jewish Yearbook of International Law* (1948).

Rubin, B., PLO violence and legitimate combatancy: a response to Professor Green, 19 *Israel Yearbook on Human Rights* (1986).

Schermers, H. G., *International Institutional Law*, vol. 2, Leiden, Sijthoff, 1972.

Schindler, D., Commentary on Hague Convention XIII 1907, in Ronzitti, N. (ed.), *The Law of Naval Warfare*, Dordrecht, Martinus Nijhoff, 1988.

Schindler, D. and Toman, J., *The Laws of Armed Conflicts*, Dordrecht, Martinus Nijhoff, 1988.

Schmitt, M., The International Court of Justice and the use of nuclear weapons, 51 *Naval War College Review* (1998)

Schmitt, M., State-sponsored assassinations in international and domestic law, 17 *Yale International Law Journal* (1992).

Schmitt, M. (ed.), *The Law of Military Operations*, Newport, Naval War College, 1998.

Schmitt, M. and Green, L. C., *The Law of Armed Conflict: into the Next Millennium*, Newport, Naval War College, 1998.

Schmitt, M. and Green, L. C., *Levie on the Law of War*, Newport, Naval War College, 1998.

Schwarzenberger, G., *International Law, vol. 2, The Law of Armed Conflict*, London, Stevens, 1968.

Schwarzenberger, G., Jus pacis ac belli?, 37 *American Journal of International Law* (1943).

Schwarzenberger, G., *Legality of Nuclear Weapons*, London, Stevens, 1957.

Schwelb, E., Crimes against humanity, 23 *British Yearbook of International Law* (1946).

Shamgar, M., The observance of international law in the administred territories, 1 *Israel Yearbook on Human Rights* (1971).

Scott, J. B., *The Catholic Conception of International Law*, Washington, Georgetown University Press, 1934.

Shafirov, P. P., *A Discourse concerning the Just Causes of the War between Sweden and Russia*, [1717], Eng. tr. Butler, W. E., Dobbs Ferry, Oceana, 1973.

Shakespeare, W., *Henry V*.

Singh, N. and McWhinney, E., *Nuclear Weapons and Contemporary International Law*, Dordrecht, Martinus Nijhoff, 1988.

Sleeman, C., *The Gozawa Trial*, Edinburgh, Hodge, 1948.

Sleeman, C. and Silkin, S., *The Double Tenth Trial*, Edinburgh, Hodge, 1951.

Smith, H., *The Force of Law: International Law and the Land Commander*, Canberra, Australian Defence Studies Centre, 1994.

Smith, H. A., *The Crisis in the Law of Nations*, London, Stevens, 1974.

Spaight, J. M., *Air Power and War Rights*, London, Longmans, Green, 1947.

Spaight, J. M., *War Rights on Land*, London, Macmillan, 1911.

Speer, R. T., Let Pass Safely the *Awa Maru, 100 Naval Academy Proceedings* (1974).

Squibb, G. D., *The High Court of Chancery*, Oxford, Oxford University Press, 1997.

Stacey, R. C. 'The age of chivalry', in Howard, M., *The Laws of War*, New Haven, Yale University Press, 1994.

Stone, J., *Legal Controls of International Conflict*, London, Stevens, 1959.

Stowell, E. C., *Intervention in International Law*, Washington, John Byrne, 1921.

Sultan, H., The Islamic concept, in UNESCO, *International Dimensions of Humanitarian Law*, Dordrecht, Martinus Nijhoff, 1988.

Sun Tzu, *The Art of War*, 500 BC Eng. tr. Griffiths, S. B., Oxford, Oxford University Press, 1971.

Tanaka, Y., *Hidden Horrors: Japanese War Crimes in World War Two*, Boulder, Westview Press 1996.

Taube, M., de, L'apport de Byzance au Développement de Droit Occidentale, 67 *Hague Recueil*, 1934.

Thomas, A. V. W. and Thomas, A. J., *Legal Limits on the Use of Chemical and Biological Weapons*, Dallas, Southern Methodist University Press, 1970.

Toland, J., *The Rising Sun*, New York, Bantam, 1970.

Tolstoy, N., *The Minister and the Massacres*, London, Century Hutchinson, 1986.

Tomuschat, C., Crimes against the peace and security of mankind and the recalcitrant state, in Dinstein/Tabory.

Treece, H. and Oakshott, R., *Fighting Men*, New York, Putnam, 1963.

Tucker, R. W., *The Law of War and Neutrality at Sea*, Newport, Naval War College, 1957.

Twiss, Sir Travers, *The Black Book of the Admiralty*, London, Monumenta Juridica, 1871–76.

United Nations, *The Blue Helmets*, New York, United Nations, 1985.

UNESCO, *Humanitarian Dimensions of Humanitarian Law*, Dordrecht, Martinus Nijhoff, 1988.

UNWCC, *Law Reports of Trials of War Criminals*, London, HMSO, 1947–49.

UNWCC, *History of the United Nations War Crimes Commission*, London, HMSO, 1948.

US, *The Law of Land Warfare*, FM27–19, Washington, Department of the Army, 1956.

US, *International Law*, vol. 2 Code of Conduct for Members of the US Armed Forces, Washington, Dept. of the Army, Pamphlet 27–161–2, 1962.

US, *The Geneva Conventions and Hague Cnvention IV 1907*, Washington, Dept. of the Army, ASubjScd 27–1, 1970.

US, *International Law: The Conduct of Armed Conflict and Air Operations*, Washington, Dept. of the Air Force, AFP 110–31, 1976.

US, *Commander's Handbook on the Law of Armed Conflict*, Washington, Dept. of the Air Force, Pamphlet AFP 110–34, 1980.

US, *Commander's Handbook on the Law of Naval Operations*, Washington, Dept. of the Navy NWP 9 (Rev.), 1989, Annotated Supplement, 1997.

US, *Conduct of the Persian Gulf War*, Final Report to Congress App. O, Washington, Dept. of Defense, 1992.

US, *Operational Law Handbook*, Charlotteville, JAG School, 1996.

Vattel, E., *Le Droit des Gens*, London, 1758, Eng. tr. Fenwick, C. G., Washington, Carnegie Institution, 1916.

Venturini, G., Commentary on Hague Convention VII 1907, in Ronzitti, N. (ed.), *The Law of Naval Warfare*, Dordrecht, Martinus Nijhoff, 1988.

Villiger, M. E., *Customary International Law and Treaties*, Dordrecht, Martinus Nijhoff, 1985.

Voge, R. G., Too Much Accuracy, 76 *Naval Academy Proceedings* (1950).

Waldock, C. H. M., The release of the *Altmark's* prisoners, 24 British Yearbook of International Law (1947).

Walzer, M., *Just and Unjust Wars*, New York, Basic Books, 1977.

Ward, R., *An Enquiry into the Foundation and History of the Law of Nations in Europe*, London, Butterworth, 1795.

Walters, F. P., *A History of the League of Nations*, London, Oxford University Press, 1952.

Webb, A. M., *The Natzweiler Trial*, Edinburgh, Hodge, 1949.

Wheaton, H., *Elements of International Law* 1, 8th ed. by Dana, R. H., London, Sampson Low, 1866.

White, N. D., *The United Nations and the Maintenance of International Peace and Security*, Manchester, Manchester University Press, 1990.

Whiteman, M., *Digest of International Law*, Washington, Dept of State, 1963–73.

Williams, P. and Wallace, D., *Unit 731*, London, Hodder & Stoughton, 1989.

Williams, S., The Polish art treasures in Canada 1946–60, 15 *Canadian Yearbook of International Law* (1977).

Wilson, B. W., and Tsouros, P. G., *Operation Just Cause: the US Intervention in Panama*, Boulder, Westview Press, 1991.

Winthrop, W., *Military Law and Precedents*, New York, Anro Press, 1986.

Wedalis, R. J., Burning of the Kuwaiti oilfields and the laws of war, 24 *Vanderbilt Journal of International Law* (1991).

Weyas, A. M. de, *The Wehrmacht War Crimes Bureau 1939–1945*, Lincoln, University of Nebraska Press, 1989.

Wolfrum, R. 'Enforcement of International Humanitarian Law', in Fleck, *Handbook*.

Table of cases

R. *v*. Casement (1917) 45
R. *v*. Finta (1994) 292
R. *v*. Keyn (1876) 278
R. *v*. Perzenowski (1947) 95, 209
R. *v*. Sawoniuk (1998) 278
R. *v*. Smith (1900) 306
R. *v*. Steane (1947) 149
R. *v*. Werner (1947) 95, 202, 209
Rebecca, The (1811) 172
Rhode, Re (1946) 150, 211, 302
Ruchteschell, Re (1947) 175

Schaefer, Re (1918) 78
Schneiderman *v*. Metropolitan Casualty Co. of New York (1961) 55
Schumann, Ex p. (1966) 297
Shimoda *v*. Japan (1963) 38, 40, 100, 128, 130, 155, 191
Singapore Oil Stocks (1955) 153
Spanish Civil War Pension Entitlement (1978) 77
Stalag Luft III Case (1947) 206
State *v*. Mogoerane (1982) 45
State *v*. Sagarius (1983) 45

Tatesham *v*. Garenserres (1351) 24, 102
Thorington *v*. Smith (1868) 54
Three Friends, The (1897) 54
'Tokyo Rose' (1951) 149
Tokyo Trial (1948) 13, 41, 73, 291
Trent, The (1861/2) 164

US *v*. Calley (1969/71/73) 33, 292, 309
US *v*. Fleming (1957) 149
US *v*. Keenan (1954) 35
US *v*. Ohlendorf (1947) 53

Victoria Nyanza, Craft Captured on (1919) 163
Vrow Anna Catherina (1803) 275

Waldeshef *v*. Wawe (1383) 102
Walton *v*. Arab American Oil Co. (1956) 133
Wilkinson *v*. Equitable Life Insurance (1956) 71

Yamashita, Re (1945) 214, 280, 303

Zamora, The (1916) 36, 166, 351

Table of treaties

Index

nuclear, 2, 48, 49, 51, 128–32, 192,
193
Wheaton, H., 104, 105
white flag, 91–2, 127, 175
William II, Kaiser, 4, 290
women
combatants, 22, 103, 145, 210
treatment of, 21, 22, 25, 27, 29, 103,
121, 132, 199, 202, 203, 210, 211,
230, 235, 237, 238, 242, 264, 314,
327, 329
wounded and sick, 88, 105, 206, 216–28,
230, 246, 329–30; *see also* prisoners
of war
civilian assistance, 221–329
collection, 217, 218, 221, 223, 231
crimes against, 297–8

hospital ships, 35, 174, 217–18, 223–4
hospital zones, 226, 246
medical aircraft, 80, 225–6
medical treatment, 218, 219–20, 327,
328, 329
neutral territory, in, 220, 271–2
protection of, 26–7, 329–30
removal of, 220, 225, 226–7
reprisals against, 228
treatment of, 26–7, 174, 218
warship sickbay, 174–5, 224

Yugoslavia, 9, 10, 45, 55, 63, 66, 67, 73,
88, 109, 116, 155, 185, 197, 227,
232–3, 277, 282, 292, 310–12, 318,
320, 322–3, 325, 332–4, 342, 343;
see also Bosnia; Kosovo